THE EVOLUTION
OF USAF
AIR AND SPACE POWER

THE EVOLUTION OF USAF AIR AND SPACE POWER

Editors Rohan Sinha, Pankhoori Sinha
Designers Mitun Banerjee, Neha Ahuja, Tannishtha Chakraborty
Picture Researcher Kingshuk Ghoshal

DTP Coordinator Sunil Sharma
DTP Designers Pushpak Tyagi, Jagtar Singh
Production Controller Man Fai Lau, Silvia La Greca Bertacchi

Art director Shefali Upadhyay

Head of publishing operations Aparna Sharma

Associate publisher-custom Nigel Duffield

Project Manager Anna Streiffert Limerick

First American Edition, 2008
2 4 6 8 10 9 7 5 3 1

Published in the United States by
DK Publishing
375 Hudson Street
New York, New York 10014

A Cataloging in Publication Record is available from the Library of Congress

ISBN: 0-536-56331-4

Reproduced by Colourscan, Singapore
Printed and bound in Ohio by The Lakeside Press

Discover more at
www.dk.com

CONTENTS

MODULE III
Airpower Through the Cold War:
Strategic Airlift, Birth of the Nuclear
Triad, Introduction of Jet Aircraft

CONTENTS

MODULE IV
Airpower Through the
Post-Cold-War Period

MODULE V
Airpower Today

ACKNOWLEDGMENTS

The subject matter in *The Evolution of USAF Air and Space Power* was based on suggestions received from OTS and ROTC instructors. The Jeanne M. Holm Officer Accession and Citizen Development Center Curriculum Division team involved in the production effort was under the direction of Dr. Charles Nath III, Director of Curriculum, at Maxwell Air Force Base, Alabama, and Mr. Jim Wiggins, Chief of Curriculum Development. This exceptional leadership team resulted in an outstanding product for the OTS/ROTC program. Special thanks go to Mr. Stan Hammonds and Mr. Kevin Lynn, Curriculum Area Managers for OTS/ROTC Curriculum. Mr. Hammonds and Mr. Lynn were the primary editors for the textbook and conducted a persistent and thorough review of the material. We commend them for their efforts to produce the best academic materials possible for more than 145 units nationwide.

We would like to express our gratitude to the team at High Stakes Writing, LLC, including Lawrence J. Goodrich, Katherine Dillin, Linda Harteker, and Ruth Walker for all their hard work in publishing this new book. Their production team included personnel from Dorling Kindersley Limited, including Nigel Duffield, Rohan Sinha, Pankhoori Sinha, Mitun Banerjee, Neha Ahuja, Tannishtha Chakraborty, Kingshuk Ghoshal, Sunil Sharma, Pushpak Tyagi, Jagtar Singh, Suresh Kumar, Shefali Upadhyay, Aparna Sharma, and Anna Streiffert Limerick; and personnel from Pearson Custom Publishing, including Christopher Will and Karen Whitehouse.

The Jeanne M. Holm Officer Accession and Citizen Development Center mission is to "Develop the best Air Force leaders and citizens of character, dedicated to serving the Nation." Our goal within OTS/ROTC is to create materials that provide a solid foundation for producing officers able to productively fulfill their roles as Air Force leaders. We believe this course continues the precedent set with the previous curriculum materials. All the people identified above combined their efforts on this project to form one great team providing "world class" curriculum materials to all our schools.

MODULE I

AIRPOWER THROUGH WORLD WAR I:

The introduction of aircraft to military operations

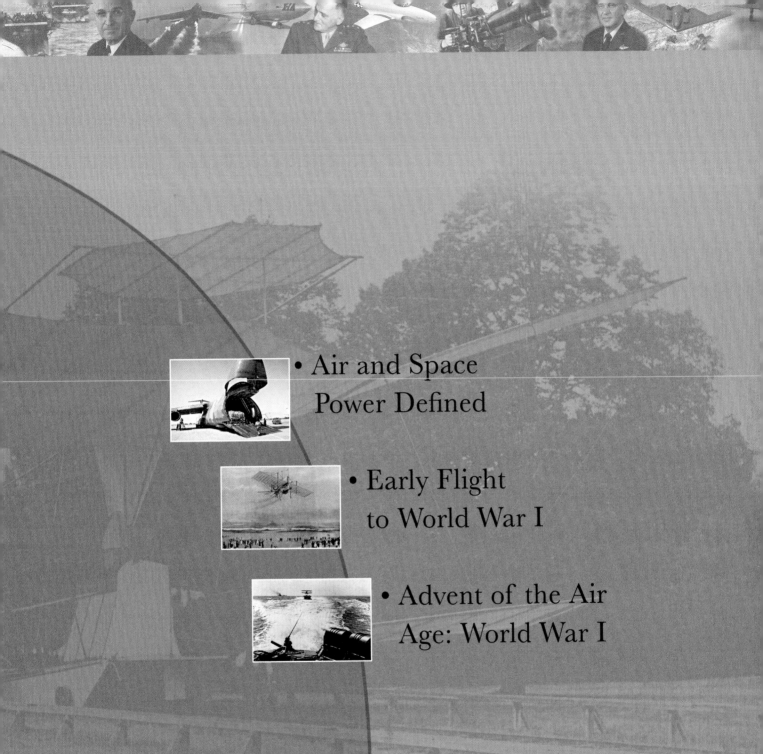

- Air and Space Power Defined

- Early Flight to World War I

- Advent of the Air Age: World War I

AIR AND SPACE POWER DEFINED

AIR AND SPACE POWER is the synergistic application of air, space,
and information systems to project global strategic military power.
A synergistic application combines the actions of two or more
forces so that their combined effect is greater than the sum
of their individual effects. The Air Force's role is to defend
the United States and protect its interests through air,
space, and cyberspace power.

IN THIS BOOK you will study how air and space power evolved to be what it is today. It is a remarkable story of great victories as well as serious setbacks. Both taught lessons that today's Air Force officers must master if the service is to meet the expectations of the president, Congress, and the American people.

But this course is not just a chronological history of airpower. It aims to review historical events to determine how they contribute to Air Force doctrine—including the principles of war; the tenets of air and space power; the Air Force's roles, missions, and functions; and its core competencies and distinctive capabilities.

While the textbook will review the events and people that shaped history, your instructor will review with you the lessons learned about what airpower can and cannot do, and their effect on today's Air Force.

First, however, you must understand what doctrine itself is. Air and space doctrine is a statement of officially sanctioned beliefs, war-fighting principles, and terminology that describes and guides the proper use of air and space forces in military operations. Doctrine shapes the manner in which the Air Force organizes, trains, equips, and sustains its forces. Doctrine consists of the fundamental principles

by which military forces guide their actions in support of national objectives.

Doctrine should be used with judgment, however. It must never be dismissed out of hand or through ignorance of its principles, nor should it be employed blindly without due regard for the mission and the situation at hand.

Air and space doctrine, then, is an accumulation of knowledge gained primarily from the study and analysis of experience. This may include actual combat or contingency operations, as well as experiments or exercises. What follows are the pillars on which air and space doctrine stands.

NEXT GENERATION STEALTH
The F-35 Lightning II Joint Strike Fighter.

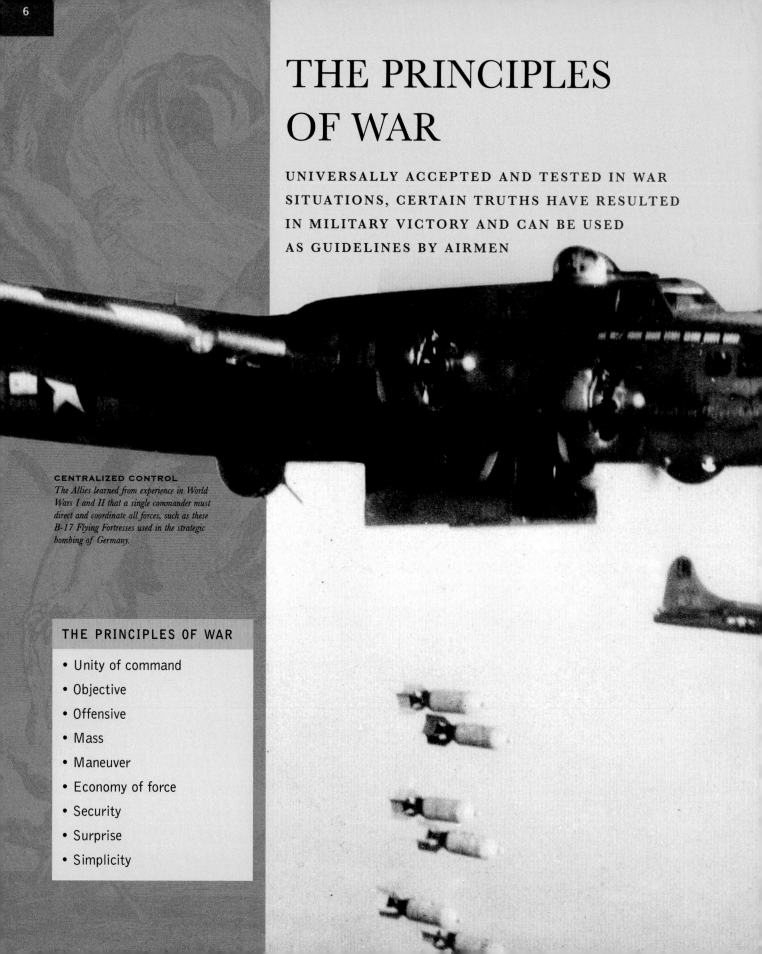

THE PRINCIPLES OF WAR

UNIVERSALLY ACCEPTED AND TESTED IN WAR
SITUATIONS, CERTAIN TRUTHS HAVE RESULTED
IN MILITARY VICTORY AND CAN BE USED
AS GUIDELINES BY AIRMEN

CENTRALIZED CONTROL
The Allies learned from experience in World Wars I and II that a single commander must direct and coordinate all forces, such as these B-17 Flying Fortresses used in the strategic bombing of Germany.

THE PRINCIPLES OF WAR

- Unity of command
- Objective
- Offensive
- Mass
- Maneuver
- Economy of force
- Security
- Surprise
- Simplicity

THROUGHOUT HISTORY, military leaders have noted certain principles that tend to produce military victory. The *Joint Doctrine for the Armed Forces of the United States* (JP 1) calls these *principles of war* "those aspects of warfare that are universally true and relevant." As a member of the joint military team, you should grasp how these principles apply to all warfare, but as an Airman, you must fully understand them in relation to air and space forces. Regardless of which service operates them, air and space forces provide unique abilities.

These principles, listed in the box, represent generally accepted truths that have shown themselves to be effective throughout history. You can use these guidelines to develop and select courses of action and concepts of operation. Of course, even valid principles are no substitute for sound professional judgment. The principles of war are not a checklist that guarantees victory. But if you ignore them, you will assume unnecessary risk.

While the principles are independent, never consider one without considering all the others. The art of developing air and space strategies depends on your ability to view these principles from a three-dimensional perspective and apply them accordingly.

Unity of command

Unity of command ensures concentration of effort for every objective under one responsible commander. That commander must direct and coordinate all efforts toward a common objective. Experience, especially that of the Allies in World Wars I and II, shows this is best achieved by giving a single commander the authority to direct all forces.

Unity of command is vital in using air and space forces. Given the multiple abilities of air and space power, centralized command and control is *essential* to fuse them. Since Airmen best understand the full range of air and space power, the ability of airpower to range on a theater and global scale imposes responsibilities that require central control under an Airman.

Objective

This principle holds that political and military goals should complement each other and be clearly stated. It involves directing military operations toward a defined and attainable objective that contributes to strategic, operational, and tactical aims. Given the versatility of air and space forces, these forces can pursue tactical, operational, and strategic objectives in any combination, and simultaneously.

Offensive

The purpose of offensive action is to seize, retain, and exploit the initiative. It means US forces should be dictating the action on the battlefield rather than reacting to enemy operations. US forces should seize the initiative as soon as possible and impose the time, place, purpose, scope, intensity, and pace of operations. This is especially significant to Airmen because air and space power is best used as an offensive weapon.

That does not mean that you will never fight defensively. But success in war is generally attained only when you are on the offensive. Even such a highly defensive air campaign as the Battle of Britain was at its heart a series of individual offensive actions by Royal Air Force pilots attacking Nazi bombing formations.

From the beginning of an operation, air forces can seize the initiative by flying over enemy lines and around massed defenses to attack the enemy directly. They cause enemy forces to react instead of act, deny them the offensive, and shape the rest of the conflict.

BATTLE OF BRITAIN
The RAF Hawker Hurricane fighter played a huge role in the Battle of Britain, downing hundreds of German bombers and fighters and, significantly, their crews.

Mass

The purpose of mass is to concentrate combat power at the most advantageous place and time to achieve decisive results. Airpower is uniquely able to launch an attack from widely dispersed locations and mass combat power at the objective. Air and space forces achieve mass through effectiveness of attack, not just overwhelming numbers. The rapid mobility of airlift enabled the airborne assault during Operation Just Cause, and played a pivotal role in massing US forces in Panama.

Maneuver

Maneuver puts the enemy at a disadvantage through the flexible application of airpower. Air and space power's ability to maneuver comes not only from its speed and range, but also from its flexibility and versatility during planning and execution of operations. Maneuver forces the enemy to react, allowing the exploitation of friendly operations, and reducing the vulnerability of friendly forces. Air maneuver allows engagement anywhere, from any direction, at any time, forcing the adversary to be on guard everywhere. The versatility and responsiveness of airpower allow the simultaneous application of mass and maneuver.

Economy of force

Economy of force is the judicious employment and distribution of forces. This principle calls for the rational use of force by selecting the best mix of air and space power. To ensure that overwhelming combat power is available, you must devote maximum effort to primary objectives and use as few resources as possible on secondary efforts. The misuse of air and space power can reduce its contribution even more than enemy action.

Security

The purpose of security is never to let the enemy gain an unexpected advantage. Gaining and maintaining control of the air, space, and information media gives friendly forces a significant advantage. Since air and space power is most vulnerable on the ground, force protection is an integral part of employing it. The Japanese had to destroy Army and Navy aircraft in Hawaii before they could attack the Pacific Fleet at Pearl Harbor in 1941.

Protecting friendly forces and their operations from enemy action is essential. Security embraces both physical security and security of information. While information has always been part of warfare, with the proliferation of information technologies, it is even more central to a conflict.

Surprise

Surprise consists of attacking enemy forces at a time, place, or in a manner for which they are not prepared. The speed and range of air and space forces, coupled with their flexibility and versatility, allow them to achieve surprise more readily than surface forces.

Surprise is one of air and space power's strongest advantages. On November 11, 1940, the Royal Navy delivered a crushing carrier-based air attack on the Italian naval base at Taranto. While losing two of 21 attacking aircraft, they left three battleships sinking, two cruisers badly damaged, and two fleet auxiliaries sunk. The Japanese attack on Pearl Harbor, the US raid on Libya, and the opening day of the air campaign during Operation Desert Storm are other examples in which airpower achieved resounding surprise.

Simplicity

Military operations are often complex. Simplicity calls for avoiding unnecessary complexity in organizing, planning, and conducting military operations. This ensures that guidance, plans, and orders are as simple and direct as the objective allows. Simple guidance allows subordinate commanders the freedom to operate creatively.

SURPRISE AND SECURITY
By catching Army and Navy air forces off guard at Pearl Harbor, the Japanese were able to eliminate them and go on to deal a deadly blow to the US Pacific Fleet.

THE TENETS OF AIR AND SPACE POWER

REFLECTING THE EVOLUTION OF AIRPOWER, FUNDAMENTAL GUIDING TRUTHS GOVERN THE APPLICATION OF AIR AND SPACE POWER

TENETS OF AIR AND SPACE POWER

- Centralized control and decentralized execution

- Flexibility and versatility

- Synergistic effects

- Persistence

- Concentration

- Priority

- Balance

SEVERAL FUNDAMENTAL guiding truths govern the application of air and space power. These truths are called *tenets*. They reflect both the historical and doctrinal evolution of airpower and the current understanding of air and space power. These tenets, listed in the box, complement the principles of war, and provide more-specific considerations for air and space forces. As with the principles of war, these tenets require a commander to use informed judgment in applying them. War is incredibly complicated, and no two operations are identical. The tenets required skillful blending to tailor them to the ever-changing operational environment.

Centralized control and decentralized execution

Centralized control and decentralized execution of air and space power are critical to its effective employment. Decades of experience have shown them to be the most effective and efficient means of employing air and space power.

Centralized control is the planning, direction, prioritization, synchronization, and integration of air and space abilities to achieve the joint force commander's objectives. An Airman at the component commander level who has a broad theater perspective should accomplish it. Centralized control makes the best use of air and space power, but it must not become a recipe for micromanagement, stifling subordinates' initiative to deal with combat's uncertainties.

Decentralized execution is delegating authority to responsible and capable lower-level commanders. This achieves effective span of control and fosters disciplined initiative, situational responsiveness, and tactical flexibility. It allows subordinates to exploit opportunities in rapidly changing situations.

KOREAN WAR FIGHTERS
The F-86 Sabrejet. The Air Force learned during the Korean War that it had put too much emphasis on building bombers to deliver atomic bombs. It needed more fighters to give it more flexibility in fighting limited wars.

F-117 NIGHTHAWK
Stealth technology and precision weapons have allowed the Air Force to send fewer planes at less risk to attack specific targets.

BLOCKADE BUSTER
The C-54 was the primary cargo plane the Air Force used in the Berlin airlift.

Flexibility and versatility

Air and space power is flexible and versatile. *Flexibility* allows air and space forces to exploit mass and maneuver at the same time. It allows air and space power to shift from one objective to another. *Versatility* is the ability to employ air and space power effectively at the strategic, operational, and tactical levels of warfare. Air and space forces, unlike other military forces, can achieve this unmatched synergy of flexibility and versatility through asymmetric and parallel operations. (Parallel operations are those coordinated to occur simultaneously and continuously against a broad range of targets.)

Synergistic effects

Air and space power produces synergistic effects—effects that exceed the contributions of forces employed individually. In other words, the whole can be greater than the sum of the parts. The destruction of a large number of targets is rarely the key objective in modern war. Rather, the objective is the precise, coordinated application of air, space, and surface power to pressure enemy leaders to comply with the US national will. Operations Deny Flight and Allied Force in the Balkans are good examples of the synergistic effects of air and space power.

Persistence

Air and space power offers a unique form of persistence. A commander can conduct air, space, and information operations against a broad range of targets. Air and space power's speed and range allow its forces to visit and revisit wide ranges of targets nearly at will. Air and space power does not have to occupy terrain or remain near areas of operation to bring force upon targets. The Berlin airlift and Operation Northern Watch, enforcing a no-fly zone in Iraq, are examples of persistent operations.

Concentration

Air and space power must achieve concentration of purpose. Airmen must guard against diluting air and space power effects through high demand. Remember that the principles of mass and economy of force call for concentrating overwhelming power at the right time and in the right place. With forces as flexible and versatile as air and space forces, the demand for them often exceeds the available forces. This may result in fragmenting the air and space effort in attempting to fulfill the many demands.

Priority

This highlights the requirement for commanders to prioritize the needs for air and space power. Without prioritization, demands for air and space power will likely overwhelm air commanders in future conflicts. Only theater-level commanders of land and naval forces can effectively prioritize their air and space requirements to the joint force commander (JFC). The air component commander should assess the possible use of his or her forces to ensure they make the greatest contribution to the most critical JFC requirements. In setting priorities, the Airman employs the principles of mass, offensive, and economy of force, as well as the tenet of concentration.

Balance

Air and space operations must be balanced. An air commander should balance combat opportunity, necessity, effectiveness, efficiency, and the effect on accomplishing objectives against the risk to friendly air and space forces. An air commander is uniquely suited to determine the proper theaterwide balance between offensive and defense operations, and among strategic, operational, and tactical applications.

ROLES, MISSIONS, AND FUNCTIONS

IT IS UP TO THE AIR FORCE TO ORGANIZE, TRAIN, AND EQUIP AVIATION FORCES TO CARRY OUT THEIR ORGANIZATIONAL AND OPERATIONAL FUNCTIONS

ROLES ARE THE BROAD and enduring purposes for which Congress established the services by law. According to the 1947 National Security Act, the Air Force's role is to organize, train, and equip aviation forces "primarily for prompt and sustained offensive and defensive operations."

Missions are tasks that the president or the secretary of defense assigns to the combatant commanders. Those commanders take these tasks and develop mission statements, operational objectives, and concepts of operations. Based on these, they assign specific tasks to subordinate commanders.

The military departments' *functions* are those responsibilities that enable the service to fulfill their legally established roles. While Department of Defense Directive 5100.1 charges Air Force forces to "conduct … prompt and sustained combat operations in the air" and to "gain and maintain general air supremacy," it does not set forth exactly how the Air Force is to accomplish these functions. These details are left to the service to develop.

You can divide Air Force functions into two types: *organizational functions* ("organize, train, and equip") and *operational functions*. You will find a list of the operational functions of air and space power in the box. Remember that these are not exclusive to the Air Force; the Army, Navy, and Marines may perform them too.

OPERATIONAL FUNCTIONS OF AIR AND SPACE POWER

- Strategic attack
- Counterair
- Counterspace
- Counterland
- Countersea
- Information operations
- Combat support
- Command and control (C2)
- Airlift
- Air refueling
- Spacelift
- Special operations
- Intelligence
- Surveillance and reconnaissance
- Combat search and rescue
- Navigation and positioning
- Weather services

B-2 SPIRIT BOMBER
These aircraft flew dozens of sorties in Operation Iraqi Freedom, which opened with an air and ground campaign known as "Shock and Awe."

Strategic attack

Strategic attack is an offensive action conducted by command authorities aimed at generating effects that most directly achieve US national strategy objectives by affecting the enemy's leadership, conflict-sustaining resources, and strategy. Understanding strategic attack is critically important to future joint operations. Air and space power is inherently a strategic force and an offensive weapon. Unlike other forms of military power, air and space power may simultaneously hold all an enemy's instruments of power at risk—military, economic, and diplomatic.

Strategic attack, as envisioned today, is more than just a function—it is also a different approach for thinking about war. It is the manifestation of the Airman's perspective: thinking about defeating the enemy as a system.

Counterair

Counterair consists of operations to attain and maintain a desired degree of air superiority by the destruction, degradation, or disruption of enemy forces. Offensive counterair consists of operations to destroy, degrade, or disrupt enemy air and missile power as close to its source as possible and at a time and place of US choosing. Defensive counterair entails detection, identification, interception, and destruction of attacking enemy air and missiles and normally takes place over or close to friendly territory.

Counterspace/land/sea

Counterspace involves operations to attain and maintain superiority in space and includes both offensive counterspace operations against enemy space forces and defensive counterspace operations to preserve US space capabilities. *Counterland* is air and space operations against enemy land forces to achieve the JFC's objectives, and includes both air interdiction of enemy land forces and close air support of friendly land forces. *Countersea* functions are an extension of Air Force capabilities into a maritime environment.

Information operations

Information operations are actions taken to influence, affect, or defend information, systems, and/or decision making. This can include *influence operations, electronic warfare operations*, and *network warfare operations*.

Combat support

Combat support is the essential capabilities, functions, activities, and tasks necessary to create and sustain air and space forces. It is those activities designed to field and support a specific military ability across the full spectrum of military operations. For the Air Force, this includes logistics, personnel, communications, financial management, security forces, services, safety, civil engineering, health services, the historian's office, public affairs, legal services, and the chaplaincy. Agile combat support (ACS) is the timely concentration, employment, and sustainment of US military power anywhere that US adversaries cannot match. Expeditionary combat support is the expeditionary subset of ACS.

Command and control

Command and control (C2) is the exercise of authority and direction by a properly designated commander over assigned and attached forces to accomplish the mission. It includes both the process by which the commander decides which action to take and the systems that facilitate planning, execution, and monitoring of those actions. Centralized C2 of air and space forces under a single Airman is a fundamental principle of air and space doctrine.

Airlift, air refueling, and spacelift

Airlift refers to transportation of personnel and materiel through the air, which can be applied across the entire range of military operations to achieve or support objectives and can achieve tactical through strategic effects. *Air refueling* is the inflight transfer of fuel between tanker and receiver aircraft. By increasing the

SPEEDY RECONNAISSANCE
The SR-71 Blackbird could reach 2,193mph (3,530kmph) and attain an altitude of 85,000ft (26,000m). No other reconnaissance aircraft could fly faster or higher.

range or endurance of receiving aircraft, it is a force enabler. By allowing aircraft to take off with higher payloads and not sacrifice payload for fuel, it is a force multiplier. *Spacelift* delivers satellites, payloads, and material to space. Assured access to space is a key element of US national policy and a foundation upon which US national security, civil, and commercial space activities depend. The Air Force is the Defense Department service responsible for operating US launch facilities.

C-5 GALAXY
US Airmen flew cargo planes like the C-5, C-141 Starlifter, and the C-130 Hercules to deliver 6,000 tons of food and medicines to countries of the former Soviet Union in 1992 and 1993.

Special operations

Special operations are operations such as unconventional warfare, direct action, special reconnaissance, counterterrorism, foreign internal defense, psychological operations, and counterproliferation. Air Force special-operations forces are normally organized into small formations.

Intelligence

Intelligence is the product that results from collection, processing, analysis, and interpretation of information about foreign countries or areas. Its purpose is to provide commanders and combat forces information about what is happening in the battlespace. This allows them to successfully plan, operate, and assess results across the range of military operations.

Surveillance and reconnaissance

Closely related to intelligence is surveillance and reconnaissance.

Surveillance is the function of systematically observing air, space, surface, or subsurface areas, places, persons, or things. This can be done by visual, aural, electronic, photographic, or other means. Air and space-based surveillance assets exploit their elevation to detect enemy initiatives at long range. Reconnaissance complements surveillance by obtaining specific information about the activities and resources of an enemy or potential enemy. It does this through visual observation or other detection methods, or by securing data about the meteorological, hydrographic, or geographic characteristics of a particular area.

Combat search and rescue

Combat search and rescue is a specific task performed by rescue forces to recover isolated personnel, such as downed pilots, during war or other military operations. It is a key element in sustaining the morale, cohesion, and fighting ability of friendly forces. It also preserves critical

RESCUE
Members of the 90th Space Wing from F.E. Warren AFB, Wyoming, execute a rescue scenario during the Guardian Challenge competition at Vandenberg AFB, California. The annual four-day event tests the readiness of Air Force Space Command's Airmen.

combat resources and denies the enemy potential sources of intelligence.

Navigation and positioning

Navigation and positioning provide accurate location and time of reference in support of strategic, operational, and tactical operations. They are key elements of information superiority and global awareness.

Weather services

Weather services supply commanders and other Airmen timely and accurate environmental information, including both the space environment and atmospheric weather.

CORE COMPETENCIES AND DISTINCTIVE CAPABILITIES

THE AIR FORCE'S FUNDAMENTAL SERVICE TO THE NATION IS TO DEVELOP, TRAIN, SUSTAIN, AND INTEGRATE THE ELEMENTS OF AIR AND SPACE POWER SO IT CAN EXECUTE ITS FUNCTIONS

CORE COMPETENCIES

- Developing Airmen
- Technology-to-war fighting
- Integrating operations

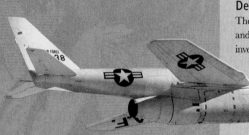

FROM EXPERIMENT TO DEPLOYMENT
The Bell X-5, which first flew in 1951, featured wings that could sweep back 60 degrees. The F-111 that dropped bombs over Libya in 1986 had the same swing-back wing design.

DISTINCTIVE CAPABILITIES

- Air and space superiority
- Information superiority
- Global attack
- Precision engagement
- Rapid global mobility
- Agile combat support
- Surprise

THE AIR FORCE'S core competencies, shown in the box (center left), and their supporting distinctive capabilities are at the heart of the service's strategic perspective.

Developing Airmen
The ultimate source of combat ability is the men and women of the Air Force. The force's largest investment and most critical asset is the total force of active, Guard, Reserve, and civilian personnel. The service's abilities stem from the collective abilities of its personnel; the abilities of its people stem from a career-long focus on developing professional Airmen.

Technology-to-war fighting
As a leader in the military application of air, space, intelligence, and surveillance and reconnaissance technology, the Air Force is committed to innovation. Just as powered flight revolutionized war fighting, recent advances in low-observable technologies, space-based systems, manipulation of information, precision, and small smart weapons offer equally dramatic advantages to combat commanders. The Air Force nurtures its ability to translate its technology into operational ability—to prevail in conflict and avert technological surprise.

Integrating operations
Effectively integrating the diverse abilities found in all four service branches remains pivotal to joint war fighting. The Air Force contributes to this objective as each element of air and space power brings unique and successful abilities to the joint force. Effective integration requires

more than investing in technology. It also requires investigating efficient joint and Air Force organization and innovative operational thinking. Continued investing in Air Force people to foster critical analysis and intellectual flexibility is just as important as developing technology.

Distinctive Capabilities
The distinctive capabilities are the basic areas of expertise the Air Force brings to any military operation, whether as a single service or along with other services in joint operations. While not unique to the Air Force, they represent what the Air Force does better than any other organization. You can find the distinctive capabilities in the box (bottom left).

Air and space superiority
Gaining air and space superiority is a vital first step in military operations. It gives friendly forces freedom of action on land and sea as well as in air and space. It provides freedom *to* attack as well as freedom *from* attack.

Relaxing pressure on the enemy's air forces may allow them to gain air superiority, with disastrous results. For example, Hitler's decision during World War II to divert the Luftwaffe from directly attacking the Royal Air Force—and bomb cities instead—gave the RAF the breathing space it desperately needed to rebuild and reorganize.

Information superiority
Information superiority is the ability to collect, control, exploit, and defend information while preventing an enemy from doing the same. While today you might think of this in terms of electronic information and networks, information superiority was actually the

MASTER OF THE SKIES
*The P-51 Mustang helped clear the
European skies of German aircraft and
establish Allied air superiority in the last
year of World War II.*

Air Force's first function. Early balloons and airplanes became spotters for Army commanders who wanted information to gain an advantage over their adversaries and improve their battlefield decisions. Today the Air Force operates sophisticated air- and space-based intelligence, surveillance, and reconnaissance systems and is the service most able to respond quickly to the information they provide.

Information superiority enabled the United States to respond quickly to the October 1994 Iraqi buildup, possibly preventing a second invasion of Kuwait. In 2003, it enabled coalition air forces to respond remarkably quickly and target the senior Iraqi leadership.

Global attack

Only the Air Force can attack rapidly and persistently with a wide range of munitions anywhere on the globe at any time. With the decline of the total force structure and worldwide bases, the US military has become primarily an expeditionary force. The Air Force, with its space forces, intercontinental ballistic missiles, and fleet of bombers and attack aircraft, is ideally suited to such operations. Air Force operations can be the first and potentially the most decisive element in countering an adversary's aggression.

Precision engagement

Increasingly, air and space power is providing the "scalpel" of US military operations—the ability to apply measured force precisely where required.

GLOBAL RANGE
*Despite its age, the B-52 still gives the Air Force
strike capability anywhere on Earth.*

While it's not the only service that can precisely employ its forces, the Air Force is the service with the greatest ability to apply the technology and techniques of precision engagement anywhere on Earth in a matter of hours. Precision engagement represents an ability not only to win wars, but also to drive crises to peace.

Rapid global mobility

Rapid global mobility refers to the timely movement, positioning, and sustainment of military forces across the range of military operations. It has increased in importance to the point that today virtually every US military operation requires it. Operations Enduring Freedom and Iraqi Freedom showed just how quickly US air forces can mobilize, deploy, and prepare for war. US air forces provided advanced elements within hours of the decision to deploy.

Agile combat support

How the Air Force supports the forces it deploys is as critical as which forces it deploys and how they get there. A force poised to respond to global missions within hours must also be able to support that force with equal ease. But agile combat support is not just a concept for deployed operations.

Every facet of the Air Force must focus on providing combat support—whether it is better-educated warriors, better home-base support for Airmen and their families, better management of the personnel system, or more-efficient conduct of business.

Conclusion

Now you have reviewed some basics of Air Force doctrine: the principles of war; the tenets of air and space power; the Air Force's roles, missions, and functions; and its core competencies and distinctive capabilities. More and more often, US leaders are calling upon air and space power as the military instrument of first choice. They are asking it to accomplish tasks previous generations thought unworkable.

To support the national leadership, you as an Air Force officer and a military professional must think about how to accomplish a broad range of missions. You must understand the potential of air and space power and be able to plan and employ it to its maximum. You must remain aware of the lessons of the past while staying alert to the future technologies and trends that will alter the art of air and space warfare.

The lessons of the last war are always suspect, because all conflicts are different. Certain principles—like unity of command, objective, and offensive—have stood the test of time. Other ideas—like unescorted daytime bombing, decentralized command, and the preeminence of nuclear weapons—have not. The doctrinal points you have studied in this chapter are derived from those ideas that experience has proven valid. Keep them in mind as you read this book, and consider carefully how historical events illustrate their basic truth.

PREDATOR AND HELLFIRE
The MQ-1 Predator, carrying the Hellfire missile, represents the wave of the future because it can strike remotely and accurately, keeping US forces far from combat and casualties down.

FUTURE TRANSPORT
This artist's conception shows the Pelican cargo plane, which will be able to fly as low as 20ft (6m) over water and carry the equivalent of 17 battle tanks.

EARLY FLIGHT TO WORLD WAR I

HAVING SPENT CENTURIES WATCHING BIRDS with admiration and envy, when humans eventually took to the air—in the late 18th century—it was, in fact, in a balloon rather than on the wing. Nevertheless, the desire to soar through the air like a bird remained. In the course of the 19th century, scientists and inventors worked on the basic principles of flight, experimenting with gliders and ungainly steam-powered flying machines and models. But it took the persistent efforts of the Wright brothers, in experiments between 1899 and 1905, to achieve practical powered airplane flight. The period up to 1914 brought spectacular progress. The public was enthralled by flying races and displays of aerobatics, while new speed and altitude records were posted yearly, although at the cost of the lives of many early aviators.

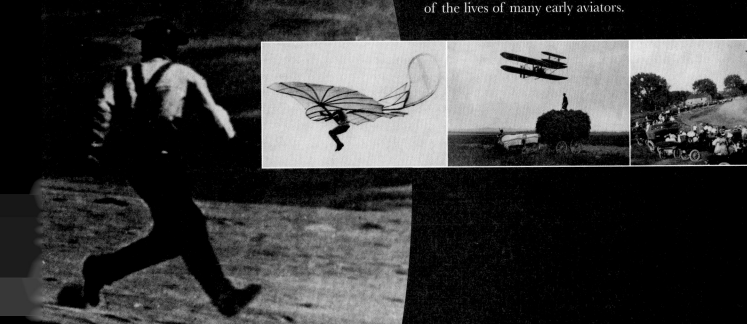

THE PREHISTORY OF FLIGHT

THE PATH TO POWERED FLIGHT WAS OPENED UP BY DREAMERS AND ODDBALL INVENTORS WHO BRAVED BOTH PUBLIC RIDICULE AND PHYSICAL INJURY

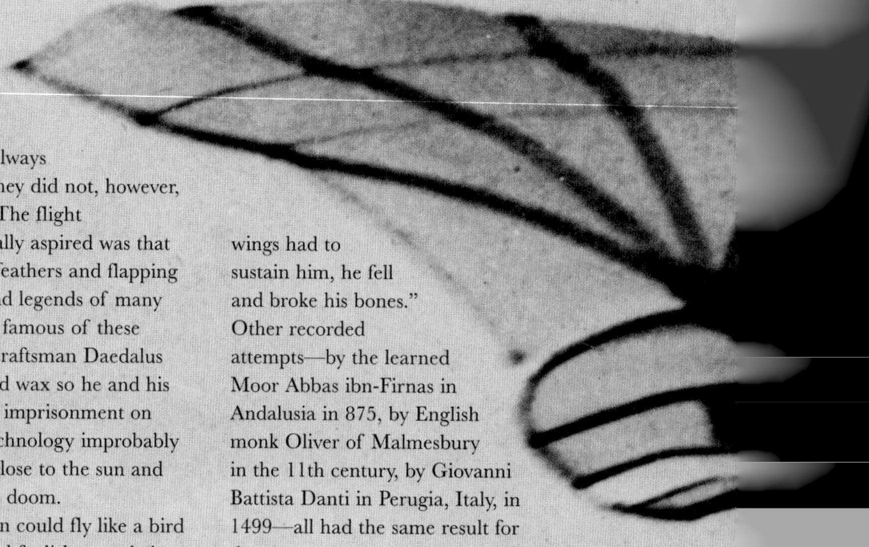

> "The desire to fly is an idea handed down to us by our ancestors who... looked enviously on the birds soaring freely through space... on the infinite highway of the air..."
>
> WILBUR WRIGHT

HUMAN BEINGS HAVE always dreamed of flight. They did not, however, dream of the Boeing 747. The flight to which humans traditionally aspired was that of the birds, a business of feathers and flapping wings. To this the myths and legends of many cultures testify. In the most famous of these ancient stories, the skilled craftsman Daedalus makes wings of feathers and wax so he and his son Icarus can escape their imprisonment on the island of Crete. The technology improbably works, but Icarus flies too close to the sun and melts the wax, falling to his doom.

The illusion that a person could fly like a bird or a bat cost some brave and foolish men their lives or limbs. The historical record is scattered with "tower jumpers" who launched themselves into the air supported only by blind faith and poorly improvised wings. In 1178, for example, in Constantinople, a follower of Islam chose the moment of a visit to the Christian Byzantine Emperor by a Muslim sultan to demonstrate his powers of flight, jumping off a high building in a copious white robe stiffened with willow sticks. In the words of a later flight experimenter, Octave Chanute, "the weight of his body having more power to draw him downward than his artificial wings had to sustain him, he fell and broke his bones." Other recorded attempts—by the learned Moor Abbas ibn-Firnas in Andalusia in 875, by English monk Oliver of Malmesbury in the 11th century, by Giovanni Battista Danti in Perugia, Italy, in 1499—all had the same result for the same reason.

"Instruments to fly"

Myth and folklore were also rich in tales of airworthy vehicles that might carry the weight of a human, from various "chariots of the gods" to witches' broomsticks. The idea of a "flying machine" was picked up by English philosopher-monk Roger Bacon in the 13th century—a man regarded as one of the founders of the modern scientific tradition. Bacon declared himself certain that humans could build "instruments to fly," involving a mechanism that would flap wings. Such "ornithopters" also obsessed the imagination of Italian Renaissance genius Leonardo da Vinci. "There is in man [the ability] to sustain himself by the flapping of wings," Leonardo wrote. He was wrong. In the many sketches of flying machines found in Leonardo's notebooks, the only truly promising idea is a screwlike propeller that he hoped would spiral into the air—a remote foreshadowing of a helicopter.

LEONARDO'S VISION
Leonardo da Vinci believed that the secrets of flight could be learned by studying birds. His concept of a flying machine (model shown here) was as impractical as all other devices for muscle-powered, flapping-wing flight.

BIRDMAN PIONEER
German engineer Otto Lilienthal made over 2,000 flights in the 1890s using hang gliders of his own design. Although he was the author of an influential work on bird flight, Lilienthal believed that "a proper insight into the practice of flying" could only be achieved "by actual flying experiments."

If no one could see how to make a machine that would fly, they could possibly see why you would want to—especially in militaristic Europe, which was divided into states that were more or less permanently at war with one another. In 1670, proposing yet another impractical design—this time for an airship lifted by spheres from which the air had been pumped to create a vacuum—Italian Jesuit Father Francesco de Lana pointed out that such a vehicle could be used to land troops to capture a city in a surprise attack, or to destroy houses and fortresses by dropping "fireballs and bombs."

Lighter-than-air flight

Although de Lana's vacuum-lifted airship was a nonstarter, it did point the way to the first successful human flight. De Lana's goal was "to make a machine lighter than the air itself." This could not be done with vacuum spheres, but it could with a balloon filled with hot air or a light gas such as hydrogen. As usual in the history of invention, the solution to a problem became apparent to several inventors at once. When Joseph and Etienne Montgolfier, paper manufacturers from the French town of Annonay, brought a hot-air balloon to Paris in 1783, they faced competition from gentleman-scientist Jacques Charles, who was ready to demonstrate a hydrogen-filled balloon.

FIRST BALLOON FLIERS
In June 1783 the Montgolfier brothers conducted the first public display of a hot-air balloon, and the following November François Pilâtre de Rozier and the Marquis d'Arlandes made the first manned ascent (above). Early French aeronauts achieved some spectacular flights. In February 1784 Jean-Pierre Blanchard soared to over 12,500ft (3,800m) in a hydrogen balloon.

FLIGHT OF FANTASY
In 1843 William Henson formed the "Aerial Steam Transit Company." Despite the circulation of optimistic images such as this one, the Aerial Steam Carriage never flew.

Engine housing

Tailplane

Wing brace

Pusher propeller

Rudder

But it was the Montgolfiers who established precedence and their place in the history books. As would happen in the exploration of space two centuries later, they sent animals up first on a test flight—a duck, a sheep, and a rooster. All landed safely, although according to one account "they were, to say the least, much astonished." The first free manned flight followed on November 21, when physician François Pilâtre de Rozier and the Marquis d'Arlandes, an army officer, drifted over Paris covering 5 miles (8km) in about 25 minutes. Ten days later Jacques Charles and a companion flew 25 miles (40km) in a hydrogen balloon.

Ballooning captured the public imagination much as flying machines would in the early 20th century. Crowds flocked to demonstration flights and the fliers became national heroes. French aeronaut Jean-Pierre Blanchard, with American expatriate John Jeffries on board, flew across the Channel from England to France in January 1785, 124 years before Louis Blériot.

Scientific progress

One of the many individuals fascinated and inspired by reports of the early balloon flights was a young boy growing up on his father's estate in Yorkshire, England. He was George Cayley, who was to make the first serious practical and theoretical progress toward heavier-than-air flight. Cayley could easily be considered as an eccentric—a member of the landed gentry using his privileged leisure time to pursue a fanciful hobby. But he, in fact, worked within a maturing scientific tradition, which enabled him to define precisely the challenge of heavier-than-air flight: "The whole problem is confined within these limits," he wrote, "to make a surface support a given weight by the application of power to the resistance of air."

Cayley addressed himself to these problems of lift and drag through observation of bird flight, systematic experimentation, and mathematical calculations. He used an ingenious device known as a "whirling arm"—a precursor of the wind tunnel—to test the lift created by different airfoils, or wings, at various angles and speeds.

IMAGE OF THE FUTURE
Sir George Cayley engraved this image of a flying machine on a silver disk in 1799. Cayley's design was the first to resemble the configuration of a modern airplane.

SIR GEORGE CAYLEY
Basing his theories on experimentation and observation, Cayley (1773–1857) pioneered the conquest of flight with his works on aeronautics.

As early as 1799 Cayley engraved on a silver disk an image of a flying machine that marked a crucial step forward in design from Leonardo-style ornithopters: The wing had ceased to be the means of propulsion, becoming instead purely a device to generate lift. Through the next decade he built both model and full-size gliders. His full-size glider had a wing attached to the front end of a pole, and at the rear of the pole a vertical rudder and horizontal tailplane. "When any person ran forward in it with his full speed," Cayley wrote, "taking advantage of a gentle breeze in front, it… would frequently lift him up and convey him several yards together."

In 1809–10 Cayley made the results of his work public in a three-part paper, "On Aerial Navigation." His calculations of lift and drag, and his comments on how an aircraft could be stabilized and controlled, constituted a solid basis for potential progress toward heavier-than-air flight. Unfortunately, they were largely ignored. As Cayley himself admitted, flight remained "a subject rather ludicrous in the public's estimation."

The awakening of a more sustained interest in heavier-than-air flight did not come for another 30 years. It was provoked by the success of the steam engine applied to transportation systems. By the

Wing brace

Silk-covered wings
with 20ft (6m) span

Launching wheels

AERIAL CARRIAGE
This reconstruction of William Samuel Henson's proposed Aerial Steam Carriage displays more elements of a modern-day flying machine than any machine before it. Although a full-size version was never built, its cambered wings and separate tail with rudder and elevator were later widely adopted. Its two pusher propellers would have been driven by a light steam engine of up to 30hp.

1840s, railroad construction was booming as steam trains transformed journey times by land. At sea, steamships were a growing threat to the dominance of the sail. Jumping on the bandwagon, in 1843 ambitious English inventor William Samuel Henson patented an Aerial Steam Carriage "for conveying letters, goods, and passengers from place to place."

Steam-driven airline

Basing his ideas on Cayley's published research, Henson imagined a monoplane with a cambered wing for extra lift, a rudder and tailplane for control, and two six-bladed pusher propellers. This contraption was to be powered by a 30hp steam engine in the fuselage. Henson's grandiose plans for an Aerial Steam Transit Company momentarily attracted the interest of investors, the proposal for passenger flights spanning the globe rendered credible by fanciful illustrations of the Steam Carriage soaring over exotic locations. But doubt and ridicule soon followed. Although Henson built a small model of his aircraft, he could not find anyone ready to put up the cash for a full-size version and rapidly abandoned aerial experimentation for good.

LIGHTER-THAN-AIR FLIGHT

THE BALLOON FLIGHTS OF 1783 began a tradition of lighter-than-air flight that ran parallel with—and for a long time ahead of—experiments with heavier-than-air flight. The drawbacks of balloons were obvious. A huge balloon was needed to carry even a small weight, and then it was only marginally controllable and at the mercy of the winds. Yet serious practical uses were found for balloons in the 19th century: they were employed as observation platforms during the Civil War, and during the Franco-Prussian War they were used to carry messages.

The first controlled powered balloon—a dirigible or airship—was demonstrated by Frenchman Henri Giffard in 1852. Mounting a steam-driven propeller under a cigar-shaped bag filled with coal gas, he flew 17 miles (27km) at around 6mph (10kmph). His example inspired other enthusiasts, although they were hindered by the lack of alternatives to the steam engine. In the 1880s electric motors came into vogue, and the La France, built by Charles Renard and A.C. Krebs, managed controlled flights at speeds of around 12mph (20kmph).

The advent of the internal combustion engine brought a further leap forward. In 1898 Alberto Santos-Dumont, the son of a Brazilian coffee-plantation owner, embarked on a series of highly successful experiments in the skies of Paris, France, where he lived. He became a well-known and popular figure, responding to mishaps, such as crashing on the roof of a hotel, with admirable panache. He built 14 airships in all before transferring his enthusiasm to heavier-than-air flight. Meanwhile, the Germans entered the airship field when Count von Zeppelin flew his first airship LZ 1 in 1900.

BALLOON MEN
The first manned flight was made in a Montgolfier balloon (left, on a cigarette card) on November 21, 1783, but balloon flight had a limited potential. It could not, for example, be used to create a viable transportation system.

TRIP AROUND THE TOWER
In 1901 Alberto Santos-Dumont flew his dirigible from the Parisian suburb of Saint-Cloud around the Eiffel Tower and back in under 30 minutes to win a 100,000-franc prize.

BOY FROM BRAZIL
Paris-based Brazilian Alberto Santos-Dumont stands in his balloon basket ready for an ascent. Although an eccentric dilettante, he proved an outstanding pioneer of airship and airplane flight.

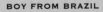

Yet interest in flight had been stimulated afresh—not least in the heart of Sir George Cayley, who now embarked on a new round of experiments that culminated in the world's first manned heavier-than-air flight in a glider in 1853. The "pilot" was Cayley's coachman. He was reluctantly persuaded to climb into the boatlike fuselage of a glider, which then rolled down one side of a valley, lifted into the air, and briefly flew before coming down uncomfortably. The coachman is said to have immediately put in his notice, on the grounds that he had been "hired to drive, not to fly." Cayley's success, achieved in the privacy of his estate, had less public impact than Henson's failure. The story of the coachman's flight only came to light long after Cayley's death in 1857.

High society

The growing respectability of flight research was exemplified by the foundation of the Aeronautical Society of Great Britain in 1866, a dignified association of scientists and engineers who staged the world's first exhibition of flying machines at London's Crystal Palace two years later. None of them flew. However, there were some notable efforts to advance understanding of aerodynamics.

Francis Wenham, a distinguished marine engineer and a founding member of the Aeronautical Society, built the first wind tunnel and produced improved data on the lift provided by different wing shapes. In the 1870s the brilliant

> "Give us a motor and we will very soon give you a successful flying machine."
>
> HIRAM MAXIM, 1892

FRENCH CANDIDATE
In the 1890s French electrical engineer Clément Ader built two steam-powered flying machines with wings modeled on a bat. Although his first, the Éole (below) managed to hop for 165ft (50m) the Avion III, seen above, failed to get off the ground.

young French engineer Alphonse Pénaud made significant progress in wing and tail design through experiments with model aircraft powered by a twisted rubber band. And Louis-Pierre Mouillard's book *The Empire of the Air*, published in 1881, was an inspirational work based on the author's observations of bird flight.

Practical efforts to progress in heavier-than-air manned flight in the late 19th century divided into three approaches. One focused on power: Was it possible to find an engine powerful enough, or rather with a favorable enough power-to-weight ratio, to lift a machine and a man into the air?

A second focused on unpowered flight as a means of understanding the secret of flight as exhibited by birds. A third, like Pénaud's, focused on model building. Success would only be achieved when the traditions of powered and unpowered flight came together—in the Wright brothers.

Engine power

Early experimenters in powered flight were unfortunate in that their only feasible power plant was a steam engine. The first of the steam-powered experimenters to make a serious attempt to get off the ground was a French naval officer, Félix du Temple de la Croix. In the 1850s, with his brother Louis, he designed and flew a model airplane powered first by clockwork and then by a miniature steam engine. He then patented a design for a full-size monoplane with a lightweight steam engine and the surprising refinement of a retractable undercarriage. His man-carrying airplane was finally built and ready to test in 1874. With a French sailor on board, it ran down a sloping ramp, briefly lifted into the air, and immediately came back down to earth.

A decade later, du Temple's "hop" was matched by a Russian experimenter, Aleksander Mozhaiskii. In 1884, at Krasnoe Selo outside St. Petersburg, Mozhaiskii tested a two-engined monoplane with a mechanic at the helm. Spouting smoke from its ship-like funnel, it momentarily lifted, then crashed to the ground.

The first claim to have actually cracked the problem of powered flight came from French electrical engineer Clément Ader. After testing his bat-winged, steam-powered Éole in 1890, he claimed: "I have resolved the problem after much work, fatigue, and money."

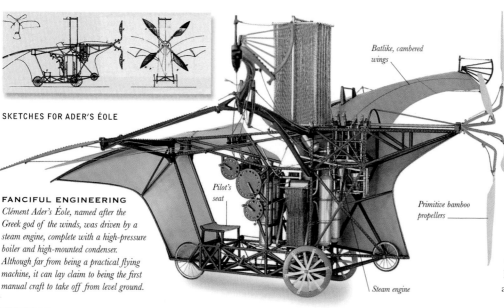

SKETCHES FOR ADER'S ÉOLE

Batlike, cambered wings

Pilot's seat

Primitive bamboo propellers

Steam engine

FANCIFUL ENGINEERING
Clément Ader's Éole, named after the Greek god of the winds, was driven by a steam engine, complete with a high-pressure boiler and high-mounted condenser. Although far from being a practical flying machine, it can lay claim to being the first manual craft to take off from level ground.

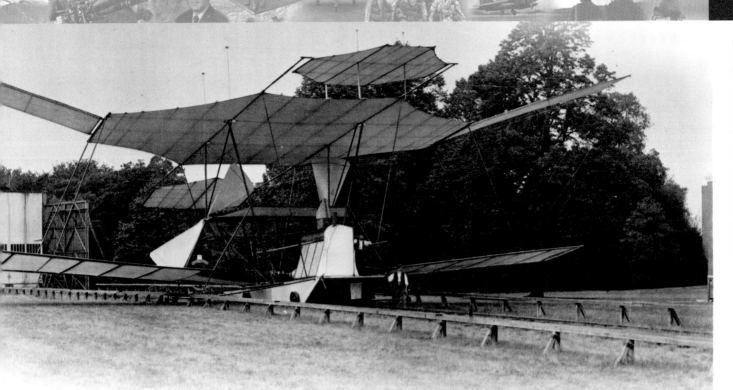

This test rig, built by the American-born Hiram Maxim in the 1890s, was a truly huge aircraft. With a wingspan of 107ft (33m) and weighing more than 3.9 tons (3.6 tonnes), it took two 180hp steam engines, each driving a propeller 18ft (5.5m) in diameter, to drive it along its restraining rails.

What he had achieved, as far as can be ascertained, was to skim the ground at a height of around 8in (20cm) for a distance of 165ft (50m). This could not be called controlled, sustained flight, but it was a start. To fund further experiments, Ader turned to the French Ministry of War, which was eager to explore any "secret weapon" that might give France an edge over its neighbor, Germany. Armed with the first military budget for airplane development, Ader built a twin-engined aircraft, the Avion III. But when tested in front of military observers in October 1897, it failed to get off the ground. Funding was cut off, and Ader's experiments came to an end.

The most prominent advocate of the power-centered approach to flight was Sir Hiram Maxim, the American-born inventor of the Maxim machine gun. He wrote that it was "neither necessary nor practical to imitate the bird… Give us a motor and we will very soon give you a successful flying machine." In the 1890s, Maxim devoted a large part of his fortune to developing a huge biplane on his estate in Kent, England. Maxim did not intend this giant to fly in any conventional sense. It sat on a test track consisting of two sets of rails. The airplane was to run on the lower rails while gathering speed for takeoff; the upper rails were to prevent it from rising into free flight, which would inevitably result in a crash. In July 1894 Maxim's machine rose from its rails after accelerating to 42mph (67kmph), only to collide with the upper rails, sustaining heavy damage. His experiments progressed no further.

Maxim, Ader, and other power-centered flight experimenters had given little or no thought to how they would actually fly their machines should they take to the air. Contemporary experimenters in unpowered flight, by contrast, hoped to make progress through building up experience of flying. Their acknowledged leader was the German "flying man," Otto Lilienthal.

BALLOONS AND THE BIRTH OF MILITARY AVIATION

PERHAPS THE FIRST AMERICAN to realize the potential of airpower was Benjamin Franklin, who observed the first balloon flights in 1783 while stationed in France. The following year, the French first used balloons for military purpose at the Battle of Mauberge against the Austrians. Their reconnaissance from balloons contributed to the French victory by allowing them to observe the Austrian forces' makeup and activities.

Interestingly, the Austrians themselves conducted the first air raid in 1849, when they launched 200 unmanned balloons, each carrying a bomb released by a time fuse, against forces defending Venice. Unfortunately, unfavorable winds sent the balloons back over Austrian troops. Both France and Austria tried unsuccessfully to use air-filled balloons in the 1859 Italian campaign.

Union and Confederate forces used balloons during the Civil War, with the Union Army conducting America's first use of airpower for observing Confederate troop movements and spotting artillery fire. But the Union gave up on balloons as early as 1863.

The French returned to using balloons in various colonial campaigns; for example, employing them as bombers during the capture of Dien Bien Phu, Vietnam, in 1884. The grandfather of US military aviation, Adolphus Greeley, revived American interest in balloons in the 1890s, and integrated aviation into the Army Signal Corps. In 1892, one of Greeley's balloons was used to direct artillery fire at the Battle of San Juan Hill, Cuba, during the Spanish-American War.

With the development of powered, lighter-than-air craft such as the Zeppelin, the world's militaries turned away from balloons as weapons in favor of more-maneuverable craft. Still, the Japanese used balloons to bomb Russian forces in Manchuria in 1904 and 1905, and the Italians used them in the capture of Tripoli, Libya, in 1911 and 1912.

Finally, the Japanese used balloons as the first intercontinental strategic weapons system during World War II, when they sent 9,000 gas-filled balloons in an attempt to start fires in US and Canadian cities and forests near the West Coast.

OTTO LILIENTHAL

Born in Pomerania (part of present-day Poland) in 1848, Otto Lilienthal was fascinated from an early age by bird flight. Although he trained as an engineer and ran a factory building steam engines, he remained convinced that ornithology held the key to human flight—a belief reflected in the title of his 1889 publication, *Birdflight as the Basis of Aviation*. Although he became famous for his experiments with what would now be called hang gliders, flying his first one in 1891, he never abandoned the idea of flapping wings as a means of propulsion. In his systematic work on wing shapes, Lilienthal showed a genuinely scientific temperament, but he also possessed a streak of showmanship that helped publicize the pursuit of human flight. He was also a man of great physical courage who had a huge impact on the development of flight. Lilienthal died on August 10, 1896, following a glider crash.

PIONEERING BIRDMAN
Despite his uncompromising methods and "birdman" reputation, Lilienthal's intelligent and systematic approach to flying made him a powerful inspiration to other serious researchers.

The flying man

In some respects Lilienthal was a direct descendant of the medieval "birdmen" and "tower jumpers." Lilienthal's flights—pacing down a hill into the wind, encumbered by his wide birdlike wings, and lifting into a glide that carried him high above the ground—were an impressive spectacle but not consonant with the notion of progress as understood in the late 19th century. It is easy to see why Hiram Maxim, with his powerful state-of-the-art steam engines and expensively constructed test track, dismissed Lilienthal as a "flying squirrel." Yet the apparently eccentric Lilienthal was far more scientific and practical in his exploration of flight than either Maxim or Ader. From a scrupulous study of bird flight and bird anatomy, he concluded that a curved, or cambered, wing was essential to produce lift. He proceeded to carry out experiments with specially constructed test equipment to see which precise wing shape, or airfoil, would give maximum lift.

Even more striking than Lilienthal's systematic study of aerodynamics was his commitment to practical experiment through flying himself. He began by trying out ornithopters, but these inevitably futile wing-flappings were soon succeeded by a more fruitful exploration of the potential of fixed-wing gliders. Between 1891 and 1896, Lilienthal designed and built 16 different gliders, mostly monoplanes but some biplanes. They were light and flimsy structures, made by stretching cotton material over willow and bamboo ribs. But, unlike Maxim's ponderous machine, they actually flew.

In all, Lilienthal carried out more than 2,000 flights, the longest covering a distance of 1,150ft (350m). A key lesson he learned from these experiences was that the air could be a treacherous medium to move through. Since Lilienthal's gliders had no control system, he was obliged to throw his body around to maintain balance and stability amid the shifting air currents. A visiting American journalist described Lilienthal's energetic mode of flight: "He went over my head at a terrific pace, at an elevation of about 50 feet [15m]...The apparatus tipped sideways as if a sudden gust had got under the left wing... then with a powerful throw of his legs he brought the machine once more on an even keel, and sailed away across the fields at the bottom."

The ultimate sacrifice

Repeated flights in such unstable machines involved an astonishing level of risk. Lilienthal did devise a shock absorber to protect him if he crashed, but only used it fitfully. On August 9, 1896, caught in a sudden gust of wind, his glider stalled and crashed. He died of his injuries the following day. By then Lilienthal was a famous man. Photographs of him in flight had inspired a great deal of public interest, and his writings had been translated into several languages. His most successful glider, the No. 11 standard monoplane, had been sold to a number of enthusiasts, making it the first aircraft to be produced in quantity. Inspired by his example, experimenters including Britain's Percy Pilcher and Americans Octave Chanute and the Wright brothers continued to explore glider flight in the last years of the century.

Yet there were serious limitations to Lilienthal's work. Although his experiments had demonstrated how essential a control system would be to any flying machine, he had failed to progress beyond control by the shifting of the pilot's body weight. Moreover, his gliders were only suitable for sport. If flight were ever to have any practical use, it would have to involve powered machines. But when Lilienthal turned his attention to powered flight, he reverted to the hopeless notion of using an engine to power flapping wings.

IMPRESSIVE SPECTACLE
Otto Lilienthal's glider experiments attracted substantial crowds and won him a reputation as "the flying man." Most of the tests were carried out at Lichterfelde, outside Berlin, where Lilienthal built a conical hill that allowed him to take off from any side, responding to the direction of the wind.

LAUNCHING THE GREAT AERODROME

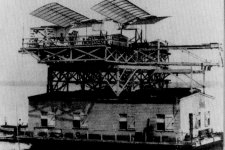

DASHED DREAMS
The first attempt to fly the Great Aerodrome was made in October 1903. Catapulted on a trolley along a track atop a houseboat, the flying machine headed downward the moment it reached the end of the track and plunged into the Potomac. The "pilot" was rescued and the wreck of the Aerodrome towed away for repair.

ON OCTOBER 7, 1903, engineer Charles Manly climbed aboard a massive flying machine perched on top of a houseboat on a stretch of the Potomac River 40 miles (65km) south of Washington, D.C. The machine was Samuel Pierpont Langley's Great Aerodrome, the product of a costly four-year project to achieve manned heavier-than-air flight. An audience of journalists and military and scientific observers had been invited to witness its first takeoff.

Manly was a mechanical wizard who had devised the airplane's innovative 52hp lightweight gasoline engine. He was expected to function as more of a passenger than a pilot, since Langley's machine was supposed to be so stable it would fly itself.

With the engine running sweetly, Manly raised his arm and a laborer wielded an ax, cutting a retaining cable. The catapult trolley shot forward, accelerating the Aerodrome to the end of its launch track. Langley described the fiasco that followed: "Just as the machine left the track, those who were watching... noticed that the machine was jerked violently down at the front... and under the full power of its engine was pulled into the water, carrying with it its engineer." Manly struggled clear of the plane to be rescued.

Langley was now under enormous pressure to deliver on his promise of manned flight. By the time the Aerodrome had been repaired it was winter. On the afternoon of December 8, conditions were far from favorable but, as Langley wrote, "the funds for continuing the work were exhausted, rendering it

As the 19th century drew to a close, the attaching of an engine to some form of glider had suddenly become more feasible through the development of the internal combustion engine, which had the potential to generate more power per weight than any steam engine. Lilienthal's disciple Percy Pilcher was the first would-be aviator to develop a gasoline aero-engine. He intended to use the 4hp power plant to drive a propeller attached to one of his gliders. But in September 1899, while the powered machine was still being assembled, Pilcher was killed when his glider fell apart during a demonstration flight.

The deaths of Lilienthal and Pilcher were a major setback for those who believed in gliding as the route to powered manned flight. The road seemed open for followers of the power-focused tradition to triumph, in the person of distinguished American scientist Samuel Pierpont Langley. Dismissive of Lilienthal and his followers, Langley believed that the application of sufficient power to an aerodynamically stable machine would solve the problem of flight. In 1896, he felt he had proved his point by flying steam-powered model aircraft off the roof of a houseboat on the Potomac River. The models, which he called Aerodromes from the Greek for "air runners," had a wingspan of around 14ft (4.25m). One flew for 1 minute 30 seconds and another for 1 minute 45 seconds.

Had Langley ended his work there, his contribution to aviation history would have been a resounding success. But the temptation to pursue manned flight proved too strong. In 1898 the United States went to war with Spain. The US War Department offered Langley generous funding to produce a flying machine, regarded as a potential weapon of war. With a budget of $50,000, plus the resources of the Smithsonian to call on, Langley fondly expected to achieve manned flight by the end of 1899. Yet delay followed delay. Langley settled on a gasoline engine to power his airplane, but it took years to develop one with the power-to-weight ratio he required. Building a full-scale version of his Aerodrome models also proved taxing for the Smithsonian workshops.

SAMUEL PIERPONT LANGLEY

Samuel Pierpont Langley (1834–1906) rose to prominence as an astrophysicist working at the Allegheny Observatory in Pennsylvania. Recognized as one of America's leading scientists, he was appointed to the prestigious position of Secretary of the Smithsonian Institution in Washington, D.C., in 1887.

Langley began investigating the practicality of flight in the 1880s and continued his experiments at the Smithsonian, exploiting its resources. He progressed from building small models powered by rubber bands to larger steam-powered "Aerodrome" models. In stark contrast to the Wright brothers, Langley developed no hands-on experience of either building flying machines or piloting them. His manned airplane, the Great Aerodrome, was the product of money and bureaucratic organization applied to the problem of flight. Its very public failure in 1903 was a crushing blow to the vanity of a proud man.

MAN OF LETTERS
A respected public figure with an impressive reputation as a scientist, Langley was humiliated by the Aerodrome fiasco.

The project ended up way over budget and four years behind schedule. And the huge flying machine that resulted simply did not work. Aerodynamically and structurally unsound, with no adequate control system, it twice plunged straight from the launch into the Potomac, taking Langley's reputation with it.

The failure of this government-funded project conducted by America's leading scientist caused many people to conclude that heavier-than-air flight would never be a reality. Ironically, a mere nine days after Langley's last failed attempt with the Great Aerodrome in December 1903, two bicycle makers from Dayton, Ohio, proved the skeptics wrong.

UNDER CONSTRUCTION
Workmen assemble Langley's Great Aerodrome on its launch track on top of a houseboat, ready for the first flight. An elaborate catapult mechanism had been created to propel the flying machine along the track and into the air.

impossible to wait until spring for more suitable weather for making a test…" This time the attempt took place off Anacostia, at the edge of Washington, where crowds of onlookers lined the riverside. The brave Manly once more shot along the launch track and for a moment the huge machine lifted into the air, before the whole tail section sadly crumpled and broke away. Plunged into the icy water, Manly was trapped under the wreckage, but pulled himself free.

Stung by the ridicule heaped upon him, Langley blamed the failure on a faulty launch mechanism, insisting his Aerodrome could have flown.

BRITISH EXPERIMENTER
British pioneer Percy Pilcher demonstrates his Bat glider, which he developed under the influence of Lilienthal. At the time of his death in 1899, he was experimenting with putting an engine on a glider—the path to powered flight that the Wrights would follow.

FIGHT TO BE FIRST

BY 1900, THE DREAM OF ACHIEVING POWERED FLIGHT WAS CLOSE TO BECOMING REALITY. THE QUESTION BEING ASKED WAS—WHO WOULD GET THERE FIRST?

"For some years I have been afflicted with the belief that flight is possible to man. My disease has increased in severity and I feel that it will cost me an increased amount of money if not my life."

WILBUR WRIGHT, 1900

LATE IN THE AFTERNOON of Saturday, August 8, 1908, on a racetrack at Hunaudières outside Le Mans in western France, Wilbur Wright unhurriedly settled himself at the controls of a flying machine. Dressed in a gray business suit, a high starched collar, and a golf cap, this phlegmatic man was preparing for his first flight in Europe. He hoped to establish in the eyes of the world that he and his brother Orville had been the first to achieve heavier-than-air powered flight.

Watching from the stands was a handful of flight enthusiasts, most of whom had come in the hope and expectation that the American would fail. They all knew that the Wrights claimed to have flown as long ago as 1903, but there was widespread skepticism about this alleged conquest of the air. France had its own claimants to the title of "first to fly"— including Alberto Santos-Dumont, who had briefly lifted off the ground in a heavier-than-air machine in 1906, and Henri Farman, who had flown a

A RESERVED MAN
Although Wilbur Wright was a man of austere and reserved temperament, his private letters reveal a caustic sense of humor, as well as piercing intelligence.

full kilometer (three-fifths mile) circuit earlier in 1908. Since Wilbur Wright's arrival in France, the press had been running articles deriding his claims to primacy; he was, they said, "not a flier, but a liar."

Wilbur Wright cannot have been certain that he was about to prove the skeptics wrong. He had never operated this particular machine, the Type A. He seemed to take forever over his preparations, ignoring the crowd's mounting impatience, until he finally announced: "Gentlemen, now I'm going to fly." Wright's assistants set the two propellers whirling, weights dropped from the catapult derrick, and the flying machine sped along its launch rail and lifted into the air. Traveling at a height of about 30ft (10m), Wright approached the end of the racetrack and put his machine into a graceful banked turn to come back over the heads of the spectators. After completing one more circuit of the track, he brought the machine gently down on its skids. There was an uproar. Clapping and cheering, the spectators ran forward to mob the pilot. Lasting just 1 minute 45 seconds, the flight had exceeded any display of flying the French had ever seen.

Since that day at Le Mans, it has been generally—though not always universally—accepted that the Wright brothers were indeed the inventors of the first heavier-than-air machine capable of sustained, controlled, powered flight.

THE WRIGHT BROTHERS' 1903 FLYER
On December 17, 1903, Orville Wright made the world's first powered heavier-than-air flight at Kill Devil Hills, Kitty Hawk, North Carolina. The Flyer flew for 12 seconds over a distance of 120ft (37m). On the fourth and final flight, with Wilbur at the controls, it flew for 59 seconds over a distance of 852ft (260m).

WRIGHT SILENCES CRITICS
Wilbur Wright showed off the Type A Flyer in a series of demonstration flights in Europe in 1908. The flights received popular acclaim and persuaded most European air enthusiasts that the Wrights had indeed been the first to fly. One French journalist wrote of the "masterly assurance and incomparable elegance" of Wilbur's flying displays.

But it still seems one of history's more mischievous twists that a goal that had eluded distinguished scientists and engineers, as well as rich enthusiasts, should have been attained by two brothers who ran a bicycle shop in Dayton, Ohio.

Men of their time

Although they lived far from the centers of power and fashion, Orville and Wilbur Wright had grown up very much in touch with contemporary currents of thought and innovation. Their formative years were a time when new inventions proliferated —the telephone, automobiles, electric light, wireless telegraphy, and the movies. Inventors such as Thomas Edison and Alexander Graham Bell were the heroes of the age. It would have been surprising had the Wrights not taken some interest in the widely publicized flight experiments of the 1890s. Interest seems to have blossomed into committed research through the perception that flight was, as Wilbur wrote, "almost the only great problem that has not been… carried to a point where further progress is very difficult."

From the outset, the Wrights displayed the systematic approach that was to characterize their entire endeavor. Their first need was to absorb existing knowledge. In May 1899, Wilbur wrote a letter to the Smithsonian Institution, asking for any papers it might have on flight and a reading list of books on the subject. "I wish to avail myself of all that is already known," Wilbur wrote, "and then if possible add my mite to help on the future worker who will attain final success." The letter received a prompt and helpful response.

When the Wrights had acquainted themselves with the works of, among others, Cayley, Pénaud, Chanute, Lilienthal, and Langley, they identified an area that seemed to have been neglected: control. Men such as Langley had imagined a flying machine to be rather like a car—an essentially stable machine

> "… I have some pet theories as to the proper construction of a flying machine…"
>
> **WILBUR WRIGHT**
> LETTER TO THE SMITHSONIAN INSTITUTION, 1899

to be switched on and then steered. However, the Wrights instinctively felt that a flying machine was more like a bicycle, and would need to be flown with constant adjustments of balance. From the start they posed the problem not simply of how to build a flying machine, but also how to fly it.

First experiments

Their first breakthrough came from a more traditional direction. Watching soaring buzzards, Wilbur was struck by the movement of the feathers on their wingtips, which kept the birds' lateral balance. The brothers puzzled for a long time over achieving a similar effect on an aircraft wing, until Wilbur had a sudden moment of inspiration. Absent-mindedly twisting the ends of a narrow cardboard box in opposite directions, he saw that the same could be done with a wing. "Wing warping" had been devised.

By 1900, the Wrights were ready to begin experiments with a glider, which they built in their bicycle workshop. Glider experiments required wind, and having contacted the US Weather Bureau, they established that Kitty Hawk, a small beach settlement on the coast of North Carolina, would provide a suitable location. In September 1900, the Wright brothers pitched camp at Kitty Hawk and assembled their first glider.

TESTING THE GLIDER
Intended as a man-carrying glider, this kite-glider (their second) had a wingspan of 17ft (5.2m) and a forward elevator. However, tests at Kill Devil Hills, now Kitty Hawk, in September 1900, soon revealed that the efficiency of the airfoil was insufficient to support a man's weight, unless the wind was very strong.

WILBUR AND ORVILLE WRIGHT

WILBUR (1867–1912) AND ORVILLE (1871–1948) were the third and fifth sons of Milton Wright, a bishop in the evangelical Church of the United Brethren in Christ, and his wife Susan. Wilbur would have attended college but for a freak sports accident at the age of 18 that undermined his health for several years. In any event, neither brother had a college education and both stayed at home, running several businesses before moving into the bicycle business in 1892. Originally setting up just to rent bicycles, they soon expanded into building their own, which they sold for a remarkably low price ($18 compared to the $160 that Orville paid for his first bicycle in 1892). Inspired by the death of Otto Lilienthal in 1896, the Wright brothers started to finance their aeronautical experiments from 1899 onward with the profits from the bicycle business. They calculated that it cost them $1,000 to crack the problem of powered flight. Their experiences dealing with something as inherently unstable as a bicycle, and the insights it gave them into combining lightness with strength to achieve balance and control, gave them a novel approach to the problem of creating a workable heavier-than-air flying machine.

Inventive and self-reliant, the brothers not only had the practical skills to make their own tools and engines, they were also voracious readers with the intellect to work out complex theoretical problems. Their ingenuity and persistence as methodical experimenters was matched by their physical bravery as test pilots. Yet they were cautious individuals—Wilbur, in particular, flew only when absolutely necessary for experimental or demonstration purposes.

Neither brother had any taste for luxurious living. They did not smoke or drink, and they were rarely seen with any women other than their sister. When Wilbur carried out his demonstration flights in France in 1908, he was cheered by crowds and courted by princes and businessmen, but he cooked his own meals and slept in a hangar with his flying machine.

The brothers combined supreme self-confidence with a deep mistrust of everyone outside their family circle. They were stubborn, hard-headed businessmen, relentless in the legal pursuit of those they thought had wronged them. Essentially private people, they coped very well with the immense fame they earned. Wilbur tragically died of typhoid fever in 1912; Orville lived on into the jet age, dying in 1948.

WRIGHT CYCLE SHOP
The bicycle became fashionable in the 1890s, and the Wright brothers combined their entrepreneurial and engineering skills when they opened up their own "Wright Cycle Co." in Dayton, Ohio, in 1892.

THE TOAST OF EUROPE
Wilbur (left) and Orville are pictured during their 1909 European tour, when they were feted by kings, politicians, and generals in France, Italy, and England.

IN THE WORKSHOP
Orville (right) is shown with a worker at the Wright Cycle Company workshop in 1897. The availability of raw materials and machinery in their well-equipped shop helped the Wright brothers with their investigations into the flying problem.

Testing the gliders

In many ways, this biplane resembled the machine in which they would eventually achieve powered flight. The pilot lay face down in a gap in the lower wing, a position that minimized drag. Sticking out in front of him was a movable elevator with which, using a hand lever, he controlled horizontal pitch. The wing-warping mechanism was operated by the pilot's feet. When the weather was right for a glide, the contraption was dragged to the top of a high dune. Either Wilbur or Orville climbed on board, while the other brother and a local assistant—usually the helpful Dan or Bill Tate—each held a wingtip. When the pilot was ready, they ran the glider downhill into the wind until it lifted off into skimming flight.

To their immense satisfaction, the Wrights found that the controls operated well, achieving balanced flight and smooth landings.

Back in Dayton, through the winter of 1900–01, they worked on a new glider that would be the largest anyone had yet flown. The most unsatisfactory feature of the 1900 glider had been the lift, which had fallen short of expectations. The Wrights had worked out the wing size and shape—crucially, the degree of camber—in line with Lilienthal's published calculations of lift and load. Now they had a second try, based on the same figures, almost doubling the surface area of the wings and using a deeper camber.

The Wrights returned to the North Carolina dunes for a second, more prolonged stay in the summer of 1901, this time setting up at Kill Devil Hills some miles from Kitty Hawk. They had by then become established members of the scattered fraternity of flight enthusiasts and were in regular correspondence with its expert, the veteran Octave Chanute, who came to witness their new round of experiments. These did not go smoothly. It took many attempts before the glider would fly at all, and when it did get off the ground, the nose proved liable to pitch dangerously upward or downward. Substantial changes to the shape of the wing restored control, but the risks of these experiments were becoming very apparent.

On one occasion Wilbur suffered a stall reminiscent of the one that killed Lilienthal. Fortunately the front elevator proved an excellent safety device, producing a cushioned fall instead of a fatal crash.

One of the Wrights' objectives in the 1901 flights was to achieve controlled banked turns using the wing-warping mechanism, but these experiments led to a side-slipping crash in which Wilbur was injured. The brothers struggled to understand why their turns would not work, eventually deciding that the wing warping was creating drag effects that upset the machine's aerodynamics. Wilbur later wrote: "When we left Kitty Hawk at the end of 1901… we considered our experiments a failure."

> "We could not understand that there was anything about a bird that could not be built on a larger scale."
>
> ORVILLE WRIGHT

UNSTABLE BUT RESPONSIVE

Wilbur (left) and Orville (at the controls) launch their No. 3 glider, on which they tested and mastered their control systems, in 1902. A movable rear rudder worked with wing warping to give the craft lateral control, allowing smooth banked turns.

But the brothers did not give up. Instead, deciding that "the calculations on which all flying machines had been based were unreliable," they set out to produce their own data for the lift created by various wing shapes moving at different speeds and angles. The results of these experiments with a homemade wind tunnel were then applied to a completely new glider, ready for the 1902 flying season.

AN IMPORTANT VISITOR

The picture above shows the Wrights' camp at Kill Devil Hills, North Carolina, during the visit of Octave Chanute (seated second from left) in August 1901. A pioneer of glider design, Chanute took much interest in the Wrights' glider experiments (right).

THE WRIGHTS' RIGOROUS EXPERIMENTS

IN THE WINTER OF 1901–02, the Wright brothers carried out a remarkable set of experiments that overturned accepted wisdom on wing design. Their goal was to test a wide range of potential wing shapes in order to establish their aerodynamic characteristics.

First, they conducted fairly rough-and-ready experiments on a bicycle. As one of the brothers cycled along to create an airflow, he then adjusted the angle of the airfoil until it balanced the wind pressure on the flat plate. Although the bicycle experiments showed that previously published figures (by Lilienthal and others) were wrong, they lacked precision. The key experimental challenge was to create a perfectly controlled airflow and an exact record of the resulting performance. For this the Wrights built a wind tunnel, in which they tested airfoils for two months under controlled conditions. This gave them a highly accurate series of figures that they were then able to apply to wing design.

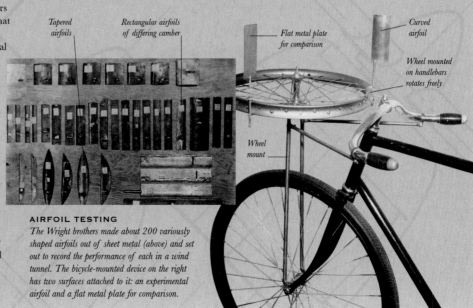

Tapered airfoils

Rectangular airfoils of differing camber

Flat metal plate for comparison

Curved airfoil

Wheel mounted on handlebars rotates freely

Wheel mount

AIRFOIL TESTING

The Wright brothers made about 200 variously shaped airfoils out of sheet metal (above) and set out to record the performance of each in a wind tunnel. The bicycle-mounted device on the right has two surfaces attached to it: an experimental airfoil and a flat metal plate for comparison.

THE WORLD'S FIRST POWERED FLIGHT

WAITING EXPECTANTLY
The Wright's Flyer sits outside the makeshift hangar at their Kill Devil Hills camp (left). Below, the brothers' ground crew and audience are pictured next to the Flyer, which has been transferred to its wooden rail just before Wilbur's flight of December 14, 1903.

ON THE MORNING OF DECEMBER 17, 1903, the wind at Kill Devil Hills was gusting at up to 30mph (48kmph). This would help the Wright Flyer get off the ground, but was sure to create problems in controlling the untested machine. Although Wilbur Wright's first brief hop into the air with the Flyer three days earlier had ended swiftly and ingloriously, the Wrights were certain their powered machine could fly.

The brothers had agreed to alternate at the controls, so it was Orville's turn first on this occasion. At 10:00am a flag was run up to signal to the helpful personnel of the nearby Kill Devil Hills lifesaving station, who had agreed to act as witnesses and helpers. The brothers then set about laying a wooden launch track alongside their campsite. The Flyer was too heavy to be launched like a glider—by two men holding the wings—and wheels would have sunk into the soft sand. So the machine was to be launched from a

> "It was only a flight of 12 seconds, and it was an uncertain, wavy, creeping sort of flight… but it was a real flight at last and not a glide."
>
> **ORVILLE WRIGHT**
> ON THE FIRST POWERED HEAVIER-THAN-AIR FLIGHT

trolley running along a wooden rail. Wilbur and Orville stood by the machine while the engine warmed up. Then, as one of the lifesavers, John Daniels, later recounted, "they shook hands, and we couldn't help notice how they held on to each other's hand… like two folks parting who weren't sure they'd ever see each other again." A camera had been positioned to capture the scene and Daniels was entrusted with operating the shutter. Orville mounted the machine, lying face down. Then, amid the racket of the engine and excited shouts from the onlookers, the machine was released from its restraining rope and set off along the track. As it lifted into the air, Daniels took the picture below.

Like his brother three days earlier, Orville found it hard to control the Flyer, and after 12 seconds in the air, he came down with a bump. Whether this or two subsequent attempts constituted true powered flights was rendered irrelevant by the fourth attempt. Orville, this time an onlooker, described what happened in his diary: "At just 12 o'clock Will started on the fourth and last trip. The machine started off with its ups and downs as it had before, but by the time he had gone over three or four hundred feet he had it under much better control,

AN HISTORIC IMAGE
On December 17, 1903, the Wright Flyer lifted off the sands in the first-ever manned flight. Orville was at the controls and Wilbur, caught midstride, watches in amazement. This photograph, taken by John Daniels, became one of the most reproduced images of the 20th century.

and was traveling on a fairly even course." Wilbur flew for 59 seconds, traveling a distance of 852ft (260m), before the Flyer pitched down to a bone-jarring landing, breaking the elevator support. The Flyer had spent less than a minute in the air, but it was enough to constitute sustained, controlled, powered flight!

Shortly after this momentous event, the Flyer was caught by a gust of wind as it was being carried back to the camp and rolled over, taking with it Daniels, who was lucky to end the day with no more than cuts and bruises. The flying machine was a wreck, but the brothers did not let the incident spoil their delight in their achievement. After lunch the brothers walked over to the Kitty Hawk weather station to telegraph home the news of their success and imminent return.

CAUGHT IN TIME
This handheld stopwatch was used to time the four flights made by the Wrights on December 17, 1903. Below is the understated telegram that Orville sent their father asking him to inform the press of their successful flight.

HARD LANDING
At the end of the fourth flight, which lasted for almost a minute, Wilbur landed hard and broke the Flyer's elevator support. It was then transported back to the Wrights' campsite, where they intended to repair the damage.

The new data led the Wrights to design a wing that was longer and slimmer, with a flatter camber. For the first time they added a tail—two fixed vertical fins that they hoped would prevent the machine from going out of control in banked turns.

The 1902 No. 3 glider proved that the Wrights' calculations were correct. Aerodynamically, it was the most efficient machine yet built, but at first it was even more tricky to control than their previous model. After a few dangerous spills, the Wrights took stock and came up with a solution. The culprit was the fixed tailfins. They needed to be movable so they could be turned to counterbalance drag. With typical ingenuity, the brothers created a control system that linked the rudder to the wing-warping mechanism. By the summer's end they were making controlled glides of up to 600ft (200m), staying airborne for up to 26 seconds.

Now the Wrights were ready to embark on the momentous step to powered flight. For this they needed an engine and a propeller. When automobile companies proved incapable of supplying a suitable engine, the Wrights had one made by their assistant Charlie Taylor, who delivered a remarkable gasoline engine weighing 180lb (82kg) and delivering 12hp. In contrast, the problem of propeller design proved astonishingly complex, forcing the brothers to tackle intricate questions of theoretical physics and mathematics.

The Wrights returned to Kill Devil Hills in late September 1903, well aware that, at that very moment, Samuel Pierpont Langley was preparing for the first flight of his Great Aerodrome. When news came through that his first attempt had failed, Wilbur wrote: "It seems to be our turn to throw now, and I wonder what our luck will be."

For a time, luck seemed to be against them. In stationary tests, the engine proved temperamental and eventually damaged the propeller shafts. They were sent for repair, but when tests resumed at the end of November, one of the repaired shafts was found to be cracked. Orville returned to Dayton to make completely new steel shafts.

PRESS MISREPRESENTATION
Typical of the stories circulating in the days following the Kitty Hawk flights was this headline from the Norfolk Virginian-Pilot. Such wild inaccuracies provoked the brothers into issuing a press release containing exact details of their achievement.

Langley's second attempt to fly his Aerodrome failed on December 8, and the way was now open for the Wrights. On their first attempt, on December 14, Wilbur could not control the machine, which came down heavily just after takeoff. But on Thursday, December 17, the goal of so many dreamers was finally attained.

Although the event did not go unreported —the Wrights themselves issued a press release—the public response was muted. The Langley Aerodrome fiasco had created a climate of skepticism, and most newspaper editors were inclined to dismiss claims of heavier-than-air flight out of hand. The attitude of the Wright brothers themselves did nothing to allay skepticism. In their January 1904 statement they concluded: "We do not feel ready at present to give out any pictures or detailed descriptions of the machine." The Wrights had not originally pursued a policy of deliberate secrecy, but once they achieved powered flight, they were determined to stop anyone else from stealing their invention before they could profit from it.

After December 17, 1903, the Wrights still faced a daunting technical challenge. Transferring their operations back to Dayton, they worked

Derrick

Take-off rail

ASSISTED TAKEOFF
From 1904, the Wright brothers used the device shown above to assist takeoff. A weight, attached to the front of the airplane by a rope, was raised to the top of a derrick. When the airplane's engine had started and the pilot was ready, the weight was released and its fall jerked the machine along the rail.

on building and testing improved models of their flying machine. The 1904 Flyer II had trouble getting off the ground under the very different weather conditions of Ohio. With the help of a catapult-assisted takeoff system, Flyer II proved capable of staying in the air for more than five minutes. However, between June and October 1905, in the much-improved Flyer III the Wrights made flights of up to 38 minutes' duration, covering more than 20 miles (30km) at a time. If anyone wanted to question whether the Wright

1903 Wright Flyer

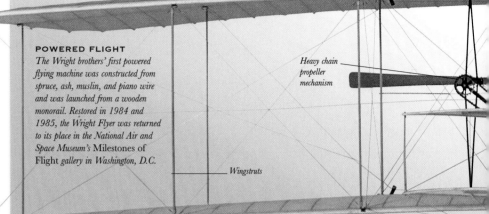

POWERED FLIGHT
The Wright brothers' first powered flying machine was constructed from spruce, ash, muslin, and piano wire and was launched from a wooden monorail. Restored in 1984 and 1985, the Wright Flyer was returned to its place in the National Air and Space Museum's Milestones of Flight *gallery in Washington, D.C.*

Heavy chain propeller mechanism

Wingstruts

EACH OF THE FLIGHTS made by the Wright brothers at Kitty Hawk in December 1903 was marked by instability, since the nose (and therefore the entire aircraft) would slowly bounce up and down. Sharp contact with the ground on the last flight broke the front elevator, ending that season's flying.

Between 1903 and 1908 the Wrights developed their original Flyer into a more robust and powerful machine, without making any fundamental changes to its configuration or control systems. All the Wright flying machines were controlled in pitch by the front elevator, in yaw by twin vertical rudders, and in roll by the twisting of the wing tips, known as wing warping.

Flying like cyclists, the Wrights kept the airplane balanced with continuous small adjustments of the controls and leaning the machine into turns. This required considerable experience—a "feel" for flying that had to be learned. The trickiest feature was the front elevator, which tended to be overly sensitive. Any slight error of judgment could cause the aircraft to climb or dive alarmingly.

UNDER CONSTRUCTION
Orville Wright attaches wing-warping wires to a wing in the primitive hangar at Kill Devil Hills. Wing warping was devised by Wilbur to control the Flyer in roll. Twisting the wings to lift one side or the other allowed it not only to fly level, but also to make banked turns, rather like a bicycle cornering.

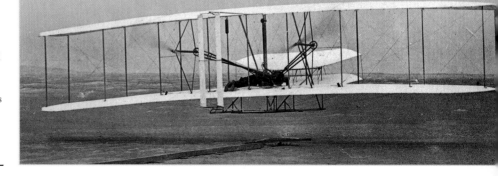

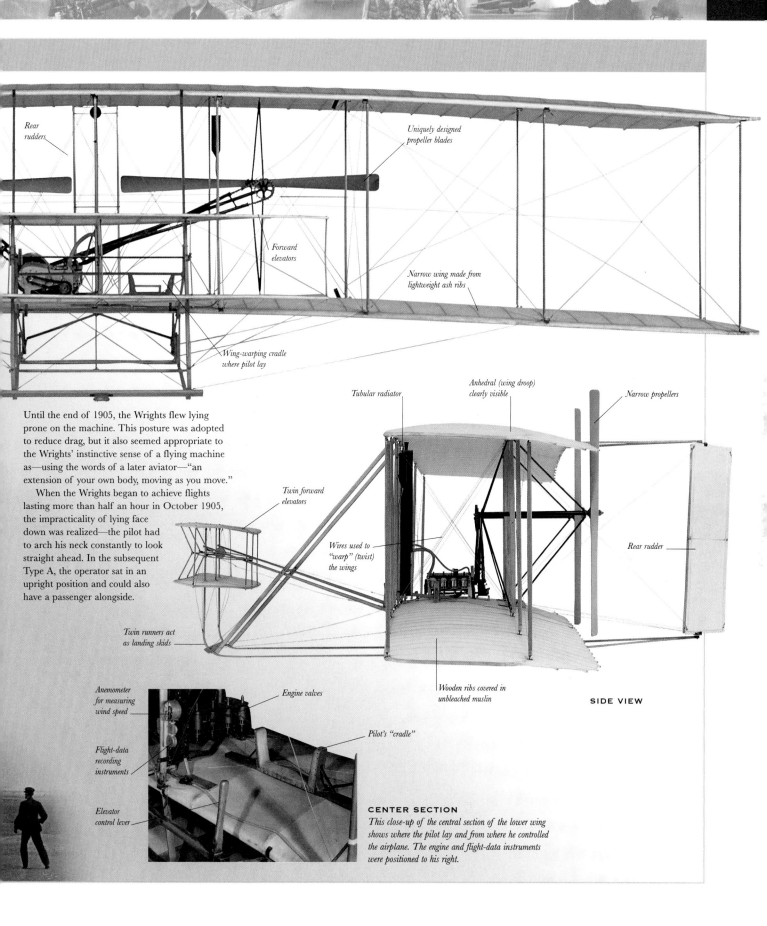

Rear rudders

Uniquely designed propeller blades

Forward elevators

Narrow wing made from lightweight ash ribs

Wing-warping cradle where pilot lay

Until the end of 1905, the Wrights flew lying prone on the machine. This posture was adopted to reduce drag, but it also seemed appropriate to the Wrights' instinctive sense of a flying machine as—using the words of a later aviator—"an extension of your own body, moving as you move."

When the Wrights began to achieve flights lasting more than half an hour in October 1905, the impracticality of lying face down was realized—the pilot had to arch his neck constantly to look straight ahead. In the subsequent Type A, the operator sat in an upright position and could also have a passenger alongside.

Twin forward elevators

Twin runners act as landing skids

Tubular radiator

Anhedral (wing droop) clearly visible

Narrow propellers

Wires used to "warp" (twist) the wings

Rear rudder

Wooden ribs covered in unbleached muslin

SIDE VIEW

Anemometer for measuring wind speed

Engine valves

Flight-data recording instruments

Pilot's "cradle"

Elevator control lever

CENTER SECTION

This close-up of the central section of the lower wing shows where the pilot lay and from where he controlled the airplane. The engine and flight-data instruments were positioned to his right.

PORTABLE PLANE

Brazilian pioneer Alberto Santos-Dumont's tiny 19 Demoiselle monoplane, built in 1907, had a wingspan of just 18ft (6m) and was perhaps the first ultralight. It was designed as an aerial "runabout" and easily separated into two parts (the tail, and the wings and propeller), to allow for easy transportation.

brothers' flights in 1903 deserved to be called "the first," there could be no doubt whatsoever that by the end of 1905 they were the only people in the world with a practical flying machine. At this time, the brothers took the extraordinary decision to cease all further flying experiments, devoting much of their effort to a search for lucrative business contracts. The obvious potential customer for the new flying machine was the Army.

The brothers suggested in a letter to their congressman, Robert Nevin, in January 1905, that the machine could be used for "scouting and carrying messages in time of war." But when Nevin raised the matter with the US War Department, the official response was dismissive. Faced with rejection at home, the Wrights approached the British and French military

establishments. A French delegation visited Dayton to negotiate with the Wrights in the spring of 1906, but no agreement was reached. The crux of the problem was that the Wrights would not demonstrate their flying machine until someone had signed a contract to buy it, but potential buyers were reluctant to commit without seeing the machine in action.

The Wrights' decision to stop flying was extremely risky. Details of most aspects of their work were known to aviation enthusiasts. Other experimenters had a serious chance of catching up with or overtaking them. In 1907, the inventor Alexander Graham Bell set up the Aerial Experiment Association in Hammondsport,

GLENN H. CURTISS

ONE OF THE FOUNDING FATHERS of American aviation, Glenn H. Curtiss (1878–1930) was born in Hammondsport, New York. Like the Wright brothers, Curtiss started in the bicycle business, before moving on to building and racing motorcycles. His skill in producing lightweight motorcycle engines attracted the attention of inventor Alexander Graham Bell, who in 1907 invited Curtiss to join his Aerial Experiment Association—where he played a leading part in designing a series of aircraft controlled by ailerons, rather than the wing warping used by the Wrights. On Independence Day 1908, Curtiss made the first public flight in the United States in *June Bug*.

A fearless pilot, Curtiss was often found at early aviation meetings, specializing in speed events. He eventually set up his own aircraft manufacturing company, pioneering seaplane and flying boat designs. By 1914 he was the leading aircraft manufacturer in the United States.

RACING MAN

Before turning to flying in 1907, Glenn Curtiss was a successful racing motorcyclist. After winning many prizes for his flying skills, Curtiss went on to organize his own flying displays (right). His new career was hampered by a bitterly contested patent dispute with the Wright brothers over their wing-warping technology.

OFFICIAL SOUVENIR BOOK & DAILY PROGRAM

Glenn H. Curtiss Aviation Meets

PRICE 10 CENTS

FIRST EUROPEAN FLIGHT
Renowned for his inventiveness and courage, France's first aviation hero was the Brazilian Alberto Santos-Dumont. He made the first powered heavier-than-air flight (little more than a hop) in Europe three years after the Wright brothers. Standing upright in his unwieldy 14bis box-kite aircraft, Santos-Dumont flew 722ft (220m) on November 12, 1906, in Bagatelle, Paris.

New York, bringing together a talented team—including motorcycle manufacturer Glenn H. Curtiss—with the avowed goal of building "a practical airplane which will carry a man and be driven through the air on its own power."

Main competition

The most potent challenge to the Wright brothers came from France. In a tradition dating back to the Montgolfier brothers, the French considered themselves the natural leaders in world aviation. Reports of the Wright brothers' achievements greatly perturbed the French enthusiasts centered on the prestigious Aéro-Club de France. Some reacted by disparaging what the Wrights had done; all felt that it was their patriotic duty to prove that the French could do better. Fortunately

for the Americans, France's would-be aeronauts had more enthusiasm than method. Despite the existence of clear published accounts of the Wrights' wing-warping system, no French aviator understood the need for control in roll. Yet, stimulated by the offer of large cash prizes for variously defined "first flights" from rich enthusiasts, the French began to create successful flying machines.

A FAMILY BUSINESS
Brothers Gabriel (left) and Charles Voisin established one of the world's first airplane factories, in the Parisian suburb of Billancourt, in 1906. By 1918, it had produced over 10,000 aircraft.

The first man to claim some of this prize money was the popular Brazilian-Parisian, Alberto Santos-Dumont, already famous for his airship exploits. In 1906, Santos-Dumont built the 14bis,

HENRI FARMAN

HENRI FARMAN (1874–1958), the son of a British journalist, was brought up in France. Although he sometimes wrote his first name as "Henry," he never spoke English. Farman originally sought to satisfy his adventurous and unconventional temperament in the Bohemian lifestyle of a Parisian art student, but soon found headier excitement in the pursuit of speed. In the 1890s he took up the new sport of bicycle racing, and from there progressed to automobile racing. In

1907 he transferred his sporting prowess and mechanical know-how to the new craze for heavier-than-air flying machines. His successes as a pilot soon made him one of the most famous men in France and reasonably wealthy. He used his money to set up an aircraft factory, enjoying immediate success with a box-kite biplane. His brother Maurice became a partner in the enterprise, and in 1912 the Farmans became France's largest aircraft manufacturers, producing over 12,000 military aircraft during WWI. The company was taken over by the state in 1936.

CHECKING THE CONTROLS
Henri Farman, at the controls of a Voisin-Farman biplane, prepared to take two passengers for a ride (left). The postcard above commemorates Farman's historic first "town-to-town" flight from Bouy to Reims on October 30, 1908.

an ungainly, impractical biplane, with its fuselage and front elevator sticking out in front of the pilot, who stood upright in a wicker balloon basket. Its design owed much to the box kite developed by Australian Lawrence Hargrave in the 1890s—an influence that was present in many early European flying machines. Santos-Dumont's public demonstrations during the autumn of 1906 caused a sensation. Progressing from tiny hops in September to a longer hop of about 70ft (50m) in October, he ended with a triumphant 722ft (220m) flight on November 12. Although negligible compared with the Wright brothers' flights of the previous year, Santos-Dumont's efforts were greeted in Europe as a major breakthrough. *Le Figaro* trumpeted: "What a triumph! … The air is truly conquered. Santos has flown. Everybody will fly."

French engineering

French aviators had at their disposal the excellent aero-engine, the Antoinette, developed by Léon Levavasseur, and the world's first factory dedicated to aircraft manufacture, set up by the Voisin brothers in 1906. During 1907, both Louis Blériot and Robert Esnault-Pelterie achieved short flights in tractor (powered from the front) monoplanes, a configuration that would soon play a crucial role in the evolution of flight. But the outstanding French performances of

CHEERED TO THE FLAG
Henri Farman made aviation history when he won the Grand Prix d'Aviation by completing the first three-fifths-mile (1-km) circular flight in Europe on January 13, 1908. Wilbur Wright had already made a similar circuit—with banked turns—on September 20, 1904.

In June, Delagrange stayed aloft for more than 18 minutes, and the following month, Curtiss won the Scientific American trophy in his June Bug, for the first flight of over a mile. Then on October 30, 1908, after further modifications, including the addition of four large ailerons to his wings, Farman made the first cross-country flight (between two points, rather than circuits around a field), covering the 17 miles (27km) between Bouy and Reims in 20 minutes.

Success at last

In the winter of 1907–08, pushed into action by the increasingly successful flights of other experimenters, the Wright brothers finally agreed to deals to market their machines. In the United States the agreement was with the Army Signal Corps, and in France with a business syndicate. Each would buy Wright machines if they successfully fulfilled stringent performance criteria in public trials. While Orville stayed behind to prepare for the US military trials, Wilbur set off for France, having shipped an unassembled Flyer ahead of him. However, it turned out that the machine had been severely damaged in customs, and Wilbur had to spend weeks making repairs. Had the aircraft not flown on August 8, 1908, Wilbur would have faced utter public humiliation. Instead, his triumphant demonstration at the Hunaudières racetrack brought instant celebrity. Over the following months he flew repeatedly, attracting huge crowds. Gradually he extended his time in the air, culminating with an extraordinary flight of 2 hours 20 minutes on the final day of the year.

1908 were achieved in modified Voisin biplanes. These basically resembled the Wright flying machine—pusher biplanes with a forward elevator—but they had a box-kite tail structure and lacked any form of lateral control. During 1907, Parisian sculptor Léon Delagrange and sportsman Henri Farman each turned up at the Voisin factory, coming away with his own individually modified version of the biplane. Both men quickly taught themselves to fly, logging up a series of increasingly impressive flights.

As a competitive sportsman, Henri Farman's chief target after learning to fly was to win the 50,000-franc Deutsch-Archdeacon prize for the first person to fly a three-fifths mile (1km) circuit. On January 13, 1908, at Issy-les-Moulineaux outside Paris, a committee of the Aéro-Club de

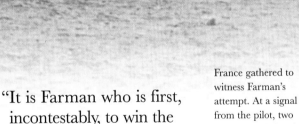

> "It is Farman who is first, incontestably, to win the mastery of the air by airplane."
>
> **ERNEST ARCHDEACON**
> FRENCH AVIATION ENTHUSIAST, JANUARY 13, 1908

France gathered to witness Farman's attempt. At a signal from the pilot, two assistants holding the aircraft by its wingtips let go and the airplane raced forward, lifting into the air. Using the rudder alone, Farman made a wide, flat turn around a pylon placed one-third mile (0.5km) from the start, returning safely to his starting point. The feat was hailed throughout Europe as an historic first, even though the Wrights had achieved the same feat—with smooth, banked turns—in 1904.

ROYAL INTEREST
England's King Edward VII (right), with Orville and Wilbur Wright (wearing his trademark flat cap), watches a flight in France in March 1909. Wilbur wrote: "Princes & millionaires are as thick as fleas."

He also set a new altitude record of 360ft (110m), and carried over 60 passengers, demonstrating that flight had become both practical and safe. Orville's experience in the military trials at Fort Myer, Virginia, was less reassuring. His flights were a resounding success until September 17, when his Flyer crashed with a military observer on board, killing the passenger and injuring Orville. Despite this setback, the army had seen enough to confirm its interest. In France, hostility toward the Wrights largely disappeared, for Wilbur's perfect control over his machine surpassed anything Europe had previously seen. Taken as sufficient proof of the Wrights' claims to earlier flights, aviation journalist François Peyrey expressed the opinion of the over-whelming majority when he wrote: "The Wright brothers are the first men who have succeeded in imitating the birds. To deny it would be childish." French aviators now rushed to incorporate the key Wright characteristic, control in roll, into their machines.

The Wrights were now among the most famous men in the world. In 1909 they were immensely busy, demonstrating flight to the rich and powerful, dealing with the business offers that flooded in from all directions, and training pilots—a necessary part of sales contracts since Wilbur and Orville were the only people who knew how to fly their machines. Early in the year Wilbur was joined in Europe by Orville and their sister Katherine. When they returned to the United States in late spring, they were belatedly feted at home. Dayton celebrated its local heroes with fireworks and a parade; the president received them at the White House; senators adjourned the Senate so that they could see them fly when they came to Fort Myer to complete the Army trials; and an estimated one million people turned out to watch Wilbur make a spectacular flight along the Hudson River. Yet amid this whirlwind of celebration and publicity, the Wrights were already showing signs of pulling back from the aviation circus. They refused to compete for the large cash prizes offered for the first man to fly from London to Manchester, or across the Channel, showing a dislike of such publicity stunts. And in August 1909, the Wrights were the only significant fliers not to attend the Reims air meeting—a defining moment for the future of aviation. Instead they tried to put their aircraft manufacturing business onto a more solid footing.

ORVILLE WRIGHT'S ARMY TRIALS

WHILE WILBUR WAS DEMONSTRATING in Europe, Orville prepared for the all-important US Army tests, arriving in Fort Myer, Virginia, on August 20, 1908. During September, Orville and his Military Flyer set nine new world records, including two for altitude and one for endurance (flying for just under an hour).

However, disaster struck on September 17, when Orville took an official army passenger, Lieutenant Thomas Selfridge, for a ride. On his fourth circuit, he heard a tapping noise, followed by two loud bangs, announcing the loss of a faulty propeller. Orville lost control of the airplane and it smashed into the ground, crumpling into a twisted wreck. Selfridge died a few hours later from a fractured skull. Orville was lucky to escape with serious injuries, including a fractured thigh, broken ribs, and serious scalp wounds.

FIRST CASUALTY
When Thomas Selfridge became the first person to die (right) in a powered aircraft, safety straps had not yet been thought of. Pilots and passengers simply grabbed one of the wing struts to keep themselves on board.

In 1910, the Wright aircraft company was set up by a consortium that included some of the country's wealthiest businessmen, and a factory was opened in Dayton. In Europe, Wright flying machines were made by a number of companies under license. But despite successful new models such as the Baby Wright racer, the Wrights soon ceased to be market leaders, for instead of concentrating their efforts on the development of their airplanes, they spent much of their energy on legal action against their competitors in Europe and the United States for infringement of patents. Their most bitterly fought case, against Glenn Curtiss, dragged on until 1914. Curtiss retaliated by taking part in an attempt, backed by the Smithsonian Institution, to prove that Samuel Pierpont Langley should be credited with creating the first viable flying machine. The endless litigation undermined Wilbur's morale and health, and he died suddenly of typhoid fever in 1912. Orville continued aeronautical research, but his relationship with the Wright company ended in 1915. He stayed in Dayton, living long enough to see the Smithsonian finally, in 1943, accept the Wrights' claim to have been the first to fly.

WOWING AMERICA

On his return from a successful tour of Europe, Wilbur Wright made a demonstration flight, on October 4, 1909, along the Hudson river from Governor's Island in New York Harbor to President Grant's tomb and back, witnessed by over a million spectators.

AT THE WHITE HOUSE

This photograph shows US president William Howard Taft, flanked by Wilbur, Orville, and Katherine Wright, standing on the White House terrace after an honors ceremony in 1909. Wilbur and Orville received the Congressional gold medal (left) the same year.

FLYING TAKES OFF

GERMAN AVIATION CHARTS A DIFFERENT COURSE, AND EUROPE DEMONSTRATES THE POTENTIAL OF AIRCRAFT AS WAR MACHINES

AIRSHIP PASSENGERS
The LZ 11 "Viktoria Luise" produced at Zeppelin's Friedrichshafen base, made its first passenger flight on March 4, 1912. In total it made 1,000 trips, flying between Hamburg, Heligoland, and Copenhagen.

MILITARY TRIALS
Army Airship "Beta" passing over British troops during maneuvers in Micheldever in 1910. This was a trial to test the potential use of airships as aerial scouts for recording troop positions. However, it was unsuccessful—the airships were too big and cumbersome, and kept landing in "enemy territory."

AS FAR AS MOST Germans were concerned, the dominant form of aircraft before 1914 was the Zeppelin, named after its creator, Count Ferdinand von Zeppelin. Although airships were also developed in other countries, it was only in Germany that they attained the status of a national icon.

Zeppelins were "rigid" airships—that is, the shape of the hydrogen-filled envelope was maintained by a solid framework rather than by the pressure of the gas inside. The LZ 1, von Zeppelin's first airship, tested in 1900, was 420ft (128m) long. Eventually these aerial monsters would grow to almost twice that size. Inevitably, such dimensions made them hard to handle on the ground, and expensive to manufacture—it was estimated that in 1914 you could make 34 airplanes for the cost of one Zeppelin.

Germany's love affair with the Zeppelin really began in 1906 when the count first achieved sustained flight with his LZ 3. Carrying out flights of up to eight hours' duration, he won official support from both the army and the royal family. Patriotic fervor rose to fever pitch when Zeppelin's next airship, LZ 4, was destroyed on the ground by a storm during a highly publicized journey up the Rhine valley in 1908. The German public spontaneously underwrote the sum of six million marks to allow von Zeppelin to continue his work, and Zeppelin airships began passenger services in 1910. Under the direction of chief engineer Ludwig Durr, Zeppelin design steadily improved. From 1912, goldbeater's skin—a fine membrane from a cow's intestine—replaced rubberized cotton as the material used to make the gas cells inside the airship's envelope. It was lighter and removed the risk of igniting the hydrogen with static electricity that could be generated by cotton surfaces rubbing together. For the framework, a new aluminum alloy called duralumin was in use by 1914, offering the strength of steel at one third of the weight. These improvements, plus more powerful engines, allowed the LZ 26 to carry a 14.2-ton (13-tonne) load at more than 50mph (80kmph).

Instruments of war

Although Zeppelins had carried more than 37,000 passengers by 1914, passenger transportation in airplanes was an idea whose day had yet to come. They were to find their first practical use in war. In the summer of 1911, a standoff between France and Germany over their interests in Morocco brought Europe to the brink of war. The crisis was resolved after much saber-rattling, but a major conflict seemed likely—a question not of whether, but of when. Stirred up by a jingoistic press, popular opinion demanded that governments back aircraft development, both as a symbol of national pride and an instrument of war.

Europe's army and navy officers were more skeptical than the public about the effectiveness of flying machines. French general Ferdinand Foch, a gifted military strategist who could certainly not be dismissed as a blinkered conservative, nonetheless expressed the opinion that aviation was a fine sport, but a worthless instrument of war. Yet there were some senior officers who embraced aviation with enthusiasm. In 1910 the French War Ministry was informed by one of its generals that airplanes were "as indispensable to armies as cannon or rifles." Even those who did not welcome the revolutionary new technology soon bowed to its inevitability. The British general staff regretfully acknowledged that it was impossible to "arrest or retard the perhaps unwelcome progress of aerial navigation." Expecting a major war at any moment, no army or navy could afford to neglect exploring the potential of flight.

But what precisely were military aircraft to be used for? One of the most influential fantasy novels of the period, H.G. Wells' *The War in the Air* (1908), imagined German airships crossing the Atlantic to attack New York. Wells' vision of an air raid was apocalyptic: "As the airships sailed along they smashed up the city… Below, they left ruins and blazing conflagrations and heaped and scattered dead." But although the Germans hoped to create a Zeppelin bombing fleet, cooler heads realized that aircraft of the period were neither reliable enough nor capable of carrying a large enough bombload to wreak such devastation on enemy cities. While experiments were carried out by dropping bombs and firing guns from airplanes—the majority of which were aimed at enemy troops—such offensive uses of aviation made relatively little progress before 1914. Instead more modest, but still vital, military roles were emphasized, centered on reconnaissance, message carrying, and artillery spotting—that is, helping gunners hit their targets by telling them where their shells were landing. By 1912 aircraft fulfilling these roles had become a standard feature of military maneuvers, and experiments had begun in air-to-ground communication (including the use of radio) and aerial photography.

Military demand

Although airships were added to the resources of both navies and armies, airplanes generally proved themselves more useful and reliable. They were also far cheaper to produce—a very important consideration. It was only in Germany that Zeppelin advocates held their ground, diverting major resources away from airplane production.

Between 1911 and 1914, European military establishments became major buyers of airplanes and the main influence on the development of the air industry. Military competitions set manufacturers targets to aim at, with lucrative contracts at stake. The lure of profits brought substantial investment from the likes of German banker Hugo Stinnes, arms manufacturer Gustav Krupps, and Russian industrialist Mikhail Shidlovski. Some private firms experienced rapid growth. Henri Farman was employing around 1,000 workers by 1914, and the Gnome aero-engine company operated on a similar scale. Governments also set up their own establishments to encourage aircraft development—notably Britain's Royal Aircraft Factory at Farnborough.

FLYING IN TO HAMBURG
The LZ 13 "Hansa" is pictured looming over Hamburg harbor in 1912 on the last leg of a journey from Scandinavia. From 1910, Zeppelins made regular flights and carried over 37,000 passengers before World War I, mostly on sightseeing trips.

COUNT FERDINAND VON ZEPPELIN

AN UNLIKELY AERIAL PIONEER, Ferdinand von Zeppelin (1838–1917) was born into the military aristocracy, and served as a cavalry officer until his fifties. His interest in airships was inspired by a visit to the United States during the Civil War, where he witnessed the use of tethered balloons as military observation posts. From 1891, he devoted his personal fortune to the development of powered rigid airships. Despite numerous setbacks, his first airship, LZ 1, made its maiden voyage on July 2, 1900. When the LZ 4 was destroyed by a storm in 1908, the popular response revived von Zeppelin's fortunes. He lived long enough to see his airships being used as bombers during World War I.

NATIONAL HERO
The success of Count von Zeppelin's airships revived national pride and made him a celebrity.

AIRSHIP DISPLAY
This German poster of 1913 depicts a heaving crowd attending a Zeppelin airshow. From 1908, Zeppelins made routine flights, carrying mail and passengers throughout Germany.

ZEPPELIN
IN DEUTSCHLAND SCHAUFLUG

However, the situation in the United States was strikingly different. America was not preparing for a major war. Its armed forces were under no pressure to embrace cutting-edge technology, and its politicians were reluctant to allocate funds for military hardware. By the summer of 1913, when the biggest European military air arms were numbered in hundreds, the US Army had 15 airplanes. Without substantial military contracts, the American air industry stagnated. In 1914, only 168 Americans were employed making aircraft.

Aircraft designs

The domination of European aviation by military contracts brought a distinct change in priorities. Since they did not yet take seriously the prospect of combat in the air, the armed forces demanded sturdy, reliable aircraft that could be flown in most weather conditions by average pilots and still carry a reasonable payload. Sporting pilots willingly risked their lives in treacherous high-performance machines built for speed or for stunting, but the military wanted stable airplanes that would survive prolonged use and keep their newly trained pilots alive. Although light monoplanes continued to be ordered for army use—for example, Taubes in Germany and Morane-Saulniers in France—there was a strong prejudice in favor of solid biplanes. A typical example was the two-seater B.E.2, designed by Geoffrey de Havilland for the Royal Aircraft Factory in 1912.

The record-breakers for speed around 1912–13 were the light monoplanes produced by French manufacturers Nieuport, Morane-Saulnier, and above all, Deperdussin, all of which made an attempt at streamlining with a fully enclosed fuselage and engine cowling. In comparison, a biplane such as the Farman Shorthorn, used for military training, was described by a cynical trainee pilot as looking "like an assemblage of birdcages." Although the monoplanes were sleek and fast, their thin single wing generated inadequate lift for carrying much weight. It was also structurally frail, and was still braced by external wires attached to struts on the fuselage. Their control systems also made these aircraft difficult to handle.

At the time, a thin wing section was considered obligatory by airplane designers. In fact, as aerodynamic research would soon reveal, a thicker wing section provided improved lift, as well as a stronger structure. In 1910 a German high-school professor, Hugo Junkers, took out a patent for "an airplane consisting of one wing, which would house all components, engines, crew, passengers, fuel, and framework." This flying wing was never built, but the idea led the way to the cantilever wing, requiring no external struts or bracing wires, that Junkers would incorporate into aircraft design during World War I. The cantilever wing would eventually make the monoplane the aircraft of the future. But in 1913–14 the machine that established a new benchmark for performance was a biplane, the Sopwith Tabloid—the first British-designed aircraft to compete successfully for speed with the French. The Tabloid pointed forward to the leading fighter-aircraft design of World War I.

The question of size

Perhaps the greatest technical breakthrough immediately before World War I concerned size. While small, well-designed monoplanes and biplanes were breaking speed and altitude records, to be of any practical use, both in peace and war, airplanes simply had to get bigger. But no one had any clear idea of the feasibility of large flying machines. Greater size implied the use of more than one engine, yet many people doubted that a multiengined aircraft could ever fly safely. Concern centered on how the airplane would behave in the extremely likely event of one of its engines failing. Would this throw the machine into a spin, with fatal consequences? The question was resolved by the young Russian designer and pilot Igor Sikorsky. In 1913–14, he repeatedly flew his large four-engined airplanes—first the Grand and then the Il'ya Muromets—proving that they could remain stable in the air with one or even two engines shut down. The path was open to the design of viable passenger-transport aircraft and heavy bombers.

Sikorsky's remarkable 1,600-mile (2,600-km) round trip from St. Petersburg to Kiev and back in the Il'ya Muromets provided a fitting finale to an era in which heavier-than-air flight itself had traveled a vast distance from its tentative origins.

FIRST BOMBING RAID

IN THE FALL OF 1911, Italy declared war with Turkey in a dispute over the territory now known as Libya, then part of the decaying Ottoman Empire. The Italian army possessed a number of foreign aircraft—French Blériots, Farmans, and Nieuports, and German Taubes. An air flotilla, initially comprising just nine airplanes and 11 pilots, was sent off with the Italian force that embarked for the Libyan coast in North Africa. In the short but brutal war that followed, the airplanes performed creditably, carrying out reconnaissance missions, mapping areas of the desert, and dropping propaganda leaflets promising a gold coin and sack of wheat to all those who surrendered. On November 1, Lieutenant Giulio Gavotti dropped four grenades over the side of his Blériot on to an Ottoman military encampment at the Taguira oasis, in the first-ever bombing raid by an airplane. Despite the fact that they faced little opposition, the aviators were hailed as heroes by patriotic Italians. Although the 1899 Hague Convention banned aerial bombing from balloons, Italy argued that this ban could not be extended to airplanes.

BATTLE OF DERNA
This propaganda poster shows three Italian monoplanes circling the battle of Derna during the Italo-Turkish war (1911–12).

THE SPECTACULAR FLIGHT OF THE IL'YA MUROMETS

APPROACHING KIEV
This painting shows the Il'ya Muromets over Kiev during its remarkable round trip between St. Petersburg and Kiev from June 30–July 11. By the end of July, Russia was mobilizing for a war in which Sikorsky's giant aircraft would be put to work as heavy bombers.

JOURNEY'S END
This photograph shows the Il'ya Muromets landing at Korposnoi aerodrome, outside St. Petersburg, after completing its epic round trip on July 11, 1914. Two figures can be seen standing on the outdoor observation platform.

ON JUNE 30, 1914, pilot and designer Igor Sikorsky took off on one of the most spectacular flights of the prewar, pioneering era of aviation. In his four-engined Il'ya Muromets, Sikorsky intended to fly from St. Petersburg over the forests and swamps of northern Russia to Kiev and back—a round trip of 1,600 miles (2,600km).

Working for his wealthy patron Mikhail Shidlovski at the Russo-Baltic Wagon Works in St. Petersburg, Sikorsky had first designed a four-engined airplane, the Grand, in 1913. With a wingspan of 88ft 7in (31m), it was a giant aircraft for its day. Foreign aviation experts, convinced the monster plane would never fly, dubbed it the "Petersburg Duck." But in May 1913, fly it did, and the "Duck" soon proved itself airworthy in test flights with eight passengers aboard.

In October 1913 Sikorsky built the even-larger Il'ya Muromets. Its wingspan was 105ft (37m), its fuselage was 77ft (27m) long, and fully loaded it weighed over 12,000lb (5,400kg). Even with four 100hp engines driving four tractor propellers, this was a lot of weight to get off the ground. The airplane could carry 16 people, including the crew, and by the spartan standards of the day, offered remarkable comfort.

It had a heated passenger cabin with electric lights powered by a wind-driven generator, a bedroom, and the first airborne toilet. There was a balcony at the front, allowing passengers spectacular aerial views, and (for the brave) an observation platform on the rear fuselage. The 1914 flight of the Il'ya Muromets was intended to demonstrate beyond any doubt that Sikorsky had created a truly practical large aircraft. It took off at first light on June 30 carrying Sikorsky, three other crew, and substantial supplies of spare parts, food, and fuel.

> "Aeronautics was neither an industry nor a science. It was a miracle."
>
> **IGOR SIKORSKY**

They were going to fly over a wilderness with no accompanying trains or cars.

After an uneventful eight hours, the aircraft made its first stop at a refueling site at Orsha. The next leg of the journey, to Kiev, was, by contrast, dangerously exciting. An engine caught fire and two of the crew had to climb onto the wing to beat out the flames with their coats. Sikorsky made an emergency landing for repairs. Taking off the following morning, he soon ran into rain and low clouds. Turbulent air currents pitched the giant aircraft around, at one point throwing it into a spin from which it emerged only after dropping over 1,000ft (350m). It was with immense relief that Sikorsky eventually brought the aircraft down from the clouds in sight of the golden domes of Kiev, landing to an enthusiastic reception. The return flight to St. Petersburg was less dramatic, and the total flying time for the remarkable 1,600-mile (2,600-km) round trip was 26 hours. Among the awards and acclaim showered upon Sikorsky came a personal expression of gratitude from Czar Nicholas II.

IGOR SIKORSKY

BORN IN KIEV, IGOR SIKORSKY (1889–1972) grew up in a household where intellectual curiosity was encouraged. As a boy he developed an interest in flight through reading the science fiction of French novelist Jules Verne and accounts of Leonardo da Vinci's designs for helicopters. After studying engineering, he failed in his attempts to make a helicopter and turned to more conventional fixed-wing designs. In 1913 he constructed the world's first four-engined airplane to fly. Known as the Grand, it formed the prototype for the Il'ya Muromets, later adapted as a long-range bomber for World War I. In 1918 Sikorsky emigrated to the United States to escape the Bolshevik Revolution. After some years teaching, he founded his own engineering company, producing many successful flying boats. In the 1930s he returned to his original obsession, producing the prototype of the first mass-produced helicopter in 1939.

RUSSIAN PIONEER
Igor Sikorsky stands in front of his S-22 Il'ya Muromets. Sikorsky's tried-and-tested designs proved that larger multiengined airplanes were viable.

Legacy of the pioneers

Flying machines and the adventurers who flew them had conquered the hearts and imaginations of millions of people. Although those who had experienced what Grahame-White called the "great, curious sense of power" conferred by piloting an airplane still totaled only a few thousand, vast numbers of individuals from all sections of society had been caught up in the romance of flight. It was famously embraced by poets and painters, who adopted the airplane as a symbol of the modernism to which they aspired. Italian poet Gabriele d'Annunzio himself became a pilot after hymning the aviator as "the messenger of a vaster life." But the excitement about aviation stretched far beyond intellectuals. In 1911 a school in provincial England asked its pupils to state their greatest goal in life. One seven-year-old, the future novelist Graham Greene, wrote: "To go up in an airplane."

By 1914 this era was drawing to an end. Aeronautics was rapidly becoming an industry, and, a little more slowly, a science. More disturbingly, to those who had hoped aviation might by its nature transcend national frontiers and bring different peoples together, aviation had become a branch of the armaments business and was about to turn into a major instrument of war.

GIANT BIPLANE
The Sikorsky S-27 Il'ya Muromets Ye had an enclosed glass cockpit, which is clearly visible above. The postage stamp, right, was issued by the Soviet Union in 1976 to honor the ground-breaking flight of the Il'ya Muromets.

DOCTRINE AND HISTORY—PRE-WORLD WAR I		
DISTINCTIVE CAPABILITIES	**FUNCTIONS (MISSIONS)**	**DOCTRINAL EMPHASIS**
• Information Superiority	• Surveillance and Reconnaissance • Artillery Spotting	• Gathering Military Information to Support Land Forces

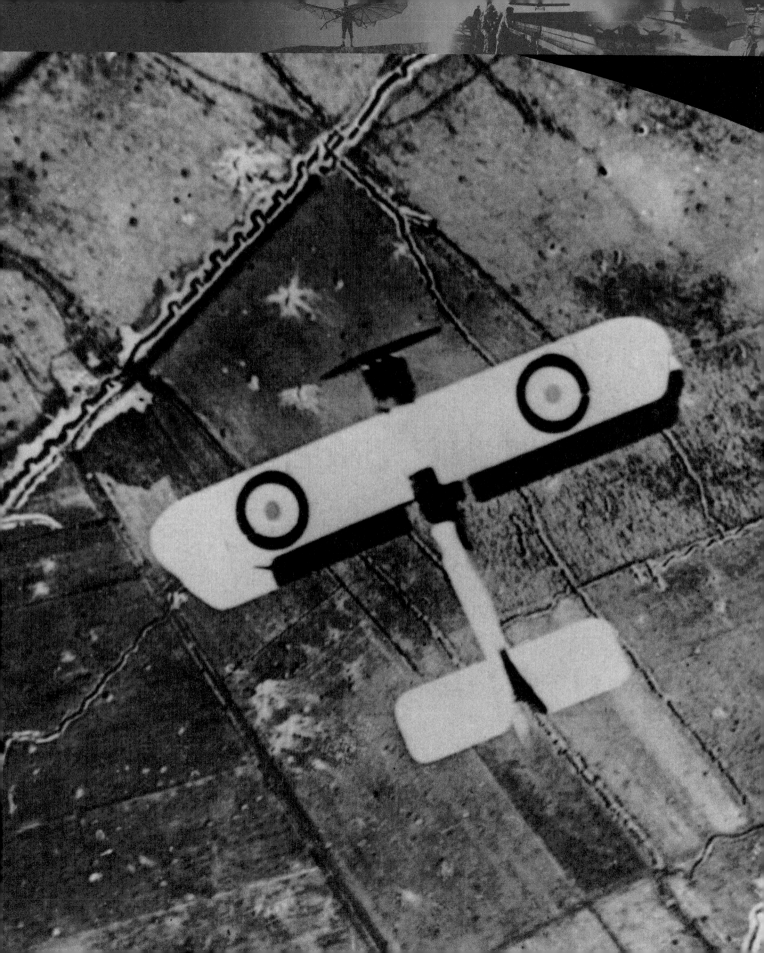

ADVENT OF THE AIR AGE: WORLD WAR I

3

AIRCRAFT FOUND THEIR FIRST PRACTICAL USE as instruments of war. Between 1914 and 1918, aviation matured under the stress of combat. For the first time, aircraft were operated on a daily basis, with regular servicing and a focus on reliability. More powerful engines and sturdier airframes improved performance. There was also a change of scale: Aircraft had been produced in hundreds before the war; now they were manufactured in thousands. Militarily, World War I identified different roles that aircraft could perform and the design of specialized aircraft to fulfill them—including bombers, which later developed into the first airliners. The air aces consolidated the tradition of pilots as popular heroes.

"Men were going to die in the air as they had for centuries on the ground and on the seas, by killing each other. The conquest of the air was truly accomplished."

RENÉ CHAMBE
AU TEMPS DES CARABINES

WORKING FOR THE GENERALS

THE PRINCIPAL ROLE OF AIRCRAFT IN WORLD WAR I WAS TO SUPPORT THE ARMIES IN THE TRENCHES— AIRMEN GAVE THEIR LIVES FOR MEN ON THE GROUND

A T THE OUTBREAK OF WAR in Europe in August 1914, aircraft did not seem set to play a serious part in the conflict. The ground forces of the major European armies were counted in millions; the frontline aircraft deployed by all combatants amounted to little over 500 fragile, unarmed monoplanes and biplanes. Caught up in the patriotic fervor of the moment, civilian pilots rushing to join up included such well-known stars of peacetime aviation as Roland Garros and Jules Védrines. But the military establishments initially had little use for the skills of the daredevil sportsman-aviators who had so recently enthralled the public.

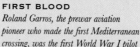

FIRST BLOOD
Roland Garros, the prewar aviation pioneer who made the first Mediterranean crossing, was the first World War I pilot to shoot down an enemy plane by firing through his propeller blades.

Aerial chauffeurs
Army pilots were essentially aerial chauffeurs. Their job was to ferry an observer—sometimes a senior officer—over the countryside to report on the movement of enemy troops. In the first months of the war there was plenty of movement to observe, with rapid advances, encirclements, and desperate retreats. In the west, the German forces overran Belgium and advanced on Paris, while in the east the Russians marched menacingly into East Prussia. Flying mostly from improvised airstrips (any unplowed field) close to the ever-shifting front line, pilots and observers roamed the thinly populated skies, seeking out bodies of enemy troops and recording their size, location, and direction of march in scribbled notes and hastily sketched maps. It was no easy task to locate the enemy in unfamiliar

territory while trying to avoid becoming hopelessly lost and coping with unpredictable weather. Low clouds hampered observation, and the sheer flimsiness of the machines led to frequent accidents and forced landings. The appearance of aircraft was greeted with volleys of rifle fire from friend and foe alike. And after undergoing these hazards, airmen sometimes saw their reports simply disregarded by the crustier generals who distrusted information from such a novel source.

A vital role
Nonetheless, aerial reconnaissance made a decisive contribution to both fronts. In the east, the Russians failed to make effective use of the few aircraft they possessed, while the Germans employed their Taubes to crucial advantage. Ranging over the forests and lakes of East Prussia, German aviators located the advancing Russian armies, giving the high command time to move reinforcements to the front. When battle was joined at Tannenberg, information from aerial observers let the numerically inferior Germans concentrate their forces in the right place at the right time to carry off an epic victory.

In the west, French and British aviators were caught up in a rapid retreat across France as the gray columns of the German army swept toward Paris. Anticipating triumph, on August 29, 1914, a German pilot flew around the Eiffel Tower and dropped a single bomb on the city. But on September 3, French aircraft assigned to the defense of their capital reported that the enemy's armies had turned away from

ELEGANT GERMAN FIGHTER
Over 3,000 Albatros D.Vs (replica shown) were built in 1917–18, providing a mount for many German aces. But despite its streamlined monocoque fuselage and elegant lines, the D.V was outclassed by Allied fighters. In July 1917, a German pilot wrote: "The D.V is so antiquated and laughably inferior that we can do nothing with it."

A NEW KIND OF WAR
A squadron of French cavalry watches a biplane passing overhead in 1915. Aircraft largely replaced the cavalry in its traditional role of scouting, since they could cover more ground more quickly. Many of the best World War I pilots were men who transferred from the cavalry, sensing its irrelevance on the Western Front.

RECONNAISSANCE BRIEF
A British officer briefs the pilot of a B.E.12 on the areas to be photographed on his mission. Most photo-reconnaissance was entrusted to two-seater aircraft, with an observer operating the camera. The pilot of a single-seater B.E.12 would have had a tricky time taking pictures while flying in hostile airspace.

WORLD WAR I RECONNAISSANCE AIRCRAFT

AT THE START OF WORLD WAR I, the German General Staff stated that "the duty of the aviator is to see, not to fight." Given that reconnaissance and artillery spotting were seen as the central purpose of military aviation, it is perhaps surprising that the aircraft dedicated to this role often had such poor performance— from frail monoplanes, such as the Taube, used at the outset of the war, to the many unexciting biplanes that trundled over the trenches. Stability was regarded as the chief virtue of reconnaissance machines, in order to provide a platform for observation and photography. But this meant they were slow and clumsy to maneuver, making them easy prey for enemy fighters and vulnerable to ground fire. Some, such as the Renault A.R. and the RAF R.E.8, had a particularly poor reputation. After a spate of accidents, the R.E.8 was temporarily withdrawn from service, but investigations revealed inadequate training rather than poor design to be the culprit. Late in World War I, progress came on the

Allied side with the introduction of the Bristol F.2B fighter for reconnaissance. Improved cameras allowed the Germans to initiate high-altitude photo-reconnaissance outside the range of most fighter aircraft.

VULNERABLE DOVE
Already outdated by the outbreak of World War I, the Rumpler Taube had a top speed of only 60mph (97kmph) and was extremely vulnerable in the air.

AERIAL VIEW
This photograph (above) was taken on a reconnaissance mission over France. Once trench warfare set in on the Western Front at the end of 1914, army commanders became totally dependent on aerial reconnaissance for information on what was happening on the other side of no-man's land. "Photo-recce" was a risky business for airmen, requiring slow, straight-and-level flights over enemy positions, repeated many times to build up a complete picture.

HANDHELD BOX CAMERA
A Royal Flying Corps observer demonstrates a Thornton-Pickard "A" Type photo-reconnaissance camera (right). Cameras were initially handheld, using straps or handles (right). Later they were mounted on the aircraft itself.

Paris to the east. This information enabled General Joseph Gallieni, who was in charge of the defense of the city, to launch an attack on the exposed German flank on the Marne that turned the tide of the war. By the end of the fall, the Germans had been driven back toward the Belgian frontier, and the war of movement on the Western Front had come to an end. The armies dug in along a line from the English Channel to Switzerland, where they would stay for the next three and a half years.

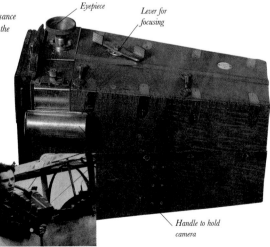

Eyepiece

Lever for focusing

Handle to hold camera

During the long agony of trench warfare, with its monstrous artillery barrages and its massed infantry offensives, in which hundreds of thousands of lives were sacrificed for pitifully small territorial gains, aviation dutifully played the role assigned to it by army commanders. As far as they were concerned, the function of aircraft was to carry out reconnaissance and the closely related role of artillery spotting, as well as to inflict damage on the enemy's soldiers and materiel through tactical bombing and ground attack.

Building a picture

From 1915, photography replaced sketches and notes as a technique for aerial reconnaissance. Aircraft with unwieldy box cameras were dispatched day after day over the front to build up an exact picture of the enemy's trench systems and gun emplacements. Initially the cameras were like those found in photographers' studios, with large glass plates that had to be changed by hand after every shot. This was ghastly work for observers with freezing fingers operating in the gale of the aircraft's slipstream. Later, cameras with a mechanically operated plate change made the observer's job more practical, but photo-reconnaissance remained as hazardous as it was unglamorous. An aircraft held steady and straight for photography presented an inviting target

EINDECKER IN ACTION
This rare aerial photograph captures a Fokker
Eindecker in action over France. The aircraft
had a metal tubular frame that gave it
strength in a high-speed dive, but in other
ways it was not of an advanced design.
It was one of the last important
aircraft to use wing warping, rather
than ailerons, for lateral control.

for ground fire, and the
underpowered obsolescent
aircraft usually thought suitable
for reconnaissance were easy prey
for enemy fighters. But, at the cost of
heavy loss of life, comprehensive
photomontages of trench systems were built
up and used for selecting targets for the artillery.

When the heavy guns opened up, again the
aircraft came into play. The gunners needed
observers to tell them where the shells were landing
so they could correct their range and direction. In
decent weather, airborne observers could usually
see where a shot was falling but there was no
efficient way of communicating this to the ground
until 1916, when some new aircraft were capable of
carrying radio transmitters. Combining the use of
radio with the "clock system"—a code of number

and letter coordinates that identified where a shell
had fallen in relation to the target—created a
reasonably efficient spotting technique. At the static
battle of the Somme in 1916, the British found that
no amount of aerial observation could make the
artillery barrages actually work against troops in
deep fortifications. In the mobile battles of 1918,
however, thousands of airmen sacrificed their lives
in an artillery-bombardment strategy that, alone,

would have failed, but employed with other arms
and methods was very effective.

Toward the end of the war the Germans at last
introduced a reconnaissance aircraft that gave its
crew a reasonable measure of safety. The Rumpler
C.VII could fly at 20,000ft (6,000m) and had an
automatic camera that took a series of pictures
when triggered. The downside was the lack of
protection for high-altitude flight. Rumpler
crews suffered from freezing cold (they
were in open cockpits), and had to be
supplied with oxygen.

Arming the airplanes

For the generals, the main reason for
putting guns in aircraft was to protect their
own reconnaissance aircraft and shoot
down the enemy's. But the initial impetus
toward arming aircraft came from pilots
and observers who simply wanted to "have
a go" at the opposition. Firing pistols and
carbines at passing aircraft had limited
effect, while attempts at dropping grenades
on them from above were a total failure.
Machine guns were what were needed. But
carrying such a weapon was a considerable
burden for the lightweight, underpowered
aircraft of 1914. It was also hazardous:
There was a serious risk of blowing parts
off your own machine, with its array of

FACING THE FLAK

GERMAN ANTIAIRCRAFT FIRE, known to the Royal Flying Corps as "Archie,"
took a heavy toll on unmaneuverable reconnaissance aircraft. Pilot
Lieutenant William Read wrote: "I wonder how long my nerves
will stand this almost daily bombardment by 'Archie'... I would
not mind quite so much if I were in a machine that was fast and
that would climb a little more willingly. Today... some of
the shells burst much too near and I could hear the pieces
of shell whistling past... Well, I suppose the end
will be pretty sharp and quick." Most
antiaircraft commanders believed shrapnel
was best for bringing down an aircraft.
Others preferred high explosive or
incendiary shells.

GOOD ODDS
*German antiaircraft gunners had a fair
chance of hitting an observation aircraft
if traveling at below 5,000ft (1,500m).*

struts and wires. The first recorded aerial victory is credited to a French aviator. On October 5, 1914, observer Louis Quénault shot down an Aviatik with a Hotchkiss machine gun mounted on a Voisin 8—a pusher aircraft (with the propeller at the rear). Affording a clear field of fire to the front, pushers were one option for air-combat machines. They proved especially attractive to the British, who introduced the Vickers "Gun bus" in 1915 and the F.E.2 and single-seat D.H.2 pushers the following year. But while pusher machines were by no means ineffective, tractor machines (propeller at the front) were faster and more maneuverable.

What the more skillful and adventurous pilots instinctively yearned for was a gun they could aim simply by pointing their aircraft at the target. Before the war, French and German designers had discovered that it was feasible to create an interrupter gear that would pause a machine gun each time a propeller blade was in its line of fire. Raymond Saulnier, designer of the Morane-Saulnier monoplane, was one of those who experimented with interrupters, but he had not been able to make one work in practice. So it was Dutch designer Anthony Fokker who fitted the first effective interrupter gear to one of his Eindecker monoplanes. The Germans went on to use guns firing through the propeller arc on all their fighters for the rest of the war. Interrupter gears and other forms of synchronizing mechanism tended to reduce the rate of fire of the machine gun, but in later German aircraft, such as the Albatros D.V and Fokker D.VII, the use of twin guns compensated for this drawback.

The Allies' first effective riposte to the Eindecker's interrupter gear was to mount a machine gun on the upper wing of a biplane so that it fired over the top of the propeller. Even after the Allies developed their own synchronizing mechanisms to allow firing through the propeller arc, they remained attached to the concept of the wing-mounted gun. Successful solo fighters such as the Nieuport 17 and the S.E.5a were usually equipped with both. In tandem with new armaments, new tactics were also being developed.

Early in the war individual fighters prowled the skies as lone hunters in search of unsuspecting enemy aircraft. By 1916, fighter aircraft were being grouped in squadrons as tactics were developed for fighting in formation. During the titanic battles of Verdun and the Somme, Allied and German airmen fought for air superiority; losses on both sides were heavy in an aerial combat that mirrored the war of attrition on the ground. Numerically inferior,

INVENTING THE FIGHTER PILOT

ON APRIL 1, 1915, FRENCH PILOT Roland Garros positioned his Morane-Saulnier Parasol monoplane behind the tail of a German observation aircraft and fired a burst from his machine gun through the propeller arc. As the German machine plummeted to earth, Garros could claim to have become the first solo fighter pilot. The secret of his success—the ability to fire forward through the propeller—had been achieved by attaching metal plates to deflect any rounds that struck the blades.

Garros had shot down three aircraft by April 18, when engine failure forced him to land behind German lines. His exploits had been highly publicized and the Germans rushed to examine his downed plane. Dutch designer Anthony Fokker was called to Berlin and told to imitate the metal deflectors. Instead, he equipped one of his Eindecker monoplanes (an unarmed reconnaissance aircraft) with an 08/15 Maxim ("Spandau") machine gun and an interrupter gear copied from a prewar German patent design. The interrupter allowed the pilot to fire through his propeller with less risk to the machine and himself.

German commanders were slow to realize that an important new weapon had been placed in their hands. Eindeckers were introduced in small numbers and were initially spread out in ones and twos, supporting reconnaissance units, which limited their effectiveness. Some German pilots instantly recognized the potential of the new machine. Through the winter of 1915–16, using the simple tactic of swooping down on their enemy from behind in a steep dive, the Eindecker pilots shot down unprecedented numbers of Allied aircraft. The British called it the "Fokker Scourge." Yet the Eindecker was in fact seriously flawed. It was underpowered, not especially nimble,

Swivel

Cord

Ammunition drum

Foresight

Mounting pivot

7.62-mm barrel fires 600rpm

WING-MOUNTED GUN
A Lewis Aerial Gun mounted on the top wing allowed pilots to shoot in the line of flight, over the propeller. The gun was fired by pulling on a cord that led down into the cockpit. The pilot's problem with this arrangement was changing the ammunition drum in flight, a perilous moment requiring him to take his hands off the controls.

and had structural weaknesses. With careful handling it was effective, but it could be a death trap even for an experienced pilot if he put too much stress on the airframe.

The Allies responded with their own solo fighter aircraft. In July 1915, France introduced the small Nieuport 11, affectionately known as the "Bébé" ("Baby"). Originally designed for racing, this light biplane was fast and extremely maneuverable. Its only major weakness was the single-spar lower wing, which allowed the wings to twist in a dive. Although it lacked a synchronized machine gun, it carried a wing-mounted Lewis machine gun, and virtually drove the Eindeckers from the skies. The scourge had finally been scourged.

BOUNCING BULLETS
A Morane monoplane (far left) displays metal plates on its propeller blades. When its machine gun fired, about one in 10 bullets hit the deflectors, bouncing off. This poster shows a German ace in an Eindecker firing through his propeller. The image captures the essence of the solo fighter pilot—the welding of man and aircraft into a single fighting machine.

FOKKER SCHWERIN

the German aircraft tended to stay on their own side of the trenches and concentrate their resources in ever-larger units capable of winning local air superiority on crucial sectors of the front.

Rapid expansion

A battle for production intensified in step with the struggle at the front. The growth in volume of engine and airframe output was spectacular. Very early in the war, military contracts allowed small manufacturers to grow into major industrial concerns. The French company Nieuport was not untypical in seeing its turnover grow from 285,000 francs in 1914 to 26.4 million francs in 1916. New players entered the aero-engine and aircraft industries, notably automobile manufacturers such as Renault and Fiat. Expansion was most rapid in Britain, which had entered the war with a weak aircraft industry almost entirely dependent on imported French engines. By the end of the war, Britain had the largest aircraft industry in the world, employing an estimated 270,000 workers.

Plagued by shortages of skilled labor and of vital materials, Germany critically lost out in the battle for volume production. In 1917, the Germans undershot a production target of 1,000 aircraft a month—at a time when the British and French between them were manufacturing about 30,000 aircraft a year.

Quantity was not, of course, the same as quality. Delays and bureaucratic incompetence sometimes led to aircraft being manufactured that were obsolescent before they were ever flown—the notorious R.E.8s and Renault ARs delivered to the front in 1917 were cases in point. The twin goals of maximizing output and improving aircraft performance often proved contradictory. Aircraft that had been good in their day were kept too long in production so that the demand for numbers could be met.

Necessity breeds invention

But there was also a built-in conservatism through the need to exploit existing resources and tried-and-tested techniques. Throughout the war the vast majority of Allied aircraft remained strut-and-wire biplanes, with a fabric skin stretched over a wooden frame. They achieved improved performance largely through the use of more powerful and reliable engines. The Germans were more innovative in their use of materials, partly because of shortages of good quality wood and of skilled workers required to build wooden-frame aircraft. For their fabric-skinned machines, the Germans mostly adopted welded steel-tube frames, which were strong, light, and easier to make. On aircraft such as the Albatros D-series fighters, they took plywood and wrapped it in strips around an inner framework to create wooden-skinned monocoque fuselages.

Although the Albatros fighters were fine machines, their evolution showed the increasing difficulties the Germans ran into, trapped between the demands of quantity and quality. Aiming to achieve its 1,000-aircraft-a-month target for 1917, Germany opted for mass production of the Albatros D.V, a variant of the D.III. But by the summer of that year, the Albatroses were being outclassed by a new generation of Allied fighters, especially the S.E.5 and the SPAD XIII. Yet dedicated to meeting their production targets, German factories went on churning out Albatroses into 1918.

The skies over the Western Front were an essentially Darwinian environment in which aircraft constantly evolved to survive—sometimes by straight imitation. When the French Nieuport 17 scout threatened the predominance of the German Albatros D.II fighter in 1916, for example, the Germans simply copied the Nieuport's single-spar lower wing—and with it, its tendency to twist and fail—to create the Albatros D.III. Similarly, after the Sopwith Triplane flown by Britain's Royal Naval Air Service shocked German fliers with its agility in 1917, Fokker copied it to create its own Dr.I triplane as a mount for Baron Manfred von Richthofen.

The entry of the United States into the war in April 1917 inspired Germany with a desperate urge to achieve victory before the overwhelming might of American manpower and industry could be brought to bear. The German high command planned an ultimate offensive on the Western Front for the spring of 1918. Evaluation trials were held to find the aircraft that would win the war. Both Claudius Dornier and Hugo Junkers put forward radical designs that looked to the future—aircraft with metal skins and, in Junkers' case, a cantilever wing that required no external struts or bracing. But again conservatism prevailed. The aircraft adopted for mass production were the Fokker D.VII and Pfalz D.XII, superb fighting machines but representing only a limited degree of innovation.

> "Aviation has assumed a capital importance… It is necessary to be master of the air."
>
> GENERAL HENRI PÉTAIN, MAY 1917

POWERING UP

THE POWER OF ENGINES USED IN combat aircraft grew from around 80hp at the start of the war to a maximum of 400hp by 1918. The two main families of World War I power plants were rotary and in-line water-cooled engines. Rotary engines were lighter and more compact, but ran into problems when required to deliver over 150hp. With their cylinders whirling around a fixed crankshaft they created a powerful gyroscopic effect that made an aircraft tricky to fly, but they worked well on maneuverable dogfighters such as the Sopwith Camel and Fokker Triplane. In-line engines powered stronger, faster aircraft.

The Allies won the battle for engine development because they had a wider range of suppliers, mostly French. The Americans produced the most powerful engine of the war—the 12-cylinder, 400hp Liberty engine—in 1918.

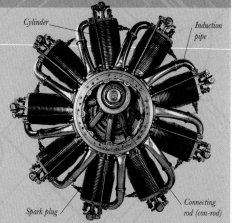

Cylinder

Induction pipe

Spark plug

Connecting rod (con-rod)

LE RHÔNE 9B ROTARY ENGINE
Many of the rotary engines used by the Allies were produced by the Gnome and Le Rhône companies. Despite some disturbing characteristics, including spraying the pilot with castor oil, they were light and powerful. The best tribute to their quality is that the Germans often installed captured Allied rotary engines in place of their own.

Cooling jacket around cylinder

Exhaust

Laminated wooden propeller

Brass-sheathed leading edge

"HISSO" IN-LINE ENGINE
The in-line Hispano-Suiza V8 is often regarded as the outstanding engine of World War I. It was powerful, compact, durable, and light for its size. The engine was used in aircraft like the SPAD XIII and the S.E.5.

SUPERIOR S.E.5A

When the British-built S.E.5a entered the war in 1917 it proved itself superior to all its German opponents. Faster than the Sopwith Camel and easier to fly, it developed a formidable reputation in the hands of celebrated aces like Edward Mannock. Designed by H.P. Folland at the Royal Aircraft Factory in Farnborough, it combined a strong airframe with good, solid performance. Over 5,000 were produced.

Wing-mounted Lewis gun

Faired headrest behind cockpit

F 938

Elevator

Laminated wooden propeller

Metal engine cowling

SKILLED HANDS

Workers construct S.E.5s at the Royal Aircraft Factory, Farnborough, Britain. Despite mass production, making aircraft remained a labor-intensive job, as it had been in the artisan workshops of the prewar era. Processes such as attaching the wire rigging needed a high level of skill and were very time-consuming.

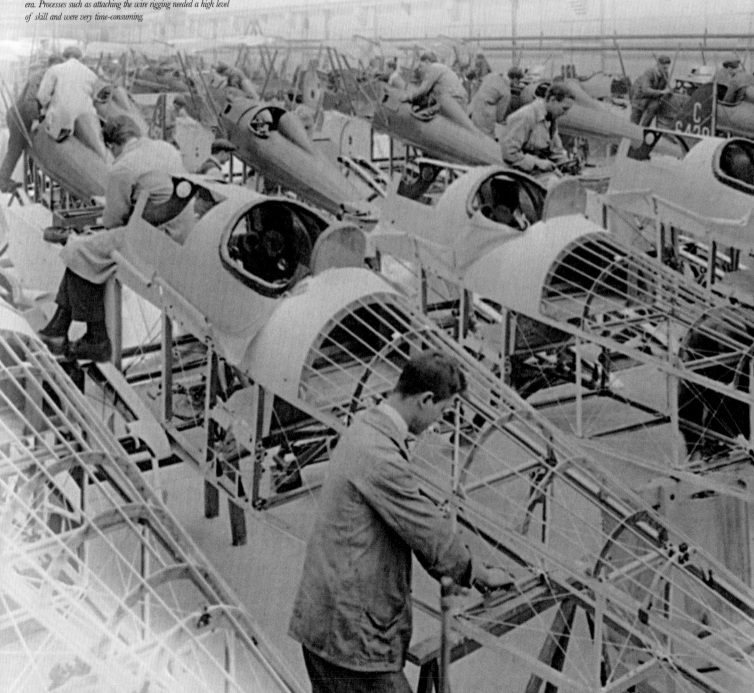

Racing to catch up

The expectation that America's entry into the conflict would swiftly swing the air war in the Allies' favor failed to take into account the degree to which American aviation had fallen behind that of Europe. The sole viable combat aircraft under production in the United States in 1917 was the Curtiss flying boat. The US Army had about 50 obsolete combat aircraft. But if the United States lacked an aircraft industry, it did have an automobile industry that was using assembly-line techniques to transform output. Confident that if America could make cars it could make airplanes, Congress enthusiastically approved funds for the mass manufacture of aircraft. Optimistic plans saw the US equipping not only its own air service but those of Britain, France, and Italy. That is not how it worked out. Assembly-line methods proved hard to apply and differences between European and American standard measurements posed retooling problems. By the war's end, US factories had delivered only around 1,400 combat aircraft, mostly versions of the D.H.4 bomber.

Similar frustrations were experienced in engine manufacturing. Seven automobile manufacturers were contracted to make the Liberty aero-engine, but an original eight-cylinder design was declared obsolete before it went into production and had to be replaced

by a heavier 12-cylinder model. Delays meant that only 1,300 Liberty engines had been delivered by June 1918. At 400hp they were the most powerful engines in the war—in fact far too powerful for existing airframes. American pilots who flew the Liberty-powered D.H.4s complained that if they ran the engine at full throttle it would shake the aircraft to pieces.

The final push

Germany launched its final offensive of the war, the Kaiserschlacht, on March 21, 1918. Using ground-attack aircraft in support of small groups of "shock troops," the Germans punched holes

MODERN WARFARE
During the Second Battle of the Marne in July 1918, a German biplane patrols the trenches as a British tank looms into view. The ubiquity of aircraft and tanks at this time was a foretaste of the type of mobile warfare that would predominate in World War II.

in the Allied lines, ending the stalemate of trench warfare. In a repeat of 1914, Allied troops fell back toward Paris. The battle in the air was every bit as intense as on the ground. The Germans even threw their heavy Gotha bombers into the fray, attacking ammunition dumps behind the lines. The arrival of the superb Fokker D.VII at the

FALLEN WARRIOR
Allied soldiers examine the wreckage of a German aircraft after one of the last battles of the war. Although the German pilots were often better trained than their opponents and had at least marginally superior aircraft, they could not cope with the number of Allied machines filling the skies.

> "What is the point of shooting down five out of 50 machines? The other 45 will… bomb as much as they want. The enemy's material superiority was… dooming us to failure."
>
> LIEUTENANT RUDOLF STARK
> GERMAN PILOT DESCRIBING THE BATTLES OF 1918

end of April meant that German pilots had their best fighter of the entire war.

Yet with victory apparently in sight, the German war effort began to crumble. By June, flying missions were being cut back due to lack of fuel. While the Allies were mostly able to replace their losses of aircraft and pilots, the Germans could not. American fliers were arriving in the thousands and their number would continue to increase. In July 1918, the Allies went on the offensive. In the air, they swamped the Germans with their sheer weight of numbers. France had grouped together aerial divisions of 700 bombers and fighters. By the time of the St. Mihiel offensive in September, US General William "Billy" Mitchell commanded a force of 1,500 French, British, and American aircraft in his sector of the front. Exhausted, short of fuel and spares, and with their airfields increasingly exposed to air attack, the German airmen never gave up the fight and, indeed, inflicted heavier losses than they suffered. But it was a struggle driven by despair rather than hope.

World War I ended with the armistice of November 11, 1918; the Germans surrendered without truly accepting defeat. The war had cost an estimated nine million lives. Of those, probably some 15,000 were airmen. This may seem a relatively small figure in absolute terms, but individually a pilot probably stood no better chance of surviving the war than an infantryman in the trenches. Aviation had come of age in a war of mass slaughter driven by industrial technology. Although many people saw airmen soaring above that impersonal butchery, they had fully played their part as victims and killers. Flight had lost its innocence.

BOMBS FROM THE AIR

DROPPING EXPLOSIVES ON PEOPLE on the ground was one of the first conceived uses for aircraft. During World War I this primitive urge was refined into strategic bombing (such as factories and cities); tactical bombing of targets behind the front line (including railroads or supply dumps); and frontline attack. The earliest bombs were artillery shells dropped over the side of aircraft by hand.

By 1917 sturdier, specialized bomber aircraft had appeared with bomb racks, bomb sights, and release systems. Raids were carried out by day when air superiority allowed it, or by night with much-reduced accuracy. By the final stages of the war, aircraft roamed the front, bombing bridges and airfields, and strafing troops and trucks, proving beyond a doubt the vital importance of air superiority.

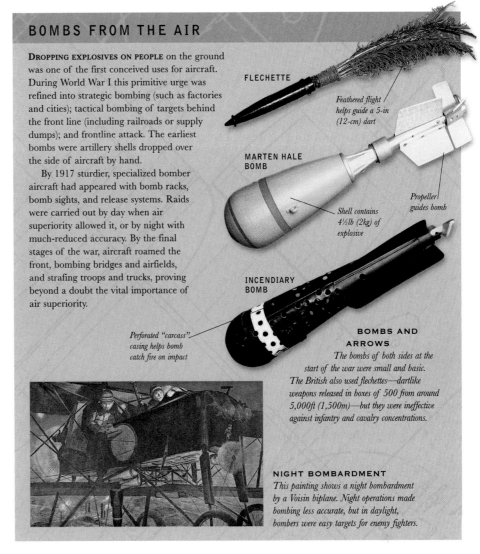

FLECHETTE

Feathered flight helps guide a 5-in (12-cm) dart

MARTEN HALE BOMB

Shell contains 4½lb (2kg) of explosive

Propeller guides bomb

INCENDIARY BOMB

Perforated "carcass" casing helps bomb catch fire on impact

BOMBS AND ARROWS
The bombs of both sides at the start of the war were small and basic. The British also used flechettes—dartlike weapons released in boxes of 500 from around 5,000ft (1,500m)—but they were ineffective against infantry and cavalry concentrations.

NIGHT BOMBARDMENT
This painting shows a night bombardment by a Voisin biplane. Night operations made bombing less accurate, but in daylight, bombers were easy targets for enemy fighters.

THE BATTLE OF ST. MIHIEL

ON SEPTEMBER 12, 1918, American forces under General John J. Pershing launched an offensive to reduce the St. Mihiel salient—a 24-mile-wide, 14-mile-deep bulge formed by a German advance south of Verdun, France. In an excellent example of a joint and combined operation, Pershing commanded the Allied First Army, which contained US Army air and ground units, a large number of US Marines, and other Allied forces. French colonial troops made up one ground corps, and French, Italian, Portuguese, and British air units joined their American counterparts.

St. Mihiel represented the first large-scale massing of airpower under central command. Colonel William "Billy" Mitchell, Pershing's air commander for the battle and later a brigadier general, had some 1,500 aircraft at his disposal—600 flown by US

personnel. He seized the initiative, gained air superiority, attacked ground forces, and interdicted German supplies, helping Allied ground forces achieve their objectives.

Mitchell believed that airpower's first task was to achieve air superiority. He was determined to use his pursuit planes in offensive counterair operations rather than defensive operations over friendly lines. He meant to attack the Germans deep in their own territory and drive them from the air while his bombers attacked targets deep in the German rear. His approach was extremely successful and helped the Allies gain and maintain control of the air throughout the offensive. Meanwhile, the 91st Aero Squadron focused on the counterland campaign, conducting close air support and interdiction missions against road and rail junctions in the German rear.

During the four days of the offensive, American Airmen made 3,300 flights over battle lines, logged 4,000 hours, and made 1,000 individual bombing attacks dropping 75 tons (68 tonnes) of high explosive. They destroyed 12 enemy balloons and 60 enemy planes.

The experience at St. Mihiel not only paid immediate dividends in World War I—it was invaluable to the future development of US airpower. Many of the future leaders of US air forces gained invaluable experience in large-scale air operations in the battle. In addition to the famous American aces like Eddie Rickenbacker and Frank Luke, US Airmen involved in the St. Mihiel offensive included three future four-star generals in the US Air Force: George C. Kenney, Joseph T. McNarney, and Carl A. Spaatz, who also became the first Air Force chief of staff.

KNIGHTS OF THE AIR

WHILE BRUTAL TRENCH WARFARE BOGGED DOWN THE ARMIES, THE MYTH OF FIGHTER PILOTS AS "KNIGHTS OF THE AIR" SUPPLIED A PUBLIC NEED FOR HEROES

AMERICA'S TOP ACE
A former racing driver and military chauffeur, Captain Eddie Rickenbacker was the most successful American fighter pilot of World War I, with 26 kills.

W ORLD WAR I was the first total war, in which the entire human resources of industrialized societies were mobilized in the drive for victory. The mass slaughter in the trenches put an immense strain upon social solidarity and morale. Even with deep reserves of patriotism to draw upon, political and military leaders recognized that popular support for the war might evaporate. Fighter pilots offered a welcome supply of heroes to be used as a focus for patriotic enthusiasm.

The French and Germans created a formalized system for allotting "ace" status to a flier based on a certain number of confirmed kills—a number that had to be raised in the course of the war as air combat intensified. The British high command never formally accepted the existence of aces but awarded a few of the highest scoring pilots the Victoria Cross, their most coveted military decoration. Aces were turned into celebrities by patriotic publicity

machines. Their faces decorated the front pages of newspapers; they were filmed for movie newsreels; they were showered with honors; and their funerals were occasions of national mourning. When French ace Georges Guynemer was killed in 1917, his name was inscribed on the walls of the Panthéon, alongside France's greatest philosophers and poets.

Soaring above the trenches

The propaganda worked because it fed a widely felt nostalgia for a cleaner, nobler form of warfare. The idealism felt by some at the start of the war—poet Rupert Brooke described entering the conflict as "like swimmers into cleanness leaping"—found no satisfaction in the squalid attrition of the trenches. Airmen seemed, morally as well as literally, to soar above the cratered mud of Flanders. This was war as it was meant to be —an opportunity to demonstrate the

"I hate to shoot a Hun down without him seeing me, for although this method is in accordance with my doctrine, it is against what little sporting instincts I have left."

JAMES MCCUDDEN VC, 1917

RED BARON'S MOUNT
Anthony Fokker based his highly maneuverable 1917 Dr.I triplane, of which the above is a modern replica, on the Sopwith Triplane, whose three wings gave it extra lift and agility. It gained notoriety as the mount of Baron Manfred von Richthofen, who claimed 19 of his 80 victories in it.

DOGFIGHT OVER THE WESTERN FRONT
*This painting shows a de Havilland D.H.4. Fighter taking on
an Albatros D.II biplane, depicting similar planes and fights
with Baron von Richthofen's "Flying Circus." In a tradition
dating from 1917, all pilots from the Flying Circus displayed
some red coloring to show their solidarity with their leader,
whose triplane was completely red.*

GERMANY'S FIRST ACES

MAX IMMELMANN (1890–1916) and Oswald Boelcke (1891–1916) were members of Flight Section 62 stationed at Douai, France, in August 1915. They were among the first pilots issued the Fokker Eindecker, and they used it to deadly effect. As their victories mounted, they were trumpeted in German propaganda as examples of fearless devotion to the Fatherland. They were courted by the aristocracy, lauded by journalists, and deluged with fan mail.

Immelmann, a fitness fanatic and teetotaller, was killed in June 1916, probably by a faulty interrupter gear in his Eindecker—causing him to blow off his own propeller. His legacy was a tricky maneuver, the Immelmann turn, which consisted of pulling upward out of an attacking dive, performing a half-roll, and dropping on the enemy from above a second time.

PENETRATING STARE
People who met Boelcke were struck by the intensity of his gaze. As squadron leader, he trained many of Germany's greatest fliers.

Of the two, Boelcke was the more attractive and the more important; he was highly intelligent —a born leader and educator. He successfully argued for the grouping of hand-picked pilots in fighter squadrons, or Jagdstaffeln. As the leader of the first of these, Jasta 2, he passed on his knowledge to many of Germany's greatest fliers, including Manfred von Richthofen. Boelcke also set out the principles of air combat—known as Boelcke's Dicta—that were taught to all German pilots. He said, among other things, that pilots should attack from behind and out of the sun; fire only at close range; and when attacked from above, turn to face the enemy instead of trying to escape. In the fall of 1916, Jasta 2 was thrown into the intense air combats over the Somme. In two months, Boelcke downed 21 Allied aircraft, to give him a total of 40 victories. On October 28, during a fierce dogfight, he collided with one of his own colleagues and spiraled to earth, fatally fracturing his skull.

THE BLUE MAX
The Pour le Mérite was the highest German military decoration. The British nicknamed it the "Blue Max" after the first airman to win it, Max Immelmann.

SECTION 62
Flight Section 62 at Douai, France, in January 1916, including Boelcke (front, fourth from left) and Immelmann (front, third from right). German airmen were infused with a formal military discipline that contrasted strongly with the individualism of French elite pilots.

masculine virtues of physical courage, skillful aggression, chivalry, and noble sacrifice.

Britain's prime minister David Lloyd George told a wartime audience that airmen were "the knighthood of the war, without fear and without reproach." Airmen were by no means immune to this elevated view of their own activities. There are many recorded instances of self-consciously chivalrous behavior—for example, pilots who declined to finish off a brave and skillful enemy whose gun had jammed. Gestures of respect for the enemy were common. When the German ace Oswald Boelcke was killed in 1916, British fliers dropped a wreath at his burial site inscribed to "the memory of Captain Boelcke, our brave and chivalrous foe." But gestures of that kind were

only a veneer on the ruthlessness of aerial warfare. The aces did not spend much time fighting aerial duels with skillful opponents, choosing to prey on lone reconnaissance aircraft instead. During dogfights they picked on the least experienced pilots, exploiting their errors for an easy kill. Top British ace Edward "Mick" Mannock once chanced upon six German aircraft on a training-school flight; he shot down the instructor and then picked off the five defenseless pupils one by one.

Souvenir hunting

Mannock was noted for his hatred of Germans and contempt for gestures of chivalry—his comment on the death of Germany's most

PUBLIC IDOL
Albert Ball was a fearless pilot and excellent marksman who became the first British ace to be idolized by the public. He was still only 20 when his plane crashed under mysterious circumstances in May 1917.

There is no doubting the adrenalin rush that many individuals experienced through combining the thrills of fighting and flying—even though "laughing in the face of danger" is an attitude found in postwar memoirs rather than in contemporary letters or diaries. Many soldiers stuck in damp verminous trenches undoubtedly looked on airmen with envy. A flier had a warm, dry, lice-free bed 10 or 15 miles behind the lines; there was never any shortage of volunteers for the air services. Yet the war in the air had more in common with the war in the trenches than is often recognized. There was a grueling attrition of pilots and aircraft. Freshly trained British pilots arriving at the front in 1917 had an average life expectancy of a little over two weeks. Like "shell-shocked" infantry, airmen were prone to nervous breakdowns as the strain of combat intensified and losses mounted. Every ace was first and foremost a survivor.

Pilot material

Fighter pilots were of varied origins. A good number, like Richthofen, transferred from the cavalry, which had lost its function in the face of barbed wire and the machine gun. Some, like the British ace James McCudden or the German Werner Voss, were drawn to aviation because of an interest in machines and worked their way up from ground

crew to pilots. Some of the best fliers, including the indomitable French ace Charles Nungesser, had been sportsmen. Pilots in general were extremely young. British ace Albert Ball was a squadron leader at the age of 19. Many of them were also quite short—cockpits were small and weight was a prime factor in aircraft performance. Guynemer was a case in point: He weighed less than 132lb (60kg) and had been rejected as too frail for service in the infantry.

Many would-be fighter pilots never made it as far as the front line. The air services were largely unprepared for the challenge of training thousands of new pilots. The result was a great waste of young lives. Almost 500 American Air Service volunteers died learning to fly, more than twice the number killed in combat. Most cadets were introduced to the controls of an aircraft either through being taken up by an instructor or, in France, "flying" on the ground in flightless "aircraft" known as Penguins. But at some point they had to take the controls themselves. Although training aircraft were chosen for their inherent stability, one moment of panic could be fatal. Many novices forgot the simplest principles

famous ace, Baron von Richthofen, was, "I hope he roasted the whole way down." But even those who were less savage in their rejection of the ethic of chivalry took great pleasure in a "kill." Fighter pilots drove to view the wreckage of aircraft they had shot down over their own lines, to examine the bodies and collect souvenirs. Richthofen himself was a renowned collector of mementos of his victories.

SHOOTING PRACTICE
An airman undergoes weapons training as his "cockpit" moves along rails in a primitive attempt to simulate the difficulty of hitting enemy aircraft in a dogfight. Many pilots were sent to the front without ever having fired a gun.

CHARLES NUNGESSER

FRENCH ACE CHARLES NUNGESSER (1892–1927) was a fearless individualist in love with danger, and perhaps more than half in love with death. A champion boxer and swimmer, he began the war in the cavalry but soon transferred to the air service. Flying for the N65 squadron based in Nancy, his bravery and flare soon became legendary, achieving 10 victories during the battle of Verdun. In 1916, he crashed while testing a new aircraft, breaking both legs; the joystick smashed into his face, breaking his jaw and perforating his palate. Two months later, still walking on crutches, he was back in the air. More crashes followed, and more injuries. By the summer of 1917 he was so ill he had to be carried to his cockpit. His decorations included the Military Cross and Legion d'Honneur. Yet he never gave up trying to improve his score, and ended up with 43 victories.

His death in 1927 has remained a mystery, after his biplane, L'Oiseau Blanc, was lost at sea between Paris and New York during an attempted nonstop Atlantic crossing.

SKULL AND CROSSBONES
Nungesser decorated his Nieuport with a macabre array of symbols of mortality, including skulls, coffins, and candlesticks. He miraculously survived World War I, only to disappear, along with his airplane, in 1927.

that had been drummed into them. For instance, every trainee was told that if his engine failed after takeoff, he should under no circumstances attempt to turn back to the airfield. But hundreds did just that, going into a fatal spin.

When losses at the front were heavy, replacements were sent to combat units with 10 hours or fewer of flying time to their credit. This was not a certain death sentence, but came close. Any aircraft of the time was difficult to fly. Basic errors in landing and takeoff cost hundreds of lives. And in the air you needed to learn quickly what maneuvers your aircraft was able to stand without falling apart. Many fighter pilots started their combat careers with a stint as an observer or reconnaissance pilot. Those sent directly into fighter units at first had little idea what was going on around them. Some testified to going through their first dogfight without seeing the enemy at all—everything happened too fast. The lack of radio contact between aircraft meant that once a pilot was in the air, even flying in formation, he was essentially on his own. Some squadrons protected novices, but others developed a ruthless attitude toward them, regarding them as disposable. They were given the unit's worst machines and left to fend for themselves.

MEN AND MACHINES
A Royal Air Force squadron is pictured at its base in northern France in 1918. The airmen are in flying gear; as usual, the ground crew are relegated to the background. The aircraft are Royal Aircraft Factory S.E.5as, probably the best British fighter of the war.

LICENSE TO FLY

This pilot's certificate was issued to a British officer by the Royal Aero Club in 1916. Pilots fresh from flight training had a low survival rate at the front— at the height of the fighting their average life expectancy could be as low as two to three weeks.

Combat style

As the war went on, all sides got better at readying pilots for the shock of the war, but it was the Germans who made the most effort to prevent deaths in training and who prepared their trainee pilots best for combat. They disseminated knowledge of the principles of air combat worked out by Boelcke in 1916, and built up a body of highly skilled fighter pilots through careful selection of suitable individuals and their integration into fighter squadrons that fought in formation. The system did not begin to break down until the end of the war, when heavy losses forced Germany to throw thousands of inexperienced pilots into the fray.

There was always a tension in fighter units between the practical advantages of fighting in formation and the individualist temperament of most of the best pilots. Many of the early aces were often loners who developed their own secrets for success in combat that they were not eager to share with their colleagues. Werner Voss, for example, was a noted success as leader of Jasta 10 in 1917, but he would still head off on his own at dawn or dusk to track down enemy observation aircraft. Canadian pilot Billy Bishop for a time commanded Britain's 85th Squadron yet still fought his own personal war, recording most of his victories on solitary missions.

The French were the first to create self-consciously elite formations of fighter pilots, the Cigognes (Storks). Originally a single squadron, N.3, fighting at Verdun in 1916, the Cigognes had expanded to five squadrons by the following year. Despite being grouped together, however, top French pilots were often reluctant to fight as part of a team.

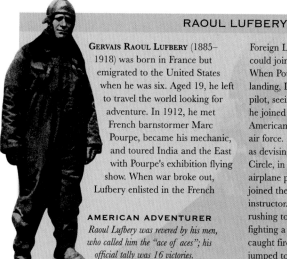

RAOUL LUFBERY

GERVAIS RAOUL LUFBERY (1885–1918) was born in France but emigrated to the United States when he was six. Aged 19, he left to travel the world looking for adventure. In 1912, he met French barnstormer Marc Pourpe, became his mechanic, and toured India and the East with Pourpe's exhibition flying show. When war broke out, Lufbery enlisted in the French

Foreign Legion—the only unit that foreigners could join—before teaming up with Pourpe again. When Pourpe was killed attempting a night landing, Lufbery graduated from mechanic to pilot, seeing his first service in 1915. In May 1916, he joined the Lafayette Escadrille, composed of American volunteers who had joined the French air force. He soon became its leading ace, as well as devising fighter tactics such as the Lufbery Circle, in which fliers formed a circle with each airplane protecting the one in front. In 1918 he joined the US Army Air Service as a combat instructor. He was killed in May 1918 after rushing to the aid of an inexperienced pilot fighting a German Rumpler. Lufbery's Nieuport caught fire in sight of the squadron airfield and he jumped to his death rather than burn alive.

AMERICAN ADVENTURER
Raoul Lufbery was revered by his men, who called him the "ace of aces"; his official tally was 16 victories.

One observer, Jean Villars, wrote that "the veterans want to hunt individually, through overconfidence and a desire to work on their own; the novices imitate them through vanity and ignorance."

High living

Fighter squadrons were never noted for their respect for formal discipline. During any lull in the action at the front, French elite pilots were in the habit of flying off to Paris, where they would be familiar figures in the best restaurants, always with attractive women in attendance and a stylish automobile parked outside.

British fighter squadrons were more noted for their drunken sprees and riotous behavior in the mess, a traditional way of coping with the fear and

personal loss that were inseparable from combat. Yet under a firm squadron leader, such behavior would be kept carefully within limits. Few pilots relished the idea of embarking on a dawn patrol with a stinking hangover—it tended to be an experience that a man would have once and never again.

The relaxed style of the fliers was hard for more traditional army officers to accept. A US military intelligence report in 1917 identified indiscipline in the British flying corps as a problem caused by "the fact that the service, owing to its picturesque nature, is very likely to attract the wrong class of men." No doubt the author of the report would have included among "the wrong class of men" the courageous American volunteers who fought for France in the famous Lafayette Squadron.

Lafayette Squadron

It was in April 1916 that the French allowed New Englander Norman Prince to group seven American pilots into a high-profile squadron, reasoning that this might encourage the United States to enter the war on the Allies' side. The American volunteers earned a deserved reputation for high living and rough partying. But thrown into the thick of the fighting at Verdun in June 1916, they flew four or five patrols a day, until all seven original pilots were either dead or wounded. The Lafayette Squadron continued in existence, never numbering more

OUTER HELMET — Hole aids hearing

INNER HELMET

LEATHER GLOVES — Sheepskin lining

FLYING JACKET — Soft, supple leather; Turned-up collar keeps neck warm

SHATTERPROOF GOGGLES — Tinted, anti-splinter glass

FLYING BOOTS — Thick lining; Leather straps

FIGHTING THE COLD
Flying in open cockpits, cold was one of the major enemies all airmen faced. Wearing two layers of helmet and gloves, plus a leather coat and sheepskin boots, offered some protection. Goggles shielded the eyes against freezing wind, dust, and oil sprayed from the engine. Parachutes and oxygen equipment for high-altitude flight became available late in the war, but only for German airmen.

DUELS IN THE SKY

"THE WHOLE SQUADRON WOULD ENTER the fight in good formation," British pilot Lieutenant Cecil Lewis remembered, "but within half a minute the whole formation had gone to hell. Just chaps wheeling and zooming and diving. On each other's tails… a German going down, one of our chaps on his tail, another German on his tail, another Hun behind that… People approaching head-on firing at each other as they came and then just at the last moment turning and slipping away." This was the classic "dogfight," the result of the meeting of two fighter formations on the Western Front. Committed to a policy of "offensive patrols" over enemy lines, the pilots of the Royal Flying Corps directly invited their German enemies to such combat.

Typically a dozen aircraft of a fighter squadron flew toward the enemy lines in a well-rehearsed close formation, each pilot craning his neck and straining his eyes to pick out distant black specks or a flash of sunlight on a windshield that might reveal the enemy. Whichever side spotted the other first would, if they felt they had the advantage, maneuver into a favorable position and dive. As Lewis described, the sky then filled with whirling aircraft as the engagement broke up into individual combats. Lieutenant Norman Macmillan recalled: "Our machines could turn in such tiny circles that we simply swerved round in an amazingly small space of air, missing each other sometimes by inches." In this chaos, pilots sometimes shot down or collided with their own colleagues. Guns jammed or ran out of ammunition at crucial moments.

> ## "Fighting in the air is not sport, it is scientific murder."
>
> CAPTAIN EDWARD V. "EDDIE" RICKENBACKER, USAS
> *FIGHTING THE FLYING CIRCUS*

Combat was close up and personal. Macmillan recalled how, as he closed in on a Fokker, the pilot looked around: "I was close enough to see his keen blue-gray eyes behind his goggle glasses… He saw I was dead on his tail and instantly banked and curved to the right… My tracers passed close over his central left wing, just outside his cockpit and in line with his head." Some aircraft returned to base with a film of blood on the windshield from an enemy shot at close range. Pilots also saw their own colleagues go down, at worst enveloped in flames. Lieutenant Ira Jones recalled being overcome by "a sudden feeling of sickness, of vomiting" as a comrade's machine blazed in the sky nearby.

At the end of a dogfight, pilots often found themselves heading back to their airfield alone, pursued by the enemy. An Australian flier, Lieutenant George Jones, remembered the experience of "being chased without any ability to retaliate" as the most nerve-shattering of all: "Every time I thought of it I could hardly hold a knife and fork if I was having a meal." But most pilots kept a stiff upper lip: According to Lieutenant John Grider, after evading enemy fighters, you "roll in derision as you cross the lines and hasten home for tea."

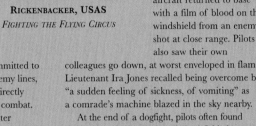

PULP HEROES
The dogfights of the Western Front were a popular topic for pulp magazines in the 1920s and 1930s. Colorful pilot memoirs were often combined with outright fiction. Ironically, many pilots later made a living as stunt fliers in Hollywood movies about the romanticized exploits of the aces.

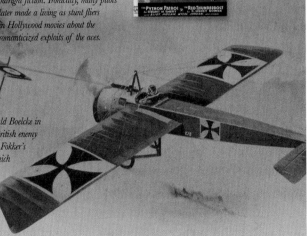

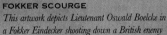

FOKKER SCOURGE
This artwork depicts Lieutenant Oswald Boelcke in a Fokker Eindecker shooting down a British enemy in 1915—the first victim of Anthony Fokker's synchronized forward-firing system, which allowed the pilot to fire though the propeller blades. It was a great success and allowed Boelcke to lead an aerial reign of terror known as the Fokker Scourge.

than 20 members, with fresh entrants drawn from the hundreds of other American volunteers serving with more mundane French air units.

Almost a year after the United States entered the war, the Lafayette Squadron was integrated into the US Army Air Service—with a sharp warning that discipline would have to be tightened. Other American pilots serving with the French were also invited to transfer to US units. An exception was African-American flier Eugene "Jacques" Bullard. Blacks were not accepted as pilots in the US force.

Despite their late arrival in the war, some Air Service pilots were enthusiastic in the pursuit of ace status. The most successful, Eddie Rickenbacker (a former "pupil" of Lufbery's), lent himself tirelessly to the demands of celebrity and publicity, even staging a fake dogfight for the movie cameras while the war was still on—a stunt that nearly turned sour when French pilots unaware of the filming tried to join in the fight.

Aces high

But beyond all the flim-flam of propaganda and publicity, fighter pilots had a real job to do, and the aces were the pilots who did it best. Broadly, the job was to win air superiority. At different times this might involve flying escort to reconnaissance or bomber missions; carrying out offensive patrols to challenge the enemy's forces; or picking off enemy reconnaissance aircraft or bombers. It was in the last of these roles that aces amassed most of their victories. The many qualities that made a successful fighter pilot included keen eyesight, fine reflexes, and perfect coordination; dedication to the task at hand, including a meticulous attention to the detailed preparation of their machine and guns; cool nerve when under fire; and utter ruthlessness in executing a kill. Air combat was about winning, not about giving the other side a fair chance. British ace James McCudden wrote that "the correct way to wage war is to down as many as possible of the enemy at the least risk, expense, and casualties to one's own side."

The ruthlessness of air combat was never better exemplified than by one of the very few recorded meetings of two aces in single combat. On November 23, 1916, British ace Major Lanoe Hawker found himself isolated from his formation and targeted by the Red Baron, Manfred von Richthofen. The German was flying an Albatros D.I, Hawker a markedly inferior pusher D.H.2. The two machines, in Richthofen's words, "circled round and round like madmen." Hawker performed small miracles of agility, side-slipping his aircraft downward each time the German was about to capture him in his sights. But, inevitably, he eventually ran out of height. Down to treetop level and over enemy lines, Hawker desperately headed for home, zigzagging all the time.

MANFRED VON RICHTHOFEN ("THE RED BARON")

AN OFFICER IN THE GERMAN CAVALRY when the war started, Baron Manfred von Richthofen (1892–1918) transferred to the air service in 1915. Having flown as an observer and bomber pilot on the Eastern Front, he was chosen by Oswald Boelcke to join his elite fighter group in France. He soon proved himself to be one of Boelcke's ablest pupils, and the deaths of Boelcke and Max Immelmann in 1916 cleared the way for Richthofen's emergence as Germany's most prominent ace. He was given command of his own squadron, Jasta 11, and then of the first Jagdgeschwader, grouping four squadrons in a fighter wing of about 50 aircraft. With its garishly colored machines, this was the formation the British christened

THE HIGHEST ACE
In 1917 the Red Baron painted his planes red to mark him out to friend and foe alike. He was a ruthless hunter and, with 80 kills, achieved the highest tally of the war.

Richthofen's Flying Circus. Richthofen was a fine leader of men, but lacked personal warmth. His closest relationship was with his wolfhound, Moritz. Arrogant and ruthless, he showed few signs of chivalry or respect for his enemies—he was known to especially despise the French. Where many pilots used sport as a metaphor for air combat, Richthofen saw it in terms of hunting—his favorite leisure activity. He once wrote: "When I have shot down an Englishman my hunting passion is satisfied for a quarter of an hour."

On leave from the front, Richthofen was a celebrity, pursued by photographers and journalists, and dining with the Kaiser. He even took time out to write his memoirs. Having survived a head wound during a dogfight in

CLOSING IN
One of von Richthofen's hunting strategies was to let fly a short burst of fire while still far away from his target: "I did not mean so much to hit him as to frighten him… He began flying curves and this allowed me to draw near."

July 1917, Richthofen came under pressure from his superiors to withdraw from combat. It was felt that his death would be a severe blow to morale. However, during the 1918 spring offensive he headed back into the fray. On April 21 he was shot through the heart while pursuing a potential victim over enemy lines. Whether the fatal shot was fired by an Australian machine-gunner or by Canadian pilot Roy Brown is still a matter of dispute.

HONORED DEATH
On April 21, 1918, Baron von Richthofen was shot down over a sector of the front manned by Australian troops. The Commonwealth troops buried the famous enemy with full military honors.

BARON'S MOUNT
Although it is the highly maneuverable "blood-red" Fokker Dr.I triplane with which Richthofen is associated, he spent most of his time flying biplanes like the Albatros D.II (right) and D.III.

ANTHONY FOKKER

FRIEND OF ACES
Fokker was a pilot before he became an airplane maker. He got along well with German aces, who often called the shots in decisions over aircraft procurement.

BORN INTO A WEALTHY DUTCH family in Kediri, Java, Anthony Fokker (1890–1939) was caught up in the prewar flying craze. He learned to fly in 1910 and soon designed his first monoplane, setting up a factory at Schwerin in Germany in 1912. The war made his fortune. Wily and ambitious, he formed close ties with German bureaucrats and ace pilots alike. Orders flooded in for aircraft such as the Eindecker E.III and the D.VII.

Fokker had a pilot's feel for airplanes and a businessman's ability to organize large-scale production, but he was not an innovative designer. The Fokker trademark welded steel-tube frame was, in fact, dreamed up by his chief technician, Reinhold Platz. At the war's end, Fokker moved to the Netherlands, smuggling airframes, engines, and parts across the border. He produced successful civil and military aircraft in the postwar period, moving to the United States, where he headed the Fokker Aircraft Corporation.

BRAVE WARRIOR
Werner Voss, killed in 1917, was described by British ace James McCudden as "the bravest German airman whom it has been my privilege to see."

was acting up. Pilots suffered from repeated nightmares, began to behave oddly, and sometimes lost their nerve completely.

In this context it is perhaps just possible to understand the mentality of British commanders who opposed the development of suitable parachutes for pilots because it might encourage them to jump out unnecessarily—in effect deserting in the face of the enemy. Yet the lack of parachutes contributed to the worst moments of the air war. A pilot might spiral down for minutes, out of control but uninjured, with nothing to do

> ## "Fight on and fly on to the last drop of blood and the last drop of fuel, to the last beat of the heart."
>
> **MANFRED VON RICHTHOFEN**
> DRINKING A TOAST TO HIS FELLOW PILOTS

but wait to hit the ground. Or, worse, be trapped in a burning aircraft with no better options than jumping to his death or blowing his brains out with a revolver.

The best fighter pilots were far from immune to such pressures of combat flying. Before they died—and most of them did die—many of the aces were harrowed men, flying too many missions and living on the edge of their nerves. Some deliberately drove themselves beyond the limit. Guynemer, for example, feared that if he withdrew from combat, people would say it was because he had "won all the awards." Thus he died flying while patently unfit, physically ill, and racked by paranoia and insomnia.

TOP ALLIED ACE
With 75 victories to his name, French pilot René Fonck was the top Allied ace of the war. He twice shot down six German aircraft in a single day. A boastful individual, Fonck never won the popular affection granted to his compatriots Nungesser and Guynemer.

A few aces died what could be called a hero's death. One such ace was German Werner Voss. On September 23, 1917, flying a Fokker triplane, Voss was jumped by a flight of S.E.5s led by James McCudden. As the S.E.5s dived down on his tail, Voss spun his aircraft to face them. McCudden wrote: "By now the German triplane was in the middle of our formation, and its handling was wonderful to behold. The pilot seemed to be firing at all of us simultaneously, and although I got behind him a second time, I could hardly stay there for a second. His movements were so quick and uncertain that none of us could hold him in sight…" Two British machines were forced to withdraw, shot up by Voss' bullets, but then the German's luck ran out. One pilot, Arthur Rhys Davids, latched on to his tail and raked the triplane with repeated bursts of fire. McCudden saw Voss' aircraft "hit the ground and disappear into a thousand fragments… it literally went to a powder."

Inglorious deaths

Such a death was rare indeed. McCudden himself died in a mundane flying accident when returning from a spell in Britain to take command of a squadron in France. Guynemer simply vanished on a mission—no trace of him or his aircraft was ever found. Boelcke's funeral oration declared that there could be for him "no more beautiful way to end his life than flying for the fatherland," rhetoric that contrasted sadly with the manner of his death as victim of a collision with one of his own men.

But however much the reality of their mostly brief, brutal, nerve-racked lives might contrast with a romantic view of air war, the legend of the aces as "knights of the air" proved durable and an inspiration to a future generation of fliers. Charles Lindbergh, famed for the first solo, nonstop Atlantic crossing, recalled how, as a child during the war, he had "searched newspapers for reports of aerial combats—articles about Fonck, Mannock, Bishop, von Richthofen, and Rickenbacker," who were to him the modern equivalent of "King Arthur's knights in childhood stories." This myth was the aces' legacy.

But Richthofen's machine was faster. Unable to shake him off, Hawker made a last attempt to turn and face his pursuer, but Richthofen opened fire as the Englishman banked and shot him through the head. Recounted in Richthofen's memoirs, this story hardly conforms to the chivalric stereotype. In effect, Richthofen ruthlessly hunted down a pilot who, for all his courage and skill, had no chance because his machine was inferior. It reads more like an assassination than a duel.

Mental torture

Whether aces or not, fighter pilots were subjected to unbearable strain at peak periods of the war. When men were flying three or four missions a day, seeing friends and colleagues dying before their eyes, often in the most gruesome fashion, they would pray for the relief of a "dud" day, when weather conditions made flying impossible. If losses were high, there would be a sharp rise in the number of pilots aborting missions, alleging that their magazines had jammed or their engine

"Those deaths must have been the most dramatic in the world's history. They fell—a cone of blazing wreckage —watched by eight million of their enemies."

MURIEL DAYRELL-BROWNING
EYEWITNESS TO THE DESTRUCTION OF
ZEPPELIN SL 11 OVER LONDON, 1916

ZEPPELINS AND BOMBERS

GIANT AIRPLANES AND AIRSHIPS BROUGHT THE TERROR OF WAR TO THE CITIES OF EUROPE

EVEN BEFORE World War I, the airship was fixed in the popular imagination as a symbol of terror. In his 1908 book, *The War in the Air*, H.G. Wells had described an airship raid on New York leaving "ruins and blazing conflagrations and heaped and scattered dead." It was a vision that appealed to some military commanders. Captain Peter Strasser, head of the German navy's airship fleet, believed that Britain could be "overcome by means of airships… through increasingly extensive destruction of cities, factory complexes, dockyards…"

The Germans had no monopoly on the intent to bomb enemy cities and factories. But they did have the lead in airship technology, and in 1914 airships were the only aircraft capable of carrying a significant bombload far enough to hit strategic targets.

AIRSHIP COMMANDER
Peter Strasser, Commander of the German Navy Zeppelin Fleet during World War I, was an ambitious officer who made the Zeppelin an effective weapon of war. He died when the L 70 was shot down over England.

However, at this stage they were not capable of fulfilling apocalyptic visions of mass destruction. Whether metal-framed Zeppelins or plywood-framed Schütte-Lanzes, German airships revealed serious drawbacks early in the war. The army found that they could not survive over the battlefield. Traveling at under 50mph (80kmph), they presented large, tempting targets for gunners on the ground; four army airships were shot down in the first month of the war. They were also distressingly accident prone, especially in bad weather.

Stealthy raiders

However, an answer to the airship's vulnerability in combat was sought in stealth. On a moonless night, despite their bulk, Zeppelins could evade detection and pursuit. Out of necessity they became night raiders. The German army and navy used airships to bomb a variety of strategic targets under cover of darkness, including Paris and other French cities. But their most prized target was Britain, and above all London. In those bitter, hate-filled days of war, German schoolchildren learned to sing: "Zeppelin, fly! Fly to England! England will burn in fire!"

SHADOW OVER THE WESTERN FRONT
The Zeppelin Staaken R.IV, of which the above is a model, flew on the Western Front in 1917–18. This six-engined monster had a wingspan of 138ft 6in (42.2m) and, when fully loaded, weighed over 14 tons (13 tonnes).

NIGHT BOMBER
Introduced in 1917, the four-engined Zeppelin Staaken R.VI was mainly used for night bombing raids on London. It was unusual in its day for having a fully enclosed cabin, but during bomb runs the commander stood in the open observation post in the nose.

AIRPOWER THROUGH WORLD WAR I

AIRSHIP FIRE BOMB
This incendiary bomb was dropped by Zeppelin LZ 38 in the first airship raid on London, on May 31, 1915. The German airship crews initially dropped fire bombs by hand over the side of their gondola; automatic release mechanisms were added later. The incendiary bombs of the time were too small, unreliable, and easily extinguished, to have much destructive effect.

The sporadic arrival of airships over Britain from 1915 onward made a deep impression on the civilian population. None who heard the sinister thumping of the Maybach engines or witnessed the dark silhouette passing overhead in the night ever forgot the experience. A Londoner who was a child at the time later remembered having been "conscious of an unspoken fear around me… as I watched those sinister shapes slipping in and out of the searchlight beams." Yet airship commanders found mounting a sustained bombing campaign beyond their capabilities. Even before effective air defenses were in place, flying from a base in north Germany or occupied Belgium to Britain and back in pitch darkness was an awesome challenge. Once the British deployed night-flying aircraft and ground batteries armed with incendiary ammunition, traveling to London under a vast bag of inflammable gas began to seem like a very bad idea.

Aerial sailors
A fundamental limiting factor on airship operations was weather. Heavy clouds, strong winds, or storms made missions impossible. Yet when they set off, the airship commanders had no idea what the weather was like over Britain.

NAVAL PATROL
This rare photograph (left) shows German naval airships in flight. Naval airship crews spent much of the war on patrol over the North Sea. Although their usefulness was limited by the inability to operate in bad weather, airships were more effective on these reconnaissance missions at sea than in their role as a strategic bombing force.

PUTTING OUT FIRES
Firemen douse rubble on the morning after a Zeppelin air raid on London in 1917. Kaiser Wilhelm II initially refused to allow the bombing of cities, but then permitted it with the proviso that residential areas and cultural monuments should be spared. In 1915, a further amendment allowed the bombing of any part of London. In practice, airship commanders had little control over where their bombs landed. Bombing cities meant killing civilians.

Time and again they set off in promising conditions only to encounter fog or strong head winds as they approached their targets.

Just flying the huge aircraft posed complex problems. They were more like warships than airplanes. The commander strode about his control cabin with binoculars around his neck while a coxswain steered the ship with a nautical-style wheel. Another coxswain monitored altitude and gas pressure. The engines were tended in flight by mechanics in the engine cars, and a sailmaker checked for damage to the outer fabric.

The commander and his officers were constantly engaged in complex calculations about the airship's altitude. A variety of factors made the craft rise or fall. For instance, when it rained, the water on the vast cover of the airship would increase its weight, making it lose height. Constant fine-tuning of ballast and gas pressure was needed to maintain a steady height.

But this was nothing compared to the problem of navigation. On night raids, Zeppelins often did well to find the right country, let alone a city the size of London. The best means of

navigation available was by a radio fix: The airship transmitted a signal to two ground stations, each then identified the direction of the signal, and the two direction lines allowed the airship's precise position to be calculated. But airship commanders mostly preferred to keep radio silence for fear of revealing their position to the enemy. They fell back on the age-old nautical technique of dead reckoning. If you knew how fast you had traveled, for how long, and in what direction, you could plot your position on a chart.

SHOOTING DOWN AN AIRSHIP

AT AROUND 2:30AM ON SEPTEMBER 3, 1916, a woman in north London, woken by explosions, looked out of her window and saw sailing close above "a cigar of bright silver in the full glare of about 20 magnificent searchlights." It was the Schütte-Lanz SL 11, one of 16 naval and army airships sent against London in the largest raid of the war. Also in the night sky was a B.E.2c biplane, piloted by Lieutenant William Leefe Robinson, part of the Home Defence Wing assigned to protect Britain against airship raids. Leefe Robinson and his colleagues had grown used to the unnerving experience of night flying. When an airship raid was detected, they took off

"I saw, far behind us, a bright ball of fire… Poor fellows, they were lost the moment the ship took fire."

ZEPPELIN CAPTAIN ERNST LEHMANN
RECALLING THE LOSS OF THE SL 11

from airstrips lit by flares and, once in the air, relied on the faintly visible line of the horizon to keep their sense of balance and hold the aircraft true. Looking for airships in total darkness was, however, a frustrating experience. Leefe Robinson had been on patrol for three hours without seeing anything when the SL 11 was suddenly lit up for all to see. Armed with explosive and incendiary ammunition, he dived toward the airship and came up under its nose, raking it with fire from bow to stern. He had shot off three drums of ammunition before he saw it begin to glow: "In a few seconds the whole rear part was blazing," he wrote. "I quickly got out of the way of the falling, blazing Zeppelin." The event was visible for miles around. Londoners cheered as the airship fell. The blaze was witnessed with very different sentiments by Captain Ernst Lehmann, commander of a Zeppelin at that

MACABRE MEMENTOS- *Pieces of the SL 11, the first airship shot down over London, were made into souvenirs such as these cufflinks and pin, which were sold to raise money for the Red Cross.*

moment heading for home. "I saw, far behind us, a bright ball of fire," he wrote. "Poor fellows, they were lost the moment the ship took fire." The SL 11 was the first airship shot down over London. Leefe Robinson was awarded the Victoria Cross for this feat, only to be killed the following year on the Western Front.

ZEPPELIN DESTROYER
The Ranken dart was designed to be dropped on an airship from above and explode after penetrating its outer cover. Explosive and incendiary ammunition eventually made airships fatally vulnerable to attack.

BURNED-OUT SHELL-
The Zeppelin L 33 was one of two German airships shot down over Britain on the night of September 23-24, 1916. It was destroyed by a combination of antiaircraft fire and air attack.

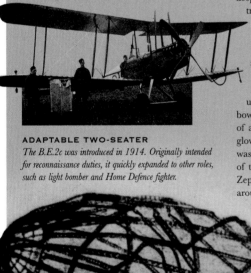

ADAPTABLE TWO-SEATER
The B.E.2c was introduced in 1914. Originally intended for reconnaissance duties, it quickly expanded to other roles, such as light bomber and Home Defence fighter.

FLYING THE GIANTS

THE LARGEST AIRPLANES THAT FLEW in the Great War were the heavy bombers the Germans called Riesenflugzeug ("giant aircraft"). The most famous of these "R-planes," the Zeppelin Staaken R.VI, was introduced into Germany's arsenal in September 1917, to join the smaller Gothas in their mass raids on Britain. These huge machines had two pilots sitting side by side operating steering wheels like those on airships. They also carried

mechanics on board, who tended the engines in flight. Arthur Schoeller, commander of an R.VI, wrote a vivid account of a night raid on London.

He described how 40 ground crew prepared the "giant" for action, loading the bomb bay, filling the vast fuel tanks, and tuning the four 250hp engines. After a light supper, the eight-man crew headed out to the aircraft, "whose idling engines sing a song of subdued power." Six R-planes taxied out on to the takeoff strip. Their engines at full throttle emitting a deafening roar, the heavily laden machines slowly rose into the air and headed out across the sea into black nothingness. With only calculations of time, speed, and direction to tell them where they were, Schoeller and his observer had begun to suspect they might be lost when, to their relief, they saw searchlights probing the sky: "bright beams making glowing circles in the thin overcast clouds." They must be over England. An airfield, lit by flares

for use by British night fighters, appeared startlingly bright beneath them. They bombed it in passing, while their machine gunners blasted away at the searchlights. Then, through a break in the cloud, they spotted the Thames River. Soon the observer, who had moved to the open observation post in the nose of the aircraft, was pressing the bomb-release keys, hoping to hit the London docks somewhere below. After dropping their bombload, they turned for home along the Thames with bursts of antiaircraft fire dangerously close. A shell splinter tore the fabric of the upper wing but caused no serious damage. Heading back across the sea, they found their troubles were far from over. In sight of the Belgian coast, all four propellers stopped because of a frozen fuel line. They glided as far as dry land, where their flares lit up a cratered terrain. Schoeller stalled the aircraft just above the ground and pancaked, smashing the landing gear and a wing. His crew was safely home.

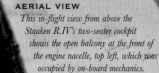

AERIAL VIEW
*This in-flight view from above the
Staaken R.IV's two-seater cockpit
shows the open balcony at the front of
the engine nacelle, top left, which was
occupied by on-board mechanics.*

Yet these calculations could be thrown off completely by the effect of wind. If navigators failed to realize that they had been blown off course, they were lost and had no way to regain their bearings.

Of course, a fair number of airships heading for London did find it. The city's lights were hidden by a strictly enforced blackout, but they were able to use the Thames River as a navigational aid, since it offered a readily indentifiable shape for them to follow. They also had searchlight and gun batteries marked on their maps, not only so they could avoid them but also so they could use them for orientation around the darkened city.

Airships did not attack a target in formation. Each came from a different direction, at staggered intervals. Once through the ring of defenses around London, the method of attack was simple—to fly as fast as possible in a straight line across the city, releasing their explosive and incendiary bombs as they went.

The first airship raids on Britain were carried out in January 1915; the first raid on London the following May. Up to the late summer of 1916, although sporadic, the raids could be counted a success. Some inflicted a substantial amount of damage—for example, on September 8, 1915, Captain Heinrich Mathy's L 13 killed 22 people and injured 87 in a single pass across London. Even wandering lost over England in the middle of the night was not necessarily a waste of energy. One of the worst raids of the war came in January 1916, when nine airships trying to bomb Liverpool became confused in the darkness and arrived instead over the cities of the Midlands, where no blackout was in force. Seventy people were killed in the bombing.

The British were forced to divert valuable resources of aircraft, pilots, and guns from the Western Front as the public demanded better protection. But these resources, accompanied by the crucial introduction of explosive and incendiary ammunition, succeeded in tipping the scales fatally against the Zeppelins. In late August and September 1916, the Germans launched their most ambitious airship bombing offensive. It was a disaster. In a series of raids, four airships were lost to ground fire or pursuit aircraft. Among those who died was the experienced Mathy; he jumped to his death from his burning Zeppelin rather than roast alive.

High fliers
The Germans responded to this setback with a new type of airship that was bigger but lighter than previous ones. These "height-climbers" regularly flew at over 16,000ft (5,600m), out of reach of ground fire and difficult for aircraft to attack. But for the unfortunate crews, missions at high altitude were a severe trial. For hours on end they endured freezing cold; they found it hard to breathe in the thin air, but using their crude oxygen equipment made them feel nauseated; rapid changes of pressure in ascending and descending gave them the bends. And for all this suffering they inflicted only limited damage.

However, the technical achievements of German airships were extraordinary. In November 1917 the L 59 flew 4,200 miles (6,760km) nonstop on an abortive mission to Africa. In the same year, L 55 established an enduring altitude record of 24,000ft (8,400m).

But turning technical capability into military effectiveness proved impossible. To the end, naval airship leader Peter Strasser still dreamed of a decisive coup—an airship raid across the Atlantic to devastate New York. However, in August 1918 he was shot down on a final hopeless mission over the North Sea.

> "Inside the fuselage the pale glow of dimmed lights outlines the chart table, the wireless equipment, and the instrument panel… Under us is a black abyss."
>
> **HAUPTMANN ARTHUR SCHOELLER**
> COMMANDER OF AN R-PLANE, DESCRIBING A NIGHT FLIGHT TO BRITAIN IN MARCH 1918

SKY JUMPER
In this stereoscopic photograph, British soldiers look at the hole left in the ground by the body of a man who jumped from a burning Zeppelin over Billericay, Essex, England. Using a stereoscopic viewer, it is possible to see the hole in 3-D.

Arrival of the Gotha

From the start of the war, the Germans had wanted to use heavier-than-air aircraft for strategic bombing, but lacked a suitable machine until the advent of Friedrichshafen and Gotha twin-engined bombers. The Gothas began raids on Britain in the summer of 1917 with impressive effect. Both the air defenses and the civilian population were unprepared for formations of bombers attacking in broad daylight. When 14 Gothas appeared over London for the first time on June 13, crowds of people ran out into the streets to watch them. The bombs falling on unsheltered civilians killed 162 people.

The Gothas flew faster than Zeppelins and were far harder to shoot down. When flying in formation, they could dish out heavy punishment to pursuing aircraft from the combined firepower of their machine guns. This relative invulnerability meant that they could operate initially in daylight and later, when air defenses improved, on moonlit, rather than moonless, nights. This made it much easier for them to locate their targets. Also, because they could be produced much more quickly and cheaply than airships, they could be deployed in far greater numbers—43 were used in the largest single raid on London.

Sporadic night attacks on London by Gothas and the even larger R-planes continued through the winter and spring of 1917–18. Paris also became a regular target for the German bombers. Parisians and Londoners grew used to a routine of air-raid warnings and all-clears, huddling through the dangerous hours in the cellars and basements of their houses or in the tunnels of underground railroad stations. The raids petered

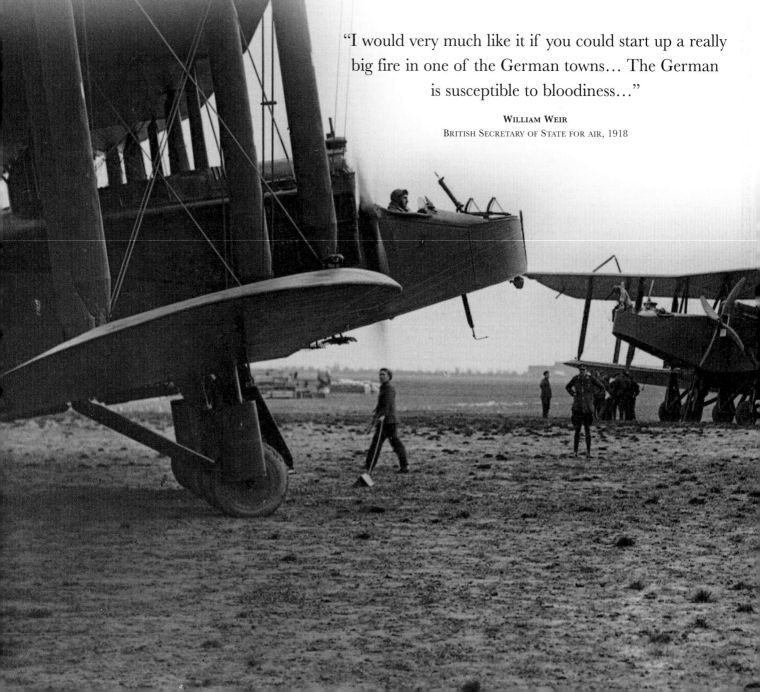

"I would very much like it if you could start up a really big fire in one of the German towns… The German is susceptible to bloodiness…"

WILLIAM WEIR
BRITISH SECRETARY OF STATE FOR AIR, 1918

out in May 1918 since, from this time on, all Germany's resources were devoted to the desperate battle on the Western Front. But airplanes had proved their relative effectiveness: In 51 airship raids on Britain, 557 people were killed and 1,358 injured; in 52 airplane attacks, 857 were killed and 2,508 injured.

Hitting back

The damage inflicted by both airships and bombers was, in truth, a puny return for the investment of men and material. But its psychological impact was far-reaching. Shrill demands for a more effective defense of the civilian population caused a crisis in British policy on the air war. And the demand for revenge against the Germans gave fresh impetus to moves toward creating an Allied strategic bomber force.

Throughout the war, debate raged among both politicians and military commanders in the Allied countries as to the merits or demerits of bombing enemy cities and factories. The stalemate and heavy losses on the Western Front naturally encouraged speculation that bombers might be able to end the deadlock by breaking the enemy's will to fight or destroying his industrial capacity. It was certainly tempting to grasp at any alternative to yet another apparently futile infantry offensive. But those

GIANNI CAPRONI

GIANNI CAPRONI (1886–1957) WAS ITALY'S most prominent aircraft designer and manufacturer during World War I. After building his first aircraft in 1910, his efforts to win contracts from the Italian army were frustrated until he was befriended by the air-minded Colonel Giulio Douhet. By 1914 Caproni had already designed an innovative prototype monoplane fighter, the Ca 20, with a forward-firing gun mounted on top of the wing. Under the influence of Douhet, however, Caproni devoted himself primarily to the production of large bomber aircraft.

By the time Italy entered the war in 1915, Caproni three-engined biplane bombers (Ca. 42s) were coming into service. By 1918 an estimated 70,000 workers were building Caproni biplanes and triplanes, not

only in Italy, but also under license in France and the United States.

Caproni joined Douhet in advocating a strategic air offensive that would have used thousands of heavy bombers to batter Germany into submission. This did not happen, but his arguments were influential, not least with American military aviation enthusiasts. After the war Caproni went on building civil and military aircraft.

BOMBER MAN
Caproni designed a number of heavy bombers, including the Ca 33, which played a major role in the allied bombing campaign.

CAPRONI CA.42
The Ca 4 series of triplanes were used on Italian bombing missions against Austria. Despite being less common than the Caproni biplanes, they were more powerful.

who saw the trenches of the Western Front as the place where, inevitably, the war would eventually be won and lost, argued against any diversion of aerial resources away from direct support for the hard-pressed armies on the ground.

At first the debate was largely theoretical, since the Allies simply did not possess the equipment to carry out a strategic bombing campaign. French airmen made a brave attempt at bombing Germany from 1915 using slow, clumsy Voisin 8s, first by day and then by night, but their losses were high and the damage they inflicted negligible. Strangely, at first those Allied countries who generally had less-strong air forces possessed the most powerful bombers. Russia deployed Sikorsky's four-engined Il'ya Muromets as bombers

HEAVY BOMBERS
Entering service in the late summer of 1918, the Handley Page O/400 bomber was the key aircraft in the newly formed independent air force. Large formations of O/400s—up to 40 bombers at a time—carried out night raids deep inside Germany. The aircraft's bombload could include a 1,650lb (750kg) "blockbuster" bomb.

and reconnaissance aircraft. Italy, which joined in the war on the Allied side in 1915, was at that time the only power to have an aircraft specifically designed for bombing, the Caproni Ca.1. Italy also had one of the most aggressive and influential advocates of strategic bombing in Colonel Giulio Douhet. His outspoken views and undisciplined behavior brought him in conflict with his superiors, and he spent part of the war in prison. But Italy nonetheless used Caproni bombers to attack the cities of its nearest enemy, Austria-Hungary.

Call for action

By 1918 there was a solid weight of opinion in the Allied countries calling for a bombing offensive against Germany, and frustration among political leaders at the military's failure to deliver it. In April 1918 Britain created the world's first independent air force, the Royal Air Force, to replace the army's Royal Flying Corps and the navy's Royal Naval Air Service. It was intended, among other things, to help give Britain more effective air defenses, and to promote a strategic air offensive against Germany. The independent force of bombers was set up in June to carry out this offensive. Meanwhile the French commander-in-chief, Marshal Henri Pétain, called for a fleet of heavy bombers to "paralyze

AIR WAR AT SEA

IN THE EARLY YEARS OF AVIATION, navies were, on balance, more aware of the potential of aircraft than were armies. This was especially true of Britain's Royal Navy, where the influence of an imaginative, progressive-minded First Lord of the Admiralty, Winston Churchill, made itself felt. But when the war started, there was no effective way of taking aircraft to sea with the fleet. In September 1914, the Royal Navy converted three cross-Channel steamers into seaplane carriers. The seaplanes were winched off the ship to take off from the sea, and lifted back on board after their mission. It sounded simple and effective, but it was not. The seaplanes found taking off and landing at sea impossible, except under highly favorable conditions—they needed exactly the right degree of swell.

Before the war, both the US and British navies had experimented with launching aircraft off a platform on the deck of a ship. The Royal Navy resumed these experiments in earnest in 1917. A light battlecruiser, HMS *Furious*, had its forward guns removed and replaced by a takeoff deck. The idea was that the latest land-based aircraft, superior in performance to seaplanes, would take off and land from the ship.

The maneuver was undertaken by Squadron Commander E.H. Dunning flying the highly agile Sopwith Pup biplane. Taking off was relatively easy if the ship sailed into the wind, but landing was another matter. Dunning managed it twice by matching his speed to that of the ship

PLATFORM LAUNCH
One system for launching aircraft at sea was to put them on a lighter—a sort of barge—towed behind a light, speedy vessel (left). When traveling fast enough, this would generate the windspeed, and hence the lift, needed for takeoff.

HOISTED OVERBOARD
Seaplanes offered a way of carrying aircraft with a fleet. Machines like this Short seaplane were winched overboard from a ship, took off from the sea, and might with luck land safely alongside and be lifted back on board.

so he could effectively hover down like a helicopter, helped by other pilots on deck who grabbed rope toggles on the wings and pulled him down as he cut his engine. But his third attempt proved fatal. The aircraft stalled and cartwheeled overboard after a tire blew, and the unfortunate Dunning drowned. *Furious* was then equipped with a rear deck for landing, but the turbulence created by the smokestack and central superstructure of the ship tossed the aircraft around too much. Nevertheless, Sopwith Camels launched from *Furious* carried out the first-ever successful air-strike by carrier-borne aircraft, bombing Zeppelin sheds at Tondern in July 1918. In the last months of

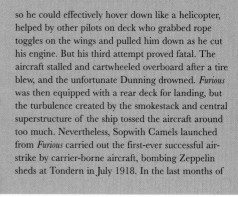

the economic life of Germany and its war industries by methodical and repeated action against principal industrial cities…" In 1918 the Allies had the de Havilland-designed Airco D.H.9 and excellent Breguet Br.14 as day bombers and the Handley Page O/400 and Caproni biplanes and triplanes as night bombers. The Handley Page, although nothing like as big as the German R-planes, could carry a maximum bombload of 2,000lb (900kg), and formed the backbone of the independent force. Other heavy bombers, including the French Farman Goliath and the British Vickers Vimy, were under construction in 1918 but arrived too late to see service.

Lesson in terror

In the summer and fall of 1918, formations of up to 40 Allied bombers flew raids deep into Germany. Predictably, bad weather and unreliable aircraft limited the effectiveness of the bomber offensive. But civilians in cities such as Frankfurt and Mannheim were taught the terror of air raids that had already been experienced by inhabitants of Paris and London. Allied airmen were always under orders to aim for precise targets, such as factories or communications centers. But Allied political leaders were eager to affect civilian morale. The British Secretary of State for air, William Weir, told Hugh Trenchard, the commander of the independent force, not to be scrupulous in respect for civilian life: "If I were you," he wrote, "I would not be too exacting as regards accuracy in bombing railway stations in the middle of towns. The German is susceptible to bloodiness, and I would not mind a few accidents due to inaccuracy."

In fact, the air commanders were generally more skeptical about strategic bombing than the politicians. Trenchard knew he was supposed to use his force to bomb German cities and factories, but more often he directed it against tactical objectives such as airfields

FIRST INDEPENDENT AIR FORCE
This recruiting poster invites volunteers to join the Royal Air Force (RAF), the world's first independent air force. Created by combining Britain's army and navy air arms in April 1918, the RAF was intended to prioritize the protection of Britain against air attack and promote the strategic bombing of enemy factories and cities.

and communications centers behind the front.

The same is true of US Brigadier General Billy Mitchell. Both Trenchard and Mitchell later became advocates of strategic bombing, but they devoted themselves in the last months of the war to the tactical use of airpower.

The evidence of World War I was that, at current levels of technology, strategic bombing could neither seriously disrupt industrial production nor significantly weaken a population's will to fight. Bombing was costly and inaccurate. Its chief positive effect lay in forcing the enemy to divert resources to air defense.

The building and operation of large bomber aircraft was nonetheless an important step in the progress of aviation. Bomber aircrews had accumulated extensive experience of long-distance flight and night flying, and the large aircraft they flew carrying bombs could, with relatively small modifications, carry passengers or freight instead. Strategic bombing in World War I helped pave the way for the development of commercial aviation—as well as the devastation of Dresden, Tokyo, and Hiroshima.

> "It is probable that future war will be conducted by a special class, the air force, as it was by the armored knights of the Middle Ages."
>
> BRIGADIER GENERAL WILLIAM "BILLY" MITCHELL
> *WINGED DEFENSE*, 1924

FIRST DECK LANDING
On August 2, 1917, pilot E.H. Dunning made the first successful landing on the deck of a moving ship. He was flying a Sopwith Pup, a popular, highly maneuverable airplane. An unsuccessful attempt five days later ended in his death.

the war, an ocean liner was converted into HMS *Argus*, the first true aircraft carrier. The smokestack was hidden away at the back of the ship, allowing a long, unobstructed flight deck. British naval commanders planned to use Argus for a Pearl Harbor-style strike against the German fleet in port. Modern naval aviation had been born.

DOCTRINE AND HISTORY—WORLD WAR I

DISTINCTIVE CAPABILITIES	FUNCTIONS (MISSIONS)	DOCTRINAL EMPHASIS
• Information Superiority • Precision Engagement • Air Superiority	• Surveillance and Reconnaissance • Counterair • Strategic Attack	• Strategic Attack of Military Targets

MODULE II

THE INTERWAR YEARS AND WORLD WAR II:
Strategic attack

- The Development
  of Air Doctrine

- Airpower in Early
  World War II

- The European Theater in
  World War II

- The Pacific Theater
  in World War II

4

THE DEVELOPMENT OF AIR DOCTRINE

THE UNITED STATES Army and Navy struggled after World War I to assimilate the meaning and role of airpower. The assistant chief of the Army Air Service, Brigadier General William "Billy" Mitchell, became such a forceful advocate of an independent air force that he offended his superiors and was court-martialed. While Mitchell's demonstrations of airpower's potential swiftly persuaded the Navy to begin building aircraft carriers, the admirals could not agree on the role of naval aviation—some saw it as a primary attack force, while many others believed it was useful only in support of battleships or in a reconnaissance role. As war clouds gathered in both Europe and East Asia, the US Army's air force went through a series of reorganizations that gradually increased its autonomy.

Deutſchlandflug 1937

> "...would not the sight of a single enemy airplane be enough to induce a formidable panic? Normal life would be unable to continue under the constant threat of death and imminent destruction."
>
> GENERAL GIULIO DOUHET
> *THE COMMAND OF THE AIR*, 1921

IMPORTANT AIRCRAFT
Introduced in 1937, the Seversky P-35 was a vital steppingstone in the development of American fighter technology. It was the first single-seat, all-metal pursuit plane with retractable landing gear and enclosed cockpit to go into service with the US Army Air Corps.

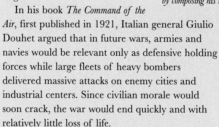

THE SHADOW OF WAR

DURING THE 1920S AND 1930S, AVIATION DEVELOPED INTO A POTENTIALLY DEVASTATING WEAPON THAT WOULD CHANGE THE NATURE OF WAR

THE EXPERIENCE of World War I set in motion an idea that was to have a potent influence on the future of warfare: the notion that wars could be won by airpower alone. The appalling casualties endured by the infantry in the long stalemate in the trenches provided a powerful motive for seeking some other way of fighting a war. And the example of aerial bombardment, especially by airships and Gotha bombers on London, suggested what that new way of fighting might be.

In his book *The Command of the Air*, first published in 1921, Italian general Giulio Douhet argued that in future wars, armies and navies would be relevant only as defensive holding forces while large fleets of heavy bombers delivered massive attacks on enemy cities and industrial centers. Since civilian morale would soon crack, the war would end quickly and with relatively little loss of life.

Although Douhet's writings were little known outside his own country, they expressed an attitude shared by many leading figures in military aviation. They included Sir Hugh Trenchard, Britain's chief of air staff, who had commanded the unified bombing force intended to launch a major aerial offensive on Germany in 1919, before peace intervened. Trenchard ensured that the bombing of cities was the central plank in British air strategy between the wars. In the United States, the most strident propagandist for military airpower was Brigadier General Billy Mitchell, commander of the US air forces in Europe in 1918 and postwar assistant chief of the Army Air

"IL DUCE"
Italy's fascist dictator Benito Mussolini was keen to identify himself with the modernity and dynamism that aircraft symbolized. This 1933 portrait by Gerardo Dottori flatters the dictator by composing his image of airplanes.

Service. To Trenchard and Mitchell, the great appeal of heavy bombing—whether used for destroying cities or, as Mitchell advocated, to sink enemy ships approaching America's shores—was that it provided a rationale for a powerful air force, independent of, and with equal status to, the other armed services. Trenchard was fortunate in already having the world's only independent air force, the RAF, although in the 1920s, he could not secure it more than the most meager funding. Mitchell had to go out and campaign for the force that he felt destined to lead. It was a campaign that brought him into political entanglements and a conflict with his superiors that eventually led to his court-martial for insubordination in 1925.

Disappearing funds
The pressing problem for military aviation in the immediate postwar period was to persuade tight-fisted governments to fund it adequately. The US air service contracted from 190,000 men in 1918 to 10,000 in 1920; the RAF shrank from a force of almost 300,000 to under 40,000 in the year after the war. The French, worried about Germany, kept a larger air arm—enabling Trenchard to use the "threat" of French aerial strength as an argument for building up the RAF in the 1920s.

In the postwar period, the RAF had a chance to practice the use of airpower in a series of small-scale colonial conflicts.

LUFTWAFFE FLYOVER
In an ominous show of strength, a formation of German Dornier Do 17 bombers fly over a Tag der Wehrmacht rally in 1938. Germany's Nazi regime took every opportunity to show off its bomber force, seeking to intimidate Britain and France with the threat of aerial destruction.

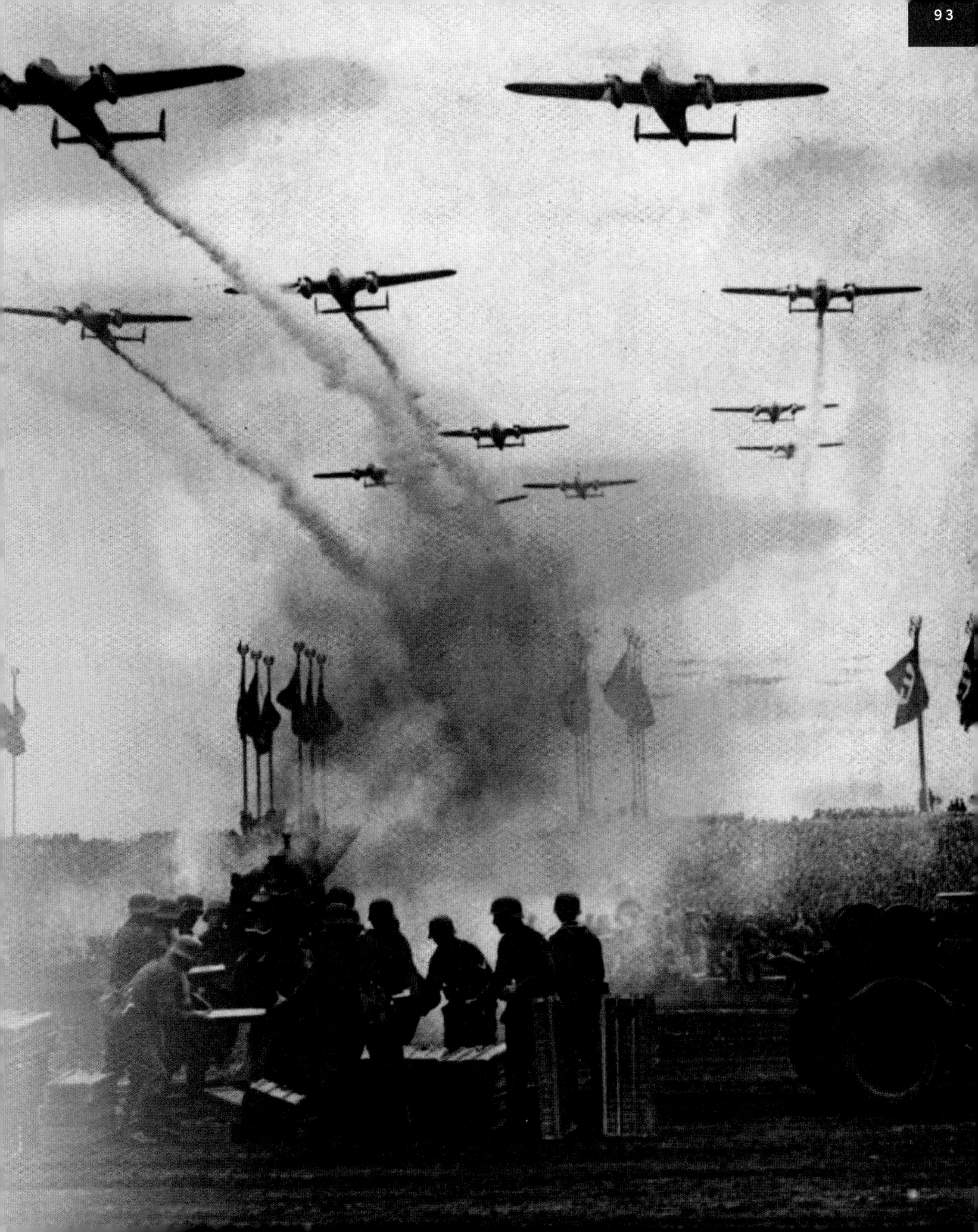

ITALO BALBO

LIKE THOUSANDS OF OTHER disillusioned young men who fought for Italy in World War I, Italo Balbo (1896–1940) joined Mussolini's violent Fascist Blackshirts in the early 1920s, playing a prominent part in Mussolini's rise to power. In 1929, he was appointed head of Italian aviation. Only then did he learn to fly. In 1928, Balbo became famous beyond Italy's frontiers for the mass-formation flights he staged—60 seaplanes across southern Europe in

DASHING PIONEER
As minister of aviation from 1929–33, Italo Balbo helped modernize Italian aviation, gaining it an international reputation with his mass-formation flights.

ITALIAN GLORY
This booklet, dedicated to the "Brave and Intrepid Italian Aviators... and Italo Balbo... who led the glory of Italian wings...," celebrates their internationally acclaimed flight from Rome to Chicago.

ITALIAN ARMADA AND THE GLORIES OF ROMA CAPT^T MVNDI

1928; 10 seaplanes across the southern Atlantic to Brazil in 1931; and 24 seaplanes to Chicago in 1933. Jealous of the acclaim Balbo received for the Chicago flight, Mussolini then packed him off to govern the Italian colony of Libya. Balbo subsequently opposed Mussolini's alliance with Nazi Germany in 1939, proposing instead a rapprochement with Britain. He was killed in 1940 when his airplane was mistakenly shot down by an Italian antiaircraft battery.

Faced with a rebellion in Afghanistan in 1919, the British bombed Kabul and Jalalabad, also dropping leaflets warning Afghani troops and tribesmen of the dire fate that awaited them if they did not surrender. This had no appreciable effect. But the use of airpower against rebels in Iraq between 1922 and 1925 was judged a major success, showing that the RAF could act as a cheap imperial policeman. France and Spain both used airpower against Berber rebels led by Abd al-Karim in their respective colonies in Morocco in the 1920s—the French achieving particular success employing their aircraft in tactical support of mobile columns of troops in trucks and armored cars.

Symbols of power

Whatever the tactics employed and the practical results achieved, there was something profoundly satisfactory to the European psyche in the deployment of aircraft against "primitive" peoples. At a period when the unbridled assertion of white racial superiority and Western technological prowess was starting to be challenged by anti-colonial movements, aircraft stood as a comforting

FASCIST FRIENDS
Italo Balbo (left) was the closest ally and heir-apparent of Benito Mussolini (right) until the acclaim following his transatlantic flights aroused Mussolini's jealousy. This photograph was taken in Italy in the mid-1930s.

REDA CC 20

IMPERIAL POLICING
A local soldier stands guard in front of an RAF Hawker Hardy in northern Iraq in the 1930s. British aircraft were sent to Iraq to protect the Kirkuk oilfields and pipelines from hostile tribes, a cheaper option than sending imperial troops.

symbol of the dominance of the "civilized" peoples over the "uncivilized." Not surprisingly, airpower appealed especially to the militaristic right-wing nationalist movements that came to power in much of Europe between the wars, for which Italian dictator Benito Mussolini's Fascists established the pattern.

When Mussolini's black-shirted followers bullied their way to power in 1922, several Italian World War I air aces were prominent in their ranks. Mussolini himself idolized aviation, revering it as a symbol of power and modernity. "Not every Italian can or should fly," he declared, "but all Italians should envy those who do and should follow with profound feeling the development of Italian wings."

In 1923, an independent Italian air force was created, the Regia Aeronautica, and the scale of Italy's airpower rapidly expanded. Mussolini's dictatorship gloried in the incredible stunts that drew world attention to Italian aviation, from the individual achievement of naval officer Francesco de Pinedo's flight from Rome to Tokyo in 1925, to the mass flying-boat spectaculars staged by Italo Balbo between 1928 and 1933. The Italian air force got to carry out its own colonial campaign against rebels in the deserts of Libya and, in 1935, was used against the forces of Emperor Haile Selassie when Italy invaded the independent African state of Ethiopia.

German rebirth

Germany was another country where no questions were raised about the importance of airpower. Formally denied the right to maintain an army or naval air force by the terms of the Treaty of Versailles, throughout the 1920s German military leaders, aviators, and aircraft makers worked, often covertly, to maintain pilot training and keep up with advances in military aviation technology and tactics. This was partly achieved through the development of German civil aviation, in which former World

WINGS OVER CHICAGO

ON THE EVENING OF JULY 15, 1933, a mass formation of 24 Italian Savoia-Marchetti S.55X flying boats, commanded by General Italo Balbo, flew over Lake Michigan toward Chicago after a 15-day, 5,750-mile (9,200-km) transatlantic flight from Orbetello, Italy, via Iceland.

That month Chicago's population was swollen with visitors to the Century of Progress World's Fair, staged to celebrate the city's first centenary. Hundreds of thousands of spectators lined the lakefront for the arrival of the Italian squadron. In perfect formation, three by three, the twin-hulled Savoia-Marchettis circled over the city and then descended gracefully onto the lake, while an escort of 43 American fighter aircraft spelled out the word "Italy" in the sky.

Balbo received a hero's welcome, and was feted with celebratory dinners and parades—he even had a major avenue named after him. The Chicago flight was a sensational propaganda coup for the Italian Fascist dictatorship, helping to project an international image of an efficient and technologically advanced regime.

RECORD-BREAKING FLYING BOATS
Originally designed in 1925 as a torpedo bomber, the huge 79ft (24m) wingspan Savoia-Marchetti S.55 was later adapted for passenger service. Identified by its back-to-back engines above the wing, it broke 14 flying-boat records for speed, altitude, distance, and load-carrying.

TRANSATLANTIC TRIUMPH
This postcard, commemorating the 50th anniversary of Italo Balbo's transatlantic flight, depicts Savoia-Marchetti S.55 flying boats approaching the New York skyline with the Statue of Liberty looming.

FORMATION FLYING
General Balbo's S.55 flying boats alight in Jamaica Bay, New York, during their epic 48-hour transatlantic crossing to Chicago. The 24 S.55s completed the entire flight in a tight V formation. Even today, pilots refer to a large formation of aircraft as a "Balbo."

War I air commanders and pilots inevitably played a major role. As director of Luft Hansa from 1925, ex-squadron commander Erhard Milch was in constant contact with top officers in the Reichswehr, ensuring that they were fully informed of the latest navigation techniques and flight instrumentation. Air clubs and flying schools also played their part, acting as a training network for future military pilots under the cover of sports aviation.

A major German military-aviation program took place in the newly established Soviet Union. In 1922, the Germans and Soviets signed the "Rapallo Treaty," finding common ground in their status as

pariah states in postwar Europe. Under secret military provisions of the treaty, Germany was allowed to carry out army and air force training in Russia, in return for providing Soviet forces with training and the latest military technology.

A substantial German base was established in Lipetsk, 220 miles (350km) outside Moscow, where, from 1925 to 1933, German pilots were secretly trained to fly state-of-the-art military aircraft, practicing bombing, fighter tactics, and maneuvers.

CIVIL AND MILITARY
Erhard Milch, a World War I fighter pilot, was head of Deutsche Luft Hansa from 1925 until 1933, when he was given the task of rebuilding the Luftwaffe.

DEMONSTRATION OF AIRPOWER
In July 1921, General Billy Mitchell used Martin MB-2 bombers, similar to the Martin MT (above), to sink the captured German battleship Ostfriesland, in the Chesapeake Bay, off the Virginia Capes. In September that year he followed up this demonstration by bombing the USS Alabama (below).

Junkers and Rohrbach set up factories in the Soviet Union where they produced military aircraft prototypes in defiance of the peace treaty. At the same time, the transfer of technology from Germany boosted the development of Soviet military aviation, which became especially dependent on German aero-engines.

American isolationism

In the United States, the 1920s were a lean period for military aviation. In a reaction against America's involvement in World War I, public sentiment was overwhelmingly "isolationist." Determined to keep out of foreign quarrels, Americans saw their military needs as purely defensive. Since the only credible threat to the United States was an attack from the sea, the navy received the lion's share of a much-reduced military budget. Advocates of a powerful independent air force with equal status to the army and navy had a hard furrow to plow, taking on both the chiefs of the established services—eager to keep control of their own air forces—and the general perception of America's defense needs.

The leading advocate of an independent US air force, General Billy Mitchell, made what was under the circumstances a pretty effective job of advancing his cause. The argument for aviation as the offensive arm that would win a major war had little impact, since that was not the kind of conflict the United States intended to get involved in. So Mitchell took it upon himself to demonstrate that aircraft could take over responsibility for the defense of America's coastal waters. The idea won some backing in Congress after Mitchell pointed out that a large fleet of bombers could be built for the price of a single battleship. The navy was forced to allow Mitchell the chance to prove his point.

Mitchell's demonstrations

In July 1921 Mitchell assembled some Martin MB-2 bombers and, in front of naval observers, undertook to sink three German warships that had come into American hands at the end of the war. Armed with 600-lb (270-kg) bombs, the Martins made short work of a destroyer and a light cruiser. The key test was whether they could sink the third vessel, a captured, heavily armored battleship, the *Ostfriesland*. Their first attempt failed. The following morning, a series of attacks with 1,100-lb (500-kg) bombs left the battleship damaged but still afloat. Finally, a strike by seven bombers carrying 2,000-lb (900-kg) bombs sent the battleship to the bottom of the sea. Mitchell was triumphant and some naval observers reportedly watched with tears in their eyes as the

WILLIAM "BILLY" MITCHELL

WILLIAM "BILLY" MITCHELL (1879–1936) earned rapid promotion in the US Signal Corps in the years leading up to World War I. In 1912, aged 32, he became the youngest officer ever posted to the General Staff. Mitchell was an early enthusiast for aviation and in 1917 emerged as the leading combat commander of the US Army's air forces on the Western Front. He struck up a close relationship with RAF chief Sir Hugh Trenchard and became, like Trenchard, an advocate of independent airpower. As assistant chief of the Army Service, Mitchell campaigned tirelessly for a well-funded US air force, lobbying Congressmen, writing

popular books and articles, and staging publicity stunts such as the sinking of the *Ostfriesland* and the flight of the Douglas World Cruisers.

But Mitchell's vigorous self-promotion and his public denigration of senior officers who disagreed with him went far beyond what was acceptable from a serving officer. In 1925 he was court-martialed and suspended from duty, after accusing his superiors of "incompetence [and] criminal negligence." Mitchell has remained a controversial figure in America, regarded by many aviation enthusiasts as an inspired prophet of airpower.

HIGHLY DECORATED COMMANDER
The decorations and medals of General William "Billy" Mitchell, recognized as the top American combat commander of World War I, included the Distinguished Service Cross and Medal, several foreign decorations, and a posthumous Congressional Medal of Honor for outstanding services to military aviation.

pride of the oceans succumbed to airpower. Others must have reflected on whether it was in fact so impressive to sink a tethered and undefended warship at the third attempt.

Mitchell's efforts may have had some effect in advancing the cause of naval aviation, but his

> ## "In the development of air power, one has to look ahead and not backward and figure out what is going to happen…"
>
> ### WILLIAM "BILLY" MITCHELL

advocacy of an independent air force came to nothing. The Army Air Service was officially upgraded to the Army Air Corps in 1926, but remained in practice an underfunded, subordinate branch of an underfunded Army—during the 1930s, United States land forces were smaller than those of Poland or Romania.

The deficiencies of the Air Corps were publicly revealed when the army briefly took over flying US airmail routes in the winter of 1934. The Army aircraft—mostly small, open-cockpit

biplanes—were inferior to civil aircraft, and army pilots generally had little or no experience of flying in bad weather conditions or at night. In short, American military aviation had fallen years behind the most advanced civil aviation. Air Corps pilots averaged more than one accident for every 1,000 hours of flying time. It was normal for them to die at the rate of about one a week. By bringing the spotlight of publicity to bear on these deficiencies, the attempt to fly the mail led to some improvements in equipment and training.

Seaborne aviation

Naval aviation in the United States made better progress, despite financial stringencies. The example of Britain suggests that this progress may have been partly due to the absence of an independent air force. For, at the end of World War I, Britain had led the way in the development of carrier-borne aviation. HMS *Eagle*, which joined the Royal Navy in 1924, set the template for future aircraft carriers, with an "island" set to one side of the flight deck incorporating a bridge

A PACKED FLIGHT DECK
The flight deck of the USS Saratoga (CV-3) could carry up to 81 aircraft. Here it is shown crowded with Vought O2U-1 Corsair reconnaissance fighters, Boeing F2B-1 fighters, and long-range Martin T4M-1 torpedo bombers.

and funnel. But until 1937 the aerial element of the Fleet Air Arm was under the direct control of the RAF and consistently starved of funds and first-rate aircraft by air commanders for whom naval aviation was a peripheral concern.

In the United States, the pivotal debate was not about the virtues of independent airpower as opposed to an air force under naval command, but rather about the relative importance and roles of aircraft carriers and battleships. As early as 1921, one American naval commander, Admiral William Sims, predicted that "the airplane carrier, equipped with 80 planes," might be "the capital ship of the future." The Navy's Bureau of Aeronautics, led by Admiral William Moffett, worked vigorously to

establish the importance of naval aviation. But less air-minded admirals, although aware of the usefulness of aircraft, believed they should be employed in support of battleships, in a reconnaissance or air-defense role, and tended to dismiss the idea of using seaborne aircraft as a prime attack force.

The first US aircraft carrier, USS *Langley*, entered

PIONEER CARRIER
The USS Saratoga was one of the US Navy's first fleet carriers, with a top speed of almost 34 knots and a capacity for 81 aircraft. A converted battle cruiser, she was commissioned in 1927 and participated in numerous task-force exercises that helped to develop American carrier strategy and doctrine.

AIRCRAFT FOR CARRIERS

DURING THE INTERWAR YEARS, US naval air tacticians worked out a basic mix of aircraft for carriers. The three main types were fighters, for the defense of the fleet and to achieve air superiority; dive-bombers to attack enemy ships from above; and low-flying torpedo aircraft.

On the whole, naval air forces lagged behind land-based forces in making the transition from slower biplanes to higher performance monoplanes. The Royal Navy was especially archaic in introducing the Fairey Swordfish biplane—top speed 138mph (222kmph)—as its latest torpedo bomber in 1934, but the US Navy still had the Boeing F4B biplane as its main fighter through most of the 1930s. There were some good reasons for sticking to biplanes: They could land at lower speeds, a useful attribute at sea, and tended to take up less deck space than monoplanes (which needed a greater wingspan to achieve the same lift). However their slow speeds made them vulnerable to antiaircraft fire during their long approaches on target when delivering their torpedoes.

LEGENDARY "STRINGBAG"
Introduced in 1934, the Fairey Swordfish was a three-man torpedo bomber that could also be used for antisubmarine warfare. Remarkably, this open-cockpit biplane performed admirably in World War II.

service in 1922. It was not an impressive vessel—a converted collier with a top speed of 14 knots—but it was a start. The next two were much larger and faster. USS *Lexington* and USS *Saratoga* were originally meant to be battle cruisers. But at the Washington Conference in 1922, the leading naval powers agreed to limits on warship numbers. The battle cruisers could not be built—but two fleet carriers could. *Saratoga* and *Lexington* were each capable of carrying up to 81 aircraft and had a top speed of 34 knots—faster than any warship of comparable size. In naval exercises from 1929 onward, they proved their ability to play a key role as an offensive strike force. Notably, in 1932 more than 150 airplanes from the two carriers executed a mock attack on the naval base at Pearl Harbor, which achieved total surprise and would have had a devastating effect if really carried out by an enemy power—the Japanese, for example.

Naval airships
Carriers were not the only means of providing aerial support at sea that were explored by the United States.

BIPLANE LANDING
Sailors standing in the USS Langley's safety nets watch as a US Navy Aeromarine 39-B biplane successfully lands on the carrier's deck in October 1922.

In the early 1930s, experiments were also conducted with the naval airships *Akron* and *Macon*. They were designed to carry fighter planes, which they would launch and recover in the air—the returning airplane had to adjust its speed to that of the airship, position itself below the airship's hull, and then fly upward to hook itself to a support sticking out from the hull. These airborne aircraft carriers could accompany the fleet, acting as command and control centers for their airplanes, which would carry out reconnaissance missions and provide air defense. This bizarre-seeming idea might have worked but for the vulnerability of airships, not only to enemy action but also to the weather. The *Akron* was lost at sea in 1933 and the *Macon* suffered a similar fate in 1935. The only lighter-than-air aircraft the US Navy continued to use were nonrigid blimps.

Carrier fleets
Despite financial stringencies, the US Navy achieved a respectable development of its carrier force in the 1930s, with the addition of the USS *Yorktown* and USS *Enterprise* thanks to money from Roosevelt's New Deal programs. But the exact role of carriers remained undecided, with many senior commanders still convinced that traditional warships held the key to sea victory. The Japanese, already identified as America's most likely enemy in a naval conflict, also prevaricated about the role of carrier aviation. But they accepted that aircraft would have to be used to weaken the US fleet before Japan's heavy warships could deliver a knockout blow. On this basis the Japanese developed the world's most effective carrier force in the 1930s, with better aircraft and better-trained aircrews than their American counterparts.

During the 1930s, the world shifted from a period of aspiration toward disarmament into widespread rearmament. By the second half of the decade, an arms race was under way, with the militaristic governments of Germany and Japan and their potential enemies pumping money into military aviation. Advances in aircraft design, engines, and general aviation technology already seen in commercial and racing airplanes were applied to a new generation of military aircraft, while wars in China and Spain gave some air forces the chance to try out their new airplanes and tactics for real.

The Luftwaffe returns

After Adolf Hitler's rise to power in 1933, Nazi Germany began what would soon become a general rearmament in Europe. Like his fellow dictator Mussolini, Hitler found in aircraft an image of dynamism, modernity, and power that reflected his own vision of the Nazi state, as well as a practical tool for achieving his military ambitions. He ordered an immediate and massive program of expansion in military aviation that was already well under way by the time the re-creation of the Luftwaffe was publicly announced in 1935. The official head of Nazi German aviation was Hermann Göring, but the true mastermind behind the rapid resurgence of the Luftwaffe was former Luft Hansa director

"OUR LUFTWAFFE"
Secretly re-formed in 1923 in defiance of the terms of the Treaty of Versailles, the Luftwaffe's resurgence after the Nazis came to power in Germany in 1933 was masterminded by Erhard Milch. In 1935 its existence was publicly announced with posters such as this, promoting "Our Luftwaffe" in German.

sufficient resources were not really available, led to chaotic inefficiency and disorganization—characteristics in any case typical of all parts of the Nazi system.

Former World War I ace and stunt flier Ernst Udet, appointed as Luftwaffe technical director and later head of aircraft production, became a wild card within the system. Among the many decisions by Udet that caused consternation, the most famous is probably his demand that the impressively fast Ju 88 medium bomber, ready to enter production in 1938, should be modified so it could also act as a dive-bomber. The result was a redesign that cut the bomber's speed from 310mph (500kmph) to 185mph (300kmph) and delayed its introduction by two years. With Udet and Milch at loggerheads and Göring pursuing his own erratic and self-serving course, it is a tribute to the abilities of German designers, scientists, and fliers that the Luftwaffe still proved an impressive force.

> "Germany is once more a world power in the air. Her air force and her air industry have emerged from the kindergarten stage. Full manhood will still not be reached for three years."
>
> **MAJOR TRUMAN SMITH**
> US MILITARY ATTACHÉ IN BERLIN, 1936

decade—the Luftwaffe was never quite as strong as its potential enemies thought it to be. Nazi propagandists ensured that the image of German airpower was stamped on the imagination of foreign peoples and their leaders, undermining the will to resist Hitler's ever-escalating demands. But after 1936, the pressure to create a numerically massive air force, for which

Erhard Milch. Despite all that had been done to keep the "shadow Luftwaffe" in existence, Milch faced a daunting task in creating the large air force Hitler demanded. Between 1933 and 1936, he expanded Germany's aircraft production by a staggering 800 percent, as well as training an entire new generation of pilots.

Although Milch's achievement was impressive—especially when new designs such as the Messerschmitt Bf 109 fighter and the Junkers Ju 87 Stuka dive bomber began to roll off the production lines in the second half of the

PROPAGANDA PLANE
A Tupolev ANT-20 "Maksim Gorkii" flies over a 1935 May Day parade in Moscow's Red Square. The propaganda plane was fitted with loudspeakers, a printing press, and a pharmacy.

Allied developments

From 1935 onward, Britain and France were acutely aware of the threat posed by the resurgence of the Luftwaffe. It coincided with the realization that their existing air fleets were rapidly becoming obsolescent because of technological developments. The RAF's new fighter ordered into production in 1935 was the Gloster Gladiator biplane (which won fame during the defense of Malta in 1940–41), but fortunately a prototype of the Hawker Hurricane flew in the same year and the Supermarine Spitfire was taking shape on the drawing board. More sensible, if less dynamic, than the Nazis, the liberal democracies embarked on a longer term but relatively slow development of new models and the industrial setup to manufacture them. By 1938, state-of-the-art monoplanes were reaching RAF squadrons in growing numbers, and production accelerated rapidly as an uneasy peace turned to war. Unfortunately for the

REGINALD MITCHELL

IN 1933 REGINALD MITCHELL (1895–1937), chief designer at the Supermarine aircraft company, took a vacation in Europe to convalesce after undergoing surgery for cancer. A conversation with some German aviators convinced him that war was on its way, and from that moment he devoted himself single-mindedly, and against medical advice, to the creation of the fighter that would be called the Spitfire.

Born in Stoke-on-Trent, in England's industrial Midlands, Mitchell was an apprentice railroad engineer before joining the Supermarine Aviation Works in Southampton in 1917. Within two years he had become the company's chief designer, and when Supermarine was taken over by Vickers in 1928, it was mainly because they wanted Mitchell's services.

He made his reputation designing seaplanes for the Schneider Trophy; his 1925 S.4 gave the world its first view of the kind of fast, streamlined monoplane that was to be his specialty. Known for his attention to detail, he went on to design the Schneider-winning S.5 and S.6—one version of which became the first aircraft to top 400mph (640kmph) in 1931. Exhausted by his work on the Spitfire, Mitchell died at the age of 42, shortly before it went into production, but he was already sure of the aircraft's success. His only regret was the name "Spitfire," dreamed up by Vickers.

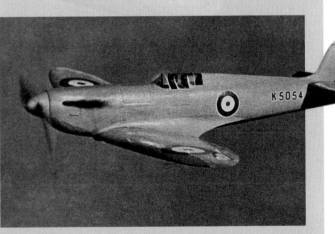

SUPER SPITFIRE
Mitchell's design for the Spitfire was revolutionary in its use of an elliptical wing, designed for maximum aerodynamic efficiency. The Spitfire evolved through many versions, late models being substantially different from the 1937 prototype (right).

French, their progress was slower and new models, such as the Dewoitine D.520 fighter, had only just begun to come into service when the German Blitzkrieg struck in 1940.

Soviet innovators

Hitler had made it clear throughout his political career that the "Jewish Bolsheviks" of the Soviet Union were intended for destruction. His rise to power brought a definitive end to the links between the Soviet and German aviation establishments that had served both so well in the 1920s and early '30s. Even in that decade, the Soviet Union had put considerable resources behind the creation of its air force and nascent air industry. Many of the leading talents in Russian aviation, including Igor Sikorsky, Alexander

Seversky, and Alexander Kartveli, had gone into exile after the revolution, contributing instead to the progress of aviation in the United States— Kartveli, for example, designed the Republic P-47 Thunderbolt, one of the great American aircraft of World War II. But a tradition of aircraft design and aerodynamic research was firmly implanted. Andrei Tupolev, who as an engineering student in prewar Russia had been arrested by the czarist police for his revolutionary activities, emerged in the 1920s as the prime mover in Soviet aviation. Other talented individuals who rose through the Soviet system included Sergei Ilyushin (eventually assigned exclusively to the development of long-range bombers), Nikolai Polikarpov, Alexander Yakovlev, and Syemyen Lavochkin, creator of the Lavochkin La-5 fighter.

Through the 1930s, these designers had to cope with working under the increasingly paranoid rule of Soviet dictator Joseph Stalin. As early as 1929, Polikarpov was arrested for "sabotage" when his department's development of a new fighter fell behind schedule. Along with his entire design team, he was consigned to the prison section of a state aviation factory (the use of prison labor was an important element in the Soviet economy), where they designed the Polikarpov I-5 fighter, earning their release in 1933. Tupolev himself was one of the thousands of prominent individuals "purged" by Stalin in the second half of the 1930s, spending six years working on aircraft design in one of the "special camps" of the Gulag. He was only released in 1943.

Yet within this bizarre system some excellent innovative aircraft design was achieved. Polikarpov, for example, was responsible for the I-16 which, along with the Messerschmitt Bf 109, was one of the very first single-seat, low-wing monoplane fighters. And Stalin's ruthless drive to industrialize the Soviet Union in the 1930s, although carried out at the expense of great human suffering, did create the basis for an effective mass-production aircraft industry.

But the impact of the Stalinist purges of the late 1930s on the Soviet air force was devastating. About three-quarters of senior officers were either executed or sent to the Gulag labor camps. The effects of this blow were still being felt when Germany invaded the Soviet Union in 1941.

New generation of fighters

In all the major air forces, the 1930s saw the same progress from biplane fighters—the sort of airplanes seen attacking King Kong on the top of the Empire State Building in the famous 1933 movie—to sleek cantilever-wing monoplanes such as the Spitfire, Bf 109, or the Fiat G.50 Freccia. The new generation of fighters consisted mostly of metal airplanes (although the Hurricane, one of the most successful, had a fabric-covered fuselage supported in part by wooden strips). They mounted a powerful engine in a lightweight frame and were designed with a scrupulous eye to reducing drag, not only abolishing the old biplane struts and wires but also having a retractable undercarriage and guns that were built into the wings or fuselage. From a traditional pilot's point of view, their most controversial aspect was an enclosed cockpit and an implied dependence on instrumentation. When Udet first sat in the cockpit of a Messerschmitt Bf 109, he is said to have remarked that "this would never be a fighting airplane" because "the pilot has to feel the air

WILLY MESSERSCHMITT

WILLY MESSERSCHMITT (1898–1978) built gliders as a teenager before World War I. Exempted from war service due to ill health, in the 1920s he began designing powered aircraft. From 1926 he had his aircraft built by BFW (Bayerische Flugzeugwerke), and he subsequently took over the company. During the vicious infighting of the Nazi regime after 1933, Messerschmitt had to cope with the hostility of the powerful state-aviation boss Erhard Milch and the bitter rivalry of designer and manufacturer Ernst Heinkel.

The adoption of the Bf 109 by the Luftwaffe in 1935 made Messerschmitt's reputation, and he renamed the BFW as Messerschmitt AG in 1938. He experimented with mixed success at the cutting edge of aviation technology, producing, among other models, the Komet rocket aircraft and the Me 262 jet fighter. After the defeat of the Nazis, Messerschmitt took refuge in Argentina, but in the 1950s he returned to Germany to continue his career.

INSPIRED DESIGNER
An inspired designer, Willy Messerschmitt was also capable of basic errors and miscalculations.

Messerschmitt Bf 109

IN 1935 THE MESSERSCHMITT BF 109 was selected as the Luftwaffe's new single-seat monoplane fighter after demonstrating its excellent handling and a high performance in competitive flight trials. It was a remarkably advanced example of the all-metal monoplane designs being introduced at that time— small, with a lightweight construction and a thin wing section to give the highest possible performance. Novelties, compared with the previous generation of fighters, included the enclosed

"The new Bf 109 simply looks fabulous. The takeoff is certainly unusual but... its flight characteristics are fantastic."

JOHANNES TRAUTLOFT
CONDOR LEGION PILOT

Transmitter/receiver package in rear fuselage

Aerodynamic balance at top of rudder

Metal monocoque fuselage structure

Metal-framed fabric-covered rudder

Non-retractable tailwheel

to know the speed of the plane." It was a prejudice shared by many old-school pilots, brought up on "flying by the seat of your pants." But they could not argue with the speed—typically 300–350mph (480–560kmph)—or rate of climb of the new models, which was combined with a breathtaking capacity to dive, spin, and roll that made them among the most exciting aircraft to pilot that have ever been created.

Heavy bombers

For most American and British air commanders, however, the crucial airplanes in their force were not the fighters but the heavy bombers. The US Army Air Corps (USAAC) and the RAF held that strategic bombing could be a war-winning use of airpower, given the right aircraft to do the job. In Britain, Trenchard and other commanders drew support for this view by arguing that a bomber fleet would allow the British to fight a war in Europe without sending an army across the Channel—and a repeat of the trench warfare of 1914–18 was what, above all else, the British wished to avoid. It was even argued that the existence of bombers might maintain peace by acting as a deterrent to would-be aggressors through a threat to attack their cities. Since, as British Prime Minister Stanley Baldwin said, "the bomber would always get through," the outbreak of war would be followed by the immediate destruction of cities—surely a prospect that would deter any country from breaking the peace.

Whereas the British concept of strategic bombing was essentially as a form of psychological warfare, centered on terrorizing civilians, American air commanders developed a notion of bombing as economic warfare. By precision bombing of factories and transportation systems, the air force would undermine the enemy's capacity to continue a war. The USAAC was of necessity committed to the accurate bombing of precise targets because its chief function in the eyes of its political paymasters was to defend America's coasts. In other words, it had to claim to be able to sink ships—small, moving targets.

cockpit and electric starter for the propeller. Leading-edge slats and slotted flaps were used to alter the shape of the wing (optimized for maximum speed) to perform adequately at slow speed for landing.

The Bf 109 was bloodied in the Spanish Civil War, where it won air superiority for the German Condor Legion. The 109E, developed in 1938, was the first true mass-production model of the basic design and became the most famous model, proving itself a match for RAF Spitfires and Hurricanes during the Battle of Britain. It was fast and maneuverable, although above 300mph (480kmph)

the controls became heavy. While it lacked the tight turning circle of the Spitfire, it was faster in a dive. About 33,000 Bf 109s were built, a record for a military aircraft. By the end of the war they had been outclassed by more modern fighters, yet many Bf 109s remained in service with foreign air arms into the 1950s.

Three-blade metal propeller

Blast troughs for twin machine guns mounted on engine crankcase

Aerial mast

Back armor protects pilot

Exhaust stubs of inverted V-engine low on nose

Navigation light on wingtip

Outward-retracting undercarriage

Aileron mass-balance

STEADY FLIER
Although the Bf 109 became unpopular with pilots as the war went on, it climbed better than any RAF fighter and flew steadily in combat, making it a good gun platform for its excellent armaments. It was also small, light, and aerodynamically efficient.

Bomber prototypes

If strategic bombing was to have any credibility, the American and British air forces needed the aircraft to do the job. They had to have the range to reach distant targets deep within enemy territory, the capacity to carry enough bombs to cause substantial damage, and the speed and firepower to brush aside air defenses—there was no place in either British or American doctrine for the concept of an escort fighter.

The development of bombers was rapid. In 1932, the state-of-the-art machine was the Martin B-10, a twin-engined monoplane with a respectable top speed of around 200mph (320kmph). But three years later, the Boeing company came up with the four-engined Model 299, the prototype of the B-17 Flying Fortress. The Model 299 crashed in October 1935, almost aborting the project and threatening Boeing with bankruptcy, but the Air Corps ordered 14 of them anyway. Capable of flying at 300mph (480kmph), the Flying Fortress was regarded by the United States as the first credible strategic bomber. The RAF, after starting the war with twin-engined long-range bombers, followed on with the four-engined Sterling, Halifax, and Lancaster.

Strategic bombing

To the countries of continental Europe and Japan, strategic bombing did not seem such an attractive use of airpower. Whether primarily defense-oriented, as in the case of France and the Soviet Union, or bent on aggressive expansionism, as were Germany and Japan, they believed that in any war the crucial battles were going to be fought between armed land forces. Although they did not ignore the potential for

DIVE-BOMBING

IN THE 1930s, DIVE-BOMBERS attracted a lot of interest because they could deliver a bombload with far greater accuracy than normal bombers. This made them especially suitable for attacking ships and close air support of ground troops. Their effectiveness was first demonstrated by American pilots supporting the Nicaraguan government against leftist rebels in the late 1920s. They were then adopted by the US Navy as a key element of the carrier air force.

On a visit to the United States in 1934, Luftwaffe official and air ace Ernst Udet got a chance to fly a US Navy Curtiss Hawk dive-bomber, becoming a vigorous advocate of this novel form of air attack. Udet backed production of the Ju 87 Stuka and insisted that all new German bombers be capable of dive-bombing. But dive-bombers were slower and heavier than other warplanes of similar size because they had to be robust enough to withstand the stresses of a diving attack. This made them too easy a prey for enemy fighters. They were eventually upstaged by high-performance fighter-bombers that could hold their own in air-to-air combat.

WAILING DIVE-BOMBER
The Junkers Ju 87 resembled a bird of prey, with its inverted gull-wing and "Jericho trumpet" sirens attached to the landing gear. Its reputation was made during Germany's successful Blitzkrieg ("lightning war") campaigns of 1939–41. The "trousered" landing gear of early models can be seen below.

direct air attacks on enemy cities or economic targets, they felt that the essential role of airpower must be to increase the chances of victory on the ground.

In the 1930s Germany was ahead of any other country in its appreciation of the most effective use of airpower. The Luftwaffe grasped the importance of seeking the destruction of the enemy's air forces—either in aerial combat or by attacks on airfields and aircraft factories—as a prelude to other air operations. It was trained to give close support to tanks and motorized infantry in mobile warfare, but also prepared for more independent operations, from

attacks on tunnels and bridges along key road and rail routes behind the enemy front line, to the bombing of arms factories and fuel depots. Troop transportation and logistical support were other areas to which the Luftwaffe paid close attention, in line with the German armed forces' general preoccupation with mobility and shock tactics.

Far from ignoring strategic bombing, the Luftwaffe gave careful consideration to issues such as the guidance of bombers on to distant targets at night—a problem that the RAF, for all its obsession with bombing cities, had omitted to take seriously at all.

But the Germans failed to develop a successful four-engined heavy bomber, largely because of the inability of German industry to produce adequate engines. For any strategic bombing campaign, they would have to rely on twin-engined medium bombers such as the Dornier Do 17 and the Heinkel He 111.

BOMBER FORMATION

A formation of Keystone bombers flies down the Hudson Valley in a display of America's aerial force. At the start of the 1930s these lumbering biplanes represented virtually the entire bomber strength of the Army Air Corps.

Nazi Germany found a chance to try out its aircraft and tactics when a civil war broke out in Spain in 1936. Right-wing "Nationalist" Spanish officers, who had failed to overthrow the country's left-wing Republican government in an insurrection, asked for the Nazis' help to mount a sustained military campaign. The Luftwaffe immediately sent a score of Ju 52 transport aircraft to airlift soldiers from Spanish Morocco to Nationalist-controlled Seville in southern Spain. This was an unprecedented operation—the movement by air of a major military force. Between July and October 1936, some 20,000 soldiers with their equipment, including artillery, were airlifted into Seville, enabling the Nationalists to take the offensive.

Aerial artillery

While Nazi Germany and Fascist Italy provided air support for the Nationalists, the Soviet Union sent pilots and aircraft to fight for the Republican side. By the end of 1936, Soviet I-15 and I-16 fighters had won air superiority and were able to inflict serious damage on ground forces, notably with the destruction of an Italian motorized column at Guadalajara in March 1937. The Luftwaffe responded by sending in the Condor

Legion, a force of around 100 of its latest aircraft and best-trained pilots, with Colonel Wolfram von Richthofen, cousin of the Red Baron, as its chief of staff. Wherever the Messerschmitt Bf 109s appeared, Soviet aircraft were driven from the skies. With air superiority assured, the Condor Legion experimented with close air support, acting as "aerial artillery" to prepare the way for ground offensives, and interdiction—air attacks on enemy reserve troops and communications behind the front line. This use of airpower proved decisive, allowing the Nationalists to achieve victory by 1939. While the Luftwaffe was drawing invaluable insights and accurate conclusions from the actual experience of combined-arms operations, the attention of the world at large was fixed upon a single issue: The terror-bombing of civilians. This was somewhat

TERROR-BOMBING
A Spanish Republican propaganda poster makes a powerful attack on the German bombing of Guernica in 1937: "This is the health/ salute [Heil] they bring."

peripheral to air operations in the civil war but central to the fears and anxieties of the citizens of London, Paris, and even New York, who could not help but see events in Spain as prefiguring their own possible future fate. Both sides in the Spanish conflict at times bombed enemy-held towns and cities, but the German and Italian air forces had far more opportunity to do so and caused the most loss of life. Apart from the devastation of the small Basque town of Guernica in April 1937, Republican-held Madrid came under intermittent aerial bombardment from 1936 onward, and the Catalan city of Barcelona was heavily bombed by the Italians for three days in March 1938, killing around 1,300 people.

Civilian reaction

There was no question that air attack frightened people. Esmond Romilly, a British volunteer fighting with the Republican International Brigades, described being trapped in a subway station during an air raid in Madrid: "A panic-stricken crowd made it impossible to move… women screamed and on the steps men were fighting to get into the shelter." US military attaché Stephen O. Fuqua, in Barcelona during the March 1938 raids, reported that economic and industrial life was "completely paralyzed" and "semipanic permeated every form of city life." Fuqua graphically described civilians suddenly blown to pieces while sitting on buses or at the tables of sidewalk cafes—afterward he saw the cafe waiters "sweeping up the human bits into containers."

Yet for all this horror, it was evident that civilians soon learned to cope psychologically with the threat of bombing. The Condor Legion's assessment of the effect of "destructive bombardments without clear military targets," based on its experience in Spain, was that in the

WATCHFUL CIVILIANS
Civilians in the Republican port of Bilbao, in Spain's Basque country, walk in fear as aircraft appear overhead. In April 1937 Bilbao was bombed by warplanes from the German Condor Legion and the Italian Aviazione Legionaria, supporting the Nationalist side in the Spanish Civil War.

long run they were more likely to stiffen popular resistance than to undermine morale. This was not the conclusion drawn by most political and military leaders worldwide. What people expect is what they see, and Guernica in particular was widely interpreted as confirming the expectation of a swift devastation of cities in the early stages of any major war.

Theories of war

Meanwhile in 1937 Japan had invaded China, giving another demonstration of the effectiveness and frightfulness of airpower. Cities such as Shanghai and Nanking were subjected to

THE DESTRUCTION OF GUERNICA

ON MONDAY APRIL 26, 1937, it was market day in the small but ancient Basque town of Guernica. At around 4:30 in the afternoon, when the town was at its most crowded, 43 aircraft of the Condor Legion—Heinkel He 111 medium bombers, He 51 fighters, and Ju 52 transport aircraft used as bombers—launched the first wave of an attack that lasted more than three hours. Strafing and dropping high-explosive bombs and incendiary devices, the German aircraft destroyed about half of the town.

A Basque Catholic priest, Alberto Onaindia, described the apocalyptic scene: "Five minutes did not elapse without the sky's being black with German planes. The planes descended very low, the machine-gun fire tearing up the woods and roads, in whose gutters, huddled together, lay old men, women, and children… Fire enveloped the whole city. Screams of lamentation were heard everywhere,

CONDOR LEGION
This postcard image shows the flags of Spain and the Condor Legion paraded side by side. The Condor Legion, which attacked Guernica, consisted of the best airmen from Hitler's developing Luftwaffe.

and the people, filled with terror, knelt, lifting their hands to heaven…"

Foreign journalists were on the scene the following day and filed graphic descriptions of the carnage and destruction. The Nationalists and Germans for a long time denied that Guernica had been bombed at all. They later more plausibly argued that Guernica had been a valid military target, since it housed reserve troops and was a major crossroads. But the Republicans won the propaganda war, establishing Guernica as a symbol of the evils both of Nazism and of terror bombing from the air. Artist Pablo Picasso, who had been commissioned to produce a large work for the Spanish Republic's pavilion at the Paris World Fair, created an iconic painting that was to prove the event's most lasting memorial.

SYMBOL OF DESTRUCTION
Guernica was reduced to ruins when 100,000lb (45,000kg) of explosives were dropped by German bombers in what was widely regarded as the deliberate terror bombing of a civilian target. Up to 1,600 people may have perished.

BILBAO
LEQUEITIO

bombing on a significant scale. This brought forth vigorous protests from the US government, which was inclined to head for the moral high ground as examples of the bombing of civilians multiplied. Secretary of State Cordell Hull said of the bombing of Barcelona: "No theory of war can justify such conduct." And in June 1938, the Senate passed a resolution condemning "the inhuman bombing of civilian populations." Yet the Roosevelt administration also sought increased funds for the American long-range bomber force, reasoning that the best way to stop an enemy from bombing your cities was to threaten credibly to flatten his in reprisal.

The other answer to the threat of bombing was to prepare air defenses to block an attack and civil defense to limit casualties. The concept of air defense was not popular with air commanders committed to war-winning strategic bombing—it was hard for them to argue that their bombers would "always get through" without accepting that enemy bombers would inevitably do the same. But the Germans had found in Spain just how vulnerable bombers would actually be—every bombing raid needed a fighter escort. In Britain, the government overruled the RAF and, in the second half of the 1930s, insisted on giving high priority to building fighters and preparing a coordinated air-defense system.

Defensive measures

One reason Douhet had given for believing that bombers could not be stopped was that their raids would come as a surprise, striking before fighters could be scrambled to intercept them. But in the 1930s, forms of radar were being developed and refined in all advanced countries—though not all were being applied to air defense— along with primitive IFF (Identification

MONSTER EAR TRUMPETS
Emperor Hirohito inspects the huge trumpetlike aircraft detectors/audible rangefinders that were part of the air defense in Japan, and other countries, in 1935. Designed to pick up the low rumble of approaching enemy aircraft, they worked in conjunction with antiaircraft guns, visible on the right.

Friend or Foe) systems that allowed ground controllers to distinguish between enemy aircraft and their own. Controllers adapted the techniques developed during World War I—keeping track of aircraft movements by pushing models around on a chart and using two-way radio links to give instructions to pilots in the air—to direct interceptors against intruding bombers.

Britain was especially well placed to develop a radar-based defense system because its front line was the coast, and radar worked much better

> "We thought of air warfare in 1938 rather as people think of nuclear warfare today."
>
> HAROLD MACMILLAN
> FORMER BRITISH PRIME MINISTER

over the uncluttered sea than over land. The British were also highly motivated by fear of air attack. The age of the bomber had come as a far greater psychological shock to Britain than to any other country because, protected by the Royal Navy, its people had long thought themselves immune to attack from abroad. The British government was told by its aviation chiefs that it could expect 20,000 civilian casualties in London on the first day of a war with Germany, and 150,000 in the first week (in fact, there were 295,000 casualties from air attacks in the whole of Britain in six years of war from 1939 to 1945). Not surprisingly,

THE FIRST JETS

ON AUGUST 27, 1939, four days before the start of World War II, the first jet aircraft took off from Marienehe airfield in Germany. Test pilot Erich Warsitz kept the diminutive Heinkel He 178 in the air for just six minutes, but it was enough to open a new era in aviation. Aircraft manufacturer Ernst Heinkel commented: "The hideous wail of the engine was music to our ears."

The wailing turbojet engine was the brainchild of Hans von Ohain, a graduate of the University of Göttingen, Germany's most prestigious center of theoretical aeronautics. It used a gas turbine to generate thrust in accordance with Newton's Third Law of Motion. The aircraft scooped up air as it moved along; this air was compressed, combined with fuel, and ignited; and the jet of hot gas forced out of the back of the engine propelled the aircraft forward.

Ohain was only one of a number of researchers in the 1930s investigating the use of gas turbines to create jet propulsion. Another was Flight Lieutenant Frank Whittle of the RAF, who filed his first patent for a

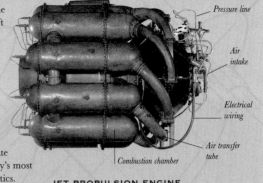

Pressure line
Air intake
Electrical wiring
Air transfer tube
Combustion chamber

JET PROPULSION ENGINE
Whittle's jet engine worked by sucking in air, then compressing and burning it with fuel, to create thrust. Faster than the propeller engine, it was also more economical on fuel.

jet engine as early as 1930. But whereas Whittle struggled to develop his engine in the face of financial difficulties and official indifference, Ohain and his assistant, Max Hahn, were backed both by Heinkel and the German Air Ministry. As a result, by the time Britain's first jet prototype, the Gloster E.28/39, flew in 1941, Germany was already developing practical jet-propelled warplanes.

FIRST JET AIRCRAFT
In August 1939 Erich Warsitz flew the world's first jet aircraft, an He 178, reaching a top speed of over 400mph (640kmph).

faced with such alarmist predictions, the defenders of democracy in Europe were unnerved by fears of air attack as Hitler pressed for advantage in 1938. The last thing they wanted was a war that would begin with the immediate destruction of cities and hundreds of thousands of civilian casualties.

Looking back on that time, British politician Harold Macmillan commented: "We thought of air warfare in 1938 rather as people think of nuclear warfare today." In other words, it was expected to lead swiftly not only to mass slaughter but also to a total breakdown of civilization. With war on the horizon, plans were finalized in 1939 for the distribution of gas masks, provision of bomb shelters, and evacuation of children. In the run-up to the war, filmgoers who saw the popular science fiction movie *Things to Come* (1936), based on a

1933 novel by H.G. Wells, found in its image of a world laid to waste by aerial bombardment a very plausible version of their own future. Watching warplanes maneuvering over rural England in 1932, British poet Siegfried Sassoon had predicted that, one day, "fear will be synonymous with flight." For many, that day had come.

AERIAL APOCALYPSE
The film version of H.G. Wells' novel The Shape of Things to Come *vividly depicts the earth laid waste by aerial bombardment in a 20-year war.*

WT 34

EXECUTIVE ORDER
President Woodrow Wilson used his executive powers to create the Army Air Service in 1918.

EVOLUTION OF US AIRPOWER

IN THE UNITED STATES, meanwhile, the political debate over how best to organize US airpower raged within the War Department, the US Army, and in Congress throughout the interwar period. As a result, airpower in the United States went through a number of makeovers in the struggle between those who favored an independent air force and those who did not.

Even before the US government bought the Wright Flyer in 1909, it had set up the Aeronautical Division within the US Army Signal Corps. Many consider this action in 1907 the birth of the US Air Force. In July 1914 the Aeronautical Division became the Aviation Section, US Army Signal Corps.

BARLING BOMBER
The Witteman-Lewis XNBL-1, designed by Walter Barling, was the largest aircraft in the world when it first flew on August 22, 1923. It could reach 95.5mph (154kmph), but at 42,569lbs (19,309kg), it could not gain enough altitude to fly over the Appalachian Mountains.

The creation of the Army Air Service

One of the first major steps toward an independent air service took place around the time the Great War ended. President Woodrow Wilson used his executive powers to create the Army Air Service in May 1918. Under this order, the Air Service left the tutelage of the Signal Corps and became a combat arm of the Army. Although it was still part of the Army, the Air Service was a step closer to separate-but-equal footing with the other services. With the Army Reorganization Act of 1920, Congress wrote the change into law. The Army Air Service became its own branch within the Army and was no longer auxiliary to the ground forces. This change gave the Air Service more autonomy, but it still answered to the Army.

The National Defense Act, also passed in 1920, established the number of men and ranks in the Air Service—ranks today's Air Force still uses. The law called for 16,000 enlisted Airmen, but Congress had so reduced defense spending that the service did not have the funds to enlist them all. Given this short

THE DIFFERENT STAGES OF THE US AIR ARM FROM 1907 TO PRESENT

• Aeronautical Division, US Army Signal Corps	1 August 1907–18 July 1914
• Aviation Section, US Army Signal Corps	18 July 1914–20 May 1918
• Division of Military Aeronautics, Secretary of War	20 May 1918–24 May 1918
• Army Air Service	24 May 1918–2 July 1926
• Army Air Corps	2 July 1926–17 September 1947
• General HQ Air Force	1 March 1935–1 March 1939
• US Army Air Forces	20 June 1941–17 September 1947
• US Air Force	18 September 1947–Present

supply of funds, the Army was tight-fisted in how much it passed along to its air arm. This only increased the Air Service's yearning for independence. Brigadier General Mitchell and others believed that winning any future wars or defending American soil would depend greatly on airpower. They reasoned it would be easier to direct airpower if the Air Service were an equal branch of the armed forces. In addition, an independent service would have its own appropriation and not have to beg each year for its share of scarce Army funds. The US Department of War, the civilian overseer of the Army, saw matters differently. Its doctrine

PRESIDENT CALVIN COOLIDGE
Coolidge created the Morrow Board, which recommended creating the Army Air Corps.

rested on a three-pronged national defense based on the Navy's battle fleet and the Army and Navy's coastal defenses.

The advocates of an independent air force believed airpower had advantages the generals were not taking into account. First, casualties from trench warfare would decrease if bombers could cross enemy lines to hit supply routes and factories. Soldiers would no longer be stuck in one place or die in waves of assaults. Second, as the Battle of Saint Mihiel showed, a mass of aircraft could overwhelm the enemy and bring the battle to him. Finally, planes could now carry heavier loads and

fly greater distances. Before long, the Atlantic and Pacific oceans would no longer guarantee America's safety.

Further demonstrations

Although the sinking of the *Ostfriesland* convinced the Navy to build aircraft carriers, it had little effect on the organization of the Army's air arm. So Mitchell tried new tactics, believing that if he could catch the public eye, Americans might pressure their representatives in Congress to support airpower.

In 1922 Mitchell arranged for two pilots, 1st Lieutenant Oakley Kelly and 1st Lieutenant John Macready to fly nonstop across the United States. After two failed attempts, they finally succeeded on their third try in 1923. Kelly and Macready flew from New York to San Diego—2,520 miles (4,055km)—in 26 hours and 50 minutes in a Fokker T-2 aircraft with a 400hp engine. In 1924 Mitchell tried an even bigger stunt—an around-the-world trip with four airplanes. Two of them—the Chicago and the New Orleans—finished the 26,345 mile (42,400km) journey in 175 days. The pilots visited cities around the globe, starting and finishing in Seattle, Washington. Also in 1924, Mitchell sent 1st Lieutenant Russell Maughan in a Curtiss PW-8 from New York to San Francisco. To the public's astonishment, Maughan finished the trip in a single day. This demonstrated that if the country were attacked, airplanes could fly in one day to defend the area under assault.

In 1923 Mitchell conducted a second series of bombing tests against ships. This time, the Navy let him use two World War I battleships, the USS *New Jersey* and the USS *Virginia*. Ten of Mitchell's 11 bombers missed the *New Jersey*. Then from 6,900 ft (2,103m) in the air at 85 miles per hour, Sergeant Ulysses S. Nero released his first ordnance through the *New Jersey's* smokestack,

THE USS NEW JERSEY
The USS New Jersey *after Sergeant Ulysses Nero's hit on September 5, 1923.*

THE CHICAGO
Commanded by 1st Lieutenant Lowell H. Smith, this Douglas World Cruiser and its sister the New Orleans flew around the world in 175 days in 1924.

PRESIDENT FRANKLIN D. ROOSEVELT
Worried about the weak state of the US military as war threats grew in Europe and East Asia, he persuaded Congress to increase the number of Air Corps officers.

FLYING FORTRESS
Boeing's B-17, first flown in 1935, made long-range bombing missions a reality and became a workhorse in World War II.

sinking the vessel immediately. Next he loosed a bomb that struck the deck of the *Virginia*, sending it, too, to the bottom of North Carolina's coastal waters.

In 1925, about the time of Mitchell's court-martial, President Calvin Coolidge instructed a group of experts led by banker Dwight Morrow to find the "best means of developing and applying aircraft in national defense." Among the Morrow Board's proposals were three of great significance to the future of US airpower:

1. Rename the Army Air Service the Army Air Corps

2. Give the Army Air Corps a seat on the Army General Staff
3. Appoint an assistant secretary of war for airpower.

Congress adopted these recommendations, passing the Air Corps Act on July 2, 1926.

How the Army Air Corps developed

Changing the name of the Army Air Service to the Army Air Corps was more than just a name change—it signified that the air arm was no longer only in "service" to ground troops. The corps could now conduct independent missions.

But tinkering with the air force continued. In 1933, Major General Hugh Drum headed an Army board that explored possible changes in the Air Corps's structure. The board recommended that the War Department form a General Headquarters Air Force (GHQ). The GHQ would command the aerial combat arm, while the Air Corps would retain training and logistical duties. Secretary of War George H. Dern endorsed the plan.

Before the Drum plan could be implemented, however, the War Department set up another

MAJOR GENERAL BENJAMIN FOULOIS: FROM ARMY'S FIRST PILOT TO AIR CHIEF

BENJAMIN FOULOIS (1879–1967) started his military career as an enlistee. He spent the last four years of his career as chief of the Air Corps—quite a leap. Like Brigadier General Billy Mitchell, he spoke out for an independent air force.

Even in his early years of service, Foulois achieved several milestones. He became the Army Signal Corps' first pilot when he flew Dirigible No. 1 in 1908. He rode with Orville Wright in 1909. With the Wrights' help, he learned to pilot a plane while stationed at Fort Sam Houston, Texas.

Foulois served in World War I at home and abroad. After the war, he testified before the Senate Military Affairs Committee, urging Congress to create an air department.

Foulois held strong opinions, which helped and hurt him throughout his career. In oral and written statements, he criticized the Army and Navy for failing to support an independent air force. Nonetheless, he ended up as chief of the Air Corps from 1931 to 1935. He resigned in 1935 when he came under attack for the Air Corps' mishandling of the airmail mission.

FIRST ARMY PILOT
Major General Benjamin Foulois (left) was the Army's first pilot. He served as chief of the Air Corps from 1931 to 1935.

board in 1934, chaired by former Secretary of War Newton Baker. It also proposed a combat group separate from training and logistical duties. The recommendations of the Drum and Baker boards were implemented in March 1935, when the GHQ set up camp at Langley Field, Virginia. GHQ remained within the Air Corps and answered to the Army. Brigadier General Frank Andrews was the senior officer of GHQ. In the past, Air Corps commanders had shared responsibility for tactical units. Now all combat aircraft would fall under Andrews's command. During peacetime, Andrews would answer to the Army chief of staff. In war, he would report to a regional combat commander. Meanwhile, ominous changes were taking place overseas. By the late 1930s many people feared that Europe was on the brink of another war. American reaction to this threat led to a growth spurt in the Air Corps.

On January 12, 1939, President Franklin D. Roosevelt spoke to Congress about the need to rebuild the US military, which he characterized as "utterly inadequate." Three months later, Congress approved increasing the number of Army Air Corps pilot officers from 1,200 to 3,203.

The Air Force's course toward independence

The foundation of Mitchell's airpower theory was the long-range bomber. Once Boeing built the B-17 in the late 1930s, long-range bombing missions could become a reality. Here was a concrete reason for an independent air service. Airpower was an offensive weapon; it could strike at military bases and factories in enemy lands. It could do much more than protect ground troops, and there was no objective reason to remain under Army command.

As long as airpower was a part of the Army, air advocates believed it would remain underfunded and underdeveloped. Events over the years proved them right: Airpower suffered greatly between the wars. As late as 1928, the Army placed greater emphasis on observation aircraft than on bombers.

The Army General Staff was the biggest proponent of keeping the Air Corps in the Army. The Army was, after all, steeped in history. Ground forces had been a part of war for thousands of years. Many in the Army saw airpower as no more than long-range artillery. They wanted the Army to keep total control of its

air arm, just as the Navy controlled its own aviation. But with major advances in technology such as the B-17, such reasoning was already obsolete.

The air force took another step toward independence on June 20, 1941, when, under Army Regulation 95-5, the Army Air Corps officially became the Army Air Forces. With Major General Henry "Hap" Arnold in command, the new air force remained under Army control. But it could now oversee its own functions in combat, training, and maintenance. Less than a year later, Army Chief of Staff George C. Marshall took a further step, raising the Army Air Forces to equal status with the Ground Forces and Services of Supply. With the formation of the Army Air Forces in

June 1941, the Air Corps and GHQ now fell under unified control. Major General Arnold was in charge of the Air Forces; under him was Major General George Brett, chief of the Air Corps. Lieutenant General Delos C. Emmons headed the new Air Force Combat Command (formerly known as the GHQ).

This last change came not a moment too soon. By the end of the year, the United States would find itself fully engaged in war in both Europe and the Pacific. The experiences gained during that war, and the performance of the Army Air Forces, would finally lead to complete autonomy of the US Air Force with the passage of the National Security Act of 1947.

GENERAL HENRY "HAP" ARNOLD

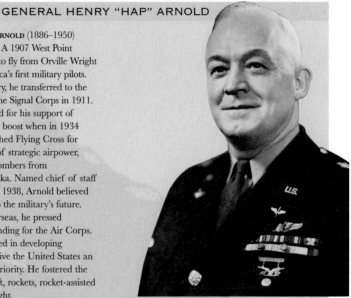

GENERAL HENRY "HAP" ARNOLD (1886–1950) served in both world wars. A 1907 West Point graduate, he learned how to fly from Orville Wright and became one of America's first military pilots. After starting in the infantry, he transferred to the Aeronautical Division of the Signal Corps in 1911.

Arnold's career suffered for his support of Billy Mitchell. But it got a boost when in 1934 he received the Distinguished Flying Cross for demonstrating the range of strategic airpower, leading a flight of B-10 bombers from Washington, D.C., to Alaska. Named chief of staff of the Army Air Corps in 1938, Arnold believed airpower to be essential to the military's future. With trouble brewing overseas, he pressed Congress for increased funding for the Air Corps. He was especially interested in developing aerospace technology to give the United States an edge in achieving air superiority. He fostered the development of jet aircraft, rockets, rocket-assisted takeoff, and supersonic flight.

During World War II, Arnold wore two hats: He served as commanding general of the Army Air Forces and was the air representative on the US Joint Chiefs of Staff. In 1944 he was promoted to five-star general, the only US air commander to achieve that rank. Poor health began to take its toll on him, however, and he retired less than a year after Japan surrendered. While he was a difficult taskmaster, his drive, vision, and sense of initiative

GENERAL HENRY "HAP" ARNOLD
A tough boss who drove himself as hard as he drove his subordinates, Arnold was the first air commander to become a five-star general. His efforts set the stage for an independent air force.

were indispensible in leading the air arm during the war and setting the stage for creation of the US Air Force shortly afterward.

DOCTRINE AND HISTORY—INTERWAR YEARS AND AIR DOCTRINE

DISTINCTIVE CAPABILITIES	FUNCTIONS (MISSIONS)	DOCTRINAL EMPHASIS
• Precision Engagement • Information Superiority • Limited Air Superiority	• Survillance and Reconnaissance • Counterair • Strategic Attack	• Strategic Attack on Enemy Homeland (Enemy War Machine)

AIRPOWER IN EARLY WORLD WAR II

5

THE OUTSET OF WORLD WAR II saw the German *Blitzkrieg* roll over Europe from Poland in the east to the English Channel in the west. In this battle, the Luftwaffe's close air support of Germany's mobile infantry and armor played a key role; the Germans also demonstrated the power of airborne troops parachuted in at the point of battle. After the fall of France, British pilots bore the brunt of the Luftwaffe, to be joined in 1941 by Soviet pilots after Germany invaded the Soviet Union. As the war expanded further with Japan's attacks on Allied positions in the Pacific, the Americans developed newer aircraft whose sheer numbers, along with their technical prowess, would gradually overwhelm the ability of the Axis to keep up. Allied air superiority ensured the invasion of Normandy and allowed the Americans to take the offensive in the Pacific.

COMMAND OF THE AIR

FROM THE START OF WORLD WAR II, AIRCRAFT WERE CRUCIAL TO THE SUCCESS OF ARMY OPERATIONS AS TROOPS WERE EXPOSED TO FIRE FROM THE SKY

"Anyone who has to fight… against an enemy in complete command of the air fights like a savage against modern European troops… with the same chances of success."

FIELD MARSHALL ERWIN ROMMEL
FROM THE POSTHUMOUS *ROMMEL PAPERS* (1953)

ON SEPTEMBER 1, 1939, Germany invaded Poland. Four weeks later the Polish forces surrendered, and their country was divided between Germany and the Soviet Union. If anyone still had doubts about the importance of airpower in warfare, this lightning campaign ended them. The Luftwaffe sent about 2,000 aircraft into Poland—a relatively small force compared with air operations later in World War II, but more than enough to overcome the few hundred airplanes of the Polish air force, despite

the skill and gallantry with which its pilots fought. In command of the air, German aircraft battered Polish ground troops, clearing a path for advancing armor, shattered Polish rail and road networks, and, in a climactic gesture of terror and destruction, reduced much of Warsaw to burning ruins.

The Polish campaign was the first example of *Blitzkrieg*, the "lightning war" of short devastating mobile campaigns, which would give the Germans control of Denmark and Norway in April 1940, France and the Low Countries in the following

THUNDERBOLT FIGHTER-BOMBER
The Republic P-47 Thunderbolt was produced in greater numbers than any other American fighter in World War II. A large, heavy single-seater, the P-47 proved effective both in air-to-air combat and as a ground-attack aircraft. It was flying in Thunderbolts that Francis S. Gabreski, the war's top American ace in Europe, recorded his 28 kills.

May to June, Yugoslavia and Greece in the spring of 1941, and the Soviet Union as far as the outskirts of Moscow by the end of that year. These German victories were, to an important degree, triumphs of airpower. It was not until later in the war that the awesome destructive capacity of strategic bombing, imaginatively envisaged in the 1930s, would become a reality. But from the outset airpower held the balance between victory and defeat. A country beaten in the air found its army and navy fighting at a hopeless disadvantage. The only serious setback that the Germans experienced in the first two years of the war was the failure to subdue Britain—a direct result of the Luftwaffe's inability to establish air supremacy over southern England in 1940.

STUKA PILOT
A German dive-bomber pilot sits in the cramped confines of his two-man cockpit—the rear gunner covered his back and the aircraft.

German dominance

The dominance of the Luftwaffe early in the war was not simply a result of overwhelming superiority of numbers or high quality of equipment. Luftwaffe methods could be very unsophisticated—during the bombing of Warsaw, Ju 52 crews scattered incendiaries over the city by shoveling them out of the airplane's side door. In the early days of the war, Messerschmitt Bf 109s were not even equipped with radios, so the pilots communicated with one another by waggling their wings. But the Luftwaffe pilots' training and numerical and technical superiority gave them a clear edge over their opponents. And, above all, German tactics were supremely well judged in the direction of airpower to affect the course of battle.

The experience of the Battle of France, in May to June 1940, came as a profound shock to British and French airmen and their commanders. Expecting a long-drawn-out contest in the manner of the Western Front in 1914–18, they found themselves outfought and outthought, facing abject defeat in a matter of days. The Germans achieved air superiority from the outset, destroying Allied aircraft by attacks on airfields, the effective deployment of flak guns, and air combat. German commanders with a firm grasp of the principle of concentration of force assigned substantial numbers of aircraft to key points on the battlefield, so that British and French airmen, scattered in "penny packets" along the front, were overwhelmed. The Allies' problems were compounded by the inferior performance of many of their machines. Aircraft such as the RAF's Fairey Battle light bomber and the French Morane-Saulnier M.S.406 fighter proved little more than cannon fodder for the Luftwaffe's

AGENTS OF BLITZKRIEG
During the lightning offensives of the early years of the war, Junkers Ju 87 Stuka dive-bombers like these operated as flying artillery in support of the German panzers. Despite their fearsome reputation, Stukas were slow and vulnerable to enemy fighters.

GROUND SUPPORT
German ground crews carry out maintenance and refueling on a Dornier Do 17. The Luftwaffe was superbly organized on the ground to support operations from airstrips on a rapidly moving battlefield.

BREATHLESS COMBAT

AIR COMBAT IN WORLD WAR II monoplane fighters was conducted at a speed that pushed a pilot's reaction times to the limits. In 1941, future author Roald Dahl was flying with the RAF in Greece when the Luftwaffe arrived in strength:

"Over Athens on that morning, I can remember seeing our tight little formation of Hurricanes all peeling away and disappearing among the swarms of enemy aircraft. They came from above and they came from behind and they made frontal attacks from dead ahead, and I threw my Hurricane around as best I could and whenever a Hun came into my sights, I pressed the button. It was truly the most breathless and in a way the most exhilarating time I have ever had in my life. I caught glimpses of planes with black smoke pouring from their engines. I saw the bright red flashes coming from the wings of the Messerschmitts as they fired their guns, and once I saw a man whose Hurricane was in flames climb calmly out onto a wing and jump off..."

Landing at his airfield after surviving this experience, Dahl found he was perspiring so heavily the sweat was dripping to the ground, and his hand was shaking so much he could not light a cigarette.

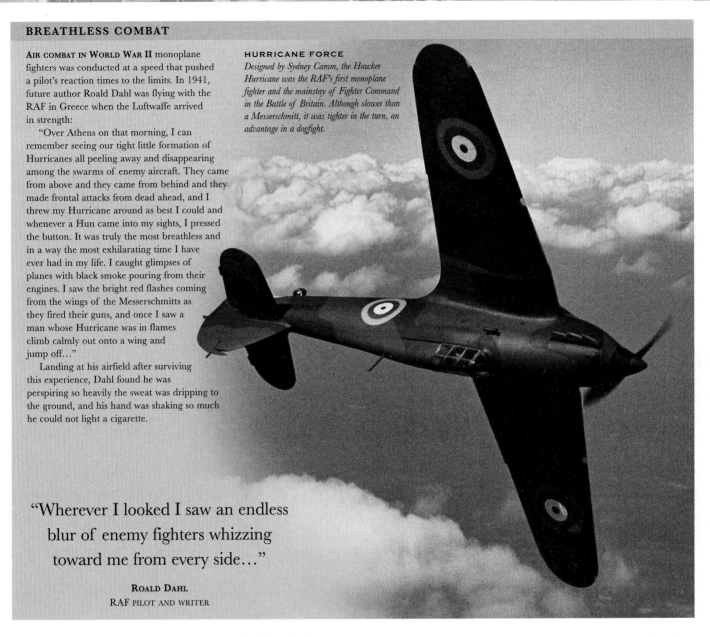

HURRICANE FORCE
Designed by Sydney Camm, the Hawker Hurricane was the RAF's first monoplane fighter and the mainstay of Fighter Command in the Battle of Britain. Although slower than a Messerschmitt, it was tighter in the turn, an advantage in a dogfight.

> "Wherever I looked I saw an endless blur of enemy fighters whizzing toward me from every side..."
>
> ROALD DAHL
> RAF PILOT AND WRITER

Messerschmitts. The Hurricanes and Spitfires that were a match for the German fighters soon had to be withdrawn to Britain because there were no airfields left from which they could operate.

Whereas the RAF and the Armée de l'Air had failed to establish any effective system for coordinating air and ground operations, the Luftwaffe was integrated into an overall strategy of shock and mobility. Avoiding sterile disputes about whether or not an air force should be "independent" or subordinate to the other arms, the Luftwaffe used its airplanes sometimes in direct support of army operations and sometimes on wide-ranging interdiction duties shading into strategic attacks on factories and cities.

Flying artillery

The most striking aspect of the *Blitzkrieg* strategy was the use of aircraft as "flying artillery" in support of armored and motorized forces. On the ground Luftwaffe liaison officers were assigned to panzer units to coordinate air attacks with army operations, while the Luftwaffe's logistical organization kept air units supplied with fuel and munitions as they moved to keep up with the rapidly advancing front line.

The Germans showed a keen appreciation of the psychological factor in warfare, especially the demoralizing effect of air attack on ground troops. The Ju 87 Stuka, the most famous and feared aircraft of the war's *Blitzkrieg* phase, was in some ways a backward airplane for its time, a poorly

armed two-seater with a fixed undercarriage. But the wailing soundtrack of its siren in the attack dive struck terror into its victims. Its bombing was accurate enough to destroy communications links such as bridges and railroad junctions, and concentrated in tight formation, it could deliver a devastating attack on ground troops or on ships— as during the Battle of Norway in April 1940.

Stuka pilots attacked in formation, rolling over and peeling off into the dive in an accelerating cascade behind the group commander. The Stuka dived at near to vertical, accelerating to over 300mph (480kmph) before the air brakes activated to stop it from reaching a velocity that would cause it to break up.

Enemy pilots and flak-gunners soon noticed that the Stuka was especially vulnerable pulling out of its dive. At that moment its speed was at its slowest, and the pilot was preoccupied with resetting the machine for level flight. The aircraft was in any case vulnerable to enemy fighters, flying around 100mph (160kmph) slower and with poor maneuverability. As the Luftwaffe lost its ability to guarantee air superiority, the Stuka's usefulness declined.

A general lesson of the first years of the war was the vulnerability of all bombers to attack by fighters. During the Dunkirk evacuation in June 1940, it was not only Stukas but also He 111s and Ju 88s—the latter fast and agile enough to later become a night fighter—that suffered heavily under attack from RAF Spitfires and Hurricanes. It was a lesson confirmed by the Battle of Britain. The single-seat fighter ruled the air (at least by day) and, as in World War I, dogfights pitted fighter against fighter in aerial combat where split-second reaction times determined life or death.

Airborne invasions

In its support of army operations, the Luftwaffe experimented with using aircraft to deliver troops to the point of battle, either by parachute or

glider. One of the most successful early examples of this novel military tactic was the taking of the apparently formidable Belgian frontier fortress of Eben Emael on May 10, 1940. Forty-one Ju 52s, each towing a glider with a contingent of troops on board, flew over German territory toward the Belgian border under cover of darkness, guided by beacons spaced out on the ground below. The gliders were released at very first light and most landed on top of the fortress or alongside nearby strong points. Taken completely by surprise, Eben Emael's garrison of over 1,000 soldiers soon meekly surrendered.

The most spectacular German airborne assault was the invasion of the Mediterranean island of Crete in May 1941—the first exclusively airborne invasion in history. Some 5,000 paratroopers were dropped on the island, occupied by almost 30,000 British and Commonwealth troops. They seized and held the airfield at Maleme, where Luftwaffe transport aircraft were then able to land with large-scale reinforcements and heavy equipment. However, even the operation at Crete showed the drawbacks of airborne assault. Many of the first wave of paratroops were killed either as they drifted defenselessly downward or immediately on landing as they disentangled themselves from

their parachutes. More determined action by the British forces could have wiped them out. Success in Crete depended on aircraft also providing effective close air support and flying in fresh men and supplies to reinforce the initial attack.

Global conflict

By the end of 1941 the war had widened from a European conflict into a genuinely global struggle, with not only the Soviet Union but also the United States and Japan (already at war with China since 1937) entering the fray. There was a distinct difference in approaches to warfare on the two sides in the conflict. Germany, Italy, and Japan all had regimes that encouraged a warrior spirit and praised war as a beneficent furnace in which men would be tempered to hardest steel. Their airmen were expected to triumph as the embodiment of the martial virtues—physical courage, ruthless aggression, patriotic self-sacrifice. Attitudes in the United States, Britain, and even the Soviet Union were more practical and pragmatic. The Soviets were second to none in the sacrifices they demanded of their people, but like the other Allied leaders, Stalin knew the war would be won more by economic organization than by martial spirit. Victory in the air required great courage and skill from aircrews, untiring support from ground crews, the work of engineers constructing airfields, and the inventiveness of scientists and aircraft designers. But in the end the air war was won by industrial output.

Levels of productivity

The gulf in productivity between the major combatants was ultimately overwhelming. Japan and Italy simply did not have the industrial capacity or sophistication to keep up as the demands of aerial warfare intensified. The Germans in principle had both the factories and the expertise, but poor use was made of these assets. Disorganization, failure to commit resources, and bad decision making meant that Germany only moved into top gear in 1943–44, by which

REICHSMARSCHAL GÖRING
Hitler invented the special title of Marshal of the Reich for his World War I ace Hermann Göring (front row, second from right) in the summer of 1940. But the morphine-addicted pilot later fell from favor as the Luftwaffe lost air superiority.

Junkers Ju 52/3m

NICKNAMED "TANTE JU" ("Auntie Junkers"), the Ju 52/3m was an aircraft that inspired a special affection in those who flew them. With its corrugated alloy skin and old-fashioned tri-motor configuration, the airplane won no prizes for elegance. Furthermore, it was deafeningly noisy to fly in and desperately slow—the Douglas C-47 could easily outpace it. Yet over 4,800 Ju 52/3m aircraft were produced, outnumbering any other European transport model.

Originally designed as a passenger airliner, the Ju 52/3m was a versatile, rugged, and reliable workhorse, whose main role was carrying troops and supplies. At the start of the Spanish Civil War, they were used to airlift Franco's troops from Morocco into Spain. During World War II, it was the Luftwaffe's major transport aircraft, operating in all weather conditions and over the most inhospitable terrain, from the snowbound Russian steppes to the Tunisian desert, from the Norwegian

NARROW CORRIDOR
The Ju 52/3m's long, narrow cabin, with a single row of seats on each side, had a maximum passenger capacity of 18. The original single-engined Ju 52s, which first flew in 1930, were used as civil transport craft.

fjords to the mountains of Crete. In May 1941, nearly 500 were used to fly German paratroopers from mainland Greece and drop them over Crete in a spectacular aerial assault. In the terrible winter of 1942–43, they flew supplies into the frozen airstrips around Stalingrad and evacuated the wounded. As their world fell apart during the final years of the war, German servicemen took comfort from flying in an aircraft that had become so familiar and never seemed to let them down.

German invasion of June 1941. Despite the primitive conditions and a lack of skilled personnel, raw materials, and machine tools, the Soviets turned out increasingly effective aircraft in remarkable quantities.

No one, however, could match the United States in mass production. The story of the US air industry in World War II is one of expansion

at breakneck speed conducted with, on the whole, astonishing efficiency. The Douglas company offers a good example of the scale of output achieved. Where it had built fewer than 1,000 DC-3s up to 1941, during the war it made some 10,000 C-47s—the military transport version of the aircraft. In all, Douglas produced almost 30,000 aircraft between 1941 and 1945. In addition to expanding the output of aircraft manufacturers, the Americans turned automobile factories to aircraft production.

The result of rapid expansion might have been a sharp drop in quality, since large numbers of previously untrained workers had to be taken on. But the design of aircraft was intelligently modified to facilitate mass production and reduce the need for special skills in the workforce. The achievement of America's wartime aircraft industry did not come automatically from the United States being the world's leading industrial power. It was a feat of organization and applied intelligence that earned the success it deserved.

Although in retrospect the entry of the United States into the war in December 1941 doomed both Germany and Japan to eventual defeat, it took a long time to bring productivity and manpower to bear on the battlefield. The Americans and their Allies had to follow an arduous learning curve before their use of airpower could match that of the Germans. In general, the Allies succeeded in sharply improving the performance of their aircraft and the training and experience of their pilots, while their enemies lost experienced pilots they could not adequately replace and often had to continue fighting in much the same aircraft with which they had started the war. In the spirit of "anything you can do, we can do better," the Allies learned to match and surpass the Germans in such areas as close air support and interdiction, and to mount even bolder airborne offensives.

War in Asia
One aspect of the widening war was the need for airmen and ground crews to operate in the world's most inhospitable terrains and climates. It was in the Sahara that the Allies learned the effective use of airpower against ground forces during their battles against the Afrika Korps in 1942–43. Here, flying conditions were usually good, but keeping aircraft engines free of clogging sand was another matter and taxed the ingenuity of technicians.

time it was being asked to perform miracles under intensive air bombardment and with severe shortages of essential materials.

On the other side, Britain's air industry performed remarkably well—its ability to recover from the losses of front-line aircraft was one of the keys to the country's survival in the Battle of Britain. The achievements of the Soviet wartime aircraft industry would have been outstanding under any circumstances, but were doubly so given the conditions that prevailed after the

BURMESE AIRDROP

GEORGE MACDONALD FRASER,
a Scottish soldier at Meiktila
in the Burmese jungle in 1944,
had a ground-up view of a
supply drop by Douglas C-47s:
"The first of the big Dakotas
was droning in, circling the drop
zone just above our heads, the Sikh
unloaders visible in its open doorway.
Behind came the other planes,
following the slow circle, banking slightly
while the Sikhs thrust out the big bales. It
was a spectacular sight, the aircraft
glittering in the sunlight, the bales falling
in a continuous shower... Most of the great
canvas bundles fell in what was called 'free
drop,' hitting the paddy with resounding
thumps and clouds of dust...

"I saw one misdirected bale come streaking
down to hit a jeep on the edge of the zone;
it struck fair and square on the bonnet,
flattening the vehicle in a tangled wreck..."

AERIAL LIFELINE
*Allied troops fighting the Japanese in the jungles
of Burma in 1944 were kept supplied by airdrops.
Transport aircraft operated with impunity as the
Japanese air force had been chased from the skies.*

The Burma-China theater was more demanding
still, becoming the site for some of the epics of
World War II air combat. There, operating first out
of Rangoon and then southern China, the Curtiss
P-40s of Claire Chennault's truculently independent
American Volunteer Group—better known as the
Flying Tigers—inflicted heavy losses on numerically
superior Japanese air forces in 1941–42. There also
the remarkable guerrilla operations of General
Orde Wingate's Chindit long-range penetration
force were carried out in the Japanese-occupied
Burmese jungle. Set up under Colonel Philip
Cochran, the American Air Commando Group
supported Wingate's imaginative forays with an
array of aircraft, from gliders and C-47 transports
to North American P-51 Mustang fighters and even
a few early Sikorsky helicopters.

In their boldest operation, in March
1944, 67 of Cochran's Dakotas towed
gliders carrying Chindit soldiers and
American engineers, plus bulldozers and
other heavy equipment, into Burma,
releasing them to fly down to jungle
clearings. There they built
landing strips so that
transport aircraft could
return the following night,
landing troop reinforcements,
artillery, jeeps, and more than a
thousand mules. It did not work
smoothly—half of the first wave of
gliders was lost—but it did allow
Wingate to, in his own words, "insert
himself in the guts of the enemy."

BUILDING FOR VICTORY
*Over 18,000 four-engined Consolidated B-24 Liberator
bombers rolled out of American factories during the war—an
average of more than 10 a day. The ability to make aircraft
in such unprecedented numbers was highly advantageous in
terms of air superiority over enemies incapable of gearing up
on the same scale.*

FLYING SHARK
*This distinctive sharkmouth decoration was adopted by
112 Squadron of Britain's Royal Air Force (RAF) in
North Africa in the second half of 1941.*

The American and British transport aircraft based in northern India not only had to supply Allied troops, but also, after the Japanese cut off the "Burma Road," became the only means of supplying the Chinese Nationalists and supporting US forces holed up in southwest China. Between 1942 and 1945, every single vehicle, weapon, round of ammunition, or drum of fuel was delivered "over the hump" from Dinjan in Assam across the Himalayas to Kunming. This was generally recognized as the most demanding route flown by transport aircraft anywhere during the war—a journey of 500 miles (800km) that took the C-47s, C-54s, and other transport planes over mountain ridges more than 16,000ft (5,000m) high.

If they hugged the mountain valleys, pilots ran into violent turbulence; if they put on their oxygen masks and flew high, they risked severe icing. During the monsoon season, dense clouds engulfed mountain ridges and valleys alike; pilots mostly flew on instruments, without sight of the ground, for the entire length of the journey. Flying the hump cost hundreds of aircrew their lives—the route was strewn with the wreckage— yet some 700,000 tons of supplies were delivered by the war's end. Nor was the experience necessarily a grim one for airmen. One RAF pilot recorded the exhilaration of flying a Dakota over the Himalayan peaks on a moonlit night, with his radio tuned to a fine program of classical music from the BBC.

FLYING THE HUMP
A C-47 flies the India-to-China supply route over the Himalayas. Operating a transport service across some of the world's most unforgiving terrain was an unprecedented challenge. At the cost of many lives Allied airmen proved that it could be done, keeping the Chinese Nationalist forces supplied with food, fuel, and munitions.

Russian winter

The most inhospitable environment in which any fliers had to operate was Russia in winter. The Luftwaffe, like the German army in general, was poorly prepared for the challenge of temperatures as low as -58°F (-50°C). Hard snow did not make a bad landing surface, but keeping aircraft operational was a nightmare. Fuel tanks and engine lubricant froze, hydraulic pumps broke down, rubber tires went brittle and cracked, flight instruments and radios refused to function. Often as few as one in four aircraft was fit to fly.

Yet under these conditions the Luftwaffe achieved some notable feats of air supply. At Demyansk in the winter of 1941–42, an army of 100,000 soldiers that had been encircled by the Soviets was kept supplied for three months by a fleet of Ju 52s and bombers, pressed into service as transport aircraft. But the following winter Hitler's demand that the Luftwaffe repeat this achievement at Stalingrad was simply beyond its capability. The 250,000 men of General Friedrich Paulus's Sixth

Army, trapped in Stalingrad by Soviet forces in November 1942, needed an airlift of at least 300 tons of supplies a day to survive. At best the Luftwaffe managed a third of this total, and on many days they could deliver nothing at all.

Stalingrad airlift

For German airmen the Stalingrad airlift developed into an epic of personal heroism, collective suffering, and organizational chaos. Despite the bitter cold, both ground and aircrews lived in makeshift unheated shelters, alongside airstrips that came under repeated Soviet air attack. The hastily assembled transport fleet consisted chiefly of Ju 52s and Heinkel 111 bombers, but also included a motley collection of training and communications aircraft, and even 18 four-engined Focke-Wulf Condors. Working in the open in the snow and ice, ground crews struggled around the clock to make these aircraft flyable—on occasion mechanics were frozen fast to an engine as they tried to service it. Pilots routinely took off and landed in almost zero visibility. During the flight to Stalingrad's Pitomnek airstrip and back, the transport aircraft were harassed by Soviet fighters and flak. They sometimes landed under artillery fire, dodging wrecked aircraft and craters.

Harrowing incidents abounded: The transport plane packed with wounded soldiers that crashed immediately after takeoff, apparently because the wounded had slid to the back of the plane as it rose; or the last-minute evacuation of Tazinskaya airstrip as it was overrun by Soviet tanks, in which a third of a fleet of 180 Ju 52s were lost, many crashing into their own colleagues as escape descended into chaos.

WINTER WAR
Soviet ground-crew members load up a bomber under the trying conditions of the Russian winter. The aircraft is a British-built Handley Page Hampden twin-engined bomber in Soviet markings.

PARACHUTES AND GLIDERS

"Thousands of white parachutes dropped through an
inferno of flak, while Dakotas crashed in flames."

PILOT PIERRE CLOSTERMANN
AIRBORNE ASSAULT ON THE RHINE, 1945

OPERATION MARKET GARDEN
*On September 17, 1944, some 10,000 Allied airborne
troops were sent into German-occupied Netherlands by
parachute and glider to take key bridges over the rivers Maas,
Waal, and Rhine. It fell short of its full objectives because of
the failure to capture the heavily defended bridge at Arnhem.*

ONE OF THE MOST IMPRESSIVE sights in the
war was the departure for a major airborne
operation, the air thick with hundreds of
transport aircraft carrying parachutists and
towing gliders. Unfortunately, this vision of
order and power had a tendency to degenerate
into something approaching chaos over the
drop zone. Pilot Pierre Clostermann described
the Allied airborne assault on the east bank of
the Rhine in March 1945 as "an apocalyptic
spectacle. Thousands of white parachutes dropped
through an inferno of heavy, medium, and light
flak, while Dakotas crashed in flames and gliders
rammed high-tension cables in showers of
blue sparks."

German successes early in the war convinced the
Americans and British of the value of airborne
operations. But airborne assaults were technically
difficult to carry off. A man floating down on a
parachute was desperately vulnerable if surprise
had not been achieved. Despite rigorous training,
paratroops were often widely scattered by the
time they reached the ground and separated
from their equipment. When the enemy reacted,
the paratroops either needed to join up rapidly
with friendly forces advancing on the ground
or be backed up by close air support and
aerial resupply.

Gliders could carry in equipment such as jeeps
and light artillery as well as troops. A glider had a

pilot and copilot sitting side by side,
communicating with the "tug" pilot by a telephone
wire in the tow rope. They did not have an easy
job. If there was turbulence, or the glider
inadvertently strayed into the tug's slipstream, the
tow rope could break, leaving the glider to an
uncertain fate. Those that reached the target zone
had to land at upward of 70mph (110kmph) on
whatever clear strip of land they could locate.
Inevitably, landing accidents were common.

Allied large-scale airborne operations—for
example, during the D-Day landings and in the
ill-fated Operation Market Garden in September
1944—rarely went according to plan, but they
sometimes proved useful.

In all, between November 1942 and Paulus's surrender at the end of January 1943, the Luftwaffe lost 490 machines, including 266 Ju 52s and 165 He 111s.

The Eastern Front

From 1943 onward, the Luftwaffe suffered an ultimately unsustainable rate of attrition on the Eastern Front and during the Allied strategic bombing offensive over Germany. Because German aircraft production belatedly expanded under the direction of new Nazi industrial chief Albert Speer, German airmen were able to continue inflicting heavy losses on their enemies, but it was a losing battle against mounting odds.

The Germans on the whole sent their less experienced pilots and more obsolescent aircraft to the Eastern Front, reserving the latest and best for the defense of Germany. Yet Luftwaffe pilots in Russia recorded astonishing kill rates: Top ace Erich Hartmann claimed 352 victories, and six other German pilots are credited with over 200 each. However, Soviet fighters were increasingly a match for their enemy—the Yakovlev Yak-9 could hold its own against Focke-Wulfs and Messerschmitts and denied the Luftwaffe superiority over the battlefield.

"Tank-busting" aircraft on both sides—the Soviet Il-2 Shturmovik and Lavochkin La-5, and the Luftwaffe's Henschel Hs 129s and Ju 87 Stukas equipped with armor-piercing cannon—played a major part in the great tank battle of Kursk in July 1943 and in the other armored clashes that followed as the Soviets rolled the German armies back. A single Stuka pilot, Hans-Ulrich Rudel, was estimated to have destroyed more than 500 Soviet tanks. But the German panzers also suffered grievously under air attack, and the Soviets were better able to replace lost armor. It was the same story in the struggle for the air. In all, the Luftwaffe claimed to have shot down 44,000 Soviet aircraft, yet German airplanes were still outnumbered on the Eastern Front throughout the later stages of the war.

The D-Day landings

In the west, airpower was central to the success of the D-Day invasion of Normandy in June 1944 and the Allied drive across Europe that followed. At the start of the war the American and British air forces were ill-prepared for providing direct support to ground forces. Even if they accepted the goal of achieving air superiority over the battlefield, they were little interested in providing air support. Senior air commanders, who resented the idea of being at the service of the army, had done nothing to develop techniques for cooperation between the forces. Such techniques eventually evolved in action, first in the North African desert and then in Italy after the Allied invasion of 1943. These

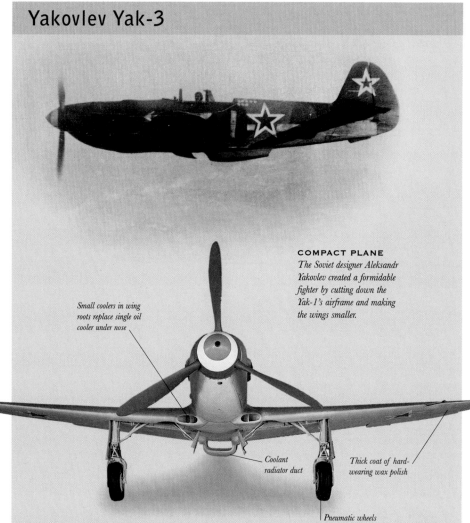

Yakovlev Yak-3

COMPACT PLANE
The Soviet designer Aleksandr Yakovlev created a formidable fighter by cutting down the Yak-1's airframe and making the wings smaller.

Small coolers in wing roots replace single oil cooler under nose

Coolant radiator duct

Thick coat of hard-wearing wax polish

Pneumatic wheels

SOVIET DESIGNER ALEKSANDR YAKOVLEV'S Yak-3 fighter earned its reputation as a supreme dogfighter in the desperate large-scale battles on the Eastern Front in 1944–45. To its shock and dismay, the Luftwaffe found that, at least at lower altitudes, it was superior to both the Focke-Wulf Fw 190 and the Messerschmitt Bf 109. On one occasion in July 1944, a squadron of 18 Yak-3s that encountered a force of 30 Luftwaffe fighters is claimed to have succeeded in shooting down 15 of them for the loss of only one of its own aircraft.

One of a family of fighters that stretched from the Yak-1 of 1939 to the impressive late-war Yak-9, the Yak-3 was the smallest, lightest Allied fighter flown during World War II. It was created by paring down the original Yak-1 in every conceivable way to reduce drag and weight, including replacing the oil cooler under the nose with twin coolers at the wing roots. The result was an aircraft with quick

acceleration, a fine rate of climb, and excellent maneuverability. Its main drawback was its very light armament, which often prevented a kill when a Luftwaffe fighter was in a Soviet pilot's sights.

Like many successful Soviet aircraft, Yak-3s were no-frills machines, economical both to produce and to operate, and capable of flying from icebound, snow-covered airfields in the depths of the Russian winter. Almost 4,900 Yak-3s were manufactured in the course of the war, under the extremely primitive and trying conditions that prevailed in Soviet aircraft factories, relocated beyond the Ural mountains after the German invasion. The ultimate accolade was awarded to the Yak-3 by the pilots of the Free French Normandie-Niémen Squadron who fought with the Soviets on the Eastern Front from 1942 onward. In September 1944, given a choice of any American, British, or Soviet fighter to fly, they picked the Yak-3.

experiences left the Allies reasonably well prepared for the large-scale use of aircraft in support of the armies in Normandy.

Without air superiority the D-Day landings could not even have been attempted. As it was, Allied fighters largely insulated their ground forces and shipping from air attack, while the first wave of the invasion included the flying in of three airborne divisions by parachute and glider. Allied bombers and fighter-bombers had destroyed bridges and other

communication links in northwest France so comprehensively that the region was virtually cut off. German attempts to move in reinforcements and supplies encountered constant harassment from marauding aircraft, until movement was hardly possible. On the front line, heavy bombers were used for the first time to "carpet-bomb" enemy positions in preparation for an offensive. By 1944 no artillery barrage could match the awesome quantity of explosives delivered by a bomber squadron.

Close air support was not without its problems. Determined efforts were made to bring airpower to bear on the right targets at the right time, but under battle conditions this was never easy. Forward air controllers, either on the ground or airborne in light aircraft over the front (another innovation of this period), would call in and direct air strikes, while various indicators such as smoke or flares were used to help identify targets. But response times were often too slow and accuracy lacking. Time and again, Allied aircraft hit their own troops instead of the enemy—making soldiers inclined to fire on any airplane, whether "friendly" or not. Airmen were sometimes made to spend time with troops in the front line to gain an appreciation of the ground forces' perspective, but it made little difference. But this is not to deny the impact ground-attack aircraft had on the battles in western Europe in 1944–45. Fighter bombers such as the Hawker Typhoon and P-47 Thunderbolt earned a fearsome reputation for their striking power with machine guns,

NORMANDY LANDINGS
American troops wade ashore on D-Day, June 6, 1944. This vast amphibious operation would have been impossible to attempt without air superiority. Extensive bombing of bridges, roads, and railroads in northern France before the invasion made it impossible for the Germans to rush reinforcements to Normandy.

THE GODFATHER OF CLOSE AIR SUPPORT

ELWOOD R. "PETE" QUESADA, son of a Spanish businessman and an Irish-American mother, was the foremost proponent of "the inherent flexibility of airpower," a principle he helped prove during World War II. His military career spanned aviation history from post-World War I era biplanes to supersonic jets.

Born in April 1904, in Washington, D.C., Quesada entered the Air Service as a flying cadet in September 1924. In 1927, he received a regular commission and was assigned as an engineering officer at Bolling Field in Washington, D.C. At Bolling, Quesada served on the same staff as two legendary Air Force leaders—Carl A. Spaatz, then a major, and Ira C. Eaker, then a captain. In 1929 Quesada participated in the endurance flight of the "Question Mark," along with Spaatz and Eaker. The three men flew a Fokker C-2A tri-motor continuously for nearly seven days, flying round trips between San Diego and Los Angeles and covering more than 11,000 miles. The flight demonstrated the possibilities of air-to-air refueling and foreshadowed long-range strategic bombing.

During classes at the Air Corps Tactical School and the Army's Command and General Staff School, Quesada began to evolve a concept of close air support for ground forces that would become his hallmark. The Air Corps officer correctly foresaw that "future war will require all sorts of arrangements between the air and the ground, and the two will have to work closer than a lot of people think or want."

In July 1941, Quesada received his first command, the 33d Pursuit Group stationed at Mitchel Field, Long Island. The unit flew the Army's "hottest" plane, the P-40. In December 1942, a year after the attack on Pearl Harbor, Quesada took the First Air Defense Wing to North Africa and the heat of battle. Shortly thereafter, he was given command of the XII Fighter Command and in this capacity would work out the mechanics of close air support and Army-Air Forces cooperation.

The successful integration of air and land forces in the Tunisia campaign forged by Quesada and the Allied leaders became a blueprint for operations incorporated into Army Air Forces field regulations—FM 100-20, "Command and Employment of Airpower," first published on July 21, 1943—and provided the Allies with their first victory in the European war. Principles such as the co-equality of ground and air force commanders, centralized command of tactical aircraft to exploit "the inherent flexibility of airpower," and the attainment of air superiority over the battlefield as a prerequisite for successful ground operations formed the core of tactical air doctrine. In October 1943, Quesada assumed command of the IX Fighter Command in England, and his forces provided air cover for the greatest invasion in history, the landings on Normandy Beach.

Over the course of his career, Quesada would achieve the rank of lieutenant general and serve as the first commander of Tactical Air

INFANTRYMAN'S FRIEND
Lieutenant General Elwood "Pete" Quesada refined his concept of close air support in North Africa.

Command. After retiring from the Air Force in October 1951, Quesada remained active and was appointed the first director of the Federal Aviation Administration by President Dwight Eisenhower. Quesada died in 1993.

ROCKET ATTACK
This is the view from an RAF Typhoon as it fires a rocket at German vehicles on a road in Normandy in 1944. The Typhoons became renowned for the tank-busting power of their rocket attacks, though with unguided weapons the odds were always against a direct hit.

VIEW TO A KILL

FRENCH PILOT PIERRE CLOSTERMANN flew both with the Free French Air Force and the RAF during World War II. Clostermann described leading an attack by four Tempest fighter-bombers on a train in the winter of 1944—a kind of operation he said was one of "those inhuman, immoral jobs we had to do because… war is war."

"The four Tempests slid down to 3,000ft [900m] in the frozen air and their polished wings caught the first gleams of a dingy dawn. We obliqued toward the train and instinctively four gloved hands, benumbed by the cold, were already pushing the prop lever to fine pitch. We could now make out the locomotive and the flak truck in front of it and the interminable mixed train dragging painfully behind."

"Without dropping our auxiliary tanks, we went into a shallow dive at full throttle… 350… 380… 420… 450mph [550… 600… 675… 725kmph]. The blood throbbed in my parched throat—still that old fear of flak. Only about a mile or two [1.5–3km] now. I began to set my aim for about 20 yards [18m] in front of the locomotive."

"Now! I leant forward, tensed. Only 800 yards [730m]. The first burst of tracer—the staccato flashes of the quadruple 20-mm flak mounting—the locomotive's wheels skidding with all brakes

jammed on… I was skimming over the snow-covered furrowed fields. Rooks flew off in swarms. My cannon roared—the engine driver jumped out of his cabin and rolled into the ditch. My shells exploded on the embankment and perforated the black shape which loomed in my sights."

"Then the funnel vomited a hot blast of flame and cinders, enveloped in the steam escaping from the punctured pipes. A slight backward pressure on the stick to clear the telegraph wires, a quick dive through the smoke, then, once again, the sky in my windshield, covered with oily soot. A glance backward. The locomotive had disappeared, shrouded in soot and spurting steam. People were scrambling out of doors and tearing down the embankment like agitated ants."

FRENCH FIGHTER ACE
French fighter pilot Pierre Clostermann settles into the cockpit of his Hawker Tempest, marked with a cross for each of his kills. Clostermann regarded the Tempest as the best Allied fighter aircraft of the war.

WORLD WAR II FIGHTERS AND FIGHTER-BOMBERS

WORLD WAR II FIGHTER AIRCRAFT were asked to perform in a variety of roles. Fighters had to battle for air superiority with their opposite numbers on the enemy side; act as interceptors against enemy bombers; fulfill a ground attack role in support of armies; act as bomber escorts; and operate as night fighters. Although many aircraft worked well in several roles, none could excel at them all. In general, the best air-superiority fighters were light single-seaters, fast in a dive and tight in a turn, such as the Spitfire and Messerschmitt Bf 109. The interceptor role suited aircraft that provided a stable gun platform with heavy firepower, such as the Hurricane. Heavier fighters that could take punishment and carry a substantial armament—such as the Hawker Typhoon and P-47 Thunderbolt—excelled at ground attack. The best night fighters were two- or three-seaters, because the pilot needed someone to operate complex radio and radar equipment.

SUPER SPITFIRE
The Supermarine Spitfire first entered service with the RAF in 1938 and remained in production during World War II.

Escort fighters required the range to accompany bombers to their targets plus the fighting ability to fight off enemy interceptors. The North American Mustang was peerless in this role.

cannon, bombs, and rockets. Napalm was also part of the ground-attack armory. As on the eastern front, even heavily armored tanks proved vulnerable to air attack. The final German counter-attack in the Ardennes at Christmas 1944 was only possible because bad weather prevented Allied aircraft from operating.

As Allied fighters and fighter-bombers ranged over enemy-held areas—preying on trains, attacking airfields, shooting up convoys of trucks—they rarely suffered substantial losses at the hands of the heavily outnumbered German aircraft. But flak took a severe toll. Flying in at low altitude to strafe or bomb a target defended by antiaircraft guns required nerve and luck. Apart from the chances of being hit by enemy fire, there was always a risk of flying straight into the target, or into a building or power pole. If the target exploded—because it was an ammunition truck, for example—the pilot might find himself careering through flying slabs of road or pieces of chassis. Most airmen

consistently preferred the active challenge of air-to-air combat to the sense of passive vulnerability they felt in the face of ground fire.

Overwhelming airpower

By the end of the war, both the German and Japanese air defenses had been totally overwhelmed by Allied airpower. The scale of Allied air operations was quite phenomenal. In the American and British strategic air offensive in Europe, thousand-bomber raids became commonplace. The first day of the Arnhem airborne offensive in September 1944 involved more then 4,000 Allied transport aircraft, fighters, bombers, and gliders. In March 1945, during its final drive on Berlin, the Soviet air force carried out over 17,500 flights in a single day.

Throughout the whole period of conflict, the United States had built almost 300,000 military aircraft, and pilots were trained by the hundreds of thousands. The war left a sorrowful legacy of destruction, much of it caused by the deployment of airpower. But another legacy of the war was flight on an unprecedented scale.

DOCTRINE AND HISTORY—EARLY-WORLD WAR II

DISTINCTIVE CAPABILITIES	FUNCTIONS (MISSIONS)	DOCTRINAL EMPHASIS
• Precision Engagement	• Surveillance and Reconnaissance	• Strategic Attack
• Information Superiority	• Counterair/land	• Counterland
• Air Superiority	• Strategic Attack	• Counterair
• Agile Combat Support	• Airlift/Special Operations	• Atomic Weapons

BOLT FROM THE BLUE
An American ground crew services a P-47 Thunderbolt in England in 1943. Under the fuselage is a drop tank, providing extra fuel for increased range. The engine cowling was painted white to avoid confusion with the rather similar German Focke-Wulf Fw 190, which put Thunderbolts at risk from friendly fire.

THE EUROPEAN THEATER IN WORLD WAR II

6

GERMANY'S ATTEMPT TO batter the British into submission by aerial bombing ran into a British air-defense system that included courageous pilots, fine aircraft, and a radar-equipped ground-control system. Yet it was a close call, and the Allies would encounter many of the same problems as British and American strategic bombing carried the battle to German factories and cities. Heavy losses proved that bombers alone could not accomplish the job—long-range fighter escorts would be necessary to defeat Luftwaffe defenses. Meanwhile, the rough treatment raw American forces received at the hands of the Axis in North Africa taught important lessons about unified air command and the coordination of close air support.

THE BATTLE FOR BRITAIN

SMALL IN SCALE COMPARED WITH AIR OPERATIONS LATER IN THE WAR, THE BATTLE OF BRITAIN AND THE BLITZ WERE CRUCIAL MOMENTS IN WORLD HISTORY

"Never in the field of human conflict was so much owed by so many to so few."

WINSTON CHURCHILL
BRITISH PRIME MINISTER, REFERRING TO RAF FIGHTER COMMAND, SEPTEMBER 1940

LEGENDARY FIGHTER
The Supermarine Spitfire entered aviation legend with its performance in the Battle of Britain in 1940. Although not the most numerous aircraft in Fighter Command, it was in many ways the best. Without it, RAF pilots would not have been able to take on the Messerschmitt Bf 109 so successfully.

THE BATTLE OF BRITAIN was raised to heroic status even before it began. On June 18, 1940, Prime Minister Winston Churchill told the House of Commons: "I expect that the Battle of Britain is about to begin. Upon this battle depends the survival of Christian civilization… The whole fury and might of the enemy must very soon be turned on us… Let us therefore brace ourselves to our duties and so bear ourselves that, if the British Empire and the Commonwealth last for a thousand years, men will still say, 'this was their finest hour.' "

Such grandiloquence invites deflation, and there have been plenty of mockers dedicated to demolishing the "myth of the finest hour." Yet more than 60 years after the event, the drama of the "Spitfire summer" shows no sign of losing its grip on the popular imagination. It still stands as the first major battle fought entirely in the air, just as the Blitz that followed was the first sustained campaign of strategic bombing.

The Battle of Britain was an aerial contest for which the British had prepared and the Germans had not. Since the mid-1930s the defense of Britain against an attack by the Luftwaffe had been a central focus of British military planning.

For the Germans, the campaign was an improvised response to finding themselves, with surprising suddenness, in control of western Europe. Hitler was nervous about invading Britain, but something had to be done to make the British accept that they were beaten. An air offensive seemed to have every advantage. It might in itself force the British to negotiate a surrender, especially if backed up by the threat of an invasion; and if it went particularly well, the invasion might be possible for real.

WARTIME LEADER
In June 1940 Britain's prime minister Winston Churchill gave the airborne defense of his country its famous name, proclaiming: "The Battle of Britain is about to begin."

Since early July 1940, the RAF and the Luftwaffe had been clashing over the English Channel, as British ports and merchant convoys came under air attack from German aircraft. The main German onslaught on England, in response to Hitler's directive to the Luftwaffe "to overcome the British air force with all means at its disposal and in the shortest possible time," began on August 13. Fleets of bombers, escorted by fighters, carried out daylight raids with special concentration on destroying airfields, aircraft factories, and radar installations. The determined resistance of RAF Spitfires and Hurricanes in the first days of the offensive led the Luftwaffe to focus increasingly on raiding Fighter Command airbases and on wearing down the fighter force in the air. Then on September 7, at a time when Fighter Command was under maximum pressure, the focus of Luftwaffe operations shifted again, turning to mass bombing raids on London. By the end of October the Luftwaffe had given up its dream of air superiority, settling for nighttime bombing raids on London and other British cities—the Blitz.

St. Paul's Cathedral stands unscathed amid the smoke of burning buildings after a Luftwaffe raid on the City of London. The British people took what comfort they could from such symbols of defiance during the dark months of the Blitz in 1940–41.

OPERATIONS ROOM
Members of the British Women's Auxiliary Air Force push wooden blocks and arrows representing enemy bombers around a map as information from Observer Corps Centres comes through on their headsets. Above them, controllers watch the progress of the enemy.

CODED CLOCKS
Clocks in operations rooms had color-coded segments. Arrows placed on map tables used the same color coding, showing when their position was last updated.

While the German commanders were confused in their objectives, the British were focused and organized to a single end. Fighter Command Chief Hugh Dowding recognized that for the RAF, surviving as a coherent defensive force was enough to constitute victory. By avoiding committing too large a part of his resources to the combat prematurely, and making his fighters concentrate on knocking out German bombers, Dowding conducted a ruthless and calculating campaign of attrition.

British defenses

The British air-defense system was the most sophisticated in the world, a triumph of organization and applied technology. In its front line were the radar stations that identified Luftwaffe aircraft approaching Britain's shores. Radar operators provided a dense flow of raw data that was processed at a centralized "filter room" and forwarded to the people who controlled operations. In the operations rooms, members of the Women's Auxiliary Air Force converted the information into 3-D graphic form by pushing wooden blocks around on a map with croupier's rakes, watched from a balcony above by the controllers. The controllers at the headquarters of the four fighter groups—each responsible for the defense of an area of the country—decided when, where, and at what strength aircraft should be sent up to meet the Luftwaffe. Controllers at sector level, with typically three or four squadrons under them, were responsible for directing the fighters on to their targets by radioed instructions.

This system was fallible. The problem of distinguishing between friendly and enemy aircraft was tackled by equipping RAF fighters flying in a radar zone with IFF (Identification Friend or Foe) devices, which gave them a distinctive radar signature; but there were often not enough IFF sets to go around, and they did not always work. Also, the Bf 110s of the Luftwaffe's Erprobungsgruppe 210 discovered that by flying close to ground level they could creep under the radar unobserved. But the system was also efficient and robust, with most communications depending on standard telephone lines that were impossible to jam and easy to repair.

The call to scramble

The radar-based early-warning system relieved Fighter Command of the need to mount continuous combat air patrols, for which it simply did not have the resources. Nevertheless, response times were very tight. Fighter pilots always ran to their aircraft when the call to "scramble" came through, because every second meant a chance to gain more height before encountering the enemy. It typically took five minutes for a squadron to get airborne, which was rarely quick enough to avoid beginning the fight at an altitude disadvantage.

Once airborne, the pilot in a Spitfire or Hurricane—or for that matter in a Messerschmitt Bf 109—was effectively welded to his machine. Strapped tightly into the small

metal cockpit, with its plexiglass hood, a bulletproof windshield in front of him, and, in most cases, an armor plate behind his back, he could barely move. He sat with his right hand on the control stick, his left on the throttle, and his two feet on the rudder bar. His right thumb rested on the gun-firing button, which was on top of the control column. The guns were as immobile as the pilot, and in combat the pilot aimed the plane at the target. He had enough ammunition to fire for about 13 seconds on each sortie.

The Luftwaffe fighter-escort pilots, in their Messerschmitt Bf 109s or 110s, liked to function as marauding hunters with their bomber force as bait. Lurking at high altitude in the loose "finger-four" formation—two pairs, each consisting of a lead pilot and his wingman—they would dive down to "bounce" the RAF fighters advancing in threes in tight V formations, especially picking off the vulnerable aircraft at the back of the V. This kind of combat could be over in seconds. The victim of a Messerschmitt diving out of the sun would probably never see the aircraft that shot him down. Exploiting the accumulated speed of the dive, the Messerschmitts could make their escapes before any response was possible.

If the RAF fighters could engage the Messerschmitts in a dogfight, they stood a much better chance. On the whole, the Spitfires and even the slower Hurricanes could outmaneuver the Bf 109s, and they were certainly more agile than the Bf 110s. In combat, where the key maneuver was a tight turn to get on the enemy's tail, a good RAF pilot would probably come out on top.

Dowding's orders were that the fighters should concentrate on shooting down bombers. A division of labor developed, with the Spitfires holding off the Luftwaffe fighter cover while the Hurricanes went for the fleets of Heinkels, Junkers, and Dorniers. Bombers were not easy targets. The He 111s—the most numerous Luftwaffe bombers—were by this time partly armored, and the Ju 88s were sturdy and fast. Their skillful gunners downed substantial numbers of RAF fighters. The most effective way of attacking a bomber formation was to fly

SUCCESSFUL INTERCEPTION
A Messerschmitt Bf 110 is shot down by a Hurricane over southern England. The heavy German twin-engined fighter was no match for RAF Spitfires or Hurricanes in a dogfight.

straight at it from the front, an especially unnerving experience for bomber crews clustered in the nose of their aircraft behind plexiglass. However, few fighter pilots had the nerve to risk collision, and most attacked bombers from behind or, occasionally, the flank. It was relatively easy to score hits on a bomber, but bringing one down was more difficult. Many made it back to their airfields riddled with bullet holes, often carrying one or two seriously injured or dead crew members.

The Messerschmitts were not really suited to the role of bomber escort. The Bf 109 had inadequate range, allowing the briefest spell in the combat zone. The Bf 110 had the required range, but was not a good enough dogfighter. When mounting bomber losses forced the Messerschmitts to take their escort duties more seriously, making some fly in close support, instead of 10,000ft (3km) above, this was extremely unpopular with Messerschmitt pilots. RAF fighter pilots had their own discontents. Some chafed at the discipline imposed by ground controllers, fuming when their hunting instincts were frustrated in the interest of some wider tactical scheme.

SCRAMBLE FOR THE SKIES
This photograph (taken in Duxford, England, before World War II) is of a demonstration given for the press by the RAF. The purpose of the exercise was to show the speed at which the airmen could reach their aircraft when called upon.

"The few"

As in World War I, a disproportionate number of kills in the Battle of Britain were recorded by a few gifted individuals. The required combination of flying skills, sharp eyesight, fast reaction times, and killer instinct was rare. The top Battle of Britain ace in the RAF, credited with 17 kills, was a Czech pilot, Josef Frantisek, flying with a Polish squadron. The highest score for a British RAF pilot was recorded by Sergeant Ginger Lacey. In the Luftwaffe, the two most trumpeted aces, Adolf Galland and Werner Mölders, vied with Major Helmut Wick in a highly publicized contest for top score. Although some pilots in Britain achieved fame—for example, the legless Douglas Bader—the RAF discouraged competition over kills and individual hero-worship. Even in Germany, the aces did not have the same public status as in World War I. The need for air heroes to cement public support for the war was not felt as keenly.

Fighter Command pilots were definitely, as Churchill dubbed them, "the few" to which so much was owed. The number killed in the Battle of Britain was 544—about one in five of those RAF pilots who took part. Luftwaffe airmen died in much greater numbers—around 2,700 of them. The difference was mostly due to the toll taken on bomber aircrews. Overall, the RAF is estimated to have shot down around 1,900 Luftwaffe aircraft for the loss of just over a thousand of their own.

There were days in late August and early September when Fighter Command was severely stretched. Luftwaffe raids on airfields had ground crew and civilian support services battling heroically to fill craters and restore communications. Repeatedly scrambled to meet harrying attacks, RAF pilots suffered periods of demoralization and exhaustion. But to win, the Luftwaffe had to break Fighter Command's resistance and, despite stretching it severely, the Germans never achieved that goal.

The turning point in the battle came on September 15, which is celebrated as Battle of Britain Day in the United Kingdom. Indeed, this was a day of heavy fighting, with Luftwaffe bombers and fighters arriving in two waves, the largest comprising almost 500 aircraft. It was also spectacular for Londoners—a good deal of the combat happened right above their heads. But RAF claims to have shot down 185 enemy aircraft were grossly inflated; the actual figure was probably 56, about twice the RAF's own losses.

> "If you are new to the game and if you are required to fly within a few feet of your neighbor's wingtip, it is a dicey experience."
>
> ROALD DAHL
> ON FORMATION FLYING IN A HURRICANE

And the battle in no sense stopped—roughly the same number of German aircraft were downed on September 27. But the continued ability of the RAF to put up a fighter defense in strength, along with the onset of fall weather, meant that German invasion plans were definitively called off, and by the end of October the Luftwaffe was devoting all its resources to the night bombing of Britain's cities.

DOUGHTY INTERCEPTORS
RAF Hawker Hurricanes fly in close formation. During the Battle of Britain, Hurricanes were the bomber-killers of choice—intercepting Dorniers and Heinkels—while Spitfires engaged the Bf 109s that shadowed the German bombers at high altitude.

THE BLITZ

FROM THE FIRST MAJOR daylight bombing of London—on September 7, 1940—through to May 1941, Britain's cities were subjected to sustained aerial bombardment on a scale never before attempted. This was Douhet's concept of air war at last put to the test—an attempt to break civilian morale by using fleets of bombers to devastate enemy cities and industrial centers. Not only London was battered, but also ports such as Plymouth, Portsmouth, Cardiff, Liverpool, Glasgow, and Belfast, and inland industrial cities such as Birmingham and Coventry. It was an unprecedented experiment, with the British people as guinea pigs. Would their morale hold or would social order fall apart in some catastrophic manner under the strain of bombardment? The result is now known, but at the time it could not be comfortably predicted.

The scale of the bombing during the Blitz was later dwarfed by Allied bombing operations against Germany and Japan—in the heaviest raids of 1940–41 the Luftwaffe never dropped more than 500 tons of bombs, whereas as early as 1943 the RAF was dropping over 2,000 tons on a single night over Germany. But the Luftwaffe raids were no powder-puff punch. Some 40,000 civilians were killed in the Blitz, and local devastation—for example, in London's East End and at Coventry— could be of awesome intensity.

The impact of the Luftwaffe's campaign was undoubtedly limited by the lack of a heavy bomber. The Heinkel He 111 had a maximum bombload of around 4,500lb (2,000kg), well under half that of a four-engined RAF bomber such as the Halifax, and even the Junkers Ju 88 had a maximum load of only 6,600lb (3,000kg). But in other ways the Luftwaffe was much better prepared for a strategic bombing campaign than the RAF.

GAS MASKS
Civilian gas masks differed from the military models (left), but their purpose was the same. However, gas bombs were not used by either side, chiefly for fear of retaliation.

KEEPING WATCH
Bofors antiaircraft gunners keep watch over a seaside town on the southern coast of England as a friendly aircraft flies by. Sneak raids were an insoluble problem along the Channel coast.

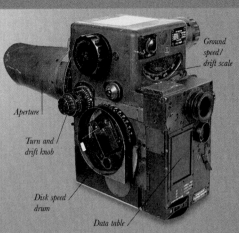

JUNKERS JU 88 BOMBSIGHT
*German bomb-aiming systems were far
superior to those of the RAF in the early
stages of the war. German bombers were
often fitted with two bombsights—one
for level bombing, and one for dive or
glide bombing.*

*Ground
speed/
drift scale*

Aperture

*Turn and
drift knob*

*Disk speed
drum*

Data table

LUCKY ESCAPE
*This still taken by a gun camera shows what is probably the
pilot of a Heinkel He 111 jumping out of his cockpit seconds
before a direct hit. Despite their vulnerability, He 111s formed
the core of the German bomber force in the Blitz.*

FIREPROOF
*A British poster publicizes the Fire Guard, an organization set
up in 1941 to counter the effect of incendiary bombs. Many
urban areas were destroyed by fire in the Blitz.*

Beat
'FIREBOMB
FRITZ'

BRITAIN
SHALL NOT
BURN
BRITAIN'S FIRE GUARD IS BRITAIN'S DEFENCE

MORNING AFTER
*The morning after the bombing raid on Coventry in
November 1940, local people go about their business.
Over 500 civilians died in the raid, a small number
compared with the mass deaths in German and Japanese
cities later in the war but a severe shock at the time.*

Remote-controlled bombing

In particular, the Germans had given considerable thought to finding and hitting a target, a problem that the RAF's Bomber Command had strangely neglected to take seriously. The Luftwaffe's experience in Spain had underlined the importance of night flying and had led to the adaptation of civil radio-navigation techniques. The result was that, unlike the airships and Gothas of World War I, German night bombers did not always have to feel their way blindly through the darkness over a blacked-out Britain.

All German bombers were equipped to follow a Knickebein ("dog-leg") radio beam to reach their targets. The elite Kampfgruppe 100, sent in first to mark targets with incendiaries, had even more sophisticated target-finding equipment, the X-gerät and Y-gerät. The Y-gerät system, introduced in December 1940, constituted fully remote-controlled bombing. The aircraft flew along a usual beam, but reradiated the beam back to its source, so the ground station could precisely track its progress. When the bomber arrived over its target zone, it went on to automatic pilot, and as soon as it reached the map coordinates of its target, the ground station transmitted a signal that released the bomb. This technique was estimated to be able to put a bomb within a radius of 100 yards (90m), at a distance of 250 miles (400km).

Luftwaffe superiority

In practice, the Luftwaffe's radio-navigation systems did not always run smoothly. The British rapidly developed countermeasures, jamming or distorting the beams in a secret electronic war. The bombers still always preferred to attack on a clear night, when they could orient themselves by the stars and by features on the ground—the Thames Estuary proved as useful a marker for German navigators in 1940 as it had in 1916. And, for all the technical wizardry, most bomb-aiming remained very approximate.

Whatever might be the case by day, by night the Luftwaffe had air superiority over Britain. Their fleets of 100 to 500 bombers roamed over Britain virtually unscathed. Antiaircraft batteries made a lot of noise and reassured people on the ground that something was being done, but in practice they stood little chance of hitting their targets. RAF night-interceptor squadrons operated with increasing success, especially using two-seater Bristol Beaufighters or Boulton Paul Defiants, which either flew blind, directed on to their targets by ground controllers, or used air-interception radar sets. But either way, their chances of a kill were modest. A German bomber crew, tightly packed inside the perspex nose of a Junkers, Heinkel, or Dornier over the shadowy flaming confusion of a British city, could be reasonably confident of returning home intact.

BUTTERFLY BOMB
This small antipersonnel bomb is an example of the thousands dropped by German bombers over Britain. It has two folding wings that revolved, slowing the rate of descent and arming the fuse.

Victory in survival

Some of the most ferocious nights of the Blitz came in April and May 1941, but this was deceptive. The Germans were by then thoroughly engaged in preparations for the invasion of the Soviet Union. As spring turned to summer, the bombers shifted eastward, and the British people, wary and watchful, slowly realized that they had come through.

London, the most frequently battered target, had been subjected to 57 nights of aerial bombardment. This had imposed a sometimes near-intolerable strain on the civilian population and on the emergency services. Yet there had been no general breakdown of society or popular pressure on the government to surrender. In the Blitz, as in the Battle of Britain, survival had amounted to a kind of victory.

SHOOTING AT V1S
British antiaircraft guns open fire at night against V1 flying bombs. The V1s were visible in the dark because of their fiery engine exhaust. Many were shot down, exploding either when hit or on impact with the ground.

BEHIND THE LUFTWAFFE'S DEFEAT

UNTIL THE BATTLE OF BRITAIN, German airpower—the Luftwaffe—seemed unstoppable. But the Luftwaffe faced its first defeat over Britain.

The Luftwaffe made a series of fatal mistakes. First of all, Germany had not counted on a drawn-out campaign over the island nation. It thought British morale would cave before a threatened German invasion. To effectively conduct what became known as the Battle of Britain, Germany needed long-range bombers and long-range fighter escorts. But the Luftwaffe included mostly short- and medium-range aircraft.

Second, Britain had its own secret: radar. The British could detect Luftwaffe aircraft before they reached English shores. British fighters picked away at German airplanes as they crossed the Channel. Even so, by September 1940, the RAF was maxed out as the Luftwaffe destroyed one British airfield and factory and radar installation after another.

Poor intelligence was Germany's third lethal flaw. The upshot was that Germany inexplicably decided to bomb London and turn away from its previous success with targets such as the airfields right when Britain was at its most vulnerable. This mistake gave Britain much-needed breathing space to rebuild its air force.

US Lieutenant Colonel (later General) Carl Spaatz went to England to study the course of the air war. He made these observations:

1. The Luftwaffe was primarily a ground-supporting air force.
2. The Luftwaffe was tactically ill-prepared for strategic bombing, which was the only way to defeat Britain.
3. The Luftwaffe lacked a strategic bombing doctrine. In fact, in less than six months during the Battle of Britain, Luftwaffe leaders developed and used four different plans.

The Battle of Britain stopped the German advance. British resolve and poor German planning contributed to the outcome. The Luftwaffe and, for that matter, Germany never fully regained momentum in the West.

SECRET WEAPONS

IN THE SUMMER OF 1944 London was subjected to a second Blitz, this time by unpiloted V1 flying bombs. The Allies had been aware for some time that the Germans were developing "secret weapons," and devastating bombing raids both on the experimental center in Peenemunde, Germany, and on launch sites under construction in France delayed the V1's deployment. But by June 1944 the Germans had switched to smaller launchers that were not detected by Allied reconnaissance aircraft. Shortly after D-Day, Hitler ordered a flying-bomb offensive against London.

In the summer of 1944 about 100 V1s a day crossed the Channel, by day and night, and in all weather conditions. Although they were unarmed and unescorted, the flying bombs posed a novel challenge to air defenses. A combination of early-warning radar, antiaircraft guns, and fighters was deployed, as against any intruders, but Spitfires, Typhoons, and Mustangs found it hard to cope with such a fast, small target. Only the new high-performance Hawker Tempests could easily catch the flying bombs; jet-powered Gloster Meteors were also sent up as interceptors, the first operational use of jets by the Allies. Shooting down a V1 was a hazardous action, since if it exploded it could easily destroy its attacker. Tempest pilots developed a technique of flying alongside a V1, lifting their wing under the flying bomb's wing, and tipping it over so that it spiraled down out of control.

After V1 launch sites in northern France were overrun by Allied troops in August 1944, the Germans began air-launching them from Heinkel He 111s flying in at low level over the North Sea. About half of the 8,000 V1s launched against Britain were shot down by aircraft or ground fire.

Hitler's other secret weapon, the V2 ballistic missile, was not interceptible, although Allied air forces made heroic efforts to destroy heavily defended V2 launch and production sites. Fortunately, the Germans did not have an atomic warhead to put on the end of it. In all, the V weapons killed almost 9,000 people in Britain in 1944–45.

V1 AUTOPILOT
This autopilot from a V1 flying bomb fed signals to the bomb's elevators and rudder to control altitude and direction. The terminal dive was initiated when a preset distance had been flown.

SPOILS OF WAR
After the war's end, an American soldier studies a V2 in the underground rocket-assembly plant in Nordhausen, Germany. Slave laborers worked under appalling conditions to produce the rockets, and many thousands died of ill-treatment.

Warhead

Controls compartment

Alcohol tank

Liquid-oxygen tank

Rocket engine

Stabilizing fin

V2 ROCKET
The V2 rocket, here stripped of its outer casing, was the first ballistic missile used in warfare. Traveling at up to five times the speed of sound, it exploded before its victims could hear it coming. Some 3,200 V2s were launched in the war.

FLYING-BOMB LAUNCH
A German V1 flying bomb captured by the Allies at the end of the war—and bearing US insignia—is test-fired. Propelled by a primitive jet engine and flying at over 400mph (640kmph), the V1 was packed with a ton of explosives. When it hit the ground, the destructive effect was impressive. Yet V1s killed only 5,475 people in Britain—less than one for each V1 launched.

"There are a lot of people who say that bombing cannot win the war. My reply to that is that it has never been tried… and we shall see."

AIR CHIEF MARSHAL
SIR ARTHUR HARRIS
HEAD OF RAF BOMBER COMMAND, 1942

DEATH FROM THE AIR

ALLIED BOMBING REDUCED ENEMY CITIES TO RUINS BUT AT A COST THAT SHOCKED THOSE WHO BELIEVED THAT "THE BOMBER WOULD ALWAYS GET THROUGH"

THERE ARE FEW MORE apocalyptic images of total war than the mass bomber formations of World War II in action—at times more than a thousand aircraft filling the sky, some stretch of earth beneath them battered into an inferno of dust, smoke, and fire. Yet if the bomber raid offered a spectacle of power and impersonal destruction on a grand scale, the men who crewed the bombers were very far from invulnerable. For much of the war, Allied bomber crews had a higher chance of dying than the people they were bombing.

USAAF 15th Air Force bombardier Howard Jackson recalled his feelings before flying in a raid over Germany in World War II: "The terror starts on the night before the mission. This should not be confused with fear. Fear is when you have to ask a girl to dance who might say no… Terror is anxiety, dreams, rationalization of excuses not to fly, headaches, loose bowels, shaking and silence." Such feelings were almost universal, and perfectly rational. No one in the American and British armed forces had a more dangerous job than bomber crews. The USAAF Eighth Air Force—the "Mighty Eighth"—which carried out a daylight bombing offensive against Germany from 1942 to 1945, lost 26,000 men—one in eight of those who flew into action—as well as another 40,000 either wounded or shot down and made prisoners of war. RAF Bomber Command lost a staggering 56,000 of its British and Commonwealth crew members—more than half of those who took part in its nighttime

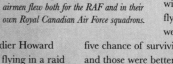

READY FOR ACTION
A Canadian crew stands ready for a mission in their Wellington bomber. Canadian airmen flew both for the RAF and in their own Royal Canadian Air Force squadrons.

strategic bombing campaign. At times the youthful bomber aircrews—typically men aged between 19 and 22—faced a tour of duty with little more chance of survival than a World War I infantryman sent "over the top" at the Somme or Verdun. In late June 1943, the USAAF's 381st Bomb Group entered combat with 36 crews, flying B-17s out of Ridgewell in eastern England. By the second week in October, only 10 of the original crews survived. In the winter of 1943–44, airmen flying for Bomber Command were estimated to have a one in five chance of surviving a 30-mission tour of duty, and those were better odds than they had sometimes faced earlier in the war.

Strategic bombing

The bomber crews were asked to take this punishment because senior commanders believed that strategic bombing could make a vital contribution to winning the war, or even win it outright. Men such as Sir Arthur Harris, in charge of Bomber Command, and General Carl Spaatz of the USAAF were convinced that if they were only given the resources, they could end the war without the need for land battles that would cost hundreds of thousands of soldiers' lives.

The RAF's bombing campaign got off to a slow start. Before the war, RAF commanders had argued for the "deterrent" effect of a strategic bomber force—the threat of having his cities destroyed from the air would stay the aggressor's hand. But when Hitler invaded Poland, no attempt was made to force a German withdrawal by bombing cities. Britain's political leaders were anxious to avoid provoking German reprisals and eager to curry favor with President Roosevelt,

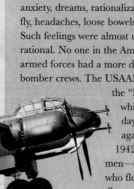

JUNKERS NIGHT FIGHTER
Designed as a fast bomber, the versatile Junkers Ju 88 also gave excellent service as a night fighter defending Germany against Allied bombing raids. The aerials protruding from the nose are part of the Lichtenstein airborne radar system.

BOMBING THE OILFIELDS
*Consolidated B-24 Liberators of the USAAF
15th Air Force bomb the Romanian Ploesti oilfields in
May 1944. More than 3,000 American Airmen lost
their lives in raids on Ploesti, but the eventual destruction
of the oil facilities was a crucial blow against the Nazi
war machine.*

SIR ARTHUR HARRIS

THE REPUTATION OF Air Chief Marshall Sir Arthur Harris (1892–1984), head of Bomber Command from 1942 to the end of the war in Europe, has become the subject of impassioned public controversy, yet among the men he led, respect for his leadership was almost universal.

Harris had been a pilot in the Royal Flying Corps during World War I. He understood and fought for things his airmen needed—for better aircraft and equipment, for proper pay and leave, and for official recognition of their efforts—even if he had no hesitation in sacrificing their lives by the thousands in pursuit of victory. Harris never wavered in his advocacy of the bombing of cities as a war-winning strategy.

His stubborn refusal to disown the February 1945 bombing of Dresden when it had become politic to do so was a piece of plain honesty that cost him dearly. He was shunned by the British establishment at the end of the war and was subsequently vilified for having carried through a policy that, in the war years, had enjoyed widespread support.

MAN ON A MISSION

Harris was a blunt and aggressive man, often to the point of rudeness. The force of his personality was felt through Bomber Command, stiffening aircrews' resolve to keep going in the face of heavy losses.

WALLIS' WELLINGTONS

Designed by Barnes Wallis, the twin-engined Vickers Wellington was the RAF's most advanced bomber at the start of the war. Hopelessly vulnerable in daylight raids, it proved a reasonably effective night bomber, taking part in raids on Germany until withdrawn from front-line service in 1943.

NAVIGATIONAL EQUIPMENT

Bomber Command's twin-engined bombers had to rely, for the most part, on maps and compasses to navigate to their targets. The map is Sheet N53, Berlin, of a British wartime series intended for both aircrews and ground troops. The astro-compass used the sun, the moon, and other heavenly bodies to help aircrews plot accurate courses.

EVENING TAKEOFF

As the light fades, RAF Short Stirlings line up to take off for a night raid on Germany. Stirlings could not reach the altitude achieved by Handley Page Halifaxes and Avro Lancasters and were often hit by bombs dropped by higher flying colleagues.

who had called on all combatants to refrain from using aircraft as a weapon of terror. Until May 1940, RAF bombers were restricted to attacks on naval targets and to dropping propaganda leaflets.

In any case Bomber Command was woefully ill-equipped to carry out a strategic bombing campaign. Its twin-engined Bristol Blenheim, Armstrong Whitworth Whitley, Handley Page Hampden, and Vickers Wellington bombers were inadequate in

bombload, speed, and armament. Their crews were mostly short on training and had to operate with poor bombsights and navigational equipment limited to a compass and a map. Yet it was presumed that they would simply fly to their targets in daylight without fighter escorts and drop their bombs on designated spots. This fantasy cost hundreds of young men their lives. Losses rose to as high as 50 percent on a single mission. And even if the bombers reached

their targets, they could not bomb accurately enough to hit them.

From the spring of 1940, the unsustainable losses in daylight operations led to a switch to night bombing, for which Bomber Command was even more ill-prepared. Britain's political leaders were still reluctant to envisage attacks on civilians, authorizing raids against targets such as synthetic oil plants and railroad yards. But an official survey carried out in 1941 estimated that, groping blindly through the darkness over enemy territory, only one bomber in three managed to drop its bombload within 5 miles (8km) of its target.

CITY DESTRUCTION

Hamburg was one of the most heavily damaged German cities. Until very late in the war, however, Allied bombers only rarely managed to inflict devastation on this scale.

Navigational aids

The development of Bomber Command's night offensive against German cities and industrial areas through 1942 and 1943 was aided by major advances in equipment and operational tactics. First, they had much better aircraft in the four-engined Halifax and Lancaster bombers, capable of carrying an impressive bombload into the heart of Germany. Second, there were navigational aids that allowed them to match the night-bombing accuracy that the Luftwaffe had achieved during the Blitz.

The first of these navigational aids was Gee: A grid of radio beams projected over Germany from sites in Britain were picked up by aircraft receivers, allowing navigators to plot their progress accurately. This was enough to ensure that the average bomber crew could find a German city in the dark. Next came Oboe:

One beam guided a bomber to its target, while a series of crossbeams told the crew when they were drawing near to their goal and when to release their bombs. Finally, in 1943, there was an airborne lookdown radar, H2S, which improved chances of identifying targets on the ground even at night and in heavy clouds.

INTERROGATION SCENE
RAF Flying Officer G. Dunbar (second from left) leads a group of officers through a debriefing following a night raid on Berlin in late November 1943.

Oboe and H2S were mostly used by elite squadrons of the Pathfinder Force (PFF). Flying Wellingtons or Stirlings (and, later, de Havilland Mosquitos), their job was to mark targets accurately with incendiaries for the less skillful pilots and bomb-aimers to home in on. The main bomber force followed the pathfinders in

RADARS

THE NIGHT FIGHTING over Germany during World War II accelerated the development of compact airborne radar sets. The Luftwaffe, for example, equipped Bf 110 and Ju 88 night fighters with Lichtenstein interception radar, which greatly improved the aircraft's effectiveness. Manned by the radio operator, it had a range of 2 miles (3km), and was used when the aircraft were closing in on targets. British bombers were equipped with H2S radar sets to help them find their targets. Various radar-jamming devices were also deployed by both sides. Radar detectors enabled the Germans to locate enemy bombers by their H2S emissions, while similar equipment warned bomber crews of the approach of radar-guided night fighters.

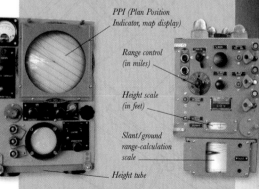

PPI (Plan Position Indicator, map display)

Range control (in miles)

Height scale (in feet)

Slant/ground range-calculation scale

Height tube

H2S RADAR SYSTEM
The RAF's H2S airborne radar helped night bombers identify targets on the ground. It was also used by the USAAF on daylight raids when there was heavy cloud cover.

a "bomber stream" that hopefully would overwhelm the German defenses by sheer numbers. By the end of 1943, bombers had VHF radio for air-to-air communication, so a pathfinder "master bomber," circling the target during the attack, could direct the operations.

GENERAL CARL A. "TOOEY" SPAATZ

CARL SPAATZ WAS APPOINTED to the US Military Academy in 1910, graduated June 12, 1914, and was commissioned a second lieutenant of Infantry. He served with the Infantry until 1915, when he was detailed as a student in the Aviation School at San Diego, California.

Spaatz went to France with the American Expeditionary Forces in command of the 31st Aero Squadron and, after November 15, 1917, served in the American Aviation School at Issoundun continuously, except for one month at the British Front, until August 30, 1918.

He joined the Second Pursuit Group in September 1918, as pursuit pilot in the Thirteenth Squadron, and was promoted to flight leader. He was officially credited with shooting down three German Fokker planes, and received the Distinguished Service Cross. Then-Major Spaatz commanded the Army plane "Question Mark" in its refueling endurance flight over Los Angeles and vicinity from January 1–7, 1929.

During the Battle of Britain in 1940, Lieutenant Colonel Spaatz spent several weeks in England as a special military observer. In August 1940 he was assigned to the Office of the Chief of the Air Corps, and two months later was appointed assistant to the chief of the Air Corps, with the temporary rank of brigadier general. The following July he was named chief of the air staff at Army Air Force Headquarters.

A few weeks after Pearl Harbor, in January 1942, Spaatz was assigned as chief of the Army Air Force Combat Command at Washington and promoted to the temporary rank of major general. In May 1942 he became commander of the Eighth Air Force, transferring to the European theater of operations in that capacity in July 1942 to prepare for the American bombing of Germany. On July 7 he was appointed commanding general of the US Army Air Forces in the European theater, in addition to his duties as commander of the Eighth.

On December 1, 1942, General Spaatz became commanding general of the Twelfth Air Force in North Africa. In February 1943 he assumed command of the Northwest African Air Force, which he organized.

After Rommel's Afrika Korps had been driven out of North Africa and the invasion of Italy was launched, Spaatz became deputy commander of the Mediterranean Allied Air Forces, including the 12th Air Force in Africa and the 15th Air Force and the Royal Air Force in Italy. He returned to

GENERAL CARL A. SPAATZ
Both General Dwight D. Eisenhower and General Omar Bradley considered Spaatz the best combat leader in the European theater.

England in January 1944 to command the US Strategic Air Forces in Europe, which he headed throughout the pre-invasion period and the ensuing campaign that culminated with the utter defeat of Germany.

Spaatz received a temporary promotion to general on March 11, 1945, and was assigned to Air Force Headquarters in Washington, D.C., in June 1945. The following month he assumed command of the US Strategic Air Forces in the Pacific, with headquarters in Guam. There he supervised the final strategic bombing of Japan by the B-29s, including the two atomic bomb missions. He was present at all three signings of unconditional surrender by the enemy—at Rheims, Berlin, and Tokyo.

In October 1945 General Spaatz returned to Army Air Force Headquarters. In February 1946 he was nominated to become commander of the Army Air Forces. In September 1947 President Harry S. Truman appointed him the first chief of staff of the new United States Air Force, a position he held until April 30, 1948.

He retired with the rank of general on June 30, 1948. Spaatz died July 14, 1974, at the age of 83, and was interred at the US Air Force Academy.

THE BATTLE OF HAMBURG

IN THE CAT-AND-MOUSE GAME that was night war over Germany, a new move giving a temporary advantage could have devastating results. This is what happened over the port city of Hamburg in late July 1943. The RAF had a new trick called "window," the scattering of strips of aluminum foil out of the bomber's flare chute to confuse German radar. Without radar, the antiaircraft guns, the night fighters, and their controllers were blinded and let the bombers through. During the short time it took the German defenders to adapt to the new situation, a series of raids by the RAF laid Hamburg to waste.

On the night of July 27–28, 735 bombers dropped 2,564 tons (2,326 tonnes) of explosives and incendiaries in little over an hour, starting fires that killed over 40,000 people. The devastation of Hamburg represented the ideal to which Bomber Command aspired—an act of destruction on such a scale that, if repeated night after night, might have made the Germans think seriously about ending the war. But the bombers could not achieve this. They were not to repeat such destruction until Dresden in 1945.

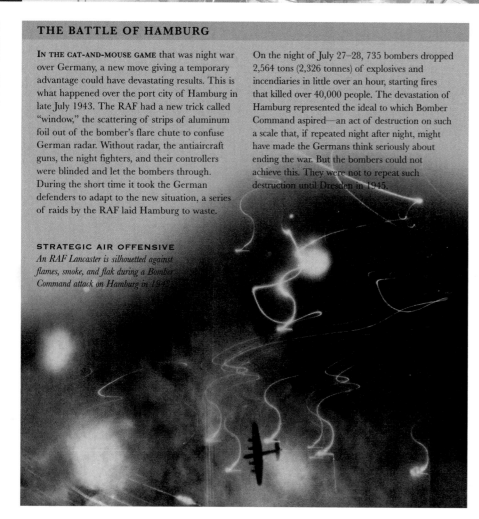

STRATEGIC AIR OFFENSIVE
An RAF Lancaster is silhouetted against flames, smoke, and flak during a Bomber Command attack on Hamburg in 1943.

two-seater Bf 110s or converted bombers such as the Ju 88. These aircraft had the crew to operate the radio and radar equipment that made night flying reasonably safe and effective, and were fast and nimble enough to take on unescorted bombers.

The deadly battle of wits in the night war brought both complex technical advances and inspired improvisations. For example, to exploit the fact that RAF bombers had no gun under the fuselage, some German Bf 110s were equipped with two upward-firing cannon, known rather bizarrely as *Schräge Musik*—a slang term for jazz. The interceptor positioned itself in level flight underneath a bomber and, using a reflex sight for aiming, fired directly upward, ideally trying to hit the fuel tanks. The RAF never really found an answer to *Schräge Musik*, but they did develop a whole range of countermeasures to jam or confuse German radars and radios, as well as equipping bombers with short-range radars to detect incoming fighters.

The effectiveness of German air defenses could be measured by Bomber Command losses. Between August 1943 and March 1944, a period when the main target of the RAF night offensive was Berlin, on average about one in 20 bombers was lost on each raid. And there was, from the RAF's point of view, no sign of improvement. Right at the end of March 1944, in one particularly disastrous raid on the city of Nuremberg, 95 out of 795 bombers sent out did not return.

American strategy

On the eve of its entry into the war, America's air doctrine called primarily for daylight strategic bombing. Soon after Germany invaded the Soviet Union, President Roosevelt asked the Army and Navy for estimates of the production requirements needed to defeat the Axis. A group of majors and lieutenant colonels in the Air War Plans Division received the task of developing an independent Army Air Forces estimate. The result was Air War

German defenses

But none of these technical improvements could give the RAF air superiority in the night skies over Germany. A chain of radar stations denied the bombers any chance of surprise. Night fighters stood ready to scramble from their airfields and intercept the attackers from whichever direction they came. Potential targets were surrounded by a dense barrier of searchlights and defended by radar-directed antiaircraft guns. It was no wonder that Bomber Command losses remained high.

Early in the war, German night fighters, guided toward the bombers by ground controllers, had to rely on their eyesight to close in for the kill. The introduction of the Lichtenstein airborne interceptor radar greatly improved their effectiveness, even if the strange assembly of direction-finding antennae attached to the fighter's nose—dubbed the "barbed wire fence" by German pilots—produced drag that slowed the aircraft down. Later still, the Germans were equipped with infrared detectors that could pick up on a Lancaster's engine exhausts.

Until mid-1943 the German night fighters were committed to a rigidly planned sector defense, staying within "boxes" under strict ground control. During the crisis of the Battle of Hamburg, however, more flexible tactics began to be adopted. Pilot Hajo Herrmann pioneered what became known as *Wilde Sau* ("Wild Boar") tactics, in which single-seat day fighters roamed freely over the target area at high altitude, swooping down on bombers they spotted silhouetted against ground fires. This was so successful that special *Wilde Sau* squadrons were established. After *Wilde Sau* came *Zahme Sau* ("Tame Boar"), in which night fighters with onboard radar shadowed or mixed with the bomber stream, picking off targets at will.

Single-seat fighters like the Bf 109, used by *Wilde Sau* squadrons, were not equipped for night fighting. Most night operations were entrusted to

AIRCRAFT RECOGNITION
Luftwaffe recruits use models to learn to identify German and Allied aircraft. Airmen on both sides suffered from "friendly fire" when misidentified by antiaircraft gunners or fellow fliers.

Plan Division plan No. 1, or AWPD/1, a plan for defeating Germany using aerial bombardment.

The AAF planners accepted the basic Anglo-American strategy of containing Japan in the Pacific, defending the Western Hemisphere, and defeating Germany first. Only with Germany out of the way would the United States begin decisive action against Japan. AWPD/1 declared that 6,800 medium, heavy, and very heavy bombers based in Europe and North Africa could knock Germany out of the war by destroying 154 industrial targets. These bombers could strike at Germany even though

German forces dominated the Mediterranean, Europe, and the western Soviet Union.

Realizing the time that would be needed to produce 6,800 bombers, the planners proposed an interim force of 3,800 to carry the war to Germany while the main force grew to its planned level. Even this was ambitious, because in the summer of 1941, the AAF had fewer than 700 bombers of all types. The AWPD believed that a growing force of American bombers could neutralize the Luftwaffe's fighter force by destroying engine and airframe plans and shooting down interceptors in aerial combat. Having won air superiority, the AAF would then attack Germany's electrical grid, cripple the transportation network, and destroy the oil industry.

AWPD/1 suffered from several flaws, as events in 1943 would make painfully clear. First, of all the targets proposed in the plan, only the oil industry proved vital enough and vulnerable enough for high-altitude strategic bombing to exact a significant toll. The German electrical grid proved too dispersed and too easy to repair, and hydroelectric dams required low-level attack using bombs too heavy for a B-17 or B-24. The offensive against German transportation never got under way until late in the war, when continental bases became available to tactical aircraft and Allied air superiority allowed heavy bombers to attack with greater accuracy from lower altitudes.

In addition, AAF planners believed that bombers could hit their targets despite northern Europe's

NOCTURNAL PREDATORS
The two-seater Messerschmitt Bf 110 was a failure as an escort fighter in the Battle of Britain, but a resounding success as a night interceptor, playing a leading role in the defense of Germany.

THE LESSONS OF KASSERINE PASS

THE BATTLE FOR KASSERINE PASS in central Tunisia, fought in February 1943, was the first serious encounter between Germans and American-led armored forces in World War II. The battle, which began badly for the Americans, has been generally regarded as a military embarrassment to the United States and the American commander, General Dwight D. Eisenhower. It exposed American Soldiers and Airmen as ill-prepared, ill-equipped, and often poorly led. American units suffered thousands of killed, missing, and captured, especially in the first two phases at Faid Pass and Sidi-bou-Zid. Interestingly, however, in the last phase of the battle at Kasserine Pass itself, the combined American, British, and Free French forces held their ground against German Field Marshall Erwin Rommel, the "Desert Fox." The Germans were forced to pull back, and pressed by British Field Marshall Bernard Montgomery in the east, soon left Africa altogether.

The battle revealed serious flaws in US combat air support. During the earlier phases of the battle, fragmented American air units got so worn out in the futile attempt to support the ground forces and gain air superiority that they were forced to retire from action before the last fighting at Kasserine Pass. Poor coordination with ground forces led to several incidents of US planes bombing their own troops and at least one fell to friendly antiaircraft fire. Air units were split among ground units and directed by ground commanders who decided which missions to fly and did not share their airplanes. This fragmentation of Allied airpower led to a defensive posture that allowed the Luftwaffe to concentrate when and where it wanted. Desperate conditions forced General James Doolittle to take centralized control of all Twelfth Air Force assets. Bad weather also played a role, preventing effective use of airpower. But Doolittle sent medium and heavy bombers to turn the tide, and in the last days as Rommel pulled back, fighters and bombers finally hit the German trucks and tanks, dealing a serious blow to enemy armor.

The importance of Kasserine Pass transcended the actual combat, however. General Eisenhower and others analyzed the results closely and made several significant changes to Army and AAF doctrine and tactics. In addition to lessons learned on the ground, Allied leaders recognized the importance of the long-held doctrinal point of gaining air superiority before undertaking a land battle. They also accepted another historic point of doctrine—that central command of air assets by Airmen was a necessity.

By the time of the D-Day invasion the following year, Allied pilots would be able to talk directly to the ground units they were supporting, and tactical air commands would work closely with the field armies. Air operations became totally offensive in nature.

Meanwhile, Rommel came away from the North African fight with a low estimate of American tactics and equipment. This view would serve him badly in Normandy.

THE PLOESTI RAID

THE OIL REFINERIES AT PLOESTI, Romania, provided 35 percent of Germany's oil. Air planners thought it would take high-level attacks by huge fleets of heavy bombers to destroy them. But Colonel (later General) Jacob E. Smart believed a low-level attack could succeed—it would increase aircraft bombing accuracy and mitigate the refineries' extensive antiaircraft defenses. Not everyone agreed, but President Roosevelt and General Hap Arnold supported the idea.

The plan called for a 2,700 mile (4,345km) mission by more than 300 bombers to attack seven refineries. Because they were busy with other missions, the units tapped for the attack were not able to train for it until 11 days beforehand.

On August 1, 1943, 177 B-24s took off from Libya to bomb Ploesti. The 367th Bomb Group, led by Colonel Keith Compton, led the attack, which ran into trouble almost immediately. Several planes had to turn back. The lead

navigator was in another plane that ditched into the Mediterranean Sea several hours after takeoff. The attackers were accidentally split into two groups when they encountered dense clouds over Greece. Colonel Compton then misidentified his initial point—a ground feature used to coordinate the attack—and led his group to a point 30 miles south of Ploesti. Three of the five attack groups were already behind schedule. The error eliminated any remaining attack coordination.

Still, 164 B-24 Liberators reached Ploesti and attacked at levels often lower than the refineries' towers. Bombers flying through oil-tank explosions were raked by merciless flak trains and machine-gun fire. B-24 gunners dueled with gunners in towers and church domes. In addition, more than 120 German and 200 Romanian aircraft defended the refineries. The 198th Bomb Group, let by Colonel John Kane, was the only one that flew its assigned course and arrived on schedule.

Only the courage and determination of the aircrews prevented the raid from failing. The bombers took heavy losses. Often they had to ascend to avoid smokestacks 210ft (60m) high. Of the B-24s participating in the raid, 54 were lost and 55 suffered major damage. Despite the odds, the USAAF Airmen managed to destroy 42 percent of the refineries' production capacity. The raid illustrated the dangers of low-level strategic bombing, and since a follow-up raid was not practical, the Germans were able to repair the facilities rapidly. But the Ploesti raid, undertaken long before mid-air refueling was perfected and made part of standard military practice, demonstrated that strategic bombing was not only possible, it was inevitable in the context of modern war.

Five Airmen, including Colonel Kane, received the Medal of Honor for bravery during the raid— the most of any single engagement of World War II.

FIERY DEATH
A B-24 Liberator erupts in flames in a raid over Austria in 1944. The USAAF photographer who took the picture said: "I felt guilty, helplessly snapping a death picture while the men were burning inside."

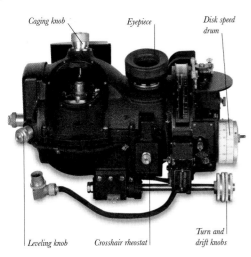

NORDEN BOMBSIGHT

The bombardier fed the Norden bombsight with data on airspeed, wind direction, and other relevant factors, and waited for two crosshairs to fix on the target several miles ahead. The Norden then told him how to fly the aircraft and when to drop the bombs.

Caging knob   Eyepiece   Disk speed drum

Leveling knob   Crosshair rheostat   Turn and drift knobs

notoriously bad weather. They reckoned that bombers could level German industry because 90 percent of the bombs directed at a target would fall within 1,250 feet of the aiming point. This proved impossible in practice—even using the Norden bombsight, bomber formations could place 90 percent of their bombs no closer than a mile from the aiming point.

But the biggest flaw in American thinking was that massed bombers could repel an attacking force of enemy fighters. Once again, events would paint a very different story.

American involvement

During 1942 the USAAF joined in the European bombing campaign. Despite the discouraging British experience earlier in the war, American commanders were convinced that their unescorted bombers could penetrate the German defenses in daylight, carrying out precision raids on key strategic targets. In theory, the Boeing B-17s and Consolidated B-24s would fly too high to be hit by flak and the interlocking gunfire of their mass formations would face off enemy fighters. Attacking targets in Germany, the bombers would "shoot their way in and shoot their way out again."

The air and ground crews of the US Eighth Air Force arriving at airbases in the east of England had more to get used to than just tea and warm beer. The reality of war in Europe proved radically different from training in Texas or Arizona. First, there was the weather. One Airman said of Britain: "I love that country. The people are fighters and made of the right stuff, but the climate was not my cup of tea and hell to fly in." The advantage of day bombing over night bombing resided in visibility. But in Europe, cloud cover was so common and so unpredictable that this advantage often did not exist.

The key to USAAF expectations of hitting precision targets was the Norden bombsight, a sophisticated proto-computer that could "drop a bomb in a pickle barrel." These bombsights were considered so vital a secret device that between missions they were removed from aircraft and kept under armed guard. Bombardiers had strict orders to destroy them before bailing out if shot down over enemy territory. But the Norden bombsight was so sophisticated that only a highly trained bombardier could operate it successfully. The USAAF soon adopted a system in which only the lead bomber of the formation had the bombsight; the other bombers in the formation dropped their bombs when he did. But even the best of bombardiers needed to be able to see the target to use the bombsight. Clouds, mist, and smoke could wreak havoc with bombing accuracy.

Through 1943 the USAAF daylight offensive gathered momentum, launched from bases not only in England but also in North Africa and, later, in Italy. But the bombers took heavy punishment. For instance, on August 17, 1943, B-17s from bases in England carried out simultaneous raids on the ball-bearing factory in Schweinfurt and the aircraft factory in Regensburg. Of 376 aircraft that set out on the dual mission, 60 were shot down and another 11 so badly damaged on their return that they were written off to be cannibalized for spare parts. It is a tribute to the courage and commitment of American aircrews that they held steady in the face of such losses.

CURTIS LEMAY

GENERAL CURTIS LEMAY (1906–90) was known as the toughest officer in the USAAF—his men were reputed to look forward to a spell in an enemy prisoner-of-war camp as a soft option compared with working for "Old Iron Ass."

It was a toughness that brought results. LeMay had been born on the wrong side of the tracks, and forged a path into the air force and up through its ranks by hard work and willpower. He took the B-17s of 305th Bomb Group to England in the fall of 1942 and proved his outfit the most effective in the "Mighty Eighth," with the tightest bomb pattern and lowest losses. He was transferred to the Pacific theater in 1944 and

personally led missions against Japan to take stock of the task. He devised the strategy of low-level night incendiary raids that reduced Japanese cities to ashes in the spring of 1945. After the war LeMay commanded the US nuclear bomber force.

TOUGH LEADER

As head of US Strategic Air Command in the early years of the Cold War, LeMay's hawkish personality contributed to the credibility of nuclear deterrence—here was a man who was definitely ready, if required, to unleash nuclear war.

Boeing B-17 Flying Fortress

THE WARTIME MODELS OF the Boeing B-17—the B-17C, D, E, F, and G—were extraordinary fighting machines. Also known as the "Flying Fortress," the B-17 was bristling with machine guns, could fly at an altitude of over 30,000ft (9,000m), and—when in mass formation—was capable of delivering a staggering tonnage of explosives. In clear weather, the sophisticated Norden bombsight allowed the B-17 to strike a relatively small target; otherwise the USAAF came to rely on blind bombing techniques.

"The B-17 was a very sturdy, easy-to-fly airplane that would take lots of damage and get you home..."

DICK ATKINS
USAAF PILOT

Hamilton Standard propeller

Plexiglas nose

Viewing panel for aiming bombs

Navigation light

Outer wing panel

Remote-controlled chin turret

Deicing strip

TURBO ENGINES
The B-17G had four turbo-supercharged engines, each with a 11ft 6in (3.5m) diameter propeller. This enabled it not only to carry a heavy bombload but also to cruise at high altitude.

Fabric-covered rudder

124485

Handheld waist gun

Rudder tab

Tail gun turret

Tailwheel

Twin Browning machine guns

For the B-17's crew of 10, conditions were cramped and uncomfortable. The aircraft was not pressurized, and the effects of altitude sickness were highly unpleasant. The crew also had to sit for hours in the freezing cold—the tail- and waist-gunners sometimes suffered frostbite. Fortunately the B-17 was robust: Many B-17s were able to return to base despite losing large chunks of wing, fuselage, or tail.

Since the B-17 was employed in large fleets, mass production of the craft was essential. For every B-17 the Germans shot down, American factories produced more than two. As a result, there were more B-17s available in the last months of the war than at any time before.

ESSENTIAL PREPARATIONS
This B-17 is undergoing essential preflight preparations at a US bomber/fighter base in England. The B-17 was able to transport a bombload of up to 6,000lb (2,742kg) a distance of approximately 2,000 miles (3,200km).

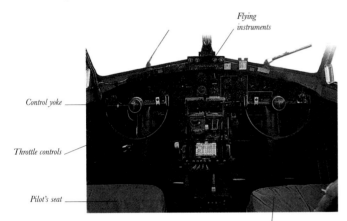

Flying instruments

Control yoke

Throttle controls

Pilot's seat

Copilot's seat

B-17 COCKPIT
The pilot and copilot of a B-17 were afforded excellent front and side visibility from the cockpit. The most important flying instruments are situated between the two control yokes, so that both pilots can see them.

CREW CONDITIONS
Conditions were cramped in the B-17. This waist-gunner —wearing full flying gear, including an oxygen mask and flak jacket—is unable to stand upright. And the only way to reach the rear gun turret was to crawl on all fours.

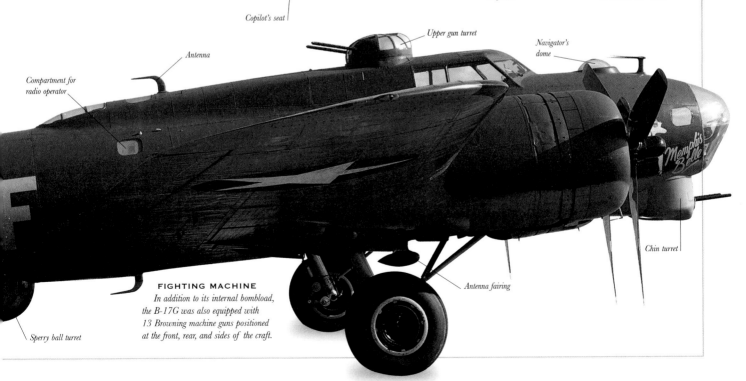

Upper gun turret

Navigator's dome

Antenna

Compartment for radio operator

Chin turret

Antenna fairing

Sperry ball turret

FIGHTING MACHINE
In addition to its internal bombload, the B-17G was also equipped with 13 Browning machine guns positioned at the front, rear, and sides of the craft.

FLYING FORTRESS RAID

AT THE START OF THE WAR, US commanders believed that formations of B-17 Flying Fortresses would be immune to fighter attack, because of their speed, high altitude, and the weight of fire from their many guns. But German fighters were not easily deterred. They discovered that the best way to attack a B-17 was from straight ahead. The glass nose provided no protection and, until the chin gun was introduced in the B-17G, there was no forward-firing armament. Fighters attacking head-on sometimes shot a tail-gunner in the back with fire passing down the inside of the fuselage. Coming under fighter attack brought an intense experience of terror mixed with adrenaline-fueled excitement. Lieutenant Robert Morrill, a B-17 pilot in the raid on Regensburg, August 17, 1943 recalled: "Time after time my entire ship shook as every gun fired. The air was filled as the formation fired thousands upon thousands of tracers. I glanced behind me and found the top turret-gunner standing in a heap of shell cases that covered the entire floor. In the cockpit my hands were glued to the wheel and throttles. I don't believe I could have let go if I had tried. In spite of the cold, sweat was running from my hair under the helmet and down across the oxygen mask, falling on to my jacket and freezing there. But none of us ever thought of turning back."

Fortunately the B-17 had a remarkable ability to survive punishment. Robust and reliable, many B-17s made it back to base even after receiving hits that took off large chunks of wing, fuselage, or tail. This was the key to its popularity with aircrews. As one American officer put it: "The B-17 was a very sturdy, easy-to-fly airplane that would take lots of damage and get you home."

> ## "None of us ever thought of turning back."
>
> LIEUTENANT ROBERT MORRILL
> B-17 PILOT

FLAK JACKET
To protect them from antiaircraft fire, US aircrews wore reinforced flak jackets, which were introduced in 1942.

KEEPING OUT THE COLD
Like all the crew, the B-17 waist-gunners wore heated flying suits to protect them from the cold at high altitudes. The temperature inside the aircraft could drop to -50°F (-45°C).

OFFICER PILOTS
The pilot and copilot of a USAAF bomber were always officers, and usually college graduates. The B-17 afforded them an excellent view of the sky and ground.

Bombing routine

The routine of a US Eighth Air Force bomber operation started early. The men would be roused at around 2:00am by an operations officer snapping on the light in their hut and calling off the crews that were to fly on the day's mission. They stumbled out into the darkness of a raw East Anglian night to walk to a briefing session, where the announcement of the target for the day, almost inevitably deep inside Germany, was greeted with a traditional groan and cursing. By 4:00am the aircrews were eating breakfast, if they had the stomach for it, while ground crews swarmed over the B-17s readying and loading them for the mission. An hour later the Airmen would be in the dispersal tent by their aircraft, waiting for the red flare from the control tower that meant "start engines." Although each member of the crew meticulously carried out the practical preparations for his role on the mission, most also carried a lucky coin or a love letter on their person—faced with the lottery of death, superstition flourished.

The "Forts" took off at 30-second intervals, lifting off sluggishly, loaded with around 50 bombs, 2,500 gallons (9,500 liters) of fuel, and heavy crates of ammunition for the guns. Then the ball-turret gunner climbed into his position and at 10,000ft (3,500m) the crew went on oxygen, while the aircraft continued climbing, taking up its place in the formation. Setting off for Germany, the bombers were an awesome sight. A pilot recalled his "exhilaration and pride" at the spectacle: "The great battle formations were something to see! As far as the eye could see there were B-17s, some of them olive-drab Fs,

others the new silver Gs." The flight was cold and uncomfortable, especially for the ball-turret gunner suspended in space with his knees pulled up almost to his chest.

Facing the flak

As soon as the day bombers were beyond the range of fighter escort, they came under attack from swarms of German fighters, mostly Bf 109s and Focke-Wulf Fw 190s. Discomfort and cold were immediately forgotten as the terror and excitement took over. The Luftwaffe pilots assigned to defense of the fatherland were the cream of the service and quite undeterred by the bombers' bristling guns. They often attacked head-on, trying to break up the bomber formation and exploiting the lack of armor and armament on the B-17's nose. Or they would launch beam attacks, raking the bombers with machine-gun and cannon fire as they cut across them. Gunners blazed away as the German aircraft buzzed around the formation. Soon parachutes would be peppering the sky as Airmen jumped from their burning B-17s; some Fortresses exploded in midair, giving the crews no chance of escape.

LOADING THE FORTRESS
An American ground crew loads the bombs onto a Boeing B-17E Flying Fortress. The B-17's normal bombload of around 6,000lb (2,700kg) was about half that of an RAF Lancaster, making the B-17, in British terms, a medium rather than heavy bomber.

THE REGENSBURG/SCHWEINFURT RAIDS

THE GROWING STRENGTH of German fighter operations in Europe was a great concern to the Allies in 1943. On June 10 the combined chiefs of staff issued a directive, "Pointblank," making attacking German fighter strength the top strategic priority. To implement this directive, Allied air planners decided to attack production facilities at Regensburg—where a large percentage of German fighters were built—and Schweinfurt, a major ball-bearing production center.

At this point in the war, the Americans' fighter escort could only reach as far as Germany's western border. So the plan was for General Curtis LeMay's 4th Bomb Wing to bomb the Messerschmitt plant in Regensburg, then fly across the Mediterranean and land in North Africa. The greater range of the new B-17F made this possible. The Allies thought the Luftwaffe would meet the attack early, then land and refuel for the attack on the bombers

as they headed back to England. The Allied plan would counter this by having the 1st Bomb Wing follow the 4th by only 15 minutes along the same flight path before breaking off to hit Schweinfurt. By the time the Germans figured out that the 4th Bomb Wing was not returning to England and the 1st was headed for Schweinfurt, they would be on the ground, low on fuel and ammunition. In addition, the plan called for three B-26 groups to raid coastal Luftwaffe airfields to divert German fighters from the 1st Bomb Wing.

On August 17 146 B-17s led by General LeMay crossed the Dutch coast and headed for southeast Germany. The group lost 17 aircraft en route, but conducted a very accurate mission from less than 20,000ft (6,096m). As at Ploesti, however, timing went awry. As the 4th left Regensburg, the 1st was still over the North Sea, five hours behind schedule because of weather. The Luftwaffe,

meanwhile, expected the 4th to head back to England and massed fighters in unprecedented numbers. The 230 B-17s of the 1st Bomb Wing flew right into the teeth of 300 enemy planes. By the time it reached Schweinfurt, it had lost 24 bombers. It then had trouble locating the ball-bearing plants and scattered its bombs all over the town while the Luftwaffe refueled and rearmed its fighters. The return trip to England for the 1st Bomb Wing was as hellish as the flight in.

The Regensburg/Schweinfurt raids cost the AAF 60 B-17s and 601 Airmen. (The Eighth Air Force would lose 60 more in a raid on Schweinfurt the following October.) "The Raid" showed how difficult and costly it was to conduct air warfare, but it foretold the day when the Luftwaffe would not be able to stop Allied bombing. Before that could happen, however, the Americans would have to find a way to extend the bombers' fighter escort into Germany.

Approaching the target, inevitably through heavy flak, the bombardier and his Norden bombsight took over control of the B-17 from the pilot. Holding straight and steady on the run into the target was essential to bombing accuracy, but a gift to German gunners on the ground. The relief was palpable when the crew felt the bomber lift upward as the weight of the bombs dropped away—and then there was the small question of getting home. Many of the B-17s would by then be carrying significant damage; some would have dead or wounded crew members on board. The hours would seem long before, in midafternoon, the bombers returned to their airfields, counted in by anxious ground crews.

Fighter support

The only way that the effectiveness of day bombing, and the survival rate of bomber crews, could be improved was through fighter escorts to protect them from attack. But the P-38 Lightnings and P-47 Thunderbolts used as escorts in 1943, with a range of about 450 miles (725km), there and back, could only accompany the B-17s and B-24s as far as the German border. Obviously, the German fighters waited until the escorts had turned away and then attacked the bombers at will. The Americans desperately needed an aircraft with a range nearer to 1,000 miles (1,600km), yet capable of holding its own in air combat with the Messerschmitts and Focke-Wulfs.

PREPARED FOR TAKEOFF
A ground crewman gives the signal for a Mustang to take off. The use of a Merlin liquid-cooled engine, like that in the Spitfire, gave the Mustang a very different look from most US fighters, which had air-cooled radial engines.

The need for a long-distance escort fighter had not been foreseen before the war and, given the long lead time involved in developing and putting into production a new aircraft, it was, on the face of it, unlikely that the need could be met. A fortuitous solution came from an unlikely quarter. The North American P-51 Mustang was a fighter aircraft that had failed. Produced in the United States to a British design and specification, early models performed poorly in combat and were relegated to a ground-support role.

That is how it might have remained, had not a Rolls-Royce test pilot, Ron Harker, suggested replacing the Mustang's Allison engine with the Merlin used in Spitfires. Combining the American airframe with a British engine created probably the finest fighter aircraft of the war.

Equipped with drop tanks, the Mustang could fly to Berlin and back. And with a top speed of over 440mph (700kmph), plus an impressive rate of climb and operational ceiling, it outclassed the Bf 109s and Fw 190s in combat performance. Introduced into the fighter-escort role in December 1943, the Mustang soon shifted the balance of the air war in favor of the American intruders, reducing bomber losses and sharply increasing the number of Luftwaffe aircraft shot down. By the spring of 1944 the USAAF was sending its bombers into Germany with up to 1,000 fighters in support.

Allied success

During 1944 the Allies won air superiority over Germany—the precondition for truly effective strategic bombing. Although the diversion of bombers to prepare for and support the D-Day

THE RED TAILS

THE 332ND FIGHTER GROUP, operating out of Italy, had a singular distinction: All its pilots were black. The African-American aviators only won the right to fly in combat through a hard battle against prejudice. Even after the USAAF reluctantly agreed to train them, in Tuskegee, Alabama, senior commanders stubbornly resisted sending them into combat, convinced that blacks were only suitable for use as ancillary staff. Protest and political pressure finally saw the first all-black fighter unit sent to North Africa in 1943.

The four-squadron 332nd, commanded by Lieutenant Colonel (later General) Benjamin O. Davis, assumed escort duties in mid-1944, flying on missions to well-defended targets such as Berlin and the Ploesti oilfields. Because of the color of the paint on their Mustangs, bomber pilots called them the Red Tails. In the strictly

99TH SQUADRON
The 99th Pursuit Squadron (whose insignia is shown here) was awarded two Presidential Unit Citations before joining the 332nd.

segregated US armed forces, the black pilots faced humiliating restrictions—they had to use separate R&R facilities and messes. But bomber crews soon learned that they were safer with the Red Tails than with any other escorts.

ALL-BLACK SQUADRON
Pilots of the 332nd Fighter Group pose beside one of their Mustangs in Italy in 1944. The Tuskegee airmen were credited with destroying 261 enemy aircraft, and black pilots earned 95 Distinguished Flying Crosses during the war.

LIEUTENANT GENERAL IRA EAKER

IRA C. EAKER MET HAP ARNOLD and Carl Spaatz at Rockwell Field in 1918 and became a lifelong friend of both. In 1929 he piloted the *Question Mark*, with Spaatz and Pete Quesada aboard. He joined Spaatz in England during World War II, where he headed VIII Bomber Command and then the Eighth Air Force.

The task of organizing the Eighth was extremely daunting. Strategic bombing was not a proven concept, the green Eighth was entering combat against a battle-tested enemy, and America's prodigious production capacity was not yet manifest.

The heavy losses suffered during the raids on Ploesti, Regensburg, and Schweinfurt raised doubts about whether the Americans should continue daylight raids or should switch to nighttime attacks, as RAF Bomber Command had done. But Eaker and his colleagues gave no serious thought to such a shift: Retraining crews and modifying aircraft for nighttime raids would have been a formidable task,

and Eaker believed strongly that doctrine would prevail. He was convinced that given enough airplanes and crews, the Eighth Air Force could fight its way in daylight to any target within range and return without suffering crippling losses.

But the heavy losses continued, requiring the Eighth to regroup. It needed time to repair aircraft and especially to train new aircrews. General Arnold came to believe that the Eighth was recovering too slowly from the October 1943 battles. He moved in new fighter aircraft, including the first P-51s, to better protect the bombers, but he also moved Eaker to the Mediterranean, where he became commander of all Allied air forces in the theater. General Doolittle took command of the Eighth Air Force.

Eaker was named deputy commander of the Army Air Forces in 1945 and retired from active duty in 1947. In 1985 Congress passed special legislation awarding him a fourth star. He died in August 1987.

LIEUTENANT GENERAL IRA EAKER
Eaker's efforts with the Eighth Air Force bore fruit after he was transferred: The Allies gained air superiority over the Luftwaffe in the spring of 1944 allowing Allied bombers to strike more effectively.

MIGHTY MUSTANG
The North American P-51 Mustang was the most renowned American fighter of World War II. Its range and high performance enabled it to give Allied bombers an effective escort to targets deep inside Germany.

landings temporarily reduced the pressure on Germany in the early summer, the subsequent liberation of France rendered the Germans' defensive position ever more desperate. Even so, it took a long time and a lot of bombs to seriously affect Germany's ability to continue the war. Damage to transport links was countered by swift reconstruction; damage to industrial sites was limited by the relocation of key factories underground. But the targeting of fuel supplies,

both through raids on the Ploesti oilfields of Romania and on factories in Germany manufacturing fuel out of coal, did eventually begin to cripple the German war machine.

Even before the fuel began to run out, the once-proud Luftwaffe was a shadow of its former self. Despite the destruction of aircraft factories in Allied raids in the spring of 1944, German aircraft output actually reached its peak in that year, with 40,000 planes produced. But losses of pilots could

not be made good as readily as losses of aircraft. As the war of attrition in the air took its toll, the Luftwaffe began throwing its pilots into combat with inadequate training. In general, neither German aircraft nor the men flying them were any longer a match for their enemies. Outnumbered and outfought, with their airfields coming under attack and their fuel reserves shrinking, by 1945 the Luftwaffe was more or less a spent force.

Seaplanes and flying boats

Airpower played a decisive role in the battle for the Atlantic, as well. Warships were generally equipped with catapult-launched seaplanes for reconnaissance—aircraft such as the slow and ungainly Supermarine Walrus, much loved by its British crews, or the German Arado Ar 196. And large flying boats such as the American Consolidated Catalina and Martin Mariner and the British Short Sunderland (a military version of the Empire flying boats that cruised to Cape Town and Sydney before the war) also patrolled the oceans, searching for enemy submarines and ships, as well as fulfilling an invaluable air-sea rescue role. Although slow by the standards of most World War II aircraft, the Catalinas and Sunderlands had invaluable range—the Catalina could stay in the air for 24 hours. These giants were not so gentle either, packing considerable defensive firepower, along with their bombs and depth charges. The Sunderland became so noted for fending off harrying attacks by Luftwaffe fighters over the Bay of Biscay that the Germans nicknamed it "the Porcupine."

Convoy protection

One of the most important uses of aircraft in World War II was for the defense of merchant convoys. German U-boats and aircraft took a heavy toll on merchant shipping sailing to and from Britain. In the winter of 1940 Fw 200 Condors based in occupied Norway and France launched long-range bombing raids on Atlantic convoys. Where shipping sailed closer to land—for example, the Arctic convoys from Britain to the Soviet ports of

LOCKHEED P-38 LIGHTNING
The Lockheed Lightning, designed for long-range missions, was the first fighter aircraft equipped with turbochargers and a tricycle undercarriage. It was complex and expensive to produce, and initially most went to the Pacific theater where long flights over water made the twin-engine arrangement desirable. Many Lightnings reached Europe in 1944 and were used by the tactical air forces for ground attack and photographic reconnaissance.

Murmansk and Arkhangelsk passing Norway—shorter range Ju 88s and He 111s also struck with devastating effect.

The convoys needed air cover to stop these attacks. One desperate measure in the early days was to catapult a Hawker Hurricane from a merchant ship—a once-only mission, since the pilot's only recourse when he ran out of fuel was to ditch in the sea and hope to be picked up. Later, escort carriers provided a less wasteful solution, although there were never enough of

them. Long-range flying boats, like the Catalinas and Sunderlands, patiently quartered the ocean in search of submarines. At first they were mostly limited to deterring U-boats from surfacing, but by 1942–43, the Allied aircraft were equipped with improved radar and depth charges, and they became more aggressive.

Allied commanders were slow to devote adequate air resources to the Battle of the Atlantic, but the allocation of long-range Consolidated B-24 Liberator bombers to the ocean in 1943 marked a decisive turning point. From then until the end of the war Allied aircraft imposed such heavy losses on the German U-boat fleet that it ceased to pose a major threat to merchant shipping.

COMPACT WALRUS
A ship-borne Walrus Flying boat is brought out of its hangar, wings folded for compact storage. The Walrus would be launched by catapult from the deck and land alongside the ship on returning from its mission.

AIRCRAFT AGAINST SUBMARINES
Aircraft proved an effective answer to German U-boats in the Battle of the Atlantic. This crew of an RAF Coastal Command Sunderland flying boat keeps watch on patrol over the Atlantic.

FLYING GUARDIANS
An American aircraft escorts a convoy of merchant ships bringing vital supplies across the ocean from the United States to beleaguered Britain.

WORLD WAR II ANTISUBMARINE AIRCRAFT

AIRCRAFT PLAYED A DECISIVE ROLE in antisubmarine warfare during the Battle of the Atlantic from 1940–43. The protection of merchant ships bound for Britain from attack by German U-boats was crucial to the country's survival. Although antisubmarine duties were also undertaken by ship-borne aircraft, the major burden was carried by long-range aircraft flying from coastal bases. Under the circumstances, Britain gave surprisingly low priority to RAF Coastal Command, which was responsible for Atlantic antisubmarine patrols. Advocates of strategic bombing wanted long-range aircraft allocated to the bombing offensive against Germany, resenting the diversion of resources to help keep shipping lanes open. One of the major requirements in antisubmarine warfare aircraft was range. Until late 1942 the Allies had no aircraft patrolling the mid-Atlantic, and this gap in convoy air defense was ably exploited by German U-boats. The gap was closed by the introduction of a maritime version of the B-24 Liberator, the Consolidated

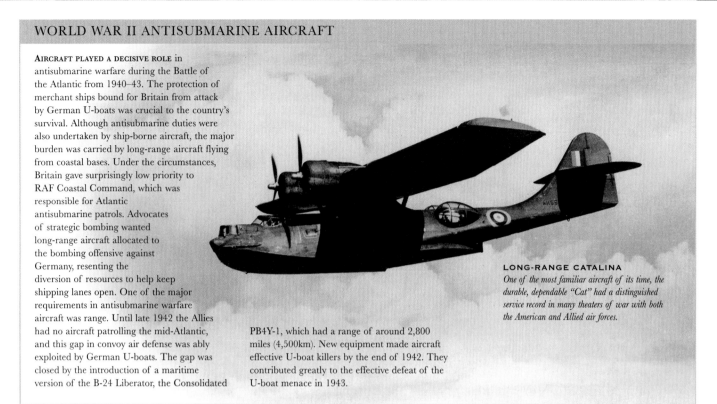

PB4Y-1, which had a range of around 2,800 miles (4,500km). New equipment made aircraft effective U-boat killers by the end of 1942. They contributed greatly to the effective defeat of the U-boat menace in 1943.

LONG-RANGE CATALINA
One of the most familiar aircraft of its time, the durable, dependable "Cat" had a distinguished service record in many theaters of war with both the American and Allied air forces.

WORLD WAR II GERMAN JET AND ROCKET AIRCRAFT

ALTHOUGH THE GERMANS ACHIEVED the first jet flight, with a Heinkel He 178, a week before the outbreak of World War II, they experienced many difficulties and delays in developing practical military jets. Experience led to essential design advances such as replacing the standard tail wheel on piston-engined aircraft with a nose wheel, to stop the jet efflux hitting the runway at takeoff. But producing a sufficiently reliable jet engine that gave enough thrust proved time-consuming. Junkers

eventually made their Jumo 004 an effective turbojet engine and supplied it to Heinkel, Messerschmitt (whose Me 262 emerged as the most prominent jet aircraft of the war), and Arado. Jets remained essentially experimental aircraft, difficult to fly and unreliable, but were not without impact late in the war.

LATE ENTRY
Introduced in 1944, the jet-propelled Me 262A-1 fighter hit top speeds of more than 100mph (160kmph) faster than conventional Allied fighters.

Survivors search through the ruins of the city of Dresden, destroyed by Allied bombers in February 1945. An estimated 60,000 people died in the raids on Dresden, which became a focus for critics of the morality of strategic bombing.

when Bf 109s and Fw 190s were being shot down in the hundreds by the numerically superior Allied fighters. In the final months of the war, out of favor with the Nazi hierarchy, Galland reverted to a role as squadron commander, and, grouping some of the few surviving Luftwaffe aces around him, formed Jagdverband 44 (JV44) to fly jets in a final self-consciously futile gesture of defiance. Nothing, however, could disguise the fact that German cities were by then wide open to bombing by day or night. The destruction of Dresden in February 1945 and the reduction of Berlin to gaunt smoldering ruins constituted a belated fulfillment of the apocalyptic vision of the advocates of strategic bombing.

Postwar analysis

In the postwar period, Allied strategic bombing retrospectively came under criticism on practical and moral grounds. Practically, it was said to have wasted resources that could have been better used to other military purposes. Morally, it was attacked for deliberately or inadvertently causing the deaths of hundreds of thousands of civilians. Certainly, it had taken a long time to achieve air superiority and to field the numbers of bombers and develop the bombs needed to devastate the enemy's heartland. Yet in the end it had, and few Germans or Japanese would be inclined to minimize the bombing's impact. As for morality, in wartime it soon comes to seem natural to harm your enemy as much as you can and in any way that you can, and this truth governed the use of bombers from Warsaw and Rotterdam to Hiroshima and Nagasaki.

Morality of war

The bomber commanders were hard men. A story is told of Arthur Harris that once during the war he was stopped by a British policeman for speeding in his car: "You'll kill someone if you go on driving like that," said the policeman. "Young man," Harris replied, "I kill hundreds of people every night." When LeMay was asked after the war about

German jet fighter

German fighter ace and air-defense chief Adolf Galland always held that the outcome could have been different if Germany had correctly played its trump card: the Messerschmitt Me 262 jet fighter. When he first flew an Me 262 in May 1943, he described the experience as like being "pushed by angels." Flying at 550mph (917kmph), around 100mph (160kmph) faster than any propeller-driven fighter, the jet was the defensive weapon Galland had been looking for, capable of penetrating any fighter cover that the bombers might receive.

The Me 262 project had been subject to frustrating delays—the airframe had been ready in 1941, but it had taken a long time to settle on a suitable engine and tackle problems with takeoff and landing. Now, Galland hoped that it would be mass-produced and deployed as an impenetrable shield around Germany. Hitler did not agree.

Obsessed with his search for an offensive "secret weapon" to win the war, the Führer insisted that the Me 262 be developed as a bomber. Against his wishes, a small number of the jet fighters were produced and an experimental combat unit was set up in Lechfeld in southern Germany to try them out. The Me 262 had many problems. It was difficult to fly and downright dangerous to land—the landing speed was high, requiring a long runway and putting excessive strain on the tires, which were liable to burst. Engine "flameouts" were disturbingly common. And although the outpaced Allied fighter pilots could not pursue the Me 262s, they found that they could pick them off by waiting over their airfields and pouncing as the jets returned to land.

Yet despite its faults, the Me 262 did take its toll on Allied bombers. In the last months of the war, the jets proved they could survive in the air

THE STRATEGIC BOMBING SURVEY

WORLD WAR II was the first conflict to use strategic bombing, but as the war drew to an end the effectiveness of strategic bombing was hotly debated. In 1944 Secretary of War Henry L. Stimson formed the United States Strategic Bombing Survey (USSBS), enlisting hundreds of civilians, officers, and enlisted men to research the matter. Beginning in 1945, they combed Germany and other previously German-occupied countries for information. They came up with four major conclusions:
1. The United States did not closely enough

examine its target list to meet the Allies' needs during bombing campaigns.
2. The best targets would have been the petroleum, oil, and lubricant industries, as well as the electric system. Attacks on submarine pens and ball-bearing plants were not effective.
3. British bombing of civilians was ineffective and did not lower morale.
4. Bombers needed fighter escorts to and from targets to minimize losses. While Allied bombers were primarily long-range at the start of the war, fighters were not.

WORLD WAR II BOMBERS

WORLD WAR II bomber aircraft were powerful machines, capable of delivering a far heavier punch than their World War I predecessors. Vulnerable to ground fire and enemy fighters, bombers relied on substantial firepower along with fighter escorts or night cover for their survival. The United States and Britain were committed to using bombers as a strategic weapon and invested heavily in long-range heavy bombers that could be used for mass-formation raids by day or by night. Their goal was to cripple the opposing war effort.

However, the impact of the Allied bombing effort on German morale was limited, but the attacks on industry—particularly oil and communications—and cities, from April 1944

onward, eventually paid off, despite high losses. Japan suffered even more heavily under American air bombardment during 1944 and 1945.

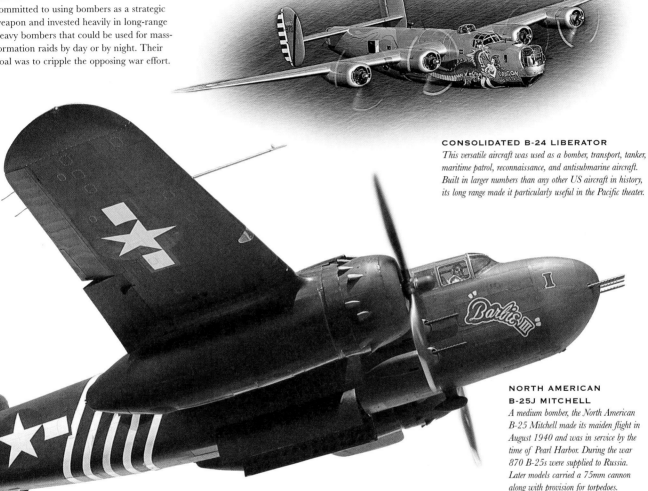

CONSOLIDATED B-24 LIBERATOR
This versatile aircraft was used as a bomber, transport, tanker, maritime patrol, reconnaissance, and antisubmarine aircraft. Built in larger numbers than any other US aircraft in history, its long range made it particularly useful in the Pacific theater.

NORTH AMERICAN B-25J MITCHELL
A medium bomber, the North American B-25 Mitchell made its maiden flight in August 1940 and was in service by the time of Pearl Harbor. During the war 870 B-25s were supplied to Russia. Later models carried a 75mm cannon along with provision for torpedoes.

the morality of what the bombers had done, he was typically forthright: "To worry about the morality of what we were doing? Nuts! A soldier has to fight. We fought. If we accomplished the job in any given battle without losing too many of our own folks that was a pretty good day." Airmen have expressed similar views. Melvin Larsen, who flew in B-17s, stated that bombing never gave him concern because: "I knew that each time we dropped our bombs… helped to bring the ending of the war that much closer." The Airmen had a job to do, and they did it, at great risk to their lives.

DOCTRINE AND HISTORY—THE EUROPEAN THEATER IN WORLD WAR II

DISTINCTIVE CAPABILITIES	FUNCTIONS (MISSIONS)	DOCTRINAL EMPHASIS
• Precision Engagement • Information Superiority • Air Superiority • Agile Combat Support	• Surveillance and Reconnaissance • Counterair/land • Strategic Attack • Airlift/Special Operations	• Strategic Attack • Counterland • Counterair • Atomic Weapons

PACIFIC ADMIRALS
Admiral Chester Nimitz (right) held command in the Pacific area from 1941 to 1945. Vice Admiral Marc Mitscher notably led Carrier Task Force 58 in the 1944 Battle of the Philippines Sea.

At first light on May 8, the Americans sent off reconnaissance patrols and soon located their enemy. The two carrier forces were 100 miles (160km) apart. At 8:30am, about 90 US Navy aircraft took off from the carriers. As they headed for their target, the Japanese carrier aircraft headed toward the US ships. The American fliers found the Japanese carriers in a tropical rainstorm. The *Zuikaku* slipped away into the mist, but the *Shokaku* was repeatedly hit by the American dive-bombers and was left still afloat but ablaze. Unfortunately for the *Yorktown*

and *Lexington*, the sky over their patch of ocean was clear as Lieutenant Commander Kuichi Takahashi led his Aichi D3A (Val) dive-bombers and Nakajima B5N (Kate) torpedo bombers into the attack. As they flew into an intense barrage of antiaircraft fire, Takahashi's aircraft was blown to pieces and so were a number of others. But too many of the airplanes got through.

It was momentarily a curiously personal close-range encounter as the torpedo bombers came in at just above flight-deck height: A Japanese pilot remembered seeing "American sailors staring at my plane as it rushed by." Both carriers took punishment, especially the "Lady Lex." Racked by fires and internal explosions, she had to be abandoned. The *Yorktown* struggled back to Hawaii for repair. The Battle of the Coral Sea was not a decisive encounter, but it was a turning point in the history of warfare. For the first time, two naval forces had fought using carrier aircraft alone, far beyond the range of even the most powerful warship's guns.

ATTACKING PEARL HARBOR

TIME FOR ACTION
Japanese sailors stand by watching as a Mitsubishi Zero takes off from their flight deck. Seaman Iki Kuramoti, on the carrier Akagi, *said of the attack on Pearl Harbor: "An air attack on Hawaii! A dream come true!"*

"THIS IS NO DRILL"
This message, telling the US fleet that Pearl Harbor was under attack, was broadcast minutes after the raid began. It was no news to personnel already fighting for their lives.

AT DAWN ON DECEMBER 7, 1941, Japanese pilots for the first wave of the attack on Pearl Harbor climbed into their cockpits, each carrying a rations pack for the flight—rice and plums, chocolate, and pep pills. Propellers spun and engines roared into life as the leader of the attack, Commander Mitsuo Fuchida, donned the traditional *hachimaki* headband.

Despite a choppy sea, 183 aircraft took off without incident and formed up to set course for Oahu island, observing strict radio silence. For much of the flight there were low clouds. Fuchida corrected his bearing as he closed on the target by taking a fix on a music program broadcast by a Honolulu radio station—which also gave an update on the local weather conditions. Then the clouds broke and the pilots were looking down on the lush green island. As Pearl Harbor came into view, Fuchida saw "the whole US Pacific Fleet in a formation I would not have dared to dream of in my most optimistic dreams." A total of 90 ships lay at anchor or in dry dock, including eight battleships.

In the excitement of the moment, Fuchida radioed the carrier force with the signal for victory—"Tora, Tora, Tora"—as the first strike went in, the

> ## "The moment has arrived. The rise or fall of our empire is at stake…"
>
> **ADMIRAL YAMAMOTO**
> MESSAGE TO THE FLEET BEFORE PEARL HARBOR

torpedo bombers skimming in low over the water and dive-bombers sweeping down from 12,000ft (3,500m). The air was thick with the smoke of explosions by the time the horizontal bombers, led by Fuchida, advanced in single file through antiaircraft fire, while Mitsubishi A6M Reisen (Zero) fighters swooped down to strafe the military airfields below. Almost 300 American planes were damaged or destroyed on the ground, and the Japanese had the air almost to themselves. In the midst of the mayhem, a flight of B-17 bombers arriving from the United States was badly shot up.

The Japanese pilots were oblivious to the human drama unfolding on the ships and ground below, concerned only with carrying out their tasks successfully. Many returned to their carriers in personal shame amid the general euphoria, convinced they had missed their targets, letting down their colleagues and their emperor. But Fuchida stayed over Pearl Harbor during the 170-plane second wave of the attack and was able to report to Admiral Nagumo on the damage caused. The admiral commented, "We may then conclude that anticipated results have been achieved." That just about summed it up.

BLAZING WARSHIPS
A rescue launch attempts to pick up survivors from US warships surrounded by burning oil. Eighteen ships were sunk or severely damaged at Pearl Harbor, including five battleships. (This is a colorized version of a black-and-white print.)

STRIKING SWORDFISH
The strike on the Italian fleet at Taranto by Swordfish biplanes from the Royal Navy carrier Illustrious in November 1940 partly inspired the subsequent Japanese attack on Pearl Harbor.

Warship defenses

No one could accuse traditional naval commanders of ignoring airpower in their war preparations. They had taken great trouble to arm their warships against air attack—the density of antiaircraft fire a battleship or cruiser could throw up was daunting. But the vulnerability of surface ships to air attack, in the absence of adequate air cover, still came as a shock. One of the worst days of the war for the Royal Navy was on December 10, 1941, when the battleship *Prince of Wales* and the battle-cruiser *Repulse* were attacked by Japanese Mitsubishi G4M (Betty) medium bombers and Nakajima B5NC (Kate) torpedo bombers off the coast of Malaysia. The *Prince of Wales* alone had 175 antiaircraft guns capable of firing 60,000 shells a minute, and the capital ships and their destroyer escorts were in open water, able to maneuver at speed. Yet in little over two hours, the *Prince of Wales* and the *Repulse* had been sunk, for the loss of only three Japanese aircraft.

Even Britain, which had lost its preeminence in carrier development, was able to score major victories by using aircraft against surface ships. The German battleship *Bismarck*, racing through

the stormy North Atlantic for the safety of Brest Harbor in May 1941, would have eluded the pursuit of the Royal Navy had it not been spotted by a Catalina from RAF Coastal Command, and then damaged by Fairey Swordfish-delivered torpedoes from the carrier *Ark Royal*. That these slow-moving, open-cockpit biplanes were sent to attack the world's most high-tech battleship seems extraordinary in itself, let alone that they should have given it a crippling wound.

The Swordfish's other memorable success was the raid on the Italian fleet at Taranto in November 1940. Attacking a heavily defended shallow harbor by night, 21 of these seemingly obsolescent torpedo bombers from the carrier *Illustrious* sank three battleships and a destroyer. A result out of all proportion to the force applied, the Taranto raid was studied with interest by naval experts around the world—including the Japanese.

Tora! Tora! Tora!

The surprise Japanese attack on Pearl Harbor on December 7, 1941, is one of the most celebrated, or infamous, uses of aircraft in the history of aviation. It was devised by senior Japanese commanders in a spirit of desperation,

since Japan's determination to control China and Southeast Asia had put it on a collision course with the United States, a country that they could not realistically hope to defeat. Admiral Isoroku Yamamoto, the naval commander in chief, hoped that if he could take out the American Pacific Fleet at the same time as grabbing Southeast Asia, Japan might at least buy time to organize a defense of its conquests. Admiral Nagumo, entrusted with commanding the surprise attack, was opposed to it and doubted that it would work.

Although Americans were understandably outraged at an attack timed to coincide with a declaration of war rather than follow it, the Pearl Harbor raid has to be recognized as a technically masterful naval air operation, in both its preparation and its execution. Japanese technical experts developed a torpedo that worked in the shallow water of the American harbor—normal torpedoes would have stuck in the seabed—and a bomb to pierce the battleships' armored decks, made by adding fins to an artillery shell. Their pilots, an elite group who had survived a harsh process of elimination, rehearsed the attack meticulously. And a fleet of 31 ships, including six aircraft carriers, was assembled and sailed undetected across 1,000 miles (1,600km) of ocean

JAPANESE STRATEGY AND WHY IT FAILED

JAPAN IS MADE UP of a series of islands short on natural resources, particularly oil. Beginning in 1931, the island nation invaded countries throughout Asia to compensate for this paucity. Eventually, the United States and Britain imposed a trade embargo on Japan to put a stop to the Japanese expansion plans. In response, Japan attacked Pearl Harbor on December 7, 1941, to take out its biggest threat: the US Pacific Fleet. Japan thought that if it could deliver a knockout blow, it could keep the United States out of action for 18 months to two years. Japan could then get hold of all the oil it needed to spread its empire. Its strategy was threefold:

1. Quick military domination would enable it to establish a strong, defensive perimeter.
2. The United States would never unite, since it was a democracy. The resulting chaos would result in a long—and therefore, ineffective—offensive against Japan.
3. Striking with mobility, surprise, and massing at unexpected times, Japan hoped to sue for peace from a stronger position.

But the Japanese plan had two weaknesses:

1. Japan grossly underestimated American resolve and anger after the Pearl Harbor attack.
2. Instead of taking advantage of its victory at Pearl Harbor and implementing a defensive perimeter, Japan kept on the offensive. As a result, it lost the Battle of the Coral Sea in

May 1942 and suffered a strategic defeat at Midway in June 1942. After Midway, the Japanese were forever on the defensive.

Japan also had to deal with two other problems. First of all, because of geography, the country depended on long supply lines to get petroleum, oil, and lubricant materials and products to the homeland and to its forces in the Pacific. Furthermore, the Allies worked out a three-pronged strategy to cut Japan off from oil and its occupied territories. These actions were:

1. To use China, Burma, and India as a back door to attack Japanese forces scattered throughout Asia. For instance, the Allies' Flying Tigers did battle with Japanese air forces in Burma and southern China from 1941–42. And many US and British airmen supplied Chinese Nationalists with everything from weapons to fuel from 1941–45 by flying a dangerous route over the Himalayas often referred to as flying "over the hump."
2. In the early stages of the war, Japan conquered many Central Pacific islands. But with concerted effort and at a great cost in lives, the Allies pushed the Japanese back north toward Japan and out of the Central Pacific, beginning with Guadalcanal in 1942–43.
3. With naval action and airpower, the Allies cut off oil supplies flowing to Japan from the Japanese-controlled Dutch East Indies.

AMERICAN VENGEANCE
The "sneak" attack on Pearl Harbor created a desire for instant revenge that was partially satisfied by the air raid on Tokyo in 1942.

to within striking distance of Hawaii, refueling from tankers in heavy seas.

While the Japanese were greatly aided by the peace-numbed laxness of American defenses, their pilots carried through the two-wave attack with skill and determination. They had the best naval aircraft in the world at that time, in the Mitsubishi A6M Reisen (Zero) fighter and the Nakajima Kate attack aircraft, used as both a torpedo bomber and a conventional horizontal bomber. The other type used in the Pearl Harbor operation, the Aichi Val dive-bomber, was broadly similar in its strengths and weaknesses to the German Stuka.

The practical impact of the Japanese action was limited by the absence of US carriers from Pearl Harbor on that day and by their failure to destroy oil tanks, which allowed a faster American recovery than might otherwise have been the case. Still, 18 ships were sunk or seriously damaged and some 164 aircraft destroyed on the ground, with the loss of only 29 Japanese aircraft out of a strike force of 353 planes.

Pearl Harbor convinced most remaining doubters of the power of carrier-borne aircraft as the decisive strike force in naval warfare. Also, the destruction or temporary disablement of so much of the United States' surface fleet left the carriers as the US Navy's key warships in the Pacific. The carriers' intended role had originally been a subordinate one, as providers of air support for the fleet. Now they would

BOMBERS ON DECK
Sixteen North American B-25 Mitchell bombers are parked nose to tail on the deck of the USS Hornet, *on their way across the Pacific for the April 1942 Doolittle bombing raid on Tokyo. The B-25s were too large to be stowed below decks.*

steal center stage, with the chief function of the surface warships to provide a protective screen for the carriers.

The Tokyo raid

The Pearl Harbor raid and the setbacks that followed in its wake left Americans thirsting for vengeance and in need of a lift to morale. Looking for a spectacular way of hitting back at the Japanese, the Americans hatched the plan of a carrier-launched bombing raid on Tokyo. Because no carrier aircraft had the range to strike Japan from far enough out, the USAAF was called on to provide North American B-25 Mitchell bombers. No one had ever thought that one of these aircraft could be flown off a carrier flight deck, but now they would have to.

> "The raid had a great many things going for it, but… the biggest thing was morale for the American people."

> **REAR ADMIRAL HENRY L. MILLER**
> ON THE DOOLITTLE RAID

Volunteer USAAF crews led by the renowned Lieutenant Colonel James Doolittle were put through an intensive course of training in short takeoffs and low-level, long-distance flight before sailing from San Francisco on the carrier *Hornet* in April 1942. Sixteen bombers were tethered on the flight deck because they were too big to be stowed below, leaving no room for the *Hornet's* own aircraft to take off or land. The carrier *Enterprise* joined up to provide air cover. The plan was for the bombers to take off late on April 18, when the *Hornet* would be about 400 miles (640km) from Tokyo. They would raid the city under the cover of darkness and fly on to land at Chuchow airfield in China, which was held by friendly forces. But early on the morning of the 18th, the task force was spotted by Japanese patrol boats. It was decided to launch the bombers immediately, although Tokyo was now 650 miles (1,050km) away and the raiders would arrive in daylight.

Doolittle was the first to take off. With the aircraft laden with bombs and extra fuel, and the carrier pitching in a heavy sea, conditions were hardly ideal for the first sea launching

TAKING OFF FOR TOKYO
Doolittle takes off from the USS Hornet *on April 18, 1942. Each B-25 had to lift off just as the pitching deck swung up toward the crest of a wave.*

THE THACH WEAVE

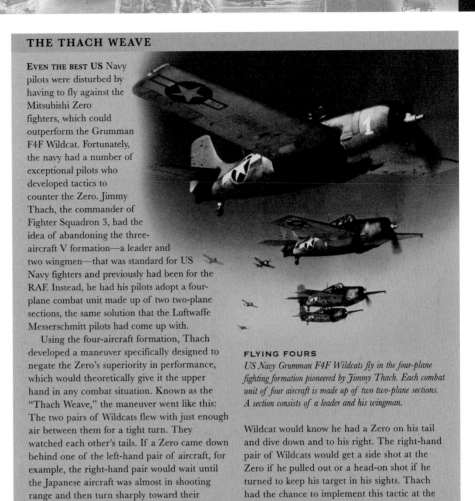

EVEN THE BEST US Navy pilots were disturbed by having to fly against the Mitsubishi Zero fighters, which could outperform the Grumman F4F Wildcat. Fortunately, the navy had a number of exceptional pilots who developed tactics to counter the Zero. Jimmy Thach, the commander of Fighter Squadron 3, had the idea of abandoning the three-aircraft V formation—a leader and two wingmen—that was standard for US Navy fighters and previously had been for the RAF. Instead, he had his pilots adopt a four-plane combat unit made up of two two-plane sections, the same solution that the Luftwaffe Messerschmitt pilots had come up with.

Using the four-aircraft formation, Thach developed a maneuver specifically designed to negate the Zero's superiority in performance, which would theoretically give it the upper hand in any combat situation. Known as the "Thach Weave," the maneuver went like this: The two pairs of Wildcats flew with just enough air between them for a tight turn. They watched each other's tails. If a Zero came down behind one of the left-hand pair of aircraft, for example, the right-hand pair would wait until the Japanese aircraft was almost in shooting range and then turn sharply toward their colleagues. Seeing the turn, the targeted

FLYING FOURS
US Navy Grumman F4F Wildcats fly in the four-plane fighting formation pioneered by Jimmy Thach. Each combat unit of four aircraft is made up of two two-plane sections. A section consists of a leader and his wingman.

Wildcat would know he had a Zero on his tail and dive down and to his right. The right-hand pair of Wildcats would get a side shot at the Zero if he pulled out or a head-on shot if he turned to keep his target in his sights. Thach had the chance to implement this tactic at the Battle of Midway.

of a B-25. Fortunately there was a 30-knot wind, which, with the 20-knot progress of the carrier, gave a windspeed of 50 knots to aid liftoff. Doolittle made it look easy and the other 15 somehow got off behind him with only one minor incident.

The sea-skimming flight to Tokyo took four hours and achieved total surprise. The B-25s did not have a sufficient bombload to cause much damage, but their sudden appearance was a severe shock to the Japanese. The aftermath to the raid unfortunately did not go as planned. Most of the

bombers ran out of fuel and all were lost, as crews either bailed out or crash-landed. Of the 80 aircrew, 73 survived, including Doolittle who returned to make a further distinguished contribution to World War II as a commander in the European theater. Of little tactical significance, the Doolittle raid shocked the Japanese into rushing their Pacific expansion plans.

The Battle of Midway

The instructions to the US Pacific Fleet in 1942 were to "hold what you've got and hit them when you can." There were only six full-size American carriers when the war started and their numbers were soon reduced by the enemy action. The Japanese enjoyed superiority both in the quantity and overall quality of their naval aircraft and pilots. The Battle of the Coral Sea was a setback for Japan—a lesson that the Americans were still in the ring and fighting. But Japanese naval commanders remained convinced that if they could draw the US Pacific Fleet into battle, they could destroy the carriers and control the ocean. This was the scenario they envisaged when they invaded Midway Island in June 1942.

Because American cryptographers had cracked Japan's naval codes, the United States was forewarned of the Midway operation and so undistracted by a simultaneous Japanese move against the Aleutian Islands. Unable to assemble a naval force comparable to the 200 ships Yamamoto sent into action, Admiral Chester Nimitz, newly appointed commander of the Pacific Fleet, had to depend on his Airmen to stop the Japanese invasion. Thanks to heroic efforts by dockyard workers at Pearl Harbor, the *Yorktown*—originally estimated to need 90 days to recover from its battering in the Coral Sea— was repaired in three days, and joined the carriers *Enterprise* and *Hornet* in Nimitz's fleet. Nimitz also had at his disposal Boeing B-17 bombers stationed on Midway. The Japanese, unaware of the strength or position of US naval forces, sent four carriers to win air superiority in preparation for the invasion— Japan's other carriers had still not been refitted after the Coral Sea or were dispersed elsewhere.

The Japanese and US forces clashed off Midway on June 4, 1942. The result was an American victory, with all four Japanese carriers sunk for the loss of the *Yorktown*. But the Battle of Midway did not give the United States instant air or naval superiority in the Pacific. Although Japanese naval airpower had suffered a severe setback, American Navy fliers were still outnumbered. The loss of the *Lexington* at the Coral Sea and the *Yorktown* at Midway was followed by the sinking of the *Wasp* and *Hornet* in the fighting around Guadalcanal in the second half of 1942. During this period, the Americans had only one carrier operational in the Pacific at any given time. Some Airmen found themselves without a deck to fly off and operated alongside the Marines from the precarious airstrip at Henderson Field on Guadalcanal.

The Essex-class carriers

During 1942–43, the most powerful carrier fleet in the world was taking shape in American shipyards. Back in 1940, the US Navy had been authorized to build a new generation of heavy carriers, which emerged as the Essex class. The first of these came into operation in 1943. The design of these modern ships was based on lessons learned from previous experience of carrier warfare, and great attention was paid to the practicalities of flying and servicing airplanes in a severely limited space. Much thought was also given to firefighting and damage control, with the result that Essex-class ships had a far better chance of surviving an enemy air attack than earlier carriers.

BATTLE OF MIDWAY

TORPEDO BOMBERS
Douglas TBD Devastators (top) made up the bulk of the American torpedo-bomber force at the Battle of Midway, although half-a-dozen newer Grumman TBF Avengers (above) also took part. All suffered heavy losses—of the TBDs seen here on the deck of the Enterprise *before the battle, only four survived.*

BATTLE WAS JOINED AT MIDWAY on June 4, 1942. The Japanese carrier aircraft opened the action with an early morning raid on the airfields on Midway Island. Japanese commanders were preparing a follow-up raid before they first became aware that there might be American carriers within striking range. By that time the *Enterprise* and *Hornet* had launched their aircraft to attack the Japanese carriers. Unfortunately, the American pilots had trouble locating their target and squadrons became split up. The 15 Devastator torpedo bombers from the *Hornet* found the carriers first, but had lost touch with their fighter cover. Slow and highly vulnerable as they flew in at low altitude to deliver their attack, the Devastators were pounced on by Zero fighters. Not a single one survived.

The aircraft from the *Yorktown* had been launched well after those from the other two carriers, but now arrived in proper formation, with fighters, dive-bombers, and torpedo bombers prepared for a coordinated attack. The Wildcat fighters, led by Jimmy Thach, were hopelessly outnumbered by the Zeros

BATTLE PANORAMA
This image, from a dioramic representation of the events, shows the torpedo squadron from USS Yorktown *attacking the Japanese carriers* Soryu *and* Akagi *on the morning of June 4. Having to hold a steady course low over the sea to deliver their torpedoes, the bombers ran the gauntlet both of antiaircraft fire from warships and predatory fighters.*

DAUNTLESS DESTROYERS
Artist R.G. Smith's impression of the destruction of the Japanese carrier Akagi: *Douglas Dauntless dive-bombers turn away after releasing their bombs on to the carrier.*

"A number of black objects suddenly floated eerily from their wings. Bombs! Down they came straight toward me."

JAPANESE COMMANDER MITSUO FUCHIDA
ON THE ATTACK ON THE *AKAGI* BY US DIVE-BOMBERS

of the Japanese combat air patrol. Although they made a brave job of occupying the Japanese fighters, they could not prevent the torpedo bombers being decimated again. But concentrating on the low-flying aircraft, the Zeros missed the American dive-bombers—Douglas Dauntlesses not only from the *Yorktown*, but also from the *Enterprise*—that fortuitously arrived high above the enemy ships at that critical moment.

As the dive-bombers turned into their steep attack, Jimmy Thach remembered: "I saw this glint in the sun, and it just looked like a beautiful silver waterfall, these dive-bombers coming down... I'd never seen such superb dive-bombing. It looked to me like almost every bomb hit..." In about five minutes three Japanese carriers—the *Akagi, Kaga,* and *Soryu*— were reduced to burning hulks, blackening the sky with columns of black smoke.

Despite the shock that the Japanese had received, they still had one carrier intact, the *Hiryu.* It flew off a wave of dive-bombers followed by a wave of torpedo bombers, to deliver a counterstrike against the *Yorktown.* Since there were only half a dozen Zeros to provide cover for each wave of bombers, they were savaged by the fighters of the *Yorktown's* combat air patrol, as well as by the ship's antiaircraft fire.

But the Japanese pilots pressed their attack regardless of losses. Remembering a Japanese pilot with his aircraft on fire still holding steady to deliver his torpedo, Thach said: "As far as determination was concerned, you could hardly tell any difference between the Japanese pilots and the American pilots. Nothing would stop them..." Damaged by the dive-bombers and then crippled by air-launched torpedoes, the *Yorktown* was finally finished off by a torpedo from a Japanese submarine. The day ended with the destruction of the *Hiryu* by dive-bombers from the *Enterprise.*

The invasion of Midway was abandoned. The Japanese had lost four carriers and about 330 aircraft to America's one carrier and roughly 150 aircraft. Japan had also lost a large proportion of its most experienced and skillful pilots. This was a crushing defeat and is rightly regarded as the turning point in the Pacific War.

Vought F4U Corsair

"It got to be a very fine plane once the bugs were out of it."

HERBERT D. RILEY
ADMIRAL, US NAVY

THE F4U CORSAIR IS REGARDED by some as the best carrier-borne fighter of World War II. In some ways it was ingeniously designed for service at sea. Take, for example, the striking "inverted gull" wing shape. This allowed the designers to make the undercarriage, placed at the lowest point of the wing, short and sturdy—ideal for carrier landing, while still keeping the very large propeller clear of the deck. Yet in other ways the Corsair was unsuited for carrier service. When the first Corsairs were delivered to the US Navy in October 1942, pilots found that with the long engine stretching in front of them, they had to lean out of the side of the cockpit to see where they were going. This proved especially problematic when attempting to land on a carrier deck, which became an extremely hazardous procedure. Consequently, the Corsair was first deployed operationally in 1943 with shore-based squadrons (mostly US Marines) in the Pacific. The aircraft was not cleared for carrier service until April 1944, by which time the pilot's seat and cockpit canopy had been raised to improve visibility.

Once this and a number of other adjustments had been made and pilots had learned how to cope with the machine's peculiarities, the Corsair proved itself a truly outstanding aircraft. It was successful both as an air-superiority fighter and as a strike aircraft carrying either bombs or rockets. In combat with Japanese fighters such as the Zero, kill ratios of around 11 enemy planes shot down to every Corsair lost were achieved.

Long nose

Sliding canopy

Large diameter propeller

Undercarriage (retracts backward)

WHISTLING DEATH
The Japanese dubbed the F4U Corsair "Whistling Death," because it made a whistling sound in flight.

Landing-gear doors

Hydraulically operated flap

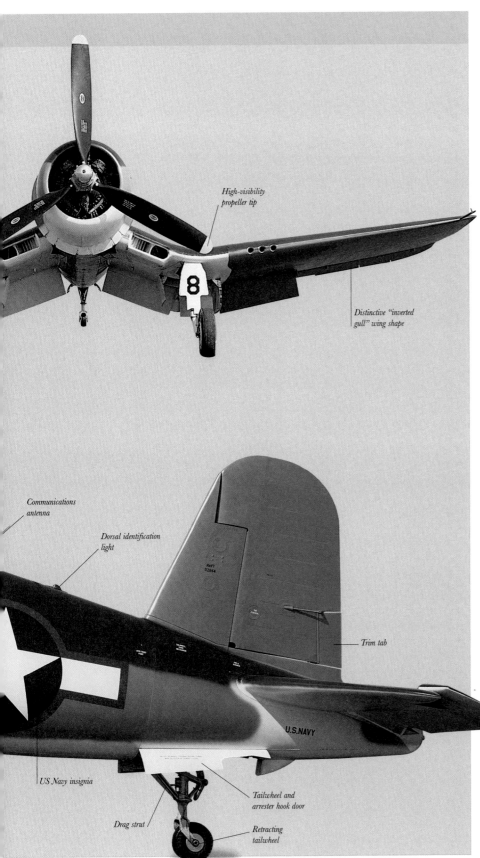

High-visibility propeller tip

Distinctive "inverted gull" wing shape

8

Communications antenna

Dorsal identification light

Trim tab

US Navy insignia

U.S.NAVY

Tailwheel and arrester hook door

Drag strut

Retracting tailwheel

Alongside these heavy carriers, new light carriers, and escort carriers, were coming into service. By the fall of 1943, the Americans had 19 carriers of all kinds in the Pacific, and the production drive was continuing apace.

There would be no point in having carriers without the aircraft to fly off them and the trained pilots to fly the aircraft. The size of the US naval air program was prodigious—the number of new airplanes needed was initially set at 27,500. To cope with pilot training on an unprecedented scale, the Navy pioneered the use of flight simulators, primitive by today's standards but good enough to allow trainees to develop the skills for deck landing, takeoff, and instrument flying far more quickly and safely than had been possible before. The mass production of a new generation of naval aircraft— the Grumman TBF Avenger torpedo bomber, the Vought F4U Corsair and Grumman F6F Hellcat fighters, and the Curtiss SB2C Helldiver to replace the Dauntless dive-bomber—required tough, practical decisions. It was no use producing an aircraft with optimal performance if it could not be cranked out in sufficient numbers with the available factories and machine tools. It is a tribute to the American genius for organization that airplanes and pilots were ready for the new carriers as they rolled off the production lines.

Not all of the new aircraft were an instant success. The Helldiver was disliked by many pilots, still attached to their old Dauntlesses that had performed so well at Midway. Helldivers were a challenge for both their pilots and maintenance crews—they were complex and often faulty, especially when they had been produced by automobile companies roped in to aircraft production for the war effort. The first version of the Corsair had a glaring defect as a carrier aircraft, in that pilots could not see over the engine as they attempted to land on deck. A simple solution was eventually found by raising the pilot's seat and cockpit canopy by 6in (16cm), but the Corsair was not authorized to fly off carriers until April 1944. Yet together, these new aircraft marked a giant stride forward in performance that was unmatched by comparable major advances on the Japanese side.

The Pacific offensive

By 1944 the United States was ready for a Pacific offensive spearheaded by carriers. The fleet was organized into carrier task groups, with two or three carriers sailing at the center of concentric circles composed of first cruisers and battleships providing a screen of antiaircraft fire, and then destroyers, primarily responsible for antisubmarine defense. A number of task groups operating together, known as a fast carrier force, constituted an impressively potent weapon of attack.

From the start of operations in 1944, it was evident that a gulf had opened up between the Americans and Japanese in terms of technology, flying skills, and tactical organization. Early in February, the heavily defended Japanese naval base at Truk was subjected to raids by aircraft from nine American carriers, including a night attack by Avengers using airborne radar to identify their targets. In addition to suffering heavy loss of shipping, the Japanese lost 10 aircraft for every one American airplane shot down—a sign of things to come.

The Japanese were without Admiral Yamamoto, who had himself become a victim of American airpower in April 1943 after the decoding of a radio intercept revealed his itinerary for a tour of Japanese forces in the southwest Pacific. Lockheed Lightning P-38 long-range fighters led by Major John Mitchell were sent from Henderson Field on Guadalcanal to eliminate the admiral. Their task was to fly over more than 400 miles (640km) of ocean and intercept a small flight of Japanese aircraft—two Mitsubishi Betty bombers carrying Yamamoto and his staff, and an escort of six Mitsubishi

Zeros—without the help of onboard radar or sophisticated navigational instruments. Mitchell found his way by dead-reckoning, using a compass, a watch, and his airspeed indicator. Thanks to his skill, and to Japanese punctuality, the P-38s found their target over the coast of Bougainville, Solomon Islands. Admiral Yamamoto's aircraft was shot down and crashed in the jungle. The admiral was thus spared from witnessing the destruction of his navy.

"Island hopping"

The Army Air Forces' primary contribution to the Pacific counterattack came from the Fifth Air Force, commanded by then Major General George C. Kenney, air deputy to General Douglas MacArthur in the Southwest Pacific Theater. While Admiral Nimitz's carrier task forces struck from the Central Pacific, MacArthur's forces struck across New Guinea toward the Philippines in a coordinated campaign known as "island hopping." The strategy was to bypass

> "Our pilots… were improving every day, and the Japanese fleet was not capable of countering our fleet again."
>
> **VICE ADMIRAL WILLIAM I. MARTIN**
> DISCUSSING THE LAST YEAR OF THE WAR

JAPANESE MASTERMIND
Admiral Yamamoto, the man who planned the Japanese attack on Pearl Harbor, was shot down by the Americans in 1943.

Japanese strongholds and strike at the enemy's weak points, thus isolating the stronger positions and allowing them to wither away. In the meantime, Allied forces would get closer and closer to Japan, enabling direct air attacks on the Japanese home islands and an invasion if necessary.

The Fifth Air Force's plan was to gain air superiority over the Japanese while interdicting their supply of reinforcements and materiel. This would allow General MacArthur's troops to advance under the cover of its fighters and bombers. It operated from primitive bases using second-string aircraft, a 10,000-mile supply chain, and low priority for equipment, since the Allied strategy put first priority on the war in Europe. But Kenney made the best of what he had: In a theater where aircraft range determined everything else, Kenney used Lockheed P-38s with locally developed 150-gallon drop tanks. He encouraged an ingenious subordinate, Major Paul "Pappy" Gunn, to mount quad .50-caliber machine guns in the nose of A-20 and B-25 aircraft, creating deadly attack planes to strafe enemy airfields. Other Fifth Air Force innovations included parachutes attached to fragmentation bombs to destroy Japanese aircraft on the ground and low-level "skip bombing" techniques used to bounce bombs off the water and into enemy cargo vessels. The Fifth Air Force eventually combined with the Thirteenth Air Force to form the Far East Air Forces (FEAF) under General Kenney. By January 1943, American air forces in the Pacific counted 1,000 planes; by December there were more than 2,000; by the end of the war, they reached 5,500. As early as the end of 1944, the number of planes flown by Kenney's FEAF exceeded the total available to Japan throughout the Pacific.

With even less priority than Kenney's Fifth Air Force, Allied forces in the China-Burma-India (CBI) theater faced logistical challenges at the end of the world's longest supply chain. Called to transport vital supplies across the Himalayas, AAF Air Transport Command (ATC) crews flying C-46s and C-47s, braved perilous

CARRIER POWER
A carrier task group, led by the USS Essex, heads into action in the Philippine Sea in 1944. The scale of US naval air operations grew to overwhelming proportions, while Japanese carrier aviation shrank to a shadow of its former power.

GENERAL GEORGE C. KENNEY
Kenney's success as commander of the Fifth Air Force and later the Far East Air Forces led to his reputation as the most accomplished combat air strategist of the war.

weather conditions to ferry 650,000 tons of supplies to Chinese and American forces. Flying the "Hump" was among the most hazardous air missions of the war. The enterprise's architect, Lieutenant General William Tunner, developed maintenance and cargo-handling techniques that later proved invaluable during the Berlin Airlift.

In addition to ATC efforts in the CBI theater, the 1st Air Commando Group (1ACG) assisted British Chindit forces that conducted long-range penetration missions against the Japanese. These first American air commandos proved that airpower could support unconventional warfare in any place, at any time. The 1ACG also demonstrated its ingenuity, conducting the first helicopter combat rescue.

Japanese disaster

The Battle of the Philippine Sea in June 1944 was planned by Japanese commanders as a masterstroke against the US fleet, which was supposed to be trapped between a powerful carrier force and airbases on the Marianas. Japanese aircraft could in theory shuttle back and forth between the carriers and the island airstrips, hitting the Americans in between. What actually happened is now known as the "Marianas Turkey Shoot."

Between 8:30am and 3:00pm on June 19, four waves of Japanese aircraft were sent in to attack the US fleet. Fed with early warning of the enemy's approach by radar operators, shipborne Combat Information Centers scrambled their fighters and vectored them on to the incoming targets. With no element of surprise, the largely inexperienced Japanese pilots were pounced on by the Hellcats. Any that slipped through were cut down by naval gunners. Meanwhile, American bombers attacked the island airfields, and their fighters preyed on Japanese aircraft trying to land there. In all, the Japanese lost over 300 aircraft in the day's fighting, while two Japanese carriers were sunk by American submarines.

Admiral Marc Mitscher, commander of Fast Carrier Task Force 58, felt that the victory would be incomplete without a counterstrike against the Japanese fleet. The enemy was located late in the afternoon of June 20. Mitscher decided to strike immediately, although it would take his aircraft to the extreme limit of their range and they would not be back before nightfall. Over 200 carrier aircraft set off, the usual mix of torpedo bombers, dive-bombers, and fighters.

NEW AVENGER
Compact and robust, the Grumman TBF Avenger became the United States' standard torpedo bomber from 1943. The Japanese could match neither the quality nor the quantity of the aircraft deployed by the Americans in the later years of the war.

THE FLYING TIGERS

CLAIRE CHENNAULT RETIRED from the Army Air Corps in 1937 due to illness and the realization that his advocacy of pursuit and tactics instead of bombardment was getting nowhere in the air force. He soon became aviation adviser to Nationalist Chinese Generalissimo Chiang Kai-shek, and in 1940–41 went to Washington to organize the American Volunteer Group (AVG), or Flying Tigers, to fly for the Chinese Air Force—with the permission of President Franklin D. Roosevelt. About 100 pilots were recruited from the Air Corps, Navy, and Marines, discharged from their service, and organized into three fighter squadrons equipped with Curtiss P-40s.

Chennault used the Flying Tigers to implement his ideas about fighter doctrine, and the group enjoyed notable success at a time when things were going badly elsewhere for the Americans. Their planes famously painted with a shark's face, the Flying Tigers were credited with bringing down some 300 enemy aircraft while losing only 14 of their own. (Some estimates put the figure of Japanese planes at around 120.) The Tigers provided hope to beleaguered Chinese cities, which had suffered uncontested Japanese bombing, and blocked the Japanese advance into China.

The AVG was disbanded in July 1942 and incorporated into what became the Fourteenth Air Force, with Chennault in command—back in the Army Air Forces and promoted to brigadier general. An outstanding tactician, the abrasive Chennault was never popular with his air force colleagues, partly because he tended to ignore the chain of command and deal directly with President Roosevelt and partly because of his advocacy of tactical bombing. He retired in October 1945; Congress made him an honorary lieutenant general in 1958, just nine days before he died.

LIEUTENANT GENERAL CLAIRE CHENNAULT
Unpopular within the Army Air Corps, Chennault found fame and career success defending the Chinese against Japanese air attacks and was given command of the American Fourteenth Air Force.

Watching their fuel levels dropping on the way out, pilots were keenly aware of the problem they were going to have getting back.

It was evening by the time the Japanese fleet was found and attacked. Lieutenant Don Lewis, flying a Dauntless, recalled the end of his dive from 15,000ft (4,500m) toward a Japanese carrier: "The last time I glanced at my altimeter it registered 3,000ft (900m). Stopped below, the big carrier looked even larger. It was completely enveloped in a sort of smoke haze. It was hard to stay in my dive this long. Under some conditions, a person can live a lifetime in a few seconds. It was time. I couldn't go any lower. Now! I pulled my bomb release, felt the bomb go away, started my pullout. My eyes watered, my ears hurt, and my altimeter indicated 1,500ft (450m)... I had already closed my dive flaps and had 280 knots, but I couldn't seem to go fast enough... Everywhere I looked there seemed to be ships with every gun blazing. The sky was just a mass of black and white puffs, and in the midst of it, planes already hit, burning and crashing into the water below...."

The fleet carrier *Hiyo* was sunk and a number of other ships damaged with the loss of only a handful of American aircraft. Exhausted by the anxiety and exhilaration of combat, the Airmen then faced the challenge of reaching home—a small flight deck far off in a vast, dark ocean. Soon aircraft began running out of fuel

and ditching in the sea. To help those with enough gas find their way back, Mitscher ordered the fleet to "turn on the lights," setting everything from searchlights to star shells ablaze in the utter darkness—a courageous action in submarine-infested waters. Some tired pilots flying into the blinding light show found it impossible to locate a carrier and ditched in the middle of the fleet. Some finally ran out of fuel within sight of a flight deck. In all, about 80 aircraft were lost in the ocean, although happily four out of five aircrews were rescued.

Japanese naval aviation never recovered from the huge losses of aircraft and pilots at the Battle of the Philippine Sea. The Battle of Leyte Gulf

> ## "We are 16 warriors manning the bombers. May our death be as sudden and clean as the shattering of crystal!"
>
> ### JAPANESE KAMIKAZE PILOT

the following October was the largest naval encounter in history, and one of the most dramatic. But from the viewpoint of carrier warfare it was a crushing walkover. The Japanese carriers were short of airplanes, incapable of launching a penetrating strike against the US fleet or defending themselves against mass attacks by US Navy aircraft. By the end of the battle, the entire Japanese carrier fleet had been destroyed. In a last effort to provide air cover for her fleet, Japan launched the 80,633-ton (73,150-tonne) *Shinano* in November 1944, the largest carrier in the world; it was sunk by an American submarine 17 hours into its maiden voyage.

FUTILE SACRIFICE
A Japanese fighter aircraft on a suicide mission is shot down by US Navy antiaircraft guns. The majority of kamikaze missions ended like this— without inflicting damage on Allied warships.

Kamikaze tactics

It was during the Battle of Leyte Gulf that Japanese naval airmen first adopted kamikaze tactics. On October 19, 1944, Admiral Takijira Ohnishi, commander of the First Air Fleet, suggested to commanders based at Mabalacat airfield in the Philippines that "the only way of assuring that our meager strength will be effective to a maximum degree" would be "to organize suicide attack units… with each plane to crash-dive into an enemy carrier." Twenty-six pilots enthusiastically volunteered to form the first "special attack unit." They were dubbed *kamikaze* ("divine wind") after a typhoon that had miraculously saved Japan from Mongolian invasion in the 13th century.

Nothing was spared in the effort to bolster morale in men effectively condemned to death. Ohnishi assured them that they were "already gods, without earthly desires." A ritual was improvised just before takeoff: The kamikaze pilots drank a glass of water or sake, sang a traditional martial song, and donned the *hachimaki* headband once worn by the samurai. Thus encouraged, they went off to die for the emperor. On October 25, a kamikaze pilot crashed a Mitsubishi Zero through the flight deck of the escort carrier *St. Lo*, dowsing the hangars in burning gasoline that ignited stored ammunition. Ripped apart by a violent explosion, the *St. Lo* sank within an hour. It was a notable success for Japan amid abject failure. Over the following months, kamikaze tactics were adopted throughout the now land-based Japanese naval air force and the army air force.

There was a clear military logic to turning their aircraft into manned, guided missiles. Technologically inferior to the Americans and forced to throw poorly trained pilots into battle, the Japanese could see no other way of reaching and hitting their targets. Japan's airmen had been flying off in the hundreds to die for the emperor without inflicting the slightest damage on the US fleet. Now they would still die, but not in vain. Kamikaze pilots were presented as an elite who proved through their sacrifice the superiority of the Japanese warrior spirit even in defeat.

The reality was different. As soon as kamikaze attacks became a general tactic, it was obvious that suicide missions would be an absurdly quick way of using up the limited number of experienced pilots. Inevitably, the suicide planes were entrusted to second-raters, dispensable and in more plentiful supply. The experienced pilots flew escort, using their skills to fend off the American fighters. So even in the early days, when suicide attacks were carried out by small groups of aircraft, the kamikaze pilot was hardly a member of an elite force.

FIGHTING THE KAMIKAZES

"THE JAPANESE AIRCRAFT DIVED THROUGH a rain of steel. It had been hit in several places and seemed to be trailing a banner of flame and smoke, but it came on, clearly visible, hardly moving, the line of its wings as straight as a sword. The deck was deserted; every man, with the exception of the gunners, was lying flat on his face. Flaming and roaring, the fireball passed in front of the 'island'… The entire vessel was shaken, some forty yards (35m) of the flight deck folded up like a banana skin…" This was the terrifying reality of being on the receiving end of a kamikaze attack, in this case a hit on the carrier *Enterprise,* described by George Blond.

The damage a kamikaze inflicted was often extreme because of the combination of the aircraft's impact, the explosion of its bombload, and burning aviation fuel. To meet this menace, in the words of US pilot Jimmy Thach: "We needed to have more than a good air defense; we had to have a completely airtight defense." The number of fighter aircraft on carriers was increased, at the expense of bombers, and combat air patrols were kept in the air over the outer line of destroyer pickets, ready to intercept intruders. A careful watch was kept on returning aircraft, because kamikaze pilots would try to sneak through the defenses with them. A system of "blanket air patrols" was instituted, to keep American aircraft over Japanese airbases almost around the clock, making it impossible for them to launch sorties.

But some Japanese aircraft always got through, and then it was up to the Navy gunners to bring them down. The Japanese pilots practiced all the tricks of any bombing attack on warships—for example, a pair coming in one high one low, to divide the antiaircraft fire, or attacking simultaneously from different directions. The problem for the American gunners was, of course, that unless the Japanese airplane was completely destroyed or rendered uncontrollable, even if it was thoroughly shot up, the kamikaze pilot would still be able to complete his mission.

CLOSE ENCOUNTER
A Japanese Zero fighter tries to crash on to the deck of the USS Missouri. *The final moments of a kamikaze attack brought a pilot virtually face to face with his enemies.*

LOW-LEVEL APPROACH
A Nakajima G6N Tensan (Jill) torpedo bomber flies in to attack a US carrier through heavy antiaircraft fire—the splashes in the water are made by American naval gunfire.

WORLD WAR II US CARRIER AIRCRAFT

THE COMPLEMENT OF aircraft on a World War II
US Navy carrier was largely made up of three
types: dive-bombers, torpedo bombers, and
fighters, whose role was to defend the fleet
and escort the bombers to their targets.
When the Pacific War began in 1941, the
US Navy had recently re-equipped with
monoplanes such as the Douglas
Dauntless, Grumman Wildcat (rushed
into British service as the Martlet), and
Brewster Buffalo. Within two years
these were being replaced by a new
generation of aircraft, including the
Curtiss Helldiver, Grumman Hellcat and
Avenger, and Vought Corsair. Although not
all immediately popular with pilots, they
gave the Americans a clear qualitative
advantage over the Japanese.

CORSAIRS READY TO GO
*Operating aircraft off the crowded deck of a carrier—pictured
here after World War II—required discipline and organization.*

THE BOMBING OF HIROSHIMA

ON AUGUST 6, 1945, AT 2:45AM local time, a
B-29 bomber took off from Tinian Island in
the Marianas carrying the world's first
operational atomic bomb. In command was
Colonel Paul W. Tibbets, head of the 509th
Composite Group, set up the previous year to
deliver America's secret weapon. Tibbets had
his mother's maiden name, "Enola Gay,"
painted on the nose.

With the 4.8-ton "Little Boy" bomb on board,
the Enola Gay was overweight and gave a few
anxious moments on takeoff, but after that the six-
hour flight went without notable incident. On the
way the Enola Gay rendezvoused with two other
B-29s that were to accompany it to the target and
observe the big event. The crew did their jobs—
navigation, preparing the bomb—and
snacked on coffee and ham sandwiches.
Weather-reconnaissance aircraft radioed
that the weather over the first-choice
target, the city of Hiroshima, was
mostly clear.

At 8:40am the Enola Gay approached
the city at over 30,000ft (9,000m). Copilot
Robert Lewis, who was scribbling a
commentary on the mission, wrote:

"There will be a
short intermission
while we bomb our
target." Bombardier
Major Thomas
Ferebee took over
control of the
aircraft through the
Norden bombsight
and released Little
Boy to airburst over
the Aioi Bridge. The
bomber jumped as
the weight dropped
away, then filled with
an unbearably bright
light. The first shock wave
struck the plane with such force that
Tibbets thought they had been hit by flak.

As the mushroom cloud rose and the ground
below boiled, Tibbets announced: "Fellows, you have
just dropped the first atomic bomb in history." The
crew had trained hard for that moment and were
relieved that it had worked. Navigator Theodore
Van Kirk thought: "Thank God the war is over and
I don't have to get shot at any more. I can go home."

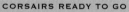

LITTLE BOY
*The atomic bomb dropped on Hiroshima was 10ft
(3m) long and weighed 9,700lb (4,400kg). It
exploded with the force of 13,800 tons of T.N.T.*

ENOLA GAY CREW
*The men who dropped the atomic bomb on
Hiroshima: The leader of the mission, Colonel
Tibbets, is third from the right in the back row,
flanked by bombardier Major Ferebee on his right
and copilot Captain Lewis on his left.*

Kamikaze legacy

Kamikaze attacks undeniably had both a psychological and physical impact on the US fleet. The bewilderment and sheer terror experienced by Sailors when they first encountered suicide bombing cannot be quantified, although it never undermined their disciplined response. The physical damage is estimated at 34 vessels sunk and 288 damaged—a considerable battering for the US Navy and, in the later stages, its British allies. After the war, the US Strategic Bombing Survey concluded that if the attacks had been carried out "in greater power and concentration they might have been able to cause us to withdraw…" But Japan did not have the resources to sustain mass suicide bombing for long. Whereas on April 6 and 7, 1945, at the height of the kamikaze frenzy, more than 300 planes a day attacked the US fleet, by June the Japanese were hard pressed to find 50 aircraft for a raid. Some 2,000 Japanese aircraft and pilots were lost in suicide attacks, far more than could be replaced.

In the end, pitting the samurai spirit of heroic self-sacrifice against overwhelming industrial might was bound to fail. The Americans organized better for production and for combat. Commanders who valued the lives of their men—and Airmen who valued their own lives—fought more effectively than those who glorified death in battle.

When the Japanese emperor broadcast his country's surrender on August 15, 1945, kamikaze commander Admiral Ugaki took off with 10 other pilots on a final suicide mission. On his aircraft radio he announced: "I am going to make an attack on Okinawa where my men have fallen like cherry blossoms. There I will crash into and destroy the hated enemy in the true spirit of Bushido…" The admiral and his pilots were never seen again.

New bomber

Japan was spared from bombing until late in the war because of sheer distance. After the one-time carrier-borne Doolittle raid of April 1942, targets in Japan were not struck again until the summer of 1944, when America's new B-29 bombers came into operation. The B-29 Superfortress marked an impressive advance in military aviation. It had a range of approximately 4,000 miles (6,400km)—double that of a B-17—and a top speed of 350mph (560kmph). The crew worked in conditions that made earlier bombers seem primitive, with heated pressurized cabins to avoid the unpleasant effects of high-altitude flight and remote-controlled guns operated by gunners using computerized sights. The downside was that the USAAF rushed the new bomber into service with inadequate testing. From June 1944 B-29s based in India, operating via Nationalist-controlled southwest China, were sent to attack Japan. Mounting these

DAYLIGHT RAIDERS
B-29 Superfortresses release their powerful bombloads on a high-level daylight mission. The American bombers achieved their maximum effectiveness in conventional raids on Japan when they were switched to low-altitude night raids with incendiaries.

raids from Asia posed formidable logistical problems, and also led to substantial losses through various kinds of equipment failure and engine fires, as well as enemy action.

Far East offensive

In late November 1944, the B-29s began a sustained offensive from bases on the Marianas Islands in the Pacific. For three months they pounded Japan from high altitude in daylight, using the same "precision-bombing" tactics as had been employed over Germany. This was of limited effect. Flying at 30,000ft (9,000m) in the Siberian jetstream, encountering winds of 200mph (320kmph), navigators frequently failed to find their targets and, with cloud cover most days, bombardiers could not hit them if they did.

In March 1945 General Curtis LeMay instituted new tactics. The B-29s were sent in by night at low altitude. Stripped of their armament to save weight, they carried a maximum load of mostly incendiary bombs. On the night of March 9, 279 B-29s started a firestorm that destroyed almost a quarter of Tokyo and may have killed 80,000 people. Bombers arrived back at their island bases blackened with soot. Night after night, other cities suffered a similar fate. Soon most Japanese people had fled to the countryside, industrial production had plummeted, and transportation links were cut. Even before the dropping of the atomic bombs on Hiroshima and Nagasaki in August 1945, strategic bombing had crippled Japan's ability to continue the war.

> "Thank God the war is over and I don't have to get shot at any more. I can go home."
>
> **THEODORE VAN KIRK**
> *ENOLA GAY NAVIGATOR*

Iwo Jima: vital air base

One of the Twentieth Air Force's biggest challenges during the bombing of Japan was the loss of B-29s that crashed into the ocean between Japan and the Marianas. General LeMay's predecessor, Brigadier General Haywood S. Hansell, created a remarkable rescue network with the Navy's help to fish downed crews out of the sea. Over the entire bombing campaign, rescue aircraft and submarines saved half of the 1,300 crew members who crash-landed at sea during missions to Japan.

More important for the survival of the B-29's crews, however, was Iwo Jima. The Japanese used the volcanic island for an early warning site and for staging attacks against the B-29 bases in the Marianas. When USAAF bombardment proved insufficient, the Marines were sent in and fought an epic battle that has passed into legend. The result of their struggle was a new air base for defending the Marianas, a radar outpost, and an emergency airfield where troubled Superfortresses could land. The island's seizure cost more than 25,000 Americans killed or wounded. But the cost in lives seemed justified by the number of Airmen's lives saved. By the war's end, more than 2,000 B-29s, each with 11 men on board, had made emergency landings on the island. One estimate is that the number of lives saved equaled or exceeded the 6,000 lost capturing Iwo Jima.

DOCTRINE AND HISTORY—THE PACIFIC THEATER IN WORLD WAR II

DISTINCTIVE CAPABILITIES	FUNCTIONS (MISSIONS)	DOCTRINAL EMPHASIS
• Precision Engagement • Information Superiority • Air Superiority • Agile Combat Support	• Surveillance and Reconnaissance • Counterair/land • Strategic Attack • Airlift/Special Operations	• Strategic Attack • Counterland • Counterair • Atomic Weapons

MODULE III

AIRPOWER THROUGH THE COLD WAR:

Strategic airlift, birth of the nuclear triad, introduction of jet aircraft

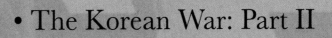

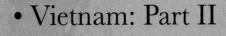

AN INDEPENDENT AIR FORCE AND THE COLD WAR

WORLD WAR II ended with both the advent of the jet aircraft and the first use of nuclear weapons. The combination of the two led many to conceive of airpower as totally strategic in nature. As military theorists grappled with what this meant for organizing attack forces, several events occurred that would greatly affect the answer—the United States rapidly demobilized; the US military was completely reorganized, with an independent Air Force equal to the other services; and the Cold War broke out in Europe. The new Air Force now had to answer an important question: How to organize a nuclear-armed strategic strike force on a tight budget?

COLD WAR WARRIORS

IN THE DECADES AFTER THE END OF WORLD WAR II, NUCLEAR-ARMED AIR FORCES TRAINED TIRELESSLY TO FIGHT A THIRD WORLD WAR THAT NEVER CAME

"The swept wings gave an impression of arrow swiftness; the shining body, of brightness and cleanness; the eight great engines, of power and pure functional efficiency… [In the bomb bay] were stored two thermonuclear bombs."

PETER GEORGE
DR. STRANGELOVE OR: HOW I LEARNED TO STOP WORRYING AND LOVE THE BOMB

"THE ENEMY OF MY ENEMY IS MY FRIEND" is an old saying that nicely sums up the World War II Allies. Despite political differences, the United States, Britain, France, and the Soviet Union banded together to fight the nearly overwhelming might of the Axis nations. But when the Allies defeated Germany, Italy, and Japan, the Soviet Union had plans that no longer jibed with the West. Moscow intended to spread its Communist empire farther and farther into Central Europe. So began a political and military struggle that lasted from 1948–89.

An American delegate to the United Nations gave this costly new "war" its name. During a speech in 1947, Bernard Baruch declared, "Let us not be deceived—today we are in the midst of a cold war."

LOCKHEED U-2R
The Lockheed U-2 high-altitude reconnaissance aircraft was used as a spy plane to overfly the USSR during the Cold War. Its altitude was supposed to put the U-2 out of reach of Soviet interceptors and missiles, but two were shot down in the 1960s.

All sides wanted to avoid another bloody conflict, or "hot" war, after 1945 and the introduction of the atomic bomb. But the Soviet Union feared that Germany would never settle for defeat, so it wanted a layer of Communist-controlled countries between it and its historical enemy. To achieve this, Soviet dictator Josef Stalin was willing to test the will of the West. He had reason to believe he could prevail: France and Britain lay exhausted after two world wars in the span of 30 years, while the United States was rapidly demobilizing and withdrawing its troops from the continent.

On the other hand, the United States was not about to give up free European nations to the Communists after it had spent so much blood and treasure to liberate them from the Nazis during World War II. What ensued was a costly buildup of arms, particularly nuclear weapons, by both sides over the next four decades. Many side conflicts would break out during the Cold War, such as the Korean War and the Vietnam War, and these would cost the lives of hundreds of thousands of men and women.

The dropping of the atomic bombs on Hiroshima and Nagasaki in 1945 had opened a new era in aerial warfare. By the 1950s, both sides in the Cold War had "the bomb." The chief function of air forces to the east and west of the Iron Curtain was to anticipate and intercept an enemy nuclear attack and penetrate enemy air defenses to deliver a nuclear strike of their own. In 1947 the independent US Air Force (USAF) was created to replace the Army Air Force (AAF). Within it, in recognition of the importance of the nuclear role, the Strategic Air Command (SAC) was established to handle the nuclear bomber force.

ROCKET-ASSISTED BOMBER
A Boeing B-47 jet bomber makes a jet-assisted takeoff. The aircraft needed the extra boost to lift off the ground with a full load of bombs and fuel. Short on range, it was turned into a credible intercontinental nuclear bomber by in-flight refueling.

MUTUALLY ASSURED DESTRUCTION

IN THE DAYS before the introduction of intercontinental ballistic missiles (ICBMs) and reconnaissance satellites—that is, through to the early 1960s—the nuclear confrontation was almost exclusively a business for aircraft and Airmen. High-altitude spy planes kept watch on enemy military preparations, providing photos of potential targets and air-defense installations. High-performance jet interceptors stood ready to scramble against incoming bombers. They would be directed by a chain of early-warning radar stations spread out across the north of Canada and Greenland down into Britain,

feeding information to control rooms in underground bunkers. And above all, there were the strategic bombers.

At the height of the Cold War, on any day or night, about 600 American nuclear-armed bombers stood fully fueled on alert, dispersed at air bases across the United States and in allied countries. Near the bombers their crews waited, studying weather briefings and mission plans, playing cards or watching movies, theoretically prepared at any moment for the call to be airborne in 15 minutes, before their bases could be vaporized by a Soviet surprise attack.

For extra insurance, between a dozen and 70 nuclear bombers were on permanent airborne alert over the Atlantic, flying exhausting 24-hour shifts that covered 10,000 miles (16,000km), ready and waiting to be directed toward the Soviet Union. If the call came, the B-52s or B-47s would go in low, ducking under Soviet radar, shuddering and bucking over the ground contours to deliver their weapons of mass destruction. This was the world of Dr. Strangelove and of Mutually Assured Destruction—in which the only rational way to keep the peace was to maintain the real threat of instant annihilation. And Airmen were the intended agents of this Armageddon.

Those theorists of aerial warfare in the 1920s and 1930s who had believed bombers were invincible and could win a war quickly on their own seemed to have been proved wrong in World War II. But the nuclear age, in an unforeseen manner, made them seem prescient. Now a bomber force really could, in principle, deliver a shock attack that would end a war in days. At least a few bombers would always get through, and armed with such destructive power, that was enough.

Yet while the focus of military spending and air force planning was on nuclear offense and defense, from the start of the Cold War very different demands were made on military aircraft and their crews as a variety of local crises and hot wars flared without escalating to nuclear conflict. The first of these was the Berlin airlift of 1948–49, which brought hardworking American and British transport aircraft briefly into the limelight usually hogged by the fighters and bombers.

The quest for independence

In the run-up to the Cold War, the struggle continued in Washington over the structure of national defense and the place of the nation's air force in that structure. Even during the chaos of World War II, many officers continued to dream of creating an air force independent of and equal to the Army and Navy. Among them was General of the Army Henry H. Arnold, who spent 39 years in the service. He recruited scientists to push aerospace science and technology forward. The better the technology, the better the chances were that the air force could stand as an equal with the other services. Arnold never led Airmen into combat, he was not a scientist himself, nor was he a mechanic or a technician—in fact, he once designed and built

BOEING B-52
The Boeing B-52 bomber was one of the aircraft the United States counted on to drop nuclear bombs on the Soviet Union if the need arose during the Cold War.

a donkey cart for his children but neglected to install brakes, with near-disastrous results—but he had a keen vision of the air force's future and the role technology would play in it.

In December 1944, Arnold called together his principal staff officers, all veteran pilots, and urged them to look 20 years into a future shaped by aeronautical science and technology. "For the last 20 years," he told them, "we have built and run the air force on pilots. But we can't do that any more." In the future, Arnold believed, the scientist and engineer who designed radical new weapons would become increasingly important, perhaps dominating the air arm as the pilot had done before.

The new air force, like the existing Army Air Forces, would emphasize strategic bombardment, including long-range fighter escort, for, as Arnold said, "It is conceivable that there will always be one industry, such as the oil industry in Germany, so necessary to all phases of the national war-making ability that its destruction would be fatal to the nation." He saw other purposes for the air force, too: It ought to be capable of defending against enemy bombers, attacking hostile ground forces, running reconnaissance,

FUTURE PRESIDENT
General of the Army Dwight D. Eisenhower, Army Chief of Staff, advocated the creation of three major operation commands: Strategic Air Command, Tactical Air Command, and Air Defense Command. Within a few years the popular war hero would become president.

transporting troops and materiel, forecasting the weather, and handling communications (think of modern-day satellites that are under Air Force control). Arnold was a thinker. He predicted many inventions people today take for granted, such as guided bombs and target-seeking antiaircraft missiles.

The Army Air Force's transition from a war footing to a peacetime function gave the soon-to-be-independent air force the space, time, and opportunity to figure out exactly what its purpose would be. Its proposed structure went through several drafts. The new Army Chief of Staff, General of the Army Dwight D. Eisenhower, thought the Air Forces should have three separate commands, each charged with one of the major airpower functions: strategic bombardment, air defense, and support of ground forces. While Eisenhower supported an independent air force, he believed that air support was essential to the success of operations on land, and that air superiority, which permitted effective support of ground forces, was best gained by aviation units operating under an air commander who knew how to employ military aircraft to the greatest advantage. General Carl A. Spaatz, Commanding General, Army Air Forces, agreed with Eisenhower's assessment. He said, "Eisenhower and I thought along the same lines about this thing." He set up three major operating commands: Strategic Air Command (SAC), Tactical Air Command (TAC), and Air Defense Command (ADC). These reflected the three basic combat missions that had evolved during World War II.

HUMBLE BEGINNINGS
General Carl A. Spaatz, Commanding General, Army Air Forces, and Lieutenant General Ira C. Eaker meet with President Harry S. Truman as he signs a proclamation designating August 1, 1946, "Air Force Day." The event marked the 39th anniversary of the birth of the air arm as part of the Army Signal Corps—with three men and no airplanes.

The peacetime reorganization took effect on March 21, 1946, with General Spaatz as commanding general, Army Air Forces. However, the final separation from the Army would not take place until 1947. In the meantime, Strategic Air Command's mission was to conduct long-range global air operations and "maximum range" reconnaissance. General George C. Kenney, based at Andrews Field, Maryland, was in charge. Tactical Air Command, under General Elwood R. Quesada, was to support ground and naval forces and, if necessary, assist Air Defense Command.

Quesada moved TAC to Langley Field in Virginia to be closer to the Army Ground Forces at Fortress Monroe in Hampton, Virginia, and the Navy's Atlantic Fleet at nearby Norfolk, Virginia. Lieutenant General George E. Stratemeyer's Air Defense Command, based at Mitchel Field, New York, was charged with defending the United States against air attack, protecting coastal shipping, training the Air National Guard, and administering and training the Air Reserve and the Reserve Officer Training Corps.

> "We did not demobilize....
> [We] merely fell apart...."
>
> **BRIGADIER GENERAL**
> **LEON JOHNSON**

Besides the three combat commands, the Army Air Forces (and later the independent air force as well) consisted of the Air Materiel Command, the Air Training Command, the Air University, the Proving Ground Command, the Air Transport Command, and the overseas theater commands.

The Army Air Forces command also had to decide what to do with its 16 wartime air forces. Because of limited resources, the Army retained only 11. SAC took over the Eighth and Fifteenth Air Forces; TAC, the Third, Ninth, and Twelfth; and ADC, the First, Second, Fourth, Tenth, Eleventh, and Fourteenth. Spaatz also formed an Air Board composed of current and retired officers to help shape postwar policy.

A military force is nothing without manpower, and as the Army Air Forces shifted to a postwar world, the commanders had to decide what to do with 2,253,000 personnel as well. Most Airmen simply wanted to go home. The Air Forces settled on a small active duty force backed up by National Guardsmen and reservists; establishing the Air National Guard in 1946. By the end of June 1947, the Air National Guard numbered 10,000 Airmen organized into 257 squadrons. Meanwhile, the ADC was administering a reserve program composed largely of inactive reservists, who were available in an emergency, though not necessarily well trained. Of more than 500,000 reservists carried on the rolls in the summer of 1947, 80 percent were inactive.

The greatest danger the Army Air Forces faced was the disintegration of the great military power that had grown up during World War II. "We did not demobilize," complained Brigadier General Leon Johnson, a Medal of Honor winner. "[We] merely fell apart ... it was not an orderly demobilization at all. It was just a riot, really." The Air Forces dropped to a postwar low of 304,000 by May 1947. The biggest problem was that the most-skilled mechanics left the service because they could easily find jobs in the private sector. That left the Air Forces with the less-experienced mechanics, and as a consequence flying accidents rose.

Finally, there was the armada of aircraft to deal with. Some 35,000 out of 79,000 aircraft of all types were treated as surplus government property. Eventually, the Air Forces' fleet fell to about 24,000 aircraft, and only 18 percent of that was ready for action.

By 1948 the situation was such that Spaatz preferred "not to speculate on what might have happened only one year after V-J Day, when the combat readiness of AAF first-line planes dropped very low, if our Air Force had been called on to resist or to suppress a recurrence of combat activity from an uncontrolled element in one of the occupied countries."

As the stampede to civilian life continued, the Joint Chiefs of Staff were fully aware of the steep decline in US military strength. Indeed, they thought it would take well over a year to reconstitute American military might to even a fraction of its recent power. General George Marshall, the Army Chief of Staff while the armed forces were in headlong decline, realized that the demobilization was injurious. Yet, even Marshall, who considered it a serious error not to have planned a more gradual and systematic reduction, conceded that it would not have been possible, in the flush of victory and with no clearly perceived danger at hand, to maintain a large standing military force.

AWAITING DESTRUCTION
Hundreds of bombers line Kingman Army Airfield in 1946. The Army Air Forces dropped from 79,000 operational aircraft in 1944 to 24,000 in 1947—with only 18 percent ready for action.

GENERAL GEORGE C. MARSHALL
The Army Chief of Staff understood the damage rapid demobilization was causing, but conceded that maintaining a large standing military force would have been difficult with no clearly perceived threat.

The Soviet threat

In spite of Americans' hopes, the postwar years ended up being anything but carefree. Tensions developed between the Western powers and the Soviet Union, as the Soviets tried to expand their empire. On March 5, 1946, two years before the recognized start of the Cold War, former British Prime Minister Winston Churchill declared in an address at Westminster College in Missouri, "From Stettin in the Baltic to Trieste in the Adriatic an iron curtain has descended across the Continent."

Two well-known American plans emerged in 1947 to combat the Soviet expansion: the Truman Doctrine and the Marshall Plan. The Truman Doctrine was a $400 million scheme to assist Turkey and Greece, which were under severe Soviet pressures. President Harry S. Truman explained that "it must be the policy of the United States to support free peoples who are resisting attempted subjugation by armed minorities or by outside pressure," indeed, to "assist free peoples to work out their own

destinies in their own way." In the aftermath of World War II, France and Italy as well faced grave dangers from well-organized Communist parties. To help Europe regain its economic strength and resist communism, now Secretary of State Marshall, the Army's wartime Chief of Staff, devised the Marshall Plan, an unprecedented financial aid program available to any country in Europe that wished to participate.

Other factors were at play in the postwar era, such as the atomic bomb. No one knew if future wars would be over in a matter of days or if conventional warfare would still reign. Since the duty to drop atomic bombs fell on the AAF, it was up to the AAF to figure out how to organize, plan, and train for its use. This was the AAF's chance to show how important its mission was to the country's defense and how wise it would be to grant it independence from the Army so it could focus on the nation's airpower needs.

In late 1945, the Army Air Forces decided all heavy bombardment units would comprise the atomic strike force. More specifically, the 58th Bomb Wing would be the first to train for this purpose. It would consist of three groups of four B-29 squadrons each. The wing's first combat element would be the 509th Bomb Group,

which had leveled Hiroshima and Nagasaki, although other groups would join as funds became available. This force was the key element of SAC. The 509th was stationed at Roswell, New Mexico, so it could be near the country's atomic bomb-building facilities at the Los Alamos complex, but far enough away that an attack on just one base could not destroy both bombs and bombers. Everything was approved by 1946, including the proposition that only the president of the United States, as commander in chief, could decide when to use an atomic bomb.

The Joint Strategic Survey Committee predicted in 1945 that the Soviet Union would have an atomic bomb within five years. That would make the United States especially vulnerable, since so many of its industrial cities were clustered along the coasts. In contrast, US bombers would have to fly thousands of miles before reaching the Soviet Union's vital inland targets. The Joint Chiefs of Staff concluded in 1946 that to successfully wage war against the Soviet Union, the United States would need forward bases in Europe to place the B-29s within range of these distant targets. Because of the limited number of bombs and the difficulty of getting them over to these European bases when an emergency arose, land and sea forces would have to seize, develop, supply, and protect the advance bases for the bombers. This interdependence argued in favor of a balance of US air, ground, and sea forces. Since the Soviet Union's ground forces were so overwhelming in number, the United States would have to resort to atomic weapons early in any conflict. But not until 1947 did the United States have spare

THE TRUMAN DOCTRINE ADDRESS
President Harry S. Truman gives his Truman Doctrine address before Congress on March 12, 1947.

B-29s to supply forward bases. Even then, the atomic strike bombers continued to train in the southwest corner of the United States.

Four major events absorbed the energies of the postwar air arm. Simultaneously with the rush to demobilize, the restructuring of the Army Air Forces, the collapse of the wartime alliance, and the first efforts to create an atomic strike force, Spaatz and his fellow Airmen took up Arnold's quest for an air force independent of the Army. It called for different kinds of personnel than the Army had. For instance, a civilian can be turned into a soldier in a matter of weeks or months. But a pilot, a mechanic, and especially personnel dealing with atomic weapons require much more training. The atomic bomb meant that the next war might well begin with a sudden onslaught, a nuclear Pearl Harbor so extensive and violent that the kind of mobilization that occurred during the two world wars would be impossible. Such a war would have to be fought by the forces under arms when the bombs began falling. In the end, the public and Congress accepted the idea that an independent air force, instantly ready for combat, was the only answer.

But the Navy continued to stoutly resist an independent air force. The admirals worried they could lose their naval aviation arm to the new air force and the Marines to the Army. The Navy also suspected that the Army would somehow hang on to the newly autonomous air force, thus wielding twice the bureaucratic power and receiving twice the funding. For General Arnold, the Army Air Force's advocate, the idea of leaving the air arm's budget within the Army was entirely unacceptable. Arnold attempted to reassure the Navy that an independent air force would not try to take away its naval aviation arm. He declared that he was opposed to bringing aircraft carriers under air force control. All these bureaucratic struggles had to be worked out and the fears of the other services laid to rest before the air force could gain control over its own destiny.

When General Eisenhower became Army Chief of Staff in 1945, he advocated for an independent air force as part of the new defense structure emerging after the war. He considered the idea so logical that he said, referring to the Army, "No sane officer of any arm would contest that thinking." He later said that although "there can be other individual opinions" concerning the status of

> ## "Airpower has been developed to a point where its responsibilities are equal to those of land and sea power."
>
> **PRESIDENT HARRY S. TRUMAN**

military aviation, it "seems to me to be so logical from all our experience in this war—such an inescapable conclusion—that I for one can't even entertain any longer any doubt as to its wisdom."

While the drive toward independence gathered momentum, the War Department underwent a postwar reorganization of its own. Many military and political leaders of the time, including President Truman, attributed the disaster at Pearl Harbor in large measure to Army–Navy rivalry and the absence of a unified command. They felt the old War and Navy Departments had failed them in 1941. Therefore, not only did Truman move swiftly to rectify this lack of unity with a reorganization, he intended that the new defense establishment should reflect his belief that "[a]irpower has been developed to a point where its responsibilities are equal to those of land and sea power." He recommended in December 1945 that Congress approve legislation to create an independent air force, an equal to the Army and Navy in a new department of defense. President Truman may have faced problems more intricate and potentially more dangerous than defense reorganization—such as the crumbling wartime alliance between communism and democracy—but he could not ignore this issue in the unsettled postwar world. As he said in retrospect, "One of the strongest convictions which I brought to the presidency was that

the antiquated defense setup … had to be reorganized quickly as a step toward insuring our future safety and preserving world peace." This restructuring included greater autonomy for the air force from June 1946 until its full independence in 1947.

But two more years of discussion and bickering ensued between the Navy, Army, and the politicians in Washington before the Senate and House passed legislation reorganizing the US defense structure. On July 26, 1947, President Truman signed the National Security Act of 1947, which created the National Military Establishment (today's Department of Defense), including the Office of the Secretary of Defense and the Departments of the Army, Navy, and Air Force. The role of the new Secretary of Defense would be to coordinate policy rather than establish it.

THE IRON CURTAIN SPEECH
British Prime Minister Winston Churchill delivers his Iron Curtain speech at Westminster College in Missouri in 1946.

The act also authorized a number of other agencies dealing with national defense. As they had during World War II, the Joint Chiefs of Staff—with representatives from each branch of the military—would provide strategic planning and direction for the armed forces. A National Security Council of Cabinet secretaries was established to advise the president on a broad range of issues; in time of crisis it would be supplemented by a War Council made up of the Secretary of Defense, the service secretaries (civilians), and the uniformed chiefs of the Army, Navy, and Air Force. To prevent a repetition of the lapses in disseminating information that had helped the Japanese achieve surprise at Pearl Harbor, a new Central Intelligence Agency would channel intelligence evaluations to the National Security Council. There would also be a Munitions Board in charge of providing arms, a Research and Development Board, and a National Security Resources Board to advise the president on questions of industrial, civilian, and military mobilization. All these components formed the framework for an integrated approach to national security without precedent in American history.

On the same day that Truman signed the National Security Act into law, he issued Executive Order 9877 "Functions of the Armed Forces," which outlined the duties of the Army, Navy, and Air Force. Basically, each was responsible for the medium—air, ground, or sea—in which it operated, although the naval establishment retained its air arm and the Marine Corps.

The Air Force had at last won its independence. Its commanders believed that strategic bombardment and atomic deterrence were the wave of future warfare. The Army and Navy had their own ideas that did not always mesh with those of the Airmen. In fact, they worried they had given up too much power and too great a share of the country's military funding to this fledgling branch. Many conflicts among the three branches were still left to be worked out under the new National Military Establishment.

MOTHER SHIP
The Bell X-1 resting in the belly of a B-29.
The X-1's conquest of the sound barrier
added a new word to the aviation dictionary:
Mach. Mach 1 means the speed of sound;
Mach 2 is twice the speed of sound.

REACHING MACH 1

Soon after the Air Force became an independent service, then-Colonel Chuck Yeager flew the Bell X-1 faster than the speed of sound for the first time. On October 14, 1947, the X-1 "Glamorous Glennis," named for Yeager's wife, reached 700mph (1,127kmph) or Mach 1.06, at an altitude of 43,000ft (13,106m).

Framing Air Force missions

The new National Military Establishment came into being on September 17, 1947, when James V. Forrestal took the oath as Secretary of Defense. On the following day, W. Stuart Symington was sworn in as Secretary of the Air Force, along with the other newly designated service secretaries; all the principal civilian authorities were now formally installed. On September 26 General Spaatz, previously the Commanding General, Army Air Forces, became the first Chief of Staff of the Air Force. Symington and Spaatz were the leaders, civilian and military respectively, who charted the course for the new service. During Spaatz and Symington's tenures, the Air Force adopted a basic organization that's still at work today: a headquarters, a network of major commands and lesser agencies, and operational commands overseas. A struggle with the Navy over the atomic mission subsided, so that by mid-1950, the Air Force assumed the primary responsibility for nuclear deterrence. The Air Force still carries out this duty, albeit with changes in equipment, emphasis, and funding.

Global realities soon demonstrated that deterrence would be only one aspect of the Air Force's evolving policy. The new service had to devote its resources to such things as the containment of communism by going to the aid of West Berlin from 1948–49, and regional collective security as seen in the creation of the North Atlantic Treaty Organization in 1949.

FIRST SECRETARY OF DEFENSE
Before taking up his new post, James V. Forrestal had served as Secretary of the Navy and argued against a single Cabinet officer controlling national defense.

The Air Force also continued to concentrate on the development of more advanced aircraft and weapons. Secretary Symington believed his job was not operational but supportive—not deciding what kinds of weapons the Air Force needed or how they should be used, but obtaining the appropriations from Congress to acquire them. As he described it, his task was "to get as much of the pie as I could for the Air Force." The pie was much smaller after World War II than it had been during the war. Bitter battles erupted between the three services for funds and over roles and missions.

Meanwhile, Chief of Staff Spaatz was divvying up the duties for the Air Force's day-to-day operations. He devised three key noncombat commands for the Air Staff: deputy chiefs for Materiel, for Operations, and for Personnel and Administration. These controlled everything from supply procurement and atomic weapons (Materiel) to guided missiles, training, and intelligence (Operations). Plus, he established the office of Air Comptroller to study the budget, cost controls, and other financial matters. Over the years, the duties have shifted numerous times, but this is how the division of labor began.

The three major combat commands inherited from the Army Air Forces—SAC, TAC, and ADC—changed once the Air Force gained its independence from the Army. Strategic Air Command emerged as the most important of the three, since it was responsible for deterrence and, should deterrence fail, for waging atomic warfare. The hitch was that SAC did not have enough atomic bombs or bombers to wage such a war and had not adequately trained enough crews to deliver the bombs. Despite the turmoil, though, SAC enjoyed a clear primacy within the Air Force. As its prestige rose, tactical aviation's declined.

The Air Force shifted TAC and ADC to serve under a new command called Continental Air Command. Continental Air Command fulfilled three duties: tactical aviation, air defense, and Air National Guard and Air Force Reserve training. This was one means to address limited funds in a postwar world. The Continental Air Command used the same personnel and aircraft for all three of its roles. The problem with this arrangement was that it did not foster a sense of teamwork. Everyone's duties could change at a moment's notice.

PRESS CONFERENCE
Stuart Symington, the first Secretary of the Air Force, appears before the press with General Carl Spaatz, first Air Force chief of staff, in 1947 to announce the setup of the new Department of the Air Force.

The flaws quickly became apparent once the United States entered the Korean War in 1950, and TAC and ADC regained their old status independent of the Continental Air Command. The Continental Air Command continued to administer the reserve components until it was disbanded in 1968.

During the Air Force's first two years of independence, support and housekeeping functions—such as maintaining records and operating bases—moved from Army oversight to the Air Force. At this time the military also began to consider integrating its forces. Many African-Americans worked in support and housekeeping units with little chance for advancement, and the all-black 332d Fighter Group (the Tuskegee Airmen) remained separate from other flight groups. Air Force officers, led by Colonel Noel F. Parrish, and including retired Lieutenant General Jimmy Doolittle, argued for integration. As a result, when President Truman issued a landmark executive order in July 1948 to integrate the races throughout the armed forces, the Air Force was already moving toward that goal.

Science and technology

Part of the AAF's legacy was an interest in science and its application to aerial warfare. In 1944 General Arnold asked an old acquaintance of his, Theodore von Kármán, to follow the advancing Allied armies to survey Germany's wartime accomplishments in aeronautical science. Von Kármán and his scientific colleagues wrote up dozens of studies over the next year or so comparing US and German progress, the importance of science and technology in a dawning era of rockets and jet aircraft, and aerospace research and development. Von Kármán said that the writings "definitely made the point that the Air Force was the major defense arm of the nation and that defense was clearly dependent on a continuous input of technological and scientific progress." Among other recommendations, he and his team called for the development of supersonic aircraft and guided missiles, and for close cooperation between the air arm and the country's scientists.

Von Kármán not only headed the group that investigated German wartime aviation, but he was chief of the Scientific Advisory Group that reported directly to Arnold. The Scientific Advisory Group disbanded in 1946, only to be revived in June the same year as the Scientific Advisory Board, again under von Kármán's leadership. This new board reported to Major General Curtis LeMay, Deputy Chief of Air Staff, Research and Development. Once the Air Force gained its independence from the Army, the board fell under the Air Materiel Command.

In another attempt to gain access to the nation's leading scientists, General Arnold proposed investing $10 million from the AAF's procurement budget in a civilian organization where engineers and scientists could study air force roles in modern war. In March 1946, the Air Materiel Command let the first contract to Project Rand (its name a contraction of research and development). According to LeMay, Rand provided "a continuing program of scientific study and research on the subject of air warfare with the purpose of recommending to the Air Force preferred methods, techniques, and instrumentalities for this purpose." While originally part of Douglas Aircraft, Rand eventually reconstituted itself as an independent nonprofit corporation, with the Air Force as its principal customer.

The creation of the Scientific Advisory Board and the launching of Project Rand were attempts to go outside the air arm and draw on the skills and wisdom of the nation's most prominent engineers and scientists. The Air Force had to decide how best to take advantage of this talent and whether research and development should remain in the Air Materiel Command. Lieutenant General Benjamin W. Chidlaw, who headed the command, thought the status quo worked. He viewed Air Materiel Command as the beginning of a unified process that included procurement, maintenance, and supply, and that anything that grew out of research and development meshed nicely with those functions. Air Force headquarters felt differently, however. By January 1950 research and development had its own command, the Air Research and Development Command. This new command conducted the never-ending quest for new and improved weapons and equipment.

Aircraft were going through some big transformations around this time as well. The jet engine was beginning to replace the piston engine because it burned cheap kerosene fuel, it was simpler to maintain, and it was more efficient than propellers at speeds greater than 450mph (724kmph). The German-developed sweptwing was gaining in popularity, since it delayed the buildup of drag as airplanes approached the speed of sound. Aerial refueling, using a technique borrowed from the British, was also introduced at this time because the early jets consumed too much fuel to reach their destinations without a mid-air, mid-flight feed. Many new aircraft were soaring around this time as well, including the Boeing B-47 bomber and the North American F-86 fighter, which both incorporated the sweptwing.

SCIENCE ADVISER
In addition to counseling the Air Force, Theodore von Kármán co-founded the Jet Propulsion Laboratory at California Institute of Technology and served as a top science adviser to NATO.

The Consolidated B-36 was powered by an array of pusher propellers and turbojets. It was so large that the crew of 15 moved from the front to the back of the bomber by pulling themselves along a tunnel on a trolley, and slept in bunks when off duty.

Although acquiring newly developed aircraft and devising techniques for their use, the Air Force could not buy them in the numbers its leaders considered necessary. Even before the National Security Act passed in 1947, Spaatz and Symington called for expansion to 70 air forces from the postwar low of 11. However, the fear of a postwar depression followed by inflation concerns in 1948 meant President Truman was more interested in cutting federal spending than in pumping additional millions into the military. The US debt was $252 billion by the end of World War II, and debt is a major factor in inflation. Expensive aircraft, such as the $3.6 million B-36 bomber at the heart of the Air Force's atomic deterrence and delivery plan, did not fit into Truman's strategies for cutting debt and inflation.

Whatever his concerns about high-cost aircraft, though, Truman could not ignore airpower. The wartime glamor of aerial warfare lingered in the public consciousness. In response, the president formed the Air Policy Commission, which heard testimony from Symington, Spaatz, and other Air Force representatives arguing in favor of land-based bombers and their exceptional performance against Japan and Germany during World War II. The Navy disagreed and pointed to its fast carrier task forces in the war against Japan as well as the folly of relying on a single weapon, the strategic bomber, for the nation's security. On this stage the Air Force continued to shape its mission as an independent service.

Secretary of Defense Forrestal, who hoped to achieve a balance among the services and avoid Air Force expansion at others' expense, warned that the nature of the next war defied prediction and might turn out to be a conflict in which land-based airpower would prove far less effective than it had in World War II. He echoed as well Truman's concerns about the possibly dangerous economic consequences of out-of-control spending for weapons and aircraft. The commission sided with the Air Force and called for 70 combat groups. Truman disagreed.

Around this time, world events intervened on behalf of the Air Force. Communists seized power in Czechoslovakia in February 1948, and the Soviets showed the first inclinations to interfere with Western access to Berlin. The US administration and Congress were more likely to fund the services when the Soviets made moves that threatened Western interests. The Air Force did not get its 70 combat groups, but the 1950 and proposed 1951 budgets gave it 48.

The Air Force, Navy, and nuclear deterrence

Since Forrestal was not having much success in keeping the peace between the services, particularly the Navy and Air Force, he convened a meeting of the Joint Chiefs of Staff in March 1948 in Key West, Florida. With General Spaatz, Admiral Louis Denfeld, and General Omar Bradley, the group more clearly defined each branch's duties. The agreement it hashed out specified that the Army was responsible for land warfare; the Navy for sea operations; the Marine Corps for amphibious operations; and the Air Force for air operations, including strategic air warfare.

Moreover, each service had to provide the maximum assistance to the others in accomplishing overall military objectives. The Air Force and Navy hit a snag, however. The Navy had long wanted its aircraft to take part in atomic deterrence and delivery. But the Air Force saw this as its domain.

In the absence of an agreement between the two branches over the nuclear issue, the Navy pursued its plans to create a carrier-based atomic strike force. The naval leadership deemed this a logical evolution from the conventionally armed carrier task forces of World War II. The Air Force leadership saw it as a wasteful attempt to duplicate Strategic Air Command's mission. Nonetheless, the Key West agreement replaced Executive Order 9877, which was the first to outline individual service responsibilities. President Truman approved the new agreement on April 21, 1948, calling it "Functions of the Armed Forces and the Joint Chiefs of Staff." Since the agreement did not resolve the issue of what the Air Force perceived as the Navy's encroachment on its atomic monopoly, bickering over the strategic air mission continued.

Four months later, Forrestal met again with the Joint Chiefs of Staff, including General Hoyt Vandenberg, who had replaced Spaatz as Air Force Chief of Staff. At the Naval War College at Newport, Rhode Island, the group discussed which service would be executive agent of atomic weapons. Whoever controlled the Armed Services Special Weapons Project controlled access to the bombs. The upshot of the meeting was that

DETERRANT FORCE
A still from a 1949 documentary, Target: Peace, *shows a crewman's view of a fleet of B-36s in operation. To stress that the purpose of the nuclear bomber force was to prevent war through deterrence, the B-36 was dubbed the "Peacemaker."*

although the Air Force continued to bear primary responsibility for strategic aerial warfare, it had to give the Navy access to nuclear bombs and allow it to participate in strategic air operations.

Another result of the Newport conference was the formation of the Weapons Systems Evaluation Group to provide the Joint Chiefs with data on the performance and usefulness of various weapons. Secretary Forrestal had strong doubts that SAC could cripple the Soviet Union, considering the limited number of available bombs, bases, and aircraft. He predicted that in any such conflict naval forces would have to control the seas so that ground forces could seize and defend advance airfields close enough to the Soviet heartland to permit airpower to attack "in a decisive, and I repeat decisive, manner." The first assignment handed to the evaluation group was a technical analysis of a strategic bombing campaign against the Soviet Union.

The group handed over a report in 1949. Its conclusions found their way into a briefing given to Truman and Secretary of Defense Louis Johnson in January 1950. The briefing listed logistical problems such as lack of overseas bases, the status of aerial refueling technique, inadequate fuel stockpiles overseas, and a shortage of airlift to supply strike forces. It also predicted anywhere from 30 to 50 percent of the bombers would be lost to enemy fire due to poor training and poor intelligence. As a result, it recommended that aircraft drop only atomic bombs rather than conventional weapons to inflict the greatest damage possible. Johnson said that the conclusion meant the long-range B-36 bomber was the choice aircraft for strategic bombing.

The B-36 in many ways encapsulated the fight between the Air Force and Navy over limited funds. The B-36 seemingly let the Air Force fulfill its atomic role. But at $3.6 million a plane, the Navy blamed it for taking money away from its dream carrier the *United States*, which would have carried a fleet of aircraft armed with atomic bombs. Both Air Force and Navy officers testified before Congress to argue for the value of each of their roles in a nuclear world. While the B-36 won the day, the biggest outcome of the Air Force-Navy clash was that Congress passed a reorganization bill that Truman signed into law in August 1949. It confirmed the office of Chairman of the Joint Chiefs of Staff. Furthermore, it redesignated the National Military Establishment as the Department of Defense, and increased the Secretary of Defense's powers. The Secretary of Defense had formerly been the first among equals with the secretaries of the Army, Navy, and Air Force. But the secretary now emerged as the president's principal adviser on all matters relating to defense with "direction, authority, and control" over the service secretaries. In addition, this law removed the Army, Navy, and Air Force service secretaries from the National Security Council and deprived them of their right of appeal to the president or the director of the Bureau of the Budget.

What also emerged during the course of the B-36 debate was confirmation of America's reliance on nuclear deterrence in the face of Soviet expansion. In November 1948 the National Security Council formally adopted deterrence as official American policy. The council said that the security of the nation required that the United States maintain, for as along as necessary, sufficient military strength

NUCLEAR GIANT
A group of mechanics stands on the horizontal stabilizer of the massive B-36 nuclear bomber, one of the largest aircraft ever built. The rudder was as tall as a five-story building.

"to act as a deterrent to Soviet aggression." American strategy looked to the atomic bomb to guarantee the peace, but these weapons and the means of delivering them were scarce as the 1940s drew to an end. Still, this declaration secured a prominent role for the Air Force in the coming decades.

The United States held a monopoly on atomic weapons until September 1949, when the Soviet Union detonated its own nuclear device. As the US stockpile grew to about 300 bombs by 1950, SAC trained crews and modified aircraft to carry the five-ton bombs. Between December 1946 and January 1949, the number of bombers grew from 23 to 121 (eight B-29s, 96 B-50s, and 17 B-36s) and crews increased from 10 to 150. Bomb assembly crews totaled seven by January 1949 as opposed to zero just three years earlier.

In this atmosphere, the West faced its first direct confrontation with the Soviet Union. The Soviets decided to block access to the Western-controlled sectors of Berlin. The question of the day for the West was how it would handle this challenge. If it resorted to nuclear weapons, untold casualties could result. And frankly, the United States still was not fully prepared for an outright atomic war. Its answer to the Soviet bullying would prove both clever and wise.

9

THE BERLIN AIRLIFT

THE COLD WAR grew out of the arrangements among the Allies for reconstructing Europe following their victory over the Nazis. For the most part, the Soviets engineered the installation of Communist governments in those territories their troops had liberated, while the Western Powers established democratic governments in the countries under their control. The Allies divided Germany into four zones—American, British, French, and Soviet—as they did the capital, Berlin, which lay deep inside the Soviet zone. Concerned that Western policies would lead to a rebirth of Germany, the Soviets tried to force the West to leave Berlin—giving the newly created US Air Force one of its first tests.

"OPERATION VITTLES"

WHEN THE SOVIET UNION TRIED TO MUSCLE THE WEST OUT OF BERLIN, THE UNITED STATES AND BRITAIN REPLIED WITH A NEW "WEAPON"—AIR TRANSPORT

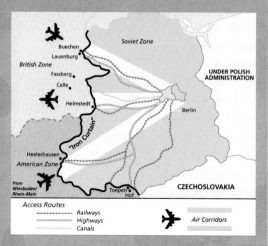

THE POST-WORLD WAR II LANDSCAPE
After World War II, the Allies split Germany into four zones: American, British, French, and Soviet. They also divided Germany's capital, Berlin, into four sectors. Berlin's location many miles inside the Soviet zone created tensions among the Allies that resulted in the Berlin airlift.

FLIGHT CORRIDORS INTO BERLIN
Despite the surface blockade, the Western powers could reach Berlin by three 20-mile-wide aircraft corridors.

IN JUNE 1948, within a few months of the Communist power grab in Czechoslovakia, the Soviets challenged Western access to Berlin. The available US nuclear retaliatory force consisted of some three dozen B-29s with crews in varying stages of training, fewer than 50 atomic bombs, and three weapons-assembly teams that were still training. The Soviets' attempt to absorb Berlin did not result in military retaliation. Instead, the West mounted the greatest supply operation in aviation history to the isolated city. The West referred to this operation as the Berlin airlift, or "Operation Vittles."

The blockade's roots grew out of the way the Allies had divided Germany and its capital, Berlin, after World War II. Under that arrangement, the Soviets controlled the eastern half of Germany and one sector of Berlin. The United States, Britain, and France administered the western half of Germany and three sectors of Berlin. The hitch was that Berlin lay deep within the Soviet zone.

Once the Soviets decided they wanted all of Berlin, they stopped all surface transportation of goods into the city's Western-controlled sectors. This put 2.5 million West Berliners at risk. German winters are harsh. Without food and coal, the people of Berlin would starve or freeze to death. In stopping the free flow of goods into the city, the Soviets were reinterpreting an understanding in force among the World War II Allies since 1945 that allowed the United States, Britain, and France to travel from western Germany through the Soviet zone to their sectors in Berlin. No written agreement covered road, rail, or barge traffic, which left these forms of transportation vulnerable to Soviet whims. However, the four powers had agreed on three 20-mile-wide aircraft corridors in and out of Berlin. With the

BERLIN AIRLIFT RINGMASTER
Lieutenant General Curtis LeMay was in charge of getting 4,500 tons of supplies a day by aircraft to US military crews and West Berliners for more than a year.

Soviet blockade in place, the Western powers could reach their sectors only by air. Because no one had ever attempted an airlift of this magnitude, the Soviets assumed that the West would release all of Berlin into Soviet hands.

Soviet pressure on West Berlin began in April 1948, when the Soviets briefly halted all cargo intended for Western troops stationed in the capital. The Soviets were at this time targeting the Allied troops, not the city's residents. In a sense it was a test run—for both sides—of what was to come in June. Lieutenant General Curtis LeMay, commander of US Air Forces in Europe, rounded up C-47 transports to keep the garrisons supplied. This first blockade lasted 10 days.

By the time the Soviets launched a more aggressive blockade of the entire western half of Berlin in June 1948, LeMay's headquarters in Wiesbaden, Germany, had already drawn up a contingency plan for resuming the airlift if the Soviet Union revived the blockade. On June 18, Soviet authorities announced new restrictions designed not only to prevent military supply deliveries but also to isolate the US, British, and French sectors

of Berlin. The Soviets explained that the expanded blockade was retaliation against the Allies for introducing a new currency into their sectors of Germany. They claimed that the new currency would destroy the value of the existing scrip, and that it was the Allies' first attempt to merge their zones to create a West German state. The Soviet Union, which had lost 28 million people during World War II, was terrified at the thought of a reemerging German nation.

The Western response

President Harry S. Truman decided that the United States should meet this challenge with an airlift, not with military force. To feed and warm 2.5 million Berliners, the West had to figure out how to deliver 4,500 tons of food and fuel to the city each day. General Lucius Clay, head of the US military government in Germany, asked LeMay to launch an airlift on June 26, 1948. Clay said that people would likely

GENERAL LUCIUS CLAY
General Lucius Clay, head of the US military government in Europe, directed Curtis LeMay to begin the Allied airlift on June 26, 1948.

call him "the craziest man in the world," yet he went forward with his plan. LeMay sent his command's C-47s on 32 flights that day from Wiesbaden and Rhein-Main Air Bases with 80 tons of food. Each plane could carry about three tons. Thus began a more than yearlong operation in conjunction with British and US Navy transports.

The C-47 workhorse transports of World War II were at first reinforced and then replaced by four-engine Douglas C-54s, which had three times the cargo capacity of the older aircraft. The Air Force marshaled the resources of the Tactical Air Command (TAC) and the Military Air Transport Service, calling in C-54s from as far away as Alaska, the Caribbean, and Hawaii. TAC also provided a few Fairchild C-82 troop transports—new, twin-boom, twin-engine aircraft that loaded through large doors in the rear of the fuselage.

GOONEY BIRD
The C-47 cargo plane transported goods to Western troops in Berlin in April 1948 and took part in the Berlin airlift later that year.

LONGTIME ALLIES

Britain's Chief of Air Staff Lord Arthur Tedder greets US Air Force Chief of Staff General Carl Spaatz at RAF Northolt in 1948. The two men played pivotal roles in their respective services during World War II and in the years immediately following.

The Fairchild C-82 could accommodate bulky cargo more easily than the C-47 or the C-54. The Royal Air Force (RAF) took part with its Sunderland flying boats, which could land on Berlin's Havel Lakes, and Avro Yorks, which were transports based on Lancaster bombers.

The Air Force rushed fighters and bombers into the region to support the mission, too. When Soviet authorities closed the surface routes, the Air Force had only one group of piston-engine fighters in Germany, along with a single squadron of B-29s on a rotational deployment from a bombardment group based at Smoky Hill Air Force Base, Kansas. General Clay asked that the rest of the B-29s, as well as an F-80 jet fighter group scheduled for deployment to Germany, be sent immediately. President Truman approved the request. In July the bombardment group's other two B-29 squadrons joined the squadron at Fuerstenfeldbruck, and the F-80s arrived at Neubiberg in August.

The question of sending B-29s to bases in the United Kingdom arose again. While the British were at first eager to accept the bombers at bases that US General Carl Spaatz and RAF Air Marshal Arthur Tedder had picked in 1946, they hesitated when the Soviets seemed willing to negotiate their way out of the sticky Berlin situation. But after Soviet attitudes

LOCKHEED P-80A SHOOTING STAR

The first operational American jet fighter, the P-80 arrived in Europe too late to see action during World War II. Although it was designed around the de Havilland Goblin engine, production models were equipped with an American power unit. By the time of the Korean War (1950), the (redesignated) F-80 was the USAF's front-line fighter.

TROOP CARRIER

CQ-581

hardened, the British agreed to the American request, and President Truman approved two group deployments.

The aircraft, however, were not equipped for atomic bombs. Throughout the crisis, the nuclear strike force remained in the southwestern United States, where it continued to train. Soviet Premier Josef Stalin presumably realized this and discounted any atomic threat from B-29s at British bases. In any event, the blockade remained in place for 10 months after the bombers' arrival in July. In other words, airlift, not strategic bombardment, was the US response to the Berlin crisis.

Truman intended to supply Berlin until the Soviet Union realized the Western powers would not abandon the city. Air Force Chief of Staff General Hoyt S. Vandenberg directed the Military Air Transport Service to join in the operation under LeMay's US Air Forces in Europe by forming a task force headquarters. Major General William H. Tunner, a staff officer of the Military Air Transport Service, headed the new

"The sound of the engines is music to our ears."

AN ANONYMOUS BERLINER
WRITING AT THE TIME
OF THE BERLIN AIRLIFT

organization. Tunner knew quite a bit about supply missions. He had maintained the flow of supplies from India across the Himalayas to China in 1944 and 1945. Late in July 1948, Tunner took over from Brigadier General Joseph Smith, whom LeMay had placed in charge when the airlift began a month earlier.

The airlift's complexity argued for a single headquarters to manage the endless stream of transports to and from Berlin. The transports would land and unload at Gatow Airfield in the British sector of Berlin, Templehof in the American sector, and Tegel in the French sector. Although located in the French sector, Tegel was built by the United States for its own use during the Berlin airlift. Since the American transports outnumbered British, some US aircraft began operating from air bases in the British zone of Germany. This reduced their flying time because the British zone was closer to Berlin, and it also spread the volume of traffic more evenly

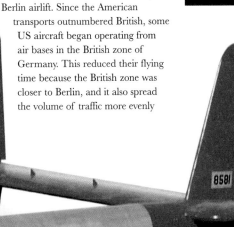

WORLD WAR II SUPPLY EXPERT
Major General William H. Tunner kept supplies flowing across the Himalayas during World War II. He put that experience to use when he headed a task force during the Berlin airlift.

over the western corridors. Regardless of the point of origin of the flight or the assigned airport, flight controllers at the Berlin traffic center handled all aircraft. Tunner had no trouble persuading LeMay that it was necessary to manage the US and British flights through one command post. However, the British preferred not to cede control to the United States. Not until mid-October 1948, when winter threatened to further complicate the airlift, did RAF Air Marshal Tedder and LeMay agree on a combined task force commanded by Tunner with British Air Commodore J.W.F. Merer as deputy. Around this time, Lieutenant General John K. Cannon, one of the most prominent tactical air commanders of World War II, succeeded LeMay as head of the US Air Forces in Europe. LeMay returned to the United States to head the Strategic Air Command (SAC).

ROOMY TRANSPORT
The C-82 troop transport could carry bulky cargo more easily than the C-47 or the C-54.

Winter challenges

Winter not only brought bad flying weather but also forced Tunner to devote a disproportionate amount of space in the cargo hold to coal. Coal was bulky and difficult to handle, yet essential to the city's survival. The change of seasons also encouraged the Soviets to harass transports in hopes of further discouraging Allied aircraft already facing winter storms and darkness. The Soviets did not shoot at the US or British aircraft, however.

WINTER OBSTACLES
The Berlin airlift continued through heavy snows and long winter nights.

The winter weather proved as bad as expected, but the American and British airmen overcame clouds, fog, and darkness by relying on ground-controlled approach radar that helped airfield controllers guide incoming aircraft. Radar cleared the way for a smooth airlift. It made it possible to synchronize operations and maintain a steady flow of aircraft, day and night, in good weather and in bad. Throughout the winter, transports arrived at Berlin's airfields in three-minute intervals. Each pilot had one chance to land; if he could not, he had to return to his point of origin and reenter the cycle. By February 1949, some 8,000 tons of food and fuel were reaching Berlin daily. The Allies were showing they had grit and determination no matter the odds.

GIANT GLOBEMASTER
USAF personnel and civilians unload flour from the cargo hold of a Douglas C-47 Globemaster at Gatow Airfield in Berlin.

In the end, the Soviet Union's blockade proved counterproductive. Rather than discouraging a union of the Western occupation zones, it forced the Western democracies toward closer cooperation. Consequently, by spring 1949, the Soviet Union entered into negotiations with the Allies to discuss access to Berlin. The chief negotiators were Phillip C. Jessup, US ambassador to the United Nations, and Jacob Malik, the Soviet representative on the United Nations Security Council. The two sides signed an agreement on May 5, 1949, that lifted the blockade just one week later. The agreement, however, did not settle the basic issue of freedom of access. Despite resumption of surface traffic into the city, the Allies continued the airlift until September 30 to build up a reserve of food, fuel, and other supplies in case the Soviets resumed the blockade. The Western democracies had won the first "battle" of the Cold War without firing a shot.

POPULAR CARGO CARRIER
Children standing on rubble in West Berlin wave to a Douglas C-47 in the early stages of the Berlin airlift. The C-47s could not carry a sufficient weight of cargo to supply the city and were soon replaced by the four-engine Douglas C-54 Skymasters.

UNLOADING AT TEMPLEHOF
C-47s unload at Templehof Airfield in Berlin.

By the time the Berlin airlift ended in September 1949, the Anglo-American effort had delivered 2.3 million tons of cargo. US aircraft carried roughly 1.7 million tons, of which 1.4 million was coal. Allied aircraft had made around 277,000 trips. The sustained operations were surprisingly safe despite crowded airways and bad weather. Flight crews, air-traffic controllers, and ground crews displayed tremendous discipline. The airlift's accident rate averaged half that of the entire Air Force. All told, 54 Allied airmen died, including 30 US Airmen and one civilian, in 12 crashes.

The airlift was a technological triumph, but its success depended on individual courage and dedication as well as Allied teamwork. Nearly every Air Force command took part to some degree. Airmen assigned to US Air Forces in Europe supported the mission at the same time that they performed their routine German-occupation duties and prepared for possible combat with the Soviets. Although TAC, the Navy, and the Royal Air Force provided transports and crews, the Military Air Transport Service did most of the flying, trained replacements, and flew spare parts and other vital cargo across the Atlantic Ocean.

The Air Materiel Command provided maintenance and logistic support in the United States, while the Air Weather Service produced forecasts. The Army Transportation Corps efficiently handled ground transportation with drivers braving Germany's icy roads to haul cargo from the Bremerhaven port to the airfields for delivery to Berlin. The Army Corps of Engineers built and maintained runways, including the new airfield at Tegel. In addition to

LUFTBRÜCKE BERLIN

REMEMBRANCE STAMP
A West German commemorative stamp celebrates the "air bridge" that kept West Berlin supplied with food and fuel through the winter of 1948–49. Only a few years earlier, Allied aircraft had been bombing the city.

transports, Navy tankers carried fuel and oil across the Atlantic. To keep the airlift going, military and civilian mechanics worked around the clock at maintenance depots in Germany and England, and technicians in the United States completely overhauled every transport after it had flown 1,000 hours in the Berlin corridors. Hundreds of French and British military personnel and civilians joined refugees displaced by World War II in loading and unloading aircraft. The airlift turned normally mundane duties such as air-traffic control and logistics into heroic efforts.

THE CANDY BOMBER

PILOTS HAD LITTLE TO DO while waiting for their cargo aircraft to be unloaded in Berlin. One day, trying to pass the time, 1st Lieutenant Gail Halvorsen talked with some German children peering through the airport fence. They asked him for candy; he told them that the next time he flew in, he would wiggle the wings of his plane and parachute them small packages of candy.

Halvorsen kept his promise. He rigged miniature parachutes with American candy bars and gum, and dropped them over Berlin. Soon other pilots were helping. German children who did not live near the airport wrote to Halvorsen asking for candy drops in their neighborhoods. To them, Halvorsen was "Uncle Wiggly Wings" and "the Candy Bomber."

1ST LIEUTENANT GAIL HALVORSEN
The C-54 pilot preparing for his next candy drop over Berlin.

BLOCKADE LIFTED
A cheer is raised at the news in May 1949 that the Soviet blockade of Berlin has been lifted. To ensure that Berliners would have sufficient supplies should the blockade resume, the airlift continued until the following September.

The consequences

One consequence of the Berlin crisis was to show radar's importance in directing aircraft in bad weather and at night. With so much attention focused on the nuclear strike force, the crisis was an important reminder of the value of transport aircraft. The airlift had other military and diplomatic consequences, as well. For one, the uncertainty of continued access to Berlin raised the possibility of a war with the Soviets. This in turn made the Air Force question how ready SAC was for war. Even before Soviet officials sealed off Berlin's western sectors, Air Force Chief of Staff General Vandenberg asked Atlantic solo pilot Charles Lindbergh to determine SAC's combat readiness and to recommend improvements. Lindbergh had been a technical adviser to the Army Air Forces during World War II. His report verified growing concerns within Air Force headquarters. He found that the attempt to model SAC after the pre–World War II Air Corps was a mistake. Some pilots and crew, forced to learn several flying and nonflying jobs, failed to master any of them. Continual training left no time to prepare realistically for combat. Lindbergh suggested greater emphasis on specialization, on training that would "simulate probable wartime missions," and on better pay and benefits to attract the best people.

Little more than 10 months later, the Allies faced a new Cold War crisis that would put these recommendations to the test: the Korean War.

DOCTRINE AND HISTORY—THE BERLIN AIRLIFT

DISTINCTIVE CAPABILITIES	FUNCTIONS (MISSIONS)	DOCTRINAL EMPHASIS
• Rapid Global Mobility	• Airlift	• Strategic Airlift • Theater Airlift

10

LEMAY AND NUCLEAR DETERRENCE

THE UNITED STATES decided early on that the Air Force's main role would be to deliver a strategic nuclear blow to any enemy; however, moving that idea from theory to reality was easier said than done. Deciding which kind of planes to use and where to base them was only part of the calculus: American and Soviet development of rockets and missiles, often using captured German technology, promised new ways of delivering a nuclear strike. In the United States, inter-service rivalries continued as the Navy sought to claim a share of the strategic mission.

THE EMERGENCE OF STRATEGIC AIR COMMAND

DETERRENCE LOOKED GOOD ON PAPER, BUT MAKING IT WORK TOOK A GREAT DEAL OF EFFORT AND ORGANIZATIONAL SKILL

IN THE YEARS immediately following World War II, the sole Air Force command charged with delivering nuclear weapons with the era's new bomber fleets was Strategic Air Command (SAC). In October 1948, war-tested General Curtis LeMay stepped in as head of SAC at Air Force Chief of Staff General Hoyt S. Vandenberg's request. Taking charge of SAC was natural for LeMay because he understood nuclear weapons and bombers. During World War II, he had commanded B-17 bombers in the European theater, then B-29 bombers in the Pacific theater. Right after the war, he served as deputy chief of staff, Research and Development, working with the Manhattan Project—which had developed the atomic bomb—and the Atomic Energy Commission on nuclear weapons development and production from 1945–47.

LeMay's new assignment gave him the chance to make nuclear deterrence work. He launched a 10-year campaign to turn SAC into the most proficient bombing command in the armed forces. One of the first things LeMay did was to move SAC's headquarters from Andrews Air Force Base in Maryland to Offutt Air Force Base in Nebraska. Completed by November 1948, the move reflected concern that coastal bases were more vulnerable to attack than inland bases. LeMay also ordered all B-29 divisions to report to him. His predecessor—General George C. Kenney—had given some autonomy to divisions

overseas, but in April 1949, LeMay assumed control of all matters relating to B-29s, no matter their location. He also emphasized training and planning. In April 1950 he realigned the Second, Eighth, and Fifteenth Air Forces by assigning bombers and reconnaissance aircraft to each one, as well as granting command of units and bases in specific US regions to each of these forces.

The North Atlantic Treaty Organization's (NATO) establishment in 1949 further defined SAC's mission. According to NATO's charter, an attack on one NATO member would be considered an attack on all. The Truman administration had two motives in joining NATO: to contain Communism and to control military spending by countries jointly defending one another through a common organization. Truman was still concerned about paying back the country's war debts. During NATO's early years, however, the battered European nations needed military assistance from the United States. Additionally, US leaders reasoned that as Europe's economy recovered in the postwar years, it would be less expensive for the United States to contain Communism by working through NATO than by fighting that battle alone.

When the Soviets detonated their first nuclear bomb in September 1949, Truman was concerned enough that he approved work on thermonuclear (hydrogen fusion) weapons.

MANY DUTIES
In the postwar years, President Harry S. Truman worked to keep the nation secure, balance its budget, and contain Communism.

STRONG INFLUENCE
General Curtis LeMay led SAC from October 1948 to June 1957. He was one of the greatest influences on the command during the tense Cold War years.

Still, he held most military spending in check. Although deterrence and SAC were key to national defense, he limited the Air Force to 48 combat groups, unchanged since the service had become independent.

Truman also called for a military policy review that resulted in NSC-68, a paper the National Security Council and Truman approved in April 1950. The document described the Soviet Union's advances in nuclear technology and its superior conventional forces. It concluded that direct, armed aggression by the Soviet Union seemed unlikely, since the United States had the nuclear advantage; nonetheless, it warned that the country must prepare for just such an act. The more likely threat NSC-68 outlined was "piecemeal aggression." This would come in the form of limited war begun by a Soviet satellite state. In that case, the United States would have to rearm for both general and local wars to meet Soviet aggression at almost any level.

This observation would prove prescient in light of the Korean War, Vietnam War, and later conflicts, but the Air Force, Army, and Navy could not get the funds to prepare for these scenarios. None had enough manpower or equipment. Despite the communist threat, the Truman administration placed its greatest emphasis on a balanced budget. Frustrated by funding shortages, Air Force Secretary Stuart Symington resigned in 1950. Air Force advocate Thomas K. Finletter took his place.

In this environment, SAC remained at best a token deterrent; however, the Berlin airlift had inadvertently given SAC some of the boost it needed. It now had a growing presence in Europe, even though its overseas bombers were not part of the atomic force. When the Berlin blockade ended, B-29s were operating from seven airfields in the United Kingdom. The British government had also agreed to share costs of rebuilding four Royal Air Force bases to accommodate the new B-36s and the jet-powered B-47s when they became available for deployment.

The Berlin airlift had other consequences. By August 1948 the Air Force's tactical air strength in Europe had doubled. Three F-80 squadrons were now stationed at Fuerstenfeldbruck. In January 1949 the US Air Forces in Europe formed the 2d Air Division at Landsberg Air Base in Germany. In May the Air Force began developing a new air-defense system with six fighter squadrons, also in Germany, and four radar stations. These formed the foundation of NATO's military arm, which would take shape in 1950.

All these changes proved that military strategy is constantly evolving. Nuclear deterrence altered the way the country planned to defend itself and to allocate its budget. US nuclear superiority over the Soviet Union was its greatest defense. When the United States entered the Korean War, General Vandenberg cautioned against wasting scarce bombers and personnel to peck at the periphery of Communist power in the Far East. The Air Force's focus, he believed, had to be on maintaining and increasing whatever strength SAC possessed through wise leadership and weapons development.

Scientific breakthroughs

While the Air Force took slow but sure steps to build up its bomber fleet, the scientific community made more rapid advances. Breakthroughs in nuclear technology came as early as spring 1948. Scientists handed the US military lighter, more compact atomic bombs after tests at Eniwetok Atoll in the Pacific. Scientists and engineers had handcrafted the early, bulky atomic bombs—such as those dropped on Japan—in their labs. But now factories could mass-produce the new, lighter atomic weapons. This had two effects. First, the advance made it possible for Tactical Air Command to at last take part in SAC's deterrence mission. Second, it paved the way for the emergence of the intercontinental missile in the late 1950s. Fitted with the new lightweight warheads, the missile could also play a nuclear-deterrent role.

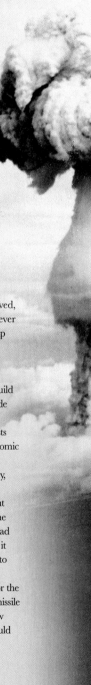

ATOMIC TESTING
Eniwetok Atoll was the site of atomic and hydrogen bomb tests in 1948, 1951, 1952, and 1954. The atoll is part of the Marshall Islands in the Pacific.

SWEARING IN
Thomas K. Finletter (left) is sworn in as secretary of the Air Force on April 24, 1950.

Another major breakthrough that occurred around this time further secured US superiority over the Soviets. After the Soviet Union tested its first atomic bomb, Truman approved work on the first hydrogen bomb. At first scientists were not sure whether they could produce this weapon, which was even more powerful than the atomic bomb. The hydrogen bomb would raise destructive yields from the range of kilotons to megatons, from the equivalent of thousands of tons to millions of tons of chemical explosives. It got its power from the energy released by the fusion of the heavier isotopes of the hydrogen atom to form new elements, a reaction occurring only when intense heat generated by a fission device acted upon those isotopes. Because of the heat needed, people sometimes referred to the hydrogen bomb as a thermonuclear weapon. But as time passed, popular use blurred the distinction between nuclear and thermonuclear. Nuclear war became a conflict involving atomic and hydrogen devices, both of which tended to be categorized, however inaccurately, as nuclear weapons.

NEW PRESIDENT
Former Army General Dwight D. Eisenhower was president of the United States from 1953 to 1961. In this photo, the president holds a press conference.

On October 31, 1952, a test explosion of a hydrogen bomb vaporized an entire island in the Eniwetok Atoll. It left a crater two miles deep and one mile wide. Scientists began wondering about the practicality of a bomb this powerful. It clearly could not be used to defend densely populated areas in western Europe, for instance. A group of scientists began advocating for greater emphasis on air defense over deterrence. Even so, the Truman administration and Secretary of the Air Force Finletter continued to focus on SAC and on high-yield nuclear bombs. The Soviets detonated their first hydrogen bomb in 1953.

Diversions for air defense

Although Truman acknowledged SAC as the key to the nation's defense, he thought additional funds should be earmarked for other defense-related purposes. He approved a bigger defense budget with additional funds put toward air-defense measures such as radar and jet fighters designed to intercept enemy bombers. The Air Defense Command regained its independence in 1951 from the Continental Air Command. Fighters developed under this larger budget included the Lockheed F-94, the Northrop F-89, and the North American F-86D. Military and civilian research groups explored ways to install a radar system that would stretch from the Arctic Circle to Greenland, Alaska, Hawaii, and Scotland, to warn of approaching Soviet bombers. The radar system would cost $370 million to install and $106 million a year to operate.

AIR DEFENSE COMMAND FIGHTER
In the early 1950s President Harry S. Truman approved a larger defense budget so the Air Defense Command could develop new fighters. Among them was the Lockheed F-94. This is the first one Lockheed built.

Finletter and SAC felt their mission threatened by these defense diversions. Finletter was not against a widespread warning network, but Air Force policy was to make changes gradually. Truman agreed. While he endorsed the Distant Early Warning Line (DEW Line), he offered no funding for it before he left office in 1953.

Former Army General Dwight D. Eisenhower, who succeeded Truman as president in 1953, also firmly believed in nuclear deterrence, but he placed greater emphasis on air defense than the previous administration had. In 1954 the Air Defense Command became the Continental Air Defense Command, and it included joint efforts by the Air Force, Army, and Navy. It reported to the Joint Chiefs of Staff. In 1957 the Continental Air Defense Command became the US component of the North American Air Defense Command, which worked with Canada

CONVAIR F-106 DELTA DART
While the F-102 problems were being fixed, a second, more complete redesign was started. Originally known as the F-102B, this became the F-106, as it was completely different, with a more powerful engine and the "wasp-waist" shape necessary for supersonic flight incorporated into the main design. More sophisticated fire-control equipment was installed, including an automatic link to ground detection systems. The F-106 entered service in 1959.

as a full partner. In 1961 construction began on an underground bunker near Colorado Springs, Colorado, to house this command. Eisenhower also got the DEW Line up and running by 1962 to detect aircraft approaching over the polar region. A second radar line in Canada would confirm aircraft course and numbers, and controllers on the ground would direct interceptors against them.

One of the big questions with which the Air Defense Command grappled in this era was whether its role was simply to support SAC or to deter an enemy attack on its own. Meanwhile, Soviet technology was improving. In 1955 the Soviet Union revealed its newest jet bomber to Western observers during a May Day parade. This bomber flew too fast for US jets to intercept it. In 1957 the Soviets sent *Sputnik*, their first satellite, into space using a rocket that could also deliver bombs to the United States if the two countries ever went to war. No air-defense system existed at the time to stop missiles. Furthermore, the US Air Defense Command was struggling with interceptor designs. Its F-102 could not even break the sound barrier until an engineer named Richard Whitcomb discovered that its straight fuselage created drag. Whitcomb then pinched the fuselage so it resembled a Coca-Cola bottle. This design, also applied to the F-106 and other supersonic aircraft, resulted in the term "Coke bottle" configuration.

Airpower boosters like former Air Force Secretary Symington began speaking publicly about a "missile gap" with the Soviet Union. Before 1957 people's fears centered on a bomber gap. Symington could easily garner attention because he had been elected a US senator from Missouri. During the 1960 presidential election, Democratic candidate John F. Kennedy pounced on the perceived missile gap as proof the Eisenhower administration was not doing enough to protect the country. His Republican opponent—Richard M. Nixon, who had served as Eisenhower's vice president for eight years—denied the existence of such a gap.

CONVAIR F-102 DELTA DAGGER
Although Convair had built the world's first delta-winged aircraft in 1948, this supersonic all-weather interceptor caused the company severe embarrassment when it failed to exceed Mach 1. However, a rapid emergency redesign program, reshaping the fuselage to reduce drag, ensured that the F-102 entered service three years late in 1956.

SPY IN THE SKY

The top-secret Lockheed U-2 spy plane was a unique source of intelligence for the United States until the advent of reconnaissance satellites in the 1960s.

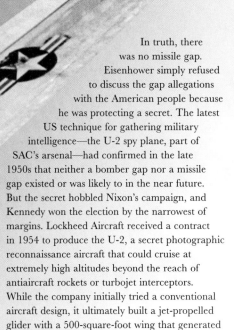

In truth, there was no missile gap. Eisenhower simply refused to discuss the gap allegations with the American people because he was protecting a secret. The latest US technique for gathering military intelligence—the U-2 spy plane, part of SAC's arsenal—had confirmed in the late 1950s that neither a bomber gap nor a missile gap existed or was likely to in the near future. But the secret hobbled Nixon's campaign, and Kennedy won the election by the narrowest of margins. Lockheed Aircraft received a contract in 1954 to produce the U-2, a secret photographic reconnaissance aircraft that could cruise at extremely high altitudes beyond the reach of antiaircraft rockets or turbojet interceptors. While the company initially tried a conventional aircraft design, it ultimately built a jet-propelled glider with a 500-square-foot wing that generated lift even in the thin air above 70,000ft (21,335m). (Air at that height is only 3 percent as dense as air at sea level.) The catch was no one had an engine that worked in such thin air. So Lockheed enlisted the aircraft-engineering company Pratt & Whitney to design one, and Shell Oil developed a special fuel. By 1955 the United States had a working U-2.

As impressive as the U-2 was from an aeronautical engineering standpoint, its ability to gather intelligence depended upon the B-2 camera. Scanning continuously, it covered the ground beneath the aircraft from horizon to horizon with such a fine resolution that a golf ball was visible from 10 miles (16km) up.

Another way to satisfy reconnaissance ambitions was through satellites. A satellite race erupted between the Soviet Union and the United States in the 1950s. The Soviets launched *Sputnik* and *Sputnik II* in 1957. The Army sent up the United States' first satellite, *Explorer I*, in 1958. While SAC did not take part in this open competition between the two countries, it had been, with the RAND

Corporation's help, looking into the feasibility of satellites as surveillance instruments since 1946. The nonprofit research organization called satellites a "world-circling spaceship."

Despite all the excitement over interceptors, radar, and satellites in the 1950s, SAC was still at the heart of the nation's military policy. During the Korean War—in which SAC participated in limited fashion with conventional B-29s—SAC grew from 59,000 officers and enlisted personnel to 153,000, a rate of growth that slightly exceeded the Air Force's overall rate of growth from 411,000 to 978,000 during that same period.

SAC aircraft

Strategic Air Command airpower went through some transformations as well. The command was slowly phasing out its B-29 and replacing it with a modern version called the B-50. It received its first shipments of B-47 Stratojets from Boeing, 45 of which SAC sent to Britain in 1953. However, the B-36 was still SAC's heaviest and longest-range bomber. Engineers fitted it with four jet auxiliary engines mounted in pairs in pods beneath its wings. Nuclear deterrence fell mostly on the B-36 and the B-50 throughout the Korean War and for some years after. The B-47 was as yet untested, and the eight-engine B-52 was in development and would not enter service until 1955.

The B-29 found a new function in its retirement: tanker aircraft. The renamed KB-29 and the new KC-97 increased

SAC FIGHTER
The swept-wing F-84F joined SAC's fighter-bomber program in 1954.

AERIAL PHOTOGRAPHY
The U-2's effectiveness depended on a camera that could take photos from more than 70,000ft (21,335km) above Earth. James Baker designed the B-2 camera.

the aerial tanker fleet from 139 to 359 in 1953. After Korea, SAC conducted reconnaissance with specially equipped versions of the B-36, B-50, B-47, B-29, and the North American B-45 jet light bomber.

In addition to bombers, tankers, and reconnaissance aircraft, the command flew fighters. Because of the B-36's operating altitude, the B-47's speed, and the availability of lighter, smaller atomic weapons, SAC freed its fighters from their escort role and enlisted them as nuclear bombers. Its fighter-escort groups (soon to be called wings) switched from Republic F-84Es to F-84Gs in 1953, and from the straight-wing G model to the swept-wing F-84F model in 1954. The F model served in the fighter-bomber program until 1957, when SAC phased out its fighter fleet.

FIRST US SATELLITE
The Army launched Explorer I *in 1958 using its Jupiter rocket.* Explorer I *was the first US satellite.*

Boeing B-52 Stratofortress

> "Moving from a B-47 bomber to the 'Buff' was like progressing from a sportster to a stretched limousine."

CAPTAIN GENE DEATRICK
1950S TEST PILOT

THE BOEING B-52, KNOWN to Airmen as the "Buff," has proved the most durable military aircraft in aviation history. First delivered to Strategic Air Command in June 1955, it is still used in frontline service today. The B-52 was designed specifically to drop nuclear bombs on the Soviet Union. But it turned out to be highly adaptable, able to change from high-altitude missions to low-level attack, to provide a platform for cruise missiles, and to operate as a conventional bomber of awesome power in regional conflicts.

The B-52 was able to carry an impressive bombload in the bomb bay or on pods under the wings. The "Big Belly" modification of the B-52D, for example, could carry 60,000lbs (27,200kg) of bombs—almost five times the capacity of a World War II "heavy" such as the Lancaster.

The B-52 features a twin-deck forward fuselage. The pilot and copilot sit above, while the navigator and radar navigator crouch in the "black hole" below. The navigators' ejection seats fire downward—a worrying fact on low-level missions. The electronic warfare officer (EWO) sits facing backward at the rear of the upper deck, with the gunner alongside, operating a tail gun by remote control. In early models of the B-52, the gunner sat in a tail turret, buffeted and shaken a good deal. Coming in to the forward fuselage (in later models) made this job less isolated and uncomfortable.

Because it was originally thought that the B-52 would be attacked by missiles, it does not feature all-around guns (and partly accounts for the small crew of six). Missiles were instead dealt with by electronic countermeasures and chaff that blocked or distracted the missiles' homing systems.

Weapons pylon attachment point

Windshield wiper

Terrain display indicator

Throttle quadrant

Attitude indicator

Control yoke

Rubber pedals

Ejection seat

CRAMPED CADILLAC
Despite the fact that the B-52 has been dubbed "the Cadillac of the skies," there is little room in the cockpit—or elsewhere. A person of average size is unable to stand upright anywhere in the craft, and only the pilots are able to see outside.

TALL TAIL
Although over the years the B-52 has progressed through a series of models and modifications, one of the constant features has been the tall vertical tail. However, on the B-52G the tail is almost 8ft (2.5m) shorter than those found on previous models.

Radar warning antenna

Escape/ejection hatches

Turbojet engines

Turret containing television scanner

Forward main undercarriage

Twin engine nacelles

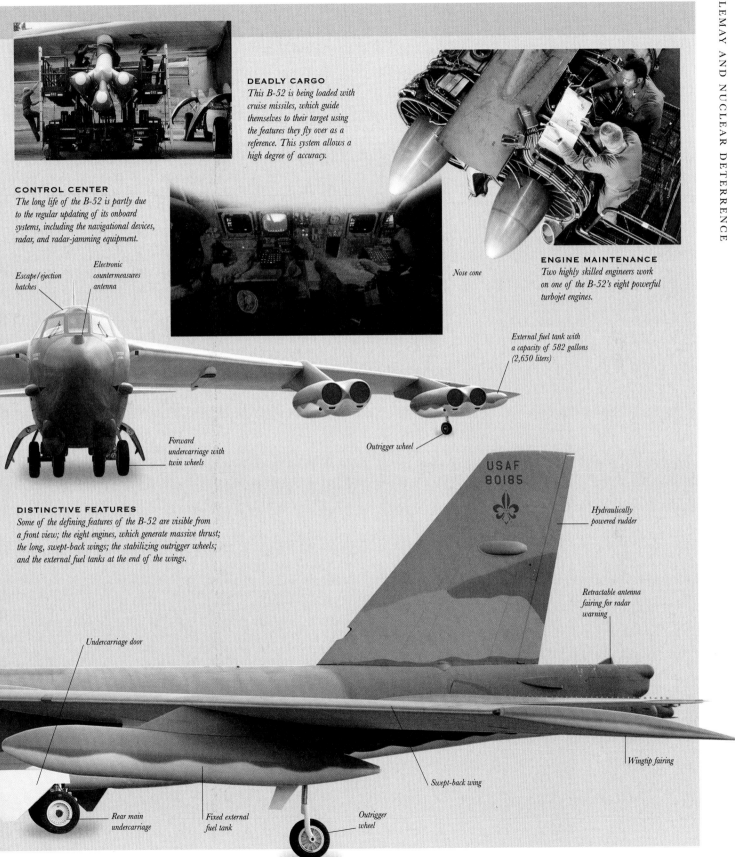

DEADLY CARGO
This B-52 is being loaded with cruise missiles, which guide themselves to their target using the features they fly over as a reference. This system allows a high degree of accuracy.

CONTROL CENTER
The long life of the B-52 is partly due to the regular updating of its onboard systems, including the navigational devices, radar, and radar-jamming equipment.

Nose cone

ENGINE MAINTENANCE
Two highly skilled engineers work on one of the B-52's eight powerful turbojet engines.

Escape/ejection hatches

Electronic countermeasures antenna

External fuel tank with a capacity of 582 gallons (2,650 liters)

Forward undercarriage with twin wheels

Outrigger wheel

DISTINCTIVE FEATURES
Some of the defining features of the B-52 are visible from a front view; the eight engines, which generate massive thrust; the long, swept-back wings; the stabilizing outrigger wheels; and the external fuel tanks at the end of the wings.

USAF 80185

Hydraulically powered rudder

Retractable antenna fairing for radar warning

Undercarriage door

Wingtip fairing

Rear main undercarriage

Fixed external fuel tank

Outrigger wheel

Swept-back wing

A new strategy

Under LeMay, mass bombing became a thing of the past. He replaced the World War II strategy with multiple attacks by independent aircraft timed to confuse enemy defenses and to hit as many targets as rapidly as possible. To do this, each crew had to be as skilled as any lead crew in one of the large formations that the Eighth Air Force dispatched against Germany during the war. He demanded realistic training exercises. During the first such exercise, staged over Dayton, Ohio, in 1949, every single crew failed miserably to find its target. With continuous, vigorous training, LeMay turned things around. By 1951 he had converted the command into a true nuclear strike force capable of prompt retaliation should deterrence fail.

Much of SAC's mission depended on access to bases overseas. These bases permitted its short-range B-47s to fly deep into the Soviet Union and its long-range B-36s to hit several targets on a single mission. By 1953 the Air Force had 16 bases in the United Kingdom, six designated for bombers. They were vulnerable, however. So even before 1953, the Air Force began reopening a string of air bases built for World War II from Newfoundland and Labrador in Canada, across Greenland, and finally to Iceland. It built others, such as Thule base in Greenland, to put the bomber force some 1,500 miles closer to Soviet territory. Along with the northern bases, the Air Force placed others in places like Spain and Morocco. In this way, the United States managed to encircle the Soviet heartland.

Eisenhower's influence

Along with the Korean War and deterrence, SAC formed a bridge linking the Truman and Eisenhower administrations. Like Truman, Eisenhower worried about driving the country into bankruptcy with too much defense spending. He wanted to achieve "security with solvency"; however, he also believed strongly in SAC's mission to deter nuclear war and contain Communism. Once the Korean War ended, the country needed a new approach to national defense that would protect the United States at an acceptable cost.

Eisenhower directed his Joint Chiefs of Staff to form a committee with members from the Department of Defense and the Bureau of the Budget and asked them to draw up a plan for national defense. Among those serving on the committee was Air Force Chief of Staff General Nathan F. Twining, who commanded the Fifteenth and the Twentieth Air Forces during World War II. The group came with a plan aptly called New Look. Boiled down, this plan declared almost exclusive reliance on SAC. No longer would the United States maintain large land and naval forces. As Twining said when New Look was modestly tweaked in much the same fashion a few years later

into the New New Look, "We cannot afford to keep in our Armed Forces conventional forces for the old type of warfare plus those for atomic warfare. We have got to make up our minds one way or the other."

The New Look concentrated on the Air Force at the expense of the other services. Eisenhower believed SAC's nuclear abilities would avert a major war as well as smaller conflicts. Until the Soviet Union built a comparable nuclear strike force, the mere threat of massive retaliation should prove adequate. Minor crises such as the Berlin blockade would not need to escalate into atomic war. Vice President Richard M. Nixon might vow that the United States would choose the time and place to retaliate against the Soviet Union rather than to allow the Communists to pester the United States with many conflicts around the world, but he was showing the world the highest card in America's hand in hopes it need never be played. In other words, the New Look relied a lot on bluff.

Although all services enhanced their firepower with nuclear weapons during the Eisenhower administration, the emphasis on deterrence and retaliation ensured SAC's dominant role. In effect, Eisenhower endorsed a belief about airpower that predated World War II—the idea that aerial bombardment could deliver the sudden shock that would disable an enemy and force his immediate surrender. Airpower had indeed proved indispensable against Germany, but not in this way. Rather than

THE NEW LOOK
Air Force Chief of Staff General Nathan F. Twining was among those Eisenhower directed to draw up a plan for the nation's defense.

an overwhelming force resulting in immediate surrender, airpower during World War II slowly wore down the enemy's air force, industry, transportation, fuel supply, and, finally, the public will. However, after the bombings of Hiroshima and Nagasaki, airpower as an instrument of shock took hold more strongly than before, and the New Look adopted this view. In this new world, the Air Force was chief among the military services, and SAC was ascendant within the Air Force.

Shortly after the United States adopted the New Look, scholars like William Kaufmann at RAND began asking how practical massive retaliation could possibly be as a deterrent, especially in the face of an expanding Soviet nuclear arsenal. How would the United States react, he asked, if told by the Soviet Union to abandon an overseas commitment or else engage in nuclear war? Would the country accept staggering damage to avoid humiliation? By 1953 the Soviets had detonated a hydrogen bomb more advanced than the earlier American device. The United States had a workable bomb by 1954. Because hydrogen bombs were so much more destructive than atomic bombs, other scholars questioned whether either side would ever dare use it. And, they continued, if neither side dared use it, could it truly serve as a deterrent? Even Nixon feared this outcome in which

AERIAL TANKER
The Boeing KC-135 made refueling in midair safer because it flew fast enough that bombers no longer risked stalling. Here a Convair F-106 refuels from a KC-135, while another fighter waits its turn.

the Communists would nibble away at the non-communist world while shielded beneath a hydrogen umbrella.

General Twining held his ground in favor of nuclear deterrence. He argued that the hydrogen bomb differed from atomic weapons only in its greater destructiveness. The New New Look emerged, which was basically the same as the 1953 New Look. Nuclear deterrence and a small land army prevailed for the balance of the Eisenhower years. Deterrence through overwhelming retaliation allowed Eisenhower to hold defense spending to about $40 billion annually throughout his eight years in office. Meanwhile, Strategic Air Command grew from 158,000 officers and airmen in 1953 to more than 254,000 in 1961, while Air Force personnel as a whole declined from 978,000 to 815,000.

NEW HEAD OF SAC
General Thomas S. Power succeeded General Curtis LeMay as commander in chief of SAC. Power served in that role from July 1957 to November 1964.

Base dispersal

LeMay left SAC in 1957 to become the Air Force's vice chief of staff. In his new post, he dealt frequently with Congress and the Joint Chiefs of Staff, so he could continue supporting his old command. His successor was General Thomas S. Power, who had served as SAC's vice commander for seven years. Throughout both men's tenures at SAC, the command refined its strategy. It originally believed overseas bases were the best way to strike back at the Soviet Union in case of war. That arrangement put US forces close to the enemy and away from what most military thinkers believed would be the Soviets' primary target—American cities. But as time went on and refueling tankers grew more sophisticated (for example, the Boeing KC-135 flew fast enough to eliminate the danger that a high-speed bomber might stall while slowing to refuel), this thinking changed.

B-58 HUSTLER
*The Convair B-58 was the Air Force's first
supersonic bomber.*

However, RAND suggested that overseas bases
were actually quite vulnerable. Pearl Harbor proved
this, as did a 1952 storm with 100mph (160kmph)
winds that struck Carswell Air Force Base, Texas,
and destroyed an entire fleet of B-36s. The Air
Force could see how quickly one small air base
could be obliterated. Therefore, SAC decided it
would be better to station its bombers around the
United States rather than overseas. The aircraft
could refuel in the air and at US overseas bases in
Morocco, Spain, and England as needed (Guam
was added in 1955). By the end of the 1950s, SAC
had 3,207 aircraft, including 1,854 bombers
comprised entirely of B-47s and B-52s. In 1960 it
received its first supersonic bomber, the Convair
B-58, but the new plane was plagued with
problems. By 1959 SAC also had 1,067 tankers,
more than a third of which were KC-135s.

The network of overseas airfields remained
largely intact, even though the emphasis shifted
from basing large numbers of bombers to using
them for tankers, to dispersing small numbers
of bombers, or to recovering aircraft returning
from nuclear strikes. LeMay further honed the
plan by placing crews' quarters close to their
aircraft when it was their turn to be on alert.
General Power extended this practice to overseas
bases in a program called Reflex Action.
Both generals prepped the command for "second
strike," that is, making sure enough bombers
survived a first Soviet onslaught to take to the
air to retaliate. In addition, SAC scattered more
and more of its aircraft to more and more bases
so that no enemy strike could take out too large
a percentage of the command's force all at once.
The bombers and tankers used Air Defense
Command bases and TAC bases; eventually
SAC started keeping some bombers in the air
at all times. This required a change in the
custodianship of the bombs. The Atomic Energy

MISSILE MASTER
*Brigadier General Bernard Schriever was in charge of the
Western Development Division that designed and built
the Air Force's first two missiles, Atlas and Titan.*

AN AROUND-THE-
COUNTRY FLIGHT
*Eight B-52s similar to this
one demonstrated US power
during a nonstop flight around
the perimeter of the United
States in 1956.*

The contractor Convair was working on a missile called Atlas. Mathematician John von Neumann, head of the Department of Defense's Scientific Advisory Board, got permission to use the substitute components to construct a second missile called Titan, in case Convair's Atlas did not work. Martin Company was the Titan contractor. Both missiles were liquid-propellant rockets that had to be fueled shortly before launch because of the fuel's volatility.

Commission had always been responsible for the nuclear weapons. But with the aircrafts' wide dispersal and possible call to retaliate at a moment's notice, that responsibility shifted to the strike forces. Now bases stored nuclear bombs, and aircraft on alert status were loaded with them. One consequence was that air bases might attract saboteurs. To prepare for this possibility, stations beefed up their security and often ran drills.

All these changes meant three things for SAC: maintaining crews on alert, expanding the command's presence and power, and training through exercises and competitions. All this work for the sake of nuclear deterrence would be worth little, however, if the Soviet Union were unaware of US power. Therefore, SAC also put on demonstrations, such as flying eight B-52s nonstop around the United States in 1956. The bombers refueled from KC-97 tankers along the way and covered 15,500 miles (24,945km) in 31 hours, 30 minutes. In this way, the United States showcased its capabilities for the Soviet Union.

Missile power

But some planners in the military and government in Washington, D.C., felt that airpower was more than bombers, tankers, and fighters. It also called for missiles. Some scientists argued for pilotless jet-powered aircraft, others for ballistic missiles. The Germans invented both during World War II. The jet-powered German V-1 killed thousands in Britain but was inaccurate and fairly easy to shoot down, but V-2s presented a bigger problem. The British could not stop them. These ballistic missiles were

guided by radio signals, traveled faster than the speed of sound, and would free fall toward Earth at speeds up to 3,600mph (5,795kmph).

Funds were short in the 1950s, so progress in missiles was slow. But in 1953 Air Force Secretary Harold Talbott's assistant for research and development, Trevor Gardner, formed the Strategic Missile Evaluation Committee. Gardner was in favor of missiles and his committee's report, issued in February 1954, did not disappoint him. Noting that the Soviet Union had detonated a hydrogen bomb the summer before and that the Soviets had access to talented German rocket engineers pressed into service after World War II, the report called for an intensified missile-development program.

Capitalizing on the sense of urgency the committee's report generated, Gardner convinced the Air Force to let him establish a special organization. The Western Development Division's duty was to rush the intercontinental ballistic missile into service. While the Air Research and Development Command would normally handle this sort of project, the Air Force considered missiles urgent enough that they got their own support group. Brigadier General Bernard A. Schriever was in charge of the new division. Since this was such a high priority program, this young yet innovative officer even got permission to use two contractors for every major component of the new weapon. Should one design fail, a substitute would be available. He had contractors working simultaneously on every missile component to speed the process. Schriever coined the term "concurrency" to describe the process.

EARLY MISSILES
*The Air Force's first two missiles were
Atlas (pictured) and Titan.*

In 1955 missiles got even more attention. James R. Killian, special assistant to the president for science and technology, suggested applying research already done to devise an intermediate-range ballistic missile that could quickly travel 1,500 miles (2,415km), from Europe to the Soviet Union. It could enter service before either Atlas or Titan, and serve as a retaliatory weapon much as could a bomber based overseas. This missile was called Thor, and Douglas Aircraft was the lead contractor. Meanwhile, the Army was independently developing its own intermediate-range missile called Redstone (and later Jupiter) with German-born scientist Wernher von Braun's leadership. Like Thor, all missiles had the same defect: reliance on highly volatile and dangerous liquid propellants. Not until Titan II did scientists begin to solve issues with fuel. Titan II used a storable liquid propellant that, although highly toxic, could remain in the missile for long periods. Therefore, Airmen no longer had to fuel missiles right before takeoff. Scientists and engineers also invented solid-propellants, an even more stable fuel. They used it for the new intercontinental Minuteman.

As the Eisenhower administration came to a close, the Air Force and Navy shared responsibility for intercontinental and intermediate-range ballistic missile development, and the Army was restricted to short-range weapons (generally under 200 miles). In 1959 the new National Aeronautics and Space Administration absorbed the Army's von Braun group, whose Jupiter rocket launched the first American satellite in 1958.

Pilotless aircraft projects did not have as much luck as those for ballistic missiles. The North American Navaho made advances in rocket technology, and Secretary of Defense Charles E. Wilson allowed work to continue on the Northrop Snark for a time. But not until the 1980s did this family of weapons become a dependable part of the deterrent force, thanks to the cruise missile and its guidance system.

The Navy's Polaris plan

With all these scientific developments maturing, the Navy also wanted to be part of nuclear deterrence. In the 1950s, it worked on nuclear-powered submarines, missile-carrying submarines, and solid-propellant missiles called Polaris. (Explosive liquid propellants were too dangerous to work with onboard ship.) The Navy argued that with enough missiles to destroy 200 targets, it could deter aggression and end an

INTERMEDIATE-RANGE MISSILE
Thor was an intermediate-range missile with a range of up to 1,500 miles and could be a deterrent to Soviet aggression.

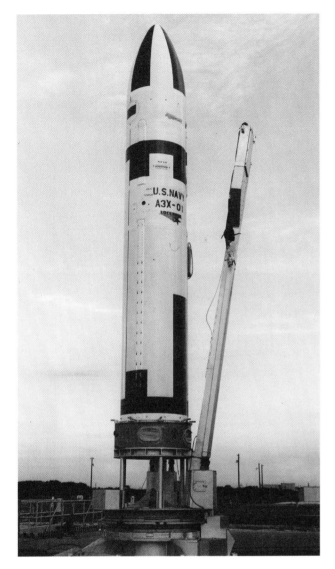

THE NAVY'S ANSWER

The Navy developed its own missile, Polaris. It planned to carry these on its submarine fleet as part of the country's nuclear-deterrent force.

Force argument, the larger, balanced bomber and missile force could minimize the damage to both Soviet and American cities.

However, SAC's General Power did not care much for the latter part of this argument that called for sparing cities. As he said, "The whole idea is to kill the bastards," for he believed in a swift and overwhelming strike against every base or city that contributed significantly to the Communist nations' war-making abilities. He instead expected his target list to expand over the years as intelligence improved. In turn, this would call for more warheads, missiles, bombs, and bombers to destroy every target identified. Furthermore, he was not opposed to Polaris. He simply saw success achieved through many simultaneous means, with SAC in charge.

It was up to Secretary of Defense Thomas S. Gates to make peace among the services. He ordered the Joint Strategic Target Planning Staff—headed by Power but including officers from the Army and Navy—to pick targets for Polaris missiles. Power stacked the group with additional SAC representatives to shut out the Navy. Nonetheless, President Eisenhower approved the staff's conclusions as the best he could hope for under the circumstances. Their plan was not much more than an enlargement of the New New Look that incorporated Polaris.

SAC at the end of Eisenhower's term

By the time Eisenhower left office in 1961, the Air Force had fewer personnel overall but Strategic Air Command had more than it had when he took office eight years earlier. The administration spared SAC principally because the dispersal policy required more security and maintenance specialists at outlying airfields. The number of aircraft decreased by 6 percent between 1959 and 1960 because the Air Force retired the B-36s and the oldest B-47s. The B-52 became king and continued in production into 1962, as did the unpopular B-58. Bomber crews were learning new tricks such as low-altitude flying, which used undulations in the terrain to avoid enemy radar.

In 1960, the last full year of Eisenhower's presidency, the bomber, rather than the missile, remained the cutting-edge means for deterrence. When that year ended, Power had 558 B-52s, 1,178 B-47s, and 19 B-58s supported by 1,000 aerial tankers, 400 of them jet-powered KC-135s. In contrast, the intercontinental missile force totaled just 30 Snarks (first tested in 1957) and 12 Atlases. The United States also had 3,500 nuclear weapons at its disposal, plus 66 bases, 20 of which were overseas. SAC reflected the country's dedication to nuclear deterrence. During the 1950s, SAC had overcome a number of challenges to its dominance. It had dispersed its aircraft and established an alert force after learning how vulnerable its bases were to surprise attack. It survived the threat that Air Force appropriations might be diverted from the deterrent force to air defense. Finally, it countered the Navy's arguments for finite deterrence. Two of the greatest influences on SAC during these years were Generals LeMay and Schriever. Both were pilots, both flew bombers, and both worked with research and development. The two complemented one another. LeMay organized, trained, and deployed a force of nuclear-armed bombers capable of destroying targets anywhere in the world. Schriever provided the deterrent force with a new weapon for keeping the peace: the intercontinental ballistic missile. Each helped SAC prepare for its national defense role during the Cold War's early, tense years—but many live tests lay ahead.

arms race between the United States and the Soviet Union. Money was still short in the postwar years, so this answer looked attractive to Eisenhower's director of the budget, Maurice Stans.

Naturally, SAC had something to say about this proposal. The Air Force and SAC pointed out that while the Navy might play a useful supporting role in deterrence, it could not replace strategic bombers and land-based missiles. These were more accurate, and accuracy was at the heart of deterrence. The Navy's finite deterrence, which had impressed Stans, could destroy only Soviet cities, since Polaris could not be as precise as bombers flying right over a target such as a small Soviet air base. If only Soviet cities were destroyed, Soviet strategic forces would remain intact and be able to level American cities in return. In contrast, ran the Air

DOCTRINE AND HISTORY—LEMAY AND NUCLEAR DETERRENCE

DISTINCTIVE CAPABILITIES	FUNCTIONS (MISSIONS)	DOCTRINAL EMPHASIS
		• Nuclear Deterrence • MAD

11

THE KOREAN WAR: PART I

THE WORLD WAR II ALLIES had divided Korea into two zones after the Japanese surrender—an American zone in the south and a Soviet zone in the north. The Soviets proceeded to set up a Communist government in their sector, which in 1950 invaded the southern Republic of Korea. The attack caught the United States off guard, with US troops in nearby Japan unprepared and undertrained; the wrong type of aircraft in the theater; and pilots with little, if any, training in tactical air support. Even so, when US and other troops fighting under the United Nations flag were backed into a small corner of South Korea by overwhelming enemy forces, US airpower provided essential help in stalling the enemy offensive.

THE AIR WAR OVER KOREA

RELENTLESS PRESSURE FROM US AIRCRAFT PREVENTS A DEBACLE ON THE GROUND AND SETS THE STAGE FOR A UNITED NATIONS COUNTERATTACK

FOR THE UNITED STATES, the Korean War (1950–53) was the first armed conflict of the Cold War. Its beginnings, like those of the Berlin crisis, were in World War II's conclusion. When Japan surrendered in 1945, it gave up its claim to Korea, a Japanese colony from 1910–45. The Allies divided Korea along the 38th parallel. All Japanese troops still stationed north of the 38th parallel were to hand over their arms to the Soviets, and all troops south of that line would surrender to the United States.

The Allies agreed that once they had repatriated the Japanese, Korea would become independent for the first time in nearly 50 years. But the Soviets had other ideas. While the Soviet Union was attempting to spread Communism west to build a buffer between itself and Germany, it also intended to protect its southern border by turning Asia Communist, too. In some places, it worked: By 1949, the Chinese Communists had won a long civil war and China became a Communist nation.

NORTH KOREAN LEADER
Kim Il Sung led North Korea beginning in 1948, with the Soviet Union's blessing.

The politics

Two Korean states emerged by 1948—a Communist North Korea and a free South Korea. With the Soviets' backing, Kim Il Sung led the Democratic People's Republic of Korea, or North Korea. He was a shadowy figure who had fought the Japanese and then fled to the Soviet Union, where he served in the armed forces. In 1948 the people of the Republic of Korea, or South Korea, elected Syngman Rhee president. He was another foe of Japan. Rhee had US support, so the United States dissolved the postwar military government and began withdrawing its occupation forces after his election. Rhee had earned his doctorate at Princeton University before World War I, and then returned to his homeland. The Japanese expelled him in 1921, however, and he spent the next 25 years in exile campaigning for Korea's independence. Now he was about to lead a free South Korea.

Each Korean leader had his own agenda, and each man pushed that agenda, regardless of what his protectors thought. Rhee's primary focus was a Korea unfettered by outside influences. Even before he became president, Rhee showed leadership abilities. He organized demonstrations in December 1945 against a US plan to create a five-year interim government in South Korea. The United States relented. Meanwhile, Kim Il Sung wanted to expand Communist control into the South and to reunify the country. He was as good at playing politics as Rhee was.

Whenever the Soviets did not support his agenda, Kim Il Sung would turn to the Communist Chinese to see if he could get help from his other neighbors. By doing so, he manipulated the Soviets as much as they tried to manipulate him. (At that time, the United States did not generally understand the divisions between the Soviets and the Chinese Communists.)

FIRST PRESIDENT
South Koreans elected their first president, Syngman Rhee, in 1948. General Douglas MacArthur flew to Seoul to meet the new president.

Although both Rhee and Kim wanted to reunify Korea, they did not want the same kind of Korea. Tensions also increased because North Korea was an industrial zone, while South Korea was thick with cultivated farmland. Each half needed what the other had. When the North Korean troops stormed across the 38th parallel on June 25, 1950, no one was totally surprised.

International reaction

The United States understood that South Korea was vulnerable to Communist armies in the north. Therefore, in the years before 1950, it trained, advised, and equipped South Korea with what it considered an adequate force to repel invasion. It deliberately did not offer South Korea enough support to retake the north from the Soviets. There had already been enough war. Where the Communists were concerned, America's main interest was in Europe, so it slighted Asia in favor of the West. The United States was also grappling with a tremendous postwar debt, and President Harry S. Truman was trying to keep military spending down.

In retrospect, the United States did not offer the South enough military aid. South Korea had only 100,000 soldiers, no tanks, no heavy artillery, a small coast guard, fewer than 20 aircraft, and only 36 fully trained pilots. In contrast, North Korea had 130,000 soldiers, 500 tanks, heavy artillery, and 132 top-of-the-line, World War II-vintage Soviet aircraft,

including the Ilyushin Il-10 attack aircraft and the Yakovlev Yak-3 and Yak-7 fighters.

With its June 1950 invasion, North Korea took advantage of this situation. The Communists assumed that even though the United States had bases in nearby Japan, it would not interfere. After all, the United States had withdrawn its occupation forces from South Korea and offered little economic aid to the country after the war. Just as important, US Secretary of State Dean Acheson gave a speech in 1950 in which he declared that the Philippines, the Ryukyu Islands of Japan, and the Aleutians formed the boundary of an American "defensive arc" in the western Pacific. In other words, it sounded as if the United States would not interfere with any attempt at a takeover.

When news of the North Korean offensive reached President Truman, he did two things. On June 25, 1950, he approved the use of American air and naval forces to help defend South Korea. He also appealed to the United Nations (UN) to come to South Korea's aid. Because the Soviet delegate to the UN Security Council had walked out in protest over the Council's refusal to admit a representative from Communist China, the Council had a freer hand in the matter—the Soviets were not there to veto action. The Council called on North Korea to withdraw all troops that were south of the 38th parallel. When North Korea refused to do so, the Council on June 27 asked all UN members to help South Korea repel the invasion. The resolution formed the basis for a UN Command, activated July 24 and headed by General of the Army Douglas MacArthur. Even though a UN commander, MacArthur was ultimately responsible to the president of the United States rather than to the UN Secretary General or the Security Council.

GENERAL DOUGLAS MACARTHUR
General Douglas MacArthur was already wearing a couple of hats in July 1950, when he was appointed to head the UN Command to save South Korea.

KOREA AND THE 38TH PARALLEL
After World War II, the Allies divided Korea along the 38th parallel.

The Far East Command

While the United States seemed to have a large force in Japan that could come to South Korea's aid, that military presence was not as powerful as it appeared. Four of the Army's 10 divisions were there, but they were only partially equipped with tanks and artillery, and were poorly prepared for combat. These divisions formed the Eighth Army under Lieutenant General Walton Walker, who reported to MacArthur. MacArthur's Far East Command was responsible for the defense of Japan, the Philippines, and the Ryukyus. Since the occupation troops' withdrawal from South Korea, the general's chief responsibility was to supply administrative and logistic support to the Korean Military Advisory Group and the American embassy in South Korea's capital, Seoul. Under Vice Admiral C. Turner Joy, the Navy's Naval Forces, Far East, assisted MacArthur's Far East Command. The Far

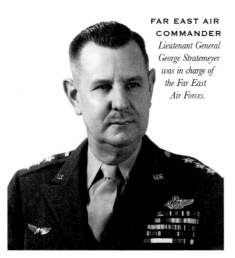

FAR EAST AIR COMMANDER
Lieutenant General George Stratemeyer was in charge of the Far East Air Forces.

LIGHT BOMBER
Air Force pilots flew the B-26 into combat during the Korean War.

East Air Forces, under Lieutenant General George E. Stratemeyer, also supported the mission.

The job of Stratemeyer's mobile strike force was to support Army and Navy operations throughout the Far East Command. He had 400 combat aircraft based in Japan, Okinawa, Guam, and the Philippines. Like the Army, the Air Force seemed well equipped. The Fifth Air Force, stationed in Japan under Major General Earle E. "Pat" Partridge, had eight F-80 squadrons, two B-26 light bomber squadrons, three F-82 Twin Mustang all-weather interceptor squadrons, plus a variety of rescue aircraft and three transport squadrons. With the exception of the F-80 jet aircraft, all were propeller-powered aircraft. Guam was home to a group of B-29s assigned to the Twentieth Air Force, also part of Stratemeyer's Far East Air Forces.

The only trouble with all this airpower was that it was not suited to the South Koreans' needs. The F-80 jet fighters did not have the range to effectively intervene from their base in Japan, and Partridge's Airmen had little practice supporting troops in combat. Since the end of World War II, the Air Force had emphasized strategic, not tactical, bombing. Furthermore, the Tactical Air Command and the Air Defense Command had lost their independence in a merger with the Continental Air Command in the 1940s, and Japan's densely populated islands left little space to train forces.

The campaign's early stages

By the time the Security Council called on UN participants to defend South Korea, American aircraft were already flying missions over the embattled country. Truman and Air Force Chief of Staff General Hoyt Vandenberg discussed and dismissed the idea of using atomic bombs. This would, they agreed, be a conventional war and would be limited to targets in South Korea.

The North Koreans and Americans did not waste time exchanging fire. On June 27 Air Force transports, escorted by fighters, began flying American civilians out of Kimpo Airfield near Seoul. Around noon, five North American F-82s ran into five Yaks

over Kimpo and downed three of the Russian-built fighters. A few hours later, eight North Korean Il-10s tried to strafe the airfield, but four F-80s operating at extreme range to protect the evacuation destroyed four of the attackers.

June 28 was no quieter. After 1st Lieutenant Bryce Poe II flew the Air Force's first jet combat reconnaissance mission in an RF-80, 12 B-26s made the first offensive American strike since the invasion. The bombers hit the rail yard at Munsan near the 38th parallel and then strafed tracks and highways nearby. Later in the day, four B-29s patrolled the advancing North Koreans' four main routes into the south and attacked suitable targets.

Although encouraged by the Fifth Air Force's initial combat victories, General Stratemeyer believed that North Korean airfields should also be attacked as quickly as possible to prevent additional incidents such as the one over Kimpo. When Yaks strafed Suwon Airfield some 15 miles (24km) south of Seoul and destroyed or damaged a B-26, an F-82, and a C-54 on June 28, this only confirmed his opinion. On June 29 MacArthur visited Suwon. The airfield was the command post for the general's liaison group assessing the Korean situation. It was also a tactical air control center to coordinate US aircraft in the vicinity. On his way there, MacArthur approved Stratemeyer's request for authority to strike airfields north of the 38th

parallel. Later that day, as MacArthur drove back to Suwon from the Han River, where he had seen the flood of South Korean troops and refugees streaming away from Seoul, 18 B-26s dropped fragmentation bombs on the airfield at Pyongyang, the North Korean capital. The B-26s returned without loss. The crews claimed that they destroyed or damaged 25 aircraft on the ground and one in the air. News of MacArthur's decision and the resulting attack had not reached Washington several hours later, when Truman approved air strikes north of the 38th parallel. That authorization reached MacArthur on June 30.

Naval ships in the area were next to join the fight. Initially they focused their attacks north of the 38th parallel. The US aircraft carrier USS *Valley Forge* and the British carrier HMS *Triumph*,

FIRST ACTION OF THE WAR
On June 27, 1950, five North American F-82s shot down Soviet-made Yaks over Kimpo Airfield, where the Air Force was attempting to evacuate civilians.

along with supporting warships, steamed toward Korea as Task Force 77 under US Vice Admiral Arthur D. Struble. On July 3 carrier-based British and American squadrons raided the airfield at Haeju and the airfield and rail facilities at Pyongyang. On July 4 Struble launched a second day of strikes against targets near the capital. The task force then headed toward North Korea's east coast to blast the oil refinery and storage tanks at Wonsan.

GROUNDBREAKING JET FIGHTER
The F-80 was the only US jet fighter in the Pacific when the Korean War broke out.

Building up the force

Partridge's Fifth Air Force had all of Korea to monitor, and it needed more aircraft. The general shifted F-80s to Japanese airfields nearer Korea, while Stratemeyer brought other F-80s from the Philippines and took steps to get F-51 Mustangs. The comparatively slow Mustang, with its liquid-cooled piston engine, was vulnerable to ground fire during strafing missions, but it could operate from the short, unpaved airstrips in southern South Korea. The Australians entrusted Stratemeyer with an F-51 squadron in Japan, which made Australia the first UN member other than the United States to come to South Korea's defense. General Vandenberg sent two B-29 groups not scheduled for atomic duty with the Strategic Air Command (SAC) to Okinawa to be nearer targets in Korea. On July 5 the first American ground unit reached South Korea. The 500-man unit placed itself in the path of an advancing North Korean division 20 times its size. By that time, 145 Mustangs had been retrieved from the

BOMBER COMMAND
General Vandenberg appointed Major General Emmett O'Donnell head of the Far East Air Forces' Bomber Command.

Air National Guard and prepared for shipment by sea to Japan, where Air Force pilots would train before flying the aircraft in combat.

Vandenberg sent Major General Emmett O'Donnell to head the Far East Air Forces' Bomber Command out of Japan. His task was to handle the strategic side of the campaign. O'Donnell had led B-17s and B-29s during World War II, and his new command initially consisted of three B-29 groups. Its mission was long-range interdiction and destruction of strategic targets. Tactical air operations fell under Partridge's Fifth Air Force.

The Pusan perimeter

On the ground, things were going badly. The American ground troops and the South Korean army were losing the battle against the overwhelming North Korean forces. Reinforcements were not arriving fast enough.

By early September the North Koreans had cornered US and South Korean forces at Pusan, a port at South Korea's southeastern tip. MacArthur and his staff believed that every available aircraft should be used to push back the North Koreans until US forces could establish a defensive perimeter around Pusan.

The decision to use bombers and fighter-bombers almost indiscriminately around the battle lines led to conflicts between MacArthur's people—principally his chief of staff, Major General Edward M. Almond—and the Far East Air Forces, especially Stratemeyer and Vandenberg. Almond wanted everything at his disposal to save the men on the ground. The Air Force argued that using B-29s on the battlefront was a waste of firepower. Vandenberg did two things. First, he explained to MacArthur the difference between tactical and strategic air operations—that is, the best way to use fighter-bombers versus the best use for bombers. Second,

---

GENERAL HOYT S. VANDENBERG

HOYT S. VANDENBERG graduated from the US Military Academy in 1923 and was commissioned a second lieutenant in the Air Service. He developed a reputation as an outstanding pilot and commander, and in 1939 graduated from the Army War College. He served on the Air Staff until late 1942, when he was appointed chief of staff of the Twelfth Air Force. He won a Silver Star for his service during the North Africa campaign.

Vandenberg returned to Washington in 1943 as deputy chief of Air Staff, but soon left for the Soviet Union, where he helped negotiate the use of Soviet bases for bombing targets in Eastern Germany, out of range of bombers from Britain or the Mediterranean. These frustrating negotiations, along with his participation in the conference President Roosevelt and Prime Minister Churchill held in Tehran, Iran, with Stalin, helped him prepare for the Cold War confrontations with the Soviets.

Vandenberg was later sent to Britain to serve as deputy air commander in chief of the Allied Expeditionary Forces. He earned an oak leaf cluster for his Distinguished Service Medal for his role in planning the D-Day invasion. Two months

after D-Day, Vandenberg assumed command of the Ninth Air Force—the largest tactical air force ever fielded—and commanded it throughout the liberation of France and conquest of Germany. He was promoted to lieutenant general in 1945, less than four years after he made major. After the war he served as director of intelligence for the War Department, and then deputy director of the Central Intelligence Group, the forerunner of the CIA.

Vandenberg returned to the Air Force in 1947 and helped work out the details of Air Force independence from the Army. He became the first vice chief of staff of the Air Force and was promoted to general. In 1948 he succeeded General Carl Spaatz as Air Force chief of staff. During his tour he led the Air Force through the Berlin blockade and the Korean War and helped strike a balance between conventional tactical forces and strategic nuclear forces. He retired in 1953 and died within the year.

FAST-TRACKER
General Hoyt S. Vandenberg went from captain to lieutenant general in less than four years.

MUSTANG TOUGH
Unlike many other aircraft, F-51 Mustangs could handle South Korea's short, unpaved airstrips.

A BRILLIANT REPUTATION
Major General Otto Weyland (back row, center)—shown here with other American World War II leaders, including Generals Dwight D. Eisenhower and Omar Bradley—became General Vandenberg's vice commander of operations early in the Korean War. He helped organize tactical airpower in defense of Pusan.

he assigned to Major General Otto P. Weyland the responsibility for continuing to make the Air Force's case. Weyland had a brilliant reputation for providing close air support during World War II, when his 19th Tactical Air Command thrust through France in 1944 as part of Vandenberg's Ninth Air Force. As Stratemeyer's new vice commander for operations, Weyland reasoned that B-29s would also be supporting the defensive perimeter if they were allowed to bomb targets that would disrupt the flow of North Korean supplies and reinforcements. Meanwhile, tactical operations could take care of troop security at the front lines at Pusan.

Almond finally relented, after gaining the right to retain control over one B-29 group, but MacArthur went a step further: As the North Koreans rushed supplies south to sustain their offensive, he agreed that all three bomber groups should be used for long-range interdiction. The B-29s heavily damaged several railroad yards and bridges during August.

Vandenberg was not done building up the Bomber Command. He laid the groundwork for a strategic-bombing campaign modeled after similar World War II operations. From Washington, Vandenberg persuaded the Joint Chiefs of Staff to send two additional B-29 groups to the Far East to attack industrial targets north of the 38th parallel. This increased the Bomber Command to five groups totaling more than 100 Superfortresses. The Joint Chiefs of Staff also provided a target list, prepared like the one that SAC intelligence specialists had given to General O'Donnell. The principal targets on the second list were chemical plants at Hungnam in the north, Pyongyang munitions factories, an oil refinery at Wonsan, and oil-storage facilities at Rashin.

B-29s like this one carpet-bombed a 27-square-mile (70-square-km) area around the Naktong River on August 16, 1950. The raid in this photo took place a year later.

NEW COMMANDER
In April 1951 General Matthew Ridgway replaced General Douglas MacArthur in Korea. He ordered B-29s to bomb Rashin in August of that year. Here he meets with Vice Admiral Turner Joy (right).

By mid-September—after about one month of systematic bombardment—Stratemeyer announced that practically all strategic industrial targets in the country had been destroyed. Since American fighters had wiped out the North Korean air force and the enemy had few antiaircraft guns, B-29 bomber crews had been able to concentrate on accurate bombing.

One major exception to that target list remained: Rashin. The northeastern town was 20 miles (32 km) from Soviet territory. Twice O'Donnell's bombers tried to hit it. Twice cloud cover foiled them. In Washington, D.C., the State Department worried that a mistaken hit on the Soviet Union could create greater problems than its satellite state, North Korea, was already causing. Rashin came off the target list. At the time, this move aroused no debate within military circles, but by spring 1951, critics of the Truman administration learned of Rashin's immunity and raised a cry that politics had interfered with military matters. By August 1951, a year after O'Donnell's two attempts on Rashin, the city's railroad yard housed an alarming volume of supplies. General

Matthew B. Ridgway, who had replaced MacArthur in April 1951, bombed Rashin. On August 25, 1951, B-29s dropped 300 tons of bombs, 97 percent of which struck within the rail complex.

Back in August 1950, before most North Korean industrial targets had been taken out, Communist troops were still pressing Pusan. When the enemy crossed the Naktong River mid-month, it threatened Taegu, an important road junction just northwest of Pusan. MacArthur directed Stratemeyer to carpet-bomb 27 square miles (70 square km) through which North Korean reinforcements and supplies were passing. If US bombers could take out the Naktong bridgehead, they could disrupt the flow of supplies. O'Donnell's planners divided the rectangle into 12 squares and dispatched a B-29 squadron to saturate each square with bombs. In less than half an hour on August

16, 98 B-29s dropped 960 tons of high explosives from 10,000 ft (3,050m). Enemy artillery fire decreased. Generals Stratemeyer and Partridge, as well as the Eighth Army's General Walker, talked MacArthur out of a second round of bombing. Since they had no recent intelligence about the situation on the ground around the Naktong bridgehead, all three insisted that B-29s be used only against known targets.

Tactical air operations

Fighter-bombers and B-26 light bombers did more to check the enemy during the successful defense of Taegu than the B-29s' massive carpet-bombing. They strafed North Korean troops as they tried to ford the Naktong. They struck bridges and supported counterattacks against hostile forces east of the river. Through interdiction and close air support, tactical aircraft helped the United States gain time to rush troops to the peninsula and stabilize the battlefront. In fact, from the very beginning of the Korean War, they strafed enemy positions and destroyed Soviet-built tanks. For example, on July 10 a flight of F-80s descended beneath the clouds and discovered a long line of North Korean tanks and trucks halted before a demolished bridge. The Fifth Air Force diverted every available aircraft—F-80s, B-26s, and F-82 interceptors—to batter the column with bombs, gunfire, and rockets. This improvised attack destroyed more than 150 hostile vehicles, including about 50 tanks.

Coordinating with other services

The reason for tactical air operations' successes were rooted in World War II, when the Army and Army Air Forces coordinated their movements through a joint operations center. In this way, they had matched requests from ground-unit commanders with available aircraft and ordnance. This worked well for routine missions as well as for emergencies. Once the center had issued an order, a tactical air control officer assigned to a particular ground unit would handle the details of an individual strike from his radio-equipped jeep. This allowed the Army Air Forces to retain control over its Airmen and the Army over its Soldiers. The tactical air officer was an experienced pilot familiar with the difficulty of locating a target from the air, with the aircraft's characteristics, and with the type of munitions each plane carried.

CRITICAL SUPPORT
Tactical air operations played a critical role during the Korean War. Planes like these B-26s supported friendly ground troops and struck bridges and tanks.

MOSQUITO

North American T.6G trainers such as these served as air control platforms in Korea. The aircraft shown have Nationalist Chinese markings.

During the Korean War, uncertain logistics on the ground meant the Air Force and Army did not always have a joint operations center. But by using radio-equipped jeeps and eventually airborne controllers, the two services managed to synchronize their forces. Both the radio-equipped jeeps and light aircraft proved easy targets for the enemy, however, so the Air Force finally put its air controllers in the North American T-6 trainer. It was fast enough to escape the Soviet-built Yaks and flexible enough to maneuver easily over the up-and-down terrain. The Mosquitos, as the T-6 controllers were called, in the end provided the principal means of controlling close-in air strikes, eclipsing the jeep-mounted control parties that had been so successful during World War II.

Partnering with an aircraft-equipped Navy complicated the Air Force's tactical duties in Korea. Troubles began on July 4, 1950, when Task Force 77's Vice Admiral Arthur Struble continued a second day of carrier-based attacks on Pyongyang. Stratemeyer had to cancel an Air Force B-29 strike also planned for Pyongyang on that day. The incident convinced the Air Force general that he needed tighter control over Navy air strikes. He asked MacArthur for operational control over the Navy's carrier aircraft, in effect assigning them a status similar to Fifth Air Force squadrons. While the Navy objected, Admiral Joy admitted that some sort of closer control was necessary. As of July 15, Joy agreed to provide Stratemeyer's headquarters with Struble's plans for carrier strikes. Joy thus avoided Air Force control but offered better coordination. While at first the flow of new communications flooded the joint operations center, the two services eventually worked out the wrinkles.

The Marine Corps offered a different kind of challenge to the Air Force. First of all, it got better press than the Air Force, and some in the Air Force felt neglected because of this. Second, Marine Corps aviation tactics differ markedly from those of the Air Force. Marines specialize in amphibious warfare; a typical action might entail seizing a small beachhead with the help of naval gunfire and air support and then bringing in artillery. For this reason, Marine Corps Airmen train in close infantry support. Pilots, air controllers, and commanders on the ground are accustomed to working together and they understand the benefits and dangers of air strikes in close proximity to friendly troops. In Korea, Marine Corps aviation thought in terms of supporting Marine ground units fighting on a narrow front, whereas the Air Force used its aircraft for wider actions such as

interdiction, reconnaissance, and close air support from the Pusan perimeter near the southern tip of the peninsula all the way to the Yalu River in North Korea. Fifth Air Force General Partridge recognized the practical differences between the Marine Corps and the Air Force, and he worked with a Marine liaison officer to find suitable targets whenever the Marines had aircraft to spare.

Air Force Generals Stratemeyer and Vandenberg also acknowledged the Marine Corps pilots' flying skills but argued that close air support alone does not win wars. Even Army General Walker declared in favor of the Air Force: "I will lay my cards right on the table and state that if it had not been for the air support we received from the Fifth Air Force we would not have been able to stay in Korea," he said.

The first phase ends

By mid-September 1950, North Korea's offensive had failed, ending the first phase of the Korean War. The UN forces had survived savage blows and grown steadily stronger. In the early days of the conflict, MacArthur told Partridge that American airpower would prevail; this turned out not to be entirely true. Fighting the North Koreans to a standstill had required air, land, and sea forces from several nations, with South Korea and the United States making the greatest contributions. Even so, airpower provided essential help in stopping the enemy, as the burned-out hulks of hundreds of tanks, destroyed bridges, and bombed railroads along the invasion route could attest.

But the North was not about to give up. Now that the United States and South Korea had secured Pusan, MacArthur's thoughts turned toward a second phase of the war. It would begin on South Korea's west coast with an amphibious assault at Inchon.

DOCTRINE AND HISTORY—THE KOREAN WAR

DISTINCTIVE CAPABILITIES	FUNCTIONS (MISSIONS)	DOCTRINAL EMPHASIS
• Air and Space Superiority • Precision Engagement • Agile Combat Support	• Counterland • Close Air Support • Interdiction • Airlift • Surveillance and Reconnaissance • Search and Rescue • Air Refueling • Strategic Attack Airlift	• Theater Attack on Military Targets • Counterair • MiG Alley • Birth of Jet Fighter

THE KOREAN WAR: PART II

12

HAVING STOPPED THE NORTH KOREAN invasion, General MacArthur turned
to the offensive with a spectacular amphibious landing at Inchon. US and
UN forces then pushed the Communist forces almost to the Chinese
border at the Yalu River, but intervention by thousands of
Communist Chinese troops sent UN forces reeling south.
While all this took place, dogfights between American fighters
and Communist MiGs became commonplace; American
dominance of the skies despite the MiG's top-notch
design and performance demonstrated the importance
of superior pilots. The war ended in stalemate, but
a new type of US aircraft came into its own—the
fighter-bomber.

DOGFIGHT IN "MIG ALLEY"

THE AIR WAR OVER KOREA ENTERS A NEW PHASE

THE FIRST STAGE of American involvement in the Korean War was a classic demonstration of the importance of airpower on the modern battlefield. The North Korean advance on the ground was stopped and then pushed back, partly through the devastating impact of attacks by bombers and fighter-bombers flying close air support and interdiction missions. The aircraft were mostly of World War II vintage—Mustangs used in a ground-attack role, US Navy Corsairs operating from carriers, and B-26 and B-29 bombers, as well as F-80 Shooting Star jets that were almost as old. In the absence of any serious opposition, these well-tried airplanes ruled the air.

Airpower played a big role in the Korean War's second stage as well. However, this time around, both sides in the conflict had a strong presence in the skies. This second phase began in the fall of 1950, with stabilization of the perimeter around Pusan and a plan that General Douglas MacArthur hatched to trap retreating North Korean troops. MacArthur opened this chapter with an amphibious Marine Corps assault at Inchon, an unlikely spot on Korea's west coast.

On September 15, 1950, 40,000 Marines and Soldiers, designated X Corps, stormed ashore at Inchon and cut off North Korean forces retreating from around Pusan. Navy and Marine Corps aviators provided cover. The Eighth Army launched its own offensive from the Pusan perimeter on September 16. The Fifth Air Force supported the Eighth Army from Pusan all the way to the North Korean border. The two assaults were meant to block 100,000 North Korean troops from escaping. They were successful: Less than a third of those troops got away.

So complete was the enemy's collapse that on September 27, President Truman authorized MacArthur to pursue the beaten forces across the 38th parallel, which separated South Korea from North Korea. South Korean troops promptly advanced into the north. The United Nations (UN) expressed concern that crossing the parallel might invite the Chinese into the war on the North Koreans' side. In fact, China warned it would retaliate if UN forces drew too near the Yalu River, which marked the border between North Korea and China. Still, the UN General Assembly passed a resolution declaring that "all appropriate steps should be taken to ensure conditions of stability throughout Korea."

The march north

Airpower performed numerous missions as UN forces marched into North Korea. The Far East Air Forces dropped the 187th Airborne Regimental Combat Team at two road junctions north of Pyongyang to cut off a retreating North Korean column and to free American prisoners of war traveling with it in two trains. The two sides fought hard, and the enemy killed 100 prisoners on one train. The other train continued north with its captives. The Far East Air Forces also parachuted supplies to advancing UN troops and flew men and cargo from Japan to airfields in Korea. Fifth Air Force fighter-bombers and Major General Emmett O'Donnell's Bomber Command did not find many worthwhile targets, since Lieutenant General Walton Walker's Eighth Army had been so successful in toppling towns and chasing the North Korean People's Army into the high country. Aerial reconnaissance, which helped chart Inchon's defenses before the assault, now faced the more difficult task of locating the enemy among northernmost Korea's mountains.

China rushes in

What happened next ensured China's entry into the war on North Korea's side. It also brought about the US Air Force's first jet combat. UN forces tried another pincer move as they had done at Inchon. While the Eighth Army pushed north, the X Corps sailed from Inchon and Pusan for Wonsan on North Korea's east coast. However, minefields delayed the X Corps from landing until November 4, even though South Koreans had captured the port. The pincer plan now became a race to the Yalu River. When South Korean troops closed in on the Yalu, the Chinese attacked piecemeal. They struck the South Koreans around the Yalu on October 25 and 26; three days later, on October 29, they hit the South Koreans at the port at Wonsan.

CARRIER STRIKE
Aircraft from the USS Valley Forge *bomb a North Korean train in July 1950.*

A BIG LEAP
Air Force C-119J Flying Boxcars drop members of the 187th Airborne Regimental Combat Team to cut off retreating enemy units south of Munsan, South Korea.

B-26 STRIKE
A light bomber hits warehouses and dock facilities in Wonsan, North Korea.

Other, more serious contacts occurred on November 1. When F-80s attacked an airfield in Sinuiju on the Yalu's southern bank, they found 15 Yaks on the ground. One F-80 was lost to antiaircraft fire. That same day, Yak fighters around Sinuiju attacked a B-26 and a T-6, but failed to down either. And four Soviet-built MiG-15 jet fighters bearing Chinese markings darted across the Yalu and jumped four F-51s, all of which also escaped. Meanwhile, Chinese infantry were pouring across the border. MacArthur's staff believed that 17,000 Chinese troops were in North Korea, but that was a serious underestimation—180,000 had already entered the country. They traveled by night to avoid detection by American aerial reconnaissance.

As all this was happening in the fall of 1950, Air Force General Weyland sought more control over aircraft in the region. He persuaded General MacArthur to place the 1st Marine Aircraft Wing under the Fifth Air Force's control. Both supported the X Corps, which was composed of Marines and Soldiers. That plan would create all kinds of communications problems. At the same time, O'Donnell's Bomber Command was short two B-29 groups, which had been withdrawn in October when victory seemed near. The command used incendiaries to multiply damage in towns and villages in the border region that might harbor enemy troops or supplies.

But Chinese troops continued to swarm across the Yalu into North Korea. On November 5 MacArthur directed Stratemeyer to take out Sinuiju, the "Korean end" of all bridges leading from Manchuria in China, and every village, town, factory, or military installation between the front lines and the Yalu River. The only targets spared were Rashin and the hydroelectric plants that supplied current to China.

President Truman learned of the plan only a few hours before the attacks were to take place. He was at first hesitant to provoke China, but MacArthur convinced him it was far more dangerous to allow the Chinese to freely build up their forces in North Korea.

Jet cover leads to jet combat
November 8, 1950, marked the first all-jet dogfight. As 79 B-29s struck Sinuiju with incendiaries, 1st Lieutenant Russell Brown, flying cover in an F-80, shot down a MiG-15. After strafing the airfield at Sinuiju, the F-80 pilots climbed to 20,000ft

(6,095m) to provide cover. It was then that the lieutenant engaged—and won—a 60-second battle with a MiG from Antung. While the bombers destroyed some 60 percent of Sinuiju, they were not able to hit the bridges because antiaircraft fire forced the bombers to fly above 18,000ft (5,485m). Throughout the rest of November, bombardiers were unable to destroy any of the 12 bridges across the Yalu. Their radio-controlled bombs were not accurate enough. When winter fell, enemy troops could simply cross the frozen river, so the Air Force suspended all attempts until March.

Lost ground
Hoping to keep China out of the war, the UN forces under American command continued to avoid crossing into China, despite the presence

of Chinese aircraft in Manchuria and Chinese troops. The UN forces also skirted the Soviet Union. No one was sure how those two countries would respond, although they suspected the Soviets would come to China's aid.

Despite their precautions, US aircraft accidentally violated Chinese and Soviet airspace three times. On August 27 two Mustangs mistook an airfield at Antung in China for one at Sinuiju in North Korea and strafed an aerodrome. On September 22 a B-29 dispatched to bomb Sinuiju hit the Antung rail yard. And on October 8 two F-80 pilots got lost and mistakenly strafed a Soviet air base in Siberia. In addition, although not authorized to enter Chinese or Soviet airspace, pilots sometimes ignored this order when in hot pursuit of a MiG seeking refuge over China.

After the first attacks by Chinese troops in late October and early November 1950, quiet settled over the North Korean battlefields. The new enemy seemed to have vanished as suddenly as it had appeared. After pausing for two weeks to regroup, MacArthur launched an offensive on November 24. The goal was to drive the enemy across the Yalu into China. About 200,000 UN forces—half of which were South Koreans—faced not the expected 70,000 Chinese supported by North Korean troops, but some 300,000 Chinese backed by North Koreans. The Chinese counterattacked with overwhelming force on November 25 against the Eighth Army and the X Corps.

FIRST JET COMBATANTS
November 8, 1950, marked the first jet-versus-jet combat. It took place between an F-80 (top) and a Soviet-built MiG.

JET COMBAT

THE FIRST SHOOTING DOWN of one jet aircraft by another took place in November 1950, when American pilot, Lieutenant Russell J. Brown, flying an F-80, downed a Chinese MiG-15. Operating from safe bases around Antung in Chinese Manchuria, the jets began to intercept US bomber missions, threatening to deny the Americans the air superiority they had previously enjoyed. In December 1950 the United States sent in the F-84 Thunderjet as a ground-attack aircraft along with its latest fighter, the F-86 Sabre, to take on the MiGs. The Sabres were deployed on offensive sweeps, engaging the Communist jets over the Yalu River in northwest Korea and effectively preventing enemy aircraft from interfering with American air operations farther south.

The Korean conflict provided strange echoes of World War I. As it had been on the Western Front in 1914–18, the most important function of airpower was to support ground troops engaged in a grim and desperate war of attrition. But once again, the fighter pilots and their contest for air superiority grabbed the headlines. The duel between MiG-15s and Sabres in "MiG Alley" over the Yalu became a classic example of aerial combat even as it unfolded.

The MiG pilots were anonymous, generally operating in formations more than 50 strong. The far less numerous Sabre pilots were a self-conscious elite—aggressive, eager for action, and intensely competitive. Not since World War I had the pursuit of ace status—the famous "five kills"—had such importance. Returning from the mission on which he recorded his fifth kill, pilot Frederick "Boots" Blesse claimed that he said a prayer: "Lord, if you have to take me while I'm over here, don't do it today. Let me get back and tell someone I finally got number five."

Competition for scores arose not only among individual pilots but also between the two Sabre-equipped formations, the 4th and 51st fighter-interceptor wings. After a mission on which he shot down two MiGs, Blesse was embraced by his commander, Colonel Harrison Thyng of the 4th Wing: "Damn, Boots," said Colonel Thyng, "it's about time somebody in this wing was the leading ace."

Many of the American pilots were World War II veterans—the average age of pilots in Korea was around 30, which would have been old for an Airman in 1941–45. The war's "top gun," Captain Joseph McConnell, conformed to the classic Korean War profile: He was 30 years old and a veteran of World War II (he served as a navigator on B-24s). Aces such as James Jabara and "Gabby" Gabreski had been fighter pilots in the earlier conflict. They were as eager to repeat or improve on earlier achievements as the younger pilots were to make their mark for the first time. Together, these World War II vets had a maximum of 100 missions to show what they were worth before being transferred back to the United States.

KOREAN WAR ACE
Major (later Colonel) James Jabara flew P-51s in World War II and shot down 15 MiGs in Korea.

Four days later, MacArthur ordered any personnel north of Pyongyang to withdraw. Aircraft covered the retreat. Fifth Air Force General Partridge turned the 1st Marine Aircraft Wing over to its Marine commander to operate independently and to speed aid to ground forces. The Fifth Air Force also placed fighter-bombers and light bombers at the Marine Corps officer's disposal. Meanwhile, Fifth Air Force General Partridge's B-29s supported the Eighth Army while the Far East Air Forces' combat cargo aircraft moved materiel from soon-to-be-abandoned airfields so it would not fall into enemy hands. Aircraft also helped by dropping components of a bridge for troops to assemble over a gorge. This not only smoothed the 1st Marine Division's retreat but also allowed it to move heavy equipment rather than abandon it.

MiG vs. F-86

The retreat resulted in talk of using atomic weapons. MacArthur approved a request for B-29s capable of dropping atomic bombs and ordered a list of targets in China and the Soviet Union. But the real trouble facing the Air Force at this juncture was the Soviet-built MiG-15. It was faster and more maneuverable than the F-51 and the F-80. The US answer was the North American F-86 Sabre, which more than matched the MiG-15's performance. Test flights of this new swept-wing jet had begun in 1947. Soon

after Chinese MiGs (manned in the earliest days by Soviet pilots) first intervened in the air war over Korea, Air Force Chief of Staff General Hoyt Vandenberg ordered that a wing of 75 Sabres be ferried by aircraft carrier to the Far East. The first F-86 encounter with a MiG occurred on December 17, 1950, when Lieutenant Colonel Bruce Hinton shot one down. Five days later, the commander of the 4th Fighter-Interceptor Wing, Lieutenant Colonel John C. Meyer, led eight Sabres against 15 MiGs. Meyer's forces downed six of the enemy at a cost of one F-86.

During the next 30 months, F-86 pilots shot down 792 MiGs and 18 other enemy aircraft. Of the 218 Sabres lost during the war, the Air Force attributed 76 to MiGs, 19 to ground fire, 15 to unknown enemy action, and 13 to unknown operational causes. The remaining losses were the result of mechanical failure or accident. Although the lighter MiG could climb faster, the Sabre could outrun it in a dive and its controls were more responsive when approaching the speed of sound. The Sabre's canopy afforded better visibility than that of the MiG, which had a restricted field of vision and an inferior defrosting system. Neither

MILITARY HELICOPTERS

COMBAT BETWEEN JET FIGHTERS was not the only airpower innovation of the Korean War. Another novelty was the first extensive military use of helicopters. Although the helicopters were not used offensively, they still had an immediate impact, primarily as a means of evacuating wounded troops from the battlefield. Sikorsky H-5s, Bell H-13s, and Hiller H-23s carried the wounded in panniers attached to the helicopter fuselage. Receiving speedy medical attention at a Mobile Army Surgical Hospital (MASH) radically improved a wounded Soldier's chances of survival. Many men had helicopters to thank for saving their lives. Many downed Airmen also owed the helicopter a debt of gratitude, for it was US Navy HO3Ss and USAF H-5s and H-19s that performed combat rescue missions when aircraft were shot down behind Communist lines or ditched in the ocean.

These errands of mercy did not exhaust the helicopters' usefulness. H-19 transport helicopters ferried troops and cargo, and helicopters were also employed as airborne command posts and used for aerial observation of the battlefield.

READY FOR ACTION
US Marines disembark from Piasecki HRP-1 tandem-rotor transport helicopters during the Korean War. The HRP-1, which first flew in 1947, was known as the "Flying Banana" because of the distinctive shape of its fuselage.

aircraft had adequate armament. The Sabre's six machine guns often did not cause enough damage to bring down the enemy, and the MiG's cannon fired too slowly to accurately hit a fast-moving jet.

Modifications to the F-86 enhanced its performance against the MiG, which improved little during the war. Engineers from North American Aviation, which had designed the aircraft, replaced the wing slats that extended automatically at low speed with a fixed leading edge to reduce drag during tight turns. Hydraulic controls were added to increase agility. But the greatest boon to maneuverability was the flying tail, a horizontal stabilizer that moved as a unit and was far more effective than the smaller elevators on the original F-86. A more powerful engine and a radar gun sight also made the updated F-86 a more formidable fighter, but the MiG still had better acceleration. As a final advantage, it enjoyed the sanctuary of the Manchurian border.

Although the F-86 was a splendid fighter, its overwhelming success against the MiG in Korea was largely due to its superior pilots. Many

DIVING SABRE
A diving North American F-86 Sabre jet fighter fires rockets at a target range at Nellis Air Force Base, Nevada, around 1953. The Sabres were not equipped with rockets or missiles when taking on MiGs during the Korean War. As in World War II, the air battles were fought with guns, although jet engines meant that combat took place at higher speeds.

of these pilots were World War II veterans. Colonel Meyer was a leading ace in the European theater of operations. He had 24 kills in that war and two victories in Korea. Lieutenant Colonel Francis Gabreski and 17 other World War II aces increased their kill totals in the Far East. Ten pilots who had a few victories in World War II became aces in Korea; among them was Major James Jabara, whose 15 kills earned him second place among Korean War aces. The leading ace, with 16 kills, was Captain Joseph McConnell. In contrast to these superb pilots, those deployed by China and the Soviet Union were largely inexperienced, particularly in the early months of the war.

While the era of aces lived on, air-combat tactics changed. World War II's big offensive fighter sweeps gave way to small defensive patrols, since policy did not permit pilots to engage the enemy north of the Yalu River. The initiative thus passed to the Chinese. This left US pilots with only one choice: to react to enemy incursions. The MiG's short range and the location of the Chinese airfields in Manchuria meant the heaviest fighting took place in "MiG Alley" in northwestern North Korea along the Yalu River from the Yellow Sea to the Sui-ho Reservoir. The F-86's short range also created limits. These aircraft could not waste time assembling in large formations. Instead, patrols of four F-86s arrived in "MiG Alley" at five-minute intervals and remained for about 20 minutes, or even less if they engaged in combat.

Although US tactics were successful, Chinese airpower remained a threat. Soviet support increased China's jet fighter strength to about 1,000 aircraft, three times the peak number of F-86s. MiGs occasionally penetrated the F-86 screen along the Yalu.

Things got even tougher early in 1951, when UN forces abandoned Seoul. The F-86s left for Japan because they were about to lose Kimpo Airfield, near the capital. Until the F-86s returned in February, defense rested solely on the bombers and fighter-bombers, which tried to interrupt the enemy's lengthening supply lines. The B-29s cratered Pyongyang Airfield after the enemy recaptured it and bombed towns suspected of sheltering Chinese troops. In January a raid on the city of Pyongyang set raging fires but failed to inflict the devastation that the Bomber Command expected. Tactical aircraft had more success. During the first five days of January 1951, the Fifth Air Force claimed that 2,500 daylight sorties by fighter-bombers had killed 8,000 Chinese. Meanwhile, bombers added to the death toll during night attacks illuminated by Navy flares dropped from Air Force C-47s.

ON PATROL
*Colonel (later General) Benjamin O. Davis Jr.,
one of the World War II Tuskegee Airmen,
leads a three-ship F-86 Sabre formation during
the Korean War. As leader of the 51st Fighter
Interceptor Wing, Colonel Davis was one of
the first African-American wing commanders.*

Stalemate

All in all, air support during the retreat was
uneven. It was weakest in the west during
December 1950, when US and UN forces
abandoned airfields such as those around
Pyongyang, and destroyed enormous
quantities of supplies and equipment. Air
support was more effective in the east, where
aircraft carriers were close at hand and the
evacuation was more orderly. A number of
measures, including attacks on the enemy's supply
lines, close air support, and interdiction, and
greater strength on the ground, slowed the
Chinese advance beyond Seoul. By mid-January,
the long retreat ended, and the front stabilized
some 40 miles (65km) south of Seoul.

The Eighth Army took advantage of the
favorable conditions to counterattack. Its troops
recaptured Seoul in June 1951 and even advanced
a short distance into North Korea. This led to
new phase of the war—a stalemate—which lasted
into 1953. Limited but vicious attacks occasionally
broke the standoff. During this time, General
Partridge decided to leave the 1st Marine Aircraft
Wing under Marine control because it was easier
for the Marine air and ground forces to work as
a team without going through the Air Force.
However, Partridge reserved the right to make
minor adjustments to plans.

Overall, airpower was invaluable in drawing
the new front line generally along the 38th
parallel. As the UN Command fought its way
north, the Far East Air Forces flew as many as
1,000 sorties in a single day. Marine Corps pilots
joined them in close air support and battlefield

interdiction. Aerial reconnaissance tracked hostile
activity. The Far East Air Forces' B-29s bombed
roads and rail junctions used by Chinese and
North Korean units to ferry supplies. The troop
carrier squadrons delivered more members from
the 187th Airborne Regimental Combat Team on
missions. Lieutenant Colonel Gilbert Check, the
27th Regimental Combat Team commander,
summed up airpower's uses in the following way:
"The close support and coordination between air
and ground units . . . can well serve as a standard
for future operations."

Truman's decision

While General MacArthur wanted to recapture
all of North Korea and unify the country,
President Truman had other plans. He believed
the United States had already spent enough
blood and treasure in Korea, and that it would
take too much more to secure the entire
peninsula. Furthermore, the White House argued
that as long as the UN Command secured South
Korea's independence from Communist China,
the countries of the free world could focus on
maintaining Europe's security in the face of
Soviet aggression. But MacArthur—who wanted
total victory in Korea—went public one too many
times with his contrary opinions, and his criticism
of the president's conduct of the war crossed into
open insubordination. Truman replaced the
popular World War II general with the Eighth
Army's General Matthew Ridgway,
who supported the administration's view.

The Joint Chiefs of Staff shared the president's
belief about Korea. They were willing to accept a

limited war in Korea because they thought that
extending the war into China would be to the
Soviets' advantage. A larger war would only tie
down the US air, ground, and naval forces
needed to support and strengthen European
allies or to retaliate against Soviet moves. The
Air Force Chief of Staff General Vandenberg
also backed the president during this debate. In
an attempt to raise more money for the Air Force
from Congress, he said that while his "shoestring
air force" could devastate China if need be, its
losses would prevent it from simultaneously
deterring or punishing Soviet aggression. In the
end, Congress and public opinion came down on
Truman's side.

The administration's views seemed justified
on June 23, 1951, when the Soviet ambassador
to the United Nations called for a truce. Since
neither the UN nor Communist forces could
win in Korea without bloody and dangerous
consequences, both sides were willing to negotiate.
However, both wished to bargain from a strong
position. So limited but ferocious battles
continued throughout the cease-fire talks as each
side jockeyed for the upper hand. In October
1951 the two sides set up a small demilitarized
zone in Korea, while simultaneously increasing
their troop numbers.

While the talks dragged on, airpower carried
out three missions: supporting UN forces at the
front lines, preparing plans to attack North
Korean targets in case negotiations collapsed, and
preventing the Chinese from amassing more men
and supplies. The F-86 was at the heart of the
efforts because it patrolled "MiG Alley."

Mikoyan-Guryevich MiG-15

THE MIG-15 WAS A PRODUCT of the Soviet design bureau headed by Artyem Mikoyan and Mikhail Guryevich. The aircraft first flew in December 1947, two months after the maiden flight of the F-86 Sabre. The two airplanes were destined to be the key players in the battle for air supremacy during the Korean War. They were similar in their swept-wing configuration but different in purpose. The Sabre was an air-superiority fighter; the MiG-15 was primarily intended as an interceptor. The MiG-15 was designed to protect the Soviet Union from the threat of fleets of American bombers flying into Soviet airspace at high altitude. The designers therefore created an aircraft with a service ceiling of about 51,000ft (15,500m) and a rate of climb of 9,000ft (2,750m) per minute. They

armed the craft with powerful cannons—preferable to machine guns for striking a bomber, but less effective in a dogfight.

The US pilots in Korea were concerned when they found out that the MiG-15 had an advantage over their Sabres of about 3,000ft (900m) per minute in a climb. Furthermore, the MiG-15s could operate at altitudes that the Sabres simply could not reach. When a North Korean pilot defected with a MiG-15 in 1953, no less a person than Chuck Yeager, the first man to break the sound barrier, was flown out to Japan to look it over. He found nothing revolutionary—just a tough, agile, well-designed aircraft with a suitably powerful engine. The Korean War ace Major James Jabara also felt that the MiG-15 was nothing special, stating, "The F-86 is the best jet fighter in the world and the MiG is the second best."

TEST FLIGHT
A US Air Force crew gives a Russian-built MiG-15 its final examination before a test flight in Okinawa in 1953. The craft fell into US hands thanks to a defecting North Korean pilot.

POPULAR FIGHTER
The MiG-15 (a trainer is shown here) was the first Soviet swept-wing fighter to be mass-produced. Thousands of MiG-15s were manufactured, not just in Russia but also in Poland and Czechoslovakia.

"It was a beautiful sports car of a fighter . . . It looked like a first-class airplane."

LIEUTENANT COLONEL BRUCE HINTON
FIRST SABRE PILOT TO SHOOT DOWN A MIG-15

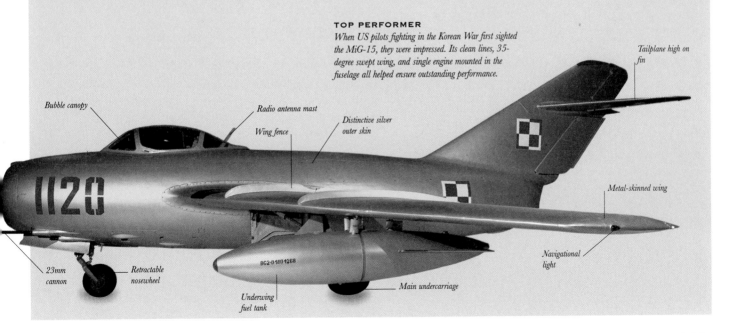

TOP PERFORMER
When US pilots fighting in the Korean War first sighted the MiG-15, they were impressed. Its clean lines, 35-degree swept wing, and single engine mounted in the fuselage all helped ensure outstanding performance.

Tailplane high on fin

Bubble canopy

Radio antenna mast

Wing fence

Distinctive silver outer skin

Metal-skinned wing

Navigational light

23mm cannon

Retractable nosewheel

Underwing fuel tank

Main undercarriage

Operation Strangle

Right before the UN and the Communists reached a stalemate in June 1951, the Fifth Air Force had drawn up a plan called Operation Strangle to push matters along. The operation was similar to one of the same name from World War II during which Allied forces bombed every possible German supply line in Italy with every available bomber and fighter-bomber to halt the flow of goods to the front lines. It forced the Germans to largely abandon railroads and even ships and rely on trucks, which turned out to be highly vulnerable as well.

The Korean version of Operation Strangle began on May 31, 1951, and continued through July. The Fifth Air Force—assisted by the Navy's carrier task force, the 1st Marine Aircraft Wing, and the Bomber Command—tried to destroy roads, bridges, and tunnels that carried truck convoys. The Chinese and North Korean supply lines stretched for 150 miles (240km) from the Yalu to the 38th parallel. The Air Force F-80s and F-84s flew most strikes. The Republic F-84 Thunderjet, which arrived in 1950 with the F-86, bolstered the Fifth Air Force's daylight ground attacks, even though it was inferior to the Sabre in air-to-air combat. The B-26s flew night patrol.

The plan was less successful than its 1944 counterpart. The emerging stalemate reduced the enemy's need for large volumes of supplies. In fact, the Chinese and North Koreans could transport

REPUBLIC F-84E
The Thunderjet was less capable in air-to-air combat than the F-86, but played an important role in ground attacks.

most of their goods at night, when the Fifth Air Force bombing was far less accurate.

Starting in October 1951 the B-29s conducted their own version of Operation Strangle. After a week in which MiGs penetrating the F-86 patrols shot down five bombers, they used the cover of night to target railroads and rail yards using a short-range navigation system (shoran) as their guide. The F-80s and F-84s joined in by attacking rail choke points, but antiaircraft fire interfered with their accuracy. Although this second Operation Strangle was not a complete success, it did manage to thwart any attempt by the enemy to build up enough supplies for a major offensive. As a result, rail interdiction continued into 1952.

The Air Force stepped up the intensity of Operation Strangle on February 25, 1952, and renamed the campaign Operation Saturate. Airmen tried to obliterate rail lines faster than North Koreans could repair them. But the high-altitude B-29 night missions were not sufficiently effective. In one six-week effort, only 1 percent of the bombs hit their mark. The Air Force needed low-altitude aircraft such as the B-26. These bombers learned to shoot off flares over their night-time targets to increase accuracy. They claimed to have destroyed thousands of trucks, but there was no way to verify this.

Since the effectiveness of night interdiction was in question, the Army began calling for more close air support. During the two Strangle operations, the Fifth Air Force flew 10 times as many interdiction as close-support sorties, which dropped to fewer than 500 a month. After the spring of 1952, the Air Force close air support jumped to 2,000 sorties a month, or nearly half the number of interdiction attacks.

UP IN FLAMES
US aircraft attack a rail yard near Wonsan, North Korea.

Furthermore, the joint operations center at Seoul improved its handling of emergency requests, so that the total time between an initial request and the resulting fighter strike was about 40 minutes.

The Air Force strategy changed yet again in May 1952, when General Ridgway ended his year-long tour as UN commander and General Mark W. Clark stepped in. Clark wanted to end the deadlock on the truce talks. Therefore, he approved General Weyland's recommendation to attack North Korea's hydroelectric plants, which would cut off power throughout the country and impress on its leaders the consequences of delaying a settlement. The Fifth Air Force and Task Force 77 drafted a plan, which the Joint Chiefs of Staff agreed with and persuaded President Truman to back. In June 1952 Air Force and Navy fighter-bombers ran 1,200 sorties and destroyed 11 out of 17 hydroelectric plants in four complexes: Sui-ho, Chosin, Fusen, and Kyosen. North Korea lost nearly all its power for two weeks and would not fully recover even by the end of the war 13 months later. Even Manchuria, China, lost a quarter of its power supply for a time. Antiaircraft fire hit only two Navy planes, and both pilots were rescued. The

LESSONS LEARNED

THE AIR FORCE ENTERED the war committed to the use of heavy bombers armed with atomic weapons, to a deterrence strategy, and—should deterrence fail—to a retaliatory strike. Three years of limited war reinforced the wisdom of these principles.

The Air Force leadership agreed that the United States should stand ready to attack the Soviet Union and not to divide its strength in another proxy war. For instance, when General Vandenberg complained about the Air Force's shoestring budget, he was more concerned about the country's ability to engage in worldwide deterrence or retaliation than tactical operations in Korea. Moreover, contrary to what circumstances might suggest, the North Korean invasion of South Korea did not mean deterrence had failed. After all, the Soviet Union did not take advantage of the Far East war by attacking elsewhere. The threat of nuclear war stayed the Soviets' hand.

Vandenberg concluded that the Soviet Union remained the biggest danger to the United States in the near future. Given the steady flow of supplies to the North Koreans from China despite the UN Command's steady interdiction sorties, he also suggested that the only way to destroy an enemy's industrial base would be through nuclear weapons. The United States adopted this platform in the middle of 1953 as the likeliest means to prevent aggression by the Soviet Union and its satellite states.

MiGs did not down a single US aircraft. In fact, the 250 MiGs stabled at Antung, Manchuria, fled farther inland. But Clark's plan did not push the talks forward as US leaders had hoped.

The UN Command continued to apply airpower to speed up the talks. In July and August 1952 Air Force and Navy aircraft carried out the two biggest raids of the war, both against Pyongyang. In July fighter-bombers flew 1,200 sorties and B-29s flew 54. In August fighter-bombers performed 1,400 sorties. These attacks did not change matters much—but other factors intervened at this time that began to turn things around.

First, a popular World War II general, Dwight D. Eisenhower, won the presidential election in November 1952 and immediately headed over to Korea to assess the situation. He discussed the possibility of using atomic weapons and announced that the US Navy would no longer protect mainland China from the Chinese Nationalists in Taiwan. In addition, the Soviet Premier Josef Stalin died in March 1953. China lost a dependable ally as Soviet leaders began fighting among themselves over who would next lead the Soviet Union. Finally, General Clark sent B-29s and Fifth Air Force fighter-bombers against North Korea's irrigation dams, immediately destroying three. Although the North Koreans quickly repaired the damage, these strikes threatened their food supply.

By June 1953, aware of all these threats, as well as of the sustained loss of men and funds if the war continued, the Chinese seemed ready to sign an armistice that would temporarily stop fighting while negotiations on a permanent peace treaty were under way. But there was a catch: South Korean President Rhee did not support a divided Korea, so he freed, rather than repatriated, North Korean prisoners of war. The Communists retaliated with a savage offensive, which resulted in some last large-scale air battles of the war. Air Force close air support sorties increased by 40 percent to almost 7,500 during June 1953. The MiGs appeared over North Korea in greater numbers than before, but suffered their greatest losses—F-86 pilots claimed more than 100 kills. The fighter-bombers and B-29s battered North Korean airfields. Finally, China, North Korea, and the United States signed an armistice on July 27, 1953.

The outcome

It is difficult to say exactly why the war ended. It might have been the threat of atomic war. It might have been Stalin's death, which distracted the Soviets and threw their support for China and North Korea into turmoil. Or it might have been that both sides had endured as much loss, both in people and in funds, as they could sustain. The UN Command counted 450,000

LOCKHEED F-80C
This Shooting Star flew combat missions in the Korean War. It was restored and appears as it did in 1950, when assigned to the 8th Fighter-Bomber Group.

dead or wounded among its troops, including 35,000 Americans killed, 100,000 Americans wounded, and 300,000 South Koreans dead or wounded. The estimated Chinese and North Korean casualties were three times that number.

As in World War II, airpower proved its worth during the Korean War. Far East Air Forces killed nearly 150,000 North Korean and Chinese troops and destroyed more than 950 aircraft, 800 bridges, 1,100 tanks, 800 locomotives, 9,000 railroad cars, 70,000 vehicles, and 80,000 buildings. This effort cost the Far East Air Forces 1,200 airmen and 750 aircraft. For the first time, the Air Force reduced its death toll through air supremacy and helicopter rescues behind enemy lines. The Air Rescue Service retrieved 170 pilots or crewmen from enemy territory, more than 10 percent of those who went down there.

Both sides showed restraint during the war. For instance, the UN Command never bombed Manchuria, so MiGs found sanctuary there. Chinese aircraft did not attack cargo moving through South Korea or touch UN forces at the front lines. And while the United States was capable of using the atomic bomb, it did not. It limited itself to a conventional war.

One other outcome was the type of aircraft developed for the Air Force. While some veteran pilots argued for a tactical machine dedicated to

close air support, strafing, and maneuverability, none emerged. What dominated—and continued to dominate—was the multipurpose fighter-bomber. During the Korean War, this was the F-86; in the late 1950s, it was the F-104. These aircraft could do it all: bomb, strafe, and engage in air-to-air combat. They were also heavier and more complex aircraft than what tactical air advocates hoped for.

DOCTRINE AND HISTORY—THE KOREAN WAR

DISTINCTIVE CAPABILITIES	FUNCTIONS (MISSIONS)	DOCTRINAL EMPHASIS
• Air and Space Superiority • Precision Engagement • Agile Combat Support	• Counterland • Close Air Support • Interdiction • Surveillance and Reconnaissance • Search and Rescue • Air Refueling • Strategic Attack	• Theater Attack on Military Targets • Counterair • MiG Alley • Birth of Jet Fighter

LAUNCH POSITION

13

THE CUBAN MISSILE CRISIS: AIR AND SPACE POWER REVISITED

MANY AMERICANS' WORST FEARS were realized when President John F. Kennedy revealed that the Soviets were stationing nuclear missiles in Cuba—90 miles (145km) south of Florida. The resulting crisis demonstrated the US ability to spy from the sky on Soviet activities, whether in the Soviet Union itself or elsewhere around the globe. The Soviets finally backed down, but the crisis highlighted the increasing importance of intercontinental ballistic missiles and launched a three-decade nuclear arms race.

MISSILE-READY TENTS

MISSILE ERECTORS

STARE DOWN IN THE CARIBBEAN

THE UNITED STATES AND THE SOVIET UNION REACH THE BRINK OF THE UNTHINKABLE

THE COLD WAR BETWEEN the United States and the Soviet Union began with the Berlin airlift in 1948–49. It continued during the Korean War (1950–53), when the Soviets backed their Communist allies, North Korea and China, while the United States and the United Nations (UN) Command supported an independent South Korea. The Cold War reached a new pitch in 1962 with the Cuban Missile Crisis. It would be the closest the two countries ever got to nuclear war.

Developments between 1953 and 1962 increased tensions between the United States and the Soviet Union and helped precipitate the crisis. For instance, as you read in Chapter 10, Lockheed Aircraft developed the photographic reconnaissance aircraft, the U-2, in 1955. The United States put this high-altitude aircraft to use over the Soviet Union in 1956. Photos from these flights proved that, contrary to popular belief, the Soviets did not have more bombers or missiles than America did. In fact, the Soviet arsenal was inferior to that of the United States. As a result of those findings, senior US officials quietly harbored a sense of military superiority.

All did not go as planned with the U-2, however. While engineers designed it to fly at around 70,000ft (21,336m)—well above the supposed range of antiaircraft rockets, turbojet interceptors, and radar—the Soviets developed surface-to-air missiles (SAMs) that could reach that altitude. In May 1960 a Soviet SAM exploded close to a U-2 flying over Sverdlovsk in the middle of the Soviet Union. The missile sent the U-2 spiraling to the ground. Pilot Francis Gary Powers, a Central Intelligence Agency (CIA) employee, parachuted to Earth. The Soviets captured him and put him on trial as a spy. They eventually sent him home in exchange for one of their own held by the United States, but the event added to the mistrust between the two countries.

Since the Soviet Union had no missiles that could reach the United States, it took the island nation of Cuba under its wing and built a military base there in 1962. Only 90 miles (145km) from Florida, Cuba was the perfect platform from which the Soviets could stage an attack. Furthermore, Cuba had

EVIDENCE
Flying two U-2s, Majors Rudolf Anderson Jr. and Richard S. Heyser took photos of Soviet missile installations like this one in Cuba on October 14, 1962.

GARY POWERS
The Soviets knocked US pilot Francis Gary Powers and his U-2 out of their skies in 1960. Powers's capture and subsequent trial increased the strain between the Soviet Union and the United States.

THE U-2

The U-2 spy plane gave the United States an edge over its Cold War enemies. With this high-altitude aircraft, the country could study its opponents' military buildup.

turned Communist as recently as 1960, and thus was a natural Soviet ally. The United States knew that the Soviets had provided Cuban Prime Minister Fidel Castro's government with defensive weapons such as antiaircraft missiles. But rumors hinted at the installation of offensive weapons as well—particularly ballistic missiles with nuclear warheads. If these rumors were true, this would mark the first time the Soviets had deployed nuclear weapons outside their own territory.

US Attorney General Robert F. Kennedy informed Anatoly Dobrynin, the Soviet ambassador to the United States, that the United States was watching activity in Cuba closely. The appearance of offensive missiles, Kennedy warned, would have "the gravest of consequences." The ambassador assured Kennedy that his country was giving Cuba only defensive weapons. He also implied that Soviet Premier Nikita Khrushchev would do nothing to embarrass the attorney general's brother, President John F. Kennedy, in the months before the November 1962 congressional elections. The administration took the ambassador at his word, since it had no evidence to disprove him.

But photos taken during flights over Cuba by U-2s stationed at California's Edwards Air Force Base would soon reveal a much different story. On October 14 Majors Rudolf Anderson Jr. and Richard S. Heyser returned with pictures of a medium-range ballistic missile launch

site in a field near San Cristobal, Cuba. Offensive weapons were present in Cuba, after all, along with 20,000 Soviet troops to install and operate them.

The Soviets' bold move served two purposes: First and more important, it allowed the Soviet Union to reach the continental United States with medium-range ballistic missiles, intermediate-range ballistic missiles, and Ilyushin-28 jet-powered light bombers at a time when Soviet intercontinental weapons were few and unreliable. Second, it protected a fellow Communist country from US invasion. The United States had already sponsored one botched invasion attempt by anti-Castro exiles. What had been an irritant to Washington now became a strategic threat.

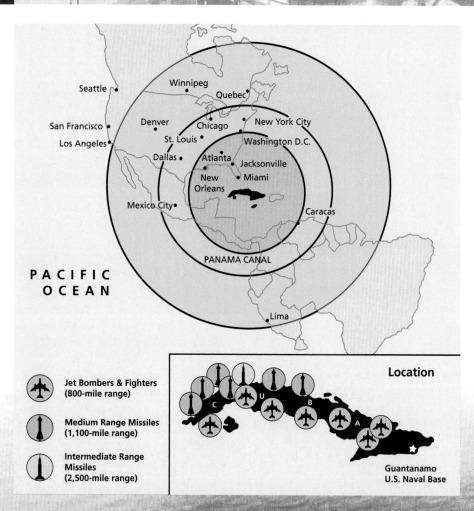

Seattle
Winnipeg
Quebec
San Francisco
Denver
Chicago
New York City
Los Angeles
St. Louis
Washington D.C.
Dallas
Atlanta
Jacksonville
New Orleans
Miami
Mexico City
Caracas
PANAMA CANAL
Lima

Jet Bombers & Fighters
(800-mile range)

Medium Range Missiles
(1,100-mile range)

Intermediate Range Missiles
(2,500-mile range)

Location

C U B A

Guantanamo
U.S. Naval Base

THREAT ASSESSMENT

The Soviets planted bombers, fighters, and missiles around Cuba in 1962. This map shows the location of each type of weapon in Cuba and its range.

The crisis

President Kennedy convened a group of officials to advise him on the matter. The committee included Vice President Lyndon Johnson, Robert Kennedy, Secretary of State Dean Rusk and other State Department representatives, CIA Director John R. McCone, Secretary of Defense Robert McNamara, and General Maxwell D. Taylor, who was chairman of the Joint Chiefs of Staff. In a series of meetings that began on October 16, the committee fashioned a national strategy to eliminate the weapons that the Soviets had installed in Cuba. The members preferred pressuring Khrushchev into removing them, but, if necessary, they would propose destroying them.

The committee explored several courses of action. One possibility was a trade—the withdrawal of Soviet weapons from Cuba in return for the recall of the American Jupiter missiles from Turkey. The Soviets seemed to favor this plan. However, President Kennedy decided it would look as if the United States could be too easily bullied into doing something it might not want to do. The irony was that the president had already authorized entering negotiations with Turkey to remove these missiles. The Jupiters were mere stopgaps until enough Polaris submarines at sea and Minuteman weapons in their silos could take over their

THE NAVAL BLOCKADE

President Kennedy ordered a naval blockade in October 1962 to halt the flow of Soviet military goods to Cuba. Here a US destroyer prepares to intercept a freighter heading toward the island.

targets. The president put the withdrawal plan on hold.

The Joint Chiefs of Staff favored a surprise aerial attack on the ballistic missile sites, the antiaircraft missiles, and other defensive weapons. The Tactical Air Command's General Walter C. Sweeney admitted that about 10 percent of the offensive weapons would survive a nonnuclear attack, and that any attack would inflict casualties among Cuban civilians and Soviet technicians. The remaining 10 percent of the offensive weapons could then be used against the United States with dire results. While some officials raised the possibility of using tactical nuclear weapons to guarantee complete elimination of the ballistic missile sites, no one seriously considered that idea.

The president rejected these options. Instead, he chose to start with a naval blockade, or quarantine. He announced the quarantine on October 22 in a televised address. Underscoring the gravity of the situation, he said that cities in the United States as far north as Washington, D.C., lay under the shadow of the medium-range missiles in Cuba. These weapons could hit any target between Hudson Bay, Canada, and Lima, Peru, he noted. Kennedy stated

US CASUALTY
Major Rudolf Anderson was the only casualty of the Cuban Missile Crisis. A Soviet SAM shot down his U-2 over Cuba on October 27, 1962.

that for the present, the quarantine seemed the best course to follow. This option avoided the possibility of a confrontation on land and moved it out to sea. It established a demarcation line where US warships would stop Soviet, East European, and charter vessels and search them for military cargo. If the United States found prohibited items on a ship, it would order the vessel to change course for a non-Cuban port. This gave Khrushchev some breathing space to figure out how he would handle the situation. He could either recall the ships or risk a violent confrontation.

The United States took further steps to secure its position. It prepared for an air attack and invasion, should the quarantine fail. Marines reinforced the US base at Guantanamo Bay near Cuba's southeastern tip and engaged in amphibious exercises off Puerto Rico. Six Army divisions went on alert, and the Air Force Reserve provided 14 squadrons of transports to carry invasion troops and equipment. Air Force RF-101 and Navy F8U-1P tactical reconnaissance aircraft began low-altitude flights over Cuba to complement the continuing U-2 surveillance. In addition, the Tactical Air Command planned strikes to destroy the missiles and support any invasion.

The Strategic Air Command (SAC) continued the U-2 flights and took steps to defend against a surprise attack on the United States, dispersing its nuclear-armed B-47s among some 40 airfields. Meanwhile, it kept 70 B-52s in the air at all times. Finally, all available ballistic missiles stood ready for a countdown. Their targets, however, would not have been in Cuba. When President Kennedy announced the quarantine on October 22, he upped the ante on the Soviets. "It shall be the policy of this nation," he said, "to regard any nuclear missile launched from Cuba against any nation in the Western Hemisphere as an attack by the Soviet Union on the United States, requiring a full retaliatory response upon the Soviet Union."

The blockade went into effect on October 24. Ships believed to be carrying offensive weapons to Cuba slowed immediately to postpone or, the administration hoped, avoid a confrontation. Nevertheless, the situation remained dangerous. Aerial reconnaissance revealed, for example, that work was proceeding on the Cuban missile sites, apparently at an accelerated pace. And on October 27, a SAM downed Major Anderson's U-2 over Cuba, killing him. He was the only casualty of the Cuban Missile Crisis. Despite

the tension, an air attack planned for October 30 and the follow-up invasion proved unnecessary. The Soviet Union did not challenge the quarantine, and on October 28 it agreed to remove its offensive weapons from Cuba. In return, the United States pledged not to invade the island.

Minuteman deployment

Unknown to the general public at the time was that on October 24—the very day the blockade went into effect—the first Minuteman missile squadron went operational. These nuclear-tipped missiles fell in Strategic Air Command's domain. Added to strategic bombers and Polaris-equipped submarines, they represented the third leg of the country's nuclear defense triad. The Air Force placed the first 10 solid-fuel Minuteman missiles in underground silos at Malmstrom Air Force Base in Montana. Meanwhile, engineers continued work to improve their design. By 1964 the Air Force deployed the more accurate Minuteman II. By 1967 SAC had 1,000 Minuteman missiles scattered around the country, and by 1968 the even more accurate and longer-range Minuteman III came on line.

THE MINUTEMAN I MISSILE
The nuclear-tipped Minuteman I missile, along with bombers and Polaris-equipped submarines, provided a defense shield for the United States. The missiles first became operational on October 24, 1962, the same day the naval blockade around Cuba took effect.

Interceptors

WHILE THE BURDEN OF US defense rested largely on its ability to deliver nuclear weapons, it required fighters to fend off an enemy's nuclear bombers as well.

Three interceptor fighters entered service in the 1950s: the F-101, which ran aerial surveillance during the Cuban Missile Crisis; the F-104; and the F-106. Designers did not build these fighters for air-to-air combat. They were not sufficiently maneuverable, but they were fast, and they had an impressive climb rate. The intent was that they would go after enemy bombers headed toward the US mainland or a US ally and shoot them down with radar-guided air-to-air missiles directed by ground controllers.

The Air Force began using the McDonnell F-101B Voodoo in 1959, and it eventually had 400 of these aircraft. But they were difficult to fly, and around 20 percent crashed; so the service phased them out by 1970. The Lockheed F-104A Starfighter was a lightweight fighter. It set a world speed record in 1958, but like the F-101, it had defects. Its range was too short to be practical, and its small wings meant it did not maneuver well. The Air Force's F-106 entered service in 1959 with a powerful engine and a thin waist, called a "wasp waist," that let it reach supersonic flight.

LOCKHEED F-104A STARFIGHTER
The F-104 broke speed records, but short wings hampered its maneuverability.

CONVAIR F-106 DELTA DART
The F-106 had a crew of one and could reach 1,265mph (2,035kmph), or Mach 1.9.

MCDONNELL F-101B VOODOO
The F-101B flew at low altitudes over Cuba to supplement the U-2 spy plane's mission.

Aftereffects

Since the Cuban Missile Crisis ended, observers have debated why the Soviet Union agreed to stop placing missiles within range of the United States. US leaders who supported nuclear deterrence argued that the country's overwhelming retaliatory force, which could ensure the destruction of Soviet cities, forced Khrushchev to back down. The Soviet Union at that point had only about 200 bombers and 35 intercontinental missiles. By contrast, the US Air Force's Strategic Air Command had 1,600 bombers and 200 missiles. But advocates of conventional forces had their own case to make. They held that Soviet leaders had reacted to the prospect of an invasion of Cuba by an overwhelming US force that included Air Force tactical aviation and the Navy. In fact, President Kennedy employed both kinds of power. He used the principles of flexible response so he could intimidate with both hands. The US military was certainly capable of waging either kind of war.

The Soviet Union learned a lesson from the crisis. Khrushchev came away convinced of the necessity of intercontinental ballistic missiles based within the Soviet Union. The country could not depend on shorter-range missiles placed outside its territory. As a Soviet official at the United Nations told an American diplomat while his country was withdrawing offensive weapons from Cuba, "You Americans will never be able to do this to us again." Meanwhile, the United States had to accept the Castro regime in Cuba, which took advantage of the crisis to achieve its own security objectives. While Castro remained in power in large part thanks to the episode's outcome, Khrushchev's hold began to slip. Two years later, his colleagues on the governing Politburo replaced him with Alexei Kosygin.

A final consequence of the Cuban Missile Crisis was that the US–Soviet arms race became even more costly. The Soviet Union focused in large part on expanding its intercontinental ballistic missile arsenal. Even though the United States already had the upper hand in long-range missiles, it continued to add to its missile and nuclear weapons stockpile. This arms race, which lasted until 1989, would strain both countries' economies.

TEST FLIGHT

An LGM-30 Minuteman III gets a test launch. The LGM-30 went operational in 1970 and production ended in 1978. Missile development continues to the present day.

VIETNAM: PART I

14

ANOTHER AFTER-EFFECT OF WORLD WAR II, the division of Vietnam into a Communist northern zone and a noncommunist southern sector, occurred after Vietnamese forces defeated French colonial troops. As North Vietnam and its sympathizers in the south battled the South Vietnamese government on the latter's soil, the Kennedy administration began providing US Army and Air Force advisers to the Saigon government. Over the next few years, the US commitment grew until some half a million Soldiers, Airmen, Marines, and Sailors were committed to the fight. The Air Force favored a swift and intense campaign to break the North's will to fight, but the Johnson administration opted for a strategy of gradually ramping up the pressure in the hope the enemy would relent.

THE WAR IN SOUTHEAST ASIA, 1961–1968

WHAT STARTED OUT AS MILITARY ASSISTANCE BECAME A FULL-BLOWN WAR AGAINST AN UNCONVENTIONAL ENEMY

> "The Vietnam War symbolized a new era of aerial technology, searing its way into public consciousness through the clatter of a helicopter or the bright yellow flame of a bomb explosion."
>
> JOHN L. PIMLOTT
> MILITARY HISTORIAN

IN JANUARY 1961, as President John F. Kennedy took office, Soviet Premier Nikita Khrushchev endorsed any and all Communist-led wars for "national liberation"—installation of a Communist dictatorship. China, a US ally from World War II had already gone Communist in 1949. The United States fought the Korean War to keep the same fate from befalling South Korea. Now that Communist forces were trying to take over South Vietnam as well, the newly inaugurated president and his advisers had to decide whether to intervene in this latest attempt.

As they had done during the Berlin airlift and the Korean War, the Soviets and the Americans avoided direct confrontation. The nuclear shadow of the Cold War made that inadvisable, but the two sides indirectly challenged one another's interests in third countries. South Vietnam was yet another example. The small Asian country was the southern half of the former French colony. France released its hold on Vietnam in 1954, when it lost a major battle at Dien Bien Phu to the forces of Communist leader Ho Chi Minh. The ensuing 1954 Geneva Accords cut the

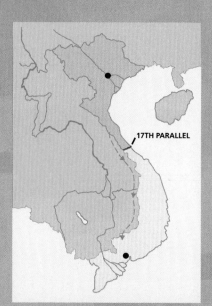

THE 17TH PARALLEL
The 1954 Geneva Accords split Vietnam into two countries along the 17th parallel. Much like the split in Korea, this divide led to tensions and eventually war.

IN TRAINING
The United States supported the Western-leaning South Vietnamese with advisers, funding, and supplies. The Air Force also trained South Vietnamese Air Force personnel (seen here).

country in two along the 17th parallel pending general elections. But the elections never took place; instead, the ruling party in each half organized separate governments. To the north was the Communist-led Democratic Republic of Vietnam, or North Vietnam. To the south was the Republic of Vietnam, or South Vietnam, led by President Ngo Dinh Diem.

The North Vietnamese wanted to reunite the two Vietnams into one Communist nation. Their principal instrument was the Viet Cong (the word is a contraction of a term that means "Vietnamese Communists"). South Vietnamese, including disgruntled peasants without farmland to call their own, originally composed the bulk of the Viet Cong. These guerillas carried out ambushes and assassinations to disrupt the south and overthrow Diem. While the Soviets and Chinese backed North Vietnam, the United States supported South Vietnam with military advisers, money, and supplies. US troops would not arrive until 1965.

Early involvement

The United States had begun sending money and personnel into Vietnam in support of the French in 1950, and the Air Force's role in Vietnam began a year later. In 1955 the US Military Assistance Advisory Group, Indochina, active since 1950, and

its air section, formed in 1951, became the Military Assistance Advisory Group, Vietnam. When France exited Vietnam in 1954, US Air Force officers and enlisted men took over work with the South Vietnamese Air Force. By early 1961 this air force had six squadrons ready for combat—one fighter, two transport, two liaison aircraft, and one helicopter. Meanwhile, North Vietnam moved people and supplies down its Ho Chi Minh Trail, a maze of roads and trails in neighboring Laos. Some 15,000 Viet Cong operated around Saigon, South Vietnam's capital, and elsewhere in the south. By this time, South Vietnam's armed forces resembled their US counterparts, with ground, sea, and air services. The Viet Cong, by contrast, fought exclusively as a guerrilla army.

Throughout 1961 the United States grew more heavily involved in South Vietnam. In September the Air Force established its first permanent unit with 67 Airmen. They installed radars at Tan Son Nhut Air Base, which also served as Saigon's airport, monitored air traffic, and trained South Vietnamese to do so. They also formed a tactical air control system for a vast fleet of South Vietnamese and US aircraft. In October four RF-101s joined the combat post. These photoreconnaissance (photorecon) aircraft began flying missions over South Vietnam and Laos within days of their arrival.

A PHOTORECON MISSION
The McDonnell RF-101 photorecon aircraft joined the mission in Vietnam in 1961. Here, technicians prepare a Voodoo for a mission in January 1967.

FARM GATE
Since the Geneva Accords did not permit the United States to supply South Vietnam with jets, the first aircraft the US military supplied to its allies included propeller-driven C-47s, T-28s (below), and B-26s (left). The Air Force's counterinsurgency unit, called Farm Gate, stabled its aircraft at Bien Hoa Air Base near Saigon.

Deniable involvement

As the Viet Cong stepped up their attacks by changing from all-guerrilla tactics using small raiding parties to all-out pitched battles using battalions, the United States increased its support for South Vietnam. It no longer limited itself to advice and technical assistance. Instead, starting in October 1961, a special Air Force detachment flew combat missions even as it trained Diem's air arm. The 1954 Geneva Accords prohibited the United States from supplying South Vietnam with jet aircraft, but they did permit provision of propeller-driven craft. In accordance with this rule, the Air Force special detachment—a counterinsurgency unit called "Farm Gate"—assembled a collection of old C-47s, T-28s, and B-26s at Bien Hoa Air Base near Saigon by mid-November. The transports conducted reconnaissance or psychological warfare missions—dropping leaflets or broadcasting from loudspeakers. The bombers and trainers attacked the Viet Cong. US Army helicopters carried South Vietnamese troops into action as US door-gunners fired at the enemy and Farm Gate bombed and strafed in support of the operations.

The Kennedy administration was not yet ready to acknowledge how rapidly the US role in the conflict was expanding, however. With no casualties or reports in the press, administration spokesmen denied that Americans were fighting the Viet Cong at all. Any interaction, they said, happened unavoidably and only in the course of their training duties. To preserve this illusion, Farm Gate aircraft wore South Vietnamese insignia and usually brought along a South Vietnamese trainee when conducting strikes or other combat missions. Moreover, Farm Gate undertook only those combat operations that officials believed were beyond the South Vietnamese Air Force's ability.

Army-Air Force wrangling

The US Air Force split its duties in Vietnam. The Air Force section of the Military Assistance Advisory Group, Vietnam, oversaw training. The 2d Advance Echelon of the Thirteenth Air Force controlled combat operations. In November 1961, Brigadier General Rollen H. Anthis, the Thirteenth Air Force's vice commander, became the first head of the 2d Advance Echelon. Eventually he would become air commander in Vietnam as well as the representative of the Pacific Air Forces for all Air Force matters in Southeast Asia.

The Air Force was not happy with the arrangement, however. The US Military Assistance Command—set up in February 1962 to oversee the entire Vietnamese theater—was largely filled with Army officers, who as the Air Force saw it, did not fully understand airpower.

BRIGADIER GENERAL ROLLEN ANTHIS
Brigadier General Rollen Anthis became the first head of the 2d Advance Echelon in November 1961. The 2d Advance Echelon would eventually become the Seventh Air Force.

Meanwhile, Air Force Chief of Staff General Curtis LeMay was skeptical of US policy in Vietnam. If the United States and South Vietnam wanted to crush the Communists, he believed, the strategy should not be to make political and economic fixes in South Vietnam. LeMay argued that the United States should exercise overwhelming force against North Vietnam. As it was, US policy was not to provoke the Soviets or Chinese, who had advisers on the ground in North Vietnam. The United States did not want a repeat of Korea, where Chinese troops flooded in

on the side of the North Koreans. LeMay believed these cautious rules tied the US military's hands.

In January 1962, as LeMay proposed his alternative approach to the war, the Air Force faced some minor changes in Vietnam. For instance, a detachment of a dozen Fairchild C-123 transports arrived in South Vietnam to deliver supplies to distant outposts and to drop paratroopers. Called "Mule Train," the unit operated 10 C-123s from Tan Son Nhut Air Base and two from Da Nang, but with the Army in charge of the US Military Assistance Command, that mission changed. Army de Havilland CV-2 Caribou transports took over the supply missions. Eventually, helicopters replaced the parachute for airborne attacks.

The C-123 found a new duty, however. When the Viet Cong began ambushing highways, the cargo aircraft could safely transport passengers and supplies (a different kind of operation than the distant outposts the Caribous serviced). Between January and June 1962, the number of C-123 sorties increased from 296 a month to 1,100. C-123s also began dropping herbicides on the jungles to kill the foliage and expose the Viet Cong operating under the canopy. At the time, no one knew that the herbicide, Agent Orange, was toxic to people.

In these early days of US involvement in Vietnam, the Air Force and Army fought a continuing power struggle over the appropriate uses of aircraft. The Air Force wanted a central tactical air control system. With such a system, they could use scarce resources to meet changing needs. The Army wanted each senior commander on the ground to control his own air units. Any effort to hand over management to the South Vietnamese—the original plan—was quickly scrapped, as Diem feared ouster in a military coup. As a result, Diem tended to decentralize his air force assets among his four corps commanders.

Air Force reorganization

Throughout 1962 the Air Force supported the South Vietnamese by attacking Viet Cong training areas, troop concentrations, supply depots, and *sampans* (small boats common in Asia); aiding ground troops with bombing and strafing; and helping with aerial reconnaissance. When the year ended, more than 11,000 Americans were serving in South Vietnam— one-third of them members of the Air Force. During the first seven months of 1963, several more Air Force units arrived, upping the total number of Air Force personnel to 5,000.

Initially, the Air Force borrowed most of its units for South Vietnam from regular outfits in the United States. But as personnel and aircraft numbers increased, General Anthis created a more formal

organization for more than a dozen units. For example, in July 1963, Anthis converted Farm Gate into the 1st Air Commando squadron, a component of the Pacific Air Forces. Mule Train units became troop-carrier squadrons. The 33d and 34th Tactical Groups performed administrative and maintenance duties.

Despite these efforts, airpower was often sidelined. This was partly because the North sent no aircraft into the South during this phase of the war. Vietnam was largely a ground war; airpower played only a supporting role. The Military Assistance Command's National Campaign Plan, drafted in 1963, focused on routing the Viet Cong using small, locally controlled ground operations rather than airpower. The plan gave the Army and Marine Corps their own air operations, which were separate from those of the Air Force. Furthermore, while the United States was beefing up its presence in Southeast Asia, the political situation in South Vietnam was falling apart. In the middle of 1963, South Vietnamese army officers overthrew Diem, executing the president and his brother. Although the United States continued to support South Vietnam throughout these changes, the junta that toppled Diem eventually collapsed, only to be succeeded by one new government after another. Instability reigned.

Stateside turmoil

The United States was undergoing its own wrenching political changes, following the assassination of President Kennedy on November 22, 1963. Vice President Lyndon B. Johnson became the country's commander in chief. In January 1964 Major General Joseph H. Moore became commander of the 2d Air Division (formerly the 2d Advance Echelon). In June

TAKING OFFICE
Lyndon B. Johnson took the oath of office of President of the United States on November 22, 1963, following the assassination of President John F. Kennedy in Dallas, Texas.

1964 General William C. Westmoreland took over the US Military Assistance Command from General Maxwell D. Taylor. Taylor stepped down as chairman of the Joint Chiefs of Staff to take the job of ambassador to Saigon. In February 1964 Admiral U. S. Grant Sharp assumed leadership of the Pacific Command, which oversaw the Military Assistance Command.

Meanwhile in Southeast Asia, the United States also was drawn into troubles in Laos—next door to Vietnam—when Communist Pathet Lao forces disrupted that country's calm. President Johnson transferred American T-28s to the Royal Laotian Air Force and established an Air Force detachment in Thailand to train Laotian pilots and maintain their aircraft. After the Pathet Lao downed a US Navy reconnaissance jet in June, eight F-100s struck an antiaircraft position on the Plain of Jars in northern Laos. This move opened a second Air Force war in the region.

For a while, things were relatively quiet in South Vietnam. During the hiatus, the South Vietnamese Air Force expanded. By early 1964, it included 13 squadrons—four fighter, four observation, three helicopter, and two C-47 transport. The South Vietnamese assigned wings to geographical areas rather than to individual corps commanders, which somewhat satisfied the Air Force's desire for more centralized control of airpower. By mid-1964 the United States had retired the T-28s and B-26s, and replaced them with A-1 Skyraiders, which reduced response time to battlefield emergencies.

NEW KID ON THE BLOCK
When the Air Force retired its aging T-28s and B-26s from Vietnam in 1964, it replaced them with the A-1 Skyraider.

During this lull in hostilities, General LeMay continued to push for a more aggressive approach toward the North. He argued for interdiction strikes in South Vietnam, air attacks on guerrillas in Laos, bombing North Vietnam, and mining North Vietnamese harbors.

For their part, the North Vietnamese were not pleased with the calm. Following Diem's execution, much of the unrest in the South faded. The Viet Cong no longer had the backing among the peasants it once enjoyed. While the Communists considered marching the regular North Vietnamese Army across the 17th parallel to stir things up and inject some discipline into the Viet Cong, an incident at sea occurred that would change everything.

MAIN AIR FORCE DUTIES IN SOUTH VIETNAM

The Air Force fulfilled seven primary duties in South Vietnam:

- Interdiction
- Close air support
- Airlift
- Reconnaissance
- Search and rescue
- Air-to-air refueling
- Command and control (supervising operations from the air)

Gulf of Tonkin incident

By 1964 support for action in Vietnam was growing thin in the United States. Johnson had an election coming up, and the Democratic Party platform promised to exercise caution in Southeast Asia. The administration was torn between the desire to administer a finishing blow to secure South Vietnam and a reluctance to become more committed than it already was. American planners were still concerned about drawing China into the conflict.

All this thinking took a backseat on August 2, 1964, when three North Vietnamese Navy torpedo boats attacked the American destroyer USS *Maddox* as it patrolled the waters five miles off North Vietnam. The torpedoes all missed

HELP AT SEA
Aircraft from the carrier USS Ticonderoga *came to the aid of the destroyer USS* Maddox *in the Gulf of Tonkin in 1964. Here, the ship refuels off the Vietnamese coast.*

their targets, but a machine gun scored a hit. In response, the destroyer and aircraft from the aircraft carrier USS *Ticonderoga* sank one of the torpedo boats and badly damaged another. After this action, the *Maddox* joined another destroyer, the USS *C. Turner Joy*, and resumed patrolling. At no time did any US reconnaissance ship get closer than five miles from North Vietnamese territory. The recognized territorial claim to offshore waters at that time was three miles, so the US ships were well outside that range. Still, on August 4, torpedo boats once again harassed the destroyers. The US ships claimed they sank two of them and damaged a third.

SOUTHEAST ASIA
A detailed look at the Southeast Asian theater.

Besides ordering carrier aircraft to bomb the torpedo boats' bases, Johnson persuaded Congress to pass the Tonkin Gulf Resolution, which gave him authority to retaliate against any future North Vietnamese attacks. He also ordered Air Force jets into Southeast Asia. Their presence would be crucial should North Vietnam or China respond to the carrier raids.

The actions in the Gulf of Tonkin and their political consequences did not immediately change the war's course. Events unfolded gradually, and it is only in retrospect that the resolution can be seen as a turning point. Congress's vote gave the president the sole authority for US policy in Southeast Asia and the right to use force as he saw fit, as long as the North was trying to conquer the South.

The Air Force quickly dispatched aircraft to their new bases in South Vietnam. Included were 12 F-102s, eight F-100s, and two B-57 squadrons. The service also sent 10 F-100s and eight F-105s to Thailand, two squadrons of Tactical Air Command F-100s to the Philippines, RF-101s to Okinawa, 48 C-130s to Okinawa and the Philippines, and 48 Strategic Air Command (SAC) KC-135 tankers to Guam to refuel jet fighters. Despite this buildup, combat remained restricted to South Vietnam, and pilots continued to fly only propeller-driven aircraft. In support of the propeller fleet, the Air Force got 25 A-1Hs from the Navy plus another squadron of 16 C-123s. The jet deployments served primarily to demonstrate American resolve, much as was done in Europe during the Berlin crisis.

On November 1, 1964, the Viet Cong attacked the US base at Bien Hoa, killing four Americans and wounding 72, while destroying five B-57s, and damaging 13 others. The United States waited to retaliate until after Johnson won reelection. Then, on December 14, the United States sent F-100s, RF-101s, and F-105s from their Thai base against the Ho Chi Minh Trail

BIEN HOA ASSAULT
The Viet Cong destroyed five B-57s like this one at the Bien Hoa Air Base in South Vietnam in 1964. The enemy damaged 13 other bombers during the raid.

in southern Laos in an operation called Barrel Roll. This was the Air Force's third war in Southeast Asia.

The United States continued to refrain from bombing North Vietnam, even though attacks on Americans persisted. But that changed after a February 7, 1965, Viet Cong strike that killed eight US Soldiers and wounded 104 near Pleiku. Johnson lifted all remaining restrictions on the use of jets in South Vietnam, and he no longer required a South Vietnamese observer or trainer to be on board a US bomber. On February 7 and 8, Air Force and Navy aircraft bombed North Vietnamese military installations in answer to an earlier attack on the South. A second bombing wave against the North took place after a February 10 guerrilla attack on US barracks at Qui Nhon that killed 23 Americans.

Rolling Thunder
On February 13, 1965, President Johnson approved an operation against North Vietnam called "Rolling Thunder." It would run from March 2, 1965, through November 1, 1968. The new operation did not satisfy General LeMay's desire for a swift and intense campaign to break the enemy's will. Johnson continued to favor a gradual response; that is, slowly ramping up the pressure on the enemy in hopes that the North Vietnamese would cave.

Rolling Thunder fighters and fighter-bombers

THE F-100, THE F-105, AND THE F-4 were among the jet aircraft most widely used in the tactical air campaign, Rolling Thunder. The planes ran interdiction against supply routes, including roads and bridges, between the North and South. Their orders were to avoid sites too politically sensitive, including important North Vietnamese cities such as Hanoi and Haiphong, as well as the border with China.

REPUBLIC F-105D THUNDERJET
Famous for their World War II Thunderbolt, Republic built the largest single-seat, single-engine aircraft ever in this long-range tactical fighter-bomber. Entering service in 1959, the aircraft carried out more air strikes over North Vietnam between 1966 and 1971 than any other USAF aircraft. Losses were heavy and since it was expensive to maintain, it was gradually phased out.

NORTH AMERICAN F-100D SUPER SABRE
The prototype Super Sabre flew in 1953, breaking the sound barrier on its first flight. With extensive use of high-strength titanium alloys, it was a radical step forward in aircraft design and soon became one of the USAF's most versatile tactical aircraft, flying over 300,000 combat sorties in Vietnam.

FIGHTING PHANTOM
The McDonnell F-4 Phantom II was the leading Western fighter of the 1960s. During the Vietnam War it served with the US Navy, Marines, and Air Force. Phantoms were adapted for a variety of roles, including reconnaissance and electronic warfare.

Rolling Thunder was a prime example of a gradual response. It focused largely on interdicting the flow of supplies from the North into the South. In any case, the Air Force now had four distinct air wars under way in Southeast Asia—the new offensive against North Vietnam, the attacks in South Vietnam, and those in northern and southern Laos.

North Vietnam responded to Rolling Thunder and its main tactical strike aircraft—F-100s, F-4s, and F-105s—by building a modern, radar-controlled air-defense system. Shortly after the bombing began, the number of North Vietnamese antiaircraft guns of all calibers doubled to 2,000. The North also acquired surface-to-air missiles (SAMs) from the Soviets. US reconnaissance aircraft detected SAMs for the first time in March 1965; by the end of that year, it had identified 56 sites. By 1966 the North Vietnamese Air Force also had about 100 Soviet-supplied MiG-17s and MiG-21s, as well as a few MiG-19s, to intercept American fighter-bombers.

The air war inside South Vietnam changed dramatically in the spring of 1965 when US ground troops began to enter the country. The Johnson administration was determined to save a faltering South Vietnam with troops and a wider air war. The tactic they would use to do so was called "search and destroy." US military forces searched for North Vietnamese regulars and Viet Cong throughout South Vietnam with the intention of wiping them out. This was intended to give the South Vietnamese room to develop their military and to increase political stability in their country. These years marked a dramatic escalation in US presence in South Vietnam—US troops increased from 23,000 in 1965 to 536,000 by 1969.

Rather than back down in the face of increased US power in the region, Ho Chi Minh moved even more men and supplies into South Vietnam. Since North Vietnam had virtually no industry, it obtained most of its supplies from the Soviet Union and China. Therefore, the Air Force had to rely on interdiction to cut the North off from its supply lines rather than to bomb factories and warehouses above the 17th parallel. The South Vietnamese government finally stabilized when Nguyen Van Thieu became chief of state in June 1965, and South Vietnamese Air Force commander Nguyen Cao Ky became premier. Thieu held power until 1975, despite many enemies and charges that he had amassed a great fortune at others' expense.

SEARCH AND DESTROY
In South Vietnam, the US military used a method called "search-and-destroy" to root out the enemy. Here, a large group of 1st Cavalry Division helicopters are on a search and destroy mission over the South Vietnamese jungles.

1965: Air Force troubles

In 1965 the US Air Force was not fully equipped, suitably trained, or doctrinally prepared for war in Southeast Asia. The transition from massive retaliation to flexible response and from nuclear to conventional weapons remained incomplete. As a result, the Air Force dropped high-explosive bombs from aircraft like the F-105, which was designed for nuclear war. The Air Force also had to build up stocks of conventional weapons in Southeast Asia. However, the service's first tasks were to set up a workable organizational structure in the region, to improve the area's air bases, to create an efficient airlift system to transport materiel, and to develop equipment and techniques to support ground troops.

The Air Force began a major facelift in mid-1965. While continuing to conduct four air wars, it adjusted its structure in Southeast Asia to absorb the increased load of incoming units. Temporarily deployed squadrons—shaped under General Anthis in mid-1963—became permanent in November 1965. In addition, a wing structure replaced groups. By February 1966 the Air Force's reconnaissance force in South Vietnam had grown to 74 aircraft based at Tan Son Nhut, and in March the 2d Air Division became the Seventh Air Force under General William W. Momyer.

PHANTOM AT NIGHT
First Lieutenant Robert W. Wickman checks the underside of his F-4C Phantom jet prior to takeoff on a night mission over South Vietnam.

One of the Air Force's biggest problems in South Vietnam was the lack of decent landing strips. Jets need good airfields, and the country had only three operational air bases—at Tan Son Nhut, Bien Hoa, and Da Nang. The airstrip shortage delayed jet deployments scheduled for 1965. The US Military Assistance Command began building three new airfields in 1965, but by the end of the year just one new field was in use. Here again, the Air Force and Army clashed because the Army-dominated assistance command persisted in giving ground troops priority over airpower.

The new Air Force chief of staff, General John P. McConnell, intervened and got permission for the Air Force to build a fourth base. For the first time, the Air Force, rather than the Army Corps of Engineers, contracted for and supervised construction of an air base. It was completed 45 days ahead of schedule and, by mid-November 1966, the first of three F-100 squadrons occupied the field. The Army also handed over 80 of its C-7 Caribous, and the Pacific Air Forces shared some C-130s to help move goods and troops.

Intensifying the air campaign

Against this background, the air war in South Vietnam intensified in 1965. While the Army asked for more ground support and the Air Force for more interdiction, so much aerial firepower was soon deployed in Southeast Asia that it did not matter which mission the Military Assistance Command gave priority to—both helped the war effort. All the services further agreed by 1966 that Army helicopters would remain under Army control and that Navy carrier aircraft would remain with their service rather than be placed at the Air Force's disposal.

No matter who controlled different portions of airpower, standing orders were to avoid killing noncombatants. This was a strategic move, because the South Vietnamese government needed local support to remain in power. The United States recognized that killing noncombatants would only alienate the peasants and drive them once again into the arms of the Viet Cong. This is where forward air controllers came in. These fighter pilots, often World War II

MORE AIRCRAFT
The Army turned over its C-7 Caribous like this one to the Air Force to help speed goods to their destination in Southeast Asia.

and Korea veterans, flew slow-moving Cessna O-1 Bird Dogs to scout out terrain. Most pilots honed their knowledge of certain geographic areas down to the minutest detail so they could spot whether the enemy was present. The air controllers could then tell fighters which sites to target. By 1966 the Air Force also had a highly accurate ground-based radar bombing system called "Combat Skyspot" at fighter pilots' disposal.

As the Air Force dropped more bombs, the need for new types of munitions for jungle warfare became evident. Its older model bombs detonated too early, at treetop level, so they did not cause enough damage among enemy troops on the ground. The Air Force Systems Command developed dozens of new munitions. They included bombs that would explode only on contact with the ground as well as cluster bombs, which dispensed

BIG BANG
B-52s joined the intensified bombing campaign over South Vietnam in 1965.

hundreds of smaller bombs. By 1968 the Air Force had an arsenal of guided bombs, the so-called smart weapons. One of these weapons sought out targets spotlighted by a laser beam.

By June 1965, B-52s had joined the bombing runs. Although they belonged to the Air Force's SAC, they operated in Vietnam at the request of the Joint Chiefs of Staff and the Military Assistance Command. B-52s flew more than 1,500 sorties in the last six months of 1965—the number rose to 15,505 by 1968—in so-called Arc Light strikes. As General Westmoreland's appetite for B-52 sorties increased, SAC grew concerned that too many of its nuclear bombers were being diverted from their nuclear-deterrence mission to conventional-weapons missions in Southeast Asia. Therefore, SAC sent some of its Pacific-based B-52s closer to the action so each designated aircraft could take part in more

missions in Vietnam, thus enabling B-52s not in the region to concentrate on their worldwide deterrence duties.

Another face of airpower during the Vietnam War was the helicopter. Although the Army flew most of these aircraft, the Air Force had its own stable of them for search-and-rescue missions as well as special operations. By the end of 1968 Air Force helicopters

had helped rescue more than 1,500 people, nearly half of them Airmen. They used Kaman HH-43s and longer-range Sikorsky HH-3s, nicknamed "Jolly Green Giants." Later, the larger and more powerful Sikorsky HH-53s were put into use. T-28s and later A-1s escorted the helicopters. Grumman HU-16s served as airborne command posts, a job later taken over by C-54s and eventually C-130s.

SEARCH AND RESCUE
Air Force helicopters had rescued hundreds of troops and downed Airmen by the end of 1968. These included Kaman HH-43s (pictured here), Sikorsky HH-3s, and Sikorsky HH-53s.

SMART BOMBS

GUIDED BOMBS made their appearance in World War II, when both the Germans and Americans experimented with attaching radio-controlled systems to conventional iron bombs. At first, the guided bombs were ineffective, because the radio link was too easy to jam and the delivery aircraft was too vulnerable to antiaircraft fire while it tracked the bomb's descent.

In the late 1950s, experiments began with bombs guided by electro-optics. The US Navy's Walleye gliding bomb, first used in 1967 in Vietnam, had a TV camera that transmitted a picture to the carrier aircraft. The aircraft's Electronic Warfare Officer could lock the bomb onto the target or guide it all the way in.

But smart weapons really came of age with the deployment of laser-guided Paveway bombs in 1968. A laser beam selects the target, and the bomb's guidance system follows the reflected beam to its source. Because the delivery aircraft is not itself the target designator, it can turn away once the bomb is released.

SMART ATTACK
The Paveway laser-guided bomb demonstrates its accuracy on a test range. The bomb requires an aircraft or a Soldier on the ground to illuminate the target by directing a beam of laser light onto it. The bomb's guidance system does the rest.

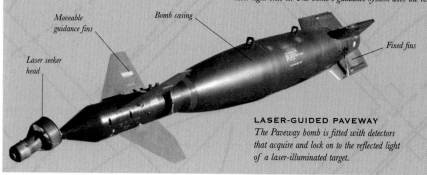

Moveable guidance fins

Bomb casing

Laser seeker head

Fixed fins

LASER-GUIDED PAVEWAY
The Paveway bomb is fitted with detectors that acquire and lock on to the reflected light of a laser-illuminated target.

In 1967 US forces saw much of the same kind of action, with the enemy changing position based on the seasonal rains that could make movement difficult. Actions included Operation Cedar Falls, Operation Junction City, and Operation Hickory. Aircraft made an even larger number of flights. Fighter-bombers flew more than 122,000 sorties, B-52s some 6,600, reconnaissance aircraft around 94,000, forward air controllers about 43,000 missions, helicopters 13,400 tasks, and airlift sorties 373,000.

MOST POPULAR HELICOPTER
The Army relied heavily on the Bell UH-1 helicopter in Vietnam to deliver and retrieve troops from the field. Soldiers also called it the Huey. Here, 1st Cavalry Division infantrymen jump from their Huey for a reconnaissance mission in 1967.

The war expands

Between 1965 and 1968, airpower supported a number of missions. The North Vietnamese and Viet Cong continued crossing the border into South Vietnam and creating havoc. A major clash took place between US Soldiers and North Vietnamese regulars in the Ia Drang Valley. This mission's success rested as much with the determination of the US Soldiers as it did on airpower. Air Force C-123s and C-130s ferried supplies to Army helicopters based near the battlefront, which then carried the materiel to the troops. The choppers also flew reinforcements in and the wounded out.

Other operations included an Air Force interdiction campaign called Tally Ho, which ran between July and November 1966. While Marine Corps units drove the enemy back into the demilitarized zone (DMZ) along the 17th parallel, Air Force tactical aircraft struck supply and communications lines. The interdiction campaign included B-52s and fighter-bombers. Seasonal rains that drove the enemy back south around Saigon triggered the start of Operation Attleboro that same November. In three weeks, US forces drove the Communists into Cambodia.

During 1966 alone, in major battles and scores of smaller skirmishes, the number of Air Force sorties was staggering. Fighter-bombers flew more than 74,000 sorties, along with B-52s (4,500 sorties), airlift units (13,600), reconnaissance aircraft (59,000), forward air controllers (27,500), and Air Force helicopters (13,500).

LESSONS LEARNED: THE FIRST HALF OF THE VIETNAM WAR

WHEN THE UNITED STATES got involved in the Vietnam War in 1961, the Air Force was in much the same shape as it had been during the Korean War. That is, the Air Force was better prepared for a nuclear-deterrence role than for a tactical one. Its bomber, fighter-bomber, and fighter crews were not as accurate as they needed to be. After all, an aircraft whose prime duty is to drop a nuclear bomb does not require the same degree of accuracy as a bomber that will drop a conventional weapon. A nuclear bomb will take out a whole city; a conventional bomb is intended for smaller targets such as a warehouse, a bridge, or a truck convoy. Since the possibility of the use of nuclear force in Vietnam was highly unlikely, the United States had to step up its tactical game.

Furthermore, the Johnson administration placed limits on the bombing campaigns of the Air Force and other branches of the armed forces, particularly in North Vietnam. At first, the Air Force was not allowed to strike at North Vietnam, even though the Communist North was the principal enemy trying to crush South Vietnam. The White House also barred the US military from hitting targets where there might be Soviet or Chinese advisers or Soviet SAM missile sites that were not yet in operation. This approach constrained the Air Force and the other military branches to such a degree that they could not pound the enemy into submission. They were limited to pinpricks.

The Johnson White House also advocated a gradual response to North Vietnamese aggression. This was wholly contrary to the war philosophy of such people as Air Force General LeMay. He advocated applying crushing blows to the enemy in its own backyard (North Vietnam) to break its will. He argued for swift and intense attacks aimed at ending the war and freeing South Vietnam, but civilian leaders in Washington, D.C., felt that a slow uptick in intensity would do the trick. The North Vietnamese, they reasoned, would see what was coming and would back down before the real onslaught came.

It turned out the military leaders were right. The gradual response applied through the failed three-year operation called Rolling Thunder (1965–68) did not work. The enemy simply used the lulls between strikes to rebuild and refortify its defenses and its offensive capabilities. Swift and intense strikes would more likely have destroyed the North's will and could have saved South Vietnam.

PHANTOM FIGHTER

Originally designed for the US Navy but also adapted by the Air Force, the F-4 Phantom II was an excellent aircraft in its performance and equipment. The ability of the apparently inferior MiGs to hold their own with the F-4s in air combat came as a shock, and in part led to the founding of the Navy's Top Gun school of movie fame. The Air Force adopted the Top Gun principle at its Fighter Weapons School in the 1970s.

Khe Sanh and the Tet Offensive

The most serious of the border threats occurred early in 1968 at the Marine outpost at Khe Sanh, where North Vietnamese troops encircled the Marines in a scene reminiscent of the French debacle at Dien Bien Phu. General Westmoreland decided to use airpower to disrupt an anticipated attack by the two enemy divisions massed around the outpost. Near the end of January, he launched a 10-week air campaign called Operation Niagara because the torrent of explosives dropping from the sky would resemble a similar volume of water at the celebrated falls. Before US forces broke the Khe Sanh siege at the end of March, Air Force, Marine, and Navy aircraft flew 24,000 tactical sorties against the enemy surrounding the base. B-52s dropped nearly 60,000 tons of bombs on trenches and artillery positions during 2,500 day and night sorties. Air Force transports landed 4,300 tons of supplies and 2,700 troops at the Khe Sanh airstrip, despite hostile mortar and artillery, and parachuted 8,000 tons of cargo to the Marines.

As seemed typical during the Vietnam War, the services had trouble coordinating their aircraft missions. Westmoreland tried to fix the problem at Khe Sanh by placing Marine tactical aircraft under the Seventh Air Force's General Momyer. But errors still occurred, and Army and Navy carrier aircraft were excluded from the arrangement.

While the siege of Khe Sanh continued, other Communist forces moved largely undetected into position and attacked five major cities, 36 provincial capitals, 23 airfields, and many district capitals and hamlets. Taking advantage of the annual Tet holidays in early February, when most South Vietnamese soldiers were on leave to celebrate the lunar new year, the enemy struck a stunning blow. The purpose may have been to provoke a popular uprising throughout South Vietnam, in which case the offensive failed. However, if the purpose was to embarrass the US political and military leadership and undermine public support in the United States, the offensive was a major success. Air Force fighter-bombers launched carefully controlled strikes, but in crowded urban areas collateral damage proved unavoidable, resulting in civilian casualties and an influx of up to 600,000 refugees that strained the Saigon government's resources. Outside the towns and cities, the aircraft bombed the enemy's

storage dumps and troop concentrations, and provided battlefield interdiction and close air support for the units fighting the Viet Cong and North Vietnamese attackers. Communist losses may have totaled 45,000, or more than half of the regulars and guerrillas who took part in the offensive. The Viet Cong ceased to exist as a serious fighting force.

SCENE OF DEVASTATION
The Cholon district of Saigon smolders after the Tet Offensive in February 1968. Although the offensive was a military disaster for North Vietnam and the Viet Cong, its effect on a shocked American public was enormous.

Costly though it was to the Communists, the Tet Offensive marked the turning point in the war. The unexpectedly savage attack by an enemy supposedly on its last legs caused the United States to reexamine its partnership with the South Vietnamese and the dominant role it had assumed in a war to preserve its ally's independence. Although repulsed on the battlefield, the attackers forced the

American public's doubts to the surface. The Southeast Asian struggle was costing the United States almost $33 billion annually, fueling inflation, and bloating the national debt. The number of Americans killed in action was approaching 20,000 troops, with nearly half of those deaths occurring in 1967. Opposition to the draft was increasing. Faced with increasing political pressure—most intensely within his own party—President Johnson refused General Westmoreland's request for 206,000 more troops, declared a halt to bombing of North Vietnam above the 20th parallel, and decided not to run for reelection.

During the air war against North Vietnam, Air Force tactical fighters flew 166,000 sorties, and the Navy's carrier aircraft flew 144,500 missions. Although the B-52s were not part of Rolling Thunder, they flew 2,330 sorties. The enemy downed 526 Air Force aircraft—54 fell victim to surface-to-air missiles, MiGs destroyed another 42, and antiaircraft fire took down the rest. Of the 745 Air Force crew members shot down on missions against the North Vietnamese, 255 died, 222 became prisoners, and 145 were rescued. The fate of the remaining 123 was unknown.

The second half of the Vietnam War, 1968–75, would look different from the first half. Bombing North Vietnam would no longer be the primary strategy of the air war, although the military did rely on bombing operations to achieve desired ends. The United States would try to find a way to relinquish its dominant role in the war and to push the South Vietnamese to play a bigger part. At the same time, the United States would also continue to try to ensure South Vietnam's freedom from Communist influences before pulling out.

DOCTRINE AND HISTORY—THE VIETNAM WAR

DISTINCTIVE CAPABILITIES	FUNCTIONS (MISSIONS)	DOCTRINAL EMPHASIS
• Air and Space Superiority • Precision Engagement • Agile Combat Support	• Counterland • Close Air Support • Interdiction • Airlift • Surveillance and Reconnaissance • Search and Rescue • Air Refueling • Strategic Attack	• Strategic Attack and Nuclear Deterrence Prior to Vietnam • Shift toward Deterrence through Strength and Global Attack

VIETNAM: PART II

15

THE TET OFFENSIVE, while a military victory for South Vietnamese and American forces, turned into a political defeat, souring the American public on the war and sapping its will to continue the fight. The Nixon administration implemented a strategy of "Vietnamization," withdrawing American forces and turning the battle over to the South Vietnamese. Still, US airpower was essential in helping turn back a North Vietnamese offensive and forcing Hanoi to agree to a cease-fire. However, in 1975 when Congress refused to come to Saigon's aid after Hanoi violated the cease-fire with another offensive, South Vietnam could not survive.

VIETNAMIZATION AND US WITHDRAWAL, 1968–1975

POLITICAL WILL WAVERED IN THE UNITED STATES AS THE US MILITARY CONTINUED ITS FIGHT TO SECURE SOUTH VIETNAM FROM COMMUNIST INFLUENCES ONCE AND FOR ALL

FOLLOWING NORTH VIETNAM'S 1968 Tet Offensive, the Johnson administration modified the partnership between the United States and South Vietnam. Although the objective remained an independent South, the United States changed the way it pursued this goal. Instead of conducting bombing campaigns in the north, and search-and-destroy missions in the South Vietnamese jungles, the United States once again began training and equipping the South Vietnamese to take over the war. This had been the United States' intent when it first sent advisers, money, and supplies to the south in 1961.

In 1968 and 1969, North Vietnam, South Vietnam, the United States, and the Viet Cong talked peace in Paris, but none of the parties was willing to give up its goals. The North still wanted all of South Vietnam, and the South still wanted its independence. Important leadership changes on both sides took place during this period. Richard M. Nixon became president of the United States in January 1969, and North Vietnamese leader Ho Chi Minh died in September 1969. In many ways, however, the status quo remained. The North stuck to its plans to conquer the South. Nixon stood by Johnson's decision to hand over the war to the South Vietnamese, a process the Nixon White House referred to as "Vietnamization."

Vietnamization included a steady withdrawal of US troops, in large part because the American public was unwilling to tolerate any more US casualties. However, placating the antiwar movement in the United States through Vietnamization inadvertently relieved pressure on the North Vietnamese to strike a truce. With the United States clearly determined to leave South Vietnam, North Vietnam had little incentive to do the same. In fact, the North spent the next few years gearing up for a large invasion, which would take place in 1972.

Vietnamization—disengagement, withdrawal, and the strengthening of South Vietnamese forces—permeated all US efforts in Southeast Asia. It affected all four air wars: the fighting over

TRANSPORTS INTO GUNSHIPS
The South Vietnamese used old C-47 (pictured) and C-119 transports as gunships during the war.

SWORN INTO OFFICE
President Richard Nixon took office in 1969 as the United States continued its difficult role in Southeast Asia.

THIRSTY FIGHTERS
A bomb-laden F-5 aircraft refuels en route to striking Viet Cong positions.

North Vietnam, South Vietnam, northern Laos, and southern Laos (an air war that came to include Cambodia). From late 1968 until the spring of 1972, when a North Vietnamese invasion of the South caused an adjustment to air operations, every Air Force undertaking was aimed at aiding the withdrawal of US combat forces, their replacement by South Vietnamese, and negotiations to end the war. In 1965, airpower had protected the buildup of US ground forces in South Vietnam. Now, airpower shielded their removal. Operations ranged from strikes by fighter-bombers to B-52s battering enemy concentrations in South Vietnam.

Modernizing the South Vietnamese Air Force

The US Air Force started modernizing the South Vietnamese Air Force in 1969. When it came to supplying South Vietnam's air arm, Vietnamization began as a matter of quantity more than quality. By 1972 the number of operating squadrons doubled—from 20 to 40. Yet the added aircraft were Northrop F-5s, which were not standard fighter-bombers for the US Air Force. The United States also handed over A-37s—modified Cessna T-37 trainers—for use as attack aircraft; helicopters provided by the Army; and old C-123 transports. The F-5 and the A-37 were short-range aircraft suitable mainly for operations within South Vietnam. For gunships, the South Vietnamese got versions of the slow and vulnerable C-47s and C-119 transports. The modernization and

expansion programs that produced the 40 squadrons excluded such aircraft as aerial tankers, the more-modern gunships, F-4s, and B-52s. Even the C-130 transport was a late addition to the growing inventory.

At Vietnamization's start, the South Vietnamese Air Force was unable to absorb the most modern equipment. This was because training required two competencies: language skills and technical know-how. Few Vietnamese trainees were fluent in English, the language of instruction, and few arrived with a deep technical background. It was easier, therefore, to begin with simpler aircraft. Also, the United States was unwilling to give away its latest technology to a foreign military, allied or not.

In 1969 South Vietnam's air arm grew from 17,500 officers and airmen and 400 aircraft to 36,000 personnel and 450 aircraft. The disproportionate growth between manpower and aircraft resulted from the time needed to train men to service and operate the planes. Even so, the South Vietnamese took on

more missions. Their forward air controllers flew 505 sorties in January 1969 and 1,083 sorties in December of that year. This represented a jump from 10 percent to 25 percent of the missions flown by air controllers. A similarly encouraging increase took place in the total number of sorties flown by South Vietnamese—from 55,000 in the first quarter of 1969 to 74,000 during the last three months of that year. By October 1969 the US Air Force had nearly completed turning over Nha Trang Air Base to the South Vietnamese, and by early 1970 airmen from both countries worked side by side at air bases at Da Nang, Pleiku, Bien Hoa, Binh Tuy, Soc Trang, and Tan Son Nhut.

Growth continued in 1970. By year's end, the South Vietnamese Air Force was up to 30 squadrons, and its arsenal of helicopters had

DRAGONFLY
To equip the South Vietnamese Air Force, the US military turned over F-5s, A-37s (below), and C-123s for its use.

grown from 112 to 310. More important than aircraft numbers, however, was that South Vietnamese airmen flew half of all strike sorties in their own country. Circumstances forced this responsibility on them. In 1969 2,500 US Airmen left Vietnam for home. In 1970 10,000 more Airmen departed, along with 11 of the 20 US fighting squadrons based in the south. Still more exited in 1971. This shifted more of the burden for providing an aerial shield for ground troops to the South Vietnamese. At the end of 1971 South Vietnam had 1,222 aircraft. Its pilots flew 63 percent of all fighter strike missions in South Vietnam and 39 percent of missions in Cambodia, where fighting had spread in 1970. And by early 1972 South Vietnam had assumed nearly full responsibility for the country's tactical air-control system. US Air Force forward air controllers also turned most of the country over to their Vietnamese allies. In fact, even US rescue forces were pushed from air bases by the expanding South Vietnamese Air Force. Because of lack of advanced equipment and training, however, the South Vietnamese remained unable to run interdiction along the Ho Chi Minh Trail or to take part in search-and-rescue missions.

Southern Laos and Cambodia: commando hunt

Even as Vietnamization was unfolding and withdrawal progressing from 1969–1972, US interdiction efforts expanded against the Ho Chi Minh Trail in southern Laos. The main purpose of this air war was to disrupt the enemy's efforts to mass troops and stockpile supplies for an assault timed to catch the Americans as their withdrawal from South Vietnam neared completion. Yet strikes on truck convoys traveling the trail were by and large unsuccessful. In addition, intelligence had little chance of scouring the ground for burned-out trucks to confirm hits that pilots claimed. The Air Force tried improved technology, such as infrared detectors, to spot what was happening under the dense jungle growth. It also employed more-powerful weapons, such as laser-guided bombs and 40-mm cannons to inflict more damage. But nothing seemed to do the trick.

Then the Defense Department proposed going after North Vietnamese manpower. China and the Soviet Union could always resupply the North with trucks and supplies, but they could not replace North Vietnamese troops killed by

HIGH-ALTITUDE PRECISION BOMBING

DURING THE FIGHTING IN 1972, cells of three B-52s were used to strike at North Vietnamese ground forces operating inside South Vietnam. The B-52s dropped their bombs from seven miles (11km) high, often through dense cloud cover. Although aircraft had been guided to release bombs on a point defined by map coordinates since early in World War II, the operation still required remarkable skill from air crews and ground controllers. Accuracy was key: a five-second delay in bomb release would translate into about a 1/2-mile (0.8-km) error in targeting.

The ground controllers tracking the B-52s on radar worked in threes, checking and double-checking one another's work. The lead B-52 was counted down to bomb release by a radio message from a ground controller: "Five, four, three, two, one, hack." The radar navigators in the other two planes hit their bomb switches a precise number of seconds later. The remoteness of the air crew from the effects of its actions was total. Bomb release was felt as a slight shuddering of the aircraft and seen as a series of lights flickering off as each of up to 66 bombs fell away. The bombs hit the ground a minute later, by which time the B-52s had turned for home. The pilot might see nothing more than a few flashes lighting up the clouds below. That was all.

US air strikes. North Vietnamese base camps proved as hard to find, however, as the truck convoys. In addition, the enemy forces began to use more antiaircraft guns, surface-to-air missiles (SAMs), and MiGs in Laos. The interdiction campaign extended into Cambodia in the spring of 1969, when the North set up military bases and storage facilities along the Cambodian border with South Vietnam.

On March 18, 1969, American B-52s began the first of 3,875 sorties over a 14-month period against the North Vietnamese bases inside Cambodia. While the Cambodian royal family opted to appease both the United States and North Vietnam by refusing to condemn the activities of either side, a group of Cambodian generals had other ideas. They tried to drive the Communists out of their country, but the enemy was too great. Since the enemy bases not only threatened the United States' Vietnamization policy but also the anti-Communist Cambodian generals led by General Lon Nol, President Nixon approved an invasion in support of the general. The US incursion began on May 1, 1970, and lasted until the end of June. The cost in American lives totaled 338, with 1,525 wounded. South Vietnamese troops took over ground operations, including a major assault in 1971, but US air support continued. Unfortunately, neither the

BLACK HOLE
The radar navigator in a B-52 was responsible for dropping the bombs. His position was on the lower deck, in the windowless "black hole" beneath the pilot and copilot.

SUPPLYING ALLIES
*The US Air Force supplied the Meo tribe in
northern Laos with T-28s similar to this one,
which has French markings. French pilots flew
this Fennec version during the war in Algeria.*

South Vietnamese army nor a hurriedly
assembled Cambodian army proved equal to their
tasks. The flow of goods over the Ho Chi Minh
Trail remained steady.

The Cambodian front sparked more antiwar
protests in the United States, and resulted in the
passage of the War Powers Act in October 1973.
This legislation required the president to report
within 48 hours if he committed US troops
overseas or "substantially" enlarged an existing
commitment. As commander in chief, the US
president would have to terminate military
actions after 60 days, plus an additional 30
days for withdrawal, unless Congress decided
otherwise. Nixon warned that such a law would
impose "unconstitutional and dangerous"
restrictions on presidential authority and
"seriously undermine this nation's ability to
act decisively and convincingly in times of
international crisis." He vetoed the legislation,
but Congress overrode him and the War Powers
Act became law.

Airpower in northern Laos

The air war in northern Laos resembled the
fighting in Cambodia. A hard-pressed ally, the
Meo tribe led by Vang Pao relied more and more
on US airpower to drive the Communists from
the Plain of Jars, where the United States first

intervened in 1964. In 1969 the US Department
of State drew a distinction between the two air
wars in Laos. Operations against the Ho Chi
Minh Trail in southern Laos were an extension
of the war in South Vietnam and would continue
as long as there was fighting in that country.
Operations in northern Laos were against the
North Vietnamese intruders and would end in
the unlikely event the Hanoi government
withdrew its forces.

On these grounds, the Air Force built up Laotian
airpower. It equipped and trained the Royal
Laotian Air Force with such aircraft as the AC-47
gunship, and supplied and trained the Meos with
fighters such as the T-28. But
because the United States was
attempting to draw down its
forces in Southeast Asia, it had
fewer and fewer aircraft and
pilots to spare in supporting
these Laotian missions against
the Communist Pathet Lao.
Victory remained elusive for the
Americans' Laotian allies. Like

A FULL TANK
*The Air Force's beefed-up fleet during
the Easter Offensive included the
KC-135 tanker.*

the fighting in the two Vietnams, the struggle in
northern Laos would eventually end in a cease-fire.

North Vietnam rebuilds: 1968–1972

US Air Force aerial reconnaissance over North
Vietnam came under fire in the post-Rolling
Thunder years. The Communists downed two
RF-4Cs and an escorting F-4 in late 1968. Quiet
followed, leading the Nixon administration to
believe that Hanoi was abiding by a tentative
agreement made during the Paris peace
negotiations not to attack unarmed reconnaissance
aircraft over the North. But then the North shot
down a US aircraft in 1969 and a second in 1970.

"There's something terribly personal about the SAM; it means to kill you...."

GENERAL ROBIN OLDS
USAF PILOT IN VIETNAM

In February 1970 President Nixon directed that fighter-bombers escort reconnaissance flights and strike back when fired upon. The Air Force and Navy took part in about 60 protective-reaction attacks against hostile gun and missile sites in 1970, twice that number in 1971, and 90 during the first three months of 1972. The mission eventually expanded to striking enemy sites that supported truck convoys moving along the Ho Chi Minh Trail.

As 1971 ended, aerial reconnaissance produced mounting evidence that North Vietnam was preparing for a major offensive. Nixon approved a new series of protective-reaction attacks on targets in North Vietnam. Starting on December 26, US aircraft launched five days of strikes, totaling more than 1,000 sorties. They hit airfields, oil-storage areas, SAM sites, supply dumps, and truck parks. When the North began firing at South Vietnamese outposts across the demilitarized zone in February 1971, the White House ordered two more days of strikes.

But the Air Force got into trouble in 1972, when General John D. Lavelle ordered his Seventh Air Force to carry out a number of strikes that seemingly went beyond what the White House requested. The Seventh raided airfields housing MiGs, radars supporting

STRIKE PACKAGE

FOR RAIDS OVER NORTH VIETNAM, the US air forces assembled "strike packages" in which support aircraft greatly outnumbered those tasked with hitting the target. Furthest from the action were KC-135 tankers, which refueled the combat aircraft. An RC-121 radar-surveillance aircraft acted as an aerial command post, giving early warning of MiGs taking off. EB-66B Destroyers, packed with electronic countermeasures equipment, flew high above the strike force, escorted by F-4s. The EB-66Bs were intended to jam ground radars, "blinding" the SAMs and antiaircraft guns. In case they failed, Wild Weasel F-105s or F-4s armed with antiradiation missiles went ahead to shoot it out with the SAMs. At the heart of the package were 20 or 30 F-105 strike aircraft armed with bombs and Bullpup missiles, surrounded by F-4s to fight off any MiGs. A single mission could easily involve 100 aircraft.

THUD STRIKE
The Republic F-105 Thunderchief, known to pilots as the "Thud," was America's prime ground-attack aircraft in Vietnam. Fast, robust, and packed with complex electronic equipment, it was designed to penetrate the most sophisticated air defenses, carrying an impressive payload of missiles and bombs.

GUIDED BULLPUP
The Bullpup was America's standard air-to-ground guided missile in the early years of the Vietnam War. It was radio-guided to its target by a controller in the launch aircraft using a small joystick. The Bullpup was superseded by fire-and-forget missiles that "locked on" to their targets.

MiG operations, SAM sites, missile storage, and missile-carrying trucks. The politicians in Washington, D.C., pushed him to retire and the Senate condemned him, but the House of Representatives praised Lavelle's bombing

ANTIAIRCRAFT DEFENSES
North Vietnamese SAMs and antiaircraft guns combined to erect a formidable barrier against American air raids. The antiaircraft guns were deadly at low altitude, forcing the American planes to fly higher, where the SAMs were most effective.

missions as "not only proper but essential." Lavelle did retire, and General John W. Vogt replaced him. Ironically, Vogt received instructions from Nixon to be even more aggressive than Lavelle in prosecuting the war in North Vietnam.

Whatever the politics, the Nixon administration was confident that airpower had forestalled a North Vietnamese offensive. Washington did not know that some major battles still lay ahead.

Mikoyan-Guryevich MiG-21

THE MiG-21, known to NATO by the codename "Fishbed," is an aircraft that benefits from a design focused on limited, attainable objectives. It was conceived in the aftermath of the Korean War, when the Soviet military decided they needed a new-generation short-range interceptor and air-superiority fighter. The aircraft had to be fast—capable of flying at Mach 2—and maneuverable, with all other features being sacrificed to high performance. It also needed to be simple, reliable, easy to maintain, and cheap enough to be manufactured in large numbers.

The design produced by the Mikoyan and Guryevich bureau was a "no frills," stripped-down, classic dogfighter and bomber-killer. In 1959, at the same time as the US was developing the F-4 Phantom—which was heavy enough to require two engines and needed an Electronic Warfare Officer to operate its array of electronic gadgetry—the MiG-21 emerged as a single-seat, single-engine, lightweight fighter, with a simple radar, two heat-seeking missiles, and a cannon. When F-4 pilots first encountered MiG-21s over North Vietnam, their craft's advanced electronics did not necessarily translate into combat victories. In fact, the MiG was more nimble and tighter in a high-speed turn, and its gun gave a definite advantage over the US fighters, which initially did not feature a gun.

Over the years, the MiG-21 evolved away from its original lightness and simplicity. Later models had more sophisticated radar and an extra fuel tank to give the aircraft greater range. The engine was modified to allow the airplane to carry more missiles as well as the extra fuel load. But the virtues of cheapness, reliability, and high performance remained. Over 13,000 MiG-21s were produced. They went into service with air forces around the world and saw action not only in Vietnam, but also in other areas, such as the Middle East. Many were still operational at the start of the third millennium.

SIMPLE BUT EFFECTIVE
Keeping in line with the MiG-21's overall ethos, the cockpit is small and retains only the essentials in terms of flight and engine instruments.

POPULAR CRAFT
Since it was first produced, the MiG-21 has been used by over 50 air forces and has seen service in at least 30 wars. The airplane shown here is a Yugoslavian Air Force MiG-21UTI, taking off in 1999 from an airstrip in Kosovo.

STRIPPED DOWN
The MiG-21 (model 21F-13 shown here) is characterized by its relatively small size, delta-shaped tail configuration, and lightness. Keeping the weight to a minimum means that it can operate with just one engine.

The Easter Offensive

General Vo Nguyen Giap was North Vietnam's most prominent military leader, having led his forces to victory against the French at Dien Bien Phu in 1954. On March 30, 1972, he sent almost his entire army—125,000 troops supported by tanks and artillery—knifing into South Vietnam for a three-pronged campaign that came to be called the "Easter Offensive." They struck first in northernmost South Vietnam and advanced toward Quang Tri City and Hue. They next attacked from the triborder region, where South Vietnam, Laos, and Cambodia converged, in an effort to move toward Kontum. Additionally, they came at the South from their bases in Cambodia to work their way toward An Loc and, ultimately, to Saigon.

For the North Vietnamese, it seemed the right moment to strike. The remaining US ground forces were largely support and advisory units. The war was still unpopular in the United States, and a US presidential election was coming up in

November. But the facts were not actually so clear cut. The South Vietnamese army was continually training on US equipment and adding to its store. A battle in the south would give the South Vietnamese the home field advantage because they had US advisers and equipment at their side. Furthermore, the tactics adopted by Giap's army and the Viet Cong were inflexible. They seemed to have abandoned the guerrilla methods that had once served them so well.

The US Air Force rallied to the South's defense with 300 aircraft and an average of 500 sorties daily. When that did not seem enough, Nixon authorized increasing aerial strength, but not ground force numbers, in the north. By June, the Air Force had 1,426 aircraft in the Pacific region, including 202 B-52s and 187 KC-135 tankers. The Navy and Marines also boosted their presence. The Navy went from two aircraft carriers in the Gulf of Tonkin to six. The Marines sent four air squadrons from airfields in Japan. The focus shifted from the

air wars in Cambodia and Laos, where efforts either ended altogether (southern Laos) or received only the sorties that the United States could spare (Cambodia and northern Laos).

Linebacker I: April–October 1972

An aerial-interdiction campaign against North Vietnam began on April 6, 1972, with attacks on the southern part of the country, and rapidly expanded. On April 16, B-52s bombed fuel-storage tanks at Haiphong. On May 8 naval aircraft began mining harbors. On May 10 the Nixon administration extended the aerial-interdiction campaign to include all of North Vietnam and named the operation "Linebacker." Meanwhile, China and the Soviet Union refrained from openly aiding North Vietnam. The strategic situation between the United States, China, and the Soviets had reversed itself. They now feared provoking the United States, since as of 1969, Sino-Soviet relations had descended into mutual hostilities. Neither wanted

AERIAL COMBAT
F-4s went after MiGs during Operation Linebacker.

ON THE OFFENSIVE
The B-52 played a major role during Linebacker, taking out military targets and enemy troops.

the United States to become too friendly with the other, a circumstance Nixon skillfully exploited.

In terms of tactics and results, Linebacker was a vast improvement over Rolling Thunder. US aircraft now had permission to attack airfields, power plants, and radio stations that did not fall into the interdiction category. However, the objective remained disrupting the flow of supplies and reinforcements to the units fighting in the south. Because radar could detect MiGs as they took off from airstrips, Air Force F-4s and Navy fighters could repel them. Electronic warfare took care of SAMs and antiaircraft guns. This new operation even had aces. Captains Charles B. DeBellevue, Jeffrey S. Feinstein, and Richard S. "Steve" Ritchie each scored their fifth kills during Linebacker.

Despite the damage inflicted on North Vietnamese targets by Linebacker air operations, interdiction closer to the battlefield tended to be more effective. This was because at the front, few civilians were available to rebuild damaged bridges, roads, and warehouses. Moreover, the Communists' supply lines narrowed like a funnel the closer they got to the front, making them prime targets. By contrast, the damage inflicted by the wider-ranging interdiction efforts in North Vietnam was quickly redressed because the Communists could easily round up civilian labor to repair the damage.

Another goal of the war to stop the three-front Communist offensive was to inflict casualties. The deadliest aerial weapons were fighter-bombers that used laser-guided weapons, B-52s, and gunships. The North Vietnamese drove the South Vietnamese from Quang Tri City on May 1. The attacking North trapped several US advisers and senior South Vietnamese officers in the city, but four Air Force HH-53 helicopters with A-1 escorts succeeded in snatching them away. Despite heavy losses to antiaircraft fire between Quang Tri City and Hue, Air Force fighter-bombers effectively used laser-guided bombs to attack bridges and artillery positions. They slowed the enemy's advance, giving the South Vietnamese time to regroup. On May 18 when North Vietnamese tanks and infantry crossed the last river barrier to reach Hue, US fighter-bombers destroyed 18 vehicles with laser-guided bombs and killed 300 soldiers. The North Vietnamese renewed their attack five days later, but the South's airpower again beat them back. The South Vietnamese forced their enemy back across the river.

On June 28 South Vietnam launched a counterattack to retake Quang Tri City. B-52s and fighter-bombers cleared the way for the

advancing forces. When the infantry attack foundered in the town, B-52s flew to the rescue. By mid-September the city was once again under South Vietnamese control. The threat to the northern provinces had ended.

In the meantime, B-52s helped blunt the two other Communist attacks along the second front of the Easter Offensive. John Paul Vann, a retired US Army officer and now a civilian adviser, informally assumed command of the defenses. As the North Vietnamese advanced on Kontum City, they encountered strong resistance at nearby Polei Kleng. An Air Force AC-130 gunship with a 105-mm howitzer rebuffed a night attack on Polei Kleng. At Kontum City, B-52s did what the gunship had done at Polei Kleng, although fighter-bombers and South Vietnamese A-37s added their firepower. US and South Vietnamese transports delivered supplies to the troops on the ground as well. Early in the battle for Kontum, a gamble paid off when the defenders fell back so that a carefully timed deluge of high explosives from B-52s caught enemy forces as they moved forward. However, the North Vietnamese succeeded in cutting off the roads into Kontum City. South Vietnamese C-123s landed cargo at the city's airfield until it, too, came under fire. Thereafter, US C-130s supplied Kontum's

> "The bombers hide above the clouds. The whistle and explosion of bombs thunder in every corner of the forest."
>
> TRAN MAI NAM
> NORTH VIETNAMESE JOURNALIST

defenders by parachute. As the battle approached its climax, South Vietnamese A-37s joined Air Force fighter-bombers and Army helicopter gunships in destroying Soviet-built tanks. But it was the B-52s that most weakened the enemy and enabled South Vietnamese ground forces to more easily check the Communists' advance. By the end of May, the South Vietnamese began expelling the Communists from some portions of the town.

The third front was around An Loc, the gateway to Saigon. The battle to defend An Loc closely resembled the battle for Kontum City. The United States orchestrated the defenses under Army Major General James F. Hollingsworth who, realizing he had devastating aerial firepower at his disposal, provided the South Vietnamese with the support they needed to hold on long enough to force the enemy to mass and present worthwhile targets. "You hold, and I'll do the killing," the general reportedly told the South Vietnamese. B-52s killed North Vietnamese on a scale that disheartened them and disrupted their plans. Moreover, the airlift allowed the defenders to cling to An Loc, since they could be supplied only by parachute. Enemy SA-7 heat-seeking missiles posed the greatest threat to US aircraft. The Communist offensive stalled by late May, and within two weeks the North Vietnamese pulled back, ending the threat to Saigon.

NIGHTTIME MISSIONS
The Air Force's F-111s flew at night in support of the B-52s. The fighter-bombers went after MiG airfields and SAM sites.

Diverging goals

Airpower helped drive the enemy back a short distance, and did so without reintroducing ground forces. In fact, the last US Army ground troops had left Vietnam in August 1972. Only 43,000 US Airmen and support personnel remained behind. Yet the very success of the air battle concerned South Vietnamese President Thieu. Recalling what had happened during Linebacker, Thieu feared that the United States' unilateral departure would leave his country at North Vietnam's mercy. Too many Communist troops remained in South Vietnam. Any settlement between the two foes, he believed, had to include a complete withdrawal of enemy troops from South Vietnam.

By contrast, the United States was focused on exiting the war. It aimed to secure a truce between the two sides. At this time, North Vietnam controlled about one-third of South Vietnam, including areas south of the demilitarized zone, the western highlands outside Kontum City, and the area along the Cambodian border. If the United States permitted the North to keep its conquests, the enemy would occupy a

position from which it could detach the northern third of the nation, if not cut South Vietnam in half, which was the very fear faced when US ground forces intervened in 1965. To encourage the South Vietnamese to agree to a truce, the United States sped military equipment to Thieu, stockpiling weapons in case the truce barred America from offering future aid. The South Vietnamese Air Force expanded to 65 squadrons with more than 61,000 officers and airmen. Other than the A-37s and C-123s, few of the 2,000 aircraft were up to the job.

Following his reelection in 1972, President Nixon took two more steps to advance US withdrawal from Vietnam. He assured Thieu that if the North ever violated the truce, the United States would take "swift and severe retaliatory action." And to force the North Vietnamese to agree to a peace deal, he ordered the Air Force to resume bombing the enemy's heartland. "This is your chance to win this war," the president told Admiral Thomas H. Moorer, chairman of the Joint Chiefs of Staff. "And if you don't, I'll consider you responsible." The president, National Security Adviser Henry Kissinger, and Army Major General Alexander Haig proposed that B-52s should hit targets at

Hanoi and Haiphong. In this way, Nixon unleashed the air campaign "Linebacker II," which began on December 18 and ended on December 29—interrupted only by a 36-hour pause for Christmas.

Linebacker II

Air Force and Navy fighter-bombers struck by day and B-52s hit at night. The F-111s attacked MiG airfields from treetop heights and, later in the operation, SAM sites. The heavy bombers followed with their payloads. Fighter-bombers patrolled, in the event MiGs should challenge the B-52s. Fighter-bombers such as the F-4 carried radar-homing missiles to suppress SAMs and scattered chaff to confuse hostile radar. Air Force EB-66s and Navy and Marine Corps Grumman EA-6s broadcast jamming signals to reinforce the chaff. The US military carefully planned its strikes to avoid hitting residential areas. While some in the press criticized Linebacker II's carpet-bombing approach, even the North Vietnamese government reported only 1,624 civilian deaths by the end of the operation. (Western newspapers had claimed that deaths numbered in the tens of thousands.)

Linebacker II's original plan called for the B-52s to fly in a long, single stream to avoid midair collisions. Experience would show, however, that this made them easy targets. North Vietnamese SAM crews downed 11 B-52s by Christmas. Therefore, during Linebacker II's final few days, B-52s no longer flew in a stretched-out stream, and only those B-52s with modern jamming equipment took part. This tactic seemed to work: the Air Force lost only four more B-52s. In addition, attacks on missile sites by F-4s during the day

and F-111s at night cut down on the number of missiles fired. Plus, the North was nearly out of SAMs. The mining of the harbors, damage to the rail system, and the unwillingness of China and the Soviet Union to risk further upsetting the delicate diplomatic balance with the United States meant that the North Vietnamese could not easily replenish their stocks. After more than 700 nighttime B-52 sorties and 650 daylight strikes by fighter-bombers and attack aircraft, the Hanoi government agreed to enter into negotiations. North Vietnam still would not withdraw its troops from the south, however.

Occasional flights continued over North Vietnam even after Linebacker ended. The purpose of most patrols was to prevent MiGs from interfering with US operations in northern Laos. On January 8, 1973, an F-4D crew made up of Captain Paul D. Howman, the pilot, and 1st Lieutenant Lawrence W. Kullman, the weapons-systems officer, shot down a MiG southwest of Hanoi with a radar-guided AIM-7 missile. This was the last aerial victory before the cease-fire's signing. The agreement, which went into effect on January 29, froze the current battle lines in South Vietnam, reestablished a coalition government of Communists and anti-Communists in Laos, permitted the withdrawal of the last US combat forces, and resulted in the release of 591 US prisoners held in North Vietnam.

Next, the United States consolidated its Military Assistance Command, Vietnam, into the much smaller Defense Attaché Office. This new office dispensed military advice and supervised equipment maintenance and technical training. US airpower remained in the region to enforce the truce, with the Air Force's regional headquarters in Thailand. The new command included 18 Air Force fighter-bomber squadrons, one reconnaissance squadron, and a Marine Corps attack-aircraft detachment. The command also coordinated with the Navy's nearby carrier task force and with Strategic Air Command, which had around 200 B-52s in the western Pacific. The purpose of this impressive

presence was to keep North Vietnam in line. With funding tight in the United States, however, the numbers steadily declined. By the end of 1974 only 25 B-52s and 12 tactical fighter squadrons were still stationed in the area.

Cease-fire

Even as the cease-fire took effect in North and South Vietnam and in Laos, US Airmen continued the fight over Cambodia, backing the government against the Communist Khmer Rouge; however, this mission ended in 1973, when Congress called a halt to the bombing. The United States was facing numerous political issues at home, including the 1971 publication of the Pentagon Papers—secret government documents that detailed the US role in the Vietnam War, including doubts about its wisdom—and the Watergate burglary revelations, which would culminate in President Nixon's resignation from office in 1974.

At 11:30 local time on July 15, 1973—the last day of bombing in Cambodia—an A-7D of the 354th Tactical Fighter Wing landed at its base in Thailand after flying the last combat mission of the war over Southeast Asia. All told, the Air Force had flown 5.25 million sorties over South Vietnam, North Vietnam, northern and southern Laos, and Cambodia. It had lost 2,251 aircraft, 1,737 of those to hostile action and 514 for operational reasons. A ratio of roughly 0.4 losses per 1,000 sorties compared favorably with a 2.0 rate in Korea and a 9.7 figure during World War II. Beginning with the deaths of Captain Fergus C. Groves II, Captain Robert D. Larson, and Staff Sergeant Milo B. Coghill in 1962, 1,738 Air Force officers and enlisted men were killed in action in Southeast Asia. Another 766 died in accidents or from illness.

As many had feared, North Vietnam consistently violated the cease-fire, but the United States did not interfere. America's political will to defend the South had evaporated, and domestic issues like inflation and a fuel shortage ruled the day. For a while, South Vietnam held its own against the North. Thieu's army would sometimes lash out to improve its position, but the North Vietnamese carved out gains as well.

South Vietnam's future looked ominous. Fuel and ammunition stocks could not keep up with South Vietnam's need for sustained air strikes and artillery barrages against the enemy. The country did not have enough trained officers, airmen, troops, or mechanics, and the North's superior antiaircraft defenses could easily wipe out what air force the South could muster. Meanwhile, North Vietnam made full use of its southernmost territories and the Ho Chi Minh Trail.

The United States was fully out of Cambodia by April 12, 1975, when Air Force and Marine helicopters completed evacuation of the American embassy at Phnom Penh. Evacuations took place on an even greater scale in South Vietnam in 1975, when North Vietnam launched a new offensive, which rapidly gathered momentum and finally overwhelmed South Vietnamese forces. In fact, more than 50,000 Americans, South Vietnamese, and other nationalities escaped by many means before the enemy reached Saigon. The last American left Saigon on April 29, and by the end of 1975, Communist governments controlled South Vietnam, Cambodia, and Laos. The long war was over.

EVACUATION
The last Americans left Saigon on April 29. South Vietnamese were scrambling to get aboard the last helicopter as it left for a US carrier offshore.

Pre-1970s Combat Aircraft

DOUGLAS A-4D SKYHAWK
The US Navy's first jet-attack bomber was so small and light that it was nicknamed "Heinemann's Hot Rod" after its designer. The aircraft was fast enough for the prototype to take the world 311 mile (500km) speed record. Entering service with the Navy and Marines from 1956, Skyhawks were frontline aircraft for 20 years.

MOST OF THE AIRCRAFT that saw action in Vietnam and in the Middle East during the 1960s and early 1970s had been designed in the 1950s. Some, like the subsonic Douglas Skyhawk, which first flew in 1954 and was still being used by the Argentineans in the 1982 Falklands War, were extremely long-lived. Aircraft such as the F-100 Super Sabre belonged to the first generation of supersonic fighters, while the slightly later F-4 Phantom showed the progression to Mach 2 as a requirement for state-of-the-art fighters.

The Phantom, originally a US Navy jet, arguably became the foremost fighter of the decade. Both the Vought A-7 Corsair II, a light attack aircraft intended to succeed the Skyhawk, and the Grumman A-6 Intruder were designed in the 1960s and first used in Vietnam. Both were still in frontline service at the time of the Gulf War in 1991.

VOUGHT F08A F8U-1 CRUSADER
The US Navy's main fleet defense fighter from 1957, the Crusader (French F8e type shown) outperformed the F-100 using the same engine. The high-mounted wing tilted up to allow slower landing and takeoff on carrier decks. Effective in combat, the F-8 was gradually replaced by the better (but more expensive) Phantom.

GRUMMAN A-6E INTRUDER
This US Navy and Marine Corps all-weather attack bomber went into combat in Vietnam in 1965. The bulbous fuselage houses one of the most sophisticated navigation and attack radar systems in the world, including automatic landing on a parent carrier. Intruders were still extremely effective in the Persian Gulf War.

VOUGHT A-7E CORSAIR
Derived from—but completely different from—the Crusader, this attack aircraft sacrificed supersonic speed for carrying capacity and range. Its stubby shape earned it the nickname SLUF for "short little ugly fella." Ordered by the US Navy and Air Force in 1966, it was still in Navy frontline service during the Persian Gulf War.

A final mission

The United States fought one final mission in Southeast Asia when Cambodian naval forces seized a US container ship called the *Mayaguez* on May 12, 1975. Air Force and Marine aircraft, including CH-3s, HH-53s, A-7s, AC-130s, and OV-10s, went to the rescue along with Marine ground troops. Because of the hurried nature of the mission and poor preparation, casualties mounted. In all, 41 Americans were killed and 49 wounded. In addition, out of 15 helicopters engaged, the enemy shot down four and damaged nine. But the United States recaptured the ship and the Cambodians released the crew.

Despite this success, the United States could no longer maintain a military presence in Southeast Asia. Even anti-Communist Thailand no longer welcomed US bases on its soil. The new US perimeter in the western Pacific extended from South Korea and Japan to the Philippines.

While the United States was not able to save South Vietnam, it could say that Communist China had not achieved dominance in the region, either. However, this outcome was primarily due to the rivalry between China and the Soviet Union. (By 1979 China actually invaded Vietnam in a short border war with tens of thousands of casualties.) The one bright spot was that Western-oriented countries like Thailand and Malaysia remained reasonably secure.

TO THE RESCUE
The Air Force and Marines rode to the rescue of 39 crew members of the Mayaguez *who were taken hostage by Cambodian Communists in 1975. Among the aircraft they used was the CH-3 "Jolly Green Giant," similar to the Air Force HH-3s shown here.*

LESSONS LEARNED: THE LATTER HALF OF THE VIETNAM WAR

EXPERIENCES DURING THE second half of the Vietnam War underscored the lessons learned during the first half. For instance, civilian leaders should, by and large, let military leaders run wars once they have begun. While President Lyndon Johnson and his staff picked the targets during Rolling Thunder, it would have been far more appropriate for the military officers on site to choose them. In addition, civilian leaders in Washington ordered only a gradual surge in violence against the enemy in hopes the North Vietnamese would back down. This did not work because it allowed the Communists to regroup again and again. This error also highlighted the fact that airpower's purpose should be to overwhelm, not to nitpick.

The United States also learned that it has to be very careful when taking part in another country's counterinsurgency; that is, when backing a government battling with rebel groups such as the Viet Cong. Rather than taking over operations, the US military should have left the effort largely to the Saigon government. In World War II, the military could use total-war tactics, but Vietnam was different; it called for limited-war tactics. Avoiding civilian casualties as much as possible was much more important. Although the United States had tremendous power at its fingertips, it could use it only to a limited extent. Therefore, before entering such a war, the leaders at home must ask themselves what their goals are and

determine whether those goals are realistic, given the circumstances. In addition, in an era when television and the Internet mean the public can keep up with every detail of what is happening overseas, civilian and military leaders need to win and keep public support before committing the country's military to an expenditure of blood and treasure.

Finally, SAMs, antiaircraft batteries, and MiGs all told the Air Force it needed even better technology than it already had. On its "want" list would be improved methods to confuse incoming missiles. And, in keeping with a lesson learned in Korea, the Air Force determined to place more emphasis on tactical aircraft.

DOCTRINE AND HISTORY—THE VIETNAM WAR

DISTINCTIVE CAPABILITIES	FUNCTIONS (MISSIONS)	DOCTRINAL EMPHASIS
• Air and Space Superiority • Precision Engagement • Agile Combat Support	• Counterland • Close Air Support • Interdiction • Airlift • Surveillance and Reconnaissance • Search and Rescue • Air Refueling • Strategic Attack	• Strategic Attack and Nuclear Deterrence Prior to Vietnam • Shift toward Deterrence through Strength and Global Attack

16

REBUILDING FOR AN AIR AND SPACE FORCE: PART I

THE VIETNAM WAR REVEALED the need for the Air Force to modernize and rethink its mission. Development began on a series of new aircraft that would prove pivotal in the coming decades. New technologies for all types of aircraft and updated missiles changed the way the Air Force operated, as did changes in American society itself. A new generation took the organization's helm, and the first women entered the service's leadership ranks.

MODERNIZING AFTER VIETNAM

SCIENCE AND TECHNOLOGY—ALONG WITH FLEXIBILITY—FORM THE NEW FACE OF THE AIR FORCE

THE DOMINANT THEME for the Air Force in the decade following the Vietnam War was modernization. This included developing and acquiring new weapons, overhauling personnel practices, and installing new leadership. The Vietnam experience and anticipation of future Air Force missions shaped these elements.

Airpower began to assume a new personality even during the Vietnam War. Yes, pilots still engaged in dogfights. But pilots also fought using more sophisticated technology, such as electronic countermeasures to throw off an enemy aircraft's air-to-air missiles, scouring the ground and air for enemy aircraft using more advanced radar than was used during World War II, and flying ever faster and more sophisticated aircraft. The need for more of these kinds of developments drove the Air Force to evolve, to expand its vision to include more science and technology, and to hire different kinds of personnel with a wider range of backgrounds.

Weapons: Development

After the Vietnam War, scientists and engineers filled many leadership positions, from secretary of the Air Force to the Air Force chief of staff. The Air Force had long been interested in science, which after all made the service's mission possible. However, as the Air Force aged, its relationships with certain scientific communities changed. For instance, while the Air Force helped set up the Rand Corporation in 1946 to study airpower's role in modern war, the nonprofit think tank eventually began to take on customers outside the air arm. Rand began to research such topics as the quality of urban life, so the ties between Rand and the Air Force became less important to both parties.

The Scientific Advisory Board's influence over the Air Force also declined in the 1970s

and 1980s. In the 1940s and 1950s, when Theodore von Kármán served the air arm as a principal science adviser and oversaw the board, aerodynamics and aircraft propulsion entered the era of supersonic flight, powerful jet and rocket engines, and orbiting or ballistic vehicles. The emphasis in those times was broad scientific investigation rather than development of specific weapons. But once the basic scientific information was in hand, the Air Force became increasingly interested in applying it to specific weapon systems.

From the dawn of the jet age during World War II until 1959, the Scientific Advisory Board and its predecessor, the Scientific Advisory Group, addressed specific weapon systems in only about 5 percent of their studies. Beginning in 1960, almost a third of the studies had this focus. Since the board's agenda increasingly leaned in this new direction, Air Force officers seemed better able to evaluate matters than scientists or engineers without a comparable military background. Therefore, officers' presence on the Scientific Advisory Board increased, as did the Air Force's control over what the board researched.

Another indication of the transition from a reliance on outside scientists and engineers to Air Force officers with scientific knowledge was the use of specially formed study groups headed by uniformed officers. The first such group issued "Project Forecast" in 1964. Researched by General Bernard Schriever's Space Systems Division of the Air Force Systems Command, the study attempted to predict the impact of probable technological advances on the Air Force. It included subjects such as new alloys and composite materials in aircraft engines and airframes. This greater trust in officers to deal with science and advanced technology signaled not only the temporary eclipse of the Scientific Advisory Board but also the emergence of science and technology careers within the Air Force.

HIDE-AND-SEEK
The B-2 bomber evades detection in part because its paint absorbs electronic pulses from radar. This stealth bomber is part of the Air Combat Command's arsenal. Air Combat Command was created in 1992 by combining Strategic Air Command and Tactical Air Command.

Weapons: Procurement

Besides becoming increasingly involved in studies such as Project Forecast, the Air Force Systems Command retained responsibility for buying weapons. It had to keep an eye on cost overruns as well. To be sure a weapon would work as planned, "Fly before buy" became the watchword. When time, cost, and technology allowed, the Systems Command held competitions between prototypes from various external developers. For instance, the Fairchild A-10 won out over the Northrop A-9 and a modified version of the A-7 already in service. And General Dynamics' F-16 bested a Northrop prototype.

However, in the 1980s there was not always enough time for competitions. Furthermore, some of the technology requested was so advanced and secret that competitions were not sensible. This was the case with the B-1, a long-range bomber intended for missions into Soviet airspace. When the Air Force could not afford to hold contests and instead had to pick a manufacturer, project officers frequently checked in with the developer on progress and costs.

Although the secretary of defense decentralized weapons development and purchases by handing over responsibility to such Air Force arms as the Systems Command, the secretary's office continued to dominate the process. The secretary had to approve projects before they could move forward. It was also up to the secretary to decide

NEW FEATURES
The C-141 was one of the aircraft that was modernized in the post-Vietnam years. Among other new features, it had in-flight refueling capability.

CONTEST WINNER
During one prototype competition, the low-altitude and highly maneuverable Fairchild A-10 Thunderbolt (above) won out over the Northrop A-9.

GUARDIAN
The B-1B bomber is another weapon in the Air Combat Command's pocket. It flies with a four-member crew.

whether to end a project. Frank Carlucci, President Ronald Reagan's deputy secretary of defense, tried to simplify the process for the commands by outlining specific steps for weapons development and procurement.

While weapons acquisition continued to be System Command's focus, the Air Logistics

Division of the Air Force Logistics Command maintained weapons. Both commands faced soaring costs in the 1970s and 1980s. Although budgets grew during the Carter and Reagan administrations, the money did not go all that far when a single B-1B bomber could cost a quarter-billion dollars and the prototype of the radar-evading B-2 cost perhaps twice that amount. In addition, both commands had to recognize that because they were not fighting a war, the American taxpayers were willing to fund the military only so far. For a while, the Logistics Command was not even getting enough money to supply Air Force bases with adequate kits of spare parts for aircraft. Funding pressure also led the Logistics Command to count its pennies carefully—in doing so, it discovered that some vendors were overcharging by tremendous amounts for supplies such as computer disks or plastic caps for navigator tools.

Weapons: Fighters, bombers, and transports

Although the Air Force faced tight funding in Vietnam's immediate aftermath, financial constraints eventually eased and airpower made some impressive advances. Easily the most revolutionary aircraft developments after the Vietnam War were the stealth variety, still a secret in 1982. Lockheed Aircraft worked on a stealth fighter, the F-117, and Northrop developed a stealth bomber, the B-2. Both companies used materials and aerodynamic shapes to make the aircraft all but invisible to radar.

The single-seat F-117 was the world's first stealth aircraft. Lockheed Advanced Development Projects, nicknamed "Skunk Works," began work on the F-117A in 1978 in Burbank, California, and flew its first model in 1981. It delivered its first aircraft in 1982 and its last in 1990. Much of the F-117A's mission can be automated, so the single pilot does not face a mission overload. The aircraft has served in numerous theaters, including "Operation Desert Storm" in 1991 and "Operation Iraqi Freedom" in 2003. As of 2008, the Air Force was in the process of replacing the F-117A with its newest stealth fighter, the F-22 Raptor.

The F-22 results from a combination of efforts. Lockheed and Boeing won the contract for the airframe, and Pratt & Whitney secured a contract for developing the engine. The fighter is a model of stealth, maneuverability, avionics, and supercruise, or the ability to cruise for long periods at supersonic speeds without afterburners. It can carry out both air-to-air and air-to-ground missions. The Air Force claims that the F-22A "cannot be matched by any known or projected fighter aircraft." Work on this fighter began in 1986, and today each carries a price tag of $142 million.

Meanwhile, conventional aircraft developments continued. McDonnell Douglas worked on the C-17. Smaller than the C-5, this aircraft was designed to deliver even the largest Army tanks to forward airstrips in a combat zone. However, when the Reagan administration made funds available for airlift, the C-17 program was not far enough along, so the Air Force contracted with Lockheed to reopen the C-5 production for 50 improved B models of that aircraft.

In 1970, a North American Aviation spinoff called Rockwell International worked on the airframe for a new bomber, while General Electric developed the engines. The first of four prototypes, named the B-1A, flew in 1974. Three years later, President Carter chose not to begin production of this aircraft, but he did permit research and development to go on. The B-1A had a variable-sweep wing like the FB-111, which was a strategic bomber modified from the tactical F-111A and introduced in the late 1960s. The B-1A also had four turbofan engines—jet engines—with three times as much thrust as the two turbofans that powered the fighter. The government canceled the project in 1977,

STEALTHY
The F-117 was the world's first stealth aircraft. It sometimes goes by the nicknames "Bat Plane" or "Stink Bug" because of its shape and color.

although testing continued until 1981. In 1981, President Reagan approved production of 100 B-1Bs, a heavier version of the B-1A with a smaller radar cross-section, improved avionics (electronic equipment for aircraft), and engine inlets redesigned for more efficient flight at high subsonic speeds and low altitude. The B-1B also has variable-geometry wings, meaning it can place its wings forward for easier takeoff, refueling, and landings, or sweep them back for faster speeds and maneuverability once in the air. The first B-1B was delivered in 1985.

While work proceeded on the B-1, the Air Force modernized its fighter force. By 1982, the twin-turbine McDonnell Douglas F-15 was replacing the F-4 as the Air Force's principal air-superiority fighter. Produced in one-seat and two-seat versions, the F-15 had basic armament consisting of Sidewinder and Sparrow missiles and a multibarrel 20-mm cannon. Later models carried up to eight tons of bombs. The smaller, less complex General Dynamics F-16, powered by a single turbofan engine, could tangle with hostile aircraft or attack targets on the ground. It also came in a one- or two-seat model. The fighter

flew at supersonic speed, and carried bombs, missiles, and a multibarrel cannon.

Besides these new aircraft, the F-111 continued to serve the Air Force in tactical fighter and electronic-warfare versions. A few F-5s did as well, either functioning as trainers for foreign

TACTICAL ADVANTAGE
The F-111 was the world's first swing-wing aircraft, entering service with the USAF in 1967. Variable geometry enables the aircraft to take off and land with straight wings, but to fly at supersonic speeds with swept wings. The F-111 was also first with automatic terrain-following radar, making it a powerful low-level strike aircraft. Used in Vietnam in 1972–73, against Libya in 1986, and then in Operation Desert Storm in 1991, F-111s were finally retired in 1993.

pilots or playing the part of hostile aircraft in aerial exercises at Nellis Air Force Base, Nevada. Although F-4s transferred from the active-duty Air Force made up most of the Air National Guard's fighter units, as late as 1982, the Guard was still flying some F-105 fighter-bombers and F-106s. The highly maneuverable Fairchild A-10 was the only aircraft developed by the Air Force exclusively to support troops on the battlefield. This twin-turbofan, subsonic attack aircraft mounted a 30-mm cannon that fired a projectile designed to penetrate tank armor, carried air-to-ground missiles and conventional bombs, and was being modified to deliver laser-guided weapons. When production of the A-10 ended in 1982, no similar aircraft was on the drawing board.

CUTTING EDGE
The F-22 Raptor is the Air Force's newest stealth fighter aircraft. It will soon be joined by the F-35.

A variant of the F-16 seemed likely to take over the ground support missions. The Air Force's Reserve component was beginning to absorb the Navy-developed A-7, which flew ground attack missions in Southeast Asia.

During much of the fighting in Southeast Asia, forward air controllers used the O-2A. This militarized light aircraft had twin booms supporting the tail surfaces, and engines mounted at the front and rear of the crew compartment. By 1982, twin-turboprop OV-10s and twinjet A-37s had replaced all but a few of the O-2As. The gunship, another Southeast Asian war veteran, also survived the Air Force's steps to modernize. The active duty Air Force had

MANY CAPABILITIES
The FB-111 is a variable-sweep wing strategic bomber.

a squadron of AC-130Hs with 20-mm cannons and a 105-mm howitzers. The Air Force Reserve maintained an AC-130A squadron armed with 20-mm and 40-mm cannons.

The Air Force's transport fleet of C-5s and C-141s also underwent modernization, but its C-130s did not. The service equipped its 270 C-141As for in-flight refueling and stretched the fuselage by 23ft (7m). These changes essentially converted the C-141A to a B model, but its greater usefulness was the equivalent of adding 90 C-141As to the fleet. The C-141B prototype flew in 1977; rebuilding the entire force to the B standard began in December 1979 and ended in June 1982. During this period, the Air Force also replaced the wings on C-5As with a stronger structure to extend the model's life and ordered 50 new C-5Bs with the redesigned wing, new engines and radar, and an improved navigation system.

In 1988, Strategic Air Command (SAC) got a new bomber, the stealth B-2. Everything about this bomber—from its paint, which absorbs and

AIR-TO-AIR COMBAT
The supersonic F-16 was smaller and less complex than the F-15. It could engage in dogfights or carry out tactical missions against targets on the ground. Most of these aircraft have now been transferred to the Air National Guard.

deflects electronic pulses from radar, to its shape—is designed to cloak it. The aircraft can fly 6,000 miles without refueling, and can carry both conventional and nuclear bombs. It complements SAC's B-52 and B-1B arsenal, and requires only a two-person crew as compared with the B-52's five-person crew and the B-1B's four-person crew. Among other duties, it flew as part of "Operation Allied Force" in 1999 and "Operation Iraqi Freedom" in 2003.

BEARING BURDENS
McDonnell Douglas developed the C-17, which could carry heavy payloads even though it was smaller than the Air Force's C-5.

McDonnell Douglas F-15 Eagle

WHEN THE SOVIETS UNVEILED their MiG-25 interceptor in 1967, American defense experts put out an urgent call for a new air-superiority fighter of outstanding performance and agility to match it. The result was the F-15 Eagle fighter-interceptor, whose lightweight construction materials and powerful, specially developed Pratt & Whitney turbofan engines gave it an excellent thrust-to-weight ratio. In a vertical climb the Eagle could reach 29,000ft (8,850m)—the height of Everest—in under a minute.

Most F-15s, which entered the service in 1974, are single-seaters, meaning that the pilot has to cope with target, identification, spotting, and tracking targets, deploying countermeasures against missile attack, and all the other complex business of modern warfare, as well as flying. The designers did an excellent job of making the pilot's task more manageable, and many of their innovations, such as HOTAS ("hands on throttle and stick") became standard on all modern fighters. Later models (the F-15C and D) carried more advanced systems, including the improved APG-70 radar.

Although not as agile in a dogfight as some smaller, lighter aircraft, the F-15's unique ability to accelerate in vertical flight provided the perfect escape route if the pilot was ever in trouble.

Engine warning lights • Airspeed indicator • Head-up Display (HUD) • Compass • HUD controls • Artificial horizon • Control stick and throttle

ACTION STATIONS
On July 27, 1988, two F-15s fulfilled their originally intended fighter-interceptor role by intercepting two Soviet Tu-95 "Bear" long-range bombers off the east coast of Canada.

BUBBLE COCKPIT
The F-15 designers created a bubble cockpit canopy for superb all-around vision, with innovative head-up display (HUD), and "hands on throttle and stick" (HOTAS) systems. These design innovations have since become standard on all modern fighters.

MULTIROLE
The Eagle was designed as a pure fighter-interceptor, but as a multirole aircraft it is better value for money. A two-seater version, the F-15E, was developed for ground attack and as a low-level penetration bomber.

EAGLE PILOT
A formation of F-15Es heads home after a training sortie. The pilot is wearing full flying gear with hard helmet and oxygen apparatus. Advanced radar provides high-resolution, ground-mapping data on the HUD and allows pilots to identify targets clearly at great distances.

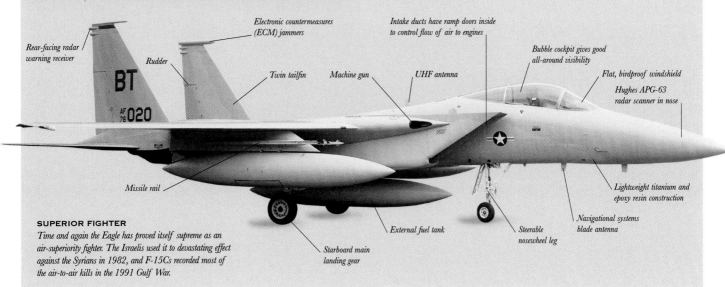

Rear-facing radar warning receiver • Rudder • Electronic countermeasures (ECM) jammers • Twin tailfin • Machine gun • Intake ducts have ramp doors inside to control flow of air to engines • UHF antenna • Bubble cockpit gives good all-around visibility • Flat, birdproof windshield • Hughes APG-63 radar scanner in nose • Lightweight titanium and epoxy resin construction • Navigational systems blade antenna • Steerable nosewheel leg • External fuel tank • Starboard main landing gear • Missile rail

BT AF 76 020

SUPERIOR FIGHTER
Time and again the Eagle has proved itself supreme as an air-superiority fighter. The Israelis used it to devastating effect against the Syrians in 1982, and F-15Cs recorded most of the air-to-air kills in the 1991 Gulf War.

Weapons: Reconnaissance

Air wars took a turn toward greater sophistication and control with the E-3 Sentry and the E-8C. These aircraft can monitor the battlefront, spot low-altitude aircraft, and gather information needed for reconnaissance, close air support, interdiction, and airlift, and report to air commanders so they can plan their operations more efficiently and effectively. Boeing Aerospace Company started work on the E-3, more generally known as AWACS (airborne warning and control systems), in 1975, and it delivered the first aircraft in 1977. The E-3 sees action to this day. In fact, in 1999, the first of the E-3s got a hardware overhaul to make it more relevant to the advanced hostile radar in the field. The E-3 is a modified commercial Boeing 707/320 with a 30-foot-wide (9m) rotating radar dome, which can decipher a scene 250 miles (402km) away.

Northrop's E-8C, more commonly known as JSTARS, or Joint Surveillance Target Attack Radar System, supports the same kind of mission as the E-3 does. The radar of this modified Boeing 707/300 surveys the ground from great ranges to offer timely information to ground and air commanders. Its missions are airborne battle management, command and control, intelligence, surveillance, and reconnaissance. It first saw action in 1991 during Operation Desert Storm.

Weapons: Missiles

The Air Force's strategic missile arsenal changed greatly in the years following Vietnam. The Minuteman remained the most numerous ballistic missile. Some of these missiles carried warheads capable of hitting multiple targets. Silos scattered around bases in Missouri, the Dakotas, Montana, and Wyoming contained two types of Minuteman: 450 Minuteman IIs, each with the F-model missile and a single nuclear warhead, and 550 Minuteman IIIs, featuring the G-model missile and able to deploy as many as three independently targeted warheads.

Under development, and about to join Minuteman, was the LGM-118A. The military called it the MX, for "missile experimental," rather than by its official nickname of Peacekeeper. It carried as many as 10 independently targeted warheads and had a range somewhat greater than that of Minuteman III. While work went ahead on the MX, the Air Force began to phase out the Titan II. Two accidents that killed three Airmen increased the pressure

DETERRENCE
Each LGM-118A Peacekeeper missile had 10 warheads that could go after different targets. Shock-absorbing tiles fall off as the Peacekeeper launches.

CAPTURING THE BIG PICTURE
The E-8A JSTARS aircraft houses its radar in a 27-foot-long (8.2m) radome under the fuselage.

to drop the Titan II. Its retirement got under way late in 1982. After the fall of the Soviet Union in the early 1990s, President George H. W. Bush cancelled the MX program.

A new breed of cruise missiles in the post-Vietnam War years radically changed the strategic force composed of such aircraft as the FB-111 and B-52. Although these new missiles functioned like small, pilotless aircraft, they differed markedly from the older, jet-propelled Snark and the rocket-powered AGM-69 short-range attack missile. The ground-launched, long-range Snark was neither reliable nor accurate. It served only a short time. B-52s and FB-111s carried the short-range AGM-69, which kept on course by inertial guidance (automated, internal navigation). It flew at supersonic speed and could use its nuclear warhead to blast a hole in the enemy's air defenses.

Far more technologically sophisticated than previous models, the new cruise missile could fly 1,500mph (2,414kmph) at high subsonic speed. It relied on inertial guidance and an automated control system that enabled it to hug the Earth's surfaces and present a small radar profile. The AGM-86 model became operational with a B-52 wing in December 1982. Engineers also designed it for the new B-1. This air-launched cruise missile had spring-loaded wings that extended to a 12-foot (3.67m) span after the 21-foot (6.4m) missile fell clear of the bomber that released it. The other Air Force cruise missile, the fixed-wing BGM-109G ground-launched cruise missile, was a mobile, truck-mounted missile.

Personnel

Personnel also had to change with the times. The Air Force began retrenching, or reducing, its personnel strength even as fighting raged in Southeast Asia. Between spring 1968 until the cease-fire in early 1973, the Air Force's active duty numbers declined from almost 905,000 officers and Airmen to fewer than 692,000. The reduction pace then slowed, with the total strength dipping below 600,000 by 1976 and reaching a low of 555,000 in 1979. The force then began to recover somewhat, reaching 578,000 in 1982.

The Air Force Reserve followed an equally erratic pattern. It approached 353,000 in 1971, its highest total in five years, only to decline steadily to 145,000 in 1979. Then it increased about 1,000 per year for the next three years. The Air National Guard went through a series of waves, too, growing from 75,000 in 1968 to almost 90,000 in 1970; dropping to 86,000 in 1971; and rising again to 95,000 in 1975. Then the Guard's numbers stabilized for three years at 91,000 before beginning an increase that carried it beyond 100,000 in 1982.

The casual observer might assume that the Reserve components generally form a mirror image of the active duty force, with one expanding as the other contracts, but such was not the case. The Air Force continued to call on reservists and the Guard to supplement the men and women on active duty. Highly trained Reserve units could be mobilized for an extended period or take over a definite task. They fulfilled duties such as airlift, air refueling, tactical flying, and air defense. Both reservists and active duty forces saw action in Southeast Asia, and were part of what Secretary of Defense Melvin Laird referred to in 1970 as "total force." Total force described the relationship between the active duty and Reserve components, one in which the Reserve and Guard duties fit seamlessly into the active duty force's routine operations.

Although the Air Force had done so since 1960, the practice of treating active duty and Reserve components as a single entity became even more important as budgets declined in the Vietnam War's aftermath. For example, the estimated operating cost of an Air National Guard fighter squadron was 70 percent that of its active duty counterpart. Consequently, the Air National Guard continued to take part in the air defense of the United States, and the Air Force Reserve extended its activity, allowing its C-124s and their crews to fly routes for the Military Airlift Command. In another Total Force program meant to make full use of aircraft, Reserve crews alternated with active duty Airmen to fly the same C-141 and C-5 transports.

Throughout the late 1970s and early 1980s, the Reserve components claimed roughly 30 percent of the Air Force's aircraft inventory and flew about 20 percent of the total flying hours. To enhance training, maintenance, and administration within the Air National Guard, the federal civil service took full-time personnel under its wing in 1969. Previously, the states employed these people, but the working conditions, pay, and retirement systems differed dramatically from state to state. This leveled the playing field for Guard and Reserve personnel. In addition, the Air Force started opening up more roles for

AN ESSENTIAL AIRCRAFT
Air commanders use the E-3 Sentry, also called AWACS, to track enemy and friendly forces during operations.

women, including flying, navigating, and, for enlistees, some 230 noncombat specialties. This occurred for two reasons: 1) women's roles in the workplace were expanding, and 2) the service needed a wider pool to recruit from as it shifted from the draft to an all-volunteer service in 1973. In 1971, Jeanne M. Holm became the Air Force's first female brigadier general, and in 1973 the Armed Forces' first female major general. In 1977, Antonia Handler Chayes became the first female assistant secretary of the Air Force, moving up to undersecretary in 1979. The Air Force also educated its personnel to reduce racial strife and drug and alcohol abuse, problems that grew during and after Vietnam.

In the post-Vietnam era, the Air Force kept its personnel primed for battle through competitions and exercises. Among the contests was "William Tell," a competition for interceptors and their ground controllers that had been held since 1958. The exercises involved airlift flights to Europe and potentially real-life experiences, such as delivering military cargo to countries in Latin America fighting Communist takeovers. The Military Airlift Command also helped out in rescue and relief operations, such as one that took place after a blizzard in Buffalo, New York, in 1977. And different arms of the Air Force engaged in what they called "flag" exercises that simulated combat conditions in terms of how quickly aircraft had to get up in the air, and mock dogfights between F-4s, F-16s, and "Soviet" F-5s. The Air Force also emphasized aircraft readiness at this time because even if a flight crew were well trained, an inoperable aircraft would make it irrelevant. Therefore, aircraft judged fully or partially mission capable improved from about 70 percent in the mid-1970s to about 80 percent during the 1980s.

This improved readiness coincided with an increase in funding for the Air Force after its initial post-Vietnam decline. Not until Carter became president did the Air Force's annual appropriation exceed $30 billion for the first time. During his final year in office (1980–81), it surpassed $40 billion. When President Reagan stepped into office, Air Force appropriations increased yet again, topping $52 billion in fiscal year 1981 and $65 billion in 1982.

MARKING A FIRST
Jeanne M. Holm was the Air Force's first female brigadier general. She achieved that rank in 1971.

Leadership

Air Force leadership went through significant changes as the country swung from war to peace, from a draft to an all-volunteer military, and from large military budgets to retrenchment. As fighting in Southeast Asia wound down, some leaders with roots in SAC and World War II began retiring. A new generation of leaders started to take their place. In particular, General Lew Allen Jr.'s appointment as Air Force

chief of staff in 1978 signaled the start of a new era. He was the first person to hold the office who had not served as an officer during World War II. He was also the first chief of staff trained as a scientist. Allen and other chiefs of staff who served in the 1970s and 1980s tended to have broader educational backgrounds and more varied experiences than did the chiefs of the 1960s. Those earlier leaders had close bonds with SAC, which had exercised a pervasive influence throughout all divisions of the Air Force almost since SAC's beginnings in 1946.

The last of the old guard to advance upward within SAC and become its commander in chief was General Joseph J. Nazzaro, who assumed that post in 1967. During World War II, he led bomber units in Europe and was a staff officer in Europe as well. In 1968, Nazzaro was replaced by General Bruce K. Holloway, a World War II fighter ace. Holloway's background included serving in the Tactical Air Command and as vice chief of staff of the Air Force. Holloway's

THE NEW GENERATION
General Lew Allen Jr. was the first Air Force chief of staff who had not been an officer during World War II.

experiences made him a break from the past, much as Allen's background made him an exception to the old rules for the office of Air Force chief of staff. Holloway's successors indicated that the Air Force was making an effort to select officers with wide experience to lead SAC.

The secretaries of the Air Force also came from a variety of backgrounds, beginning in 1961. Between 1961 and 1982, the Air Force had eight different secretaries, many with science backgrounds. Eugene Zuckert was secretary from 1961–65. An attorney, he had served as assistant secretary of the Air Force and as a member of the Atomic Energy Commission. His successor, Harold Brown, was a physicist, a teacher, and a research scientist at a number of prestigious institutions, including a radiation laboratory operated by the Atomic Energy Commission. He would also serve as director of Defense Research and Engineering for Secretary of Defense Robert McNamara and would return to the Pentagon in 1977 as President Carter's secretary of defense. Following Brown was Robert C. Seamans Jr., another scientist, who was secretary from 1969–73, and John L. McLucas from 1973–75, who was a corporate official with various engineering firms and had other science ties as well. Still others with varied backgrounds took the job: engineer Thomas C. Reed (1975–77), businessman John C. Stetson (1977–79), physicist Hans Mark (1979–81), and businessman Verne Orr (1981–85).

No matter who held the Air Force secretary's chair, the secretary of defense determined the budget for each military branch. Secretary of Defense Caspar W. Weinberger was the first in a string of defense secretaries who saw himself as an advocate for the different services. Rather than imposing his judgments on them, he pushed vigorously to fund the programs that each branch considered essential. He adopted a policy that resembled budget making in the Eisenhower years, allowing the service secretaries and his own assistants to hammer out their respective budgets within a general ceiling. This worked particularly well during Reagan's terms, when the overall defense budget grew and few difficult choices had to be made. But even then, the success or failure of an Air Force secretary's term depended in large part on the secretary of defense.

TOTAL FORCE
The Reserve component has increasingly become an operational force, fighting alongside active-duty and National Guard Airmen around the world.

The Air Force as an organization

Although its leadership went through some substantial modifications in the 1970s and 1980s, the Air Force's structure was less affected, particularly at the top. After almost four decades, the secretary of the Air Force continued to serve as civilian head of the service. The post had administrative and managerial responsibility for ensuring that the service's men and women were properly equipped, adequately trained, and appropriately deployed. The Air Force chief of staff remained ultimately responsible for the day-to-day activities of the organization and also served as one of the Joint Chiefs of Staff. (The chief of staff also delegated duties to the vice chief of staff and the assistant vice chief of staff.) The Air Staff advised the chief of staff, served as a link with the major commands, and assisted the secretary of the Air Force.

The deputy chiefs of staff—who headed the different components of the Air Staff—saw only two changes in the 1980s. The inspector general moved from special staff—which advised the chief of staff, the vice chief of staff, and the assistant vice chief of staff—to head a seventh major component of the Air Staff. And some Air Staff components got new titles. Logistics and Engineering replaced Systems and Logistics; Personnel became Manpower and Personnel; Research and Development was recast as Research, Development, and Acquisition; and Plans and Operations temporarily became Operations, Plans, and Readiness. Meanwhile, the special staff went through a large number of changes—anything from focusing on security concerns to computer science upgrades—depending on the Air Force's needs at the time.

Air Force commands likewise remained much the same, divided into two groups: operational and support. The overseas operational commands included the Pacific Air Forces, the Air Force component of the Pacific Command, concentrated in South Korea and Japan as well as housing some

OVERSEAS MISSION
This C-5 Galaxy is part of the Pacific Air Forces. Here it lands at an airport in Sri Lanka during Operation Unified Assistance, which provided relief to locals in the wake of the 2004 tsunami.

THE SCIENCE OF FLIGHT
Beginning in the 1960, many secretaries of the Air Force, including physicist Harold Brown (1965–69), had science backgrounds.

elements in Hawaii and the Philippines. The US Air Forces in Europe, the Air Force component of the European Command, kept itself primed to join the air forces of nations belonging to the North Atlantic Treaty Organization in defending a region extending from Norway to Turkey and encompassing some seven million square miles. The US Air Force, Southern Command, underwent major changes. It disbanded in the mid-1970s, was a division of the Tactical Air Command until 1987, and thereafter reported to the Twelfth Air Force.

The Air Defense Command became the Aerospace Defense Command in 1968 to reflect the Air Force's ever greater reach into the heavens. It dissolved in 1979 as priorities continued to shift from bomber defense to missile warning and space surveillance. Other commands split the Aerospace Defense Command's duties. The Air Force Communications Command took over its communications role. Strategic Air Command managed the space surveillance and ballistic missile warning systems, and Tactical Air Command took over the interceptors, radars, and control centers designed to defend against bombers.

Other operational commands in the United States survived the Air Force's evolution in the post-Vietnam period. These included the Alaskan Air Command (early warning and air defense); Tactical Air Command (air defense of the United States and prepping units for overseas deployment); SAC (nuclear-deterrent role in cooperation with the Navy's ballistic missile submarine fleet); and

Military Airlift Command (rescue and weather service and, after 1975, responsibility for the Tactical Air Command's airlift units). The newest of the Air Force commands was the Air Force Space Command, formed in 1982, which tracked orbiting spacecraft and was responsible for warning of approaching ballistic missiles.

The support commands remained largely unchanged during this era of change. The Air Force Systems Command, the Air Force Logistics Command, the Air Force Communications Command, and the Electronic Security Command continued as major commands, as did the Air Training Command, which absorbed Air University in 1978. Many other agencies and units existed to support the major commands, but these came and went more easily as they adapted to the Air Force's changing needs.

Modernization results

As the appearance of new missiles and aircraft demonstrated, the Air Force modernized following the cease-fire in Southeast Asia. The last years of Carter's administration and Reagan's first years signaled an upturn in spending and in manpower, as well as in the proportion of new missiles and aircraft acquired. The cost of running this larger and more modern Air Force also increased. When the draft ended in 1973, all services had to compete with civilian employers to attract and retain personnel. Manpower, as well as weapons acquisition and maintenance, became costlier. The tug-of-war between these needs left the Air Force with a delicate juggling act.

Both Korea and Vietnam taught the Air Force that while Strategic Air Command was essential in holding the large powers like the Soviet Union in check, the Air Force also needed to place greater emphasis on its tactical fighters. The new guard acknowledged this need by adding aircraft like the F-15 and F-16 to the Air Force arsenal and by supporting continuous research and development. A series of incidents over the next decade would show the wisdom of this approach.

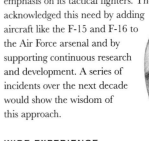

WIDE EXPERIENCE
General Bruce K. Holloway took over as commander in chief of Strategic Air Command in 1968. Much of his background was in tactical fighting.

REBUILDING FOR AN AIR AND SPACE FORCE: PART II

17

As the Air Force modernized and upgraded its equipment, the United States found itself harassed by a series of rogue-state actions. Cuban meddling and a Communist coup on the Caribbean island of Grenada led to US intervention there, while the United States responded to a terrorist attack against Americans in West Berlin with an air strike against the perpetrator, Libya. Harassment of political opponents and US forces in Panama—by the narcotics-trafficking General Manual Noriega—resulted in a US invasion that captured the dictator and installed democratic government in the Central American nation.

URGENT FURY, EL DORADO CANYON, AND JUST CAUSE

THREE OPERATIONS DURING THE 1980S, EACH UNDER VERY DIFFERENT CONDITIONS, PROVIDED LESSONS FOR THE AIR FORCE AS THE COLD WAR WOUND DOWN

IN MANY WAYS THE COLLAPSE OF the Soviet Union, which began during the 1980s, made the global security picture more complex for the United States, rather than simpler. In this post-Cold War period, the United States, as the sole superpower, had to deal with a number of "two-bit hooligans." It would have been easier if those hooligans did not often have sophisticated weapons and a willingness to use them, but they did. The US responses to these challenges ranged from a single air raid (Libya) to full-blown war (Iraq). Each episode illustrated the Air Force's capabilities and readiness for almost any contingency.

Operation Urgent Fury

One of the first of these was Operation Urgent Fury in Grenada in October 1983. It was an overall success, but both the military and the news media gave it mixed reviews.

Grenada is a part of the West Indies, in the Caribbean Sea. Relatively large among the islands there, it had a population of 90,000. It had been under British rule since 1803 but obtained independence in 1974. Its first prime minister, Sir Eric Gairy, had been a thorn in the side of the British for years—corrupt, ruthless, and a squanderer of his country's money. In 1979 Maurice Bishop, a Marxist-Leninist, took advantage of Sir Eric's absence from the country to stage a coup to oust him and install himself in power.

Under Bishop, Grenada began to cooperate with Cuba and signed agreements with Czechoslovakia, Vietnam, North Korea, Libya, and East Germany—none of them, at that point, friends of the United States.

In addition to the large amount of military equipment these deals brought Grenada, they included a deal to complete an international airport at Point Salines, on the island's southwestern tip.

To the United States, the size of the project—far larger than what Grenada needed for its tourism industry—and the involvement of Cubans on the ground were red flags. The project was a cover for the projection of communist power into the eastern Caribbean.

As the Bishop government continued with other projects that could be described only as military construction, resistance to his rule began to surface. And meanwhile, the country got into deep economic trouble, severe enough that Bishop began asking Western governments for aid.

To Bishop's deputy prime minister, Bernard Coard, this was a betrayal of the Marxist-Leninist principles the government was supposedly following. He took advantage of Bishop's absence to stage a coup. Coard, with the aid of General Hudson Austin, took over as prime minister, with the support of the armed forces, though not much of the public, since Bishop was still immensely popular.

Eventually Coard and Austin launched a military operation that captured Bishop and seven of his followers, whom they executed, burning and burying their bodies afterward. Martial law was declared.

The Organization of Eastern Caribbean States, to which Grenada belonged, was shocked at these events and voted for military intervention to restore order on the island. The organization members had no viable military forces of their own and so asked for help from the United States and the Caribbean Community, which included some of the larger entities in the region.

ON WATCH
AC-130 gunships, using a base in Barbados, played a major combat-support role in the Grenada operation.

Meanwhile, the US military had been watching the situation and making plans. On October 20 a battle group built around the carrier USS *Independence* and a Marine amphibious unit, both en route to Lebanon, were ordered to head toward Grenada and await further instructions. The Joint Chiefs of Staff gave the planners three strategic objectives: Secure the safety of American citizens on the island, restore a legitimate democratic government, and eliminate the Cuban presence.

On October 21 President Reagan signed a draft National Security Decision Directive regarding a possible invasion of Grenada. The next day, the Joint Chiefs ordered the operation, Urgent Fury, to proceed. What made the situation particularly urgent from Washington's perspective was the presence of about 1,000 US citizens on Grenada, mostly students and faculty of a medical school. The president and others were concerned about their safety, which the government in Grenada seemed unable to guarantee.

Vice Admiral Joseph Metcalf III was named commander of the organization carrying out Urgent Fury. His deputy was Major General H. Norman Schwarzkopf, later to become a household name, but at that point a little-known Army officer.

The US forces involved in Urgent Fury suffered from spotty intelligence. Grenada had not been important to US intelligence agencies up to that point. Their information on Cuban forces was good, but on the Grenadians, it was not so reliable. Despite reconnaissance flights, the US forces did not know the placements of enemy positions. They also did not know the whereabouts of the medical students and their professors.

The Cubans had 701 men on Grenada, military engineers who knew how to use heavy weapons. US intelligence had underestimated the Grenadian forces: Instead of 1,200 soldiers in the army and up to 5,000 members of the People's Revolutionary Militia, there were actually 2,179 well-armed troops in the army, plus 7,000 men and women in the militia. The Americans knew these forces had Soviet weapons— antiaircraft and antitank guns, heavy machine guns, mortars, and even a few armored personnel carriers—but they worried little about these armaments. They underestimated the willingness of the Grenadian forces to use them.

In his memoirs, General Schwarzkopf recalls listening incredulously to intelligence briefers who kept saying the Grenadians either would not fight, or would not be able to inflict much damage because they were so poorly trained. He did not say anything in the meetings, but kept worrying, "What if they do fight?" Unfortunately, they did.

GRENADA AND THE CARRIBEAN SEA
Grenada is a part of the group of islands known as the West Indies in the Carribean Sea.

RESCUED
*American students board a C-141B Starlifter on their
way out of Grenada.*

darkness, and they did not know what defenses
awaited them.

By a little before 8 a.m., the last wave of
transport aircraft started landing with the
Rangers' heavy equipment such as jeeps, and
the defenders were soon driven from the airfield.
The Americans captured more than 200 Cubans
on the way.

The Rangers also reached the first group of
medical students—about 135 of them—and
rescued them at the campus known as True Blue.
The Rangers also found out about another group
of students at the Grand Anse, south of St. George,
the capital. The US forces were able to remain in
telephone contact with the students, which proved
a vital source of military intelligence. It was not
until October 28, however, that the forces became
aware of another group of more than 200 US
citizens on the Lance aux Epines peninsula.

The lightly armed Rangers were supported by
AC-130s, on watch over the island 24 hours a day.
Usually two of the airships were on station at a
time, while the third went to replenish supplies at
the Grantley Adams airport in Barbados. The use
of this airport was a major factor in the success
of the operation. One of the problems on the
ground in Grenada was that so much of the
Point Salines airfield remained unfinished, and
there were so many piles of supplies around, that
US forces had trouble parking as many of their
aircraft as they would have liked. Hence, the
value of being able to use Grantley Adams,
some 45 minutes away by air, as a staging ground.

By the end of October 25, the first full day
of the operation, US forces held both airfields
and considerable terrain around them, but things
had not gone as the planners had predicted.
The Grenadians and the Cubans had fought back,
giving the US forces a bloody nose. Still, the
situation was not in doubt. Cuba was not coming
to the rescue, and Grenada's nominal "friends"
in the Eastern bloc were just standing by.

The next day, evacuations of the American
medical students and other civilians began.
By the end of the operation, 688 people had
been brought out of Grenada—students, Catholic
priests and nuns, missionaries, other foreign
nationals, and some Grenadians.

The US forces' attack toward Grand Anse
and St. George proceeded. The 82d Airborne
Division troopers had the toughest time
because they encountered the strongest defense
on the island. Nonetheless, they kept pushing
onward, albeit cautiously, north and east
through heavy underbrush.

Urgent Fury began late on October 24, when
a Navy SEAL team began reconnoitering the
beaches. The main assault began early the next
morning, when Marines arrived by helicopter
to take the Pearls airfield on the east side of the
island. They succeeded, sustaining no casualties
and capturing a dozen Cubans. They moved on
to the nearby town of Grenville, and soon the
entire area was under US control.

The Army Rangers at the Point Salines airfield
had a tougher time. They were short staffed
because of a need to support other operations.
The plans for the invasion were made in some
haste, and were revised on the fly—for instance,
it was decided to have the Rangers parachute
in rather than landing with the aircraft. The
attack was rescheduled to 5 a.m., which forfeited
the advantage of operating under cover of

By the end of the day on October 27, the battle for Grenada was essentially over, though neither side quite realized it. The next day, US forces launched an assault on the Calivigny barracks, the last major Grenadian camp and supposedly the center of the Cuban activities on the island. Despite some casualties, the Americans secured the barracks in about an hour. The next few days were spent mopping up. The students at Lance Aux Epines were finally discovered and returned to the United States. Finally, Bernard Coard and Hudson Austin were found and arrested, to await judgment for their role in Maurice Bishop's death and their usurpation of power.

Operation Urgent Fury was officially closed on November 2. It turned out to be no cakewalk. Eighteen Americans were killed, another died of his wounds later, and 106 were wounded. On the enemy side, 24 Cubans were killed, as were 21 members of the Grenadian army; 396 defenders were wounded, and 673 were captured. Some two dozen civilians were known to have been killed during the operation.

US forces achieved their goals in Operation Urgent Fury, but just how successful the mission was is open to debate. It had taken several days to beat back the opposition, despite the overwhelming American military advantage. The execution of the different phases of the operation was poorly

URGENT FURY

A wounded Soldier is treated by US military personnel before being placed aboard a C-141B Starlifter aircraft for medical evacuation during Operation Urgent Fury in Grenada, which occurred from October 25 to November 3, 1983.

coordinated. Most serious were the intelligence failures. The rescue of the American medical students was the most important objective of the operation, but the intelligence services did not know where they were. "We won in Grenada in spite of ourselves," is how one critic put it.

Air Force units participating in the operation received good marks, however. Some confusion cropped up in the initial loading phase and during the Point Salines drop, but the Air Force crews got the soldiers to the target and dropped them where they were supposed to. They also kept supplies and reinforcements coming in on schedule. The firepower of the AC-130 gunships was of great value in supporting the ground forces.

Perhaps the greatest value of Urgent Fury was that it was a wakeup call to the US military, showing the need for more training, better intelligence, and improved coordination of joint assets. Those lessons were learned—and heeded.

MEDEVAC

Medics load an injured Soldier from the 82nd Airborne on a chopper for evacuation on the second day of Operation Urgent Fury.

Libya

Terrorism has been a political and military tactic through the ages, but only over the past quarter century or so have individual countries institutionalized it as state policy. One of the leading practitioners of state-supported terrorism was Muammar Qadhafi, the leader of Libya.

By the mid 1980s, his virulent anti-Western rhetoric began to move from words to deeds. In October 1985 the Italian cruise ship *Achille Lauro* was hijacked and a wheelchair-bound American tourist was murdered. Two months later, terrorists attacked the airports in Rome and Vienna. The attackers in both airport assaults were killed or captured, but they left 19 civilians dead and over 100 more wounded. Countries other than Libya were involved in these assaults, but US intelligence pointed to Libya as the prime instigator.

No "smoking gun" had been found to tie these incidents to Qadhafi—for legal reasons and with an eye to world public opinion, the United States did not want to retaliate without solid proof of Libya's involvement. Planning a potential strike against Libya, however, did not have to wait.

In January and February 1986 two US Navy carrier battle groups took part in a pair of exercises in the Gulf of Sidra, off the coast of Libya. The Navy had been conducting exercises in the Mediterranean since the end of World War II, but the American presence enraged Qadhafi. In the early 1980s, he proclaimed the 32° 30' latitude the northern boundary of Libya, and he referred to this line as the "Line of Death." The two exercises in 1986 did not cross the line, but they did attract the attention of the Libyan Air Force. A number of encounters ensued, which actually left the Navy fliers feeling a little more comfortable, since it was clear that the Libyan fliers were not very good.

In March 1986 President Reagan authorized an exercise that would cross the "Line of Death." The exercise placed the Navy ships involved on a wartime footing and permitted offensive as well as defensive actions as necessary. When the task force, now including three carriers, crossed the line, the Libyans followed quickly, firing several SA-5 surface-to-air missiles, followed by SA-2s, at the Navy aircraft. All missed, and Navy aircraft soon took out the missile site using antiradiation missiles.

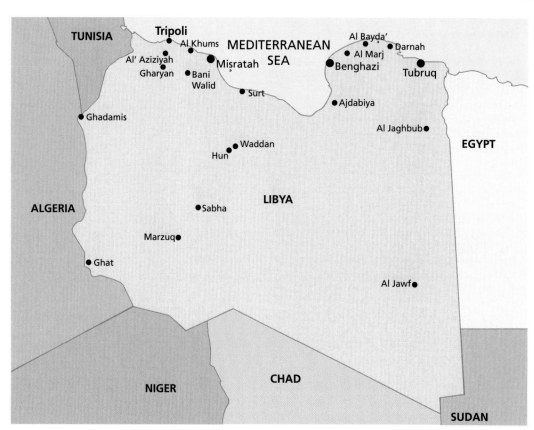

The Navy had dealt Qadhafi a severe blow, and he reacted by unleashing his terrorists again. On April 2 a bomb tore apart a Berlin discotheque, killing a US Soldier and his girlfriend and wounding another 79 Americans and 150 Germans. Intelligence agents had indications something was afoot but could not identify the target until it was too late for warnings.

US analysts had been watching messages between Libya and its embassy, called the "Libyan People's Bureau," in East Berlin. One message to Qadhafi mentioned that something would happen soon to make him happy, and then after the bombing, the bureau followed up: "An event occurred. You will be pleased with the result." It was the smoking gun intelligence agents were looking for.

After meeting with his advisers on April 9, President Reagan authorized the operation known as "El Dorado Canyon." It called for the destruction of major elements of Libya's terrorist infrastructure and the destruction and suppression of Libyan air defenses. Admiral Frank B. Kelso, the Sixth Fleet commander, was put in charge. Time was of the essence; Reagan wanted action before the Libyans could strike again.

Planning had actually been under way since the airport attacks in Rome and Vienna, but one tweak of the plan led to some concern on the

LIBYA AND THE MEDITERRANEAN SEA
Although US Navy ships had operated in the area since World War II, Libyan leader Muammar Qadhafi was particularly incensed by 1986 US exercises off the Libyan coast.

part of the Air Force units set to take part in the operation. On the target list were several facilities known to be used for training terrorists. They included two targets in Tripoli: the Aziziyah barracks—the center of terrorist activities in Libya—and the Murat Sidi Bilal camp, a Palestine Liberation Organization school. Another site, the Jamahiriyah barracks, was located in Benghazi. Libyan air force facilities and aircraft at the Tripoli and Benghazi airfields were also targeted, as were segments of the Tripoli and Benghazi air defense sectors, which had to be taken out to clear a flight path for the raiders. None of these would be easy targets, because they were all surrounded by built-up civilian areas, and the Libyans were heavily armed with Soviet-made missiles, as well as the French-designed Crotale missile.

Admiral Kelso and his team decided the best way to accomplish their purpose was by air strikes. He needed aircraft that could fly fast and low and hit their targets with pinpoint accuracy. He found them at RAF Lakenheath in England: the F-111F, known as the Aardvark, or just "Vark." Its Pave-Tack targeting pod contained forward-looking infrared radar and laser designating/range-finding systems that interfaced with the plane's avionics.

The 48th Tactical Fighter Wing, based at Lakenheath, England, got the job of carrying out the Air Force portion of El Dorado Canyon. Nine F-111Fs were scheduled to attack the Aziziyah barracks, three other Aardvarks were to hit the Murat Sidi Bilal Camp, and six aircraft would bomb the Tripoli airfields. The Navy would go after the Benghazi targets. The raiders were to follow in close succession at low level and make only one run over the target. Admiral Kelso also directed that the pilots positively identify each target before dropping bombs.

The F-111Fs were supplemented with five EF-111A Raven aircraft (nicknamed "Sparkvarks"), which supplied electronic countermeasures; that is, radio jamming. Perhaps the most critical factor to the success of the operation was the support of the tankers. Prime Minister Margaret Thatcher authorized the use of British bases for the launch of the attacks, but other countries were not so accommodating. France and Spain refused to allow overflight of their territories. The 48th's aircraft had to take a circuitous route over the Atlantic through the Strait of Gibraltar and across the Mediterranean to Libya.

Moreover, once the attack force was on its way, Italian government radio operators passed word of its passage to their counterparts on Malta, whose government passed along the intelligence to Libya—fortunately too late to help much.

Late in the afternoon of April 14, the first of 28 tankers took off, followed shortly thereafter by the F-111Fs and the EF-111s from Lakenheath and Upper Heyford. El Dorado Canyon was under way. After about six and a half hours in flight, including four refuelings, the Aardvarks streaked toward their targets, a few minutes before 2 a.m. Libya time. The Navy aircraft had launched much later, because they were based much closer, but they arrived over the target in concert with the Air Force planes.

Not all of the 18 F-111s made it to the target: Three of the aircraft set to hit the barracks had

EL DORADO CANYON

EL DORADO CANYON
A ground crew prepares a 48th Tactical Fighter Wing F-111F aircraft for a retaliatory air strike on Libya. An arming supervisor gives hand signals to the pilot of the aircraft as the crewman under the wing pulls arming pins out of the GBU-10 modular glide bombs. The crewman by the landing gear is checking for foreign objects on the runway that might be sucked into an engine before takeoff.

electronics problems and had to abort. The crew of another plane became disoriented after refueling and had to abort as well.

What happened to the last F-111F is still subject to conjecture. This plane, manned by Captain Fernando Ribas-Dominicci (posthumously promoted to major) and Paul Lorence, disappeared. Some Navy sources have been quoted saying the Navy pilots saw an Aardvark inadvertently fly into the water. Another possibility is that the missing aircraft was shot down by a surface-to-air missile, which is more likely since it was eighth in a series of nine planes and a missile battery had briefly locked in on the aircraft just ahead.

Shortly before 2 a.m., the EF-111As and their Navy counterparts started jamming Libyan radars. Those that tried to filter out the interference soon found themselves shut down by AGM-88 and AGM-45 antiradiation missiles. At 2 a.m., the Air Force and Navy planes hit their targets simultaneously. Both groups came in at an altitude of 100 ft (30m).

The Libyans struck back with unguided missiles and antiaircraft shells that lighted up the sky but did not deter the fliers. Three of the Aardvarks placed their laser-guided bombs on target. Another F-111F held its fire when the crew could not identify their aiming point. A fifth plane used a wrong aiming point and dropped three bombs near the French Embassy. Of the four F-111s set to hit the Murat Sidi Bilal camp, three laid their bombs precisely (the fourth had aborted). The last five

AIRBORNE TANKER
A McDonnell Douglas KC-10 Extender takes off on a refueling mission.

aircraft took aim at the Tripoli airfield and within five minutes had done major damage. In 19 minutes it was all over, except for some trigger-happy Libyans striking out in the darkness with more shells and missiles.

The attackers left behind two ships sunk, another probably sunk, and yet another damaged; six aircraft destroyed and several others damaged; several air defense network stations knocked out; many military and terrorist facilities destroyed or damaged; and one dictator with a severe case of nerves.

The Libyans claimed 37 people were killed and 93 injured, all but one of them civilians—a proportion US forces found a suspiciously high number. The Libyans also claimed that one of the fatalities was Qadhafi's infant daughter; later information indicated Qadhafi had "adopted" her posthumously.

The Americans and others saw El Dorado Canyon as a success in the severe jolt it gave Qadhafi and his terrorist companions. For months after, Qadhafi kept a low profile, but it was a bittersweet success. Not only was one of the F-111Fs lost with its crew, but the bombing and navigation systems on the aircraft failed to work as well as they should have. Too many aircraft had to abort for one reason or another, and too many bombs missed their targets. Still, the Airmen of the 48th had reason to be proud of their role.

Operation Just Cause

In December 1989 the United States once again had to turn its attention to the Caribbean and Central America. Six years after restoring democratic government to Grenada, the United States intervened to bring down another dictatorship. Under the code name Just Cause, the United States invaded Panama and removed its strongman, General Manual Antonio Noriega, from office.

Noriega had established himself as the leader of Panama after the death in 1981 of Omar Torrijos-Herrera, who had overthrown the elected government of Panama in a coup in 1968. Noriega had been the head of military intelligence in Panama in the late 1960s and, as such, had forged an alliance with the US Central Intelligence Agency. When he took over as leader of his country, he proved even more brutal than Torrijos.

US intelligence agencies continued to see him as useful, though less so over time, especially since much of the information he supplied seemed to be second rate. He consolidated Panama's armed services into something he called the Panama Defense Force, thinking this would give him a more positive image. In fact, his control over this force let him rule the country in more draconian ways.

Relations with the United States deteriorated as Noriega escalated a campaign of harassment against US servicemen—a campaign that eventually became a factor in the decision to oust Noriega militarily. Americans criticized his repression of dissent, and after the US Senate passed a resolution on June 25, 1987, calling for the Panamanian people to oust Noriega, he responded by ordering an attack on the US Embassy in Panama City. In early 1988, two federal grand juries in the United States indicted Noriega for drug trafficking. Things got even worse when Noriega annulled the May 1989 elections and ordered his opponents beaten by members of the so-called "Dignity Battalions" ("Digbats," or as American Soldiers called them "dingbats").

Fearing the Digbats might be turned against US citizens and their property, President Bush authorized additional forces for Southern Command, the unified headquarters for Latin America, whose primary mission was the defense of the Panama Canal. Bush also ordered several thousand Americans either to move back on base or be evacuated as a precautionary measure.

Meanwhile, more US combat troops kept arriving, under the guise of "movement exercises." These exercises were intended, in part, to draw a response from the Panamanian forces. The OA-37s of the 24th Tactical Air Support Squadron, 24th Composite Wing, based at Howard Air Base in the Canal Zone, also took part in these exercises. They flew over Panamanian installations to see what response they would get.

All these activities provided intelligence later put to good use during Just Cause.

International outcry against the nullified election continued, but this did not seem to bother Noriega. Instead, he continued to harass his opponents and to do all he could to create an anti-American attitude among the people. Harassment of Americans in Panama continued. For instance, military school buses were stopped and ticketed for not having Panamanian license plates, and American service members were often arrested and held in jail, generally for just a few hours, under various pretexts. In one particularly serious incident, on the night of April 12, 1988, the Panamanian forces (very likely aided by a Cuban special operations unit) attacked US Marines guarding a tank farm near Howard. Several of the attackers were killed or wounded.

Tensions grew, and planning for some sort of US military operation began in earnest. Another failed and bloody coup heightened tensions further, but US forces learned a lot from watching how Noriega responded to the attempt.

At this point, Noriega got his rubber-stamp legislature to declare a "state of war" between Panama and the United States. Back in Washington, members of the US Congress were concerned about the perceived "passive" response of their armed services to all these Panamanian provocations. They were worried about a failure of nerve on the part of the military—but the plans to depose Noriega was already in motion.

Lieutenant General Maxwell R. Thurman took over as head of the Southern Command on September 3, 1989. He named Lieutenant General Carl Stiner's XVIII Airborne Corps, based at Fort Bragg, to do the actual planning of the operation. Stiner and his staff came up with a plan calling for a massive simultaneous onslaught of US forces against the Panamanians. There were 13,000 US troops on the ground in Panama, but Operation Just Cause would bring in enough additional troops to double that. It was a complex undertaking—the largest US military operation since the Vietnam War.

Insofar as it was an invasion, Just Cause was an invasion from the "inside out." US troop numbers in Panama had been on the downswing and levels were set to fall even further in 1999, when control of the Canal would go to Panama. But the United States still had a number of important military installations from which attacks against Noriega could be launched—Howard Air Base, the main US airfield in the Canal Zone; Quarry Heights, the Southern Command headquarters; Fort Clayton, the home of the US Army South; Fort Davis, home to a battalion of special forces troops; and Fort Sherman, home of the US Jungle Operations Training Center.

AIRLIFT SUPPORT
C-130s like this one, along with C-141s and C-5s, carried assault forces into battle during Operation Just Cause.

The Air Force's role in Just Cause was mainly, but not only, one of support. A fleet of C-130s, C-141s, and C-5s was gathered to airdrop or land attackers, then bring in reinforcements and supplies. Other aircraft were used for close support of the ground troops, notably the AC-130A/Hs. Another type of aircraft, the recently unveiled F-117A, would support the Army Rangers later in the operation.

In the final weeks of 1989, two more incidents of harassment of US military personnel in Panama focused the attention of operation planners even further. On December 16, defense force guards stopped four American servicemen in their private vehicle. When they attempted to drive off, the Panamanians opened fire, wounding three, one of them mortally. A few hours later, a Navy lieutenant and his wife were stopped, held, beaten severely, and threatened with death before being released. These episodes

were the last straws. Noriega was about to find out what it meant to be in a "state of war" with the United States.

The new chairman of the Joint Chiefs of Staff, General Colin Powell, met with Secretary of Defense Dick Cheney and the service chiefs. Powell then went to the White House to brief President Bush, along with Vice President Dan Quayle, Secretary of State James Baker, and National Security Adviser Brent Scowcroft. After weighing the options and listening to everyone's views, the president gave the order: "Let's do it."

The operation was set to begin at 1 a.m. on Wednesday, December 20. The planners for Just Cause had more time than those for Urgent Fury, but Just Cause was a more massive operation. On December 18, Military Airlift Command aircraft began to gather at airfields in the southeastern United States. A severe ice storm threatened Pope Air Force Base in North

Carolina, so the loading of the planes took place according to a compressed schedule. When an ice storm hits a place that seldom has such weather, there is often no deicing equipment, which was the case at Pope. Emergency supplies were flown in from other bases, but it was a challenging several hours for ground crews, paratroopers, and Rangers, as they dealt with ice coatings half an inch thick. Personnel on the base picked up their pace, and they were aided by Army and Air Force retirees and Reservists living nearby who had heard "something was up" at Pope and came by to help. Commanders on the base gratefully accepted the aid of these volunteers. With everyone pulling together, all 31 C-141s were loaded and ready to depart on schedule.

Although the aircraft left at something close to their scheduled departure time, there were other problems. It became clear that the Panamanians were aware of the impending invasion. And in the

United States, CBS News reported the departure of large numbers of aircraft from Fort Bragg that might or might not be en route to Panama.

The first to arrive on the ground in Panama were the special operations units trying to capture Noriega—which proved to be harder than expected—and the units assaulting key Panamanian installations. Two AC-130Hs were assigned to the force assaulting La Comandancia, a walled compound where the Panama Defense Force had its command center. It was one of the most important objectives of the operation. The AC-130Hs soon had the building ablaze. Then the defenders set the adjacent buildings on fire, too, and the resulting dense clouds of smoke hindered both the Airmen and the US Soldiers on the ground. In the ensuing confusion, several American Soldiers were wounded by friendly fire and their M-113 armored personnel carriers damaged.

Meanwhile, other gunships were assisting with other portions of the assault. They engaged the enemy briefly on the golf course, where Panamanian and American troops used to golf together. More important action took place at the Pacora River Bridge, east of the airfields on the highway to Battalion 2000's base at Fort Cimarron. Soldiers came under fire there from the Panama Defense Force—they took few casualties, but the encounter gave the Americans an impetus to get on with their mission. For a time, it appeared that the Panamanians might break through the thinly-held US lines. A couple of AC-130s were called out to bring the Panamanians to a halt, and soon the bridge was securely under American control.

Almost simultaneously, airborne assaults were under way at Torrijos/Tocumen (the two airfields) and Rio Hato. It was the largest nighttime airdrop since Normandy. The action near Torrijos, a civilian airport, was complicated by the late arrival of a Brazilian passenger airliner with an estimated 376 passengers. These civilians were going to be right in the thick of the action, and were likely to end up as hostages.

MANUAL NOREIGA
Manual Noriega's mug shot, taken in Miami after he surrendered to the United States.

At Tocumen, General Manual Antonio Noriega, the real target of the whole operation, was consorting with a prostitute. The Army Rangers did not know how close they were to their prey, but after Noriega spotted the Americans dropping out of the sky, his aides hustled him out of the Ceremi Recreation Center at the base and sent him into hiding. It would be some days before he was captured, but his last days of freedom were spent continually on the run.

As the Rangers and paratroopers swooped down on the two airfields, the Panamanians did indeed start taking hostages, including some Americans, from among the passengers of the Brazilian airliner. The Panamanians soon realized they did not have a chance against the American forces and surrendered. But the nearly 400 passengers had to stay in the airport terminal until the battle was over.

By noon on December 20, the situation had stabilized. US troops expanded their perimeter around Torrijos/Tocumen, and civilians started to come out of their houses to welcome them. The assault on the airfields had been highly successful, with only one Ranger fatality and five troops wounded, plus another 19 injured during the jump.

HELLFIRE
Army AH-64 Apache helicopters like this one fired seven Hellfire missiles during Operation Just Cause. All were direct hits.

PAVE HAWKS

The Air Force deployed HH-60C Pave Hawk helicopters like these during Operation Just Cause. The Pave Hawk is a highly modified version of the Army Black Hawk chopper. Its main mission is combat search and rescue, day or night. Pave Hawks also provide civil search and rescue, emergency aeromedical evacuation, disaster relief, international aid, counterdrug activities, and NASA space shuttle support. They saved more than 4,300 Americans in the New Orleans area after Hurricane Katrina in September 2005.

Panamanian casualties were heavier. A major weapons cache was seized, along with 25 aircraft.

More Rangers jumped from their planes over Rio Hato. The battle there was short but vicious. Many of the Panamanians turned tail when they saw parachutes blossoming over them, but others stayed to fight. By sunrise, though, the Americans had seized all their objectives, and by the end of the day on December 20, the invasion of Panama was essentially over. The US troops fanned out to take key installations, and most of the defenders chose to surrender. From that point on, one of the biggest problems facing the US troops was the breakdown in law and order on the ground. Planners had not foreseen this, and had sent along few military police. The situation was brought under control only with the use of combat troops as police.

Operation Just Cause would not really be a success, though, until Noriega was captured, and after his close call at Tocumen, he was on the run. On the afternoon of December 24, Christmas Eve, he surfaced, in a gray T-shirt and baggy Bermuda

shorts, at the Nunciature, the Vatican embassy in Panama City. He held out in this sanctuary for 10 days. General Thurman ringed the embassy with troops. At one point, in an attempt at psychological warfare, the soldiers blasted Noriega—and the embassy—with rock music over loudspeakers. This had no effect on Noriega but irritated the ambassador and his staff, so the soldiers hit the "power off" button in short order.

On January 3 Noriega surrendered. He was allowed to wear his Panama Defense Force uniform when he did so, but he was a pathetic figure as he walked out of the Nunciature and into American custody. An Army UH-60 helicopter flew him to Howard Air Base, where Drug Enforcement Administration agents took him into custody. Now dressed in prison coveralls, he was flown to Miami to be booked at the federal courthouse there and jailed on drug charges. He was later convicted of drug trafficking and money laundering and sent to a US prison. Operation Just Cause did not officially end until January 31, but for all practical purposes, it ended with Noriega's surrender.

American losses in Just Cause were relatively light, given the size of the operation—not much more than in Operation Urgent Fury. US fatalities in Panama were 23; 324 Americans were wounded. Panamanian losses were higher—314 killed, 124 wounded, and about 5,800 captured or detained. Civilian casualties were high, in large part because of Panamanian forces setting fire to the slums around La Comandancia and firing recklessly into the night. Human rights organizations later claimed that thousands of Panamanians had died in the fighting, but there seems to be little evidence for that claim. The official US number was an estimate of 202 killed and 1,508 wounded.

For the Air Force, Just Cause reaffirmed the service's essential role in the modern US military.

Its airlift role got most of the attention, but its combat elements provided strong support to ground troops. Strategic Air Command KC-135s and KC-10s from 23 squadrons demonstrated again the value of tankers in modern warfare. Between December 20 and January 4, the tankers pumped 12,069,500 pounds of fuel to other aircraft.

Tactical Air Command had a role too, albeit less visible. As during the operation in Grenada, F-15s flew combat air patrol missions in case Cuba tried to interfere. It soon became apparent, however, that this was not going to happen. More directly involved were a pair of EC-130H Compass Call aircraft, two EF-111As, and another pair of EC-130Es. These were used for electronic warfare against Panama's communication and for psychological warfare. And two EC-130Es provided airborne command post platforms.

The Military Airlift Command shouldered the load in Just Cause. Aircraft and personnel from every active duty, Reserve, and National Guard flying unit in the command took part. So did personnel from airlift control squadrons, aerial port squadrons, the Air Force Weather Service, and aeromedical evacuation units, both in the United States and in Panama.

Just Cause was not the perfect operation, nor was it the hardest the US armed forces have ever undertaken. It took place under uniquely favorable conditions—in a country where US military forces had been stationed for years and where they were able to train for the operation under the noses of those they were about to attack. Moreover, the defending forces were weak, and the Panamanian people were ready for a change in leadership.

But even with all these advantages, some things failed to go according to plan. The Panama Defense Force found out about the impending attack, so the element of surprise was lost. Bad weather delayed the airborne assault. Noriega proved elusive for some days. Friendly fire caused some "blue on blue" casualties. The Rangers and paratroopers and their equipment did not land exactly as intended. These are minor points, though. Operation Just Cause helped lay to rest any lingering doubts about the effectiveness of the US armed forces after the Vietnam War.

The Air Force role in Just Cause was a support role, albeit a crucial one. In the next chapter of their history, the US armed forces would find themselves a conflict in which the Air Force would have the lead role in containing a foreign despot.

MODULE IV

AIRPOWER THROUGH THE POST-COLD-WAR PERIOD

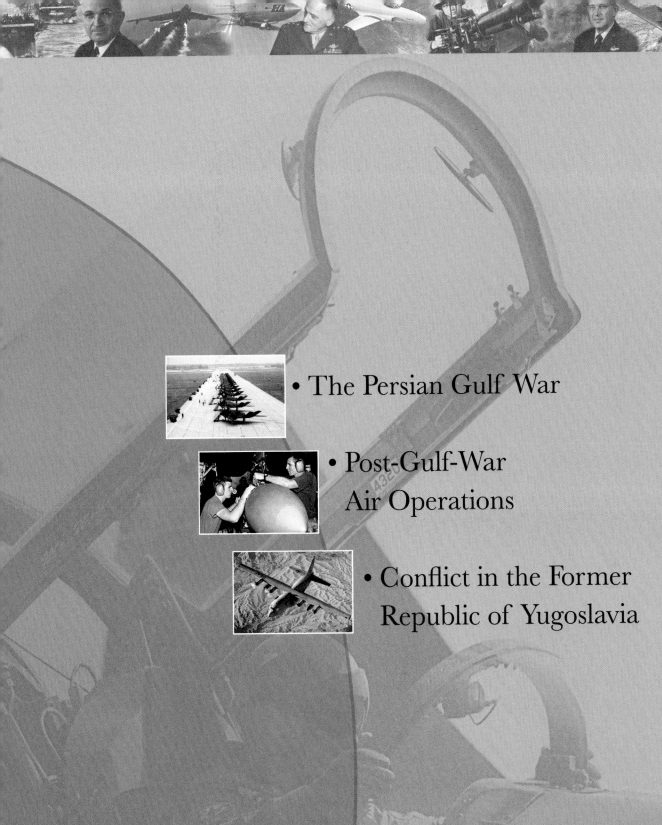

- The Persian Gulf War

- Post-Gulf-War
  Air Operations

- Conflict in the Former
  Republic of Yugoslavia

18

THE PERSIAN GULF WAR

WHEN IRAQI DICTATOR Saddam Hussein seized Kuwait in 1990, he made a historic miscalculation—that no one would respond. Instead, the United States launched its biggest overseas operation since the Vietnam War and unleashed a counterpunch that relied on airpower to an unprecedented extent. The buildup and supply operations tested the Air Force's airlift ability as much as combat operations tested its fighter pilots. The war was remarkable for the speed, flexibility, and precision of modern airpower, as well as for a remarkably low Air Force casualty rate.

DESERT SHIELD AND DESERT STORM

THE WAR FOUGHT TO EXPEL SADDAM HUSSEIN FROM KUWAIT WAS THE FIRST IN WHICH AIRPOWER WAS THE DOMINATING FACTOR AND THE AIR FORCE THE DOMINATING FORCE

THE ARMED SERVICES were still pondering the lessons of Just Cause when another geopolitical temblor shook the world. This one threatened much wider repercussions than the Panama crisis: Iraq had invaded and conquered its neighbor Kuwait. US intelligence services believed this was the first phase in a campaign by Iraqi leader Saddam Hussein to dominate the Arabian Peninsula and its oil reserves.

Kuwait had supported Iraq during the Iran–Iraq War during the 1980s, but since the creation of the modern state of Iraq in 1922, tension had simmered between Kuwait and Iraq. Britain, acting under the authority of the League of Nations after World War I, had carved the new state out of a part of the defeated Ottoman Empire. Boundary lines were drawn on a map with little regard for ethnic or religious realities

SKY SENTRY
The E-3 Sentry early-warning and control aircraft—essentially a Boeing 707 with a saucer-shaped radar antenna on its back—was the hub of coalition air operations in the Gulf War.

on the ground. Of particular significance was that the new Iraq had no ocean port—but next-door Kuwait, another chunk of Ottoman legacy, did.

From the start, Iraq had claimed Kuwait, which remained in British possession, as one of its own provinces. When the British withdrew after giving Kuwait independence in 1961, Iraq tried to seize its smaller neighbor. British troops returned in force to chase the Iraqis off, but Iraq tried again in 1973—it seized a chunk of northeastern Kuwait and returned it only after receiving an $85 million "loan" from the Kuwaitis. After that, relations between the two countries were outwardly calm but strained below the surface. Iraq remained determined to acquire an ocean port.

Meanwhile, Saddam Hussein was working his way to the leadership of Iraq. His style has been described as "gun-barrel politics." In 1979, while in his early 40s, he staged a coup against the president of Iraq and took over that position himself. He maintained his authority through murder and terror. He distrusted the United States and believed that the West was plotting to destroy him. This, however, did not keep him from accepting US assistance during his war with Iran.

During much of the Cold War, the United States had considered Iran and Iraq as bulwarks that would keep the Soviet Union from moving into the Middle East. After the 1979 Islamic revolution in Iran, however, the previously close relations between the United States and Iran shifted abruptly. Washington began to regard Iraq as a buffer against both the Soviets and the Shiite *Ayatollahs*, or Muslim religious leaders, in Tehran. Iraq was at best a lesser evil, however. American overtures to Iraq had to overlook the country's human rights abuses, its hostility to Israel, and its support of terrorism.

In October 1989 President George H. W. Bush designated the Persian Gulf area vital to US national security. He signed a directive that committed the United States to defense of its "vital interests," by military force if necessary. As part of its overtures to Iraq, Washington provided some credit guarantees. Despite congressional opposition, President Bush also signed an agreement expanding trade with Iraq, but things went downhill from there.

On February 24, 1990, Saddam shocked not only a meeting of the Arab Cooperation Council but also the United States when he railed against possible American dominance of the Persian Gulf and hailed the Soviet Union as the "key champion of the Arabs." Washington tried to smooth things over, but Saddam became only more bellicose. Among the incidents causing particular concern was the discovery by several Western governments of a shipment to Iraq of banned material that could be used to make missiles or nuclear weapons.

Things soon got worse during what a State Department official called "the spring of bad behavior." Saddam began to threaten Kuwait, charging it with engaging in economic warfare against Iraq. Kuwaiti overproduction of oil, he charged, was holding down world oil prices at a time when Iraq, deeply in debt following its war with Iran, needed them kept high.

Iraq invades

On July 16, 1990, Iraqi Foreign Minister Tariq Aziz wrote secretly to the Arab League, charging both Kuwait and the United Arab Emirates of exceeding oil production quotas to hurt Iraq. He also accused Kuwait of stealing oil literally out from under Iraq by slant drilling in the Rumaila oil field, which the two countries shared. The next day, Saddam repeated Aziz's charges publicly, and soon Iraqi troops were moving toward the Kuwait border.

FIRE FLIGHT
A group including the F-16A, F-15C, and F-15E flying over burning oil fields during Desert Storm.

Estimates of Iraqi military strength on the eve of the war vary widely. Iraq had three kinds of ground forces: the elite Republican Guard, the regular army, and the Popular Army. The Republican Guard, about 20 percent of Iraq's ground forces, was the most capable and best equipped of the three. These units were "armor heavy," with Soviet T-72 main battle tanks and a variety of modern armored personnel carriers and artillery. Most of the 50 divisions and additional brigades of the regular army were infantry. But the regular army also had several armored and mechanized divisions, consisting mainly of older Soviet and Chinese equipment. The Popular Army consisted of 250,000 men, all members of the ruling Baath Party. Its personnel were considered low-caliber and they were generally kept to the rear.

Additionally, Iraq had more than 5,000 main battle tanks, 5,000 armored infantry vehicles, and 3,000 artillery pieces of 100 millimeters or more. Iraq's ground forces, in sum, were well equipped. And, after the long years of the war with Iran, they were considered battle hardened. In retrospect, it might have been more accurate to describe them as simply exhausted.

The 40,000 men of the Iraqi air force had a somewhat lesser reputation than the ground forces did. In terms of numbers, they were the sixth-largest air force in the world, with more than 700 combat aircraft, ranging from the modern to the nearly antique. These aircraft operated from 24 primary air bases as well as 30 additional dispersal fields. These bases had extensive facilities, including shelters thought capable of withstanding even nuclear blasts.

If the equipment was good, though, the pilots were not as impressive. Even the best of them, the French-trained pilots flying the F-1 Mirages, were poorly skilled in the art of air combat. Iraq had an extensive air-defense network made up of radar, hardened and buried command and control facilities, surface-to-air missiles, interceptors, and antiaircraft artillery. The network was designed in keeping with the standard Soviet practice, which entailed mounting an intertwined, redundant, and layered air-defense system. Baghdad's defenses were so concentrated that they were actually thicker than the most heavily defended Warsaw Pact target of the Cold War. But the Iraqi network depended almost wholly on centralized control. That was a vulnerability the United States would exploit.

Besides a tiny navy, the Iraqi military also had several weapons that posed serious threats. The best known was the Soviet-designed Scud missile. The Iraqis had three versions of this weapon. The standard had a range of 180 miles (300km). The Iraqis modified the missiles to produce the Al Husayn, with a range of 360 miles (600km), and the Al-Hijarah, which could reach targets 450 miles (750km) away.

All three missiles could carry high explosives or unitary and binary nerve agents and biological warheads; however, they were poorly constructed and could not be accurately targeted. They were really terror weapons more than anything else, but the knowledge that they could carry biological and chemical agents (which the Iraqis had developed and used during the war with Iran) affected the actions of the United States and its coalition partners during the war.

Whatever Iraq's weaknesses, it clearly had Kuwait outgunned. The Kuwaiti army had 20,000 men, plus another 7,000 in the National Guard. Its tanks numbered 250, of which only 165 were considered first-line. Kuwait's air force had only 60 planes, and its navy was even smaller than Iraq's. Other countries on the Arabian Peninsula were not much better off. Most of them, notably Saudi Arabia, had modern aircraft, but they had only enough air power to delay, not defeat, an attack.

The force that was available to face down the Iraqis was the US Central Command (CENTCOM). Its area of responsibility was Southwest Asia and East Africa—from Iraq to Pakistan to Somalia. The command was normally a planning staff, but in a contingency, it could provide military muscle. The situation on the Kuwaiti border was definitely a contingency. The CENTCOM's commander in 1990 was Army General H. Norman Schwarzkopf, and Lieutenant General Charles A. "Chuck" Horner led the Air Force portion of Central Command's structure, CENTAF. Horner also commanded the Ninth Air Force, based at Shaw Air Force Base, South Carolina.

Airpower was essential to any of the command's operations, and it was also its most mobile component. In case of trouble, Air Force units could arrive on scene first, establish air superiority, interdict enemy supply lines, and provide close air support. These actions would clear the way for the safe arrival of ground forces with their equipment and supplies.

As Iraqi forces massed along and then burst across the Kuwaiti border, the Central Command was conducting a command post exercise at Eglin Air Force Base, Florida, and Fort Bragg, North Carolina. The timing of this exercise was a boon to planning for Desert Shield and Desert Storm. The exercise showed a need for a revised troop list, more armor, and more mobile forces. It also confirmed CENTAF's concept of air defense for the Arabian Peninsula.

Meanwhile, at the United Nations (UN), the international community was denouncing the invasion of Kuwait. On August 2 the Security Council passed Resolution 660, condemning the invasion and demanding Iraq's withdrawal. Other resolutions followed in subsequent months. Iraq did not budge,

LIEUTENANT GENERAL "CHUCK" HORNER
Lieutenant General Charles Horner commanded the Ninth Air Force and Central Command Air Forces.

TOP GENERAL
General H. Norman Schwarzkopf was the commander of US Central Command.

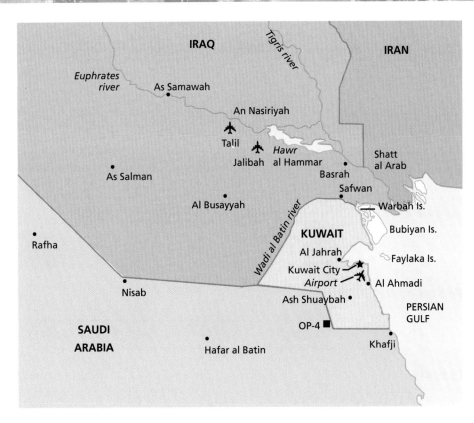

movements, leaving General Horner in Saudi Arabia to act as Central Command, Forward.

So began what eventually became known as the Persian Gulf War. (Gulf War is another name for this conflict, although during the 1980s, that term was used for what is now referred to as the Iran–Iraq War.)

Desert Shield

The deployment portion of the war, known as Desert Shield, had two phases. The first phase lasted from August 7 to November 8, 1990, and consisted of establishing a defensive posture. The second phase, a defensive-offensive stage, came after President Bush's November 8 announcement that he would increase the number of American troops on the Arabian Peninsula. The offensive portion of this phase would become Desert Storm.

Among the first units to deploy after the Joint Chiefs of Staff directed combat troops to the Gulf on August 6 was the 1st Tactical Fighter Wing from Langley Air Force Base, Virginia. The wing had been on alert since the invasion of Kuwait, so it did not take long to move. Its F-15C fighters arrived at Dhahran, Saudi Arabia, August 8 after a 14-hour flight involving seven midair refuelings. Combat air patrols started the next day. These patrols were the first line of defense should Iraq attempt to invade Saudi Arabia.

Meanwhile, the rapid airlift of soldiers of the 82d Airborne and 101st Airborne Divisions, as well as personnel of the 7th Marine Expeditionary Brigade, was under way. It would become one of the most remarkable achievements in US military annals. Not only personnel but also all manner of supplies had to be brought in by air.

however, and on November 29, 1990, the UN Security Council passed Resolution 678, which authorized the use of "all means necessary" to eject Iraq from Kuwait if it did not withdraw by January 15, 1991.

Diplomacy and military action run on different timetables. Immediately after Iraqi forces invaded, President Bush ordered two Navy carrier battle groups into the region. Other forward actions were taken as US officials considered the possibility of an Iraqi attack on Saudi Arabia.

On August 4 Schwarzkopf and Horner briefed President Bush on military options. Afterwards, the president dispatched the two generals to Saudi Arabia, along with the US Secretary of Defense Richard Cheney, to get Saudi King Fahd ibn Abd al-Aziz's consent for stationing US forces there. The king consented to the deployment, and neighboring countries followed suit. General Schwarzkopf returned to the United States to oversee initial troop

TAXIING OUT
C-5 Galaxies contributed mightily to airlifting troops and supplies to Saudi Arabia before the Gulf War. This aircraft was photographed in Iraq in 2006.

Airlift would be the critical factor in Desert Shield's success. Although heavy equipment came in by sea, 99 percent of the personnel deployed for Desert Shield arrived by air. This put boots on the ground swiftly enough to forestall any Iraqi ideas of pushing farther southward.

The whole operation stretched the Military Airlift Command to the limit. Two weeks into Desert Shield, 94 percent of the command's C-5s and 74 percent of its C-141s were occupied moving troops and supplies over the "aluminum bridge" from the United States to Saudi Arabia.

The command relied on its Air Reserve Component units and soon had to call up six Reserve and one Air National Guard C-5 squadrons, 10 Reserve and one C-141 squadrons, and five C-130 squadrons from each component. But these resources still were not enough. On August 17 General Hansford T. Johnson, commander of both the Military Airlift Command and the US Transportation Command, announced the activation of Stage I of the Civil Reserve Air Fleet. It was the first activation in the fleet's 38-year history. Stage I provided 38 long-range international aircraft and crews. Stage II, during Desert Storm, brought in another 116 aircraft, also a mix of passenger and cargo jets.

During Desert Shield's early days, 50 to 65 strategic airlift missions flew daily into the theater. By mid-September this fell to 44. The number of missions shot up to 100 by the end of the month, and then tapered to 36 a day in early October. When the president called for more troops into the region on November 8, the number of missions swelled again.

In December and January, the C-141s were flying three times as many missions as normal. The C-5s saw similar rates of increase. The pace only quickened once Desert Storm began. At the peak of the airlift, 127 aircraft were taking part, with a landing every 11 minutes. But even this

REFUELING IN THE AIR
A KC-135R Stratotanker refuels an F-16C Fighting Falcon fighter aircraft from the 614th Tactical Fighter Squadron (TFS), 401st Tactical Fighter Wing of Torrejon Air Base, Spain, as another Fighting Falcon flies alongside during Operation Desert Shield.

was not fast enough. Critical supplies were still taking as long as two weeks to reach Saudi Arabia, so on October 30 the command launched its overnight service, called Desert Express. Dedicated C-141s flew high-priority supplies from Charleston Air Force Base, South Carolina, twice a day. A second service, European Desert Express, operating out of Rhein-Main, Germany, was also introduced. During Desert Shield, the Air Force flew 17 million ton-miles daily—10 times the amount flown during the Berlin airlift.

The C-130 tactical air lifters from active-duty, Reserve, and Guard units played a role in Desert Shield as well. Like other aircraft, they rotated in and out of the theater regularly, so their numbers fluctuated. As soon as they reached the theater, the crews were hard at work moving munitions and supplies from stockpiles to the arriving units' locations. These activities became even more intense once Desert Storm began. The transports flew daily missions between staging areas and forward logistics bases. Needing to touch down where there were no airfields, they landed on narrow roads. The C-130s delivered 159,000 tons

(144,242 tonnes) of cargo, 600,000 gallons (2,271,000 liters) of fuel, and 184,000 personnel in 21,000 hours of flying.

Once the air war began and coalition forces had blinded Iraq's command, control, and communications network, General Schwarzkopf executed what he later called the "Hail Mary pass," a maneuver that trapped many Iraqis. He kept the XVIII and the VII Airborne Corps in place initially to hold the Iraqis in their positions. Then, given that the Iraqi network was out of commission, his plan was to move the XVIII Corps west to put it into position to encircle the Iraqis. The C-130s moved almost the entire XVIII Corps from the Dhahran/Ad Dammam area to near Rafha, more than 400 miles (644km) to the west.

CENTAF's original plan was to use 72 aircraft, with one landing every 10 minutes, 24 hours a day, for 14 days. As it happened, the Hercules landed once every seven minutes for 13 days, moving 9,000 tons (8,165 tonnes) of equipment and 14,000 troops.

The C-130s also continued to be used for various airdrops. For example, when the 101st Airborne Division outran its supplies, C-130s dropped 100 tons (91 tonnes) of food and water. Most of the airdrops, however, were to supply Iraqi prisoners with food and water. The C-130s also played a role in evacuating casualties, but the war ended so quickly that only 2,023 patients were airlifted out during Desert Storm—only a few more than during Desert Shield.

The need for airlift capability did not end when the shooting did, however. The C-130s were busy taking troops back from the front and airlifting 6,000 refugees from Safwan, Iraq, to relocation camps in Saudi Arabia. The capacity for air refueling was critical to the success of Desert Shield/Desert Storm. The Air Force commonly refers to air refueling as a "force multiplier," and the Gulf War showed that this cliché is grounded in fact. Air refueling made the Desert Shield buildup possible in far less time than it would have taken otherwise. Without air refueling, the buildup would have taken longer than would have been militarily sound, and it would have been impossible for coalition forces to sustain such a ferocious pace during the air war.

WORKHORSES OF TACTICAL AIRLIFT
A C-130 Hercules transport aircraft from the West Virginia Air National Guard flies over the United Arab Emirates during a troop-carrying mission in support of Operation Desert Storm.

STRATEGIC AIRLIFT
A C-5A from Military Airlift Command prepares to unload supplies from its nose ramp in support of Operation Desert Shield.

The four phases

Desert Storm was the result of planning that began in August. General Schwarzkopf asked for a conceptual offensive air plan, and the planning group, known as Checkmate, developed Instant Thunder. The name was an allusion to Rolling Thunder, the phased-in offensive of the Vietnam War.

Planners saw Instant Thunder as a blueprint for a stand-alone war-winning strategy. The idea was to attack Iraq's centers of gravity by destroying 84 strategic targets in a week. Schwarzkopf approved the plan preliminarily and sent it along to General Horner. Horner rejected the "airpower alone" argument but accepted the rest of the plan.

Somewhere along the line, the name Instant Thunder disappeared, and CENTAF started fighting with a plan known by a somewhat less exciting name—Offensive Campaign, Phase I. Despite the name change, the new campaign retained Instant Thunder's basic concepts.

On August 25, 1990, the Central Command presented General Colin Powell, chairman of the Joints Chiefs of Staff, with a proposal for

a four-phase offensive campaign:
Phase I: Strategic air campaign
Phase II: Air campaign against the Iraqi air defense in Kuwait
Phase III: Attrition of Iraqi ground combat power to neutralize Iraq's deployed ground forces and isolate the Kuwaiti battlefield
Phase IV: Ground attack to eject Iraqi forces from Kuwait.

OFF AGAIN!

A 48th Tactical Fighter Wing F-111F Raven departs for Saudi Arabia in support of Operation Desert Shield.

PREPARING TO DEPLOY

Ground crews service the F-117A aircraft of the 37th Tactical Fighter Wing on the flight line as the wing prepares to deploy to Saudi Arabia for Operation Desert Shield.

WAR AIMS

Just hours before the first bombs of Desert Storm began to fall, General Schwarzkopf issued an order restating the coalition's objectives:

- Attack Iraqi leadership and command and control facilities

- Gain and maintain air superiority

- Sever Iraqi supply lines

- Destroy nuclear, biological, and chemical weapons production, storage, and delivery capabilities

- Destroy Republican Guard forces

- Liberate Kuwait City.

Of the four phases, airpower alone would accomplish the first two; a combination of air and ground power would accomplish the latter two. A study suggested that the first three phases would last six, two, and six days, respectively. But when more coalition aircraft became available in January 1991, the planners decided to combine the first three phases. Coalition aircraft would attack all targets of each of the phases simultaneously.

General Schwarzkopf named General Horner the Joint Force Air Component Commander and gave him responsibility for planning the air campaign and for coordinating more than 2,700 aircraft from 14 countries and service components. Schwarzkopf said, "If you aren't part of the air campaign under Horner, you don't fly."

To integrate operations, Horner relied on a master attack plan and another document called the air tasking order (ATO). The latter was the daily schedule used to execute the attack plan. The two plans were very different in size. The master attack plan was only 21 pages long. The ATO was the size of a big city phone book, and it could take up to two hours to transmit it electronically to all units.

The ATO was very effective during the strategic air campaign, but it proved inflexible as the situation became more fluid and the focus shifted to mobile targets in and near Kuwait. To regain flexibility, new plans were developed.

Horner had quite a job to do. Not only was he in charge of a staggering number of aircraft, but he also had to face some resistance from

members of other service branches that were not convinced that an Air Force officer should control their forces. But Horner knew his job, worked well with other officers, and performed admirably. Using persuasion, compromise, and patience, Horner kept all parties reasonably satisfied.

Desert Storm

Desert Storm began January 17, 1991. Taking off from their base in Saudi Arabia, a trio of HM-53J Pave Low helicopters led nine Army AH-64 Apache gunships into Iraq. The first tasks were to spot Iraqi radars (for which the Pave Low helicopters were well equipped) and to knock them out (something the Apaches could do). Then 19 F-15Es slipped through the gap that had been opened in Iraqi air defenses and went to bomb Scud missile-launcher sites in western Iraq. Three EF-111As came through the gap as well. Their task was to provide electronic countermeasures for a group of F-117s on their way to attack the heart of Iraq—Baghdad.

One of the F-117s planted two Paveway III laser-guided bombs on the Nukhayb Sector Air Defense Center southwest of Baghdad. With that, Iraq's air-defense command and control system began to fall apart. As some early warning radars and an air-defense center were knocked off, the Iraqis reacted blindly. At one point, the sky over Baghdad lit up like a fireworks display, but the Iraqis were shooting at ghosts. The Americans had not arrived yet.

However, they did arrive within minutes. F-117s went directly to the "AT&T Building," the center for telecommunications, and the Abu Guryahb Presidential Palace (one of Saddam's many residences and the wartime headquarters of the Iraqi general staff), among other buildings. A cheer went through General Horner's office in

INVALUABLE SUPPORT
EF-111A Raven aircraft prepare to takeoff on a mission during Operation Desert Shield.

Riyadh when the CNN correspondent in Baghdad, whose live report by telephone they had been listening to, was cut off in midsentence. Horner's staff knew that the bombers had put a dent in Iraqi telecommunications.

Then came the blasts of the Tomahawk land-attack missiles. Fired from Navy vessels in the Persian Gulf and Red Sea, these missiles had a 90-minute journey to Baghdad, where they struck the Baath Party headquarters and the city's six electrical power plants. Without electricity, Iraqi national air defenses had to rely on a balky backup power system. Meanwhile, the remaining Iraqi radars were overwhelmed by incoming attack aircraft. In short order, Iraq's extensive radar system was knocked out. Before the week was out, Iraq's air defenses were essentially blind.

A few hours after the F-117 bombs and the Tomahawk missiles struck, there was another round of explosions. Seven B-52Gs from the 2d Bomb Wing had arrived in Baghdad, more than 11 hours after they had left Barksdale Air Force Base in Louisiana. It was the longest combat mission in the history of warfare.

These planes carried the AGM-86C, a cruise missile variant that had been kept secret to that point. The eight targets attacked by the B-52Gs were struck later by other planes, which made it harder to evaluate the success of the raid from Barksdale, but intelligence sources rated the attacks as successful. Perhaps just as important, this 35-hour round trip demonstrated the Air Force's worldwide capabilities, summed up in the phrase "Global Reach—Global Power."

GROUND STRIKE
First delivered to the US Navy in 1981, the McDonnell-Douglas F/A-18 Hornet was, as its designation indicates, a dual-role aircraft—both an agile air-superiority fighter and a powerful ground-attack aircraft. During the Gulf War in 1991, the Hornets were mostly used in a ground-attack role.

OLD RELIABLE

WHATEVER ITS ROLE, THE B-52 was a powerful aircraft that got the enemy's attention. By the third day of Desert Storm, when the Iraqi air force had been neutralized but Iraqi missiles remained a threat, the B-52s shifted to high-altitude operations out of the lethal range of most missiles. So high up that enemy troops on the ground often failed to notice them, the aircraft dropped bomb after bomb.

Although they did not necessarily kill many of the enemy, they did prompt many of the desertions that sapped the strength of the Iraqi forces. Almost universally, prisoners of war called the B-52 the weapon they feared most.

One Iraqi commander interrogated by US troops after the war said that he had surrendered because of the B-52s. When his interrogator countered that the Iraqi's position had never been attacked by the bombers, the Iraqi responded, "That is true, but I saw one that *had* been attacked."

AWAITING THE NEXT MISSION
Weapons loaders use an MJ-1 bomb loader to load Mark 117 750lb (340kg) bombs on a B-52 Stratofortress aircraft during Operation Desert Shield.

The attack from Barksdale was the most dramatic B-52 mission of the war, but it was only a small part of the planes' activity. Sixty-eight B-52Gs, from bases in England, Spain, and the Indian Ocean, as well as Barksdale, had a role in Desert Storm. They were 3 percent of the coalition's total combat aircraft, but they delivered 30 percent of the air munitions tonnage. Only one of these aircraft was lost during the war, and that was to an accident rather than hostile fire. Eight other planes were damaged.

In Desert Storm, use of precision-guided munitions and the highly sophisticated new cockpit and systems avionics blurred the traditional distinction between strategic and tactical aircraft. The B-52G was considered a "strategic" bomber, but in the Gulf War it flew mostly against ground support targets in Kuwait. The "tactical" fighter-bombers (F-117As, F-111Fs, and F-15Es), on the other hand, often attacked strategic targets during Desert Storm.

Preparing the battlefield proved to be the B-52s' forte, but it was not their only mission. One strategic target they went after was the huge Taji logistics center north of Baghdad, too vast for efficient use of precision-guided munitions. The B-52s turned the center into piles of rubble.

As this was being accomplished, coalition aircraft swept the Iraqi air force from the sky. Press reports had described it as a force to be

THE GREAT SCUD HUNT

ONE WAY THE IRAQIS did fight back was with Scud missiles. On January 17, they launched two Scuds against Israel, which was not a member of the anti-Iraq coalition. The Scuds were notoriously inaccurate, and these two were true to type: both fell into the sea.

But as a terror weapon, the Scuds packed quite a punch. Subsequent firings caused serious casualties and damage and created fear in civilian populations. The CENTAF planners had given a lot of thought to Scuds during their preparation for war. A particular concern was that Scud attacks would goad Israel into retaliation, which could shatter the fragile alliance of Arab states supporting the war.

January 18 and 19 saw further Scud attacks on Israel. It took an intense effort, but the US government managed to dissuade the Israelis from counterattacking. The United States shipped Patriot missile batteries to Israel to provide defense against further attacks, and more coalition aircraft were sent Scud hunting.

The Great Scud Hunt got off to a good start. A launch site was spotted, and F-15Es from the 4th Tactical Fighter Wing were sent against it. The planes pounded the site, apparently catching the Iraqis off guard. It was five days before the Iraqis attempted another mass Scud launch against Israel.

After that, it was not quite as easy. The Scud crews were fast on their feet. They were able to launch a missile and move their launchers to a new site within minutes. If a coalition pilot spotted a Scud as it was fired, he might be able to knock out the launcher. Otherwise, it usually got away.

Because of the extreme importance put on keeping Israel from retaliating, and because

IN SEARCH OF THE ENEMY
An Air Force A-10A Thunderbolt II aircraft flies over a target area during Operation Desert Storm.

everyone knew that these missiles could deliver chemical weapons, the Great Scud Hunt took on a life of its own. A-10 and F-16 patrols looked for Scuds during the day. At night, F-15Es equipped with low-light infrared low-altitude navigation and targeting pods, as well as F-16s and A-6s with forward-looking infrared equipment, took over. Eventually the anti-Scud effort accounted for 22 percent of all strategic air campaign sorties.

Despite some successes, especially when special operations forces on the ground could locate the missiles and their loads, the Great Scud Hunt did not

destroy a great many missiles. In fact, some reported Scud kills may have involved high-quality East German-built decoys. Postwar analyses indicated that while most fixed Scud launchers had been destroyed, the Iraqis still had at least 36 mobile launchers.

The Great Scud Hunt did blunt Iraq's use of this terror weapon and the resulting psychological effects. Sadly, on February 25, one of the last Scuds fired smashed into a building housing an Army Reserve unit in Dhahran, Saudi Arabia. The casualties—28 killed and 98 wounded—were a grim reminder of the damage Scuds could do.

---

reckoned with, but coalition intelligence had a very different picture. As noted earlier, the Iraqis had modern aircraft, but the training of their pilots left much to be desired. The fliers had not done well in the war with Iran. Still, their hardware was good enough to pose a threat.

General Horner planned to gain air superiority quickly at the outset of Desert Storm; however, it was a mild surprise to see just how quickly coalition forces gained air supremacy. Coalition fliers realized during the first night of the operation that missiles and antiaircraft fire were their biggest worry. Iraqi pilots, used to a rigid, Soviet-style air-defense system, were confused once their system's hardware had been reduced to rubble. Forty-one Iraqi aircraft fell to coalition missiles and guns, but hundreds more were destroyed on the ground.

Many US Airmen were surprised that the Iraqi air force crumpled so easily, but Iraqi doctrine considered the air force as a strategic reserve to be used at the most propitious moment. Saddam Hussein was never comfortable with his air force, believing it to be too independent. Therefore, he kept it on a tight rein. Now, at the crucial moment, most of the force hunkered down in shelters to wait out the storm—a big mistake.

Generals Schwarzkopf and Horner declared air supremacy on January 27, but coalition leaders feared the Iraqi air force might be just lying low, ready to spring back in force. To preclude that possibility, General Horner directed his fliers to go after the shelters in which Iraqi planes were being stored.

The shelter-busting campaign began January 22, before the declaration of air supremacy. The

F-111Fs, F-117As, and F-15Es took the lead, with the F-111Fs of the 48th Tactical Fighter Wing proving especially adept. Fitted with the Pave Tack targeting pod, which could acquire, track, and designate targets for an assortment of precision-guided munitions, the Aardvark proved a deadly shelter buster.

The Iraqis offered no aerial resistance. For days, their planes were hidden in "bombproof" shelters or parked next to schools, hospitals, or important archaeological sites. The allies left these planes untouched, but their GBU-10s and GBU-24s drilled through the roofs of the shelters to turn the aircraft into useless hunks of twisted metal. By the end of the war, coalition aircraft had destroyed 375 of Iraq's 594 hardened aircraft shelters; Aardvarks were credited with 245 of those.

It was not clear until after the war just how successful this campaign had been, because damage assessment was very difficult. This would become a bone of contention between the fliers and intelligence personnel.

It was during the shelter-busting campaign that an F-111F hit "the mother of all targets." When 20 Aardvarks attacked Tallil Air Base, in southeast Iraq near Nasiriyah, the first plane hit an ammunition dump. It erupted with such fury that the rest of the planes were unable to attack further. Smoke and debris flew 30,000ft (9,144m) into the air. Some analysts called this the largest nonnuclear man-made explosion ever detected by satellites.

Meanwhile, the men of the Iraqi air force were feeling they did not have much of a future there. On January 21 the Iraqis sent 25 large aircraft to safety in Iran—the very country against which they had fought an exhausting war just a few years before. Five days later, a major portion of the surviving Iraqi air force began fleeing to Iran. By February 10, 120 Iraqi aircraft were in Iran. Even more pilots tried to seek refuge in Iran; however, running low on fuel, flying experience, or both, they crashed before they got there.

F-15s shot down several MiG-23s seeking sanctuary, and this slowed the aerial exodus, but when CENTAF reduced the number of aircraft on barrier patrol, the stampede began anew. Ultimately, 148 Iraqi air force jets made it to Iranian airfields. These jets never returned to Iraqi hands.

Before the Gulf War, the Iraqi air force was a known quantity—the sixth largest in the world—but its quality was unknown. After Desert Storm, it was clear that the Iraqi air force was not very good, and was no longer very large.

Precision-guided munitions at work

The anti-Scud and the shelter-busting campaigns continued as coalition forces went after other targets. One operation stands out as, among other things, a demonstration of the value of precision-guided munitions. On January 25 Iraq deliberately released millions of gallons of Kuwaiti oil from the Al Ahmadi refinery into the Persian Gulf. The resulting slick extended for miles. Ecological disaster loomed if the oil

could not be shut off, so CENTAF worked out a two-pronged plan.

The first prong involved setting fire to the slick. This was done, though not quite as planned, and not by the Air Force—the slick was set ablaze during a gun battle between Navy vessels and an Iraqi patrol boat.

The second prong was to bomb two fuel manifolds that controlled the pressure to the main pipeline. The Air Force was going to turn off the tap by bombing it. A task force of five F-111s got the assignment. Two of the aircraft each carried a 2,000lb (907kg), precision-guided bomb. Seconds after the first was launched, the aircraft controlling it reported that it had lost its data link to the bomb. The weapons system officer in the second guidance aircraft quickly regained control of it, and directed it into the target manifold. A minute later, amid flak from the ground, another F-111 launched the second bomb. The same weapons systems officer directed it to its target.

While some observers think the Kuwaiti underground was involved with turning off the oil manifolds, the air strike was clearly a major factor in stopping the oil flow.

The Battle of Khafji

Another episode in the war in late January was a ground attack launched by the Iraqis on the small Saudi town of Ras Al Khafji. Why Saddam chose this as the place to make a stand still baffles analysts. It had no strategic, or even much tactical, value. One view is that Saddam made this move to force the Americans into fighting on the ground on his timetable. He thought that the Americans were unlikely to accept casualties, and that if he could inflict even a few on them sooner rather than later, they would lose their nerve and withdraw. It did not work out that way, however.

Even before the assault began, intelligence agencies were aware that something was afoot. An E-8 surveillance plane (a prototype still being tested at the time) picked up a convoy moving to the border. Two A-10s and an AC-130 were vectored in on the target. By the time they were through, 58 of the 71 vehicles of the convoy had been destroyed.

The Iraqis made their move against Khafji and Al Wafrah, 35 miles (56km) to the west, on the evening of January 29. They met with initial success at Khafji, capturing the town and pushing the few defenders back. But a few Marines trapped in the town were able to call in air strikes and artillery barrages. Early on January 31 Saudi and Qatari forces, assisted by the Marines, counterattacked and drove the Iraqis back across the border with heavy losses.

"TANK PLINKING"

RECONNAISSANCE PLANES had spotted many possible targets before the war. And once fighting began, crews began to identify their own ways of spotting the enemy. For instance, tanks and other armored vehicles that had dug into the desert sand held their heat until evening, making them visible to the Aardvark's Pave Tack equipment. General Horner soon started ordering F-111Fs out on missions known as "tank plinking." General Schwarzkopf and other Army officers were unhappy with that term, but the activity continued, and so, in Air Force circles at least, did the name.

Soon F-15Es, with low-level infrared navigation and targeting pods, and A-6Es joined this battle. The Strike Eagle, with its sophisticated targeting system, was an excellent tank buster.

The A-10s—officially known as the Thunderbolt II, though pilots preferred to call them "warthogs"—were dazzlingly proficient at going after armored vehicles, albeit with an unusual targeting method. The A-10 is normally a close-air support/attack aircraft. But in Iraq, it was used extensively in night antiarmor operations. The "hog drivers" found early on that the imaging infrared seekers of their Maverick missiles could be used as a sort of forward-looking infrared equipment. Using these seekers, the pilots could search for the telltale heat signature of an armored vehicle. It was like looking through a soda straw, the pilots said.

TANK-BUSTER
The A-10 "Warthog" is an aircraft specifically designed for the close support of ground forces, and in particular for taking on enemy armored vehicles. It is relatively slow-moving, but can stay over the battlefield for long periods and withstand a good deal of punishment from ground fire.

The tank plinking had a profound effect on the Iraqi tank men. They were used to seeing their tanks as a refuge, sheltering them from enemy fire and the cold. But the infrared capabilities of the coalition forces made the tanks easy to spot. The tanks became places of danger rather than of safety. Iraqi officers learned to stay as far away as possible from a tank.

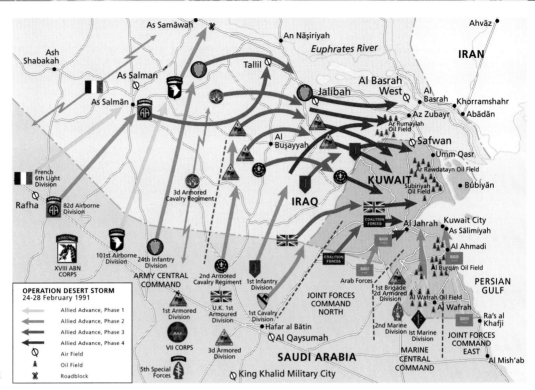

TROOP MOVEMENT
General Norman Schwarzkopf sent coalition forces straight north, then wheeled them to the east, while the 82d Airborne Division and French forces formed a blocking action to prevent Iraqi attack from the west.

The battle had not been just a ground action. Coalition aircraft waited overhead and pounced as the enemy, who lacked air support of its own, retreated.

As episodes like Khafji played out, the coalition assault on the Iraqi army and its logistical lifeline, which began on the first day of the war, continued. B-52s dropped tons of bombs in and behind the front lines in Kuwait. The Hercules, in its guise as the MC-130E Combat Talon, delivered a 15,000lb (6,804kg) bomb called the BLU-82. In contrast with the sophisticated munitions used to deal with the oil slick, the BLU-82 launch was simple: the crew opened the rear cargo door and pushed the bomb, pallet and all, out the door. Its explosion could be heard miles away. Its effectiveness as a minefield-breaching weapon (its original mission) remained undetermined, but it was clearly a potent psychological weapon.

The railroad and highway bridges across the Tigris and Euphrates rivers between Baghdad and Basra were important targets, and they were pursued with precision guidance systems. Bridges have always been important targets, but they can be hard to destroy. Here the precision guidance made a difference; it was responsible for almost all the successful hits on the bridges.

These attacks snarled road traffic, creating congestion that provided further targets. Additionally, since communication lines often ran along or under bridges, successful hits on bridges often took out communication lines at the same time.

By the end of the war, 41 major bridges, including all nine railroad bridges, had been brought down, along with 31 hastily erected pontoon bridges. The combination of ruined bridges and Iraqi truck drivers' unwillingness to drive under constant observation of coalition aircraft left the Iraqi forces unable to launch strong offensive operations.

The Iraqi skies were so full of coalition aircraft, in fact, that CENTAF planners had to take special precautions to avoid friendly fire and midair collisions. Planners came up with a system of kill boxes to "deconflict" aircraft operating in the same area and to simplify the locating of targets.

The coalition's air campaign went well until February 13, when something happened to slow it. Earlier in February, US intelligence had learned that the Al Firdos District bunker in Baghdad had been activated as a center for military communication and perhaps intelligence. This bunker had been thought to be a civilian bomb shelter. But the barbed wire surrounding it, the prominent signs forbidding public access, and the many military vehicles parked nearby all seemed to confirm it as a military, rather than civilian, facility. Accordingly, two F-117s were assigned to bomb it.

The aircraft dropped two GBU-27 penetrating laser-guided bombs on the building, killing hundreds, mostly civilians. The Iraqi propaganda machine spread the story as evidence of American barbarism, and many other countries decried the episode. Fearing a backlash that would undercut support for the war, President Bush and General Powell called an immediate halt to all bombing of Baghdad targets. From February 15 to February 22 central Baghdad was left alone while US forces pursued strategic targets farther afield. Iraqi forces in Kuwait remained under constant air attack.

In the last hours of the war, a pair of F-111Fs dropped a hot new weapon. To penetrate several hardened command bunkers, Air Force scientists and engineers developed, constructed, tested, and deployed a new laser-guided bomb in just 17 days. It was the GBU-28, machined from the barrels of surplus Army eight-inch howitzers. Two of these bombs were tested in Nevada, and

two others were shipped to the theater—their casings still warm to the touch.

Command Leadership Bunker No. 2 at Al-Taji, thought to be a favorite haunt of Saddam, was the target for the new bomb. The first GBU-28 missed, but the second pierced many feet of dirt and concrete and exploded well inside. It was a fitting end to the strategic air campaign.

Meanwhile, the ground campaign continued. The bombing at that point had been directed at the enemy's front-line troops, at the request of US ground commanders, but the Iraqis had been under fire for so long that they did not need much more "softening." Most of their army units crumbled quickly when the land assault began in earnest.

General Schwarzkopf first led his troops straight up the middle, but then shifted the XVIII Airborne Corps and the VII Corps to the west via a C-130 airlift. As his troops fronting Kuwait City rolled over the enemy ahead of them, the two corps to the west began their move into empty desert. In just hours they were threatening the enemy's rear. The French element and the 82d Airborne Division formed a blocking position to counter any enemy attack from the west, but then other units drove north and wheeled east to drive toward Basra. By the end of the second day, elements of the 101st Airborne Division had reached the south bank of the Euphrates and were astride Highway 8, one of the main supply routes into Kuwait.

As antiaircraft artillery and missile sites disappeared under this attack, the Warthogs became especially effective. On February 25 two A-10 pilots from the 76th Tactical Fighter Squadron, Captain Eric Salomonson and 1st Lieutenant John Marks, used Mavericks and the A-10's powerful 30-mm gun to destroy 23 tanks and damage 10 more.

Some of the most vivid photos of the war showed hundreds of vehicles smashed and burning on a road out of Kuwait City—the "highway of death," as it came to be called. On the night of February 25, one of the two prototype E-8 aircraft was directed to watch this stretch of highway closely. Intelligence had received word that the Iraqis were preparing to pull out of Kuwait City. Small yellow crosses, each representing an enemy vehicle, soon began to pop up on the plane's radar screen. The crosses began to overlap into a solid line showing the route the panicky Iraqi soldiers were using.

CENTAF quickly organized an attack force. F-15Es from the 4th Tactical Fighter Wing, with infrared navigation and targeting equipment, led the way. In the dark, they hit fleeing Iraqis near Mutla Ridge, forming a chokepoint that blocked further movement north. Then they turned to the tail end of the column coming out of Kuwait City, bottling up the mass of vehicles between the two points. At daybreak, Air Force and Navy planes flew up and down the line of retreat, ravaging the vehicles caught in the congestion. Photos showing the terrible destruction led many people far from the scene to think the attacks were overkill. But the highway of death was more a graveyard of vehicles. Many Iraqis simply bolted and escaped into the desert—fewer than 300 Iraqi dead were found later in the debris.

The attackers pressed onward. On February 26 the 2d Armored Cavalry ran into a brigade of the

SPECTACLE OF DESTRUCTION
Coalition air attacks on Iraqi ground forces (below, right) in the Gulf War left an awesome spectacle of destruction in their wake. Attempting to flee Kuwait City by night, the Iraqis found the road blocked by mines dropped by F/A-18s. They were then destroyed (left) by air strikes orchestrated by controllers of E-8 J-STARS air-to-ground radar aircraft.

Republican Guard's Tawakalna Division. Fighting in a sandstorm, the Americans crushed the Guards in less than six minutes, destroying them as a fighting force. The next day, Tallil and Jalibah airfields fell to the 24th Infantry Division.

The Coalition forces entered Kuwait City that day, although General Schwarzkopf had to remind the Americans that the liberation of the city was to be the task of the coalition's Arab forces.

By this point the ground war had degenerated into a rush for the border by both sides. Most Iraqis seemed intent only on escaping. At one point, the First Armored Division pulverized its foe in what has been called the biggest tank battle since the 1943 Battle of Kursk, in the Soviet Union. The division destroyed more than 300 Iraqi armored vehicles with only one American Soldier killed.

The Cease-fire
At this point, President Bush decided it was time to stop the bloodletting. The coalition had forced the invaders from Kuwait, and American, British, and French units were well within Iraq. With images of the highway of death on TV screens and front pages around the world, the president did not want to appear to be piling on a defeated foe. In consultation with Powell, Schwarzkopf, and other advisers, Bush decided to end the conflict at 8 a.m. Saudi time on February 28. Iraq agreed to a cease-fire, but heavy fighting broke out sporadically over the next couple of days.

The negotiations that concluded the war took only about an hour, on the morning of March 3, in a special tent set up at the airfield at Safwan. The war officially ended April 11, after Iraq accepted UN Security Council Resolution 687, which detailed cease-fire terms.

With the war over, the victors could begin to study the lessons learned. One of the debates was whether airpower alone had won the war. Had the air campaign been allowed its proper role, some believed, there would have been no need for a ground campaign. Others felt that Iraq was largely a ground-war victory, with some support from the Air Force and other fliers. The truth lies somewhere between these positions.

In the Persian Gulf War, unlike in previous wars, airpower was clearly the dominating factor, from

the first day to the last. US and coalition aircraft roamed Iraq and Kuwait, crippling Iraq's ability to wage war, knocking out its air force, and isolating the battlefield. Iraq was staring defeat in the face from that first night, when F-117s knocked out Saddam's command and control infrastructure.

The Gulf War was also remarkable for the low number of casualties the victors suffered: only 24 coalition aircraft were lost, including seven by the Air Force, during Desert Shield, and only 38 coalition aircraft were lost, including 14 by the Air Force, during Desert Storm. Air Force personnel losses during Desert Shield and Desert Storm came to 34. Eight Air Force fliers were taken prisoner during the conflict; all returned to US hands after the cease-fire.

Another controversy within postwar analysis has to do with which forces destroyed the most targets. The Gulf War Air Power Survey put this into perspective by saying that the "squabbling" about numbers misses the point. What mattered, the survey said, "was the effectiveness of the air campaign in breaking apart the organizational structure and cohesion of enemy military forces and in reaching the *mind* of the Iraqi soldier."

The Gulf War was remarkable for the speed, range, flexibility, lethality, and precision of modern airpower. But the United States had a number of advantages in the Gulf War that it will not necessarily be able to count on in future conflicts. Desert Shield/Desert Storm occurred before some planned cuts to defense spending took effect. It was a war against an enemy with a well-conceived airfield infrastructure in place. The terrain enhanced the effectiveness of the Air Force weapons. The war was fought against an enemy that, however strong it was militarily, was ill served by its leadership. And it must be noted: it was not just the weapons systems that won the war. It was the Airmen, Soldiers, Sailors, and Marines who served.

DOCTRINE AND HISTORY—THE PERSIAN GULF WAR

DISTINCTIVE CAPABILITIES	FUNCTIONS (MISSIONS)	DOCTRINAL EMPHASIS
• Air and Space Superiority • Precision Engagement • Global Attack • Information Superiority • Agile Combat Support • Rapid Global Mobility	• Strategic Attack • Air Refueling • Command and Control (C2) • Surveillance and Reconnaissance	• Strategic Attack (Precision Weapons/ Stealth) • Suppression of Enemy Air Defenses

19

POST-GULF-WAR AIR OPERATIONS

IN SOME RESPECTS, the Gulf War did not end with the liberation of Kuwait. Saddam repeatedly violated terms of the cease-fire and attacked his own people in the Kurdish north and Shiite Muslim south. In response, US and coalition aircraft undertook a series of operations to fence in the Iraqi dictator. The Air Force also played a significant role in attempts to relieve famine in Somalia—attempts that resulted in the infamous Battle of Mogadishu, in which US forces found themselves in a memorable urban firefight with irregular militia forces.

PEACE IS NOT ALWAYS PEACEFUL

AFTER OUSTING SADDAM HUSSEIN FROM KUWAIT,
COALITION FORCES SOUGHT TO CONTAIN HIM WITH
NO-FLY ZONES. IN SOMALIA, INITIAL SUCCESS WAS
FOLLOWED BY WITHDRAWAL AS THE
COUNTRY FELL BACK INTO CHAOS

EVEN AS THE DESERT STORM warriors returned home to victory parades, Saddam Hussein began taking revenge on his own people, many of whom had risen up against the dictator. He believed the coalition that had removed him from Kuwait would have little desire to try to control what he did against Iraqis. Just days after his generals met with the coalition forces at Safwan, he turned his attention to minority ethnic groups, notably the Kurds, and to the Shiite Muslim Arabs in the south. In the savage civil war that ensued, he ordered Iraqi national forces' helicopters to drop napalm and chemical warfare agents on insurgents trying to oust him from power.

Saddam was right in thinking that the United States and its allies would be reluctant to get involved in another war. But things took an even more serious turn when the entire Kurdish population tried to flee through the mountains into Turkey, which refused them entry. The plight of Kurdish refugees in northern Iraq and southeastern Turkey, starving and ravaged by disease, got President George H. W. Bush's attention. On April 5, 1991, he ordered Operation Provide Comfort, meant to ease the Kurds' plight by moving an estimated 350,000 of them to safe areas within Iraq and providing humanitarian aid. These numbers would later mushroom.

Moving the Kurds to safe areas involved securing a large part of northern Iraq—in effect invading a second time. To enforce the ban on Iraqi use of fixed-wing aircraft, a no-fly zone was established on April 6, 1991, which covered the entire country north of the 36th parallel. The United States and its allies were not sure how Saddam would respond to these moves, so the Provide Comfort units were well armed.

Most of the Air Force aircraft assigned to Operation Provide Comfort came under control

ON GUARD
An F-15E from the 90th Fighter Squadron at Elmendorf Air Force Base, Alaska, flies a training mission. F-15 Strike Eagles played a key role in support of Operation Northern Watch.

of the 7440th Composite Wing (Provisional) at Incirlik, Turkey. The wing controlled a range of aircraft needed to support the mission. The Air Force aircraft were soon joined by transports from Britain, France, and Italy.

The operation started on April 7, with Air Force Hercules C-130s departing from Incirlik to drop food, tents, and other supplies. Fully-armed A-10s preceded the transport planes, and F-15Cs and

F-16Cs circled over them, ready to swoop down on any enemy that tried to interfere. E-3B/C AWACS aircraft controlled and observed the operation, and KC-135s performed refueling duty. By the end of April, a forward airstrip had been built and there was less need for airdrops. Provide Comfort settled into a routine that lasted for more than five years, with supplies continuing to be airlifted for distribution into the countryside.

REFUELING ALOFT
An E-3B Sentry Airborne Warning and Control System aircraft refuels along the Iraqi border as part of Operation Northern Watch, enforcing the no-fly zone over northern Iraq.

FALCON PATROL
General Dynamics F-16 Falcons like this one flew in support of Operation Northern Watch, which succeeded Operation Provide Comfort and enforced a no-fly zone over northern Iraq from 1992 to 2003.

TEAMWORK
Two Airmen team up to load a data link pod on an F-15E Strike Eagle during Operation Northern Watch.

Operation Southern Watch

Paralleling the troubles in northern Iraq was a Shiite rebellion in the south. Air Force planes based in Saudi Arabia monitored developments there. For a year, Iraqi fighters and bombers held their fire. But eventually, provoked by Iranian aircraft that had begun crossing into Iraq, they took to the air again. A southern no-fly zone was created to keep Iraqis from attacking Shiite rebels near Basra. This zone was much harder to enforce than the northern one, because Iraqis were flying 30 sorties a day. Operation Southern Watch began August 27, 1992.

In December 1992, after a period of relative quiet, the Iraqis showed renewed aggression and went after some F-15Es. This encounter was inconclusive but a second the next day ended badly for the Iraqis. A pair of MiG-25s crossed the 32nd parallel and one fired an air-to-air missile, missing an F-16. The commander of the F-16 squadron, Lieutenant Colonel Gary North, fired an AIM-120A air-to-air missile and blasted one of the MiGs out of the sky. This was the first kill for the F-16 in Air Force service, as well as for the AIM-120A.

The situation simmered along over the next several weeks. The Iraqis made more incursions into the no-fly zones, and in a threatening gesture against the planes enforcing them, they moved missile batteries into the zones. The United States warned Saddam that these actions could have serious consequences, but he chose to strike a more defiant pose. To make sure he understood the gravity of the situation, on January 13, 1993, more than 100 American, British, and

French aircraft struck Iraqi targets between Kut and Basra. Saddam's forces attempted to strike back, but not very effectively.

Southern Watch aircraft continued to strike missiles sites and the Zaafaraniyah nuclear fabrication facility southwest of Baghdad. This continued until January 20, 1993, Inauguration Day in Washington. Perhaps realizing that he was not winning his skirmishes with the United States and its allies, Saddam Hussein used Bill Clinton's taking office as the 42nd president of the United States as the occasion for a "gesture of peace," and declared a cease-fire.

But the provocations did not end at that point. In April 1993, when former President Bush visited Kuwait, the US intelligence services reported discovering Iraqi complicity in a plot to assassinate him. To remind Iraq that such behavior would not be tolerated, President Clinton ordered a Tomahawk strike on the headquarters of the Iraqi secret police. Twenty-three missiles were launched, causing severe damage to the building.

From then on, into the summer of the following year, peace prevailed in the Persian Gulf, but it was a superficial one at best. Iraq continued to frustrate United Nations attempts to inspect its military facilities—including those where chemical and

biological warfare agents were produced—and its nuclear production sites. Then in late summer, Saddam Hussein began to threaten Kuwait again. It looked as if the Gulf War were about to repeat itself; however, the United States reacted quickly—even more quickly, in fact, than in 1990, because this time, there was already a strong American forward presence in Saudi Arabia. In November, more than 100 American, British, and Kuwaiti aircraft took part in a large-scale exercise over Kuwait and the southern no-fly zone. It included B-1s and B-52s dropping 500lb (227kg) bombs on a Kuwaiti bombing range only a few miles south of the Iraqi border. The Iraqis presumably were paying attention.

LAUNCHING FORTH
An F-16 Fighting Falcon launches for a combat air patrol mission during Operation Southern Watch.

After this show of force, Iraq pulled its Republican Guard back from the border. The Iraq-Kuwait frontier remained a troubled location, however, as Iraq continued to rebuild its shattered military and threaten Kuwait. For their part, US forces, especially Air Force elements, remained in Saudi Arabia and Kuwait to ensure that Saddam Hussein did not threaten other countries in the region.

TRACKING THE MISSION
An officer tracks an Operation Southern Watch mission inside the Combined Air Operations Center (CAOC) at a forward-deployed base. Spanning nearly 30,000sq ft (2,787sq m), the CAOC was the nerve center for all US Central Command air operations. With crews operating around the clock, CAOC officials planned, controlled, and tracked all coalition missions throughout the region.

NOSE JOB
Two Airmen lower the nose radome of a KC-10 refueler after changing the weather radar dish, during Operation Southern Watch.

To feed Somalia

Although Iraq demanded US attention well into the 1990s, the Air Force was also engaged in operations in other parts of the world through this period. One of them took place in the African nation of Somalia. This country had been wracked by famine and disease, governmental collapse, and civil war. International aid agencies had tried to help but only got caught up in the turmoil of the Somali warlords. Thousands of civilians perished.

Finally UN Secretary-General Boutros Boutros-Ghali decided that higher-order help was needed. He asked President George H. W. Bush for help, who in turn authorized "Operation Provide Relief" on August 14, 1992. Somalia fell within the geographic area of Central Command, and this operation was the first undertaken by the newly reorganized Air Mobility Command.

Personnel arrived at Moi International Airport in Mombasa, Kenya, on August 17 to establish a base from which to fly supplies to refugee camps in Kenya and certain airheads in Somalia itself. Eight C-130s and four C-141s soon followed.

The first humanitarian missions were flown on August 21 to a refugee camp in Kenya, near the border with Somalia. The 314th Airlift Wing once again proved itself a workhorse. Eventually, C-130s took over the operations, including a number of aircraft from the British Royal Air Force, along with Luftwaffe (German Air Force) C-160 Transalls.

The quality of the landing strips in Somalia posed serious problems. The first missions into Somalia touched down on a 5,700ft (1,737m) rutted dirt airstrip at Belet Uen near a relief camp. The C-130s also used a former Somali air force strip at Baidoa, which was paved but derelict—only half its 10,000ft (3,048m) was usable.

Once on the ground, the crews had to deal with roving gangs of bandits, who tore holes in the sides of aircraft as they were sitting on the ground and stole the aid supplies they contained. Eventually the crews realized they should fly only during the day and keep their engines running as they unloaded. Despite all this, in the final months of 1992, the C-130s flew nearly 1,600 missions and carried more than 13,000 tons (11,790 tonnes) of relief supplies into Somalia.

BELEAGUERED PEACEKEEPERS
UN soldiers engage in combat during a peacekeeping mission in June 1993 in Mogadishu, Somalia. During the previous year famine killed some 350,000 Somalis.

The relief efforts were hampered by violence, particularly in the port city of Mogadishu, Somalia's capital. The United Nations finally brought in a contingent of Pakistani peacekeepers to protect the supplies. Impressive Lift, as it was called, flew in almost 1,000 personnel and more than 1,100 tons (997 tonnes) of equipment from Pakistan to Mogadishu, but the force was not enough to protect supply routes to more remote areas from the warlords and their clans. When a relief ship being unloaded in Mogadishu harbor came under shellfire, the United Nations suspended relief operations until the warlords could be brought under some kind of control.

Operation Restore Hope

Hundreds of Somalis were dying daily in the violence, and once again, Boutros Boutros-Ghali appealed to the United States for help. On November 26 President Bush ordered the commitment of up to 40,000 troops to support the Somalia relief efforts—an offer which the United Nations formally welcomed in a Security Council resolution.

The force was not a UN task force, but included units from France, Italy, Belgium, Canada, Australia, and Pakistan, as well as smaller contingents from more than 20 other countries.

Lieutenant General Robert Johnston, USMC, was named commander of Joint Task Force Somalia, later known as the United Task Force. It included elements from the First Marine Expeditionary Force, the 10th Mountain Division, and Air Force and Navy units. Their operation, which began as the Provide Relief humanitarian airlift missions continued, was soon dubbed Restore Hope.

Restore Hope began on December 9 with the arrival of the first Marines, and soon became an impressive example of the Global Reach—Global Power concept. For Air Mobility Command, Restore Hope was a complex operation, involving

not just airlifters but tankers as well. This integration of airlift and tanker assets into an "air bridge," like that used during the Gulf War, saved wear and tear on the airlifters by letting them minimize the numbers of landings and takeoffs.

The aircraft involved used several fields across the region as staging bases—in Egypt, Djibouti, Saudi Arabia, and Ethiopia, as well as in Baledogle and Kismayu in Somalia. The operation even made use of a field in Aden, Yemen. Yemen had supported Iraq during the Gulf War, and so getting Yemeni permission to use the airfield, albeit sparingly, was seen as a considerable diplomatic breakthrough.

The Mogadishu airport was the center of operations throughout Restore Hope. On its busiest day, January 24, 1993, it saw 450 aircraft movements. Its peak day for cargo was December 22, when 923 tons (900 tonnes) of cargo were delivered. Its peak day for passenger delivery was December 31, when 1,470 troops arrived.

Once the US Marines landed, they scoped out the situation and then pushed inland to open roads and secure the airfields at Baidoa and Baledogle. Farther south, on December 20, the Marines, with the help of Belgian paratroopers, secured Kismayu, Somalia's second-largest city and port. Kismayu had the longest runway in the country measuring 11,000ft (3,350m).

At this point, the first phase of the operation was concluded. By December 31, the second phase was completed. This involved deployment of the United Task Force into Baidoa and the expansion of security operations throughout central Somalia. The third phase of Restore Hope—the extension of security operations into southern Somalia—was also accomplished quickly. By mid-January, General Johnston was able to turn the operation over to the UN peacekeepers. The Air Mobility Command switched from deployment to redeployment as the C-5s and C-141s returned US

troops home. Operation Restore Hope was officially declared complete on May 4, 1993.

After this, only a small US presence—4,000 personnel—remained in Somalia to support the second United Nations operation. The primary forces on the ground there were international—from Pakistan, Belgium, Australia, France, Canada, Italy, Botswana, and Morocco. Restore Hope had been a successful operation, with well-defined goals. United Nations officials had similar aspirations for this next phase of international activity in Somalia. They hoped to end tribal warfare and stop the famine, but their goals were murky, and sadly, they did not achieve them.

The Battle of Mogadishu

Once most of the US troops had departed, the Somali clan chiefs, led by Mohammed Farah Aideed in Mogadishu, fell back into their old ways of continual tribal warfare. The small contingents of UN troops were unwilling or unable to halt the violence. Then on June 5, 1993, some of Aideed's men ambushed Pakistani troops, killing 24 of them. What had begun the year before as a humanitarian mission had now degenerated into a drawn-out, costly, and deadly military action.

American forces, mostly special operations units, returned a few days later with hopes of quelling the violence, but those were soon shattered. Three AD-130Hs of the 16th Special Operations Squadron went after Aideed and his forces with their 105-mm howitzers. They pummeled his headquarters and several weapons caches over a period of days. But this was not enough to get Aideed to stop his assault on the UN relief convoys and peacekeepers.

Then on October 3, a major firefight broke out in downtown Mogadishu between Aideed's followers and Task Force Ranger, a US joint-service team. The goal of the task force was to capture a number of the leaders of Aideed's militia. Air Force combat controllers and pararescuemen from the 24th Special Tactics Squadron, based at Pope Air Force Base in North Carolina, took part in the operation, along with Army Rangers and Delta Force personnel. The assault was to take place near Aideed's headquarters, in a built-up area with structures several stories high surrounded by a warren of narrow streets and alleys. Army UH-60 Black Hawk helicopters transported the task force.

As the choppers hovered while discharging their troops down ropes, they came under intense fire. One of the Black Hawks was shot down. When combat controller Staff Sergeant Jeffrey W. Bray got to the crash site, he found two Air Force pararescuemen, Master Sergeant Scott C. Fales and Technical Sergeant Timothy A. Wilkinson, already on the scene. They had roped down from their grenade-damaged helicopter and had begun treating the wounded.

BLACK HAWK SURVIVOR
Wounded Army helicopter pilot Michael Durant is escorted to a waiting air ambulance after his release from captivity in Mogadishu.

The three men were in the thick of the action over the next 18 hours, and Fales and Wilkinson were both wounded. Several times Wilkinson darted through streams of gunfire to help the wounded. Under grenade attack, Fales shielded patients with his own body.

Meanwhile, a second Black Hawk succumbed to point-blank fire from rocket-propelled grenades. All the crew perished in the crash or the firefight that followed it, except the pilot, Chief Warrant Officer Michael Durant, who was captured (he was released a few weeks later). Two Army sharpshooters, Master Sergeant Gary Gordon and Sergeant First Class Randy Shugart, roped down to defend the survivors, but died in the firefight. For their actions, they were awarded the Medal of Honor.

At 7 a.m. the next morning, a US-Malaysian relief force fought its way to the embattled troops. The fighting finally sputtered to an end, but it had been a costly operation—18 Americans killed and 84 wounded, and more than 1,000 Somalis dead.

Bray and Fales received Silver Stars for their part in the battle, and Wilkinson was awarded the Air Force Cross, becoming the first Air Force enlistee to receive that medal since the *Mayaguez* incident in 1975. Other members of the 24th squadron were awarded medals for their actions in the fight as well.

However brave individual Airmen, Soldiers, and Sailors were on the ground in Somalia, the battle caused the Clinton administration to rethink the US role there. International efforts in Somalia had become entangled in conflicting objectives, vague directives, and growing animosity of Somalis toward the UN forces, including the Americans. It was not long before President Clinton decided to remove US forces and Secretary of Defense Les Aspin resigned. US personnel had operated under American, not UN command, but still had to operate within the limits of UN directives. They were often asked to serve as peacekeepers—a role for which they had not been trained.

The last US troops left Somalia by March 25, 1994, and at that point fewer than 1,000 Americans, mostly civilian aid workers and diplomats, remained in that troubled country. With US troops gone, clan warfare escalated again. A year later the United Nations ordered the remaining peacekeepers withdrawn. Tragically, the civil war has continued until the present day.

DOCTRINE AND HISTORY—PROVIDE COMFORT/NORTHERN WATCH/SOUTHERN WATCH/RESTORE HOPE

DISTINCTIVE CAPABILITIES	FUNCTIONS (MISSIONS)	DOCTRINAL EMPHASIS
• Rapid Global Mobility (Provide Comfort/ Northern Watch) • Air Superiority • Precision Engagement (Southern Watch)	• Airlift • Counterair • Strategic Attack • Surveillance and Reconnaissance	• Protect Northern Iraqi No-Fly Zone • Humanitarian Airdrops for Refugees • Theater Attack of Military Targets

20

CONFLICT IN THE FORMER REPUBLIC OF YUGOSLAVIA

THE END OF SOVIET DOMINATION in Eastern Europe had profound consequences in the Balkans, where the aftereffects of World War I were still playing out in ethnic conflict. As one by one, the constituent republics that made up Yugoslavia withdrew from the federation, a series of wars broke out between local Serbs and other ethnic groups—each conflict orchestrated from Belgrade by Serbian strongman Slobodan Milosevic. In an unprecedented fashion, airpower proved the most effective tool in restoring the peace.

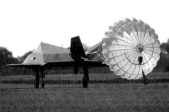

SAVING SARAJEVO

AIRPOWER BECAME THE KEY TO MAKING PEACE IN THE TROUBLED BALKANS

MANY ETHNIC GROUPS, including Serbs, Croats, Bosnians, and Albanians, inhabit the Balkans region in southeastern Europe. Three major religions are represented among them: Roman Catholicism, Eastern Orthodoxy, and Islam. Their animosity toward one another goes back centuries and grows from these religious and ethnic differences, which have resulted in countless and savage civil wars.

The Federal Republic of Yugoslavia was cobbled together by the victorious Allies following World War I. In World War II, it was the scene of bloody fighting among ethnic groups and between nationalist partisans and the Nazi occupiers. The country saw a period of calm when it fell under Communist rule after World War II, particularly during the rule of Marshal Josip Broz Tito from the 1940s until his death in 1980. But in 1991, as the Warsaw Pact dissolved—a pact of which Yugoslavia was not a member—the centrifugal forces tearing at Yugoslav unity strengthened. The de facto ruler, Serb Slobodan Milosevic, began relying on Serb nationalism to replace communism as a means of staying in power.

As Soviet troops withdrew from Eastern Europe in 1991 and Milosevic alienated the country's non-Serb nationalities, Yugoslavia's simmering hatreds began to resurface as one republic after another declared independence. On June 25, 1991, Slovenia and Croatia were the first republics to withdraw from federal Yugoslavia. The primarily Serb Yugoslav government attempted to reassert control over the breakaway republics, often using ethnic Serbs residing there, and regained some territory from Croatia. The fighting spread—Macedonia seceded in September 1991, followed by Bosnia-Herzegovina in March 1992. The Serbs soon shifted their focus from Croatia to Bosnia, where they used local Serb forces to recapture two-thirds of Bosnia by mid-July.

They also laid siege to Bosnia's capital, Sarajevo, cutting off the city's food and other necessary supplies. All sides in the affected areas began to turn on one another as Bosnian Muslims fought Serbs, Serbs fought Croats, Croats fought Bosnian Muslims, and all used the war to settle age-old grievances.

The West was watching, and over the next seven years it interceded through five different missions—two humanitarian and three military. They were Operation Provide Promise (1992–96, humanitarian), Operation Deny Flight (1993–95, military), Operation Deliberate Force (1995, military), Operation Allied Force (1999, military), and Operation Shining Hope (1999, humanitarian). The US Air Force played a major role in each.

Operation Provide Promise

The United Nations (UN) initially sent 23,000 peacekeeping troops into the region in 1992, but when it had difficulty handling the crisis, NATO joined the operation. Unlike the Gulf War, where the United States dominated the command and control apparatus, the UN and NATO ran two parallel, often competing, chains of command in the Balkans. In late June 1992 UN troops reopened the Sarajevo airport, which three months of fighting had closed. A UN relief airlift named "Operation Provide Promise" started on July 3, 1992. Until January 4, 1996, this airlift sustained Sarajevo's citizens. Lasting three times as long as the Berlin airlift, Provide Promise became the longest humanitarian airlift in history. US Air Force C-130s did much of the work, although

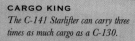

CARGO KING
The C-141 Starlifter can carry three times as much cargo as a C-130.

BEARING THE BURDEN
Once again, the reliable C-130 did much of the heavy lifting during Operation Provide Promise.

20 other countries also took part. The aircraft flew 12,895 sorties and delivered 180,000 tons (163,273 tonnes)—versus 2.3 million tons (2.1 million tonnes) for the Berlin airlift—of food, medicine, and other supplies to Sarajevo and elsewhere in Bosnia.

Leading the effort was the US Air Forces in Europe's 435th Airlift Wing, whose main arm was the 37th Airlift Squadron. The 38th Airlift Squadron—composed of active duty, reserve, and National Guard C-130 units—began assisting the 37th on January 4, 1994. Once the UN and NATO had secured ground routes around Sarajevo in February 1994, the need for C-130s was less urgent, and the Air Force ended the 38th Airlift Squadron's involvement in June 1994. However, even as the C-130s' role was slowing down, the Air Force enlisted five C-141s to help with Provide Promise because they could carry three times the cargo that a C-130 could. This effort lasted from May 8 to July 21, 1994.

When fighting again erupted around Sarajevo during the summer and damaged several aircraft, the UN and NATO suspended the operation until August 16. Hostile fire on NATO aircraft was not anything new. A missile brought down an Italian transport in September 1992, and small-arms fire and shrapnel from artillery fire damaged several cargo aircraft. C-130 crews routinely wore body armor and survival vests and carried side arms. Airmen laid sheets of Kevlar armor on cockpit floors and other vital sections of C-130s and C-141s. Most aircraft had missile countermeasure systems as well, and all crews kept a keen lookout for missile launches. Although it was a humanitarian mission, Operation Provide Promise was definitely a dangerous one.

THE BALKANS REGION
This map shows the independent former-Yugoslav republics—Bosnia-Herzegovina, Croatia, Macedonia, Montenegro, Serbia, and Slovenia—and a few neighboring countries. Serbia and Montenegro abandoned the name Yugoslavia in 2003 and formally dissolved their union in 2006.

DIRECT HITS
During NATO's first combat engagement in 45 years, Captain Robert Wright, flying his F-16C, shot down three Bosnian Serb Super Galeb light-attack aircraft on February 28, 1994. He got two of them with AIM-9 Sidewinder missiles, pictured here.

INTO ACTION
F-15s like this one flew combat air patrols during Operation Deny Flight. Air operations over Bosnia began on April 12, 1993.

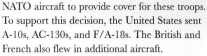

Operation Deny Flight

The next phase of US involvement in the Balkans began in 1993, when the Serbs extended their offensives into eastern and southwestern Bosnia. They ignored UN resolutions that established safe areas (Resolutions 819 and 824) and no-fly zones (Resolution 781) in the republic. In particular, they disregarded Resolution 816, which authorized the use of force against aircraft violating the ban on military flights. When Serbian helicopters continued to violate Bosnian air space, the UN asked NATO to enforce the no-fly zone in an operation subsequently named "Deny Flight."

Responsibility for Deny Flight rested with Allied Forces Southern Europe. It, in turn, handed over control of the operation to Allied Air Forces Southern Europe, initially under USAF Lieutenant General Joseph W. Ashy and then Lieutenant General Michael E. Ryan. Allied Air Forces Southern Europe delegated day-to-day control to the Fifth Allied Tactical Air Force under Italian Lieutenant General Antonio Rossetti. On April 9, 1993, General Rossetti established a combined air operations center in Italy whose director was responsible for planning and directing air operations over Bosnia. The first director was USAF Major General James E. Chambers and the second was USAF Major General Hal M. Hornburg.

Using F-15Cs, F-16Cs, F-14As, F/A-18Cs, and support aircraft, the United States provided the bulk of the airpower for Deny Flight. These aircraft came primarily from Air Force units in Europe and from Navy carriers in the Mediterranean and Adriatic, with additional units deploying from the United States. The British, French, Dutch, and Turkish also supplied air forces, and Italy lent several bases to the operation.

Deny Flight began on April 12, 1993, with NATO fighters flying combat air patrols, British and US tankers refueling them in flight, and reconnaissance aircraft keeping track of hostile activity. Serbian aircraft, mostly helicopters, violated the no-fly ban hundreds of times during Deny Flight, and Serbian aircraft shadowed NATO fighters, but these missions generally concluded peacefully. Clashes were more frequent at ground level, however, where UN troops engaged in several battles. On June 10, 1993, the UN passed Resolution 836, which authorized

NATO aircraft to provide cover for these troops. To support this decision, the United States sent A-10s, AC-130s, and F/A-18s. The British and French also flew in additional aircraft.

In February 1994 the uneasy calm ended. Serbs shelled a marketplace in Sarajevo, killing 68 civilians and wounding more than 200. NATO ordered the Bosnian Serbs to withdraw 12 miles (19.3km) from Sarajevo, and the UN negotiated a cease-fire for the city. Two NATO firsts took place shortly thereafter. On February 28 a group of Bosnian Serb Super Galeb light-attack aircraft struck Muslim facilities about 50 miles (80.5km) from Sarajevo. A pair of the 526th Fighter Squadron's F-16Cs intercepted four of the intruders, initiating NATO's first combat action in 45 years. The raiders ignored warnings to leave the area, so flight leader Captain Robert L. Wright picked off three of the quartet in quick succession. He got two with AIM-9s and the third with an AIM-120. Another pair of F-16s arrived in time to bag a fourth Galeb. The surviving aircraft scuttled from the area.

On March 18, 1994, the Muslims and Bosnian Croats agreed to a cease-fire, but the Bosnian Serbs did not. Among their offensives was an April 10 tank attack into one of the supposed Muslim safe areas in Gorazde, Bosnia. A pair of the 512th Fighter Squadron's F-16Cs responded, but because of bad weather they decided to aim for a Serb artillery command post rather than the tank. This was the second historic

PROVIDING COVER

Among other aircraft, the US military sent the Navy's F/A-18 to beef up cover for UN ground forces in Bosnia during Deny Flight. The Hornet has been given the unusual dual designation F/A as it can be used as both a fighter and an attack aircraft. Though slower than an F-14, its small size makes it extremely maneuverable. Formations of attack F/A-18s can defend themselves en route to their target and chase enemy fighters after they have dropped their bomb loads. This photo shows the NASA safety support version.

moment for NATO—the first time that its aircraft struck a ground target.

Over the next few days, more fighting took place between NATO air forces and Serb ground forces around Gorazde. A portable missile shot down a British Sea Harrier, but the pilot ejected safely and made his way back to friendly lines as US aircraft provided him with cover. The upshot of these clashes was that the Serbs managed to wrest control of the region around Gorazde.

Throughout the summer of 1994, the many opposing sides in the Bosnian conflict fought, but NATO generally kept out of the mix. The United Nations continued trying to broker a peace deal, but by November, things were getting so out of hand on the ground that the UN asked NATO for air strikes. In its first major strike since the Bosnian war began in 1992—although its seventh air engagement—NATO sent 40 aircraft to strike a Serb airfield in Croatia on November 21, 1994. The strike force included US and Dutch F-16s, F-15Es, Marine F/A-18s, and an EF-111A, British and French Jaguars, and French Mirage 2000s. An EC-130E coordinated the strike, AWACS kept watch, and several helicopters stood by for search and rescue.

LAUNCHED AT SEA

Navy carriers roaming the Mediterranean and Adriatic flew their F-14s (pictured) and F/A-18s during Operation Deny Flight.

Before the main force attacked, several F-15Es and F/A-18s had destroyed missile sites and a radar van. The other attackers aimed laser-guided bombs, cluster bombs, and iron bombs at the runway and airport support facilities. At the UN's request, they did not hit any enemy aircraft, but the damaged airstrip prevented their takeoff. The Serbs repaired the airfield by mid-December, but did not fly for some time.

Another state of limbo followed in which smaller skirmishes took place. Serb forces fired

missiles at NATO aircraft and took UN peacekeepers hostage. NATO forces at first struck back at missile sites, but when the UN ordered them not to return fire, NATO grounded its planes, because flying without the authorization to take out enemy sites exposed friendly aircraft to too much danger. Former President Jimmy Carter helped negotiate a cease-fire in mid-December 1994, but this pact fell apart on May 1, 1995, when the Croats attempted to seize territory back from the Serbs. As more fighting ensued, the Serbs took more hostages to rebuff UN and NATO actions. Still, the United Nations continued to tie NATO's hands by permitting the use of airpower, including reconnaissance and combat air patrols, only in limited instances.

On June 2, 1995, a Bosnian Serb SA-6 missile downed an Air Force F-16 from the 31st Fighter Wing's 555th Fighter Squadron, forcing Captain Scott F. O'Grady to eject from his aircraft. Bosnian Serb forces wanted nothing more than to grab an American flier, and launched an intensive search. At times, they were within a few feet of O'Grady's hiding place. The United States conducted its own intensive search, finally locating the downed flier. A rescue force of Marine Corps personnel choppered in to bring him to safety while Air Force A-10s provided cover. Between them, they executed a daring rescue on June 8, evading several antiaircraft missiles in the process.

Things only grew worse in Bosnia that summer. The UN lost all control in Sarajevo by mid-June. Srebrenica, along Bosnia's eastern border, fell in mid-July, with Serb forces rounding up, marching off, and then massacring thousands of Bosnian Muslim men and boys. The UN was losing every safe area in the war-torn country and could not even protect its troops, yet the world organization stubbornly refused to lift its restrictions on NATO airpower.

By late July US, British, and French military leaders grew frustrated and began to take matters into their own hands. They decided to rebuff any Serbian attack on the last remaining safe area, Gorazde, with immediate NATO air strikes. They extended this guarantee to Sarajevo, Bihac, and Tuzla on August 1. These were the makings of a new operation—Operation Deliberate Force. Weary of UN policies hobbling their air units, and tired of the enemy killing, wounding, or kidnapping their peacekeepers, a British-French Rapid Reaction Force went to Sarajevo to fend off Serb attacks. Under pressure from the NATO ministers, UN Secretary General Boutros Boutros-Ghali gave the UN commander, French Lieutenant General Bernard Janvier, permission to authorize NATO air strikes. NATO had been working on a plan to rout the Serbs since December; in August leaders from Allied Forces Southern Europe and Allied Air Forces Southern Europe briefed the UN secretary general and others on Operation Deliberate Force to protect UN safe areas.

Lessons learned: Deny Flight

Some 100,000 sorties by 200 aircraft during Deny Flight could not stop the Serbians or Bosnian Serbs; in fact, the operation resulted in Operation Deliberate Force. Deny Flight provided a number of lessons. The first was the difficulty of coordinating the efforts of two major organizations: the United Nations and NATO, international bodies with sometimes opposing objectives. The UN is primarily a diplomatic organization; NATO is a military one. Each organization ultimately wants peace, but each has a different way of reaching it. The second lesson came with the loss of Captain O'Grady's F-16. Thereafter, NATO air forces supported more of its missions with air-defense-suppression aircraft; that is, aircraft capable of taking out missile sites. The US Air Force also learned that its aircraft must fly in less-predictable patterns and recognized the need to increase communication between its reconnaissance and combat crews.

DASSAULT MIRAGE 2000C

Dassault's third-generation of tailless delta interceptor uses fly-by-wire controls to give far better turning ability than previously available with this wing form. The aircraft entered French air force service in 1988.

The Air Force learned three other lessons. One lesson was that the size of air forces can fluctuate dramatically during an operation; therefore, bases must be capable of handling large numbers of aircraft. One of the air bases in Italy was far over capacity, for example. Deny Flight often suffered from too few personnel and too few high-level officers. Another problem was a lack of understanding between countries. For example, Italy and France would not let their security police carry guns, which was contrary to US military policy. And finally, any modern-day campaign needs plenty of modern-day equipment. At first, Deny Flight forces did not possess enough electronic and communications gear, but this was eventually rectified. These lessons carried over into the more successful Operation Deliberate Force.

Deliberate Force

The act that finally set Deliberate Force in motion was the renewed shelling of Sarajevo on August 28, 1995. One enemy mortar round killed 38 civilians and wounded 85 others. US Admiral Leighton W. Smith, commander of Allied Forces Southern Europe, and Janvier's second in command, British Lieutenant General Rupert Smith, approved launching the air campaign.

Deliberate Force involved two main air campaigns, the first in August 1995, and the second in September of that year. The August air campaign went by the name Dead Eye and had two target lists. Its priority list named 26 air-defense targets and 68 other sites; its second target list included some 450 Bosnian Serb positions, ranging from an airfield to command posts. As usual, the UN hesitated to go after the enemy full throttle and approved only one-third of the targets. Janvier, back from leave, also showed reserve. This caution reminded some of the Americans involved of the ineffectual graduated-response policy in Vietnam. Still, Janvier and Smith selected targets on August 29 and ordered an attack for 2 a.m. on August 30. NATO aircraft began taking off from their bases in Italy or from carriers in the Adriatic Sea as soon as their orders came in.

Forty-three aircraft heading for targets in eastern Bosnia made up the first wave of attackers, designated Dead Eye Southeast.

347

CONFLICT IN THE FORMER REPUBLIC OF YUGOSLAVIA

This initial force worked over 16 air-defense sites, but before this strike force exited the target area, a second force, named Strike Package Alpha, roared in with 18 aircraft to pound Serb positions around Sarajevo, including a command-and-control bunker 12 miles (19.3km) southeast of the capital. An F-15E destroyed the underground facility with a 2,000lb (907kg) laser-guided bomb. A third wave, called Strike Package Bravo, also made up of 18 aircraft, flew in next to spend 20 minutes bombing four more targets, such as ammunition dumps and missile sites around Sarajevo. Two reconnaissance planes next flew in to assess the damage. Three more strike packages—Charlie, Delta, and Echo—completed the day's activities. In addition to the strike packages, A-10s and other aircraft provided close air support. On several occasions, forward air controllers called in the A-10s to attack artillery and mortar positions and bunkers. Meanwhile, air-defense-suppression aircraft prowled the skies and kept Serb missile sites quiet, although one portable missile downed a French Mirage 2000N. The crew ejected, but the Serbs captured them and held them until the end of the year.

Initially, this first round of Deliberate Force seemed to do the job. Serbian President Slobodan Milosevic contacted General Janvier the evening of August 30 and asked him to stop the bombing. At Milosevic's request, Janvier offered to meet with Bosnian Serb commander

Ratko Mladic to discuss conditions for halting the air strikes. Janvier also proposed a cease-fire, which did not go down well with NATO or UN officials, who felt Janvier had overstepped his authority. Nonetheless, they stopped the bombing on September 1, although they continued reconnaissance, enemy air-defense suppression, and other similar missions. When it turned out that the Serbs were only feigning interest in cease-fire, Deliberate Force was on again.

RESCUED
President Bill Clinton applauds as US Air Force Captain Scott O'Grady raises his fists during ceremonies at the Pentagon to welcome O'Grady home. The F-16 fighter pilot was shot down in June 1995 over Bosnia. He avoided capture by Bosnian Serbs for six days before a US Marine rescue helicopter plucked him out of hostile territory.

THE DELIVERY SYSTEM
An F-15E Strike Eagle, similar to these, dropped a laser-guided GBU-10 bomb during Operation Deliberate Force. The blast destroyed an underground bunker.

AIRBORNE COMMAND
Deliberate Force's September air campaign involved a host of aircraft, including the command post EC-130E.

Deliberate Force: Act II

The first attacks of the second air campaign began shortly after 1 a.m. on September 5. For the next four hours, 70 aircraft, accompanied by 50 air-defense-suppression aircraft, battered Serb storage and repair depots, ammunition dumps, and command-and-control facilities. After pausing briefly for a thunderstorm, 20 fighter-bombers, joined by air-defense suppression aircraft, plastered more storage sites. Most aircraft—F-15Es, F-16s, F/A-18Ds, Mirage 2000s, and GR-7 Harriers—dropped laser-guided bombs, such as the 500lb (227kg) GBU-12 and the 2,000lb (907kg) GBU-10. NATO AWACS and EC-130E airborne command post aircraft patrolled the skies. NATO aircraft maintained the pressure until September 14.

Among the biggest threats to NATO airpower were Serb flak barrages, similar to the box barrages that the Germans had used during World War II.

ON THE OFFENSIVE
F-16s dropped laser-guided bombs during the September offensive of Operation Deliberate Force.

The Serbs densely surrounded their antiaircraft artillery guns with missiles so NATO aircraft could not get to the target at the center of the "box" without great risk.

Meanwhile, the civil war on the ground was wearing down Serb forces. A Croat-Bosnian Muslim offensive in western Bosnia forced the Serbs to reduce their hold on Bosnian territory from three-quarters to less than one-half. In Geneva, Switzerland, Bosnian Muslim, Croat, and Serb foreign ministers met for the first time in two years to discuss a cease-fire. NATO halted bombing on September 14. Three days later, NATO and the UN agreed that no more air strikes were necessary. Operation Deliberate Force was over.

A cease-fire was not actually agreed upon until October 12, 1995. In the meantime, NATO aircraft had to intervene on a number of occasions in October to maintain what peace there was on the ground. Meanwhile, the presidents of Bosnia, Croatia, and Serbia met at Wright-Patterson Air Force Base, Dayton, Ohio, to hammer out their agreement. They initialed what became known the "Dayton Accord" on November 21 and formally signed it in Paris on December 14.

The Deliberate Force air campaign had involved more than 200 aircraft, which flew 3,500 sorties. About 750 of those flights were strike sorties. These aircraft delivered more than 600 precision weapons against 55 targets.

BUNKER BLASTER
The GBU-10 Paveway II bomb is more than 14ft (4.3m) long, has a nearly 5ft (1.5m) wingspan, and weighs 2,000lb (907kg).

INITIATION INTO COMBAT
The B-2 went into combat for the first time over Kosovo in 1999.

The US Air Force flew about 60 percent of the sorties, and the British and French split another 30 percent nearly equally. Airpower had played a vital role in Bosnia. With the cease-fire, the UN turned over control of operations in Bosnia and Croatia to NATO, which officially assumed military command on December 20. The United States, Britain, and France maintained sectors during what was called Joint Endeavor, with the US sector in northeast Bosnia. Under the terms of the agreement, NATO aircraft could use force to respond to even perceived threats. Airmen welcomed this authorization and the change from UN to full NATO control. Now airpower could respond more quickly to developing events. The Air Force spent most of its time during Joint Endeavor airlifting supplies and military equipment to support the peace.

Operation Allied Force

In a region long accustomed to civil war, it was not many years before fighting erupted again in the former Yugoslavia—this time in Serbia itself.

In 1999, Milosevic ordered his military to remove the ethnic Albanians—who formed most of the population—from the southern Serbian province of Kosovo. As refugees streamed towards the border with Albania, NATO again stepped in, both to stop a humanitarian crisis and to show that it was a credible peacekeeping force in Europe.

Operation Allied Force began in March 1999. This 78-day campaign, which would end with Milosevic's withdrawal from Kosovo, was significant for a number of reasons. NATO ultimately won the day through airpower alone. No war before or since has been fought solely with airpower. NATO chose this route because no member country felt its citizens would support a cause that would result in the deaths of its servicemen. Therefore, no country committed

ground troops. NATO air forces put out a royal effort, with more than 38,000 sorties, but did not suffer a single combat casualty. This, too, was an incredible accomplishment. Their biggest gaffe was bombing the Chinese embassy in Belgrade, Serbia's capital.

The Air Force recorded two firsts as well during Allied Force: The B-2 stealth bomber saw combat for the first time, and the Air Force dropped its first 2,000lb (907kg) GBU-31 precision weapon. Indeed, the B-2 delivered the GBU-31, which has a tail kit that guides the bomb to its target using an inertial navigational system and a global positioning system. The stealth bomber got credit for destroying one-third of the targets in Serbia during the first eight weeks of the campaign.

FIRST USE
The Air Force used GBU-31 Joint Direct Attack Munitions (JDAM) during Operation Allied Force. These bombs are being loaded onto the flight deck of the USS Harry S. Truman *to support the war in Iraq*

Lockheed F-117 Nighthawk

Color multi-functional display indicator (CMDI)

Radar altimeter and altitude instruments

Engine performance indicator

Data-entry panel

Sensor display

Infrared acquisition and designation system (IRADS) display controls

Control column

Ejection seat handles

VIRTUAL REALITY
The F-117 (modified cockpit shown) is equipped with sophisticated navigation and attack systems integrated into a digital avionics suite that increases mission effectiveness. This includes a moving-map display, head-up display, and screen for infrared imagery.

IN 1975, THE LOCKHEED Skunk Works initiated a secret program to develop a radar-proof "stealth" aircraft. Development was by no means straightforward, and the first F-117As were not delivered to the USAF until 1982. Nicknamed the "Bat Plane" or "Stink Bug," its unique appearance results from the use of flat, faceted surfaces to deflect radar emissions at an angle, especially from the front.

The airframe is covered in radar-absorbent material and the cockpit windows are coated in a gold layer that conducts radar energy into the airframe. There is even a fine mesh over the engine intakes, which might otherwise provide a radar signature for the enemy to track. Any

weaponry or fuel tanks are carried internally to maintain the stealth effect. It cannot use radar, because this might give away its position; it relies instead on a passive infrared "eye" in the nose to look forward at the ground. The result is an aircraft as near to radar-invisible as can currently be conceived. The pilot's view out of the cockpit is very limited, but this does not matter because the aircraft's subsonic speed makes it too slow for daylight combat. It only attacks by night, and the pilot never looks outside, keeping his eyes on the multi-function display screens in front of him.

The designation "F" for fighter is a strange one, as the F-117A has no guns and does not usually carry missiles. A night-penetration strike aircraft, it

is equipped instead with the most up-to-date smart weapons and targeting systems for precision attack. While the F-117A is a complex weapons system to be operated by a single pilot, who needs a lot of electronic help approaching the target, its strikes proved extremely accurate in the Gulf War in 1991.

The F-117As have established themselves as a central element in America's air armory. They justify their impressive price tag—more than $40 million each—by their accuracy of attack and near invulnerability, although one was shot down by Serbian artillery during the Kosovo campaign in 1999.

One-piece, upward-hinging cockpit canopy

Engine air intakes covered by grilles to screen compressor face from radar

FRONT VIEW
The flat undersurfaces of the F-117A's wing are blended into the fuselage, making the whole underside a lifting surface. The exterior is almost entirely covered with matte-black radar-absorbent material.

Window for forward-looking infrared (FLIR) sighting and targeting unit

Omni-directional air data sensing probe

Nose wheel

INVISIBLE NIGHTHAWK
Like many other weapons, the F-117A was developed to counter advances in an enemy's military capabilities. In this case, however, the F-117A not only raised the stakes, but also bypassed an entire class of weapons entirely—radar-directed air defenses.

All glazed panels are gold-coated to conduct radar energy into the airframe

Faceted surfaces give angular appearance

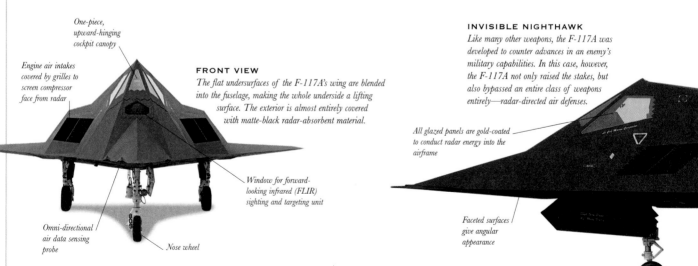

DOCTRINE AND HISTORY—CONFLICT IN THE FORMER YUGOSLAVIA

DISTINCTIVE CAPABILITIES	FUNCTIONS (MISSIONS)	DOCTRINAL EMPHASIS
• Air and Space Superiority • Precision Engagement • Agile Combat Support	• Counterland • Close Air Support • Interdiction • Surveillance and Reconnaissance • Search and Rescue • Air Refueling • Strategic Attack	• No Defined Doctrine (Deny Flight) • Strategic Attacks on Ethnic-Cleansing Serbs and Military Capabilities (Allied Force)

DESERT RANGERS

Unveiled to the public in 1988, the Nighthawk saw active service during 1991's Operation Desert Storm. Operating from their base in the Nevada desert and refueling in midair, F-117As flew more than 1,500 sorties and were the only coalition aircraft to strike targets in Baghdad.

SLOWING DOWN

The F-117A has a landing speed of 172mph (227kmph) so a drag chute is needed to reduce the length of the landing run.

Milosevic's forces were no match for NATO's. The Serbian president resorted to propaganda, to terror tactics, and to mixing his forces among civilians to make NATO operations more difficult, since he rightly calculated that NATO would try to avoid civilian casualties. Hundreds of thousands of Albanians became refugees because of the war. Milosevic counted on this flood of humanity to distract NATO from its war efforts; it did not. Rather, it resulted in a second NATO operation, Operation Shining Hope, to prevent the starvation among refugees. The US Air Force airlifted food and other supplies for Shining Hope. Like Operation Allied Force, Shining Hope ran from April to June 1999.

Lessons learned: Allied Force

Allied Force ended with some pleasant realizations and some room for improvement. On the bright side, the United States found that while it harbored concerns about coordinating an offensive with its European allies under NATO's auspices, it turned out each party brought something necessary to the battlefront. For instance, the Air Force had the military muscle (i.e., the GBU-31) and technology (i.e., the B-2). Europe delivered might as well, but it also opened its bases, offered access, provided infrastructure, and played an important diplomatic role. Furthermore, when NATO could act without the UN, it demonstrated a singleness of purpose and resolve. Milosevic's forces recognized that NATO was not going to back down, and this realization helped bring about his defeat.

Nonetheless, the US military saw it had some lessons to implement. Commitments around the globe were stretching all branches thin. Therefore, training and support would become more important than ever to the success of any offensive or humanitarian mission. The military emerged with a renewed interest in smart weapons, and with the knowledge that it must hone its force to meet future needs. To do the latter, the military realized it had to consider what future wars would look like and what future humanitarian crises would require, and then build a force—troops and materiel, tactical and strategic, strike force and airlift—around those demands. Taking these steps, the military reasoned, could help address the dangers of becoming a "hollow force"—one that seems powerful but is not actually prepared.

What no one knew, however, was that before long the American homeland itself would come under air attack—not from a hostile nation's air forces, but from a tiny group of depraved and determined terrorists.

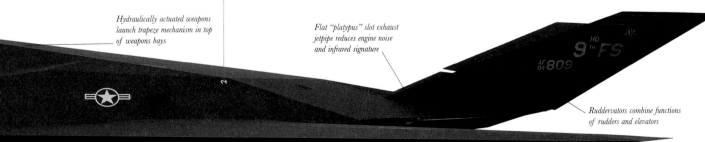

Hydraulically actuated weapons launch trapeze mechanism in top of weapons bays

Flat "platypus" slot exhaust jetpipe reduces engine noise and infrared signature

Ruddervators combine functions of rudders and elevators

Composite construction leading edge

Engine housing

MODULE V

AIRPOWER TODAY

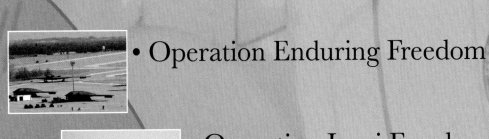

- Operation Enduring Freedom

- Operation Iraqi Freedom

- USAF CONOPS

- Air and Space
  Power Review

21

OPERATION
ENDURING FREEDOM

FOLLOWING THE AL QAEDA terrorist attacks on the United States on September 11, 2001, US forces went after the terrorist organization and the Taliban regime in Afghanistan that sheltered it. US strategy relied on air superiority and close air support, with Special Forces ground controllers—sometimes operating on horseback—calling in air strikes in a display of air-ground coordination never before achieved.

The Pentagon in Arlington, Virginia, was one of the sites targeted by terrorists on September 11, 2001.

ORIGINS OF THE GLOBAL WAR ON TERROR

AFTER SUFFERING A STUNNING ATTACK, THE UNITED STATES MOVES TO ELIMINATE TERRORIST SAFE HAVENS IN AFGHANISTAN

FOR MANY AMERICANS, the global war on terror began on September 11, 2001, when terrorists hijacked and crashed four airliners on US soil. However, 9/11 was only the culmination of a sequence of other events. These included bombings against US military personnel in Lebanon and Saudi Arabia, the US Embassies in Tanzania and Kenya, and the USS *Cole*, anchored at a port in Yemen.

The first of these bombings occurred on October 23, 1983, when a five-ton Mercedes truck crashed into the Marine barracks in Beirut and set off a 12,000lb (5,440kg) bomb that collapsed the building. A total of 241 Americans died, most of them Marines on a peacekeeping mission in war-torn Lebanon. On that same day, a second truck crashed into a French military position only a few miles away, with similar deadly results. The next attack, with an even bigger explosive, took place years later on June 25, 1996, against US military living quarters in Dhahran, Saudi Arabia. This truck bomb killed 19 Air Force personnel and wounded scores of others. The Airmen were in Saudi Arabia to enforce the no-fly zone in southern Iraq for Operation Southern Watch.

Terrorists directed another massive assault on Americans overseas on August 7, 1998, at the US Embassies in Tanzania and Kenya. These explosions killed 12 US citizens and hundreds of local citizens, and wounded about 5,000 Kenyans, 76 Tanzanians, and one American. Then on October 12, 2000, as the USS *Cole* refueled at a port in Yemen, two suicide bombers detonated their small craft next to the ship. The bomb killed 17 Sailors and wounded 39 others.

These and other acts of violence against US personnel around the world signaled with increasing intensity that certain terrorist groups had the United States in their sights. Osama bin Laden—scion of a wealthy family living in Saudi Arabia—was leader of one of these groups, al Qaeda (the Base). Among other goals, al Qaeda, a loose confederation of like-minded violent Islamists, aims to impose its twisted version of "purified" Islam, replace "corrupt" Arab regimes with Islamic theocracies, and expel all Western and secular influences from the Islamic nations.

The United States responded to these attacks in a variety of ways. For instance, after the embassy attacks, it launched cruise missiles at suspected terrorist sites in Sudan and Afghanistan. But not until September 11, 2001—when 19 terrorists hijacked four commercial airliners and crashed them into the World Trade Center in New York City, the Pentagon in Arlington, Virginia, and a field in Pennsylvania—did the United States fully embark on the Global War on Terror (GWOT).

The US government decided on a two-pronged response to September 11: Destroy the terrorists based in Afghanistan and deny terrorists sanctuary wherever else they might seek shelter. For this effort, the United States resolved to call on every resource at its disposal, including the military (active, Reserve, and Guard), intelligence (the Central Intelligence Agency, the Defense Intelligence Agency, and the National Security Agency), diplomatic avenues, and domestic law enforcement (the Federal Bureau of Investigation).

Afghanistan is a landlocked nation occupied by tribes with conflicting sets of loyalties.

TRADE CENTER TERROR
As one tower of the World Trade Center burns, a second airliner heads for the tower's twin. Using airplanes as human-guided missiles, with their fuel to wreak destruction instead of a warhead, the terrorists were able to inflict vast damage while armed with nothing more than sharp blades.

The United States also created a Department of Homeland Security to coordinate the counterterrorism efforts of all federal government agencies involved in protecting US interests.

President George W. Bush explained who the terrorists were in a speech to the Congress on September 20, 2001. "Al Qaeda is to terror what the mafia is to crime. But its goal is not making money; its goal is remaking the world—and imposing its radical beliefs on people everywhere." Afghanistan's Taliban regime gave al Qaeda sanctuary and training grounds from which to plan and launch attacks against the United States and other countries around the world. President Bush added, "Our war on terror begins with al Qaeda, but it does not end there. It will not end until every terrorist group of global reach has been found, stopped, and defeated."

The US response to the September 11 attacks began on October 7, 2001, with the start of Operation Enduring Freedom (OEF) against terrorist strongholds in Afghanistan. This operation expanded in January 2002, when the United States sent forces to crush terrorist networks in the Philippines, Bosnia, and Africa. In that same month, Bush also announced a new doctrine—the doctrine of preemption—that would mark a major break with the country's traditional approach to world affairs. Under this new

SPEECH BEFORE CONGRESS
On September 20, 2001, President George Bush addressed Congress to outline what the country faced in the post–September 11 world.

doctrine, the United States would now reserve the right to attack regimes that posed a serious threat, even though it had not been attacked.

The United States responds

The US Air Force went into Afghanistan with B-1s, B-2s, B-52s, F-14s, F-15Es, F-16s, F-18s, A-10s, AC-130s, and C-17s. These aircraft hit terrorist training camps and bases, provided cover for US ground troops, and ferried in Special Forces troops and supplies. US Navy carriers launched fighters against al Qaeda and Taliban targets, while US and British submarines joined in with missile strikes.

Air Force B-1s delivered 40 percent of the guided and unguided bombs in OEF's first six months. In the operation's first 18 months, US and allied air forces (in this operation also referred to as coalition forces) flew 85,000 sorties and 48,000 airlifts, and dropped 9,650 tons (8,754 tonnes) of bombs. These efforts helped depose the repressive Taliban regime in just a few months, and would eventually allow

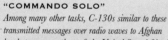

"COMMANDO SOLO"
Among many other tasks, C-130s similar to these transmitted messages over radio waves to Afghan locals to reassure them of the United States' friendly intentions. The Air Force referred to these aircraft as "Commando Solo."

LONGEST FLIGHT TO DATE
In 2001 the B-2 made its longest flight on record from its base in Missouri to Afghanistan. Here, two B-2s taxi down the runway in Missouri in 2008.

Afghanistan to install a new government. But much happened before these hoped-for developments.

One of the most important missions at OEF's start was the battle for Mazar-e Sharif, a city in northwest Afghanistan and a Taliban stronghold. US Special Forces worked in concert with the Northern Alliance, a band of native Afghan militias headed by General Muhammed Fahim. Before moving toward Mazar, however, coalition forces needed to establish air supremacy.

The Air Force began deploying for the Afghanistan theater on September 17. Air Force Lieutenant General Charles F. Wald, already in charge of US airpower in the Middle East, set up his base in Saudi Arabia. From the Combined Air Operations Center (CAOC), he coordinated air

operations, which began on October 7. For the first wave of the attack, US and British ships sent 50 cruise missiles toward Taliban sites throughout Afghanistan. In the second attack wave were F-14s, F-18s, B-2s, B-1s, and B-52s hitting hard at Taliban bases. The coalition forces owned the air by the third day, even though the Taliban had begun this battle with 45,000 troops, 450 tanks, 30 MiG-21s (a Soviet fighter) and Su-22s (a Soviet fighter-bomber), some SA-3s (surface-to-air missiles), 300 antiaircraft guns, and 100 Stinger missiles (portable, shoulder-launched missiles). In fact, General Wald claimed that the coalition forces wiped out the Taliban's air defenses "within the first 15 minutes or so." Most aircraft flew so high that they were out of range of the Stinger missiles, which could reach no farther than 15,000ft (4,572m). The Taliban could not put up much of a defense against the overwhelming US and coalition airpower.

At the start of this campaign, the B-2 stealth bomber made its longest flight to date—from Whiteman Air Force Base, Missouri, to Afghanistan. The bomber remained aloft for 41 hours. It struck Taliban targets before heading toward the British island of Diego Garcia in the Indian Ocean, where it replaced its tired crew with a fresh one. Other aircraft playing a large role in the air campaign's early days were the C-130 "Commando Solo" aircraft, which broadcast friendly messages over radio

AIR FORCE COMMANDER
Lieutenant General Charles F. Wald coordinated air operations during the early months of Operation Enduring Freedom from the Combined Air Operations Center in Saudi Arabia.

waves to local people, and C-17s, which delivered food to refugees. US Representative Ike Skelton said, "It's the first time I've ever heard of trying to feed the people while you're trying to destroy their government. I don't think it's ever been done before, but I think it's an excellent strategy." C-130s also delivered Special Forces wherever they needed to go while C-17s and C-130s dropped supplies.

The air campaign devoted the first two weeks to counterair missions; that is, to demolishing fixed targets such as airfields and communication lines. By the third week, the missions shifted to a counterland focus, with airpower zeroing in on troops and tanks.

This progress seemed promising; but as the war continued, the United States appeared to be using airpower as fitfully as it had in Vietnam. For instance, the United States was once again concerned with excessive collateral damage (civilian deaths). Rather than pounding the Taliban and al Qaeda into submission, Air Force and Navy pilots used extreme caution—they were ordered to fly over target zones once before flying over a second time to drop their loads. The members of the Afghan Northern Alliance complained that they were not receiving sufficient support from coalition airpower. They urged the United States not to demonstrate such caution, claiming that in war civilians inevitably are killed. The New York Times reported that the "concerns of American generals and politicians—to exhaust diplomatic avenues, to minimize civilian deaths, to avoid alienating the Muslim world, to stop short of being dragged into the quagmire of Afghanistan's politics—have little resonance among these men [Northern Alliance fighters]."

STAFF SERGEANT MATT

WHEN THE FIRST AIRPLANE struck the World Trade Center on September 11, Staff Sergeant Matt watched the events unfold from a training site in Kansas.

The 26-year-old Air Force combat controller was attending a close air support proficiency training course when America came under attack. Though he had completed the academic portion of the exercise, he would not get to conduct the practical portion—at least not in Kansas.

The sergeant, who does not wish to release his last name for security reasons, returned to his unit within days of the bombing. A few weeks later, Matt would be among the many Air Force Special Operations Command professionals deployed in support of Operation Enduring Freedom.

Fresh from this stateside training and with two rucksacks on his back, Matt started conducting close air support proficiency under real-world circumstances in the heart of Afghanistan.

"I was charged with supporting Northern Alliance forces in their fight against the Taliban," Matt said. "I infiltrated Afghanistan in early October, working as part of an Army Special Forces team."

For this mission, the combat controller's duty was to arrange close air support against Taliban targets. Throughout his nearly three-month deployment, Matt estimates he made hundreds of calls to US aircraft seeking their help to hinder advancing enemy forces.

OLD MEETS NEW
US Army Special Forces Soldiers gallop down a shallow riverbed during a horseback patrol through the town of Kunduz, Afghanistan, in August 2002. During Operation Enduring Freedom, Air Force combat controllers accompanied the Special Forces to coordinate close air support.

An example of the ground-to-air support Matt provided happened in early November during a decisive battle dubbed the Battle for the Balk Valley.

"After about a week of traveling on horseback with the Northern Alliance, we had made our way to the valley area about the 5th of November," he said. "From our observation point, we could see a stronghold of Taliban troops."

Matt and his Army counterparts set up an observation position on a mountainside and, looking down at the enemy troops, they began assessing the situation.

"Our charter was to assist the Northern Alliance in their advance toward Mazar-e Sharif," he said. "My specific role was to bring in the air assets to reduce the enemy threat and minimize the ground resistance."

Dug in along the mountain ridge of the Darye-Suf Valley, the controller was responsible for guiding airpower to the fight.

"The Taliban had established bunkers and basically settled in, prepared to fight and maintain control of the territory," he said. "There were vehicles, armored tanks, and personnel carriers stretched across the valley. They were holding their ground and were not about to relinquish [it] to the Northern Alliance."

Using "spotting scopes"—similar to a high-power, high-tech binocular—the controller identified the targets and began plotting positions using global positioning systems and maps.

"I had to prioritize the targets to ensure we put the bombs on the right targets first," Matt said. "Once I positively identified the targets, I passed the coordinates back to our headquarters element to request air support."

Close air support calls are a key mission for combat controllers. Using various technological equipment, a controller can pinpoint the exact location where an aircraft commander needs to put bombs on target. The type of target and various contributing factors, such as surrounding structures, will help the controller determine what type of bomb and aircraft are best suited for the mission. When passing the close air support request to the headquarters element, the controller will caveat the request with which airframe can best make the mission happen.

"Different types of munitions are better situated for different targets," Matt said. "In this case, what was needed was a [Navy] F-18 [Hornet] with precision-guided bombs."

These bombs can work in conjunction with the Special Operations Forces laser marker. The marker provides a controller with the capability to locate and designate targets.

With the Hornet overhead, Matt marked the target—a bunker—and cleared the pilot to fire.

"He put the bomb through the front door," Matt said.

Making a few more passes, the F-18 pilot took coordinates from Matt and continued the bombing campaign against the Taliban troops.

"It was then the Taliban began a counterattack," he said. "They started firing rocket-propelled grenades at our position and the fire became pretty intense. I called in for additional air support and within minutes had a B-52 [Stratofortress] en route. The [rockets] began hitting our position, exploding over our heads and impacting the berm in front of us."

Less than five miles (8km) out, the B-52 pilot made contact and the controller relayed the coordinates. Within seconds, the bomber made an initial pass over the attacking force, dropping eight bombs. The bombing gave the team enough of a break in firing so they could move down the mountain toward a ravine. Matt knew he needed more airpower, and called in for fighter support.

As a Navy F-14 Tomcat arrived on the scene, the pilot radioed the controller that Taliban troops were moving in toward his new position.

"After we verified our location, I cleared the pilot to come in hot—to begin firing on the troops moving in our direction," Matt said. "He made several passes and gave us enough support to move toward a rocky outcrop a few meters down the mountain for cover."

Looking back up the mountain, the controller could see where Taliban forces had now overrun the entrenchment he and his Army counterparts had just left. Pulling out his GPS, Matt recalled his last coordinates and passed them to the B-52 pilot still circling the area.

"In seconds, the bomber dropped two large bombs on the spot we just left," he said. "The combined effort of the B-52, F-18, and F-14 pilots cleared out the resistance and allowed the Northern Alliance to gain the ground. The next day, as [we were] making our way down the mountain, the resistance was very light.

"There is no doubt in my mind that the airpower allowed the Northern Alliance to move through that valley virtually unimpeded," Matt said. "[Close air support] actions helped cut down the amount of time it would have taken for the alliance to advance. Additionally, it helped reduce the loss of life that would surely have resulted in direct action."

EYES IN THE SKIES
The Rivet Joint aircraft was one of the reconnaissance aircraft used in the initial stages of the war against the Taliban in Afghanistan.

The battle for Mazar-e Sharif

During the third week of the campaign, American and British Special Forces began moving with Northern Alliance forces toward Mazar-e Sharif. In 1997 Taliban fighters had captured the strategically located city to expand their control into the surrounding areas. Now, with US airpower and US and British Special Forces at its side, the Northern Alliance was moving back. Many of the Special Forces rode on horseback and grew beards to blend in with the Afghan fighters, but even though they adopted nineteenth-century practices and appearances, the US and British commandos also carried high-tech equipment—including laptops and lasers—to call in air strikes.

By November 6, two separate forces of commandos and Northern Alliance troops had driven the Taliban out of Keshendeh and Ag Kupruk, two towns critical to reaching Mazar, with air strikes followed by ground attacks. Then the two groups, along with a third arm of the Northern Alliance, joined forces to fight their way north to Mazar-e Sharif. They routed the Taliban, which fled the city on November 9. With the momentum now in their favor, Northern Alliance fighters continued their push to control the entire country by seizing four more cities: Taloqan, Herat, Jalalabad, and Kabul, the capital. The Northern Alliance credited airpower for much of its success.

Finally, it used this success to take Kandahar in southern Afghanistan by December 7. The Northern Alliance had deposed the Taliban, although dangerous guerrilla forces still remained in the country.

A combination of factors led to the victories in 2001. The Special Forces could spot and relay targets to circling bombers or to command centers to arrange for air strikes. Furthermore, reconnaissance aircraft such as the JSTARS, AWACS, and P-3s, along with satellites and Rivet Joint aircraft, tracked activity on the ground. Once these spies in the sky sent data to CAOC, the command center could fly in Predator, Global Hawk, and Shadow UAVs to confirm and narrow down targets for attack aircraft. The Predators even fired Hellfire missiles on at least four occasions. In fact, UAVs fired weapons for the first time in the Afghan

FIREPOWER
Predators like this one were the first UAVs to fire missiles in a combat operation. They launched Hellfire missiles on at least four occasions during the early stages of Operation Enduring Freedom.

theater. Finally, with the information from all these sources, attack aircraft such as AC-130 gunships or B-52 bombers carried out the air strikes. This coordination permitted rapid turnaround between request and execution at a level that had not previously been achieved.

US Secretary of Defense Donald Rumsfeld summed up the strategy used to win Mazar-e Sharif—and in a sense, the conquest of the other Taliban-held towns as well—when he said in early 2002, "The battle for Mazar was a transforming battle. Coalition forces took existing military capabilities—from the most advanced (such as laser-guided weapons) to the antique (40-year-old B-52s updated with modern electronics) to the most rudimentary (a man on a horse with a weapon)—and used them together in unprecedented ways, with devastating effect on enemy positions, enemy morale." Still, as of 2008, the Taliban and al Qaeda continued to attack US and NATO forces and pro-Western Afghans.

The Taliban have shifted their base to the treacherous Afghan mountains and switched their tactics to all-guerrilla warfare.

Nonetheless, the initial phase of GWOT ended with the Taliban out of power. An interim Afghan government stepped in with Hamid Karzai at its helm in December 2001. In 2004 the country set up a new constitution with a president, vice president, and two-house parliament. Karzai was elected president in late 2004.

Lessons learned

Many things worked well in the first phase of GWOT, yet much room remained for improvements. The military and think tanks studied five categories in particular: Technology, operation formats, airlift and refueling, command and control, and intelligence-surveillance-reconnaissance (ISR).

During the Afghan conflict, a combination of old and new technologies achieved success on the ground in ways never before seen. US commandos discovered targets while traveling with Northern Alliance troops, reported these targets with their laptops to circling aircraft or to CAOC, and gunships and bombers then zoomed in and struck. In addition, reconnaissance aircraft and satellites kept a watch on ground activities 24/7. This "network-centric" approach meant responses to calls for air strikes were faster than in the past. This faster response time is also referred to as a "kill chain."

The Global Hawk and other UAVs, which soar as high as 65,000ft (19,800m) for 30 hours at a time, were among those aircraft that gave commanders greater access to what was taking place on the ground. Unmanned Combat Aerial Vehicles (UCAVs) such as the Predator perform much the same function from 24,000ft (7,315m) in the air for up to 24 hours at a time—the

Predator can also deliver the precision Hellfire missiles. The think tanks and commanders concluded that the military needed more of both types of aircraft, but both have technical problems. The Predator flies at only 90mph (145kmph), and its optimum altitude is 10,000ft (3,048m), which puts it in range of antiaircraft fire. In addition, bad weather can hamper its takeoff. At least two Global Hawks crashed in Afghanistan. Investigators determined that one crash was due to a defective bolt; the reason for the other crash is not known. Much work remains to be done on these types of unmanned aircraft, although their future is promising.

The military employed two types of operations in Afghanistan: joint and combined. "Joint" refers to coordinated efforts by the Air Force, Army, Navy, and Marines, while "combined" describes operations mounted by the United States with coalition forces, including the Northern Alliance. Considering the outcome by December 2001 in Afghanistan, these two types of operations were generally successful. Even so, experts concluded that all the services could have organized themselves more efficiently. As experience in earlier wars had shown, when a number of branches try to synchronize their efforts, sometimes there are too many leadership layers. Bureaucracy can get in the way and slow communication. Whatever the reasons, the experts recommended streamlining all coordinated efforts.

Afghanistan presented a unique challenge to airpower because of its remote location. As noted earlier, the B-2 logged its longest flight in history during that conflict. And because no forward bases were available at the start of OEF, A-10s and AV-8s could not participate, while fighters like the F-14 and F-18 had to fly long distances from Navy carriers in the Indian Ocean. Long flights require tankers, while most such operations require airlifts to get troops and supplies to the

front. Both tankers and airlift aircraft did superb jobs, the experts said.

Still, just as it had following the Bosnian crisis, the Air Force determined that it could have used more tankers, as well as more airlift capacity, in Afghanistan. In addition, OEF called for airlift aircraft able to land at rough and makeshift airstrips. One final twist to the tanker's role during OEF was that the Air Force modified some KC-135s to serve as communications platforms. These "smart tankers" relayed information to fighters and to CAOC. The Air Force decided to modify more aircraft after the early stages of OEF.

The term *command and control* relates to the sharing of information among ground forces, aircraft (including manned and unmanned reconnaissance aircraft), all services, and command centers. During the war against the Taliban, the coalition forces' command-and-control center was in Saudi Arabia—some 7,000 miles (11,265km) away. Because of modern technology, however, it was possible to track and coordinate events on the ground and in the air over Afghanistan from a distance. Advanced technology also permitted air forces to dramatically reduce their sorties—from about 3,000 a day for Operation Desert Storm to about 200 a day for OEF. While the

Department of Defense has cautioned that these numbers might be overly optimistic, they indicate how command and control, coupled with technology, can improve efficiency in the field.

One expert noted that because the modern battlefield requires so much data sharing, it also requires tremendous bandwidth. The services must make more bandwidth available, he advised, because current systems do not have the necessary capacity. In addition, the military must find better ways to use the information provided by so many sources. The problem is similar to what the average civilian deals with when surfing the Internet. A vast amount of information exists, and it is difficult to decide what to keep and what to discard. Likewise, the military must be able to sift through the abundance of information and get the relevant data to the forces in the air and on the ground in a timely manner.

Intelligence-surveillance-reconnaissance (ISR) opened new opportunities for all branches of the US military in Afghanistan. For the Air Force, new data from reconnaissance aircraft, satellites, and Special Operations Forces on the ground meant that an aircraft could change course at midmission or go after new targets as new intelligence became available. With this real-time data, provided in part by six satellites during OEF, airpower played a crucial role in routing the Taliban. That being said, human intelligence on the ground remained the most indispensable factor. As the enemy dispersed into the mountains—or as bad weather rolled in—nothing could replace the information the commandos provided. Therefore, experts stressed maintaining human intelligence and not becoming overly reliant on technology.

In some cases, however, data were not reaching aircraft in a timely manner, called "sensor-to-shooter" time. For instance, UAVs picked up data, but because no direct communication lines existed between them and fighter planes, the fighters had

DOCTRINE AND HISTORY—OPERATION ENDURING FREEDOM		
DISTINCTIVE CAPABILITIES	**FUNCTIONS (MISSIONS)**	**DOCTRINAL EMPHASIS**
• Global Attack • Agile Combat Support • Precision Engagement • Rapid Global Mobility • Air and Space Superiority • Information Superiority	• Strategic Attack • Counterair • Counterspace • Counterland • Countersea • Information Ops • Combat Support • Command and Control • Airlift • Air Refueling • Spacelift • Special Ops • Intelligence • Surveillance and Reconnaissance • Combat Search and Rescue • Navigation and Positioning • Weather Services	• Focus on Air and Space Dominance

nothing to act on immediately. The Air Force rectified this problem by installing a means of direct communication between Predators and AC-130 gunships, which would receive images in their cockpits. Work continues on these kinds of developments.

It is important to note that the Taliban was not a sophisticated enemy. While it still confronts US and friendly forces in Afghanistan with guerrilla tactics, it has never been able to disrupt data transmissions from satellite to command and control. It has

never had precision-guided bombs or stealth aircraft. The Taliban camps in caves, and it began the war with only 30 aircraft in its arsenal. The question remains: What will happen if the United States ever goes up against its equal? Will its ISR and its technology be up to the job? Will a similarly equipped hostile force allow the United States breathing room in the midst of combat to sort out its complex communication lines during joint operations? The Air Force, as much as any other service, must consider and respond to these questions.

OPERATION IRAQI FREEDOM

22

CONVINCED THAT SADDAM HUSSEIN was harboring weapons of mass destruction and supporting terrorism, President George W. Bush, in a near-repeat of the Persian Gulf War a decade earlier, launched an air campaign—"Shock and Awe" as a prelude to a ground invasion. While the first phase of the war featured conventional tactics against a regular army, the second phase—a series of urban insurgencies—provided new challenges for airpower. The war also saw increased use of unmanned aircraft.

THE UNITED STATES DEALS SADDAM A FINAL BLOW

A CAMPAIGN AGAINST A REGULAR ARMY MORPHS INTO A HIT-AND-RUN STRUGGLE WITH INSURGENTS AND SUICIDE BOMBERS

IN OCTOBER 2002, the US Congress passed the Iraq War Resolution, granting the president the authority to attack Iraq. That authority, however, was conditional—a US attack depended on whether Iraq's President Saddam Hussein agreed or refused, once and for all, to abide by United Nations (UN) Resolution 687, drawn up in the wake of the 1991 Persian Gulf War. Resolution 687 did three basic things: 1) it barred Iraq from acquiring or developing nuclear materials; 2) it warned the country not to support or engage in terrorism; and 3) it ordered Iraq to "accept the destruction, removal, or rendering harmless, under international supervision" of its weapons of mass destruction (WMDs).

WMDs and the International Atomic Energy Agency

Right from the start—in the days following the 1991 Gulf War—Iraq had thwarted attempts by the International Atomic Energy Agency (IAEA) to inspect its weapons facilities, even though such inspections were required under Resolution 687. The Iraqi government hid equipment, stalled inspections, and made half-hearted attempts to appease the inspectors by providing incomplete lists of its nuclear and other WMD-related stockpiles and laboratories. An IAEA summary of events given to the UN Security Council in October 1997 described Iraq's earliest declarations of stockpiles as "totally inadequate," and reported that the IAEA's access to designated inspection sites was obstructed.

Nonetheless, by November 1992, the IAEA had destroyed or rendered harmless most of the weapons that it did find in Iraq. In addition, the IAEA fulfilled the third part of its obligation by removing unirradiated and lightly-irradiated material between November 1991 and June 1992, and removing irradiated material between December 1993 and February 1994. However, it was not until August 1995, after a general who had a tight rein on the clandestine programs left the country, that Iraq became somewhat freer about releasing information on its weapons-development efforts and weapons-storage sites. After that, the IAEA managed to destroy, render harmless, or remove more nuclear materials from the country.

By 1997 the IAEA surmised that Iraq had no nuclear weapons, despite signs that it had attempted to develop them before April 1991. Iraqi cooperation with weapons-inspection efforts had always been erratic, however, and by the end of 1998, the country had become so unyielding that IAEA inspectors were forced to withdraw. They did not return for four years. During that interim period, they monitored the country remotely, relying on tools such as satellite photos.

In 2002 the IAEA felt it was time to push once more for on-site inspections. In addition, the United States was exerting pressure on Iraq to comply. Therefore, with the backing of UN Resolution 1441, the IAEA resumed inspections, interviews with scientists, and collection of documents in November 2002. It continued those activities until ordered to halt on March 17, 2003, in the light of looming military actions against Iraq.

The IAEA's April 2003 report to the UN Security Council stated that Iraq "provided access to all facilities requested by the IAEA, including presidential compounds, private residences, and new sites, without conditions or delay." The agency report further said, "As of 17 March 2003, the IAEA did not find in Iraq any evidence of the revival of a nuclear programme.... However, the

IAEA INSPECTIONS
In June 2003, a team of IAEA scientists inspects nuclear material that had been under its safeguard at the Tuwaitha nuclear facility before the Iraq war.

time available for the IAEA before inspections were suspended was not sufficient to permit it to complete its overall review and assessment." So while the IAEA did not find any incriminating evidence, it also did not have the time to complete its inspections and therefore could not guarantee that no nuclear weapons existed.

WMDs and US intelligence

The US intelligence community, along with the services of other friendly nations, was also offering a mixed picture about Iraq's nuclear and other WMD stores. The results of these studies remain controversial. Some of the intelligence reported Iraq was indeed hiding WMDs. Much of this information, which later proved to be false, came from controversial sources—including Ahmad Chalabi, a Shiite Iraqi exile intent on ousting Hussein, a Sunni Muslim. In a debate that split the US intelligence community, Chalabi had champions and detractors. At one point, the Central Intelligence Agency (CIA) had a relationship with Chalabi that later turned sour, so it wanted nothing further to do with him. At the same time, Vice President Richard Cheney and the Office of the Secretary of Defense held Chalabi in high regard. After the removal of Saddam, Chalabi served as a deputy prime minister of Iraq for several years. He continues to serve in a government post and has denied providing false information to the Bush administration about WMDs.

While many intelligence professionals concluded that Iraq did not have WMDs, or that the evidence was not conclusive, many senior officials in the administration (including CIA Director George Tenet) were convinced that Iraq did have such weapons, cleverly hidden. Other Western intelligence agencies shared information that seemed to support that viewpoint. Controversy continues today over the conclusions the White House eventually came to regarding the reports—namely, the assumption of Iraq's guilt and subsequent invasion of the country.

In September 2002, President George W. Bush went before the UN General Assembly to underscore Iraq's lack of cooperation with the IAEA and fears of a growing nuclear arsenal. That same month, Secretary of State Colin Powell

FINAL WARNING
President George W. Bush, seated in the Oval Office at the White House, warns Saddam Hussein in a televised address to leave Iraq within 48 hours or face war.

went before the House and Senate Foreign Relations Committees to share the same concerns. He emphasized that if Saddam Hussein possessed WMDs, he would likely arm terrorists, who in turn would target Americans at home and abroad. The two men's presentations were effective, and in October, both houses of Congress passed the Iraq War Resolution, which President Bush signed on October 10, 2002.

In November 2002, the UN Security Council unanimously adopted Resolution 1441, which gave Iraq one last chance to fully comply, within 30 days, with requests for inspections and documents by the IAEA and the UN Monitoring and Verification Commission. Iraqi compliance

began that very same month, yet chief UN inspector Hans Blix complained that Iraq continued to interfere with IAEA work. Furthermore, beginning in February 2003, Secretary Powell went before the UN Security Council on several occasions to link Iraq with terrorism, to present video and audio evidence of Iraqi WMD programs, and to ask the council to enforce Resolution 1441.

While debate continued over the conclusions drawn from the US intelligence, President Bush spoke to the American people in a televised address on March 19, 2003. He stated that "American and coalition forces are in the early stages of military operations to disarm Iraq, to free its people, and to defend the world from a grave danger." He added, "Our nation enters this conflict reluctantly—yet, our purpose is sure. The people of the United States and our friends and allies will not live at the mercy of an outlaw regime that threatens the peace with weapons of mass murder. We will meet that threat now, with our Army, Air Force, Navy, Coast Guard, and Marines, so that we do not have to meet it later with armies of firefighters and police and doctors on the streets of our cities." "Operation Iraqi Freedom" (OIF) had begun.

NUCLEAR WEAPONS CENTER
Shortly after the first Gulf War, IAEA inspectors found evidence that the Al-Atheer plant, pictured here, was the center of Iraq's nuclear weapons program. The IAEA destroyed it in April 1992. Such discoveries lent credence to later suspicions about Iraq's ultimate intentions.

The prewar air campaign

The latest US operations against Iraq had actually begun in June 2002, some nine months before the President's March 2003 announcement, with the launch of "Operation Southern Focus." Under orders from Secretary of Defense Donald Rumsfeld, Air Force and British pilots—with experience gained from the 12-year enforcement of the no-fly zones through Operations Northern Watch and Southern Watch— changed their targets. Rather than mostly going after SAMs and antiaircraft artillery in response to attacks from the ground, the coalition pilots began to zero in on more important, fixed

EARLY ORDER
Secretary of Defense Donald Rumsfeld ordered a stepped-up campaign against Iraqi air defenses in June 2002, several months before the start of OIF.

targets such as command centers. The intent of this escalation was to permanently weaken Iraq's air defenses, not just demolish one gun, missile, or radar site.

US Air Force Chief of Staff General John P. Jumper reported that during Southern Focus and the runup to OIF (June 2002– March 2003), US and allied aircraft flew about 4,000 sorties against the integrated air defense system in Iraq and against surface-to-air missiles and their command and control. Coalition aircraft delivered 606 bombs against 391 targets during Southern Focus. Iraq fought back, launching about a dozen rockets and missiles at coalition crews each day during the same period.

By the time OIF began, the Iraqis were "pretty much out of business," General Jumper said. In other words, the Southern Focus air campaign— coupled with 12 years of Operations Northern Watch and Southern Watch—had firmly established coalition air superiority before the OIF ground campaign ever began. In fact, Secretary of the Air Force James G. Roche remarked after the first phase of OIF that

SHOCK AND AWE
During the Iraq invasion, the media riveted television audiences with scenes of strikes by aircraft and cruise missiles on Baghdad. Although precisely targeted against official buildings, these air strikes were linked to the fashionable military principle of "shock and awe"—the use of a spectacular display of power to undermine the enemy's will to fight.

because of Northern Watch and Southern Watch's successes, the Iraqi Air Force did not fly a single sortie against coalition forces during OIF.

Reconnaissance flights in the prewar years also fortified the position of coalition forces when they eventually engaged in OIF. Surveillance crews had spotted repairs to damaged Iraqi air defenses as well as installations of fiber-optic networks that were critical to President Hussein's command and control centers. Fiber-optic networks are part of communication lines that help commanders send orders to their troops in the field.

The campaign

The 1999 "Operation Allied Force" over Kosovo was among those campaigns that proved airpower could play a major role—if not the sole role—in winning a war. As Operations Northern Watch, Southern Watch, and Southern Focus over Iraq showed, faith in airpower remained strong. It could deliver overwhelming power and save troops from having to single-handedly win on the battlefield. Airpower also paved the way for the start of OIF on March 20, 2003.

Coalition forces entered OIF with total air superiority, in a new campaign dubbed "Shock and Awe." Aircraft pounded Baghdad, Iraq's capital, over several days as ground troops advanced from Kuwait in the south. Thanks to Shock and Awe, the prewar air campaign, coalition ground forces reached Baghdad in a mere 22 days. This was an astounding demonstration of the US military's capability for speed, precision, and effectiveness.

While the first phase of the Iraq War was a military success, subsequent developments have deepened the political dispute in the United States between supporters and opponents of the war. The failure to find a single weapon of mass destruction in Iraq is a key factor in the debate.

PREPARATION INDISPENSABLE
Air Force Chief of Staff General John P. Jumper said that the prewar air campaign put Iraq's air defenses out of business before OIF ever began.

"RISK-FREE" AIR ATTACK

PRECISION-GUIDED BOMBS AND MISSILES constituted less than 10 percent of munitions used during the Gulf War; by 2003, around two-thirds of airborne munitions were "smart."

The use of JDAMs (joint direct attack munitions) was crucial. A JDAM was a bomb with a guidance package linked to a Global Positioning System (GPS) or an Inertial Navigation System (INS). The map coordinates of a target on the ground were fed into the bomb's control system. Once released from the aircraft, the JDAM would then steer itself to the designated coordinates without any further guidance. JDAMs were accurate to within around 33ft (10m) and could be used in weather conditions that would create problems for laser- or TV-guided munitions.

Other key factors in the 2003 invasion included the increasing use of UAVs (unmanned aerial vehicles), more than 100 of which were deployed. They mostly carried out reconnaissance missions, but Predators on occasion acted as UCAVs (unmanned combat air vehicles), executing precision air strikes with Hellfire missiles. The introduction

of "time-sensitive targeting"—directing strike aircraft lurking over the battle area to a target only minutes after it was identified—was considered a success. In one incident, a B-1 bomber struck a house where Saddam Hussein and his sons were said to be meeting less than 12 minutes after US intelligence had identified the target.

Although a number of well-known problems, including civilian casualties caused by occasional inaccuracy or mistaken target identification and losses to friendly fire, resurfaced

during the Iraq invasion, the effectiveness of the deployment of airpower was indisputable. Iraqi ground forces simply could not operate without air cover. They could not maintain command and communications in the face of precision air strikes. With its massive costs and its immense organizational and technological demands, airpower remained the clearest determinant of power differences between states in the early twenty-first century. Iraq might have given a superpower a fight on the ground, but in the air, it could not compete.

TANK DESTRUCTION
Iraqi armored forces had no defense against pinpoint air strikes once they had been identified as a target by America's "eyes in the sky." The A-10 Warthog was the United States' primary tank-busting aircraft, but any airplane armed with JDAMS or other guided munitions could be directed to strike Saddam's tanks.

Airpower's role

Airpower has played six principal roles in OIF: strategic uses, intelligence-surveillance-reconnaissance (ISR), counterair, counterland, counterspace, and airlift/refueling. Early in the conflict, airpower fulfilled two key OIF strategies—bombing military and government sites in Baghdad into submission and wiping out Iraqi command and control (C2) abilities. The purpose of these strategies was to topple the Iraqi government.

For example, on Day 1 of OIF, F-117As helped begin the new operation by attacking Baghdad. A few hundred miles away, coalition ground forces prepared to cross Iraq's southern border under cover of heavy artillery barrages aimed at targets in Iraq. The strategy's

second point—destroying Iraqi command and control—grabbed attention on April 5. Coalition aircraft bombed the home of senior Iraqi military leader General Ali Hassan Majid ("Chemical Ali") in Basra, a southern Iraqi city. Attacks on C2

continued on April 7 with a two-pronged attack in Baghdad. Aircraft dropped four bombs on a supposed meeting spot for President Hussein and his sons, and the Army's 3d Infantry Division raided government buildings and two of Hussein's palaces.

OPENING SALVOS
The F-117A played a major role at the start of Operation Iraqi Freedom by attacking Baghdad. Here, an F-117A Nighthawk from the 8th Expeditionary Fighter Squadron returns from the opening mission of OIF on March 20, 2003.

PILOTLESS HELICOPTER
*Unmanned remote-controlled helicopters
were in operation with American forces
in Iraq by 2005. These UAV
helicopters could perform a variety of
functions, including communications,
reconnaissance, and supply.*

GLOBAL HAWK
*A superstar among American UAVs, Global Hawk is a
high-altitude reconnaissance aircraft. The basic model is
44ft (13.4m) long, with a wingspan of 116ft (35.4m).
Its maximum speed is over 350mph (600kmph).*

Operation Iraqi Freedom is ongoing as of mid-2008, and airpower continues to play a strategic role. As the operation proceeds, its strategies have shifted, and they will continue to do so. For instance, with Hussein and his old guard long deposed, local insurgents and al Qaeda cells now pose the biggest threats to coalition forces and Iraq's stability. Therefore, airpower might be called in to take out an insurgent stronghold or to provide close air support for US troops ambushed on the ground.

Strategies and tactics must be flexible, and airpower must bend to meet new demands.

One of the most difficult aspects of fighting the insurgents in Iraq is that they often hide among the local population. Intelligence may pin down the precise location of an insurgent group, but those hostile headquarters might be in the middle of a neighborhood. Dropping a bomb might take out the insurgents, but it could also kill innocent civilians. The United States and coalition forces must walk a fine line in such instances. They could easily wipe out the guerrillas, but they would probably lose local favor if they killed a family or hit a nearby hospital. One observer, historian John Buckley, has argued, "Airpower was an excellent weapon of major wars, but of limited use in low-intensity conflicts restricted by political considerations." Whether that is true or not, commanders must take these types of considerations into account as the war continues.

During the first phase of the war, aircraft gathered information critical to the overthrow of Hussein and his Ba'ath Party. Twenty-four hours a day, aircraft conducted recon while staff at the Combined Air Operations Center in Saudi Arabia managed the flights and the incoming intelligence.

LONG-LIVED WARTHOG
*The A-10 Thunderbolt II, better known
as the Warthog, pummeled Iraqi armor
in 2003 as it had in 1991. First flown
in 1972, the Warthog is likely to remain
in service until 2028—a striking example of
the longevity of some of today's military aircraft.*

Intelligence has a five-step cycle—planning and direction, collection, processing and exploitation, production, and dissemination. In OIF, airpower played the "collection" role. Because events were happening so swiftly, however, the intelligence cycle could not always keep up with demands at any one of its five stages.

Whatever shortfalls the intelligence process experienced, ISR logged some significant numbers in OIF's early days. Initially, 1,801 aircraft were dedicated to the mission, of which 80 were for ISR. These included the RQ-1 Predator UAV, RQ-4 Global Hawk UAV, EP-3, P-3C Orion, U-2, E-8C (JSTARS), and RC-135 Rivet Joint. Together, these craft flew about 1,000 sorties, collected 3,200 hours of video, 2,400 hours of signals intelligence (SIGINT), and 42,000 battlefield images.

Strikes often came within minutes after recon reported findings, as B-1s and other aircraft circled over suspected sites while awaiting directions. This was yet another example of time-sensitive targeting.

Air forces undertake counterair operations to maintain air superiority; they engage in counterland operations to protect troops on the ground. While these are distinct and seemingly separate goals, success in modern warfare is really about merging efforts. Air, land, and sea forces support one another, and each is essential to the other's success. For instance, on March 21, 2003, the Army's Special Forces won control of two airfields in western Iraq to secure a platform for future counterair and counterland operations.

Both counterair and counterland missions include interdiction, but interdiction takes a different shape for each type of mission. In a counterair move on March 27, 2003, US aircraft went after Iraqi command and control sites,

DESERT PATROL
US helicopters fly over the Iraqi desert during counterinsurgency operations. The United States faced the challenge of bringing airpower to bear against an elusive enemy not only in Iraq but also on a global scale.

military divisions, and military assets, which included air defenses in and around Baghdad. During two counterland missions on March 24, B-52s struck Republican Guard positions and trucks south of Baghdad. Two days later, B-52s struck two more Iraqi convoys south of the capital city. These and other counterair and counterland strikes helped minimize casualties among US and coalition ground forces.

US military satellites also contributed to coalition air superiority over Iraq. During OIF's early days, Lieutenant General T. Michael Moseley, Combined Forces Air Component Commander (CFACC) for the Iraqi theater, worked to make sure that air, land, and sea forces benefited from the CFACCs 50-plus satellites.

These satellites played a vast range of roles— they gathered data for weather reports, conducted surveillance, warned of incoming missiles, and transmitted GPS coordinates to pilots for accurate bombing. Iraqi countermeasures included deployment of a GPS jammer, which is an indication of the kinds of challenges US commanders may face in future conflicts.

SPACE CHIEF
Air Force Lieutenant General T. Michael Moseley (shown here after promotion to general) was Combined Forces Air Component Commander (CFACC) for OIF as well as for Southern Watch and Operation Enduring Freedom.

ON A MISSION
A B-1B Lancer heads out on a mission from a base in southwest Asia. These aircraft took part in time-sensitive targeting in Iraq later in the war, just as they had in OIF's early days, when a B-1 went after a suspected meeting site of Iraqi leader Saddam Hussein and his sons.

As it had during Operation Enduring Freedom (OEF) in Afghanistan, airlift to Iraq was challenging because of the region's remoteness and its hostile terrain (for instance, sand can damage delicate equipment in aircraft). Refueling also posed a challenge, but this did not prevent the Air Force from making a supreme effort in both operations. In fact, airlift operations in support of OIF and OEF combined were the third-largest airlift in Air Force history, behind only the Berlin airlift (1948–49) and Operation Desert Shield/Desert Storm (1990–91). In the first month of OIF alone, pilots flew 24,196 sorties, of which 56 percent were airlift and refueling flights. Tankers flew 6,193 sorties during OIF's initial stages to deliver 376.4 million pounds of fuel. In the first few years of OIF, airlift moved more than 2 million passengers and flew more than 37,000 sorties.

Lessons learned—so far

No one knows how long US troops will be deployed overseas for Operation Iraqi Freedom. This will be determined by the combined inputs from American domestic politics, foreign policy, and military strategy. However, the Air Force can draw lessons from the past several years' experiences.

IRAQ CAMPAIGN MEDAL
Even high-tech campaigns such as OIF involve risk to ground troops and air crews. Among the recipients of this medal were crew members who had flown sorties over Iraq on 30 consecutive days.

When President Bush announced on May 1, 2003, that "major combat operations in Iraq have ended," few would have predicted that the United States would still be fighting an insurgency in Iraq well into 2008 and most likely some years beyond. The Air Force, along with its fellow service branches, has seen many successes during the operation thus far, but it has also found areas where improvement is needed.

One of the biggest successes has been how well all the services have operated together. In testimony before Congress on July 9, 2003, Army General Tommy Franks, then commander of US Central Command and of coalition forces, praised these joint operations. These included conventional forces (air, land, and sea) supporting special operations and vice versa. He said that decisive combat in Iraq saw a maturing of joint force operations in many ways, with some capabilities reaching new performance levels. These included what Franks called "joint interoperability," that is, how well the Army, Navy, Air Force, and Marines coordinated overall strategy and individual missions. He also pointed to better joint C4I (command, control, communications, computers, and intelligence) networks—how well the

branches gathered and shared information in a timely fashion and how efficiently their commanders delivered instructions to troops in the field.

In addition, this integrated effort resulted in a lightning-fast campaign, the proof resting in the fact that ground troops reached Baghdad in only 22 days. Although the war has not ended but rather evolved into something entirely different—urban guerrilla warfare—the initial stages demonstrated the US military's remarkable capabilities.

Finally, General Franks commended the use of precision munitions, C2, equipment readiness, state of training of the troops, and coalition support as clear "winners" during OIF.

On the other hand, General Franks listed areas needing improvement. He said that OIF, like OEF, revealed the need for more bandwidth to support its activities, in particular, sharing information among all services and with coalition partners. In addition, the United States must place more emphasis on human intelligence (as opposed to air and space reconnaissance and surveillance). He also said that to avoid friendly-fire incidents, combat identification (ID)

GENERAL ON THE SCENE
General Tommy Franks surveys the scene in Iraq on April 16, 2003. In the background are the remains of one of President Saddam Hussein's palaces, which had been struck by a Tomahawk land-attack missile.

FIGHTING FALCON

An F-16C from the 18th Fighter Squadron on its way to the bomb range with two MK-84 2,000lb (907kg) bombs. The F-16, which played a pivotal role in OIF, is one of the most widely used military aircraft in the world.

AN OLDIE BUT A GOODIE

With more than 40 years of service, the B-52 remains an essential member of the Air Force fleet. This B-52 Stratofortress, based at a forward-deployed location, is ready for a mission in Iraq.

systems should be improved and standardized. In fact, in January 2008, the Air Force announced research into combat ID, resulting in a fiber-optic cloth that lights up and should help pilots spot friendly forces on the ground. Finally, Franks said, the deployment process is cumbersome and needs to be streamlined.

Historians and military analysts will continue to pore over Operation Iraqi Freedom, in all its phases, for years to come. As time passes and the situation in Iraq evolves, a clearer picture of the runup to the war, the war itself, and the situation in Iraq following the war will undoubtedly emerge, with new lessons for the Air Force, the other branches of the US military, and the US government as a whole.

DOCTRINE AND HISTORY—OPERATION IRAQI FREEDOM

DISTINCTIVE CAPABILITIES	FUNCTIONS (MISSIONS)	DOCTRINAL EMPHASIS
• Global Attack • Agile Combat Support • Precision Engagement • Rapid Global Mobility • Air and Space Superiority • Information Superiority	• Strategic Attack • Counterair • Counterspace • Counterland • Countersea • Information Ops • Combat Support • Command and Control • Airlift • Air Refueling • Spacelift • Special Ops • Intelligence • Surveillance and Reconnaissance • Combat Search and Rescue • Navigation and Positioning • Weather Services	• Focus on Air and Space Dominance

IN A PERIOD WHEN the enemy may not be a national army but a stateless terrorist group, the Air Force cannot afford to bask in the glow of past successes. Nuclear deterrence alone will not serve—the Air Force must develop a new way to deter a potential hostile force. Warfare itself has moved into a fourth dimension— cyberspace—demanding an Air Force response in the formation of Cyberspace Command. In addition, the Air Force has developed a series of new concepts of operations (CONOPS) to guide its approach to future missions and operations.

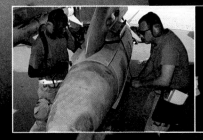

PREPARING FOR FUTURE WARS

THE AIR FORCE EVOLVES TO MEET NEW CHALLENGES

SINCE THE AIR FORCE first emerged in the days of the Army Air Service in 1918, its mission has expanded dramatically. Rapid technological breakthroughs have helped bring about the Air Force's evolution from defender of the skies, to protector of sky and space, to protector of sky, space, and cyberspace. As Air Force Chief of Staff General John P. Jumper and Secretary of the Air Force James G. Roche wrote in a 2004 paper titled *The US Air Force Transformation Flight Plan*, "[It] is essential that we remain focused on how we intend to shape our force so it is poised for the future, not for the century of World Wars and Cold Wars we left behind. We need to develop strategies and CONOPS [Concepts of Operations] appropriate for this new era and rethink our doctrinal approaches to organizing, training, and equipping."

Just as technology is ever developing, wars and warfare must reflect that change. Part of the Air Force's adaptation to twenty-first century war and conflict will involve flexibility. The service must be able to "fight and win [everything] from a major conflict to small-scale contingencies and in every phase of a campaign," wrote Jumper and Roche in their joint report. In addition, the Air Force has formed Cyberspace Command to meet new technological threats, both offensively and defensively. Perhaps most significant, the service has drawn up six new CONOPS to guide Air Force war strategies.

To decide how to meet the challenges of the future, it's often helpful to draw on lessons from the past—in this case, lessons learned thus far in the ongoing Global War on Terror (GWOT). The GWOT has taught the Air Force to prepare to meet many different challenges, including those posed by technologically advanced enemies. The Air Force must be on alert 24/7, combine its efforts with those of the other US military branches, and work more often with coalition partners. Specifically, the Air Force recognizes the following:

1. America's enemies are not what they used to be. During World War II, the country knew it had to defeat the armies of Germany, Japan, and Italy. Today's foes are more nebulous;

they are terrorists who often claim no homeland, resort to suicide attacks, train in remote desert camps, and ultimately aim to lay their hands on weapons of mass destruction (WMDs) to attack the West. The United States' old standby—nuclear deterrence—is of limited use in these scenarios. The Air Force must devise new ways to deter these nontraditional adversaries.

2. Potential adversaries around the world have access to new technologies—everything from Intelligence-Surveillance-Reconnaissance (ISR) to WMDs. For instance, as Iran and North Korea are trying to develop nuclear arsenals, China is pouring billions of dollars into expanding its military. In fact, China shot down one of its own weather satellites in 2007, a move that proved it had weapons capabilities that could reach into space. When it comes to technology, the United States is no longer necessarily leaps and bounds ahead of other countries.

3. Now that flight is commonplace and cyber attacks can be launched from anywhere in the world with an Internet connection, the United States' geographic isolation is not as great a protection as it used to be. Therefore, the Air Force's role as the country's first line of defense now includes homeland security and cyber detail, as well as overseas duty.

4. With a smaller Air Force presence overseas, the service must develop more-efficient ways to use its personnel and fleet.

5. New circumstances require the Air Force to work in more joint, allied, and coalition operations, which in turn demand greater coordination—interoperability and precise, real-time command and control (C2)—among services and friendly countries.

6. Information travels faster than ever, which compels the Air Force to step up the speed of its intelligence-gathering and decision-making processes so it can strike adversaries before they can attack US positions.

7. Precision is important in twenty-first century warfare to avoid collateral damage.

8. The Air Force's C4ISR (command, control, communications, computers, intelligence, surveillance, and reconnaissance) is vulnerable to cyberattacks. The service must devise ways to secure its information network, which guides everything from C2 to a pilot's target selection. The Air Force created Cyberspace Command to help address this problem.

20TH AIR FORCE SECRETARY
Dr. James G. Roche served as secretary of the Air Force from 2001 until 2005. He is one of the authors of The US Air Force Transformation Flight Plan.

TO SERVE AND PROTECT

Airmen honor the fallen with the flag at half-mast at Ellsworth Air Force Base, South Dakota, on May 15, 2008. The Global War on Terror is a daily reminder of the sacrifices made by service members over the decades and those who serve today.

A NEW COMMAND
Then-Secretary of the Air Force Michael Wynne tells an audience at the Pentagon in 2007 that Cyberspace Command will temporarily call Louisiana home. In 2006 he announced that the Eighth Air Force would take on the work of the Air Force's newest command.

Cyberspace Command

The GWOT has demonstrated how dangerous it would be to ignore cyberspace, when groups such as al Qaeda recruit suicide bombers over the Internet. Therefore, cyberspace—a virtual place where information is stored, such as on computer networks—is the newest addition to the Air Force's realm of responsibility. In 2005 the Air Force released a revised mission statement, which said that the service's duty is "the defense of the United States of America and its global interests—to fly and fight in air, space, and cyberspace."

In 2006 Secretary of the Air Force Michael Wynne announced the formation of Air Force Cyberspace Command to deal with threats posed by hackers, terrorists, and criminals who use the Internet to further their schemes. If any one of these three groups were to gain access to a US military computer network or file, it could disrupt communication lines between commanders and their troops. "Our ability to fight in ground, sea, air, and space depends on communications that could be attacked through cyberspace," Secretary Wynne said. He added that the "cost of entry into the cyberspace domain is low," meaning that anyone wishing to harm the United States now has an easy way to do so.

Islamist terrorists are not the only potential enemies who abuse cyberspace. Criminals use the Global Positioning System (GPS) to arrange drug

drops. Hackers pose dangers, too. For instance, in 2007, hackers from China's People's Liberation Army broke into Pentagon networks as well as British and German government networks. Their goal, experts assume, was to scour for military and trade secrets and test the networks' vulnerabilities.

In his speeches, Secretary Wynne has discussed the possibility of cyberwarfare. "One rough-and-ready demonstration that cyberspace is a true domain on a par with land, air, space, and sea is to apply the basic questions of the principles of war," he said in a 2006 address. "For example, can one mass forces in cyber? Yes. Does surprise give an advantage in cyber? Of course. Simplicity? Economy of force? Clarity of objective? Yes, yes, and yes." Since cyberwarfare adheres to the standard principles of war, it logically follows that the Air Force can apply standard defensive and offensive procedures to counter cyberattacks and to launch cyberstrikes.

Cyberplans

The Eighth Air Force became the new Air Force Cyberspace Command in November 2006, and the Air Force is mapping out career paths for Airmen who wish to enter it. The command's goals are to:
1. Protect cyberspace
2. Make sure commanders have full access to all battlefield information available through cyberspace
3. Carry out offensive missions in cyberspace
4. Support reconnaissance missions.

What would an offensive cyberspace mission look like? It might be an effort to destroy an enemy's power grid, since without power, enemy field commanders would not get orders to their troops, radar would not spot approaching US fighters and bombers, and the enemy would not interfere with US lines of communications.

Computer viruses are another weapon in the US cyberspace arsenal. Airmen could infect an enemy's computer systems and cripple its ability to wage war, but the Air Force can also use cyberspace for constructive purposes, such as training. Pilots can practice combat scenarios in a simulator, which is a piece of computerized equipment offering virtual experiences. Using the simulator, a pilot can "fly" through a severe thunderstorm or enemy fire without having to go through the real experience. As oil becomes a more precious commodity, simulators have an added benefit—they conserve fuel. A final advantage is that they reduce wear on aircraft.

Concepts of Operations

Concepts of Operations (CONOPS) are another important aspect of the Air Force in the twenty-first century. While Cyber Command is specifically focused on cyberspace, CONOPS are warfare doctrines that affect all Air Force commands. According to *Air Force Magazine Online*, CONOPS have usually been tactical, affecting narrow missions. The *US Air Force Transformation Flight Plan* provides a helpful definition. It states that "the term Air Force CONOPS has a very specific purpose: clearly convey how air and space power capabilities should be used as instruments of national military power." That is, the service must figure out how to use its strengths—aircraft, satellites, unmanned aerial vehicles (UAVs), unmanned combat air vehicles (UCAVs), advanced technology, and Airmen—to meet

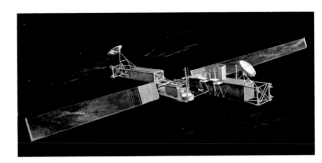

THE AIR FORCE TOOLBOX
The Air Force has many tools at its disposal to fulfill its obligations under the six new CONOPS. Satellites, such as this Milstar satellite that supports secure communications for joint forces operating in war, are one such piece of equipment.

its mission. The explanation continues, "The Air Force CONOPS are not independent forces in and of themselves (i.e., there will not be physical entities dedicated to particular CONOPS). Rather, the necessary capabilities and assets for any given CONOPS...will evolve to best meet the needs of the Combatant Commanders." In other words, CONOPS are not written for specific commands; they belong to the entire Air Force and are meant to be used across the Air Force as a way to approach any mission, operation, or problem. This includes everything from planning an operation to weapons acquisition to budget decisions. Furthermore, CONOPs will guide the Air Force's actions in joint operations with other services and coalition partners.

In their *Flight Plan* paper, Roche and Jumper put the importance of CONOPs in context: "For those of us charged with protecting the United States, new national security realities have forced us to redefine our enemies as well as our concepts of defense," they wrote. "As we prepare to fight these new enemies, we recognize the campaigns of the future will involve all elements of our nation's might—economic, diplomatic, information, investigative, and military power—and will require us to develop new CONOPS, technologies, and organizational constructs that will enable us to address these new challenges. It is these new challenges, as well as historic opportunities to exploit revolutionary technology, that underscore the absolute necessity of transforming our military capabilities."

CYBERSPACE COMMAND: THE EARLY STAGES
Cyberspace Command will help the Air Force protect its C4ISR from hackers and other cyberattackers. Here, Airmen update antivirus software at Cyber Command's temporary headquarters in Louisiana.

The most recent CONOPS are based on lessons learned from the GWOT. Within that framework, this chapter focuses on six fairly new CONOPS that are strategic and that have an impact on the Air Force's overall mission. They are:

- Homeland Security
- Space and C4ISR
- Global Mobility
- Global Strike
- Global Persistent Attack
- Nuclear Response.

Secretary Roche labeled these six CONOPS "the foundation" on which the Air Force intends to transform itself. Each will define a problem to be solved, specify the desired outcome, spell out the assets needed to resolve the problem, and address problems and answers in terms of joint operations with other US services or with coalition partners.

Homeland Security CONOPS

The Homeland Security CONOPS addresses three problems: 1) defending the United States through air and space power by coordinating with other US agencies, while abiding by US laws regarding the use of military force within the country; 2) responding to requests from local, state, and federal agencies without sapping the Air Force's strength to engage in combat; and 3) making sure

the Air Force remains capable of meeting demands overseas while fulfilling homeland security duties. Homeland Security CONOPS includes only missions within US territories or within 500 miles (805km) of its shores (a region also referred to as *littorals*).

The United States is particularly difficult to protect from a terrorist attack because of its large borders and its societal tradition of freedom of travel. The Air Force must prepare itself to meet all kinds of dangers—from CBRNE (chemical, biological, radiological, nuclear, and explosive) agents that may be smuggled into the country to cyberattacks to psychological attacks. At the same time, because homeland security is a domestic mission, any Air Force activity in support of it must occur within the US law. For instance, the 1878 Posse Comitatus Act limits military activities within the United States. This law was enacted to protect the country from a military takeover. It defines how the military services may disperse their forces and ISR assets around the country.

The Homeland Security CONOPS draws its objectives from the Department of Homeland Security's *National Strategy for Homeland Security*. The goals are to: 1) prevent terrorist attacks within the United States; 2) reduce America's vulnerability to terrorism; and 3) minimize damage and recover from attacks that do occur.

ON GUARD
An F-16 Fighting Falcon on patrol. Since 9/11, the F-16 has been a major part of Operation Noble Eagle, safeguarding the US homeland.

The Homeland Security CONOPS whittles these points down to three simple orders for the Air Force—*prevent*, *protect*, and *respond*.

To prevent attacks against the United States, the Air Force must be able to deter, detect, predict, and preempt threats to the homeland, particularly those that target friendly resources through air and space. When the country is operating under elevated threat levels, the Air Force must protect such things as critical infrastructure, as defined by the Department of Defense and the National Security Council; the continuity of government; and key national resources. In extreme cases, the Air Force may resort to its Air Sovereignty Alert network (a network meant to maintain control of US airspace), missile defense, its unique capabilities to disarm or disable CBRNE weapons, and precision conventional strikes within the United States or its littorals.

One way the Air Force currently safeguards American soil is through Operation Noble Eagle, which began shortly after the 9/11 attacks. Within the first 16 months of operation, US aircraft flew more than 27,000 sorties over American cities to look for suspicious aircraft. Fighters such as the F-15 Eagle and the F-16 Fighting Falcon shoot flares if they find an aircraft flying in prohibited space, such as over the White House. If an aircraft manages to penetrate banned airspace, Air Force fighters have the right to shoot it down if it does not respond to warnings.

Space and C4ISR CONOPS

This CONOPS' purpose is to identify and define the space and C4ISR assets that the Air Force needs to fulfill its duties. As with all CONOPS, the missions might be joint, coalition, or small-theater operations, as well as full-scale war. For this reason, the Air Force must develop a mix of tools and select those needed for the particular mission. This CONOPS also oversees research and development into advanced space, counterspace, information operations, C2 battle management, and C4ISR systems to achieve more-accurate precision attacks and a shorter sensor-to-shooter kill chain. Ultimately, the Space and C4ISR CONOPS pushes for greater strategic, operational, and tactical abilities that can engage in any necessary activity around the world. They should deliver timely intelligence to C2 so commanders can dominate the battlefield in any

PROTECTING UNITED STATES SOIL
This F-22A Raptor, the first of its type to take part in Operation Noble Eagle, takes off from Langley Air Force Base, Virginia, on January 21, 2008.

SCANNING AFGHANISTAN
An MQ-9 Reaper gets a preflight check from an aircrew before a mission over Afghanistan. This UAV can conduct reconnaissance as well as attack targets.

operation and protect Airmen, Soldiers, Sailors, Marines, and noncombatants.

Ideally, ISR keeps commanders and their personnel up to speed with a constantly changing battlefront. For instance, a UAV can alert a pilot that a mobile target has changed locations. In addition, ISR relies on manned and unmanned aircraft and on air, space, surface, and subsurface sensors. To maintain a complete picture of the battlefield, ISR requires that all services and coalition partners involved in an operation share information as well as battle plans. All this information comes together to create something called "Predictive Battlespace Awareness." Intelligence operators use Predictive Battlespace Awareness to decipher an adversary's intentions, capabilities, goals, and potential

courses of action, which in turn allows commanders to seize and maintain the initiative against a foe.

Global Mobility CONOPS

Global Mobility CONOPS is all about speed. It directs the Air Force to be prepared to rapidly deploy US military forces anywhere in the world. A quick, effective response to a crisis reduces instability and gives the adversary less time to mount a defense or offense, thereby cutting down on the number of US and allied casualties. Rapid mobilization also plays a key role in small-scale conflicts and humanitarian relief operations.

The Air Force has four ways to achieve its Global Mobility CONOPS goal:
1. Power projection through the Air Mobility Command (AMC). Organized in 1992, the AMC operates in the continental United States (CONUS), overseas, and in all operational theaters. Its airlift and refueling capabilities are indispensable to any operation. Without the capability to project (that is, deploy) forces, there is no conventional deterrent. While the number of US forces stationed overseas continues to decline, global interests remain, making the unique capabilities only AMC can provide even more in demand. AMC assets can refuel Air Force, Navy, Marine and allied aircraft.
2. Power projection through global command and control. This avenue demands advance planning by all US services to respond to a crisis in minimum time. The planning should include deployment, employment, sustainment, and redeployment.

3. Power projection through expeditionary air bases. The Air Force must be able to open a base and establish air operations anywhere and under any conditions, including environments in which CBRNE agents are present. It must also be able to mesh its work with that of other forces, such as the Army, Marine Corps, and Special Operations Forces. It should be able to handle smooth transitions from one stage to another—from airfield seizure to base opening, force employment and sustainment along with other mobility forces, and rapid redeployment.

4. Power projection through space mobility. Space mobility depends on space superiority. Therefore, the Air Force must ensure its satellites are able to move about as needed in space. It must also be able to quickly deploy and sustain space-based forces.

In summary, the Global Mobility CONOPS supports global command, control, and communications; air refueling; airlift; opening and establishing air bases; space-lift operations; and extending space operations. Doing all this requires speed, flexibility, and precision.

Global Strike CONOPS

The primary functions of Global Strike CONOPS are to take out high-value targets and pave the way for the main body of an attack. This doctrine comes into play in the early stages of a conflict. Initial strikes may include neutralizing an

adversary's defensive (antiaccess) systems, such as radar, surface-to-air missiles (SAMs), and C2. This approach relies heavily on long-range systems that can act within hours or even minutes. Sea, air, land, space, and cyberspace units do all they can to prepare the battlefield before massing their theater forces for an attack.

For smaller-scale strikes, the Global Strike CONOPS provides the assets to rapidly attack high-value targets without warning, anywhere

on the globe. A campaign against enemy antiaccess systems may or may not precede these operations. In addition, most smaller campaigns do not require a follow-up assault.

One of the biggest obstacles the Air Force may encounter during a Global Strike operation is lack of access to forward bases. Current or potential allies may deny the United States access to forward bases for political reasons, such as not wanting to get caught in the middle of a conflict between the United States and another country. A second challenge is the condition of some of the bases. The airstrips, for example, may be unpaved or rough. Additional friction may come from the absence of an easily definable enemy (i.e., terrorists with no obvious homeland) and uncertainty over who will or will not join a coalition for the operation.

The Global Strike CONOPS has two goals:
1. Access: Gain and maintain air and space superiority to open the way for joint force operations.

AN AIRBORNE FUEL STATION
The Air Mobility Command figures large in the Global Mobility CONOPS. Here, an F-15 Eagle gets ready to fill up, courtesy of a KC-135 Stratotanker.

AIMING HIGH
Airmen load a GBU-31 precision-guided bomb onto an F-16 Fighting Falcon for Operation Iraqi Freedom. Global Strike CONOPS calls for hitting high-value targets in the early stages of an operation to lessen the risks before the bulk of the forces enter a theater.

2. Rapid global response: Quickly neutralize an adversary's key, high-value targets.

A Global Strike mission requires five assets:
1. Precision, long-range, quick-reaction air- and space-based strike platforms that can operate in an antiaccess environment to jumpstart an operation.
2. Networked C4ISR to locate targets, manage the battle space, and assess damage.
3. Land forces and Special Operations Forces to enter the battlefield early to protect ports and airfields and to help find, fix, track, and destroy targets.
4. The ability to apply intelligence, cyber, and electromagnetic (electronic countermeasures such as radar jamming) tools in all phases of a crisis.
5. Counterair operations, with an emphasis on joint missile defense.

A FORCE TO BE RECKONED WITH
The F-15E Strike Eagle is among the aircraft that would play a part in any Global Persistent Attack CONOPS operation.

Global Persistent Attack CONOPS

After a commander has entered a conflict using the guidelines from the Global Strike CONOPS, the next step is to apply the Global Persistent Attack CONOPS to the battlefield. Future US conflicts will most likely be with rogue states and terrorists, rather than with stable nations. Therefore, the main purpose of the Global Persistent Attack CONOPS is to restore stability—although this CONOPS directs that the Air Force also always be ready to engage regional powers with major combat operations. This CONOPS can also address peacekeeping missions and sustainment operations; that is, supplying personnel with food, fuel, ammunition, and other necessities.

The Global Persistent Attack CONOPS sets the following goals:
1. Information dominance. In short, collect, control, exploit, attack, and defend information. Share information with other services and coalition

READY, SET, GO...
One of the Air Force's duties under the Global Persistent Attack CONOPS is to make sure joint and coalition forces are fully supplied with fuel, food, and equipment. C-17 Globemasters like those lined up below play a key role in supply efforts.

STAYING SHARP
With its ability to carry nuclear arms or conventional arms, the B-52 can easily fulfill the dual roles recommended under the Nuclear Response CONOPS.

partners, disperse it to personnel in the field in real time, and attempt to blind the enemy's attempts to gather intelligence.

2. Freedom to maneuver. Make sure joint and coalition forces can attack targets at will and from advantageous positions.

3. Persistent force application. Supply joint and coalition forces with all the tools they will need for the battlefield—that is, fuel, munitions, personnel, etc.—so they can carry out their mission.

The Global Persistent Attack CONOPS provides joint force commanders with everything they need to conduct long-term combat operations and to achieve victory with minimum loss. This CONOPS first seeks to gather information to make decisions more quickly and more intelligently than the enemy can. Second, by maintaining information, space, and air superiority, joint forces find protection and the freedom to maneuver. Third, well-supplied troops can apply uninterrupted pressure on the enemy. This persistent force places the enemy at a disadvantage. Persistent precision strikes and information operations can influence, manipulate, or dismantle an adversary's ability to act.

Nuclear Response CONOPS

During the Cold War, both the United States and the Soviet Union had nuclear weapons aimed at each other. The threat of MAD (mutually assured destruction) kept each side from any rash action. Today, things are different. Potential adversaries may be terrorists with no homeland that MAD can threaten. Their aim may be to target forward-deployed US forces, as well as US and allied population centers with CBRNE agents. To address these threats, the United States needs a new deterrent strategy.

The congressionally mandated Nuclear Posture Review, completed in December 2001, spells out such a strategy. It established a "new triad"—nuclear and nonnuclear offensive strike systems, active and passive defenses, and a revitalized defense infrastructure—all bound by enhanced C2 and intelligence. Because it includes conventional weapons, this plan reduces the US dependence on nuclear weapons. At the same time, it recognizes the importance of a nuclear umbrella under which joint conventional forces can operate. Another reason for drawing up a

plan with an increased emphasis on conventional weapons is that the United States is drawing down its nuclear forces following the collapse of the Soviet Union.

However, if deterrence and conventional weapons fail, the Nuclear Response CONOPS can link nuclear strike forces with C2 and intelligence to jointly defeat the enemy through a variety of attack options. Nuclear Response CONOPS relies on joint ISR, joint nuclear C2, joint nuclear strike forces, and joint support forces.

With the help of these six CONOPS, the Air Force can adapt to present and future threats and use all the powerful tools at its disposal to their maximum effect. Applied correctly, the CONOPS should also reduce casualties. The United States is a superpower, with the most advanced military in the world, yet its officers and personnel need guidance, just as any force does. The six CONOPS, along with Cyberspace Command and an appreciation of the principles of war, doctrine, and lessons learned from past wars, are good starting points for facing twenty-first century challenges.

AIR AND SPACE POWER REVIEW

THE AIR FORCE HAS COME a long way since the Army Signal Corps launched its Aeronautical Division with one captain and two enlisted men. Aviation has developed from a single man steering a flimsy wood-and-fabric craft by shifting his hips to the F-22 Raptor. From a secondary role in World War I, airpower became a decisive factor by World War II, and in some cases in the late twentieth century, the decisive factor. Air superiority has become everything in conventional warfare: No army or navy can even consider fighting successfully without adequate air cover. Yet the nature of warfare is ever changing, and the Air Force must change along with it.

FLYING FISH
Army Captain Harry Gwynne and his decorated Nieuport Plane, "The Flying Fish," in France. In 1912 this plane was the first aircraft fitted with a permanently installed machine gun. Nieuport 11s and 17s were used in World War I by the French and the American Expeditionary Forces as well as by the air forces of Russia, Belgium, Italy, and Britain.

AIRPOWER CHANGED THE NATURE OF WAR; WAR CHANGED THE USES OF AIRPOWER

AMONG THE LESSONS LEARNED: AIR SUPERIORITY IS ESSENTIAL; THE AIR FORCE MUST ADAPT AND EVOLVE

THE TWENTIETH CENTURY was the century of flight, when humanity at last learned how to use the third dimension. This remarkable technological and social transformation began with the Wright brothers' famed flight on December 17, 1903. That day, Orville Wright got the *Wright Flyer* into the air for 12 seconds and traveled 120ft (37m), barely half the wingspan of a C-5B Galaxy. Since that chilly and blustery morning, Air Force personnel have circled the globe nonstop, landed on the moon, successfully fought in wars and conflicts, and carried out humanitarian missions, all while exploiting incredible technologies. Revolutionary advances in flight continue to profoundly influence the United States Air Force and make it the only truly global air force in the world.

In centuries past, armies and navies sought height to control surrounding surface areas. Armies aimed to hold the high ground, and navies built ships with large masts and lookout positions to watch for enemy fleets. During the medieval period, experimenters hoisted observers aloft in kites. The invention of the balloon in 1783 allowed armies and navies to conduct the first aerial surveillance. Despite the advantages these

DAREDEVIL DOOLITTLE
James Doolittle, wearing a flying suit and parachute, refuels the center wing tank of his Laird Super Solution racing plane. Doolittle went down in history for making the first blind flight. He flew a 15 mile (24km) irregular course in a Consolidated NY-2 biplane before landing safely.

fragile forms of air capability gave armies and navies, land and sea forces still had to gain victory through short-range power projection, such as infantry that advanced sometimes only a few yards at a time. World War I is an excellent example of a war won a few feet at a time at a terrible price, as millions died in the trenches. Those who believed in airpower vowed aircraft could lessen the pain by shortening conflicts and reducing the slaughter on the battlefield.

The Air Force's evolution

In the years since 1907, when the US Army Signal Corps established its Aeronautical Division to take charge of ballooning and air machines, military aviation in the United States has evolved from an auxiliary of the Army into the independent United States Air Force. An organization that began with one captain and two enlisted men peaked in 1944 with more than 2 million personnel, dipped below 400,000 in the years immediately following World War II, and expanded for the Korean and Vietnam wars and the most intense periods of the Cold War. So far in the twenty-first century, the Air Force maintains somewhat more than 300,000 active duty Airmen. The old Signal Corps headquarters has developed into a carefully organized institution with a secretary of the Air Force, a chief of staff, appropriate staff support, and major commands and operating agencies organized according to function.

A single thread unified these many changes—a commitment to the development, acquisition, and use of aircraft as a weapon of war. The flimsy, fabric-covered aircraft used for daytime

EARLY RECONNAISSANCE MISSION
Armies used balloons as early as the eighteenth century to conduct reconnaissance missions over hostile forces. Union forces used this balloon during the Civil War (1861–65).

scouting and courier runs have given way to sleek aircraft built with exotic metals and composite materials. Pilots no longer shoot at one another with pistols and rifles; they now have multibarrel cannons and air-to-air rockets. The hand-dropped bombs of World War I foreshadowed today's laser-guided munitions, and the telescopic bombsight blazed the trail to today's radar. The newest aircraft can fly undetected, exceed the speed of sound, fly in inclement weather and at night, and deliver tons of deadly weapons in a single flight.

Increasing technological sophistication has its advantages, but it comes with burdens as well. The price tag for aircraft development has risen steadily with each technological step forward. While the *Wright Flyer* cost $30,000, a single aircraft can now cost hundreds of millions to design and build. Sophistication has introduced other inconveniences along with its great benefits. For instance, in 1919 Major Theodore C. Macauley could take out his pocketknife to whittle smooth a wooden propeller's damaged surface, but to maintain and repair an aircraft today requires the same skill and equipment needed to build them. In fact, in 1917 the Army acquired McCook Field in Ohio to conduct research and development into flight. The days rapidly disappeared when a single mechanic could learn how to fix anything that might go wrong with an aircraft. Today's aircraft mechanics must specialize and constantly train to maintain their proficiency. It took the Wright brothers only a few weeks to teach officers to fly, but now aircraft are so complex that pilots must go through flight school. The Air Force even sends some of its officers to the elite Massachusetts Institute of Technology (MIT) to learn aircraft engineering.

Since the Air Force is such a large and important part of the defense of the United States, its officers must be able to do more than fly skillfully and understand the basic principles of aircraft design. Therefore, in addition to engineering programs, the Air Force developed a system of professional military education schools to teach everything from routine administration to warfare aviation principles. The most celebrated of these was the Air Corps Tactical School, which produced a doctrine of strategic air warfare in the 1930s for accurate, long-range, daylight bombing to destroy an enemy's war-making potential. Many personnel who became leaders during World War II were either teachers or students at this school. After achieving independence in 1947, the Air Force grouped the different professional schools under the Air University and established a service academy to educate career officers.

The aircraft: bombers and fighters

Since its inception, the heart of the Air Force has remained its aircraft. The Army's Barling bomber set altitude and endurance records in 1924 while carrying loads of three or four tons. That same year, an Army transport flew nonstop across the United States, and two of four aircraft that set out to fly around the world completed the 175-day trip. It is no wonder that Airmen like Brigadier General Billy Mitchell trusted that technology could convert aircraft into fighting machines capable of crushing an enemy's morale and military industry.

In the 1930s, advances came from both commercial and military engineers. Inventions such as cantilever construction, load-bearing stressed-metal skin, streamlining, wing flaps, and retractable landing gear served both arenas. The technological cross-fertilization bore even more fruit. For example, Boeing's single-engine Monomail transport inspired the twin-engine, open-cockpit Y1B-9 bomber, which in turn taught lessons that engineers applied to the basic Model 247 transport with two engines and an enclosed cabin and cockpit. As another example, after using wing flaps to reduce the landing speed of its P-26 pursuit aircraft, Boeing adapted them to Model 247D, its most successful commercial aircraft in that series. Similarly, the Boeing 314 seaplane owed a debt to the XB-15 bomber prototype, while the Model 307 transport borrowed from the B-17.

In 1934 the Army introduced the P-26, its first low-wing, all-metal, monoplane pursuit aircraft. Even with wing flaps, the P-26 represented a bridge between the old technology and the new. It kept the open cockpit, which fighter pilots preferred over the confining Plexiglas-enclosed greenhouse; an externally braced wing; and a fixed, though streamlined, landing gear. As the 1930s progressed, fighter designs improved. Enclosed cockpits (unpopular though they were), retractable landing gear, cantilever construction, and the new liquid-cooled Allison engine streamlined the pursuit aircraft so the twin-engine P-38 and the single-engine P-39 and P-40 could outrace even the fastest bombers.

As aircraft design after World War I made impressive technological leaps that opened long-distance travel as never before, the American people reverted to an isolationist stance, which saw little reason to invest in the military or take an interest in what happened overseas. After the terrors of trench warfare, the last thing the public wanted was to get embroiled in yet another messy European war. This meant the air service not only faced technological hurdles to build better bombers and pursuits, it also had to persuade the public that spending money to

MODEL AIRCRAFT
This P-26A reproduction is painted to represent the commander's aircraft of the 19th Pursuit Squadron, 18th Pursuit Group, stationed at Wheeler Field, Hawaii, in 1938.

MARAUDER
A Martin B-26 medium bomber parked on the tarmac in 1941.

develop aircraft was in the country's interest. Despite negative public headwinds, Airmen such as General Mitchell pushed hard to develop bigger and better bombers to support strategic air warfare—defined as the decisive use of military aviation against an enemy's heartland. Since there was little chance of convincing the public of an offensive force's worth, airpower boosters framed their argument for aircraft, like the bomber, in defensive terms. They built their case around the idea that the bomber would be the perfect defensive weapon if an invading fleet headed for US coasts.

Behind the defense argument, however, Mitchell and his followers believed aircraft, particularly the bomber, could be an awesome offensive weapon. Even if a hostile country had

PRIMITIVE DELIVERY
Before anyone imagined such a weapon as the precision-guided bomb, pilots dropped bombs by hand from open cockpits during World War I as this German pilot is doing.

overwhelming land and naval forces, airpower could conquer them. For this reason, airpower advocates pushed for an independent air force, equal to the Army and Navy. The Army opposed this move, fearing that if it lost its air arm, the service would also lose its close air support, surveillance, and interdiction capabilities.

It would take World War II to prove how essential airpower was to victory in any modern campaign; only then would the Army's air arm gain its independence. Fortunately, the War Department agreed to continue funding aircraft development for strategic bombing campaigns despite the politics in the years leading up to World War II. In 1935 Boeing introduced the B-17 Flying Fortress, which flew faster than most fighters and seemed to have enough firepower to blast its way to distant industrial targets. Consolidated Aircraft completed the B-24 Liberator by 1938, and North American Aviation had the B-25 Mitchell in the air by 1940. US factories were mass-producing most of these bombers by 1941. Boeing's B-29 Superfortress made its first flight in 1942, and the Martin B-26 Marauder went into combat the same year.

The buildup to World War II

As the Army Air Forces built up some muscle despite opposition at home, Germany, Japan, and Italy were forming a dangerous alliance. Under Adolf Hitler, Germany rearmed and began a campaign of conquest, beginning with the invasion of Poland in 1939 that triggered World War II. Italian dictator Benito Mussolini led his country into war alongside Germany in 1940, and a military-dominated Japan attacked the US Navy base at Pearl Harbor on December 7, 1941, trying to cripple US naval power long enough for Tokyo to seize the natural resources needed to dominate the western Pacific, particularly China.

The B-17 and other long-range bombers, like the B-24 and B-29, inspired a group of Army Air Forces planners to draft a proposal in mid-1941 for defeating Germany by aerial bombardment. Their strategy, if the United States went to war, was to

WISE INVESTMENTS
The War Department funded research and development into strategic bombers in the 1930s and 1940s. One of the aircraft developed was the B-24 Liberator, which was employed in every combat theater during World War II.

GUARD DUTY
The P-51 began escorting bombers over Germany in 1943. This tough pursuit aircraft dramatically cut the loss of bombers during World War II.

defeat Hitler first. The Airmen believed that American bombers could fight their way deep into Germany and, using the Norden bombsight, destroy 154 industrial or transportation facilities that would knock Germany out of the war.

As it turned out, strategic bombing bludgeoned German war industries to death, rather than killing them swiftly and cleanly. The bombing was far less accurate than expected, in part because the Norden bombsight could not see through the prevailing cloud cover over northern Europe. Radar helped, but even that was problematic when bombing cluttered urban areas. In addition, the air offensive gained

momentum slowly. US industry had to build the aircraft, and the Army had to transport the bombers and pursuits to England as well as train crews. The United States did not drop bombs on Germany until January 1943, and even then, unescorted bombers suffered dismaying losses. Not until the North American P-51 Mustang started accompanying the bombers could the Allies wrest control of the daytime skies from the German Luftwaffe or the strategic bombing campaign begin the systematic destruction of vital industries like oil production and transportation.

Airpower shaped the war in the Pacific as well, from the assault on Pearl Harbor to the atomic bombing of Hiroshima and Nagasaki. Common images from this air war included duels between

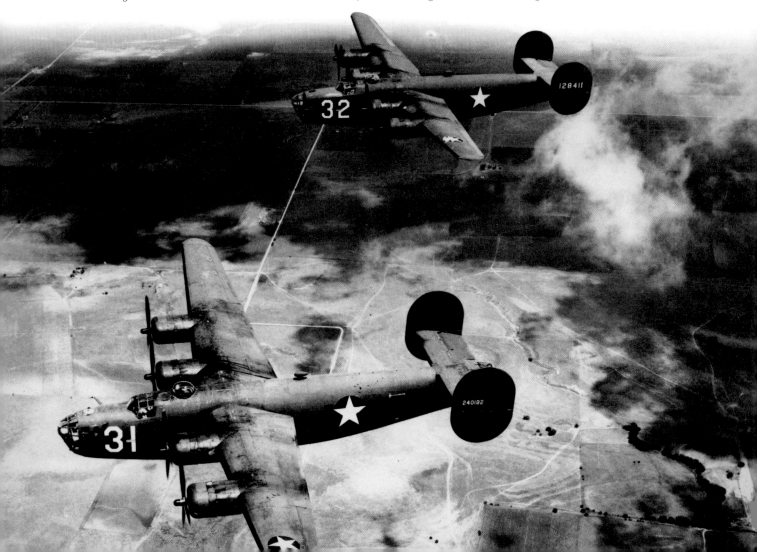

MOTHER SHIP
A B-29 bomber carries the experimental Bell XS-1, in which Chuck Yeager broke the sound barrier, under its belly. B-29 raids over Japan during World War II convinced at least one Japanese official that the war was lost.

carrier-based aircraft and firebomb raids on Japan. Much of the fighting in the Pacific focused on seizing air bases—such as the Mariana Islands—so the United States could launch air strikes against Japan. Because of the vast distances in the Pacific region, any sustained strategic bombing of Japan had to wait on a suitable aircraft, the B-29, as well as available island bases. Aerial supply runs over the Himalayan "hump" also played a critical role in keeping China effective in the war against Japan.

When strategic air attacks began against Japan, some Japanese military leaders realized the war was lost. Premier Kantaro Suzuki said, "It seemed to me unavoidable that in the long run Japan would be almost destroyed by air attack so that merely on the basis of the B-29s alone I was convinced that Japan should sue for peace. On top of the B-29 raids came the atomic bomb…which was just one additional reason for

> "It seemed to me unavoidable that in the long run Japan would be almost destroyed by air attack so that merely on the basis of the B-29s alone I was convinced that Japan should sue for peace.
>
> JAPANESE PREMIER KANTARO SUZUKI

giving in.… I myself, on the basis of the B-29 raids, felt that the cause was hopeless."

Airpower's demonstrated effectiveness during World War II convinced even the most skeptical observers that the Army's air element deserved independence. General Dwight D. Eisenhower said that "no sane man" could contest this thinking any longer. In 1947 President Harry S. Truman signed the National Security Act that established a Department of the Air Force and the National Military Establishment (today's Department of Defense), among other institutions. It was clear that a unified defense establishment and an independent Air Force were necessary for national security in the nuclear age.

Some post-World War II airpower lessons

One month later, after Truman signed the act, Air Force Captain Charles E. "Chuck" Yeager and the

Bell XS-1—an experimental aircraft—broke the sound barrier. The Air Force was a creature of the supersonic revolution as well as of the atomic era. These two prisms tended to limit the way the Air Force viewed itself, and these perspectives would haunt the service—first in Korea, then in Vietnam, and for some time thereafter.

A NEW KIND OF REVOLUTION
Captain Charles Yeager (left) broke the sound barrier in 1947 while flying the experimental Bell XS-1. The Air Force had entered the age of supersonic flight.

AIRPOWER CLEARS THE WAY
General H. Norman Schwarzkopf turned to airpower during Operation Desert Storm in advance of any ground conflicts. An A-10A Thunderbolt takes part in the air campaign during the early-1991 war.

Vietnam taught the US military, especially the Air Force, some costly lessons. All too often during the Vietnam War, the US government used airpower, not to achieve a desired military effect, but to send political messages. Leaders issued orders to avoid harming Soviet and Chinese advisers, thus sparing hostile troops in the same region. Officers and enlisted personnel vowed "never again" to fight a war in this limited way, and this mindset proved an important catalyst for vital changes in military doctrine, policy, leadership, and training in the 1970s and 1980s. It also set the stage for the successful conclusion of the Cold War and Desert Storm.

Some tactics from Vietnam bore repeating, however. Two campaigns highlighted the value of the air arm: the use of airpower to defeat the North Vietnamese spring invasion in 1972 (Linebacker I), and the application of airpower to force North Vietnam to seek serious peace at the end of the year (Linebacker II). These operations were aggressive and swift. Unfortunately, in the years following Linebacker II, national resolve to support the South Vietnamese government flagged, so what had been accomplished in the air and on the land in Vietnam withered in the face of renewed Communist advances. The Saigon government ultimately collapsed in 1975.

BACKBONE
The Navy-developed McDonnell F-4 Phantom II was a key part of the Air Force in the 1960s and 1970s.

Within a year of independence, the Air Force took the lead role in the country's first serious confrontation with the Soviet Union: the Berlin airlift. This confrontation did not involve supersonic flight or much in the way of exchanging fire, although America's atomic capability likely helped keep the situation under control. In Berlin, the speed and flexibility of airlift thwarted the Soviets' attempt at a hostile takeover. Berlin remained free because Air Force aircrews, supported by other American and Allied Airmen, managed to supply the city from the air. The pilots and their crews displayed the same determination to reach Berlin that they had over hostile territory in World War II. However, aircrews died this time, not because of flak and fighters, but because of poor flying conditions.

The atomic bomb's fury seemed to vindicate the belief that airpower could win wars by striking a single decisive blow. However, the United States exercised a monopoly over this weapon only briefly; the Soviet Union tested its own bomb in 1949, and by the mid-1950s both countries had the hydrogen bomb. The United States and the Soviet Union resembled two scorpions in a bottle, each capable of killing the other but only in the certain knowledge that both would die. The very destructiveness of nuclear weapons inhibited their use. Therefore, nuclear warheads became a force for stability, a deterrent to all-out war.

For a time, some Air Force leaders like General Nathan Twining (chief of staff from 1953–57) suggested that the threat of nuclear retaliation could deter every kind of warfare. Yet smaller wars and crises continued because the same certainty of mutual destruction that deterred an all-out attack also argued against the use

of nuclear weapons except in the case of national survival. One of the most interesting developments in the nuclear age is the centralized control that civilians in the Department of Defense exercised over the use of nuclear weapons.

War in Korea brought its own challenges, particularly the rediscovery of tactical airpower's value. The application of massive airpower countered the June 1950 North Korean invasion as well as the subsequent Chinese Communist intervention in November of that year. Even in the era before precision munitions, aircraft successfully substituted for an overwhelming ground force and dominated the air so United Nations troops could go about their work without much fear of enemy air attacks. After Korea, aerial refueling allowed airpower to reach great distances and gave them greater flexibility and value.

A sometimes inappropriate fascination for technology and nuclear capabilities in the 1950s and into the 1960s led the Air Force to increasingly turn away from the various scenarios conflicts might take. As a result, the Vietnam War quickly revealed dangerous shortfalls in strategic thinking, leadership, tactics, and weapons development. The service discovered it had to come to grips with air defense networks built around radar-controlled fighters, SAMs, and antiaircraft artillery. Thus the Air Force was forced to acquire three Navy-developed aircraft for the fight in Vietnam: the Douglas A-1 Skyraider counterinsurgency aircraft, the Ling-Temco-Vought A-7 Corsair II light attack aircraft, and the powerful McDonnell F-4 Phantom II multirole fighter, which became the backbone of the Air Force in the 1960s and 1970s.

The war in Southeast Asia was a watershed for the Air Force in many ways. The service relied on experienced veterans during the conflicts in the 1950s and 1960s. Fighter pilots seasoned by combat in World War II were the MiG killers of Korea. The Strategic Air Command built its nuclear deterrent on a force that had flown against Berlin and Tokyo. By the time of Vietnam, these core groups were the senior leaders, but after Vietnam, leadership passed to a new generation. World War II was either a childhood memory or the stuff of history books for the Vietnam-seasoned leaders of Desert Storm, so Desert Storm's success stemmed from hard lessons learned in Southeast Asia.

> "Gulf lesson one is the value of airpower."
>
> PRESIDENT GEORGE H. W. BUSH

Vietnam taught the Air Force the importance of operating strike aircraft in high-threat areas. As a result, the Air Force made several changes. It emphasized realistic training, such as the Red Flag exercises. It also developed technologies, such as precision weapons and enhanced electronic warfare systems to jam radar. Two aircraft came out of these efforts—the McDonnell Douglas F-15, which would help the Air Force achieve air superiority, and the F-16 Fighting Falcon with an all-electronic flight control system. The stealth Lockheed F-117 was also hatched at this time. It was every bit as revolutionary as the all-metal monoplane of the 1930s, the turbojet, and the swept wing that followed. The Air Force also learned that airpower works best when unrestrained by politicized rules of engagement.

Rethinking the Air Force's purpose

During the 1980s, all the military branches revisited their original principles. Creative thinkers rediscovered nineteenth-century military theorist Carl von Clausewitz, who said that the best targets were at the "center of the enemy's gravity." Air Force Colonel John Warden III pushed the theory further because Clausewitz came from an era when only land and naval forces existed. Warden focused on the uniqueness of warfare in the third dimension, with airpower's ability to strike swiftly, decisively, and simultaneously across an enemy's entire spectrum of operations and targets. His study unearthed a growing awareness within the Air Force that thought and doctrine had lagged behind technology. "Strategic" had become synonymous with "nuclear," and "tactical" had come to mean "air support." The revolutionary possibilities of a combined strategic and tactical attack proved themselves during Desert Storm.

In 1990 Secretary of the Air Force Donald B. Rice launched a study of airpower's value and use. The study examined its five innate virtues: speed, range, flexibility, precision, and lethality. Out of these strengths, the study drew five functions: to sustain nuclear deterrence, provide versatile combat forces, supply rapid global mobility, ensure control of the high ground, and guide US international influence. Based on these findings, Rice issued a report titled *Global Reach-Global Power* in June 1990 based on these findings.

Debate ensued, but was limited by the onset of the Gulf crisis in August 1990.

Within days of Operation Desert Shield's launch, airpower thwarted any hopes Iraqi leader Saddam Hussein might have entertained of entering Saudi Arabia. During Operation Desert Storm, theater commander in chief General H. Norman Schwarzkopf used an air campaign to destroy Iraq's offensive potential well in advance of any ground conflict. This operation was the test case for modern airpower in the precision-weapon era. It validated Secretary Rice's stand on the dominance of airpower in war. Critics who believed the value of air forces was only in terms of supporting land armies found their logic undone by the stealth fighters and conventional aircraft that incapacitated Iraq's military. Indeed, the Gulf War, and Operations Northern Watch and Southern Watch, showed military and political leaders how much flexibility air and space power gave them over combat zones. After Desert Storm, President George H. W. Bush said, "Gulf lesson one is the value of airpower."

Conflict in the former Yugoslavia in the 1990s was another occasion for the Air Force to flex its newly found muscles and effectiveness. While the United Nations initially tied airpower's hands for fear of collateral damage, it eventually yielded to pressure from NATO to let Air Force and NATO aircraft do their thing. As Air Force Chief of Staff General Ronald R. Fogleman said of the UN's initial tactic, "To many of us Airmen, it was very reminiscent of what we had seen in Vietnam."

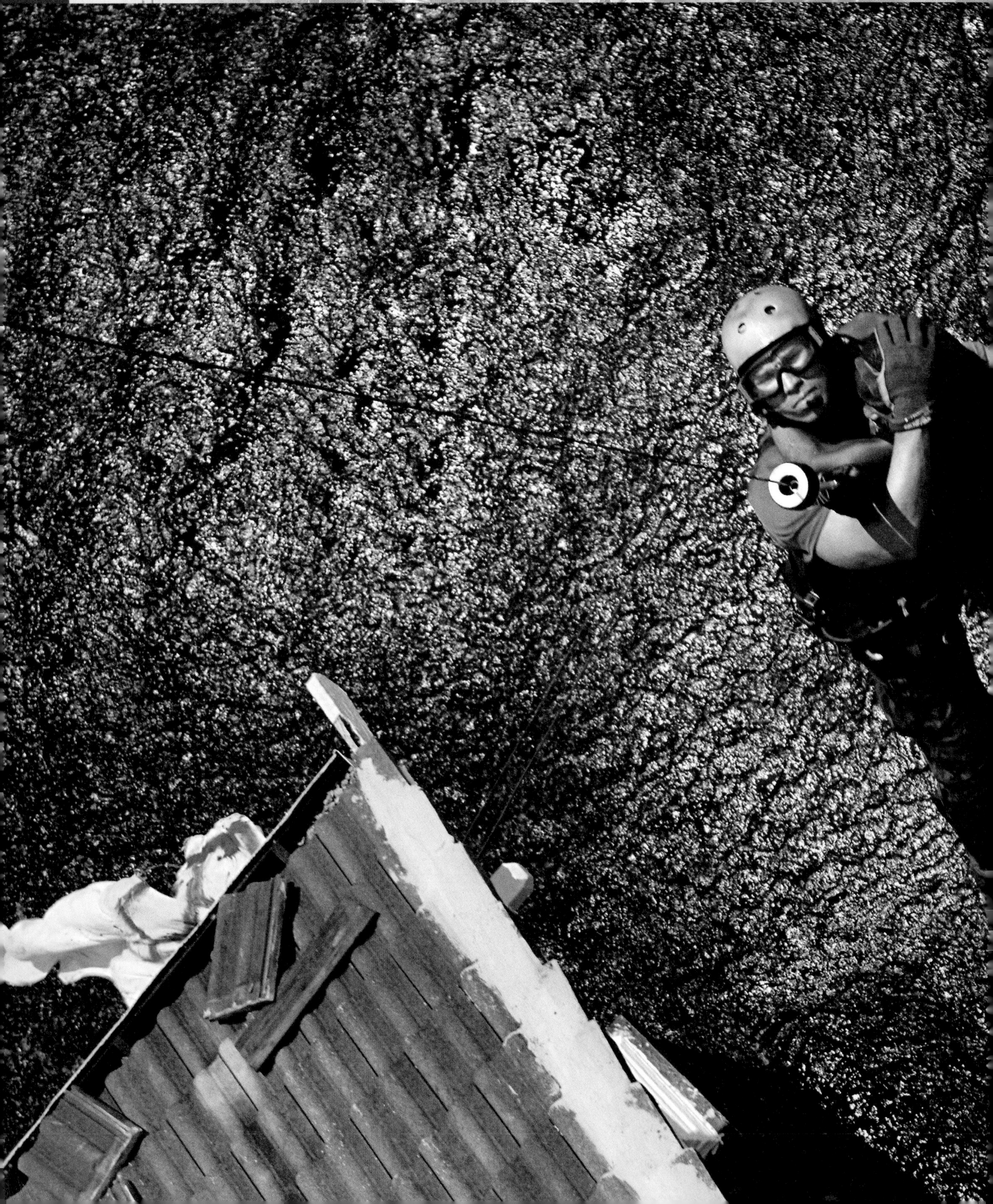

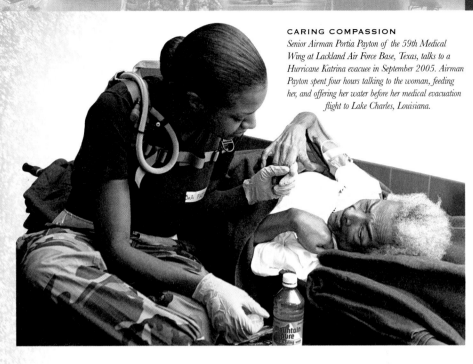

CARING COMPASSION
Senior Airman Portia Payton of the 59th Medical Wing at Lackland Air Force Base, Texas, talks to a Hurricane Katrina evacuee in September 2005. Airman Payton spent four hours talking to the woman, feeding her, and offering her water before her medical evacuation flight to Lake Charles, Louisiana.

Once the UN admitted that the half-hearted application of airpower had produced poor results, the renewed NATO air campaign became a model of how airpower should be used. Precise attacks shattered Bosnian Serb air defenses and allowed precision attacks against other military targets. Eleven days of air attacks involving 3,515 sorties by 293 aircraft from eight countries brought the first hopes for a lasting peace to a region that had seen turmoil since the end of the Cold War. Chastened, the Serbs came to the peace table in Dayton, Ohio.

Ambassador Richard Holbrooke, the assistant secretary of State, commenting on airpower in the former Yugoslavia, said, "One of the great things that people should have learned from this is that there are times when airpower—not backed up by ground troops—can make a difference. That's something that our European allies didn't all agree with; Americans were in doubt on it; [but] it made a difference."

The humanitarian missions

Besides military operations, the Air Force has also grown adept at humanitarian missions. Since 1947 the Air Force has participated in nearly 600 humanitarian relief operations. Some, such as the Berlin airlift, Operation Provide Hope in the former Soviet Union, and Operation Provide Promise in Bosnia-Herzegovina, are well known. Others—responses to plagues, floods, fires, typhoons, hurricanes, volcanic eruptions, and earthquakes—

are far less known, but may have involved an even greater need for speed.

Ironically, after the Soviet Union collapsed, more responsibilities rather than fewer fell on the United States as the sole superpower. Who else has the might, training, and funds to step in on such a grand scale? The biggest Air Force participants in these operations were the airlifters of the Air Mobility Command. In 1993 alone, Air Mobility Command aircrews operated in 96 percent of the world's countries, 186 out of 193 nations, and from 1987 to 1997, the Air Force offered aid in nearly 100 emergencies. Fortunately, the US military has state-of-the-art support systems such as aerial refueling and space-based assets to guide airlifters like the C-17 Globemaster III. These capabilities, coupled with streamlined management and a trim organization, permit the Air Force to assist relief efforts with a previously unattainable efficiency.

HEAVY LIFTER
The C-17 Globemaster helps the Air Force fulfill the humanitarian side of its missions.

HOIST RESCUE
An Air Force chopper lifts Technical Sergeant Lem Torres and a young boy to safety from the roof of the child's flooded home after Hurricane Katrina in September 2005.

Leaner and meaner

In contrast to the Air Force of the 1970s and mid-1980s, the Air Force of the early 1990s was smaller, more tightly organized, and more flexible. It had a clearer perception of its capabilities. It was largely based in the continental United States, as US forces withdrew from abroad.

The Air Force also changed the way it made decisions. While headquarters developed and offered guidance, it was up to field operations to decide how best to execute policy. Above all, the Air Force reinvented itself by returning to basic principles, commonsense structure, clear lines of authority and responsibility, and widespread empowerment of military and civilian personnel at every level.

The number of major commands decreased from 13 to eight. The number of flying squadrons fell from 240 to 205. Even though smaller and reorganized, this Air Force was more capable of fulfilling America's national security needs than at any previous time in its history. It preserved its combat edge, technological superiority, and freedom of action even as it reduced its size and resources.

Once *Global Reach-Global Power* fulfilled its purpose of moving the Air Force toward a new set of strategies, the service came up with a new publication in 1996 titled *Global Engagement*, which laid out a vision for the twenty-first century Air Force. It emphasized joint warfare and the belief that the United States would turn to air and space power to meet most future conflicts. Meeting this challenge would require the Air Force to integrate its air and space assets as never before to achieve air, space, and information superiority; to be able to attack anywhere at any time around the globe; to be capable of rapid global mobility; to carry out precision attacks; and to efficiently meet combat support needs. These core competencies would ensure that the service could continue to meet its primary mission: to defend the United States through control and exploitation of air and space.

FIGHTING SPIRIT
This F-16 Fighting Falcon, winging over Afghanistan for Operation Enduring Freedom, is part of the Air Force's precision-attack arsenal.

challenges. They are: Homeland Security, Space and C4ISR, Global Mobility, Global Strike, Global Persistent Attack, and Nuclear Response. It is doubtful that these will be the Air Force's final answer to GWOT. They are merely the service's first answer to the new environment the United States faces.

The basis for airpower's many achievements in war and peace is its professional force. This force has matured along with the service's increasingly sophisticated arsenal. Today's aircraft and the nature of warfare demand more skill, judgment, and initiative from Airmen than ever before. Although the leather jacket has survived as a symbol of an adventurous era, the individual who wears it now is better trained, more broadly educated, and more widely experienced than the typical flyer of a bygone era, when biplanes cost a few thousand dollars and nuclear weapons were science fiction. While the Air Force will continue to exhibit the same change and evolutionary patterns that have occurred since the introduction of the first military aircraft five years after Kitty Hawk, one characteristic will not—the need for perceptive, dedicated, skilled, and courageous men and women to carry on, extending the proud legacy of the past into the future. Will you be one of them?

The impact of 9/11

Then came the terrorist attacks on September 11, 2001. The Air Force once again had to rethink strategy by studying what lessons the service could learn from the evolving Global War on Terror. The enemy was no longer an obvious target like the Soviet Union of the Cold War, nor was it a European civil war to be halted as in the former Republic of Yugoslavia. Now the enemy was a fleeting shadow. Whom do you attack when the terrorist claims no homeland? In 2004 the Air Force responded with six CONOPS to address these new

EVACUATING THE SICK AND WOUNDED
Army and Air Force rescue helicopters depart on their next mission as part of a massive operation in New Orleans to evacuate victims of Hurricane Katrina in September 2005.

SEARCH AND RESCUE
Technical Sergeant Lem Torres surveys houses in September 2005 looking for victims of Hurricane Katrina in New Orleans.

ECONOMY OF FORCE

GENERAL FOGLEMAN spoke about the new Air Force during an Air Force Association symposium on air warfare in 1996. He said, "The Air Force was the first service to recognize that the post-Cold War era called for a new look at how military force would and could be applied. This was reflected in our strategic vision of *Global Reach-Global Power* that was published in 1990. We used this vision to restructure the Air Force so that we could provide the nation an economy of force capability to execute the National Military Strategy—primarily through the application of asymmetric force. This was a vision that was built on the basis of the new National Security Strategy articulated by President [George H. W.] Bush in the summer of 1990. In short, the end of the Cold War freed up assets previously immersed in the nuclear deterrent mission—bombers, tankers, post-SIOP reconnaissance aircraft, and satellites—allowing the Air Force to be responsive on a conventional, day-to-day basis to the needs of the theater commanders."

ADDITIONAL LESSONS FROM THE WAR ON TERROR

LIKE ALL SERVICES, THE AIR FORCE is studying the lessons the country as a whole has gleaned from the ongoing fight. Among them:

1. Wars in the twenty-first century will increasingly require all assets at a country's disposal: economic, diplomatic, financial, law enforcement, intelligence, and both overt and covert military operations.

2. Joint force operations are the new way to fight wars. The ability of these forces to communicate and operate seamlessly is critical. For instance, teams of US Special Forces on the ground, working with Navy, Air Force, and Marine pilots, have won victories in Afghanistan. These Special Forces identify targets and coordinate the timing of air strikes through common communications links, all with devastating effect on the enemy.

3. Coalitions must also work together to fight wars. However, they must avoid fighting wars by committee, as was done by the United Nations during the early days of the conflict in the former Republic of Yugoslavia. Furthermore, the mission must shape the coalition; the makeup of the coalition must not determine the mission.

4. Defending the United States requires prevention through such means as intelligence gathering and then acting on the data. Defense may also sometimes require preemptive strikes. However, it is not possible to defend against every threat, in every place, at all times. Sometimes the only defense is to take the war to the enemy—the best defense is a good offense.

5. The United States must rule out nothing in advance, including the use of ground forces. The enemy should understand that this country will use every means at its disposal to defeat hostile forces. In short, the new US deterrent is to be aggressive, and the enemy must see that the United States will not give up.

6. Victory in GWOT requires steady pressure on the enemy, leaving him no time to rest and nowhere to hide (a lesson learned in Vietnam). The United States should give no strategic pauses that would allow the enemy breathing room or time to regroup. Ultimately, this type of unrelenting pressure will end the war earlier, with fewer casualties on all sides.

7. The new and high-tech must work alongside the old and conventional. In Afghanistan, precision-guided bombs could not achieve optimal effect until the United States placed old-fashioned boots on the ground (and sometime on horseback) to tell the bombers exactly where to drop their munitions.

8. Military operations must include humanitarian assistance, radio broadcasts, rewards, and other efforts to help the local population and rally them to the US cause.

9. US leaders must be straight with the American public. They should tell people the truth, and when leaders cannot tell the truth either for lack of information or for national security reasons, they should admit it. The public supports its troops and the job they must do. They also understand GWOT will not be easy. And the public must also be able to believe that—good news or bad—their leaders will tell it to them straight. In this way, leaders earn public trust.

JOINT EXERCISES
Army Special Forces Soldiers train for the Global War on Terror with a "fast-roping" exercise out of the rear of an Air Force MH-53 helicopter. Joint operations are the way the United States now fights wars.

INDEX

PICTURE CREDITS

i US Air Force: (c). ii-iii aviation-images.com: John Dibbs. 1 NASM: (c) (clb); John J Ide Collection (cl); US Air Force: (r). 2-3 US Air Force: (l). 3 Corbis: George Hall (cb); EAA / Phil High: (clb); US Air Force: (r). 4-5 US Air Force. 6 NASM: Photozincograph copied from Christopher Hatton Turner, Astra Castra, Chapman and Hall (London) 1865, frontispiece (tl). 6-7 Corbis: Bettmann (c). 7 EAA / Phil High: (br). 8-9 Corbis. 10 NASM: Photozincograph copied from Christopher Hatton Turner, Astra Castra, Chapman and Hall (London) 1865, frontispiece (tl). 10-11 Corbis: Bettmann (c). 12-13 Corbis: Aero Graphics Inc. (c). 13 US Air Force: (tc). 14 NASM: Photozincograph copied from Christopher Hatton Turner, Astra Castra, Chapman and Hall (London) 1865, frontispiece (tl). 14-15 US Air Force: (c). 16 Corbis: George Hall (tr); US Air Force: (b). 17 US Air Force: (t). 18 Getty Images: Loomis Dean / Time Life Pictures (cl); NASM: Photozincograph copied from Christopher Hatton Turner, Astra Castra, Chapman and Hall (London) 1865, frontispiece (b). 19 Corbis: Neil Rabinowitz (t); US Air Force: (bl). 20-21 US Air Force: (b). 21 Boeing

Airplane Company: (tr). 22-23 NASM: (c). 23 NASM: (clb) (cb) (crb). 24 DK: Peter Chadwick (bl); NASM: Photozincograph copied from Christopher Hatton Turner, Astra Castra, Chapman and Hall (London) 1865, frontispiece (tl). 24-25 NASM: (c). 25 SS: Science Museum (br). 26 AB: Austin Brown / Science Museum (crb) (bc); DK: Mike Dunning (tr); NASM: John J Ide Collection (tl). 27 MEPL: (tc); NASM: (br) (cr). 28 AB: Austin Brown / MUS (clb); Philip Jarrett: (tc); SS: Science Museum (bc). 29 NASM: (tl). 30 Getty Images: Hulton Archive (tl). 30-31 NASM. 32 NASM: (t) (bc) (bl) (clb). 33 NASM: (tr) (br). 34 DK: (bl); NASM: (tl) (tc). 34-35 NASM. 36 Getty Images: Hulton Archive / LOC (b). 37 NASM: (tc) (br) (tr). 38 NASM: (clb) (br). 39 AB: Austin Brown (t); NASM: (br) (bc). 40 LOC: (ca); NASM: (tl). 40-41 NASM: (b). 41 LOC: (ca) (cl); NASM: (br); Photo by Eric F Long, copyright 1997 (tc). 42 NASM: (cl) (br) (c). 42-43 DK: Martin Cameron (t). 43 DK: Martin Cameron (c); AB: Austin Brown / The John Stroud Collection (cb). 44 AB: Austin Brown / Bibliotheque Nationale, Paris (tl); NASM: (crb). 45 Getty Images: (br); Hulton Archive / Illustrated London News (t). 46 Aspect Picture Library: Derek Bayes (bc); NASM: (bl). 46-47 NASM: (t). 47 NASM: (br). 48 NASM: (bl); LOC (c). 49 NASM: (t) (bc) (br). 50 Advertising Archives: (clb); NASM: Photozincograph copied from Christopher Hatton Turner, Astra Castra, Chapman and Hall (London) 1865, frontispiece (tl). 50-51 Quadrant Picture Library: The Flight Collection (c). 52 NASM: (cr); Peter Newark's Military Pictures: (bc); TRH Pictures: (tr). 53 NASM: Poster Collection (br). 54 NASM: James Dietz, Breakthrough Over Kiev (198) (tr); United Technologies Corp. (tl). 55 NASM: (tr) (c) (cl). 56-57 IWM: (cl). 57 Illustrated London News Picture Library: Postcard. 'Dueling in Cloudland' by CH Davis © The Sphere, Valentine's Series (ref.4500) (cb); NASM: (crb); Riverside Keystone Mast Collection (clb). 58 AB: Austin Brown (bl); NASM: (tl) (cr); Photozincograph copied from Christopher Hatton Turner, Astra Castra, Chapman and Hall (London) 1865, frontispiece (l). 59 NASM: Riverside Keystone Mast Collection (c). 60 IWM. 61 Corbis: Bettmann (tr);

DK: IWM / Gary Ombler (bc); IWM: (bl); NASM: World War I Photography Collection (Driggs) (cl). 62 IWM: (t) (bc). 63 DK: IWM / Gary Ombler (cr); IWM: (bl); LOC: (bc); NASM: Robert Soubiran Collection (tr). 64 DK: Gary Ombler (bl); Mike Dunning (cr). 64-65 IWM: (br). 65 Philip Jarrett: RAF Museum, Hendon (tr). 66 IWM: (tr) (b). 67 DK: IWM (tr); Peter Newark's Military Pictures: (c). 68 IWM: (c); Philip Jarrett: (bl); Peter Newark's Military Pictures: (tl). 68-69 Illustrated London News Picture Library: Postcard. 'Dueling in Cloudland' by CH Davis © The Sphere, Valentine's Series (ref.4500) (cr). 70 DK: IWM / Gary Ombler (cr); IWM: (cl); NASM: (tc). 70-71 NASM: IWM (br). 71 IWM: (tl). 72 NASM: Robert Soubiran Collection (tl). 72-73 IWM: (c). 73 DK: IWM / Gary Ombler (tr). 74 DK: RAF museum, Hendon (tl); NASM: (c). 75 NASM: (cb); Phillips Petroleum Company (bl). 76 IWM: (cr); NASM: (tc) (b) (cl). 77 IWM: (tl) (tc); NASM: (br). 78 NASM: (c); Eric F. Long (bl); Photozincograph copied from Christopher Hatton Turner, Astra Castra, Chapman and Hall (London) 1865, frontispiece (l); Peter Newark's Military Pictures: (tl). 78-79 NASM: (cr). 80 DK: IWM / Gary Ombler (tl); NASM: Douglas H. Robinson, University of Texas, Dallas (ca); IWM (bl). 81 DK: IWM / Gary Ombler (cra) (crb); IWM: (cl); NASM: (b). 82-83 NASM: (cl). 83 Deutsches Museum, München: (cl); NASM: (tl); Krainik Lighter-than-air Collection (br). 84-85 IWM: (cb). 85 Philip Jarrett: (c); NASM: (cr). 86 IWM: (tr) (clb). 87 Philip Jarrett: (tr). 88-89 NASM: Boeing Airplane Company (c). 89 Getty Images: Hulton Archive (c); IWM: (ca); NASM: (cla); R.G. Smith Douglas SBD-3 / Gift of MPD Corporation (cb). 90-91 NASM: (cl). 91 Getty Images: Hulton Archive (cl). 91 Philip Jarrett: (fclb); NASM: (crb) (cb) (clb). 92 Foto Saporetti: (cra); IWM: (l); Peter Newark's Military Pictures: (tl); US Air Force: (bl). 93 NASM: Boeing Airplane Company. 94 NASM: (tc) (b) (tl). 95 NASM: (tr) (br); Museo Aeronautico Caproni, Milan, Italy (c); Rudy Arnold Photo collection (crb); TRH Pictures: (tl). 96 Getty Images: Hulton Archive / US Air Force (tr); NASM: (c). 97 Getty Images: Hulton Archive / General Photographic Agency (cr); NASM: (c).

98 NASM: (tl). 98-99 NASM: (cl). 99 Philip Jarrett: (tr); NASM: (br). 100 MEPL: (tc). 100-101 NASM: WideWorld Photos, Inc. (bc). 101 Hugh Cowin: (tc); Peter Newark's Military Pictures: (cr). 102 AB: The John Stroud Collection (c); Getty Images: Hulton Archive (bl). 102-103 DK: Gary Ombler (b). 104 NASM: (bl) (c). 104-105 Getty Images: Hulton Archive (br). 106 MEPL: (tr); Robert Hunt Library: (bl). 107 akg-images: (bl); Peter Newark's Military Pictures: (tr) (cr). 108-109 Peter Newark's Military Pictures: (cl). 109 DK: Dave King (tr); NASM: Warren M. Bodie (c); The Ronald Grant Archive: (br). 110 Corbis: (br); The Granger Collection, New York: (tl); IWM: (l). 111 Getty Images: E. Bacon / Topical Press Agency (t). 112 Corbis: Bettmann (clb); Getty Images: Hulton Archive / Stringer (b). 113 Airmen Memorial Museum: (tl); Corbis: Museum of Flight (b); LOC: (cra). 114 US Air Force: (br). 114-115 US Air Force: (t). 115 Corbis: Underwood and Underwood (cr). 116-117 IWM: (cl). 117 NASM: (fclb) (clb); MUS (cb); US Air Force (crb). 118 IWM: (tl); NASM: (b). 118-119 NASM: (b). 119 TopFoto.co.uk: (tc). 120 MEPL: Unsere Wehrmacht. 121 AB: The John Stroud Collection (tr). 122 MEPL: Signal, January 1941 (bl). 123 DK: Gary Ombler (cb); Peter Newark's Military Pictures: (tl). 124-125 IWM: (cl). 125 IWM: (tr) (br). 126 Corbis: Yevgeny Khaldei (bl); IWM: (tc). 127 Getty Images: Hulton Archive (c). 128 DK: MUS / Gary Ombler (c); MUS: (tr). 129 Getty Images: Hulton Archive / Archive Photos / Robert F. Sargent (cla); US Air Force: (crb). 130 IWM: (cra); NASM: MUS (br); Royal Air Force Museum, Hendon: (tl). 131 AB: (tr); IWM: (br). 132-133 Getty Images: Hulton Archive (cl). 133 DK: IWM / Gary Ombler (cb); IWM: (crb); TopFoto.co.uk: (clb). 134 Getty Images: Hulton Archive / Fox Photos (bl); IWM: (cr) (l); The National Archives: Roy Nockolds (tl). 135 NASM. 136 IWM: (tl); The Museum of World War II: (tr). 136-137 Getty Images: Hulton Archive (bl). 137 Getty Images: Hulton Archive (tr). 138-139 AB: The John Stroud Collection. 140 Dungarvan Museum, Ireland: (tl). 140-141

Getty Images: Hulton Archive / Picture Post / Haywood Magee (bl). 141 DK: IWM / Gary Ombler (tl) (ca); Getty Images: Hulton Archive (br). 142 IWM: IWM / Gary Ombler (tr); Getty Images: Hulton Archive / Fox Photos (c). 143 DK: IWM / Andy Crawford (cr); NASM: (b); IWM (cl); The Museum of World War II: (tc). 144 AB: (bl); DK: IWM / Gary Ombler (tl); Getty Images: Hulton Archive / Keystone (cra); IWM: (l). 144-145 NASM: US Air Force (cr). 146 Getty Images: Hulton Archive (tr). 146-147 Getty Images: Hulton Archive (cl). 147 DK: IWM / Gary Ombler (tc); IWM: (tr) (br). 148 Courtesy of Norman Groom: (bl). 148-149 IWM: (c). 149 Getty Images: (tr). 150 IWM: (cla); NASM: (br). 151 NASM: (cl). 152-153 Getty Images: Hulton Archive (b). 153 DK: IWM / Gary Ombler (cl); NASM: Boeing Airplane Company (br). 154 DK: Gary Ombler (c); TopFoto.co.uk: (tc). 154-155 DK: Gary Ombler (b). 155 DK: Gary Ombler (cl); Getty Images: (tc); NASM: US Air Force (tr) (cr). 156 DK: IWM / Andy Crawford (cra); NASM: Boeing Airplane Company (c); Wright / McCook Field Still Photograph Collection (cl). 157 NASM: (tr). 158 NASM: (tr); US Air Force (bl) (ca). 159 NASM: US Air Force (c); US Air Force: (tr). 160 Corbis: Hulton-Deutsch collection (c) (clb); Getty Images: Hulton Archive (b); NASM: (tr). 161 Getty Images: Hulton Archive (b); Quadrant Picture Library: The Flight Collection / Aeroplane (t). 162 Getty Images: Hulton Archive / Keystone / Fred Ramage (tl). 162-163 AB: John Dibbs (cr). 163 AB: John Dibbs (tr). 164-165 Corbis: Bettmann (cl). 165 Getty Images: Hulton Archive / MPI (clb); Hulton Archive (crb); NASM: R.G. Smith Douglas SBD-3 / Gift of MPD Corporation (cb). 166 IWM: (l); NASM: Eric F. Long (bl); Peter Newark's Military Pictures: (tl). 166-167 Getty Images: Hulton Archive (cr). 167 NASM: US Navy (tl). 168 Corbis: Bettmann (tl); Getty Images: Hulton Archive (b); The Museum of World War II: (cl). 169 NASM: RAF Museum, Hendon / Charles E. Brown (c). 170 Corbis: Bettmann (bl); The Museum of World War II: (tr). 171 Getty Images: Hulton Archive / MPI (bc);

PICTURE CREDITS

NASM: (tr). 172 Getty Images: Hulton Archive (c); NASM: US Navy (tc). 172-173 NASM: US Navy (cr). 173 NASM: R.G. Smith Douglas SBD-3 / Gift of MPD Corporation (cr). 174 Corbis: Hulton-Deutsch Collection (tl). 174-175 DK: Gary Ombler (b) (tc). 176 NASM: (b); US Navy (tr). 177 Alamy Images: Pictorial Press Ltd. (br); NASM: US Navy (cr); US Air Force: (tl). 178 Corbis: Bettmann (c); Getty Images: Hulton Archive / MPI (tc); The Museum of World War II: (cra). 179 Corbis: Bettmann (cr); NASM: US Navy (br). 180 DK: IWM / Andy Crawford (bl); NASM: US Air Force (cr); Robert Hunt Library: (tr). 181 IWM: (tr). 182-183 US Air Force: (c). 183 Corbis: Lake County Museum (tl); Hugh Cowin: (cla); TRH Pictures: US Air Force / Department of Defense (clb); US Air Force: (fcla) (bl) (c) (ca) (cb). 184-185 US Air Force: (cl). 185 Corbis: Bettmann (cb); Lake County Museum (crb); NASM: Boeing Airplane Company (clb). 186 DK: IWM / Gary Ombler (b); NASM: Boeing Airplane Company (tl); US Air Force (bl). 186-187 NASM: Boeing Airplane Company. 188-189 Getty Images: Time Life Pictures / DOD Pool. 189 US Army: (tr). 190 US Air Force: (tl). 190-191 Corbis: Bettmann (br). 192 Harry S. Truman Library: (br); Department of Defense (tl). 193 Getty Images: George Skadding / Time Life Pictures (tr). 194-195 US Air Force: (b). 195 US Air Force: (tl). 196 Harry S. Truman Library: (tc); US Air Force: (bl). 197 NASA: (bl). 198 NASM: US Air Force (tl). 199 Corbis: Bettmann (tl); Lake County Museum (br). 200-201 Corbis: Bettmann (cl). 201 Getty Images: Hulton Archive / Keystone (crb) (clb); NASM: (cb). 202 DK: IWM / Gary Ombler (l); Maps.com: (tl) (bl); US Air Force: (br). 202-203 US Air Force: (c). 203 US Air Force: (tr). 204 Corbis: Hulton-Deutsch Collection (tr); NASM: (bl). 204-205 US Air Force: (b). 205 Getty Images: Robert Lackenbach / Time Life Pictures (tr). 206 Corbis: Bettmann (tl). 206-207 Corbis: Bettmann (bl). 207 Corbis: Hulton-Deutsch collection (br); Getty Images: Hulton Archive / Keystone (tl). 208 Getty Images: Hulton Archive / Keystone (tl). 208-209 Getty Images: Hulton Archive / Keystone (bl). 209 US Air Force: (tr). 210-211 DK: Gary Ombler (cl). 211 Corbis: George Hall (tr); Hugh Cowin: (clb); US Air Force: (cb). 212 DK: IWM / Gary Ombler (tl); Harry S. Truman Library: US Army (cb); US Air

Force: (bl). 213 Corbis: (r); Harry S. Truman Library: Department of Defense (bl). 214 Corbis: (cl); Bettmann (tr). 214-215 Corbis: George Hall (b). 215 Hugh Cowin: (tr). 216 Courtesy of Lockheed Martin Aeronautics Company, Palmdale: (l). 217 Corbis: (br); Bettmann (c); NASM: (tr); Eric F. Long (tc). 218 DK: Gary Ombler (crb); Getty Images: Hulton Archive / US Air Force / Archive Photos (tl). 218-219 DK: Gary Ombler (b). 219 Corbis: George Hall (tl) (ca) (tr); DK: Gary Ombler (cl). 220 US Air Force: (bc). 220-221 Corbis: George Hall (tr). 221 US Air Force: (bc). 222 Corbis: Bettmann (tr); US Air Force: (br). 223 US Air Force: (tl) (br). 224 Alamy Images: Northants Photo (l). 225 Getty Images: US Navy (tl). 226-227 Corbis: Museum of Flight (cl). 227 US Army: (cb); US Air Force: (clb) (crb). 228 Corbis: (cr); DK: IWM / Gary Ombler (tl); US Army: (bl). 229 Maps.com: (r); US Army: (bl). 230 US Air Force: (tl) (bl). 230-231 Corbis: Horace Bristol (b). 231 US Air Force: (tc). 232 Corbis: Bettmann (tc); US Air Force: (br). 233 Corbis: Bettmann (t); US Army: (bl). 234 US Air Force: (c). 235 Naval Historical Foundation, Washington, D.C.: US Navy (tl); US Air Force: (bc). 236-237 Corbis: Museum of Flight (c). 238-239 Getty Images: Hulton Archive / Archive Photos (cl). 239 NASM: Boeing Airplane Company (clb); US Air Force: (cb) (crb). 240 DK: IWM / Gary Ombler (tl); Courtesy of US Navy: (bl). 241 US Air Force: (c). 242 Corbis: Horace Bristol (crb); The US National Archives and Records Administration: (tc); US Air Force: (br). 243 Corbis: Bettmann (bl). 244 Getty Images: Hulton Archive / Archive Photos (br). 244-245 NASM: Boeing Airplane Company (c). 246 US Air Force: (t). 247 AB: Austin Brown (cl); Corbis: Museum of Flight (tr); DK: Gary Ombler (b). 248 US Army: (bl); US Air Force: (tc). 249 US Air Force: (tc). 250-251 Corbis: Bettmann (c). 251 NASM: (clb); US Air Force (crb); US Air Force: (br). 252 Corbis: Bettmann (bl); DK: IWM / Gary Ombler (tl); Getty Images: Hulton Archive / Keystone (br). 252-253 Corbis: Aero Graphics Inc. (tr). 254-255 Getty Images: Lynn Pelham / Time Life Pictures (bl). 255 US Air Force: (tl) (br). 256 NASM: (tr); US Air Force (b) (cra) (bl). 257 Corbis: (r). 258-259 Naval Historical Foundation, Washington, D.C.: US Navy (cl). 259

Corbis: Tim Page (crb); Getty Images: Hulton Archive (cb); Courtesy of US Navy: (clb). 260 DK: (bl); IWM / Gary Ombler (tl). 260-261 US Air Force: (b). 261 Getty Images: Hulton Archive (tl). 262 US Air Force: (tl) (br) (t). 263 Courtesy of US Navy: (br); US Senate Historical Office: (tr). 264 Naval Historical Foundation, Washington, D.C.: US Navy (b). 265 US Air Force: (tr). 266 Corbis: (t); NASA: DFRC (c); NASM: (b). 267 Getty Images: Hulton Archive / Archive Photos / Patrick Christain (b). 268 US Air Force: (tl) (bl) (cr). 269 Getty Images: Hulton Archive / US Air Force / Archive Photos (t); US Air Force: (br). 270 Military Picture Library: David Hunter (tc); William F. Bennett (cl). 270-271 Corbis: Bettmann (cr). 272 Corbis: George Hall (b). 273 Corbis: Tim Page (ca). 274-275 Corbis: Aero Graphics Inc. (l). 275 NASM: (cb); US Air Force: (crb) (clb). 276 Corbis: (br); DK: IWM / Gary Ombler (l); PA Photos: (bl). 276-277 US Air Force: (tr). 277 US Air Force: (br). 278 NASM: (bc). 278-279 Alamy Images: Aero / Thierry GRUN (tr). 279 US Air Force: (br). 280 Getty Images: Hulton Archive / Central Press (bl); NASM: (crb); Fairchild (tr). 281 aviation-images.com: Mark Wagner (tl); DK: Gary Ombler (b); Getty Images: Vuk Brankovic / AFP (cr); TRH Pictures: E Nevill (cl). 282 US Air Force: (bl). 283 US Air Force: (tr). 284-285 Corbis: Aero Graphics Inc. (t). 285 Corbis: Bettmann (br). 286 AB: Austin Brown (bl); Boeing Airplane Company: (tl). 286-287 Corbis: (b). 287 Courtesy of Northrop Grumman: (tr). 288-289 Corbis: George Hall (t). 290-291 Courtesy of Northrop Grumman: (cl). 291 Corbis: (crb); US Air Force: (clb) (cb). 292 DK: IWM / Gary Ombler (tl); US Air Force: (bl). 293 Corbis: Museum of Flight (b). 294 Corbis: Aero Graphics Inc. (t); George Hall (clb). 295 Corbis: Aero Graphics Inc. (tr); NASA: DFRC (cr); US Air Force: (bl). 296 NASA: DFRC (tr); US Air Force: (cr). 297 Corbis: Aero Graphics Inc. (clb); DK: Gary Ombler (b); TRH Pictures: McDonnell Douglas (tr) (cr); US Air Force / Department of Defense (cla). 298 Corbis: Roger Ressmayer (l). 298-299 Courtesy of Northrop Grumman: (tc). 299 Hugh Cowin: (br). 300 US Air Force: (bl) (cra) (bl). 301 US Air Force: (tc) (bl) (br). 302-303 US Air Force: (t). 303 US Air Force: (crb) (cb) (clb). 304 DK: IWM / Gary

Ombler (tl); US Air Force: (bl). 305 Maps.com: (br). 306 Corbis: (tl). 307 Corbis: Jean Louis Atlan / Sygma (b); US Air Force: (tr). 308 Maps.com: (tr). 309 US Air Force: (bl) (tr). 310-311 US Air Force: (tr). 312 Corbis: Bettmann (tc). 312-313 Corbis: Aero Graphics Inc. (bl). 313 US Air Force: (tr). 314-315 US Air Force: (c). 315 US Air Force: (cb) (c) (ca). 316-317 Corbis: (cl). 317 Boeing Airplane Company: (tl); US Air Force (crb) (cb). 318 aviation-images.com: John Dibbs (bl); Corbis: Bettmann (l). 318-319 US Air Force: (b). 320 US Army: (tr); US Air Force: (cl). 320-321 US Air Force: (br). 321 Houghton Mifflin Company: Taken from Crusade: The Untold Story of the Persian Gulf War by Rick Atkinson. (tl). 322 US Air Force: (tc) (bl). 323 Getty Images: 49th Pad / US Army / Time Life Pictures. 324 US Air Force: (t). 324-325 US Air Force: (bc). 325 US Air Force: (tr). 326 Boeing Airplane Company: (tl); Getty Images: AFP (tr); US Air Force: (bc). 327 US Air Force: (tr). 328 US Air Force: (c). 329 US Army: (tr). 330 PA Photos: Laurent Rebours (tr). 330-331 Corbis: (br). 332-333 Getty Images: Purestock (cl). 333 US Air Force: (clb) (cb) (crb). 334 Corbis: Bettmann (tl); US Air Force: (bl). 334-335 Corbis: George Hall (c). 335 Getty Images: Purestock (tr); US Air Force: (cr). 336 US Air Force: (bl) (tr); US Army: (cr) (bc) (tc). 338 Getty Images: Scott Peterson (br). 339 Getty Images: HOCZINE ZAOURAR / AFP (tr). 340-341 Corbis: George Hall (cl). 341 aviation-images.com: Mark Wagner (crb); US Air Force: (clb) (cb). 342 Corbis: Bettmann (tl); US Air Force: (bl). 342-343 US Air Force: (br). 343 Maps.com: (tr). 344 US Air Force: (bl); US Army: courtesy of US Navy (tl). 344-345 NASA: DFRC (tr). 345 Corbis: George Hall (c). 346 aviation-images.com: Mark Wagner (tc). 346-347 Corbis: Aero Graphics Inc. (br). 347 Getty Images: AFP (tr). 348 US Air Force: (t) (br) (clb). 349 Getty Images: US Navy / Michael W. Pendergrass (t). 350 Corbis: Aero Graphics Inc. (tl); DK: Lockheed Martin / Gary Ombler (tr) (bl). 350-351 DK: Lockheed Martin / Gary Ombler (br). 351 aviation-images.com: Mark Wagner (cl); US Air Force: (tl). 352-353 US Air Force: (c). 353 US Air Force: (cla) (c) (ca) (clb). 354-355 Corbis: George Hall (cl). 355 Getty Images: AFP / Seth McCallister (cb); US Air Force: (crb) (clb). 356 NASM: Poster Collection (l);

US Department of Defense: Cedric H. Rudisill (tl). 357 Getty Images: AFP / Seth McCallister (c). 358 Getty Images: Pool Photo (tc). 358-359 Corbis: George Hall (b). 359 Getty Images: Michael Latz / AFP (br); US Air Force: (tr). 360 Getty Images: Scott Nelson (bl). 361 Getty Images: Ethan Miller (t); US Air Force: (br). 362 US Air Force: (tr) (br). 362-363 US Air Force: (br). 364-365 Corbis: Aero Graphics Inc. (b). 365 Courtesy of Northrop Grumman: (crb); PA Photos: Empics / Anja Niedringhaus (cb); Empics / Murad Sezer (clb). 366 Getty Images: RAMZI HADIR / AFP (bl); NASM: Poster Collection (tl). 367 Corbis: Brooks Kraft (tc); Forestier Yves / Sygma (br). 368 PA Photos: Empics / Jerome Delay (bl); US Air Force: (br). 368 US Department of Defense: (tl). 369 PA Photos: Empics / Murad Sezer (cr); US Air Force: (br). 370 aviation-images.com: (bl); Courtesy of Northrop Grumman: (cr) (t). 371 PA Photos: Empics / Anja Niedringhaus (tr); US Air Force: (bl) (br). 372 PA Photos: Empics / Andrew Milligan (bl); US Air Force: (tl); US Army: (tr). 373 Corbis: Aero Graphics Inc. (t); US Air Force: (cl). 374-375 Corbis: Stocktrek Corp / Brand X (cl). 375 US Air Force: (cb) (clb) (crb). 376 NASM: Poster Collection (tl); US Air Force: (bl). 376-377 US Air Force: (r). 378 US Air Force: (bc). 378-379 US Air Force: (bc). 379 US Air Force: George Hall (t). 381 US Air Force: (tc) (b). 382-383 US Air Force: (bl). 383 US Air Force: (tr). 384 Corbis: Stocktrek Corp / Brand X (b); US Air Force: (t). 385 US Air Force: (t). 386-387 US Air Force: (l). 387 US Air Force: (clb) (cb) (crb). 388 NASM: (br); Poster Collection (l); US Air Force: (tl). 389 Corbis: Medford Historical Society Collection (l). 390 US Air Force: (bl). 391 Corbis: (bl); Museum of Flight (t). 392 EAA: Jim Koepnick (tc); US Air Force: (b). 393 Corbis: Bettmann (br); Getty Images: Keystone (t). 394 US Air Force: (tl). 394-395 Alamy Images: Gary Edwards (br). 396-397 US Air Force: (l). 397 US Air Force: (t) (br). 398 US Air Force: (tr) (br) (cl). 399 US Air Force: (b).

Jacket images: Front: US Air Force. Back: Corbis: George Hall.

All other images © Dorling Kindersley For further information see: www.dkimages.com